Companion Website Activities and Essays

Throughout the textbook, you will see references to the Companion Website in **green text**.
These refer to specific activities and essays that are relevant to the topic being discussed.
Below is the full list of activities and essays, along with the textbook pages on which they are first referred.

Sensation & Perception

THIRD EDITION

Sensation & Perception

THIRD EDITION

Jeremy M. Wolfe
Harvard University Medical School

Keith R. Kluender
Purdue University

Dennis M. Levi
University of California, Berkeley

Linda M. Bartoshuk
University of Florida

Rachel S. Herz
Brown University

Roberta Klatzky
Carnegie Mellon University

Susan J. Lederman
Queen's University

Daniel M. Merfeld
Harvard University Medical School

Sinauer Associates, Inc. • Publishers
Sunderland, Massachusetts U.S.A.

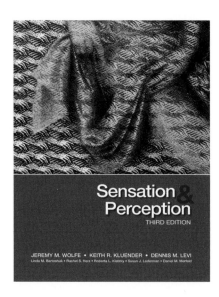

About the cover

Point of Touch: *Bathsheba*, 1995, by Lia Cook. The artist uses a combination of weaving and painting techniques to translate visual pixels into an image embedded in cloth. More of her work can be seen at www.liacoook.com. (46" x 51"; linen, rayon, oil paint, dyes; Collection of Oakland Museum of Art, California.)

Sensation & Perception

For information, address
Sinauer Associates, Inc., 23 Plumtree Road, Sunderland, MA 01375 U.S.A.
Fax: 413-549-1118
E-mail: publish@sinauer.com
Internet: www.sinauer.com

Library of Congress Cataloging-in-Publication Data

Sensation & perception / Jeremy M. Wolfe ... [et al.]. -- 3rd ed.
    p. cm.
 Includes bibliographical references and index.
 ISBN 978-0-87893-572-7 (casebound)
1. Senses and sensation. 2. Perception. I. Wolfe, Jeremy M.
 QP431.S445 2012
 612.8--dc23

                        2011036497

Printed in U.S.A.

6 5 4 3

About the Authors

JEREMY M. WOLFE is Professor of Ophthalmology & Radiology at Harvard Medical School. Dr. Wolfe was trained as a vision researcher/experimental psychologist and remains one today. His early work includes papers on binocular vision, adaptation, and accommodation. The bulk of his recent work has dealt with visual search and visual attention in the lab and in real-world settings such as airport security and cancer screening. He taught Introductory Psychology for over twenty-five years at the Massachusetts Institute of Technology, where he won the Baker Memorial Prize for undergraduate teaching in 1989. He directs the Visual Attention Lab and the Center for Advanced Medical Imaging of Brigham & Women's Hospital.

DENNIS M. LEVI has taught at the University of California, Berkeley since 2001. He is Dean/Professor in the School of Optometry and Professor at the Helen Wills Neuroscience Institute. In the lab, Dr. Levi and colleagues use psychophysics, computational modeling, and brain imaging (fMRI) to study the neural mechanisms of normal pattern vision in humans, and to learn how they are degraded by abnormal visual experience (amblyopia).

KEITH R. KLUENDER Head/Professor of Speech, Language, and Hearing Sciences and Professor of Psychological Sciences at Purdue University. His research encompasses: how people hear complex sounds such as speech; how experience shapes the way we hear; how what we hear guides our actions and communication; clinical problems of hearing impairment or language delay; and practical concerns about computer speech recognition and hearing aid design. Dr. Kluender is deeply committed to teaching, and has taught a wide array of courses—philosophical, psychological, and physiological.

LINDA M. BARTOSHUK is Bushnell Professor, Department of Community Dentistry and Behavioral Science at the University of Florida. Her research on taste has opened up broad new avenues for further study, establishing the impact of both genetic and pathological variation in taste on food preferences, diet, and health. She discovered that taste normally inhibits other oral sensations such that damage to taste leads to unexpected consequences like weight gain and intensified oral pain.

RACHEL S. HERZ is currently an Adjunct Assistant Professor in the Department of Psychiatry and Human Behavior at Brown University. Her research focuses on olfactory cognition and perception and the roles and features of emotion, memory, and language. Using an experimental approach grounded in evolutionary theory and incorporating both cognitive–behavioral and neuropsychological techniques, Dr. Herz aims to understand how biological mechanisms and cognitive processes interact to influence perception, cognition, and behavior.

ROBERTA L. KLATZKY is Professor of Psychology at Carnegie Mellon University, where she also holds faculty appointments in the Center for the Neural Basis of Cognition and the Human–Computer Interaction Institute. She has done extensive research on haptic and visual object recognition, space perception and spatial thinking, and motor performance. Her work has application to haptic interfaces, navigation aids for the blind, image-guided surgery, teleoperation, and virtual environments.

SUSAN J. LEDERMAN is Professor Emerita of Psychology at Queen's University, with cross-appointments in the Centre for Neuroscience and in the School of Computing. Her research interests span both perception and cognition, with particular emphases on psychophysics, haptic perception and recognition of objects and their underlying neural processes and representations, multisensory perception, and sensory-guided motor control. She has applied the results of her research to a number of real-world problems, including the design of haptic and multisensory interfaces for virtual environments and teleoperation.

DANIEL M. MERFELD is an Associate Professor of Otology and Laryngology at the Harvard Medical School with cross-appointments at the Harvard–MIT Health, Science, and Technology program and the Harvard Faculty of Arts and Sciences. He is also the Director of the Jenks Vestibular Physiology Laboratory at the Massachusetts Eye and Ear Infirmary. Most of his research career has been spent studying how the brain combines information from multiple sources, with a specific focus on how the brain processes ambiguous sensory information from the vestibular system in the presence of noise. Other research includes work developing a vestibular implant for patients who have severe problems with their vestibular periphery.

Brief Contents

Contents

CHAPTER 4 Perceiving and Recognizing Objects 85

CHAPTER 5 The Perception of Color 117

CHAPTER 6 Space Perception and Binocular Vision 149

Preface to the Third Edition

This is a Sensation and Perception text written by enthusiasts who have spent years working in the field because we think it is fun. Of course, there are other motivations at play as well; we work on problems like oral pain that have medical applications, or issues such as airport security that have broader societal implications. But a good part of what gets us up in the morning is the sheer enjoyment of working to find solutions to these problems.

Our goal in writing an undergraduate textbook is to spread our enthusiasm. How should we go about doing that? Collectively, the authors of this book know a great deal about sensation and perception and we could have created a really fat tome by stapling together the review chapters we have written for more advanced handbooks. While this might have been quite authoritative, we suspect it would have been more of an undergraduate sleep aid than a vehicle for transferring the enthusiasm we feel about sensation and perception. Instead, in each of the 15 chapters of this book, we have tried to tell a coherent and interesting story that will give the reader enough background and exposure to enough current research to understand why these topics are interesting and how they might be further investigated and understood. We are not naïve or immodest enough to believe that you will devour a chapter on "The Perception of Color" or "Perceiving and Recognizing Objects" in the way that you might devour a good novel. However, we do hope that you will find each chapter to be more than a compilation of facts. We hope to be like Cleopatra in Shakespeare's play: while other texts may "cloy the appetites they feed," we hope our work "makes hungry where most it satisfies." We will be satisfied if the book teaches the reader enough to inspire the reader to want to know more.

In service of these goals, we have produced a textbook that is reasonably comprehensive while still being digestible. It is possible that you, the student, may not think so at 3:00 a.m. the day before the final exam, but that was the goal. Like many textbook authors, we recognize the futility of trying to get students to learn everything about a topic from a single encounter. We want to present a coherent introduction to the important topics. We hope to leave enough time for the instructor or the interested student to dive into the endless material that lies behind, and to the side of, each point made in the actual text.

Some of that extra material can be found on the text's website, www.sites.sinauer.com/wolfe3e. There you will find a number of brief essays on topics that we brokenheartedly removed from earlier versions of our chapters. Given the chance, each of us can talk your ear off on the topics in this book, but we have sincerely tried to avoid doing this. In addition to the essays, the website features a host of great demonstrations made possible by Evan Palmer of Wichita State University, the guardian of our website.

In trying to convey our enthusiasm for this material, we wanted to create a beautiful book. If we have succeeded, it is in no small part due to our publisher, Sinauer Associates. The people at Sinauer produce beautiful books and we were fortunate enough to have their commitment to a Sensation and Perception text that is full color throughout. We have enjoyed seeing the actual pages as they came to us for proofreading. We hope that you find your experience with the book to be both aesthetically and intellectually appealing.

We were pleased by the reception of the first and second editions of our textbook and pleased that this reception warranted a third edition. For this edition, we incorporated some of the new findings from the past few years. We have also tried to note more links between chapters. In fact, we formalized this effort with "Further Discussion" boxes, as well as comments in the text. Of course, we didn't point out (or even notice) all the possible connections. That, as they say, is an exercise for the reader. Speaking of readers, it is always a question whether or not anyone actually reads the preface. If you did and you are reading this, send a note to wolfe@search.bwh.harvard.edu. We are curious. Please also feel encouraged to send us notes and comments about the actual text. We are even more curious about those reactions.

Acknowledgments

Our editor, Sydney Carroll gracefully cajoled us into doing our work more-or-less on time. Stephanie Hiebert did a fantastic job copyediting and caught our errors, improved the words, and made the text fit for public use. David McIntyre came up with an endless set of clever ideas for better images and photos (check out Figure 7.33). Laura Green oversaw the whole production process through a great flurry of emails. We also wish to thank the entire production department at Sinauer: Christopher Small, Janice Holabird, who created an elegant book design, and Joanne Delphia, who designed the cover. Mike Demaray, Craig Durant, and colleagues at Dragonfly Media Group created the beautiful art program of this text. Christian Stilp at the University of Wisconsin provided the color spectrograms for the hearing unit. Rachel Shoup and Ingrid Johnsrude deserve special thanks for their help in making the book more readable and student-friendly. The following colleagues also deserve thanks for their helpful insights and comments: Marianne Dieterich (Ludwig-Maximilians-University of Munich, Germany), Henrik Ehrsson (Karolinska Institute, Sweden), George Gescheider (Hamilton College), and Roland Johansson (Umeå University, Sweden).

The following reviewers read and critiqued drafts and/or previous versions of the text, and we are grateful for their expert assistance:

Timothy Allen (California State University, Long Beach)

Lisa M. Bauer (Pepperdine University)

Elizabeth Bowering (Mount Saint Vincent University)

Kathleen Cullen (McGill University)

Lisa Delano-Wood (San Diego State University)

Tim Donahue (Virginia Commonwealth University)

Raymond H. Dye, Jr. (Loyola University, Chicago)

Laura Freberg (California Polytechnic State University, San Luis Obispo)

Phyllis R. Freeman (State University of New York, New Paltz)

Deborah Giaschi (University of British Columbia)

Paula Goolkasian (University of North Carolina, Charlotte)

David Hall (Portland State University)

Laurence Harris (York University)

Kim Hellemans (Carleton University)

Patrick J. Hibbeler (Miami University)

Aaron Johnson (Concordia University)

Dr. Jane Karwoski (University of Nevada, Las Vegas)

Zili Liu (University of California, Los Angeles)

John S. Monahan (Central Michigan University)

Robin Morris (University of South Carolina)

Jonathan Pillow (University of Texas at Austin)

Bryan Raudenbush (Wheeling Jesuit University)

Lisa Sanders (University of Massachusetts)

James Schirillo (Wake Forest University)

Bennett Schwartz (Florida International University)

T. C. Sim (Sam Houston State University)

Mark Stewart (Willamette University)

Duje Tadin (University of Rochester)

Elizabeth B. Torres (Rutgers University)

Lee Wurm (Wayne State University)

Finally, many, many colleagues sent us reprints and answered questions about points both specific and general. We gratefully acknowledge their help even if we cannot list all of their names. We are also indebted to the users of the text, students and faculty, who pointed out errors, typos, and other short-comings in the first and second editions. We hope we caught them all and we hope that the readers of this edition will continue to offer us assistance. As noted earlier in the preface, if you find a flaw or if you have any other comment—even a positive one—please feel encouraged to let us know. You can use wolfe@search.bwh.harvard.edu as a point of contact for all of us.

Media and Supplements

FOR THE STUDENT

Companion Website (sites.sinauer.com/wolfe3e)
The *Sensation & Perception*, Third Edition companion website provides students with a wealth of study and review materials to help them master the important concepts covered in the textbook. All of the site's content is keyed to textbook chapters, and Web activities and essays are referenced in the textbook. The site is available to students free of charge and includes the following resources:

- *Chapter Overviews* introduce students to the important concepts presented in each chapter. Additionally, select key terms are linked to the relevant activities and essays allowing easy transition to explanations.

- *Interactive Activities* lead students through important processes, phenomena, and structures. These exercises give students the opportunity to explore a variety of topics in an interactive, exploratory format, including perception experiments, illusions that illustrate key concepts, models of cognitive processes, and interactive diagrams of important structures.

- *Web Essays* expand on selected topics from the textbook and provide additional coverage and examples.

- *Study Questions* are designed to give students the opportunity to test their mastery of the important concepts, processes, and terminology presented in the chapter.

- *Flashcards and Key Terms* help students master the hundreds of new terms introduced in the textbook.

- *Chapter Summaries* provide a detailed overview of each chapter's contents, and include a fill-in-the-blank review feature.

FOR THE INSTRUCTOR

(Available to qualified adopters)

Instructor's Resource Library
(ISBN 978-0-87893-661-8)

The *Sensation & Perception*, Third Edition Instructor's Resource Library includes a wide range of resources to help instructors in course planning, lecture development, and student assessment. The IRL includes the following:

Lecture Resources

- *Textbook Figures and Tables*: All of the figures and tables from the textbook, formatted and color-adjusted for optimal legibility when projected. All images are provided as both high- and low-res JPEG files.

- *PowerPoint Presentations*: For each chapter of the textbook, the IRL includes two separate PowerPoint presentations:
  - *Figures & Tables*: All of the figures and tables from the chapter.
  - *Lecture*: A complete lecture presentation that consists of a detailed lecture outline with selected figures and tables inserted.

Instructor's Manual

The Instructor's Manual includes a variety of resources to aid in course development, lecture planning, and assessment. The Manual includes the following categories for each chapter of the textbook:

- *Chapter Overview*: The big picture synopsis of what the chapter covers.

- *Chapter Outline*: The outline structure of the chapter, including headings.

- *Chapter Summary*: A detailed breakdown of all of the important concepts presented in the chapter.

- *Lecture Outline*: A suggested lecture for each chapter, presented in a slide-by-slide format designed for use in PowerPoint presentations.
- *References for Lecture Development*: A list of references for additional reading and course development on the topics presented in each chapter.

Test Bank

A complete set of multiple-choice questions for each chapter of the textbook. Questions cover the full range of material covered in each chapter, and include both factual recall and conceptual questions. Some questions also include diagrams, and all have Bloom's Category designations. The test bank is provided in several formats:

- *Microsoft Word*
- *Wimba Diploma*: This easy-to-use software allows you to quickly create quizzes and exams using any combination of publisher-provided questions and your own questions.
- *Blackboard* and *WebCT*

Value Options

eBook (ISBN 978-0-87893-951-0)
www.coursesmart.com

Sensation and Perception, Third Edition is available as an eBook via CourseSmart, at a substantial discount off the price of the printed textbook. The CourseSmart eBook reproduces the look of the printed book exactly, and includes convenient tools for searching the text, highlighting, and note taking. The eBook is available in both downloadable and online formats, and supports the iPhone and iPad.

Looseleaf textbook (ISBN 978-0-87893-876-6)

Sensation and Perception, Third Edition is available in a three-hole punched, looseleaf format. Students can take just the sections they need to class and can easily integrate instructor material with the text.

Sensation&
Perception

THIRD EDITION

CHAPTER 1

Dana Ellyn, *See No Evil, Hear No Evil, Speak No Evil (Forever Hold Your Peace)*, 2010

Introduction

Welcome to Our World

Apparently you've elected to read at least part of a textbook on "sensation and perception." You may be majoring in psychology or studying an allied field, such as neuroscience or biology, or you may be simply curious. No matter what interests you most, some large part of your understanding will be informed by sensation and perception.

This first chapter of the book gives an introduction to the sorts of questions that interest us and the sorts of methods that researchers have developed in order to answer those questions. These are useful examples. We could have picked many others. The rest of the book will introduce you to a panorama of questions that have occupied and continue to occupy the professional attentions of thousands of scientists.

Sensation and Perception

What does your phone feel as you run your finger down its touch screen (**Figure 1.1**)? What does it hear as you whisper into its receiver? We assume that these are silly questions, though it would not be silly to ask about the lightest touch that the screen could sense or the faintest vibration in the air that the microphone could sense. What does your cat feel as you run your finger down its back? That seems a more reasonable question, though you have no access to the private experience of the cat. You don't even have access to the private sensory world of a person whose back you might stroke. Only your own sensory experience is directly accessible to you.

This book is titled *Sensation & Perception*. The ability to detect the pressure of a finger and, perhaps, to turn that detection into a private experience is an example of **sensation**. **Perception** can be thought of as the act of giving meaning to those detected sensations. How do you *understand* the finger that runs down your back? Is it a gesture of affection? Is it the officer at the airport security checkpoint looking for weapons? This book will trace the path from stimuli in the world, through your sense organs, to the understanding of the world that you perceive.

Everything we feel, think, and do depends on sensations and perceptions. For this reason, philosophers have thought, talked, and written about the topic in profound and systematic ways for over two millennia. (See **Web Essay: 1.1: Senses of Reality through the Ages**.) The idea that sensation and perception are central to mental life has deep roots. The eighteenth-century French philosopher Étienne Bonnot de Condillac (1715–1780) (**Figure 1.2**) famously asked his readers to imagine the mental life of a statue with no senses, and he concluded that the statue would have no mental life. Then Condillac imagined opening the statue's nose and giving it a whiff of the scent of a rose. Now the mental life of the statue would consist of that smell. Thus, with more senses

sensation The ability to detect a stimulus and, perhaps, to turn that detection into a private experience.

perception The act of giving meaning to a detected sensation.

FIGURE 1.1 Would it make sense to ask what a cell phone feels when you stroke its screen? Why or why not?

quale (pl. qualia) In philosophy, a private conscious experience of sensation or perception.

FIGURE 1.2 Étienne Bonnot de Condillac imagined how a statue could develop a mental life.

and more experience, Condillac imagined a real mental life developing. If our mental life relies on information from our senses, then it follows that the place for the study of the senses is within the science of human behavior and human mental life—that is, within psychology. Of course, this placement is not absolute. Researchers studying topics in sensation and perception can be found in biology, computer science, medicine, neuroscience, and many other fields. Critically, however, we approach the study of sensation and perception as a scientific pursuit. As such, it needs scientific methods. That's why the next sections of this chapter are devoted to the variety of methods used in the study of the senses.

Method 1: Thresholds

What is the faintest sound you can hear? How would you know? What is the loudest sound you can hear? This last question is not as stupid as it may sound, though it could be rephrased like this: What is the loudest sound you can hear *safely*? If you listened to sounds above that limit, perhaps by blasting your music too enthusiastically, you would change the answer to the first question. You would have damaged your auditory system, and the faintest sound you could hear would now be less faint. How would you know? As we'll learn in this chapter, a variety of methods are available for measuring sensory "thresholds" of this sort.

Method 2: Scaling—Measuring Private Experience

When you say that you "hear" or "taste" something, are those experiences— what the philosophers call **qualia** (singular *quale*)—the same experiences as the experiences of the person you're talking to? We can't really answer the question of whether your qualitative experience of "red" is like my qualitative experience of "green" or, for that matter, "middle C." We still have no direct way to experience someone else's experiences. However, we can demonstrate that different people do, in some cases, inhabit different sensory worlds. Our discussion in this chapter will show how "scaling" methods can be used to perform this act of mind reading.

Method 3: Signal Detection Theory— Measuring Difficult Decisions

A radiologist looks at a mammogram, the X-ray test used to screen for breast cancer. There's something on the X-ray that might be a sign of cancer, but it is not perfectly clear. What should the radiologist do? Suppose she decides to call it benign, not cancer, and suppose she is wrong. Her patient might die. Suppose she decides to treat it as a sign of malignancy. Her patient will need more tests, perhaps involving surgery. The patient and her family will be terribly worried. If the radiologist is wrong and the spot on the mammogram is, in fact, benign, the consequences may be less dire than missing a cancer, but there will be consequences. This is a perceptual decision, made by an expert, that has real consequences. Our discussion of "signal detection theory" will show how decisions of this sort can be studied scientifically.

Method 4: Sensory Neuroscience

You're warming up for the big game, but a few muscles are feeling a bit sore and painful. You pull out a tube of smelly ointment to help make the pain go away. Your teammates can now smell you coming, but at least you don't notice the pain so much. You do, however, experience a burning sensation, or perhaps your skin feels a bit cold. The air did not get warmer or colder, and your skin is no warmer or colder either, but the feeling is unmistakable. This chapter's exploration of "sensory neuroscience" will explain how your perception of the world depends on the activity of our sensory nerves at least as much as it depends on the world itself.

Method 5: Neuroimaging—An Image of the Mind

Suppose you arrange to view completely different images with each of your two eyes. We might present a picture of a house to one eye and a face to the other (Tong et al., 1998). The result is an interesting effect known as "binocular rivalry" (see Chapter 6). The two images would vie to dominate your perception: sometimes you would see a house, and sometimes you would see a face. You would not see the two together. One reason binocular rivalry is interesting is that it represents a dissociation of the stimuli, presented to the eyes, and your private perceptual experience. Even if we cannot share the experience, modern brain-imaging techniques enable us to see that experience as it takes place in the brain. Methods of "neuroimaging" will be our final topic in this chapter.

Thresholds and the Dawn of Psychophysics

The study of the senses was always a mix of experimental science and philosophy. It is very interesting to look for precursors of the modern, scientific study of sensation and perception. We will start with the very interesting and versatile nineteenth-century German scientist-philosopher **Gustav Fechner** (1801–1887) (Figure 1.3). Fechner is sometimes considered to be the true founder of experimental psychology (Boring, 1950), even if that title is usually given to **Wilhelm Wundt** (1832–1920), who began his work sometime later.

Before making his first contributions to psychology, Fechner had an eventful personal history. Young Fechner earned his degree in medicine, but his interests turned from biological science to physics and mathematics. Though this might seem an unlikely way to get to psychology, events proved otherwise. Fechner was a very hardworking young scientist. He worked himself to exhaustion. In addition to being overworked, he suffered severe eye damage from gazing too much at the sun while performing vision experiments (a not uncommon problem for curious vision researchers in the days before reliable, bright, artificial light sources). As a consequence, Fechner fell into deep depression. Not only did he resign from his position at the university; he also withdrew from almost all his friends and colleagues. For 3 years he spent almost all of his time alone with his thoughts.

Then Fechner experienced what he believed to be a miracle, when his vision began to recover quickly. His religious convictions deepened, and he became absorbed with the relationship between mind and matter. This pursuit placed him in the middle of a classic philosophical debate between adherents of **dualism** and **materialism**. Dualists hold that the mind has an existence separate from the material world of the body. Materialists hold that the mind is not separate. A modern materialist position, probably the majority view in scientific psychology, is that the mind is what the brain does. Fechner proposed to effectively split the difference by imagining that the mind, or consciousness, is present in all of nature. This **panpsychism**—the idea that the mind exists as a property of all matter—extended not only to animals, but to inanimate things as well. Fechner described his philosophy of panpsychism in a provocative book entitled *Nanna, or Concerning the Mental Life of Plants*. This title alone gives a pretty good idea of what Fechner had in mind.

FIGURE 1.3 Gustav Fechner invented psychophysics and is thought by some to be the true founder of experimental psychology. Fechner is best known for his pioneering work relating changes in the physical world to changes in our psychological experiences.

dualism The idea that the mind has an existence separate from the material world of the body.

materialism The idea that the only thing that exists is matter, and that all things, including the mind and consciousness, are the results of interaction between bits of matter.

panpsychism The idea that the mind exists as a property of all matter—that is, that all matter has consciousness.

FIGURE 1.4 Ernst Weber discovered that the smallest detectable change in a stimulus, such as the weight of an object, is a constant proportion of the stimulus level. This relationship later became known as "Weber's law."

psychophysics The science of defining quantitative relationships between physical and psychological (subjective) events.

two-point touch threshold The minimum distance at which two stimuli (e.g., two simultaneous touches) are just perceptible as separate.

just noticeable difference (JND) (or difference threshold) The smallest detectable difference between two stimuli, or the minimum change in a stimulus that enables it to be correctly judged as different from a reference stimulus.

Weber fraction The constant of proportionality in Weber's law.

Weber's law The principle describing the relationship between stimulus and resulting sensation that says the just noticeable difference (JND) is a constant fraction of the comparison stimulus.

Fechner's law A principle describing the relationship between stimulus and resulting sensation that says the magnitude of subjective sensation increases proportionally to the logarithm of the stimulus intensity.

Inspired by what we might consider to be somewhat unconventional ideas, Fechner took on the job of explaining the relation between the spiritual and material worlds: mind and body. From his experience as a physicist, Fechner thought it should be possible to describe the relation between mind and body using mathematics. His goal was to formally describe the relationship between sensation (mind) and the energy (matter) that gave rise to that sensation. He called both his methods and his theory **psychophysics** (*psycho* for mind, and *physics* for matter).

In his effort, Fechner was inspired by the findings of one of his Leipzig colleagues, **Ernst Weber** (1795–1878) (Figure 1.4), an anatomist and physiologist who was interested in touch. Weber tested the accuracy of our sense of touch using a device much like the compass one might use when learning geometry. He used this device to measure the smallest distance between two points that was required for a person to feel two points instead of one. Later, Fechner would call the distance between the points the **two-point touch threshold**. We will discuss two-point touch thresholds, and touch in general, in Chapter 13.

For Fechner, Weber's most important findings involved judgments of lifted weights. Weber would ask people to lift one standard weight (a weight that stayed the same over experimental trials) and one comparison weight that differed from the standard in incremental amounts. He found that the ability of a subject to detect the difference between the standard and comparison weights depended greatly on the weight of the standard. When the standard was relatively light, people were much better at detecting a small difference when they lifted the comparison weight. When the standard was heavier, people needed a bigger difference before they could detect the change. He called the difference required for detecting a change in weight the **just noticeable difference**, or **JND**. Another term for JND, the smallest change in a stimulus that can be detected, is the **difference threshold**.

Weber noticed that JNDs change in a systematic way. The smallest change in weight that could be detected was always close to one-fortieth of the standard weight. Thus, a 1-gram change could be detected when the standard weighed 40 grams, but a 10-gram change was required when the standard weighed 400 grams. Weber went on to test JNDs for a few other kinds of stimuli, such as judging the lengths of two lines, for which the ratio was 1:100. For virtually every measure—whether brightness, pitch, or time—a constant ratio between the change and what was being changed could describe the threshold of detectable change quite well. This ratio rule holds true except when intensities, size, and so on are very small or very large, nearing the minimum and maximum of our senses. In recognition of Weber's discovery, Fechner called these ratios **Weber fractions**. He also gave Weber's observation a mathematical formula. Fechner named the general rule—that the size of the detectable difference (ΔI) is a constant proportion (K) of the level of the stimulus (I)—**Weber's law**.

In Weber's observations, Fechner found what he was looking for: a way to describe the relationship between mind and matter. Fechner assumed that the smallest detectable change in a stimulus (ΔI) could be considered a unit of the mind because this is the smallest bit of change that is perceived. He then mathematically extended Weber's law to create what became known as **Fechner's law** (Figure 1.5):

$$S = k \log R$$

where S is the psychological sensation, which is equal to the logarithm of the physical stimulus level ($\log R$) multiplied by a constant, k. This equation describes the fact that our psychological experience of the intensity of light, sound, smell, taste, or touch increases less quickly than the actual physical stimulus increases. With this equation, Fechner provided a mathematical ex-

FIGURE 1.5 This illustration of Fechner's law shows that as stimulus intensity grows larger, larger changes are required for the changes to be detected by a perceiver.

pression that formally demonstrated a relationship between psyche and physics (psychophysics).

Consider the similarity between Fechner's law and Albert Einstein's famous equation

$$E = mc^2$$

Like mind and body, energy (E) and mass (m) had, before Einstein, been thought of as distinct things. (The letter c corresponds to the speed of light, almost a billion feet per second.) Just as Einstein showed how to equate energy and mass, Fechner provided us with at least one way to think about mind and matter as equivalent. As you learn about the senses when reading this book, you will find that we typically make a distinction between units of physical entities (light, sound) and measures of people's perception. For example (as we'll learn in Chapter 9), we measure the physical intensity of a sound (sound pressure level) in "decibels," but we refer to our sensation as "loudness."

Fechner invented new ways to measure what people see, hear, and feel. All of his methods are still in use today. In explaining these methods here, we will use absolute threshold as an example because it is simpler to understand, but we would use the same methods to determine difference thresholds such as ΔI. An **absolute threshold** is the minimum intensity of a stimulus that can be detected (Table 1.1). This returns us to the question we raised earlier: What is the faintest sound you can hear? Of course, we could ask the same question about the faintest light, the lightest touch, and so forth. (See **Web Activity 1.1: Psychophysics**.)

absolute threshold The minimum amount of stimulation necessary for a person to detect a stimulus 50% of the time.

method of constant stimuli A psychophysical method in which many stimuli, ranging from rarely to almost always perceivable (or rarely to almost always perceivably different from a reference stimulus), are presented one at a time. Participants respond to each presentation: "yes/no," "same/different," and so on.

Psychophysical Methods

How can we measure an absolute threshold in a valid and reliable manner? One method is known as the **method of constant stimuli**. The method requires creating many stimuli with different intensities in order to find the tiniest intensity that can be detected (Figure 1.6). If you've had a hearing test, you

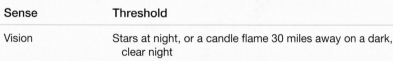

TABLE 1.1 *Some commonsense absolute thresholds*

Sense	Threshold
Vision	Stars at night, or a candle flame 30 miles away on a dark, clear night
Hearing	A ticking watch 20 feet away, with no other noises
Vestibular	A tilt of less than half a minute on a clock face
Taste	A teaspoon of sugar in 2 gallons of water
Smell	A drop of perfume in three rooms
Touch	The wing of a fly falling on your cheek from a height of 3 inches

Source: From Galanter, 1962.

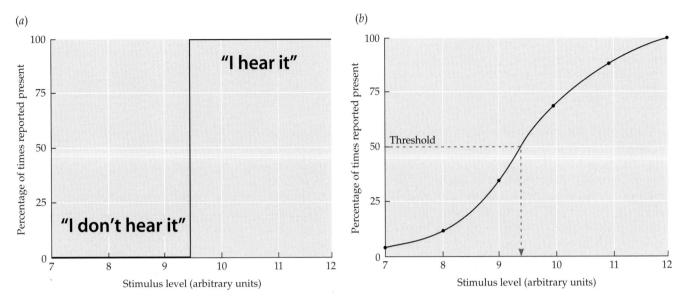

FIGURE 1.6 The method of constant stimuli. (*a*) We might expect threshold to be a sharp change in detection from never reported to always reported, as depicted here, but this is not so. (*b*) In reality, experiments measuring absolute threshold produce shallower functions relating stimulus to response. A somewhat arbitrary point on the curve, often 50% detection, is designated as the threshold.

may recall having to report when you could and could not hear a tone that the audiologist played to you over headphones. In this test, intensities of all of the tones would be relatively low, not too far above or below the intensity where your threshold was expected to be. The tones, varying in intensity, would be presented randomly, and tones would be presented multiple times at each intensity. The "multiple times" piece is important. Subtle perceptual judgments (e.g., threshold judgments) are variable. The stimulus varies for physical reasons. The observer varies. His attention waivers. His sensory systems fluctuate for all sorts of reasons. As a consequence, one measure is almost never enough. You need to repeat the measure over and over and then average responses or otherwise describe the pattern of results. Some experiments require thousands of repetitions (thousands of "trials") to establish a sufficiently reliable data point. Returning to our auditory example, as the listener your task would be to report whether you heard a tone or not. You would always report hearing a tone that was relatively far above threshold, and almost never report hearing a tone that was well below threshold. In between, however, you would be more likely to hear some tone intensities than not hear them, and you would hear other, lower intensities on only a few presentations. In general, the intensity at which a stimulus would be detected 50% of the time is chosen as the threshold.

That 50% definition of absolute threshold is rather interesting. Weren't we looking for a way to measure the weakest detectable stimulus? Using the hearing example, should that be a value below which we just can't hear anything (see Figure 1.6*a*)? It turns out that no such hard boundary exists. Because of variability in the nervous system, stimuli near threshold will be detected sometimes and missed other times. As a result, the function relating the probability of detection with the stimulus level will be more gradual (see Figure 1.6*b*), and we must settle for a somewhat arbitrary definition of an absolute threshold. (We will return to this issue when we talk about signal detection theory.)

FIGURE 1.7 The method of limits. Here the subject attends to multiple series of trials. For each series, the intensity of the stimulus is gradually increased or decreased until the subject detects (Y) or fails to detect (N), respectively, the stimulus. For each series, an estimate of the threshold (red dashed line) is taken to be the average of the stimulus level just before and after the change in perception.

	Trial series							
	↓1	↑2	↓3	↑4	↓5	↑6	↓7	↑8
20	Y						Y	
19	Y		Y		Y		Y	
18	Y		Y		Y		Y	
17	Y		Y		Y		Y	
16	Y		Y		Y		Y	Y
15	Y	Y	Y	Y	Y	Y	Y	Y
14	Y	N	Y	N	Y	N	Y	Y
13	N	N	Y	N	Y	N	N	Y
12		N	N	N	N	N		N
11		N		N		N		N
10		N		N		N		N
	13.5	14.5	12.5	14.5	12.5	14.5	13.5	12.5

Intensity (arbitrary units)

Crossover values (average = 13.5)

The method of constant stimuli is simple to use, but it can be somewhat inefficient in an experiment because much of the subject's time can be spent with stimuli that are clearly well above or below threshold. A somewhat more efficient approach is the **method of limits** (Figure 1.7). With this method, the experimenter begins with the same set of stimuli—in this case, tones that vary in intensity. Instead of a random presentation, tones are presented in order of increasing or decreasing intensity. When tones are presented in ascending order, from faintest to loudest, listeners are asked to report when they first hear the tone. With descending order, the task is to report when the tone is no longer audible. The data from an experiment such as this show that there is some "overshoot" in judgments. It usually takes more intensity to report hearing the tone when intensity is increasing, and it takes more decreases in intensity before a listener reports that the tone cannot be heard. We take the average of these crossover points—when listeners shift from reporting hearing the tone to not hearing the tone, and vice versa—to be the threshold.

The third and final of these classic measures of thresholds is the **method of adjustment**. This method is just like the method of limits, except the subject is the one who steadily increases or decreases the intensity of the stimulus. The method of adjustment may be the easiest method to understand because it is much like day-to-day activities such as adjusting the volume dial on a stereo or the dimmer switch for a light. But even though it's the easiest to understand, the method of adjustment is not usually used to measure thresholds. The method would be perfect if threshold data looked like Figure 1.6*a*. But because reality is closer to Figure 1.6*b*, it is hard to get people to reliably adjust intensity to the same value across people and time.

Scaling Methods and Supertasters

Moving beyond absolute thresholds and difference thresholds, suppose we wanted to know about the magnitude of your experiences. For example, we might give you a light and ask how much additional light you would need to make another light that looks twice as bright? That turns out to be an answerable question. We could give you a knob to adjust so that you could set the second light to appear twice as bright as the first, and you could do it.

We don't need to give the observers a light to adjust. A surprisingly straightforward way to address the question of the strength or size of a sensation is to simply ask observers to rate the experience. For example, we could give observers a series of sugar solutions and ask them to assign numbers to each sample, governed only by the rule that the numbers make sense to the observer. Sweeter solutions should get bigger numbers, and if solution A seems twice as sweet as solution B, the number assigned to A should be twice the number assigned to B. This method is called **magnitude estimation**. This approach actually works well when observers are free to choose their own range of numbers. More typically, we might begin the experiment by presenting one solution at an intermediate level and telling the taster to label this level as a specific value—10, for instance. All of the responses should then be scaled sensibly above or below this standard of 10. If you do this for sugar solutions, you will get data that look like **Figure 1.8**.

method of limits A psychophysical method in which the particular dimension of a stimulus, or the difference between two stimuli, is varied incrementally until the participant responds differently.

method of adjustment A method of limits in which the subject controls the change in the stimulus.

magnitude estimation A psychophysical method in which the participant assigns values according to perceived magnitudes of the stimuli.

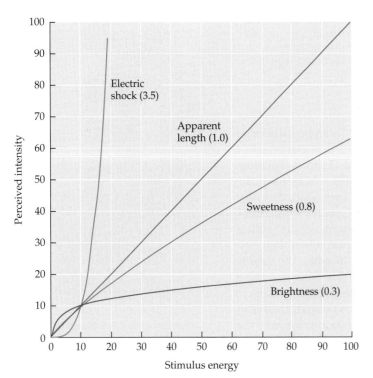

FIGURE 1.8 Magnitude estimation. The lines on this graph represent data from magnitude estimation experiments using electric shocks of different currents, lines of different lengths, solutions of different sweetness levels, and lights of different brightnesses. The exponents that describe these lines are 3.5, 1.0, 0.8, and 0.3, respectively. For exponents greater than 1, such as for electric shock, Fechner's law does not hold, and Stevens' power law must be used instead.

Harvard psychologist S. S. Stevens (1962, 1975) invented magnitude estimation. He, his students, and successors measured functions like the one in Figure 1.8 for many different sensations. Even though observers are asked to assign numbers to private experience, the results are orderly and lawful. However, they are not the same for every type of sensation. That relationship between stimulus intensity and sensation is described by what is now known as **Stevens' power law**:

$$S = aI^b$$

which states that the sensation (*S*) is related to the stimulus intensity (*I*) by an exponent (*b*). So, for example, experienced sensation might rise with intensity squared (*I* × *I*). If the exponent is less than 1, this means that the sensation grows less rapidly than the stimulus. This is what Fechner's law and Weber's law would predict.

Suppose you have some lit candles and you light 10 more. If you started with 1 candle, the change from 1 to 11 candles must be quite dramatic. If we add 10 to 100, the change will be modest. Adding 10 to 10,000 won't even be noticeable. In fact, the exponent for brightness is about 0.3. The exponent for sweetness is about 0.8 (Bartoshuk, 1979). Properties like length have exponents near 1, so, reasonably enough, a 12-inch-long stick looks twice as long as a 6-inch stick (S. S. Stevens and Galanter, 1957). Note that this relationship is true over only a moderate range of sizes. An inch added to the size of a spider changes your sensory experience much more than an inch added to the height of a giraffe. Some stimuli have exponents greater than 1. In the painful case of electric shock, the pain grows with $I^{3.5}$ (Stevens, Carton, and Shickman, 1958), so a 4-fold increase in the electrical current is experienced as a 128-fold increase in pain!

At this point in our discussion of psychophysics, it is worth taking a moment to compare the three laws that have been presented: Weber's, Fechner's, and Stevens'.

- *Weber's law* involves a clear objective measurement. We know how much we varied the stimulus, and either the observers can tell that the stimulus changed or they cannot.
- *Fechner's law* begins with the same sort of objective measurements as Weber's, but the law is actually a calculation based on some assumptions about how sensation works. In particular, Fechner's law assumes that all JNDs are perceptually equivalent. In fact, this assumption turns out to be incorrect and leads to some places where the "law" is violated, such as in the electric shock example just given.

Stevens' power law A principle describing the relationship between stimulus and resulting sensation that says the magnitude of subjective sensation is proportional to the stimulus magnitude raised to an exponent.

FIGURE 1.9 Cross-modality matching. The levels of bitterness of concentrated PROP perceived by nontasters, medium tasters, and supertasters of PROP are shown on the left. The perceived intensities of a variety of everyday sensations are shown on the right. The arrow from each taster type indicates the level of sensation to which those tasters matched the taste of PROP. (Data from Fast, 2004.)

- *Stevens' power law* describes rating data quite well, but notice that rating data are qualitatively different from the data that supported Weber's law. We can record the subjects' ratings and we can check whether those ratings are reasonable and consistent, but there is no way to know whether they are objectively right or wrong.

A useful variant of the scaling method can show us that different individuals can live in different sensory worlds, even if they are exposed to the same stimuli. The method is **cross-modality matching** (J. C. Stevens, 1959). In cross-modality matching, an observer adjusts a stimulus of one sort to match the perceived magnitude of a stimulus of a completely different sort. For example, we might ask a listener to adjust the brightness of a light until it matches the loudness of a particular tone. People can do this and, for the most part, everyone with "normal" vision and hearing will produce the same pattern of matches of a sound to a light. We still can't examine someone else's private experience, but at least the relationship of visual experience and auditory experience appears to be similar across individuals.

Not so when it comes to the sense of taste. There is a molecule called propylthiouracil (PROP) that some people experience as very bitter, while others experience it as almost tasteless. Still others fall in between. This relationship can be examined formally with cross-modal matching (Marks et al., 1988). If observers are asked to match the bitterness of PROP to other sensations completely unrelated to taste, we do not find the sort of agreement that is found when observers match sounds and lights (**Figure 1.9**). Some people—we'll call them nontasters—match the taste of PROP to very weak sensations like the sound of a watch or a whisper. A group of **supertasters** assert that the bitterness of PROP is similar in intensity to the brightness of the sun or the most intense pain ever experienced. Medium tasters match PROP to weaker stimuli, such as the smell of frying bacon or the pain of a mild headache (Bartoshuk, Fast, and Snyder, 2005). As we will see in Chapter 15, there is a genetic basis for this variation, and it has wide implications for our food preferences and, consequently, for health. For the present discussion, this example shows that we can use scaling methods to quantify what appear to be real differences in individuals' taste experience.

Signal Detection Theory

Let's return to thresholds—particularly to the fact that they are not absolute. An important way to think about this fact and to deal with it, experimentally, is known as **signal detection theory** (D. M. Green and Swets, 1966). Signal detection theory holds that the stimulus you're trying to detect (the "signal") is always being detected in the presence of "noise." If you sit in the quietest place you can find and you wear your best noise-canceling headphones, you will find that you can still hear *something*. Similarly, if you close your eyes in a

cross-modality matching The ability to match the intensities of sensations that come from different sensory modalities. This ability enables insight into sensory differences. For example, a listener might adjust the brightness of a light until it matches the loudness of a tone.

supertaster An individual whose perception of taste sensations is the most intense.

signal detection theory A psychophysical theory that quantifies the response of an observer to the presentation of a signal in the presence of noise. Measures obtained from a series of presentations are sensitivity (d') and criterion of the observer.

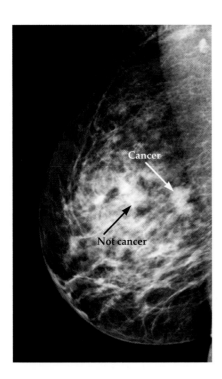

FIGURE 1.10 Mammograms, X-rays of the breast, are used to screen women for breast cancer. Reading such images is a difficult perceptual task, even for a trained radiologist. (Courtesy of Dr. Robyn Birdwell, Harvard Medical School.)

criterion In signal detection theory, an internal threshold that is set by the observer. If the internal response is above criterion, the observer gives one response (e.g., "yes, I hear that"). Below criterion, the observer gives another response (e.g., "no, I hear nothing").

dark room, you still see something—a mottled pattern of gray with occasional brighter flashes. This is internal noise, the static in your nervous system. When you're trying to detect a faint sound or flash of light, you must be able to detect it in the presence of that internal noise. Down near threshold, it will be hard to tell a real stimulus from a particularly vigorous surge of internal noise.

There is external noise too. Consider that radiologist, introduced earlier, reading a mammogram looking for signs of breast cancer. In **Figure 1.10**, it is the marked fuzzy white region that is the danger sign. As you can see, however, the mammogram contains lots of other similar regions. We can think of the cancer as the signal. By the time it is presented to the radiologist in an X-ray, it is a signal plus noise. Elsewhere in the image, and in other images, are stimuli that are just noise. The radiologist is a visual expert, trained to find these particular signals, but sometimes the signal will be lost in the noise and missed, and sometimes some noise will look enough like cancer to generate a false alarm (Nodine et al., 2002).

Of course, sometimes neither internal nor external noise is much of a problem. When you see this dot, •, you are seeing it in the presence of internal noise, but the magnitude of that noise is so much smaller than the signal generated by the dot that it has no real impact. Similarly, the dot may not be exactly the same as other dots, but that variation, the external noise, is also too small to have an impact. If asked about the presence of a dot here, •, and its absence here, , you will be correct in your answer essentially every time. Signal detection theory exists to help us understand what's going on when we make decisions under conditions of uncertainty.

Since we are not expert mammographers, let's introduce a different example to illustrate the workings of signal detection theory. You're in the shower. The water is making a noise that we will, imaginatively, call *noise*. Sometimes the noise sounds louder to you; sometimes it seems softer. We could plot the distribution of your perception of noise as shown in **Figure 1.11a**.

Now the phone rings. That will be our *signal*. Your perceptual task is to detect the signal in the presence of the noise. What you hear is a combination of the ring and the shower. That is, the signal is added to the noise, so we can imagine that now we have two distributions of responses in your nervous system: a noise-alone distribution and a signal-plus-noise distribution (Figure 1.11b).

For the sake of simplicity, let's suppose that "more" response means that it sounds more like the phone is ringing. So now your job is to decide whether it's time to jump out of the shower and answer what might be the phone. The problem is that you have no way of knowing at any given moment whether you're hearing noise alone or signal plus noise. The best you can do is to decide on a **criterion** level of response (Figure 1.11c). If the response in your nervous system exceeds that criterion, you will jump out of the shower and run naked and dripping to find the phone. If the level is below the criterion, you will decide that it is not a ring and stay in the shower. Note that this "decision" is made automatically; it's not that you sit down to make a conscious (soggy) choice. Thus a criterion, in signal detection theory, is a value that is somehow determined by the observer. A response, inside the observer, above criterion will be taken as evidence that a signal is present. A response below that level will be treated as noise.

There are four possible outcomes (Figure 1.11d–g): You might say "no" when there is no ring; that's a correct rejection (Figure 1.11d). You might say "yes" when there is a ring; that's known as a hit (Figure 1.11e). Then there are the errors. If you jump out of the shower when there's no ring, that's a false alarm (Figure 1.11f). If you miss the call, that's a miss (Figure 1.11g).

How sensitive are you to the ring? In the graphs of Figure 1.11, the sensitivity is shown as the separation between the noise-alone and signal-plus-noise

FIGURE 1.11 Detecting a stimulus using signal detection theory (SDT). (*a*) SDT assumes that all perceptual decisions must be made against a background of noise (the red curve) generated in the world or in the nervous system. (*b*) Your job is to distinguish nervous system responses due to noise alone (red) or to signal plus noise (blue). (*c*) The best you can do is establish a criterion (dotted line) and declare that you detect something if the response is above that criterion. SDT includes four classes of responses: (*d*) correct rejections (you say "no" and there is, indeed, no signal); (*e*) hits (you say "yes" and there is a signal); (*f*) false alarm errors (you say "yes" to nothing); and (*g*) miss errors (you say "no" to a real signal).

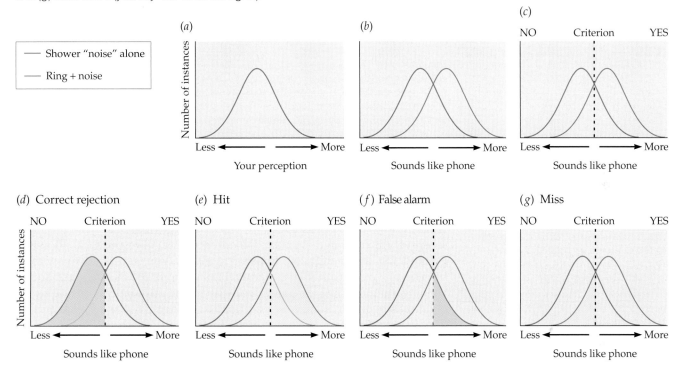

distributions. If the distributions are on top of each other (**Figure 1.12***a*), you can't tell noise alone from signal plus noise. A false alarm is just as likely as a hit. By knowing the relationship of hits to false alarms, you can calculate a **sensitivity** measure known as *d′* (*d*-prime), which would be about zero in Figure 1.12*a*. In Figure 1.12*c* we see the case of a large *d′*. Here you could detect

sensitivity In signal detection theory, a value that defines the ease with which an observer can tell the difference between the presence and absence of a stimulus or the difference between stimulus 1 and stimulus 2.

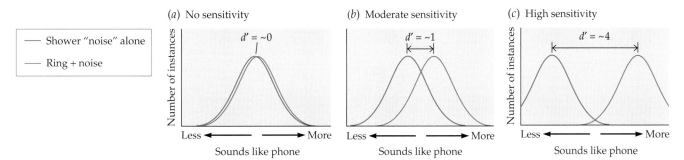

FIGURE 1.12 Your sensitivity to a stimulus is illustrated by the separation between the distributions of your response to noise alone (red curve) and to signal plus noise (blue). This separation is captured by the measure *d′* (*d*-prime). (*a*) If the distributions completely overlap, *d′* = 0 and you have no ability to detect the signal. (*b*) If *d′* is intermediate, you have some sensitivity but your performance will be imperfect. (*c*) If *d′* is big, then distinguishing signal from noise is trivial.

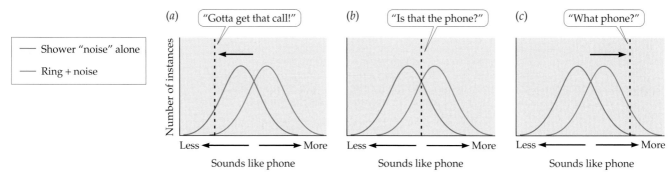

FIGURE 1.13 For a fixed d', all you can do is change the pattern of your errors by shifting the response criterion. If you don't want to miss any signals, you move your criterion to the left (a), but then you make more false alarms. If you don't like false alarms, you move to the right (c), but then you make more miss errors. In all these cases (a–c), your sensitivity, d', remains the same.

receiver operating characteristic (ROC) curve In studies of signal detection, the graphical plot of the hit rate as a function of the false-alarm rate. If these are the same, points fall on the diagonal, indicating that the observer cannot tell the difference between the presence and absence of the signal. As the observer's sensitivity increases, the curve bows upward toward the upper left corner. That point represents a perfect ability to distinguish signal from noise (100% hits, 0% false alarms).

essentially all the rings and never make a false alarm. The situation we've been discussing is in between (Figure 1.12b).

Now suppose you're waiting for an important call. Even though you really don't want to miss the call, you can't magically make yourself more sensitive. All you can do is move the criterion level of response, as shown in **Figure 1.13a**. If you shift your criterion to the left, you won't miss many calls, but you will make lots of false alarms (Figure 1.13a). That's annoying. You're running around naked, dripping on the floor, and traumatizing the cat for no good reason. If you shift your criterion to the right, you won't make those annoying false alarms, but now you will miss most of the calls (Figure 1.13c). For a fixed value of d', changing the criterion changes the hits and false alarms in predictable ways. If you plot false alarms on the x-axis of a graph against hits on the y-axis for different criterion values, you get a curve known as a **receiver operating characteristic (ROC) curve** (Figure 1.14).

Suppose you were guessing (the Figure 1.12a situation), then you might guess "yes" on 40% of the occasions when the phone rang, but you would also guess "yes" on 40% of the occasions when the phone did not ring. If you moved your criterion and guessed "yes" on 80% of phone-present occasions, you would also guess "yes" on 80% of phone-absent occasions. Your data would fall on that "chance performance" diagonal in Figure 1.14. If you were perfect (the Figure 1.12c situation), you would make 100% hits and 0% false alarms and your data point would lie at the upper left corner in Figure 1.14. Situations in between (Figure 1.12b) produce curves between guessing

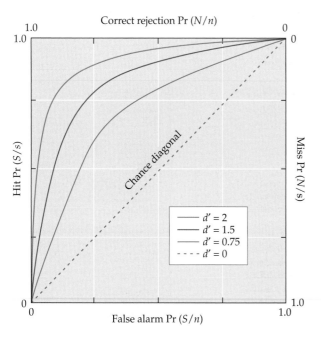

FIGURE 1.14 Theoretical receiver operating characteristic (ROC) curves for different values of d'. Note that $d' = 0$ when performance is at chance. When d' increases, the probability of hits and correct rejections increases, and the probability of misses and false alarms decreases. Pr(N/n) = probability of response "no signal present" when no signal is present (correct rejection); Pr(N/s) = probability of response "no signal present" when signal is present (miss); Pr(S/n) = probability of response "signal present" when no signal is present (false alarm); Pr(S/s) = probability of response "signal present" when signal is present (hit).

FIGURE 1.15 Joseph Fourier was a French mathematician and physicist who first showed how very complex signals could be understood more easily as a combination of simple sine wave components.

and perfection (the green, purple, and blue curves in Figure 1.14). If your data lie below the chance line, you did the experiment wrong!

Let's return to our radiologist. She has an ROC curve whose closeness to perfection reflects her expertise. On that ROC, her criterion can slide up and to the right, in which case she will make more hits but also more false alarms, or down and to the left, in which case she will make fewer false alarms but more misses. Where she places her criterion (consciously or unconsciously) will depend on many factors. Does the patient have factors that make her more or less likely to have cancer? What is the perceived "cost" of a missed cancer? What is the perceived cost of a false alarm? You can see that what started out as a query about the lack of absolute thresholds can become, quite literally, a matter of life and death.

Signal detection theory can become a rather complicated topic in detail. To learn about how to calculate d' and about ROC curves, there are many useful websites and several texts (e.g., Macmillan and Creelman, 2005; see Burgess, 2010, if you're interested in the application to radiology).

Fourier Analysis

While we're on the topic of signals, there's just one more tool in the researcher's arsenal that will prove helpful to you as you learn about sensation and perception. French mathematician **Joseph Fourier** (1768–1830) (**Figure 1.15**) developed analyses that permit modern perception scientists to better understand how complex sounds such as music and speech, complex head motions, and complex images such as objects and scenes can be decomposed into a set of simpler signals. To understand Fourier's analytical technique, let's begin with sounds, because they're easy to describe.

One of the simplest kinds of sounds is a **sine wave** (or, in hearing, a *pure tone*). The air pressure in a sine wave changes continuously (sinusoidally) at one frequency (**Figure 1.16**). The time taken for one complete cycle of a sine wave is the **period**, or **wavelength**, of the sine wave. The height of the wave is its amplitude. The **phase** of the wave is its position relative to a fixed marker. Phase is measured in degrees, with 360 degrees of phase across one period, like the 360 degrees around a circle. Thus, in Figure 1.16 the red and blue sine waves differ by 90 degrees in phase.

Sine waves are not common, everyday sounds, because few vibrations in the world are so pure. If you've taken a hearing test or used tuning forks, you may have heard sine waves. Flutes can produce musical notes that are close

sine wave 1. In hearing, a waveform for which variation as a function of time is a sine function. Also called *pure tone*. 2. In vision, a pattern for which variation in a property like brightness or color as a function of space is a sine function.

period or wavelength The time (or space) required for one cycle of a repeating waveform.

phase 1. In vision, the relative position of a grating. 2. In hearing, the relative timing of a sine wave.

FIGURE 1.16 Sine waves. (*a*) A vibrating tuning fork produces sinusoidal variations in air pressure—variations that are the stimulus for hearing. We can plot those variations as sine waves. The period, or wavelength, is the time taken for one complete cycle (marked by the gray box). The amplitude is the height of the wave. The position of the wave relative to a fixed marker is its phase—measured in degrees out of a total of 360 degrees, like the 360 degrees around a circle. The red and blue sine waves shown here are separated by 90 degrees of phase. (*b*) This tuning fork produces a sine wave that has half the amplitude and half the wavelength of the waves in (*a*). In hearing, the frequency of a sine wave is the number of cycles per second. In vision, you might have sinusoidal variation of light over space; then the frequency would be in cycles per degree of visual angle (see Chapter 3).

(*a*)

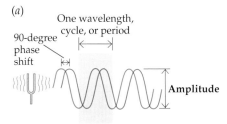

One wavelength, cycle, or period

90-degree phase shift

Amplitude

(*b*)

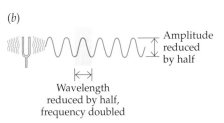

Amplitude reduced by half

Wavelength reduced by half, frequency doubled

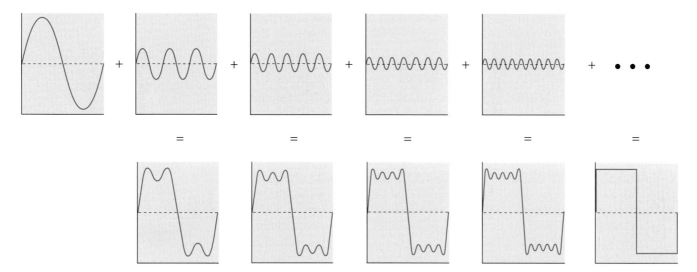

FIGURE 1.17 Every complex sound wave can be analyzed as a combination of sine waves, each with its own frequency, amplitude, and phase. Here, multiple sine waves (top) are added together to form more complex waveforms (bottom). When infinitely more sine waves with even higher frequencies are added, a square wave (bottom right) can be constructed.

Fourier analysis A mathematical procedure by which any signal can be separated into component sine waves at different frequencies. Combining these sine waves will reproduce the original signal.

spatial frequency The number of cycles of a grating per unit of visual angle (usually specified in cycles per degree).

cycles per degree The number of pairs of dark and bright bars per degree of visual angle.

to pure tones, but other musical instruments, human voices, birds, cars, and almost all other sound sources in the world produce complex sounds.

If pure tones are so uncommon, you may wonder why we're bothering to discuss them. It turns out that all sounds, no matter how complex, can be described as a combination of sine waves (**Figure 1.17**). Fourier proved that even the cacophony of a room full of people talking or the swelling sound of a full orchestra can be broken down into combinations of sine waves at many different frequencies with different amplitudes and phases. Any complex sound can be broken down into individual sine wave components through this process, which is called **Fourier analysis**. (See **Web Activity 1.2: Fourier Analysis**.)

Fourier analysis is a powerful mathematical tool that is used in many research fields. As we will see in Chapter 12, Fourier analysis is used extensively by vestibular and spatial orientation researchers. Vision researchers use Fourier analyses to explore the visual system in ways quite similar to those employed by hearing researchers. While sounds are described as changes in pressure across time, images can be described as changes in light and dark across space. Images can be broken down into components that capture how often changes from light to dark occur over a particular region in space, called **spatial frequencies**. Spatial frequencies are defined as the number of these light/dark changes across 1 degree of a person's visual field. There would be 360 degrees around the head. One degree is about the size of a thumbnail at arm's length. Thus, in vision the units of spatial frequency are **cycles per degree** of visual angle (**Figure 1.18**). Just as a complex sound can be broken down into a set of sine wave pure tones, a visual stimulus can be broken down into component spatial frequencies. We will have more to say about this in Chapter 3.

Fourier analysis is more than a mathematical curiosity. To a first approximation, your auditory and visual systems appear to break down real-world sounds and images into sine wave components. When we study how individual neurons respond to sounds and images, we find many neurons that have strong preferences for some frequency components compared to others, and this is

(*a*) High-frequency
square wave

10 cycles

(*b*) Low-frequency
square wave

5 cycles

(*c*) High-contrast
sinusoidal spatial grid

(*d*) Low-contrast
sinusoidal spatial grid

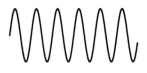

(*e*) Normal

(*f*) High frequencies filtered out

(*g*) Low frequencies filtered out

FIGURE 1.18 The spacing between dark and light stripes in (*a*) has a spatial frequency that is twice the spatial frequency of (*b*). When spatial frequency is represented as sinusoids (*c*, *d*), there are greater amplitude differences for high-contrast (*c*) than for low contrast (*d*). A photograph of penguins (*e*) illustrates how images appear when high spatial frequencies are taken away (filtered out) (*f*) and when low spatial frequencies are filtered out (*g*). (From Breedlove, Watson, and Rosenzweig, 2010.)

especially true for early stages of auditory and visual processing. Understanding how simpler sounds and images are encoded provides essential insights into how we hear and see real events and objects in our world.

Sensory Neuroscience and the Biology of Perception

During the nineteenth century, when Weber and Fechner were initiating the experimental study of perception, physiologists were hard at work learning how the senses and the brain operate. Much of this work involved research on animals. It's worth spending a moment on a key assumption here: that studies of animal senses tell us something about human senses. That may seem obvious, but the assumption requires the belief that there is some continuity between the way animals work and the way humans work.

The most powerful argument for a continuity between humans and animals came from Darwin's theory of evolution. During the 1800s, Charles Darwin (1809–1882) proposed his revolutionary theory in *The Origin of Species* (1859). Although many of the ideas found in that book had been brewing for some time, controversy expanded with vigor following Darwin's provocative statements in *The Descent of Man* (1871), where he argued that humans evolved from apes. If there was continuity in the structure of the bones, heart, and kidneys of cows, dogs, monkeys, and humans, then why wouldn't there be continuity in the structure and function of their respective senses and nervous systems?

FIGURE 1.19 Johannes Müller formulated the doctrine of specific nerve energies, which says that we are aware only of the activity in our nerves, and we cannot be aware of the world itself. For this reason, what is most important is *which* nerves are stimulated, not *how* they are stimulated.

An inescapable implication of the theory of evolution is that we can learn much about human sensation and perception by studying the structure and function of our nonhuman relatives.

At the same time that Darwin was at work in England, the German physiologist **Johannes Müller** (1801–1858) (Figure 1.19) was writing a very influential book, his *Handbook of Physiology* (1838/1912). In this book, in addition to covering most of what was then known about physiology, Müller formulated the **doctrine of specific nerve energies**. The central idea of this doctrine is that we are aware only of the activity in our nerves, and we cannot be directly aware of the world itself. Further, what is most important is *which* nerves are stimulated, and not *how* they are stimulated. For example, we experience vision because the optic nerve leading from the eye to the brain is stimulated, but it does not matter whether light, or something else, stimulated the nerve. To prove to yourself that this is true, close your eyes and press very gently on the outside corner of one eye through the lid. (This works better in a darkened room.) You will see a spot of light toward the inside of your visual field by your nose. Despite the lack of stimulation by light, your brain interprets the input from your optic nerve as informing you about something visual.

The **cranial nerves** leading into and out of the skull illustrate the doctrine of specific nerve energies (Figure 1.20). The pair of optic nerves is one of 12 pairs of cranial nerves that pass through small openings in the bone at the base of the skull. The cranial nerves are dedicated mainly to sensory and motor systems. Cranial nerves are labeled both by name and by the Roman numeral that roughly corresponds to the order of their locations beginning from the front of the skull. Three of the cranial nerves—**olfactory (I)**, **optic (II)**, and **vestibulocochlear (VIII)**—are exclusively dedicated to sensory information. The vestibulocochlear nerve serves spatial orientation ("vestibular"; see Chapter 12) in addition to hearing (discussed in Chapter 9). Three more—**oculomotor (III)**, **trochlear (IV)**, and **abducens (VI)**—are dedicated to muscles that move the eyes. The other six cranial nerves either are exclusively motor (spinal accessory [XI] and hypoglossal [XII]) or convey both sensory and motor signals (trigeminal [V], facial [VII], glossopharyngeal [IX], and vagus [X]). With respect to our study of perception, later we will return to the first six cranial nerves described here, because each one plays an important role in our ability to use our senses to learn about the world around us.

The doctrine of specific nerve energies extends beyond the cranial nerves, as illustrated especially well by our senses of hot and cold on the skin. Two special types of nerve cells are warmth fibers and cold fibers, which respond to increases and decreases in temperature on the skin. Capsaicin, a chemical that naturally occurs in chili peppers, causes warmth fibers to fire, creating a sense of increasing heat even though the temperature has not changed. On the other hand, menthol, which imparts the minty flavor in cough drops, stimulates cold fibers (Bautista et al., 2007), so skin feels cooler without getting physically colder. In sufficiently high amounts, both capsaicin and menthol stimulate pain receptors in the skin. Paradoxically, this is why ointments often contain capsaicin or menthol, where their effect is to suppress real physical pain.

doctrine of specific nerve energies A doctrine, formulated by Johannes Müller, stating that the nature of a sensation depends on which sensory fibers are stimulated, not on how fibers are stimulated.

cranial nerves Twelve pairs of nerves (one for each side of the body) that originate in the brain stem and reach sense organs and muscles through openings in the skull.

olfactory (I) nerves The first pair of cranial nerves. The axons of the olfactory sensory neurons bundle together after passing through the cribriform plate to form the olfactory nerve, which conducts impulses from the olfactory epithelia in the nose to the olfactory bulb.

optic (II) nerves The second pair of cranial nerves, which arise from the retina and carry visual information to the thalamus and other parts of the brain.

vestibulocochlear (VIII) nerves The eighth pair of cranial nerves, which connect the inner ear with the brain, transmitting impulses concerned with hearing and spatial orientation. The vestibulocochlear nerve is composed of the cochlear nerve branch and the vestibular nerve branch.

oculomotor (III) nerves The third pair of cranial nerves, which innervate all the extrinsic muscles of the eye except the lateral rectus and the superior oblique muscles, and which innervate the elevator muscle of the upper eyelid, the ciliary muscle, and the sphincter muscle of the pupil.

trochlear (IV) nerves The fourth pair of cranial nerves, which innervate the superior oblique muscles of the eyeballs.

abducens (VI) nerves The sixth pair of cranial nerves, which innervate the lateral rectus muscle of each eye.

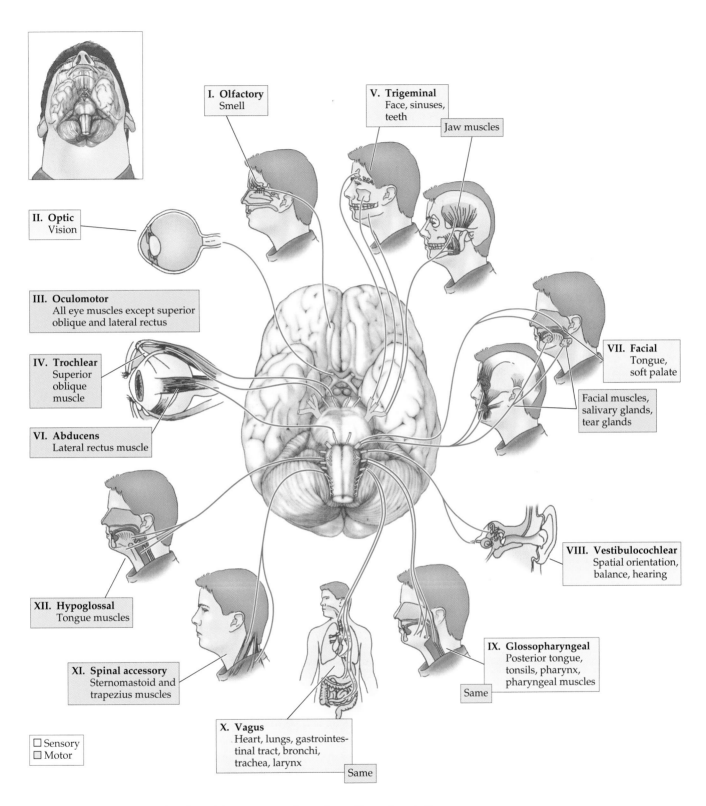

I. Olfactory
Smell

V. Trigeminal
Face, sinuses, teeth

Jaw muscles

II. Optic
Vision

III. Oculomotor
All eye muscles except superior oblique and lateral rectus

IV. Trochlear
Superior oblique muscle

VI. Abducens
Lateral rectus muscle

VII. Facial
Tongue, soft palate

Facial muscles, salivary glands, tear glands

VIII. Vestibulocochlear
Spatial orientation, balance, hearing

XII. Hypoglossal
Tongue muscles

XI. Spinal accessory
Sternomastoid and trapezius muscles

IX. Glossopharyngeal
Posterior tongue, tonsils, pharynx, pharyngeal muscles

Same

☐ Sensory
☐ Motor

X. Vagus
Heart, lungs, gastrointestinal tract, bronchi, trachea, larynx

Same

FIGURE 1.20 Twelve pairs of cranial nerves pass through small openings in the bone at the base of the skull. All of these nerves conduct information for sensation, motor behavior, or both. (After Rosenzweig, Breedlove, and Watson, 2005.)

FIGURE 1.21 Cortex of the human brain. The darkened areas show where information from four different senses first reaches the cortex.

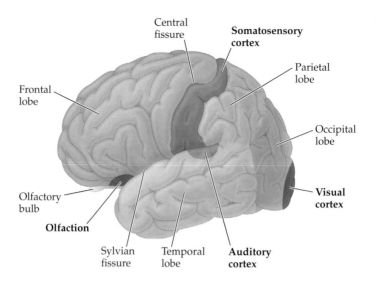

polysensory Blending multiple sensory systems.

vitalism The idea that there is a force in life that is distinct from physical entities.

FIGURE 1.22 Hermann von Helmholtz was one of the greatest scientists of all time. He made many important discoveries in physiology and perception.

Just as different nerves are dedicated to individual sensory and motor tasks, areas of the brain stem and cerebral cortex are similarly dedicated to particular tasks. Areas of the cortex dedicated to perception actually are much larger than the darkened areas in **Figure 1.21**. The areas depicted here are primary sensory areas; more complex processing is accomplished across cortical regions that spread well beyond these primary areas. For example, visual perception uses cortex that extends both anteriorly (forward) into parietal cortex and ventrally (lower) into regions of the temporal lobe. In addition, as processing extends beyond primary areas, cortex often becomes **polysensory**, meaning that information from more than one sense is being combined in some manner. (See **Web Activity 1.3: Sensory Areas in the Brain**.)

Hermann Ludwig Ferdinand von Helmholtz (1821–1894) (**Figure 1.22**), one of the greatest scientists of the nineteenth century, was greatly influenced by Müller at the Free University of Berlin. Although initially inspired by Müller, Helmholtz truly disliked one of Müller's beliefs: **vitalism**, the idea that there is a force in life that is distinct from physical entities. By contrast, Helmholtz thought that all behavior should be explained by only physical forces. Vitalism violated the physical law of conservation of energy, and Helmholtz wanted the brain and behavior to obey purely physical laws. He chose a very smart place to begin his attack on vitalism. Müller had claimed that the nerve impulse could never be measured experimentally. So, Helmholtz set out to show that the activity of neurons obeys normal rules of physics and chemistry by being the first to effectively measure how fast neurons transmit their signals. (See **Web Activity 1.4: Neurons**.)

In an early effort, Helmholtz estimated that the speed of signal transmission in the nerves in frog legs was about 90 feet per second, comfortably within the range of ordinary physical events. Later he concluded that sensory nerves in people transmitted signals at speeds of between 165 and 330 feet per second. In all cases, this transmission was slower than many people believed at the time. Helmholtz emphasized this point when he noted that a "whale probably feels a wound near its tail in about one second, and requires another second to send back orders to the tail to defend itself" (Koenigsberger, 1906/1965, p. 72). As you may already have guessed, not all neurons are equal when it comes to speed; some are faster than others. It's still interesting to realize that when you stub your toe, a measurable amount of time elapses before you feel the consequences.

(a)

(b)

FIGURE 1.23 (a) Santiago Ramón y Cajal (perhaps not on his happiest day in the lab). (b) Ramón y Cajal created these drawings of brain neurons while peering into a microscope for many hours. Because of his painstaking care and accuracy, his early drawings are still cited today.

Neuronal Connections

During the second half of the nineteenth century, when Helmholtz was making stunning discoveries concerning vision and hearing, other scientists were learning a great deal about how neurons and brains work. After nearly dying of malaria in Cuba, the Spaniard **Santiago Ramón y Cajal** (1852–1934) (Figure 1.23a) returned to his homeland to develop some of the most painstaking and breathtaking insights into the organization of neurons in the brain. Spending many hours peering into a microscope, he made the most spectacular detailed drawings of neurons and their connections ever created. Figure 1.23b shows an example.

Ramón y Cajal's drawings suggested that neurons do not actually touch one another. Instead, he depicted neurons as separate cells with tiny gaps between them. **Sir Charles Sherrington** (1857–1952) (Figure 1.24) named the tiny gap between the axon of one neuron and the dendrite of the next a **synapse** (Figure 1.25), from the Greek word meaning "to fasten together." Sherrington made very careful measurements demonstrating that the speed of neural transmission decreases at synapses, and this work helped us understand that something special happens at this junction where neurons meet to communicate.

Initially, people thought that some sort of electrical wave traveled across the synapse from one neuron to the next. **Otto Loewi** (1873–1961) (Figure 1.26), however, was convinced that this could not be true. One reason is that some neurons increase the response of the next neuron (they are *excitatory*) but other neurons decrease the response of the next neuron (they are *inhibitory*). Loewi proposed that something chemical, instead of electrical, might be at work at the synapse. This insight launched many studies about molecules that travel from the axon across the synapse to the dendrite of the next neuron. These

synapse The junction between neurons that permits information transfer.

FIGURE 1.24 Sir Charles Scott Sherrington was an English neurophysiologist who earned a Nobel Prize for his pioneering discoveries concerning neural activities.

FIGURE 1.25 A synapse. An axon terminal in the presynaptic cell binds to the dendrite of the postsynaptic cell. Neurotransmitter molecules are released by synaptic vesicles in the axon and fit into receptors on the dendrite on the other side of the synapse, thus communicating from the axon of the first neuron to the dendrite of the second neuron.

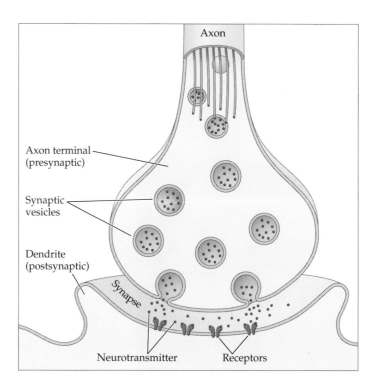

Axon

Axon terminal
(presynaptic)

Synaptic
vesicles

Dendrite
(postsynaptic)

Synapse

Neurotransmitter   Receptors

FIGURE 1.26 Otto Loewi was a German pharmacologist who received a Nobel Prize for demonstrating that neurons communicate with one another by releasing chemicals called neurotransmitters.

neurotransmitter A chemical substance used in neuronal communication at synapses.

molecules are called **neurotransmitters**. There are many different kinds of neurotransmitters in the brain, and individual neurons are selective with respect to which neurotransmitters excite them or inhibit them from firing. Drugs that are psychoactive, such as amphetamines, work by increasing or decreasing the effectiveness of different neurotransmitters. Today, scientists use chemicals that influence the effects of neurotransmitters in efforts to understand pathways in the brain, including those used in perception.

Neural Firing: The Action Potential

After Loewi's discovery of neurotransmitters, scientists learned what it really means to have a neuron "fire." Investigators made the greatest early advances by taking advantage of the fact that some squids have giant neurons as thick as 1 millimeter. **Sir Alan Hodgkin** (1914–1998) and **Sir Andrew Huxley** (born 1917) (**Figure 1.27**) conducted experiments in which they could isolate a single

(a) Hodgkin   (b) Huxley

FIGURE 1.27 Sir Alan Hodgkin (a) and Sir Andrew Huxley (b) were British physiologists who made the first recordings from inside a neuron. They moved from Cambridge to Plymouth, England, to record voltages from inside the giant axons of fresh Atlantic squid. They earned the Nobel Prize for discovering how the action potential works to conduct signals along the axons of neurons.

Na$^+$ entry locally depolarizes axon…

…which sufficiently depolarizes the adjacent region of the axon to open more of the voltage-gated Na$^+$ channels, re-creating the action potential there.

The process continues down the length of the axon.

FIGURE 1.28 An action potential (firing) of a neuron is created when the membrane of the neuron permits sodium ions (Na$^+$) to rush into the cell, thus increasing the voltage. Very quickly afterward, potassium (K$^+$) flows out of the cell, bringing the voltage back to resting voltage. This process occurs along the length of the axon until the action potential reaches the axon terminal.

neuron from the squid and test how the nerve impulse travels along the axon. With such large axons, they could pierce the axon with an electrode to measure voltage, and they could even inject different chemicals inside. They learned that neural firing is actually electrochemical (**Figure 1.28**). Voltage increases along the axon are caused by changes in the membrane of the neuron that permit positively charged sodium ions (Na$^+$) to rush very quickly into the axon from outside. Then the membrane very quickly changes again in a way that pushes positively charged potassium ions (K$^+$) outside the axon, restoring the neuron to its initial resting voltage. All of this—sodium in and potassium out—occurs in about one one-thousandth of a second every time a neuron fires.

Because even the biggest axons in mammals are much, much smaller than the giant squid axon, it is difficult and even rare to be able to insert an electrode inside a neuron. Usually we measure electrical changes from close outside mammalian neurons (**Figure 1.29**). By measuring different aspects of neurons firing, we can learn about how individual neurons encode and transmit information from sense organs through higher levels of the brain.

One way to investigate what a neuron encodes is to try to identify the stimulus that makes it fire the most vigorously. For example, a neuron in the primary visual cortex (see Chapter 3) might respond best to little lines that are vertical, less to lines tilted to the left and right, and not at all to horizontal lines. When you get to the auditory system in Chapter 9, you will learn how

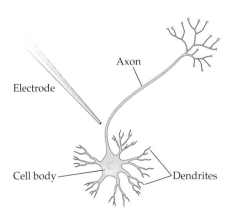

FIGURE 1.29 Neuroscientists record the activity of single neurons with electrodes close to the axons. Modern techniques permit the insertion of multiple electrodes to measure activity in multiple neurons so that we can better understand how neurons work in concert when encoding sensory information.

FIGURE 1.30 These curves were obtained by measuring responses of six different neurons to sounds of different frequencies and intensities. They are called tuning curves because they show how patterns of neural firing are selectively "tuned" to different frequencies that vary from 0 to 50 kilohertz (kHz = 1000 hertz, or 1000 cycles per second). The sound intensity required for a neuron to respond is shown in decibels (dB). (After Breedlove, Watson, and Rosenzweig, 2010.)

neural firing can be timed in ways that match timing within sounds. It's not just how fast neurons can dance, but also how well they can stay with the beat.

Sometimes we learn a lot by simply finding the threshold for getting a neuron to fire. For example, you will learn that different neurons in the auditory nerve, on the way from the ear to the brain, are most sensitive to particular frequencies of sounds. The frequency of the least intense tone that is required to make a neuron fire is a measure of that neuron's best, or characteristic, frequency (**Figure 1.30**).

Neural Firing: Populations of Neurons

electroencephalography (EEG) A technique that, using many electrodes on the scalp, measures electrical activity from populations of many neurons in the brain.

event-related potential (ERP) A measure of electrical activity from a subpopulation of neurons in response to particular stimuli that requires averaging many EEG recordings.

Modern perception researchers use other tools to understand how thousands of neurons work together within the human brain. For example, **electroencephalography (EEG)** measures electrical activity through dozens of electrodes placed on the scalp (**Figure 1.31a**). EEG does not allow researchers to learn what individual neurons are doing or to pinpoint the exact area of neural activity. However, EEG can be used to roughly localize whole populations of neurons and to measure their activities with excellent temporal accuracy.

Like a single behavioral measurement, a single EEG signal recorded for a single event is usually not terribly informative. If you want to know the brain's response to a prick of the skin or a flash of light, you record the responses to many, many repetitions of that stimulus (Figure 1.31b). You then average all the responses aligned to the moment that the stimulus was present. The resulting averaged waveform is known as an **event-related potential (ERP)** (Figure 1.31c). For example, **Figure 1.32** shows the ERPs from an experiment in which observers saw very brief flashes of light lasting from 0.1 to 5 milliseconds (ms); a millisecond is one one-thousandth of a second. Each duration was shown to the observer 400 times. The EEGs for the 300 ms after each flash were averaged together to produce the waveforms—the ERPs—shown in the figure. For the millions of neurons contributing to the particular signal, nothing happens for the first 50 ms or so. Then there is a small negative deflection of the signal, followed by a larger positive deflection. You can see how this sort of recording could tell us about the timing of nervous system responses to stimuli in the world.

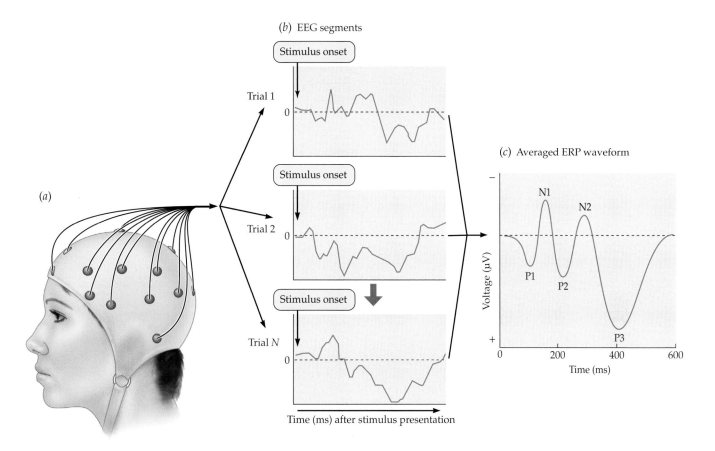

FIGURE 1.31 Electroencephalography. (*a*) Electrical activity from the brain can be recorded from the scalp using an array of electrodes. (*b*) The activity from one electrode is quite variable, even if the same stimulus (perhaps a flash of light) is presented multiple times. (*c*) However, if many such signals are averaged, a regular pattern of electrically positive (P) and negative (N) waves can be seen. (After Breedlove, Watson, and Rosenzweig, 2010.)

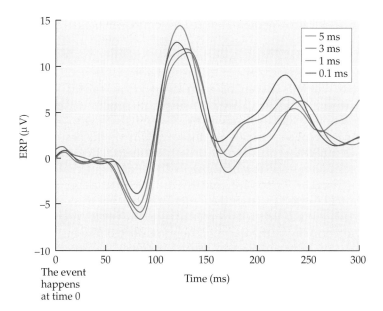

FIGURE 1.32 Event-related potentials produced in response to very brief flashes of light (After Yesilyurt et al., 2009.)

FIGURE 1.33 The massive device used for magnetoencephalography. What looks like a huge helmet contains superconducting magnets.

magnetoencephalography (MEG) A technique, similar to electroencephalography, that measures changes in magnetic activity across populations of many neurons in the brain.

computed tomography (CT) An imaging technology that uses X-rays to create images of slices through volumes of material (e.g., the human body).

A related method, known as **magnetoencephalography** (**MEG**) (Figure 1.33), maintains a good measure of the timing of populations of neurons while providing a better idea of where in the brain neurons are most active. MEG takes advantage of the fact that neurons make very small changes in their local magnetic fields in addition to small electrical changes. With MEG, researchers use extremely sensitive devices to measure these tiny magnetic fields, but superconducting quantum interference devices (SQUIDs) used to measure such tiny changes in magnetic energy are very expensive and are less common than EEG devices.

NEUROIMAGING   Surely one of the most exciting and important changes in neuroscience in the last generation has been the advent of methods that enable us to see the brain while it is still in its owner's living head. We have had X-rays for over 100 years, but an image like the X-ray in Figure 1.34 gives only a ghostly impression of soft tissues like those making up the brain.

Compare that image to the images in Figure 1.35. Figure 1.35*a* shows a **computed tomography**, or **CT**, image. To create CT images, standard X-rays are used in a different manner. A beam of X-rays is passed through the target—the head in this case. The device emitting that beam spins around the head, sending the beam on many paths through the same slice of the head. This

FIGURE 1.34 A standard X-ray of the head does not provide much of a look at the structure of the brain.

(*a*) CT (*b*) MRI

FIGURE 1.35 CT and MRI. (*a*) This CT image is one horizontal slice through the head, from the eyes at the top of the image to the back of the head. The dark areas are the fluid-filled ventricles in the brain, the bright white is bone, and the gray is the brain itself. (*b*) This structural MRI image shows a vertical slice through the middle of the head. You can see the folded cortex of the brain, the spinal cord descending down the neck, and much more.

process is repeated for many slices, until the whole head is scanned. Each time the beam passes through the head, some amount of the emitted energy is absorbed by the intervening tissue. Dense tissue absorbs more than lighter tissue. The detector on the other side of the head measures the amount of energy that was lost on the way through the head. If you have information from many, many passes through the head from many different positions, you can put the slices together to create a three-dimensional picture of the head.

Figure 1.35*b* shows an image produced by **magnetic resonance imaging**, or **MRI**. MRI uses a very different method to make spectacular images. The brain and its owner are placed in a very powerful magnetic field that influences the way the atoms spin. The physics is complicated, but by pulsing the magnetic field it is possible to measure a signal that can indicate the presence of specific elements in the tissue. If you ask about hydrogen in the brain, you are (mostly) asking about water, and your computer can use that signal to reconstruct the structure of the water-rich tissue inside your head.

For the study of the senses and, indeed, for the study of many topics in psychology, the most remarkable use of MRI technology is known as **function magnetic resonance imaging**, or **fMRI**. With fMRI, we can see the activity of the living brain. Here the critical factor is that active brain tissue is hungry brain tissue. It needs oxygen. Oxygen and other supplies are delivered by the blood, so an active brain demands more blood. The result is that there is a **blood oxygen level–dependent** (**BOLD**) **signal** that can be measured by the MRI device. Instead of looking for the presence of water, the magnetic pulses and recording are used to pick up evidence of the demand for more resources. There are some drawbacks. It takes a few seconds for the BOLD signal to rise after a bit of brain becomes more active, so the temporal resolution of the method is not as good as EEG/ERP methods, for example. The spatial resolution is not particularly fine. The machines are noisy, making auditory experiments difficult. Moreover, acquiring and running these machines is expensive. Still, none of these drawbacks have prevented the method from revolutionizing the study of the brain.

magnetic resonance imaging (MRI) An imaging technology that uses the responses of atoms to strong magnetic fields to form images of structures like the brain. The method can be adapted to measure activity in the brain, as well (see *functional magnetic resonance imaging*).

functional magnetic resonance imaging (fMRI) A variant of magnetic resonance imaging that makes it possible to measure localized patterns of activity in the brain. Activated neurons provoke increased blood flow, which can be quantified by measuring changes in of the response of oxygenated and deoxygenated blood to strong magnetic fields.

blood oxygen level–dependent (BOLD) signal The ratio of oxygenated to deoxygenated hemoglobin that permits the localization of brain neurons that are most involved in a task.

FIGURE 1.36 Functional MRI. The warm colors show places where the BOLD signal was elevated by the presence of a visual stimulus. Blues show decreases in BOLD activity. The big region of elevation corresponds to the primary visual areas of the brain (see Chapter 3).

positron emission tomography (PET) An imaging technology that enables us to define locations in the brain where neurons are especially active by measuring the metabolism of brain cells using safe radioactive isotopes.

Refer to the
Sensation and Perception
Companion Website
sites.sinauer.com/wolfe3e
for activities, essays, study questions, and other study aids.

Figure 1.36 shows some of the results from a very basic fMRI experiment. The observer was watching a screen. A visual stimulus was on for 30 seconds and off for 30 seconds in alternation. Regions of the brain that were made more active by the presentation of the visual stimulus would demand more supplies in response to the presence of the stimulus, so there would be a difference between the BOLD responses to stimulus-on and stimulus-off conditions (with that lag of several seconds). Subtracting the stimulus-on and stimulus-off fMRI signals reveals the difference in BOLD responses. Typically, these are shown as colors superimposed on a structural MRI of the brain.

Positron emission tomography (**PET**) is an imaging technique in which a small amount of a safe, biologically active, radioactive material (a tracer) is introduced into the participant's bloodstream, and a specialized camera detects gamma rays emitted from brain regions where the tracer is being used most. The logic is similar to that of fMRI: the idea is to detect activity in neurons by looking for increased metabolic activity. The most common tracer used in perception experiments is the unstable form of oxygen, ^{15}O, which has a half-life of only a little more than 2 minutes. Neurons that are most active in the brain should have the greatest requirement for this oxygen. Although PET is a somewhat inconvenient method, it has the advantage of being silent, which is helpful in studies of brain activity related to hearing.

Modern labs often use multiple methods in the same experiment or series of experiments. You might use behavioral methods to determine the nature of a particular perceptual capability, but such methods might take hours and hundreds or thousands of trials. If your observers can't spend that much time in the scanner, you might have them perform a shorter, stripped-down version of the study while being imaged. You might do yet another version of the task, specialized for the demands of EEG recording. By means of these "converging operations," you could build up quite a detailed picture of what your observer perceives and how the observer's brain gives rise to those perceptions.

Now that you've completed this brief tour of the methods of the trade, you should be ready to embark on a more comprehensive examination of sensation and perception. We hope you enjoy the journey.

Summary

1. Sensation and perception are central to, and often precede, almost all aspects of human behavior and thought. There are many practical applications of our increased understanding of sensation and perception.

2. Gustav Fechner invented several clever methods for measuring the relationship between physical changes in the world and consequent psychological changes in observers. These methods remain in use today. Using Fechner's methods, researchers can measure the smallest levels of stimulus that can be detected (absolute threshold) and smallest differences that can be detected (difference thresholds, or just noticeable differences).

3. A more recent development for understanding performance—signal detection theory—permits us to simulate changes in the perceiver (e.g., internal noise and biases) in order to understand perceptual performance better.

4. We learn a great deal about perception by understanding the biological structures and processes involved. One early observation—the doctrine of specific nerve energies—expresses the fact that people are aware only of the activity of our nervous systems. For this reason, what matters is which nerves are stimulated, not how they are stimulated. The central nervous system reflects specializations for the senses from cranial nerves to areas of the cerebral cortex involved in perception.

5. The essential activities of all neurons, including those involved in sensory processes, are chemical and electrochemical. Neurons communicate with each other through neurotransmitters, molecules that cross the synapse from the axon of one neuron to the dendrite of the next. Nerve impulses are electrochemical; voltages change along the axon as electrically charged ions (sodium and potassium) pass in and out of the membranes of nerve cells.

6. Recordings of individual neurons enable us to measure the lowest level of stimulus required for a neuron to fire (absolute threshold). Both the rate and the timing pattern of neural firing provide additional information about how the brain encodes stimuli in the world.

7. Electroencephalography (EEG) and magnetoencephalography (MEG) measure the activity of many neurons with great precision in timing, but not brain location.

8. Positron emission tomography (PET) and functional magnetic resonance imaging (fMRI) measure metabolic changes to precisely localize the activity of many neurons in the brain, but with little precision in timing.

9. Fourier analysis is a mathematical tool that helps researchers break down complex sounds and images in ways that permit better understanding of how sounds and images are sensed and perceived.

CHAPTER 2

Karl Mullen, *Cell, Cell, Cell*, 2011

The First Steps in Vision: From Light to Neural Signals

W ith the naked eye we can see stars that are up to about 2000 light-years (almost 6 trillion miles) away, and in a dark winter sky far from city lights the neighboring galaxy, Andromeda, is visible at over 2 *million* light-years away! This chapter describes the first steps in seeing. To understand how we see, we must first consider a little physics and optics, and then we'll look at how the eye is built to capture and begin to process light.

In subsequent chapters we'll see how light information gleaned by the eyes travels back through the head to the brain, and how the brain transforms this information into a meaningful interpretation of the outside world. For a preview of the entire visual process, work through **Web Activity 2.1: Visual System Overview**.

A Little Light Physics

Light is a form of electromagnetic radiation—energy produced by vibrations of electrically charged material. There are two ways to conceptualize light: as a **wave** or as a stream of **photons**, tiny particles that each consist of one quantum of energy. This dual nature of light can be confusing to physics and psychology students alike. In this discussion we'll try to avoid confusion as much as possible by treating light as being made up of waves when it moves around the world, and being made up of photons when it is absorbed.

Although the full spectrum of electromagnetic radiation is very wide, light makes up only a tiny portion of this spectrum. Figure 2.1 illustrates the electromagnetic spectrum from gamma rays (which have very short wavelengths) to radio and television waves (which have very long wavelengths). Visible light waves have wavelengths between 400 and 700 nanometers (nm; 1 nm = 10^{-9} meter), as illustrated on the right-hand side of the figure. Note that as the wavelength varies in the visible spectrum, the color we observe changes from violet at about 400 nm through the whole spectrum of the rainbow up to red at about 650 nm. (As we'll discuss in Chapter 5, however, the light waves themselves are not colored; it is only after our visual system interprets an incoming wave that we perceive the light as a specific color.)

Let's consider what happens to light on its way from a star to an eye. (See **Web Activity 2.2: From Sun to Eye**.) In empty space the electromagnetic radiation from a star travels in a straight line at the speed of light (about 186,000 miles per second). Once it reaches the atmosphere, some of the starlight's photons will be **absorbed** by encounters with dust, vaporized water, and so on; and some of the light will be **scattered** by these particles. Most of the photons, however, will make it through the atmosphere and will eventually hit the surface of an object.

wave An oscillation that travels through a medium by transferring energy from one particle or point to another without causing any permanent displacement of the medium.

photon A quantum of visible light or other form of electromagnetic radiation demonstrating both particle and wave properties.

absorb To take up light, noise, or energy and not transmit it at all.

scatter To disperse light in an irregular fashion.

FIGURE 2.1 The spectrum of electromagnetic energy (specified in nanometers), with the visible spectrum (400–700 nm) expanded at right. Note that 1 nm = 10^{-9} m.

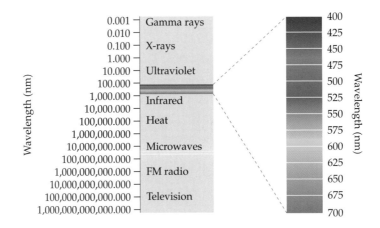

If the ray of starlight were to strike a light-colored surface, most of the light would be **reflected**. Indeed, the fact that most of the light bounces off the surface accounts for that surface's "light" appearance. However, most of the light striking a dark surface is absorbed. Light that is neither reflected nor absorbed by the surface is **transmitted** through the surface. If we are gazing at our star through a window, as the light travels from air into the glass some of the light rays will be bent, or **refracted**, as it is transmitted.

Refraction also occurs when light passes from air into water or into the eyeball. In fact, the part of an eye exam in which the eye doctor checks the patient's prescription is often called a "refraction" because the doctor determines how much the light must be bent by eyeglasses for it to be properly focused on the retina. In the next section we'll see how the optical system of our eyes performs this same kind of focusing.

Eyes That See Light

In order to see stars or anything else, we need some type of physiological mechanism for sensing light. Even single-celled organisms such as amoebas respond to light, changing their direction of motion to avoid bright light when it is detected. But eyes go well beyond mere light detection. An eye can form an **image** of the outside world, enabling animals that possess eyes to use light to recognize objects, not just to determine whether light is present and what direction it's coming from.

Before explaining how eyes form images, let's take a tour through the human eye to become familiar with its important parts. Figure 2.2 shows a front-to-back slice through a human eye, with the most important structures labeled. (See **Web Activity 2.3: Eye Structure**.)

The first tissue that light from the star will encounter is the **cornea**. Contact lenses sit on a thin film of tears in front of the cornea. The cornea provides a window to the world because it is **transparent** (that is, most light photons are transmitted through it, rather than being reflected or absorbed). It is transparent because it is made of a highly ordered arrangement of fibers and because it contains no blood vessels or blood, which would absorb light. The cornea does, however, have a rich supply of transparent sensory nerve endings, which are there to force the eyes to close and produce tears if the cornea is scratched, preserving its transparency. If you have ever scratched your cornea or worn contact lenses too long, you know exactly how painful this can be! Fortunately, the external layers of the cornea regenerate very quickly, so even when a cornea is scratched, it usually heals within 24 hours.

reflect To redirect something that strikes a surface—especially light, sound, or heat—usually back toward its point of origin.

transmit To convey something (e.g., light) from one place or thing to another.

refract 1. To alter the course of a wave of energy that passes into something from another medium, as water does to light entering it from the air. 2. To measure the degree of refraction in a lens or eye.

image A picture or likeness.

cornea The transparent "window" into the eyeball.

transparent Allowing light to pass through with no interruption, so that objects on the other side can be clearly seen.

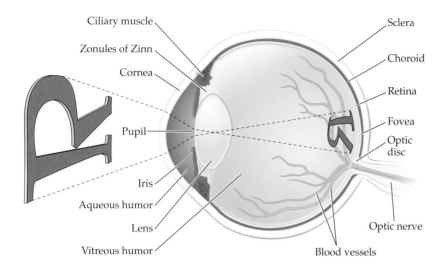

FIGURE 2.2 The human right eye in cross section (viewed from above). Note that the *R* on the retina is reversed right to left, and it is upside down. The "hole" in the retina where the optic nerve leaves the eyeball is the optic disc (where the absence of photoreceptors results in a blind spot). (From Rosenzweig, Breedlove, and Watson, 2005.)

The **aqueous humor**, a fluid derived from blood, fills the space immediately behind the cornea, supplying oxygen and nutrients to, and removing waste from, the cornea and the **crystalline lens**. Like the cornea, the lens has no blood supply, so that it can be completely transparent; and, as we'll see later, the shape of the lens is controlled by the ciliary muscle.

To get to the lens, the light from our star must pass through the **pupil**, which is simply a hole in a muscular structure called the **iris**. The iris gives the eye its distinctive color. The pupil controls the amount of light that reaches the retina, via the pupillary light reflex. When the level of light increases or decreases, the iris automatically expands and contracts to allow more or less light into the eye.

When you emerge from a dark room into bright light (e.g., coming out of a movie theater), not only does your pupil constrict, but there's a good chance that you will sneeze. Sneezing in response to being exposed to a bright light—the "photic sneeze reflex"—is not yet understood, even though it has intrigued some of history's greatest minds. Aristotle thought the heat of the sun on the nose might be responsible. However, Francis Bacon (1561–1626) showed that Aristotle was wrong. Bacon stepped into the sun with his eyes closed and did not sneeze; the heat was still there, but the sneeze was not. Bacon guessed that the sun's light makes the eyes water, and that moisture ("braine humour," in his words) then seeps into and irritates the nose. We now know that the sneeze takes place too soon after light exposure to be the result of the comparatively slow formation of tears. Current thinking suggests that the photic sneeze reflex is a result of crossed wires in the brain.

After passing through the lens, our starlight enters the vitreous chamber (the space between the lens and the retina), where it will be refracted for the fourth and final time by the **vitreous humor**. This is the longest part of the journey through the eyeball; this chamber comprises 80% of the internal volume of the eye. The vitreous is gel-like and viscous (a bit like egg white), and generally transparent. While staring up at the bright blue sky on a lazy sunny day, however, you may have noticed "floaters," small bits of debris (biodebris) that drift around in the vitreous. Floaters are quite common, and they are usually not a cause for concern.

Finally, after traveling through the vitreous chamber, the light emitted by our favorite star is (hopefully) brought into focus at the **retina**. To be a bit more precise, only some of the light will actually reach the retina. Much of the light energy will have been lost in space or the atmosphere, because of absorption

aqueous humor The watery fluid in the anterior chamber of the eye.

crystalline lens The lens inside the eye that enables the changing of focus.

pupil The dark, circular opening at the center of the iris in the eye, where light enters the eye.

iris The colored part of the eye, consisting of a muscular diaphragm surrounding the pupil and regulating the light entering the eye by expanding and contracting the pupil.

vitreous humor The transparent fluid that fills the vitreous chamber in the posterior part of the eye.

retina A light-sensitive membrane in the back of the eye that contains rods and cones, which receive an image from the lens and send it to the brain through the optic nerve.

accommodation The process by which the eye changes its focus (in which the lens gets fatter as gaze is directed toward nearer objects).

presbyopia Literally "old sight." The loss of near vision because of insufficient accommodation.

cataract An opacity of the crystalline lens.

and scattering, as described already. In addition, a good deal of light becomes lost in the eyeball, so only about half of the starlight that arrives at the cornea actually reaches the retina. The role of the retina is to detect light and "tell the brain about aspects of light that are related to objects in the world" (Oyster, 1999). In other words, the retina is where seeing really begins.

Focusing Light onto the Retina

Remember that refraction (light bending) is necessary to focus light rays. Because the cornea is highly curved and has a higher refractive index than air (1.376 versus 1), it forms the most powerful refractive surface in the eye. The aqueous and vitreous humors also help refract light. However, the refractive power of these three structures is fixed, so they cannot be used to bring close objects into focus. This job is performed by the lens, which can alter the refractive power by changing its shape—a process called **accommodation**.

Accommodation (change in focus) is accomplished through contraction of the ciliary muscle. The lens is attached to the ciliary muscle through tiny fibers (known as the "zonules of Zinn") (see Figure 2.2). When the ciliary muscle is relaxed, the zonules are stretched and the lens is relatively flat. In this state, the eye will be focused on very distant objects (like our star). But to focus on something closer—say, a wristwatch—the ciliary muscle must contract. This contraction reduces the tension on the zonules and enables the lens to bulge. The fatter the lens is, the more power it has.

Accommodation enables the power of the lens to vary by as much as 15 diopters. If your eyes were corrected for distant vision, 15 diopters of accommodation would enable you to read your watch at a distance of about 6.7 centimeters (cm), or 0.067 meter; the distance in centimeters is equal to 100 divided by the amount of accommodation in diopters, which is 15 in this case; that is, $100/15 = 6.7$ cm. To calculate the amount of accommodation using meters instead of centimeters, we start with 1 instead of 100: $1/0.067$ meter = 15 diopters. If you can read your watch at 6.7 cm (while wearing your distance correction), you are either very lucky or very young. Our ability to accommodate declines with age, starting from about 8 years old, and we lose about 1 diopter of accommodation every 5 years up to age 30 (and even more after age 30). By the time most people are between 40 and 50 years old, they find that their arms are too short because they can no longer easily accommodate the 2.5 diopters or so needed to see clearly at 40 cm ($1/0.4 = 2.5$). This condition is called **presbyopia** (meaning "old sight"), and it is, like death and taxes, inevitable!

Why do we all have presbyopia to look forward to? The main reason is that the lens becomes sclerotic (harder) and the capsule that encircles the lens (enabling it to change shape) loses its elasticity. Luckily for us, Benjamin Franklin (1706–1790) invented bifocals—lenses that have one power at the top (permitting us to see distant objects) and a different power at the bottom (allowing us to be in focus at a comfortable reading distance).

Like the other optical components of the eye, the lens is normally transparent. It is transparent because the crystallins (a class of proteins that make up the lens) are packed together very densely and therefore are very regular. Anything that interferes with the regularity of the crystallins will result in loss of transparency (areas that are opaque—that is, "opacities"). Opacities of the lens are known as **cataracts**, and they are caused by irregularity of the crystallins. Cataracts can occur at different ages and take many different forms. Congenital cataracts (present at birth) are relatively rare; but if they are dense (and therefore interfere with retinal image quality), they can have devastating effects on normal visual development if not treated promptly. Most cataracts

(a) Emmetropia

(b) Myopia

(c) Myopia with correction

(d) Hyperopia

FIGURE 2.3 Optics of the human eye. (After Oyster, 1999.)

are discovered after age 50, and the prevalence of cataracts increases with age so that by 70 almost everyone has some loss of transparency. Cataracts can interfere with vision because they absorb and scatter more light than the normal lens does. Fortunately, treatment of cataracts (in which the opacified lens is extracted and replaced with a plastic or silicone implant) has become quite routine.

To focus a distant star on the retina, the refractive power of the four optical components of the eye must be perfectly matched to the length of the eyeball. This perfect match, known as **emmetropia**, is illustrated in Figure 2.3*a*. Refractive errors occur when the eyeball is too long or too short relative to the power of the optical components. If the eyeball is too long for the optics (Figure 2.3*b*), the image of our star will be focused *in front* of the retina, and the star will thus be seen as a blur rather than a spot of light. This condition is called **myopia** (or "nearsightedness"). Myopia can be corrected with negative (minus) lenses, which diverge the rays of starlight before they enter the eye (Figure 2.3*c*). If the eyeball is too short for the optics (Figure 2.3*d*), the image of our star will be focused *behind* the retina—a condition called **hyperopia** (or "farsightedness"). If the hyperopia is not too severe, a young hyperope can compensate by accommodating, thereby increasing the power of the eye. If accommodation fails to correct the hyperopia, the star's image will again be blurred. Hyperopia can be corrected with positive (plus) lenses, which converge the rays of starlight before they enter the eye.

On average, the adult human eye is 24 millimeters (mm) long, about the diameter of a quarter. However, eyeballs can be quite a bit longer or shorter and still be emmetropic because eyes generally grow to match the power of the optical components we're born with. (Most newborns are hyperopic because the optical components of their eyes are relatively well developed at birth compared to the length of their eyeballs.)

As noted earlier, the most powerful refracting surface in the eye is the cornea, which contributes about two-thirds of the eye's focusing power. When the cornea is not spherical, the result is **astigmatism**. With astigmatism, vertical lines might be focused slightly in front of the retina, while horizontal lines are focused slightly behind it (or vice versa). If you have a reasonable degree of uncorrected astigmatism, one or more of the lines in Figure 2.4 might appear to be out of focus, while other lines appear sharp. Lenses that have two focal points (that is, lenses that provide different amounts of focusing power in the horizontal and vertical planes) can correct astigmatism.

The Retina

The preceding discussion covered how the human visual system delivers a focused image of our favorite star onto the retina, which is spread across the back of the eyeball. The optics involved are similar to those in most cameras (see Figure 2.2), which also include a mechanism for regulating the amount of light (the "stop," analogous to the iris in human eyes) and a lens for adjusting focal length so that both near and far objects can be focused on the film spread across the back of the camera. However, this is as far as we can take this analogy, because although the purpose of a camera is simply to record the image projected onto the film, the purpose of the human visual system is to interpret this image. This is the difference between taking a picture and seeing a picture. And the process of seeing begins with the retina, where the light energy from our star is **transduced** into neural energy that can be interpreted by the brain.

Eye doctors use an instrument called an ophthalmoscope to look at the back surface of their patients' eyes, which is called the **fundus** (plural *fundi*). (You probably remember all too well having that bright light shining into

emmetropia The condition in which there is no refractive error, because the refractive power of the eye is perfectly matched to the length of the eyeball.

myopia Nearsightedness, a common condition in which light entering the eye is focused in front of the retina and distant objects cannot be seen sharply.

hyperopia Farsightedness, a common condition in which light entering the eye is focused behind the retina and accommodation is required in order to see near objects clearly.

astigmatism A visual defect caused by the unequal curving of one or more of the refractive surfaces of the eye, usually the cornea.

transduce To convert from one form of energy to another (e.g., from light to neural electrical energy, or from mechanical movement to neural electrical energy).

fundus The back layer of the retina—what the eye doctor sees through an ophthalmoscope.

FIGURE 2.4 Fan chart for astigmatism. Take off your glasses (if you wear glasses) and view this "fan." If you have a significant degree of astigmatism, one or more of the lines will appear to have lower contrast.

FIGURE 2.5 Fundus of the right eye of a human. (From Rodieck, 1998.)

your eye when the doctor examines your fundus.) **Figure 2.5** shows a normal fundus. The white circle is known as the optic disc. This is the point where the arteries and veins that feed the retina enter the eye, and where the axons of ganglion cells (which we will get to shortly) leave the eye via the optic nerve. This portion of the retina contains no photoreceptors, and consequently it is blind. You can experience your own blind spot, corresponding to the optic disc, by closing your left eye, fixating on the *F* in **Figure 2.6a** with your right

FIGURE 2.6 To experience your blind spot, close your left eye, fixating on the *F* in part (*a*) with your right eye. Hold the book about 15 cm away from your eye, and adjust the distance of the book from your eyes until the red circle disappears. This is your blind spot. Ordinarily you are not aware of it, because the visual system "fills in" the blind spot with information from the surrounding area. If you fixate on the *F* in part (*b*) with your right eye and again adjust the distance, when the gap in the line falls in your blind spot, it will fill in and you will see a continuous red line.

(*a*)

(*b*)

eye, and adjusting the distance of the book from your eyes until the red circle disappears. The reason you don't normally notice this large blind spot in your visual field is that the visual system "fills it in" with information from the surrounding area (Figure 2.6*b*).

The fundus is the only place in the body where one can see the arteries and veins directly, so it provides doctors with an important window on the well-being of the body's vascular system. The vascular "tree" spreads out across the retina in a characteristic way but stops short of the fovea (the center of the brownish spot near the center of the fundus in Figure 2.5).

You can see your own vascular tree by using a simple trick that requires only a penlight. In a dark room, close your eyes and place the penlight against the outside corner of one eye. Holding the penlight against the eye, gently move the light around (up and down, and back and forth). Within a few seconds you should see the shadows cast by your blood vessels looking like the branches of a tree. We don't normally see them because the blood vessels move with our eyes, so their shadows are stabilized retinal images and, as with the blind spot, the visual system fills in behind them. The motion of the penlight makes the shadows move, enabling us to see them.

Even when viewed through an ophthalmoscope with a lot of magnification, the fundus does not provide a detailed view of the retina. To get a good look at the structure of the retina, we need a photomicrograph (**Figure 2.7**), which reveals that the retina is a layered sheet of clear neurons, about half the thickness of a credit card (Rodieck, 1998), with another layer of darker cells, the pigment epithelium, lying behind the final layer.

FIGURE 2.7 Photomicrograph of the retina. The section shown is near the fovea. (From Oyster, 1999; micrograph from Boycott and Dowling, 1969.)

photoreceptor A light-sensitive receptor in the retina.

rod A photoreceptor specialized for night vision.

cone A photoreceptor specialized for daylight vision, fine visual acuity, and color.

duplex In reference to the retina, consisting of two parts: the rods and cones, which operate under different conditions.

outer segment The part of a photoreceptor that contains photopigment molecules.

inner segment The part of a photoreceptor that lies between the outer segment and the cell nucleus.

synaptic terminal The location where axons terminate at the synapse for transmission of information by the release of a chemical transmitter.

chromophore The light-catching part of the visual pigments of the retina.

rhodopsin The visual pigment found in rods.

melanopsin A photopigment that is sensitive to ambient light.

As we'll see in the next section, together these neurons constitute a mini-computer that begins the process of interpreting the information contained in visual images. The transduction of light energy into neural energy begins in the backmost layer of the retina, which is made up of cells called **photoreceptors**. When photoreceptors sense light, they can stimulate neurons in the intermediate layers, including bipolar cells, horizontal cells, and amacrine cells. These neurons then connect with the frontmost layer of the retina, made up of ganglion cells, whose axons pass through the optic nerve to the brain.

Before we describe the function of these layers, we should address an obvious question regarding the structure of the retina: Why are the photoreceptors at the back—that is, in the last layer? This arrangement requires light to pass through the ganglion, bipolar, horizontal, and amacrine cells before making contact with the photoreceptors. However, these neurons are mostly transparent, whereas cells in the pigment epithelium, which provide vital nutrients to the photoreceptors, are opaque. Once we see that the photoreceptors must be next to both the pigment epithelium and the other neurons, the layering order makes much more sense.

Retinal Information Processing

As noted in the previous section, the retina contains five major classes of neurons: photoreceptors, horizontal cells, bipolar cells, amacrine cells, and ganglion cells (see Figure 2.7). Let's take a closer look at the functions of each of these cell types. (See **Web Activity 2.4: Retinal Structure**.)

Light Transduction by Rod and Cone Photoreceptors

The retina contains roughly 100 million photoreceptors. These are the neurons that capture light and initiate the act of seeing by producing chemical signals. The human retina contains at least two types of photoreceptors: **rods** and **cones**. These two types not only have different shapes (which is how they earned their names; see Figure 2.8), but they have different distributions across the retina and serve different functions. Because human retinas have both rods and cones, they are considered to be **duplex** retinas. Some animals, such as rats and owls, have mostly rod retinas; others (e.g., certain lizards) have mostly cone retinas.

Both types of photoreceptors consist of an **outer segment** (which is adjacent to the pigment epithelium), an **inner segment**, and a **synaptic terminal**. Molecules called visual pigments are made in the inner segment (which is like a little factory, filled with mitochondria) and stored in the outer segment, where they are incorporated into the membrane. Visual pigment molecules consist of a protein (an opsin), the structure of which determines which wavelengths of light they absorb; and a **chromophore**, which captures light photons. Each photoreceptor has only one of the four types of visual pigments found in the human retina. The pigment **rhodopsin** is found in the rods, concentrated mainly in the stack of membranous discs in the outer segment. Each cone has one of the other three pigments—which respond to long, medium, and short wavelengths, respectively.

Recent evidence suggests that there may be a third type of photoreceptor—one that "lives" among the ganglion cells, and that is involved in adjusting our biological rhythms to match the day and night of the external world (Baringa, 2002). These photoreceptors are sensitive to the ambient light level and contain the photopigment **melanopsin**, and they send their signals to the suprachiasmatic nucleus (SCN), the home of the brain's circadian clock, which regulates 24-hour patterns of behavior and physiology.

Rod   Cone

Outer segment

Inner segment

Synaptic terminal

FIGURE 2.8 Rods and cones. (From Rodieck, 1998.)

When a photon from our favorite star makes its way into the outer segment of a rod and is absorbed by a molecule of rhodopsin, it transfers its energy to the chromophore portion of the visual pigment molecule. This process, known as **photoactivation**, initiates a biochemical cascade of events eventually resulting in the closing of channels in the cell membrane that normally allow ions to flow into the rod outer segment. Closing these channels alters the balance of electrical current between the inside and outside of the rod outer segment, making the inside of the cell more negatively charged. This process is known as **hyperpolarization**. Hyperpolarization closes calcium channels at the synaptic terminal, thereby reducing the concentration of free calcium inside the cells. The lowering of the calcium concentration, in turn, reduces the concentration of neurotransmitter (glutamate) molecules at the synaptic terminals, and this change signals to the bipolar cell that the rod has captured a photon. The entire sequence of events takes only a matter of milliseconds. Cones act in a qualitatively similar fashion.

The amount of glutamate present in the photoreceptor–bipolar cell synapse at any one time is inversely proportional to the number of photons being absorbed by the photoreceptor. Thus, unlike most other types of neurons, photoreceptors do not respond in an all-or-nothing fashion. They pass their information on to bipolar cells via **graded potentials** instead of action potentials.

Humans have many more rods (about 90 million) than cones (about 4–5 million), and the two types of cells have very different geographic distributions on the retina (**Figure 2.9**). Rods are completely absent from the center of the fovea, and their density increases to a peak at about 20 degrees and then declines again. The cones are most concentrated in the center of the fovea, and their density drops off dramatically with retinal **eccentricity** (distance from the fovea).

photoactivation Activation by light.

hyperpolarization An increase in membrane potential such that the inner membrane surface becomes more negative than the outer membrane surface.

graded potential An electrical potential that can vary continuously in amplitude.

eccentricity The distance between the retinal image and the fovea.

FIGURE 2.9 Photoreceptor density across the retina. The top panels show slices through the photoreceptor inner segments at different eccentricities (distances from the fovea). The graph shows the density of rods and cones plotted as a function of distance from the fovea. Note that in the peripheral slices, the cones are always the larger cells. (After Oyster, 1999; micrographs from Curcio et al., 1990.)

FIGURE 2.10 The "rule of thumb": When viewed at arm's length, your thumb subtends an angle of about 2 degrees on the retina, assuming your thumb is about 2 cm across and your outstretched arm extends about 57 cm from your eye.

As the photographs of photoreceptors at different eccentricities in Figure 2.9 illustrate, cones are also smaller and more tightly packed in the foveal center. This "rod-free" area (about 300 square micrometers [μm] on the retina) subtends a visual angle of about 1 degree, and it is directly behind the center of the pupil. So if we look directly at an object whose image is smaller than 1 degree, the image will land on a region of the retina that has only cones. (How big is 1 degree? Here's a rule of thumb, illustrated in **Figure 2.10**: Your thumb, when viewed at arm's length, subtends an angle of about 2 degrees on the retina, assuming your thumb is about 2 cm across and your outstretched arm extends about 57 cm from your eye.) **Table 2.1** illustrates some of the fundamental differences in the properties of the fovea compared to the peripheral retina. Most important for us, the fovea has high acuity and we use it to identify objects, to read, and to inspect fine detail. On the other hand, we use the periphery to detect and localize stimuli that we aren't looking at directly (e.g., seeing a moving truck out of the "corner of the eye").

Rods and cones operate best under different lighting conditions: Rods function relatively well under conditions of dim (scotopic) illumination (which is why animals with all-rod retinas are nocturnal), but cones require brighter (photopic) illumination (e.g., sunlight or room lights) to operate efficiently. Having an area at the center of the fovea with no rods means that, under dim

TABLE 2.1 *Properties of the fovea and periphery in human vision*

Property	Fovea	Periphery
Photoreceptor type	Mostly cones	Mostly rods
Bipolar cell type	Midget	Diffuse
Convergence	Low	High
Receptive-field size	Small	Large
Acuity (detail)	High	Low
Light sensitivity	Low	High

FIGURE 2.11 Blue, green, and red represent the S-, M-, and L-cones, respectively, of a living human being in a patch of retina at 1 degree from the fovea. The pseudocolor image was made by the use of adaptive optics to measure and bypass the aberrations of the eye, and of selective bleaching to isolate the different photopigments. (From Roorda and Williams, 1999; courtesy of Austin Roorda.)

illumination, the central 1 degree or so around the fovea is effectively blind! Indeed, practiced stargazers know that it is often easier to spot a dim star by looking out of the corner of one's eye than by looking directly at it.

Rods and cones differ functionally in another important way. Because all rods have the same type of photopigment, they cannot signal differences in color. Each cone, on the other hand, has one of three different photopigments that differ in the wavelengths at which they absorb light most efficiently. Therefore, cones can signal information about wavelength, and thus they provide the basis for our color vision.

> **FURTHER DISCUSSION** of cones and color detection can be found in Chapter 5 on page 118.

The three cone photopigments are not distributed equally among the cones (Figure 2.11). Short wavelength–sensitive cones (S-cones) constitute only about 5–10% of the total cone population, and they are essentially missing from the center of the fovea. Thus, the foveal center is dichromatic (it has only two color-sensitive cones). We also know that there are more long wavelength–sensitive cones (L-cones) than medium wavelength–sensitive cones (M-cones); it has been estimated that there are, on average, about twice as many L-cones as M-cones, although the ratio of L- to M-cones varies enormously among individuals. Table 2.2 illustrates some of the fundamental differences in the

TABLE 2.2 *Properties of human photopic and scotopic vision*

Property	Photopic system	Scotopic system
Photoreceptors	4–5 million cones	90 million rods
Location in retina	Throughout retina, with highest concentration close to fovea	Outside of fovea
Acuity (detail)	High	Low
Sensitivity	Low	High

FIGURE 2.12 The panel on the left illustrates the way the right-hand panel might look to someone with age-related macular degeneration (AMD). (From National Eye Institute, 2010.)

properties of the photopic (high illumination) and scotopic (low illumination) visual systems.

When photoreceptors capture light, they produce chemical changes that start a cascade of neural events ending in a visual sensation. Photoreceptors send their signals by way of the synaptic terminals, specialized structures for contacting other retinal neurons. Figure 2.8 shows examples of rod and cone synaptic terminals. The synaptic terminals contain connections from the neurons that photoreceptors "talk to": the horizontal and bipolar cells.

The Man Who Could Not Read

Imagine not being able to read because you couldn't see well enough. What follows is the sad story of a man in this very predicament. This healthy 72-year-old loved to read. He read the newspaper religiously every day (especially Sundays), and he read approximately a book a week. But he began to notice that reading was becoming difficult. There seemed to be a blurred spot in the center of his vision that was becoming gradually worse, making it difficult for him to read and recognize faces (**Figure 2.12**). Reading was a bit better under bright lights, but reading the paper indoors, or a menu in a dimly lit restaurant, was becoming progressively more difficult. He also noticed a small—but growing—blind spot in the middle of his field of vision.

A visit to the eye doctor confirmed that the man had **age-related macular degeneration** (**AMD**). AMD is a disease associated with aging that affects the **macula**, the central part of the retina that has a high concentration of cones. The **fovea** is a small pit near the center of this area that contains the highest concentration of cones. AMD is the leading cause of visual loss among the elderly in the United States, and it gradually destroys sharp central vision, making it difficult to read, drive, and recognize faces. The man's blind spot in the middle of his visual field, also known as a **scotoma**, is a consequence of the loss of cones in the macula. You can experience a temporary foveal scotoma in **Web Activity 2.5: Simulated Scotoma.**

AMD comes in two flavors: wet and dry. In wet AMD, abnormal blood vessels behind the retina start to grow under the macula, and because they are fragile, they leak blood and fluid. The blood and fluid raise the macula, resulting in a rapid loss of central vision. Because the macula is displaced, straight lines may look wavy. Dry AMD is much more common, occurring when the macula cones degenerate. Sometimes dry AMD turns into wet AMD.

Once dry AMD becomes advanced, no form of treatment can prevent vision loss. However, fortunately for the man who could not read, treatment can delay and possibly prevent intermediate AMD from progressing to the advanced

aging-related macular degeneration (AMD) A disease associated with aging that affects the macula. AMD gradually destroys sharp central vision, making it difficult to read, drive, and recognize faces. There are two forms of AMD: wet and dry.

macula The central part of the retina that has a high concentration of cones.

fovea A small pit, near the center of the macula, that contains the highest concentration of cones, and no rods. It is the portion of the retina that produces the highest visual acuity and serves as the point of fixation.

scotoma A blind spot in the visual field.

stage. The National Eye Institute's "Age-Related Eye Disease Study" (the AREDS) found that taking a high-dose formulation of antioxidants and zinc significantly reduces the risk of advanced AMD and its associated vision loss.

Lateral Inhibition through Horizontal and Amacrine Cells

As the name implies, **horizontal cells** run perpendicular to the photoreceptors, making contacts between nearby photoreceptors. These lateral connections play an important functional role in the form of **lateral inhibition**, which enables the signals that reach retinal ganglion cells to be based on differences in activation between nearby photoreceptors. Lateral inhibition plays an important role in perception, and we will have much more to say about it when we discuss center-surround receptive fields later in this chapter.

Amacrine cells are also part of the lateral pathway. Like horizontal cells, amacrine cells run perpendicular to the photoreceptors in the inner layers of the retina, where they receive inputs from bipolar cells and other amacrine cells and send signals to bipolar, amacrine, and retinal ganglion cells. Amacrine cells come in many flavors, by some estimates as many as 40 (Rodieck, 1998). Although amacrine cells have been implicated in both contrast enhancement and temporal sensitivity (the detection of changes in light patterns over time), their precise function remains unclear.

Convergence and Divergence of Information via Bipolar Cells

If horizontal and amacrine cells form a lateral pathway in the retina, then photoreceptors, bipolar cells, and ganglion cells can be considered to form a vertical pathway. Bipolar cells are the intermediaries. There are various types of bipolar cells, and their wiring determines the information that is passed from the photoreceptors to the ganglion cells. For example, in peripheral vision a **bipolar cell** receives input from as many as 50 photoreceptors, pools this information, and passes it on to a ganglion cell. This convergence of information from many photoreceptors to a single bipolar cell (known as a **diffuse bipolar cell**) is a characteristic of the rod pathway, and the same sort of convergence occurs in the cone pathway in the peripheral retina.

Pooling of information from many photoreceptors is a very important mechanism for increasing visual **sensitivity**. Indeed, the fact that most rods communicate with ganglion cells through diffuse bipolar cells largely accounts for the ability of the rod system to function well in dim lighting conditions. However, convergence wreaks havoc on **visual acuity**: A diffuse bipolar cell may fire at the same rate in response to a single point of bright light or several spots of dim light, so a ganglion cell listening to the diffuse bipolar cell will be unable to tell which pattern of light is present.

In contrast, in the fovea, **midget bipolar cells** receive input from single cones and pass this information on to single ganglion cells. The fact that one-to-one pathways between cones and ganglions exist only in the fovea accounts for why images are seen most clearly when they fall on this part of the retina. The high degree of convergence in the retinal periphery ensures high sensitivity to light but poor acuity. The low degree of convergence in the fovea ensures high acuity but poor sensitivity to light. You can explore this trade-off of sensitivity and acuity in **Web Activity 2.6: Acuity versus Sensitivity**.

Interestingly, each foveal cone actually contacts two bipolar cells (representing a divergence of information): one responds to an increase in light captured by the cone and is called an **ON bipolar cell**; the other responds to a decrease and is called an **OFF bipolar cell**. The fact that there are both ON and OFF bipolar cells provides information about the sign (or direction) of the

horizontal cell A specialized retinal cell that contacts both photoreceptor and bipolar cells.

lateral inhibition Antagonistic neural interaction between adjacent regions of the retina.

amacrine cell A retinal cell found in the inner synaptic layer that makes synaptic contacts with bipolar cells, ganglion cells, and other amacrine cells.

bipolar cell A retinal cell that synapses with either rods or cones (not both) and with horizontal cells, and then passes the signals on to ganglion cells.

diffuse bipolar cell A bipolar retinal cell whose processes are spread out to receive input from multiple cones.

sensitivity 1. The ability to perceive via the sense organs. 2. Extreme responsiveness to radiation, especially to light of a specific wavelength. 3. The ability to respond to transmitted signals.

visual acuity A measure of the finest detail that can be resolved by the eyes.

midget bipolar cell A small bipolar cell in the central retina that receives input from a single cone.

ON bipolar cell A bipolar cell that responds to an increase in light captured by the cones.

OFF bipolar cell A bipolar cell that responds to a decrease in light captured by the cones.

ganglion cell A retinal cell that receives visual information from photoreceptors via two intermediate neuron types (bipolar cells and amacrine cells) and transmits information to the brain and midbrain.

P ganglion cell A small ganglion cell that receives excitatory input from single midget bipolar cells in the central retina and feeds the parvocellular layer of the lateral geniculate nucleus.

M ganglion cell A ganglion cell resembling a little umbrella that receives excitatory input from diffuse bipolar cells and feeds the magnocellular layer of the lateral geniculate nucleus.

koniocellular cell A neuron located between the magnocellular and parvocellular layers of the lateral geniculate nucleus. This layer is known as the koniocellular layer.

change in illumination. This information is important for visual information processing at higher levels in the visual pathway, and as we will see, the ON/OFF distinction built into the anatomical structure of the retina is present at many levels of the visual pathway.

Communicating to the Brain via Ganglion Cells

By the time signals arrive at the final layer of the retina (the **ganglion cells**), there has already been a lot of information processing. Some information has been pooled through convergence; some has been enhanced by lateral pathways. Ganglion cells receive their input from bipolar and amacrine cells, process this input further, and send messages off to the brain through their axons, which gather in the back of the eyeball and emerge together as the optic nerve.

By now you are probably getting the idea that each cell type comes in many varieties, and ganglion cells are no exception. The human retina contains about 1,250,000 ganglion cells, about one-hundredth the number of photoreceptors. Midget bipolar cells send their signals to small ganglion cells, which are widely referred to as **P ganglion cells** because they feed the parvocellular ("small cell") layer of the lateral geniculate nucleus (LGN) (discussed in Chapter 3). P cells constitute about 70% of the ganglion cells in the human retina. Diffuse bipolar cells project to ganglion cells that are known as **M ganglion cells** (**Figure 2.13**) because they feed the magnocellular ("large cell") layer of the LGN. The dendrites of these ganglion cells spread out much more than those of the P ganglion cells, giving them an umbrella-like appearance. About 8–10% of ganglion cells in the human retina are of the M variety. The dendrites of both P and M ganglion cells increase in size with retinal eccentricity, but at all eccentricities the P ganglion cells have much smaller dendritic trees than do the M ganglion cells.

The astute reader may have noticed that M and P ganglion cells together constitute about 80% of all ganglion cells. Other ganglion cell types, known as **koniocellular cells**, project to koniocellular layers in the LGN. Some of these, with input from S-cones, may be part of a "primordial" blue-yellow pathway (see Chapter 5), while yet other ganglion cells that project to the koniocellular layers are thought to correspond to "nonblue" koniocellular cells.

CENTER-SURROUND RECEPTIVE FIELDS Much of what we know about how retinal ganglion cells work comes from painstaking physiological studies in which tiny electrodes are used to study the electrical changes in individual

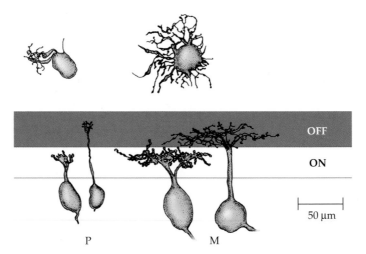

FIGURE 2.13 Different types of retinal P and M ganglion cells. The upper panel shows the cells in the flat-mounted retina; the lower panel shows them in section. (After Oyster, 1999.)

ganglion cells. Ganglion cells fire action potentials spontaneously, at about one spike per second, even in the absence of visual stimulation. However, each ganglion cell has a small window on the world known as its **receptive field**. The receptive field is the region on the retina in which visual stimuli influence the neuron's firing rate. This influence can be either excitatory, increasing the ganglion's firing rate; or inhibitory, decreasing the ganglion's firing rate.

> FURTHER DISCUSSION of receptive fields can be found in Chapter 3 on pages 68–72.

Work on horseshoe crabs and frogs provided some of our earliest information on the receptive fields of retinal neurons (Hartline, 1940). But it was Stephen Kuffler who first mapped out the receptive fields of individual retinal ganglion cells in the cat, using small spots of light (Kuffler, 1953). **Figure 2.14** illustrates Kuffler's main findings and provides some important insights into how the retina processes visual information. Kuffler's experiments are simulated in **Web Activity 2.7: Ganglion Receptive Fields**.

Let's consider Figure 2.14*a*. Kuffler's visual stimulus was a small spot of light, which he moved about on the retina, turning it on and off while recording impulses from a single retinal ganglion cell. When the spot was placed on

receptive field The region on the retina in which visual stimuli influence a neuron's firing rate.

(*a*) ON-center ganglion cell

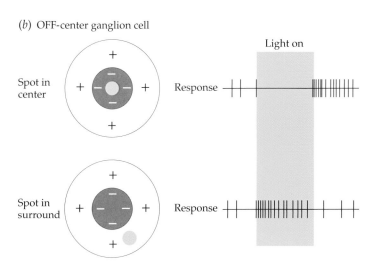

(*b*) OFF-center ganglion cell

FIGURE 2.14 Retinal ganglion cell receptive fields. (*a*) ON-center field. In each image on the left, the small white circle illustrates the region on the retina where the retinal ganglion cell increased its firing rate when the spot (small yellow circle) was turned on. The large gray circle illustrates the region on the retina where the retinal ganglion cell decreased its firing rate when the spot was turned on and increased its rate when the spot was turned off. The plots on the right illustrate the spikes fired by the associated retinal ganglion cell. (*b*) OFF-center field. In each image on the left, the large white circle illustrates the region on the retina where the retinal ganglion cell increased its firing rate when the spot was turned on. The small gray circle illustrates the region on the retina where the retinal ganglion cell decreased its firing rate when the spot was turned on and increased its rate when the spot was turned off. The plots on the right illustrate the spikes fired by the associated retinal ganglion cell. (After Kuffler, 1953.)

ON-center cell A cell that depolarizes in response to an increase in light intensity in its receptive-field center.

OFF-center cell A cell that depolarizes in response to a decrease in light intensity in its receptive-field center.

filter An acoustic, electrical, electronic, or optical device, instrument, computer program, or neuron that allows the passage of some frequencies or digital elements and blocks the passage of others.

contrast The difference in luminance between an object and the background, or between lighter and darker parts of the same object.

(a)

(b)

FIGURE 2.15 Mach bands. (a) This visual illusion gets its name from the illusory bright stripe in the region marked "B" and the illusory dark stripe in the region marked "D." (b) The actual intensity distribution of the Mach pattern illustrates a luminance ramp edge. (Part a from Cornsweet, 1970.)

a specific small region of the retina, the ganglion cell *increased* its firing rate when the light was turned on (this response is indicated by a plus sign in the figure). This area of the retina is called the "center" of the ganglion cell's receptive field. But when the spot was moved to an adjacent area of the retina, the ganglion cell *decreased* its firing rate when the light was turned on (indicated by a minus sign). Interestingly, turning the light *off* in this area surrounding the receptive-field center led to a brief surge in the cell's firing rate, after which the cell settled down to its spontaneous rate.

Kuffler found that the spatial layout of the ganglion cell's receptive field is essentially concentric; that is, a small circular area in the center responds to an increase in illumination, and a surrounding ring responds to a decrease in illumination. The ganglion cell fires fastest when the spot size matches the size of the excitatory center, and it reduces its firing rate when the spot begins to encroach on its inhibitory surround.

The cell just described is known as an **ON-center cell**. It increases its firing rate when a light is turned on in the center of its receptive field, and it decreases its firing rate when the light is turned on in the surround. However, nearly as many ganglion cells do exactly the opposite: their firing rates decrease when a spot in the center of the receptive field is turned on, and increase when the spot is turned on in the surround. These are known as **OFF-center cells** (Figure 2.14b). Most retinal ganglion cells have one of these two types of concentric center-surround organization.

This center-surround organization has two important functional consequences. First, it means that each ganglion cell will respond best to spots of a particular size (and will respond less to spots that are either bigger or smaller). In this way, retinal ganglion cells act as a **filter** by editing the information they send on to the brain. Second, ganglion cells are most sensitive to *differences* in the intensity of the light in the center and in the surround, and they are relatively unaffected by the average intensity of the light. This is a useful quality because the average intensity of the light falling on the retina varies a lot, depending on whether you are indoors or outdoors, whether it is daytime or nighttime, how far away you and the objects you're looking at are from the source of illumination, and so on. But the **contrast**—the difference in luminance or brightness between adjacent bits of the scene—will be roughly the same regardless of lighting conditions.

Phenomenologically, we have the impression that our eyes work like video cameras, capturing faithful snapshots of the world around us. Note, though, that the rest of the visual system sees only what the retinal ganglion cells show it, and the ganglion cells are not content simply to pass along the raw images encoded by the photoreceptors. Instead, the ganglion cells, together with the bipolar, amacrine, and horizontal cells, act as an image filter, transforming the raw image into a new representation. This new representation highlights certain important information, such as contrast, and largely discounts other types of less useful information, such as ambient light intensity. In fact, the whole visual system can be considered a long series of filters, with each stage in the system responsible for extracting a particular aspect of the visual world and passing this aspect on to the next stage.

SEEING ILLUSORY STRIPES—MACH BANDS Seeing is not always believing. Sometimes our eyes play tricks on us, and the illusions that we see can be quite informative about the neural operations that the visual system carries out. One well-known visual illusion was described by Ernst Mach (1838–1916), the famous Austrian physicist whose name is attached to the units that describe the speed of sound. **Figure 2.15a** shows the visual illusion that bears Mach's name. The illusion is known as "Mach bands" because there is an illusory

FIGURE 2.16   Neuronal explanation for Mach bands. (*a*) "Cartoon" showing a classic explanation. (*b*) A slightly more modern version.

bright stripe in the region marked "B" and an illusory dark stripe in the region marked "D." These bright and dark stripes (Mach bands) are illusions formed by the visual system.

The actual intensity distribution of the Mach pattern, shown in Figure 2.15*b*, is initially constant, increases smoothly over a short distance, and than remains steady at the new (higher) level. This intensity pattern is a luminance ramp edge, which contains no bright or dark stripes. Rather, the vivid perception of bright and dark stripes comes from operations performed by the visual nervous system instead of from the visual stimulus. This is an example where you can't believe your eyes—the perceptual brightness of the pattern varies where its physical intensity does not!

In 1865, when Mach first reported his observations, we had very little direct knowledge about the visual nervous system; however, Mach suggested that the illusory stripes were produced by lateral interactions in the retina. This notion gained wide support following the discovery of center-surround antagonistic receptive fields in the retina. This type of explanation, illustrated in **Figure 2.16**, has been popular for about the last 50 years.

In Figure 2.16*a*, the concentric circles represent ON-center retinal (or LGN) receptive fields (RFs). The RF on the left receives less light than the one on the right. If these receptive fields inform the brain about the intensity of light falling within their RFs, the brain will get the message that the left side of the picture is dimmer than the right side. Consider the middle RF in Figure 2.16*a*. Its center falls within the left half of the pattern; however, part of the antagonistic surround falls within the brighter right half. Thus, the middle RF will receive more surround antagonism, and therefore its response will be lower than the response of the RF on the left. The perceptual result will be that the region just to the left of the luminance step will appear as a darker stripe (or Mach band). The bright Mach band would be explained by an RF that had its center just within the bright panel but part of its antagonistic surround in the dimmer left half. The result would be less antagonism compared to the rightmost RF (where the entire surround is in the bright panel), and the perceptual consequence would be a brighter stripe (or Mach band).

Figure 2.16*b* shows an alternative way of illustrating the center-surround model of Mach bands. If a luminance ramp edge (left) is filtered by a center-surround (or lateral inhibition) weighting function (middle), the output will have an "undershoot" (a little dip to the left of the ramp) and an "overshoot" (a little bump to the right of the ramp) that seem to correspond to the Mach bands.

Although this simple "classic" explanation feels good, it is not the full story, and a complete understanding of Mach bands (and other similar perceptual illusions) will likely require a theory involving stages beyond the retina (for an excellent review, see Pessoa, 1996). For example, the classic theory fails to explain why Mach bands are less obvious at step edges than they are at ramp edges like the one shown in Figure 2.15b. However, the Mach band phenomenon reminds us that our visual system does not simply passively transmit information about the intensities of objects; it acts on that information in ways that often sharpen edges and contours.

P AND M GANGLION CELLS REVISITED   As already mentioned, retinal ganglion cells come in several types; for humans, the most important of these are the P and M cells. The receptive fields of these two types of ganglion cells differ in some important ways. First, at all eccentricities P cells have smaller receptive fields than M cells have. This isn't too surprising, because the size of the receptive field is probably determined by the size of its dendritic field (see Figure 2.13): since M cells listen to more photoreceptors (via bipolar, horizontal, and amacrine cells) than P cells do, M cells respond to a larger portion of the visual field.

An additional consequence of the differing sizes of M and P receptive fields is that M cells are much more sensitive—better able to detect visual stimuli—than are P cells under low lighting conditions (e.g., at night). However, the smaller receptive fields of P cells enable them to provide finer resolution (greater acuity) than M cells can, if there is enough light for the P cells to operate. See **Web Activity 2.6: Acuity versus Sensitivity** for more on this trade-off.

P and M ganglion cells also differ in their temporal responses. P cells tend to respond with sustained firing while light shines on their excitatory regions. M cells tend to respond more transiently: an M cell will respond with a brief burst of impulses when the spot is turned on, and then quickly return to its spontaneous rate, even if the spot remains lit. Thus, M and P ganglion cells signal different information to the brain. P cells provide information mainly about the contrast in the retinal image, and M cells signal information about how the image changes over time.

Finally, P and M cells differ in what they say to the brain about the color of the light they detect (see Chapter 5).

Whistling in the Dark: Dark and Light Adaptation

If you enter a dark room from bright sunlight, the number of photons of light entering your eye might be reduced by a factor of several billion. Initially you will have trouble seeing anything, but after about 30 minutes in the dark you will be able to detect just a few photons (Figure 2.17). And when you emerge from the dark and return to the sunlight, you will be able to see almost instantly. How does the visual system alter its sensitivity over such a large operating range?

When a flashlight is shone in someone's eye in a dimly lit room, the pupil quickly constricts. The diameter of the pupil can vary by about a factor of 4, from about 2 mm in bright illumination to about 8 mm in the dark (Figure 2.18). Because the amount of light entering the eye is proportional to the area of the pupil, the 4-fold increase in diameter accounts for a 16-fold improvement in sensitivity. In other words, 16 times as many quanta can enter the eye when the pupil is completely dilated, compared to when it is constricted. Although

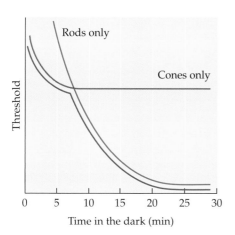

FIGURE 2.17 Dark adaptation curve. The purple curve shows the threshold light intensity required to detect a peripheral spot following several minutes of adaptation to a bright light. The red curve illustrates the rapid adaptation of the cones. The blue curve shows the slower recovery of the rods to much lower threshold intensities (that is, greater sensitivity). The purple curve represents the most sensitive of the two at any given time.

this adaptive ability certainly helps, pupil dilation accounts for only a small part of the visual system's overall ability to adapt to light and dark conditions.

A second mechanism for achieving a large sensitivity range is provided by the way photopigments are used up and replaced in receptor cells. In dim lighting conditions, plenty of photopigment is available, and rods and cones absorb and respond to as many photons as they can. As already noted, rods provide better sensitivity in such situations than do cones. Indeed, the rod system is capable of detecting a single quantum of light! (See **Web Essay 2.1: How Many Quanta Does It Take?**) After a photopigment molecule is bleached (used to detect a photon), the molecule must be regenerated before it can be used again to absorb another photon.

As the overall light level increases, the number of photons starts to overwhelm the system: photopigment molecules cannot be regenerated fast enough to detect all the photons hitting the photoreceptors. This slow regeneration is a good thing for increasing our sensitivity range. If photons are scarce, we use them all to see; if we have an overabundance, we simply throw some of them away and use the leftovers.

This light compensation mechanism is enhanced by humans' duplex retinas. Rods provide exquisite sensitivity at low light levels, but they become overwhelmed when the background light becomes moderately bright, leading to a loss in information quality. Cones are much less sensitive than rods (they function poorly under very dim light), but their operating range is much larger, stretching from about ten photons per second (just enough light to see color) to hundreds of thousands of photons per second (e.g., a snowcapped mountain in bright sunlight). So we use rods to see when the light is low, and

(*a*) Bright illumination

(*b*) Dark

2-mm pupil

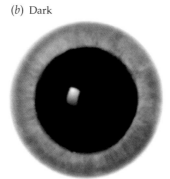

8-mm pupil

FIGURE 2.18 The black spots in the middle of these two eyeballs show the possible range of pupil sizes as we go from bright illumination (*a*) into the dark (*b*).

the cones take over when there is too much light for the rods to function well. After adapting to a bright light, cones recover sensitivity quickly (red curve in Figure 2.17) and then saturate. They are not very sensitive to very dim light. Rods recover more slowly (blue curve in Figure 2.17), but after 30 minutes or so they are very sensitive to dim light.

Although pupil size, photopigment regeneration rates, and the rod/cone dichotomy all play a role in dark and light adaptation, the most important reason we are not bothered by variations in overall light levels has to do with the neural circuitry of the retina. As we learned earlier, ganglion cells fire at their maximum rate when the centers of their receptive fields are brightly lit while the surrounds are completely dark (or vice versa) (see Figure 2.14). But the cells will still fire at an above-spontaneous rate when light falls on the entire receptive field, as long as the light is *brighter* in the ON portion than in the OFF portion of the receptive field. Therefore, as long as the photoreceptors feeding the ganglion cells are not completely saturated, the ganglion cells will encode the pattern of relatively light and relatively dark areas in the retinal image. And the pattern of illumination, not the overall light level, is the primary concern of the rest of the visual system.

To sum up, the answer to the question of how the visual system deals with such large variations in overall light levels has two parts. First, we reduce the scale of the problem by regulating the amount of light entering the eyeball, by using different types of photoreceptors in different situations, and by effectively throwing away photons we don't need. Second, by responding to the contrast between adjacent retinal regions, the ganglion cells do their best to ignore whatever variation in overall light level is left over.

The Man Who Could Not See Stars

Imagine not being able to see stars. What follows is the sad story of a man who could not. This man loved to go out at night and look at the sky when he visited the countryside. He used to find his favorite distant star by scanning the northern sky, and when he spotted its faint glow, he would look off to the side so that he could see it out of the corner of his eye. He always found it fascinating that he could see a dim star better with his peripheral vision than when he fixated it directly.

On one visit, his first in 2 years, he was very excited when he spotted his star. To his great dismay, however, when he looked off to the side, as he had done so many times before, the star disappeared. He had noticed during the preceding year that he was beginning to experience difficulty driving at night. Sometimes he didn't see cars off in the distance, or cars overtaking from the side. And he seemed to be dazzled for a long time by the headlights of oncoming vehicles. Movies were also becoming a problem. It seemed to take forever for his vision to adapt to the darkness of the theater.

He was also beginning to experience other difficulties with his vision. Just in the previous week he had walked into a table in a restaurant, and several times he had tripped over items that he simply hadn't noticed. He hadn't worried too much about these difficulties, because he was having no trouble reading and his vision in bright lights seemed just fine. But not seeing his favorite star out of the corner of his eye really shook him. He was reminded of his father, who in his later years had not been able to drive or read because he had been almost totally blind.

Retinitis pigmentosa (RP) is a family of hereditary diseases characterized by the progressive death of photoreceptors and degeneration of the pigment epithelium. In the most common form of RP, exhibited by the man who could not see stars, the rods are affected before the cones. Therefore, people suffering

retinitis pigmentosa (RP) A progressive degeneration of the retina that affects night vision and peripheral vision. RP commonly runs in families and can be caused by defects in a number of different genes that have recently been identified.

FIGURE 2.19 Fundus of a patient with retinitis pigmentosa. Compare this picture with the normal fundus shown in Figure 2.5. (From Rodieck, 1998.)

from this form of the disease first notice vision problems in their peripheral vision and under low light conditions—situations in which rods play the dominant role in collecting light. In some cases, vision loss progresses slowly and goes unnoticed until age 20 or later. However, the age of onset and rate of progression vary greatly, probably reflecting complex variations in the genetics of the disease. Eventually, visual loss spreads toward the fovea, often leading to total blindness.

Figure 2.19 shows the fundus of the man who could not see stars. A comparison with the normal fundus pictured in Figure 2.5 shows that the most striking difference is the presence of conspicuous clumps of pigment in the RP fundus that have a characteristic shape and are known as "bone spicules." These bone spicules are the hallmark of retinitis pigmentosa.

When you're reading this book, you direct your gaze (and your fovea) at the words. But if an elephant were to walk up beside you, you would see it out of the corner of your eye (your peripheral field of vision) and most likely make an eye movement to look at it directly. Luckily, the extent of peripheral vision in intact visual systems is pretty big. How big? You can test the extent of your own visual field by closing your left eye, stretching your arms out in front of you with index fingers raised, and moving your right finger around while you fixate your gaze on the left finger. The points at which you can no longer see the right finger above, below, and to the right and left of the other finger define the limits of your peripheral vision.

Normal visual fields (Figure 2.20*a*) are limited by anatomy: the upper, lower, and inside edges are set by the prominence of the eyebrows, cheekbones, and nose, respectively; and the outer edge is limited by the abrupt edge of the retina. RP sufferers typically exhibit an overall shrinkage of their visual fields (Figure 2.20*b*), as well as "ring scotomas," bands of blindness between the relatively normal central visual fields and the periphery.

At present, there is no cure for retinitis pigmentosa. Large doses of vitamins A and E evidently alter certain electrical potentials that can be measured from the retina and may slow the progression of RP by a very small amount, but it is not clear that these large vitamin doses actually improve either visual fields or dark adaptation. However, there is hope for persons with RP. On June 26, 2000, mapping of the human genome was completed, paving the way for new treatments of genetic diseases. Several genes associated with RP and related

FIGURE 2.20 Visual fields in (*a*) normal individuals and (*b*) the man who couldn't see stars. The fields are pictured as though we were looking through the back of the patient's head at the field limits on the retina. Thus, the right eye is shown on the right, and the left eye on the left. The numbers show the visual angles in degrees. The reddish-shaded areas show the outer limits of vision (the size of the visual field). The small black ovals in the center represent the physiological blind spot (due to the optic nerve head). In part (*b*), note that the outer limits of vision are somewhat shrunken, but more important, a ring of blindness (illustrated by the black ring) occupies the middle of the visual field. This ring scotoma is one of the hallmarks of retinitis pigmentosa.

diseases have already been identified, and gene replacement therapy has shown promise in mice models (Busskamp et al., 2010).

Summary

1. This chapter provided some insight into the complex journey that is required for us to see stars and other spots of light. The path of the light was traced from a distant star through the eyeball and to its absorption by photoreceptors and its transduction into neural signals. In subsequent chapters we'll learn how those signals are transmitted to the brain and translated into the experience of perception.

2. Light, on its way to becoming a sensation (a visual sensation, that is), can be absorbed, scattered, reflected, transmitted, or refracted. It can become a sensation only when it's absorbed by a photoreceptor in the retina.

3. Vision begins in the retina, when light is absorbed by rods or cones. The retina is like a minicomputer that transduces light energy into neural energy.

4. The retina sends information to the brain via ganglion cells, neurons whose axons make up the optic nerves. Retinal ganglion cells have center-surround receptive fields and are concerned with changes in contrast (the difference in intensity between adjacent bits of the scene).

Refer to the
Sensation and Perception
Companion Website
sites.sinauer.com/wolfe3e
for activities, essays, study
questions, and other study aids.

5. The visual system deals with large variations in overall light intensity by (a) regulating the amount of light entering the eyeball, (b) using different types of photoreceptors in different situations, and (c) effectively throwing away photons we don't need.

6. Age-related macular degeneration (AMD) is a disease associated with aging that affects the macula. The leading cause of visual loss among the elderly in the United States, AMD gradually destroys sharp central vision, making it difficult to read, drive, and recognize faces.

7. Retinitis pigmentosa (RP) is a family of hereditary diseases characterized by the progressive death of photoreceptors and degeneration of the pigment epithelium. In the most common form of the disease, patients first notice vision problems in their peripheral vision and under low light conditions—situations in which rods play the dominant role in collecting light.

CHAPTER 3

Christopher Small, *Untitled #25*, 2011

Spatial Vision: From Spots to Stripes

n Chapter 2 we learned that the macroscopic structures of the human eye function essentially as a biological camera: the iris regulates the amount of light entering the eyeball; and the cornea, lens, and aqueous and vitreous humors focus these rays so that a clear image is formed on the retina. The rod and cone photoreceptors capture this image in a way that is roughly analogous to the way the film in a camera captures photographic images.

It is here, however, that the analogy between visual system and camera ends. Cameras take pictures. Visual systems see. How do we get from an image of the world in front of us to an interpretation of that world—what is out there, where it is, and what we can do to it? This process starts in the eyeball itself, where the postreceptor layers of the retina translate the raw light array captured by the photoreceptors into the patterns of spots surrounded by darkness, or vice versa, detected by the ganglion cells (see Figure 2.14). As we discussed in Chapter 2, this retinal translation helps us perceive the pattern of light and dark areas in the visual field, regardless of the overall light level (e.g., it enables us to see almost as well at dusk as we can at noon).

In this chapter we follow the path of image processing from the eyeball to the brain (Figure 3.1). Ganglion cells in the retina respond preferentially to spots of light. As we will see, neurons in the cerebral cortex prefer lines, edges, and stripes. Furthermore, this portion of visual cortex is organized into thousands of tiny computers, each responsible for determining the orientation, width, color, and other characteristics of the stripes in one small portion of the visual field. In Chapter 4 we will continue this story by examining how other parts of the brain assemble the outputs from these minicomputers to produce a coherent representation of the objects whose reflected light started the photoreceptors firing in the first place.

Visual Acuity: Oh Say, Can You See?

The King said, "I haven't sent the two Messengers, either. They're both gone to the town. Just look along the road, and tell me if you can see either of them."

"I see nobody on the road," said Alice.

"I only wish I had such eyes," the King remarked in a fretful tone. "To be able to see Nobody! And at that distance, too!"

— Lewis Carroll, *Through the Looking Glass*

Since we'll be talking in this chapter about how the visual system codes images in terms of oriented stripes, let's start by determining just how well we see stripes when they are very close together and/or when the difference in

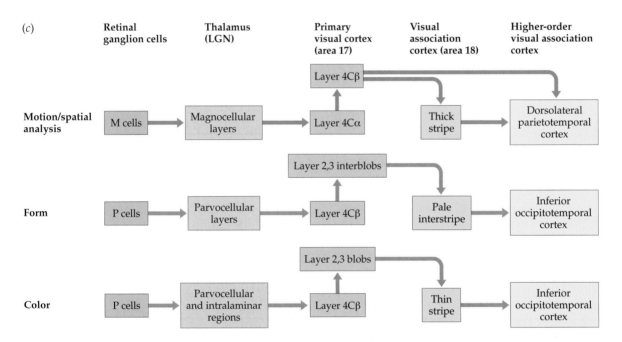

FIGURE 3.1 Cortical visual pathways. (a) The basic organization of the primary visual pathway from eyeball to striate cortex, in coronal section. (b) A lateral view of the brain, illustrating early visual areas and showing the putative *where* (dorsal) and *what* (ventral) streams. (c) The flow of information for motion, form, and color analysis from retinal ganglion cells to higher-order visual association cortex. (Part *a* after Purves et al., 2008; *b* and *c* after Blumenfeld, 2002.)

contrast The difference in luminance between an object and the background, or between lighter and darker parts of the same object.

illumination between the stripes and the background (the **contrast**) is very low. In addition to setting the boundary conditions for how well we should expect the visual system to be able to perform, we will use this section to introduce some important jargon that we'll need in the rest of the chapter.

FIGURE 3.2 A visual acuity test. See the text for details.

Get a tape measure, prop your textbook up, and, while looking at the *X* in the middle of **Figure 3.2**, back up until you cannot tell the orientation of the black and white stripes. Measure how far your eye is from the page. Now walk forward a bit until you're sure you can see which grating includes vertical stripes and which horizontal stripes, and again measure your distance from the page. Congratulations! You just completed a fast (but not terribly accurate) measurement of your own visual resolution **acuity**.

Eye doctors specify acuity in terms like *20/20* (more about this in a moment), but vision scientists prefer to talk about the smallest visual angle of a cycle of the grating that we can perceive (**Figure 3.3**). A **cycle** is simply one repetition of a black and a white stripe (both of the gratings in Figure 3.2 have 25 total cycles). **Visual angle**, which we mentioned briefly in Chapter 2, is the angle that would be formed by lines going from the top and bottom (or left and right, depending on the orientation of the stripes) of a cycle on the page, through the center of the lens, and on to the retina. You can learn more about this concept in **Web Activity 3.1: Visual Angle**.

More precisely, to calculate the visual angle of your resolution acuity, divide the size of the cycle in Figure 3.2 (which was 2 millimeters, or 1/16 inch) by the viewing distance at which you could just barely make out the orientation of the gratings (average your first and second measurements to get a rough estimate of this distance), and then take the arctangent of this ratio. Under ideal conditions, humans with very good vision can resolve gratings like those in Figure 3.2 when one cycle subtends an angle of approximately 1 minute of arc (0.017 degree).

This resolution acuity represents one of the fundamental limits of spatial vision: it is the finest high-contrast detail that can be resolved. The limit is determined primarily by the spacing of photoreceptors in the retina. To see why, imagine that we're projecting the **sine wave gratings** shown in **Figure 3.4** onto the retina. The light intensity in such gratings varies smoothly and continuously across each cycle (unlike the gratings in Figure 3.2, in which intensity changes abruptly from black to white and back to black). However, the

acuity The smallest spatial detail that can be resolved.

cycle For a grating, a pair consisting of one dark bar and one bright bar.

visual angle The angle subtended by an object at the retina.

sine wave grating A grating with a sinusoidal luminance profile.

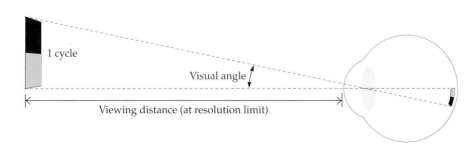

FIGURE 3.3 Visual angle. Shown here is the angle size of one cycle of a grating at the retina.

FIGURE 3.4 Sine wave gratings. (a) The stripes are wider than the photoreceptors (pink circles in the top panel), and the grating can be reconstructed vertically. (b) The stripes are narrower than the photoreceptors, so both black and white bars will fall inside a single receptor (top panel), resulting in a uniform gray field (bottom panel).

aliasing Misperception of a grating due to undersampling.

visual system "samples" the grating discretely, through the array of receptors at the back of the retina (in this respect the eye is more like a digital camera than like a traditional camera that uses film). If the receptors are spaced such that the whitest and blackest parts of the grating fall on separate cones (Figure 3.4a), we should be able to make out the grating. But if the entire cycle falls on a single cone (Figure 3.4b), we will see nothing but a gray field (or we may experience a phenomenon called **aliasing**, in which we misperceive the cycles to be longer than they actually are).

Cones in the fovea have a center-to-center separation of about 0.5 minute of arc (0.008 degree), which fits nicely with the observed acuity limit of 1 minute of arc (remember that we need two cones per cycle to be able to perceive the grating accurately). Rods and cones in the periphery are packed together less tightly (recall that in the periphery rods are physically more tightly packed [denser] than cones, as shown in Figure 2.9), but here many receptors converge on each ganglion cell. As a result, visual acuity is much poorer in the periphery than in the fovea. For a demonstration of the difference between foveal and peripheral vision, see **Web Activity 3.2: Foveal Acuity**. (See also **Web Essay 3.1: Hyperacuity**.)

A Visit to the Eye Doctor

Eye doctors don't describe acuity in terms of visual angles and cycles. The last time you visited your eye doctor, she may have asked you to read letters, decreasing the size of the letters until you made several errors. Then she may have told you that your visual acuity was 20/20 if your vision was good, or 20/30 if you needed glasses, or possibly 20/10 if you could read the smallest letters on the eye chart. This method for designating visual acuity was invented in 1862 by a Dutch eye doctor, Herman Snellen (1834–1908). Snellen constructed a set of block letters for which the letter as a whole was five times as large as the strokes that formed the letter (**Figure 3.5**). Note that the resulting patterns are reminiscent of the gratings in Figure 3.2. He then defined visual acuity as follows:

$$\frac{\text{(distance at which a person can just identify the letters)}}{\text{(distance at which a person with ``normal'' vision can just identify the letters)}}$$

In later adaptations of the Snellen test, the viewer was positioned at a constant distance of 20 feet, and the size of the letters, rather than the position of the viewer, was altered. So normal vision came to be defined as 20/20. To relate this measure back to visual angle, a 20/20 letter is designed to subtend an angle of 5 arc minutes (0.083 degree) at the eye, and each stroke of a 20/20 letter subtends an angle of 1 arc minute (the familiar 0.017 degree). Thus, if you can read a 20/20 letter, you can discern detail that subtends 1 minute of arc. If you have to be at 20 feet to read a letter that someone with normal vision can read at 40 feet, you have 20/40 vision (worse than normal). Although 20/20 is often considered the gold standard, most healthy young adults have an acuity level closer to 20/15.

Acuity for Low-Contrast Stripes

Up to now we've been discussing the tiniest high-contrast details that we can resolve. We learned that high-contrast sine wave gratings can be distinguished from a uniform gray field, as long as adjacent pairs of light or dark stripes are separated by at least 1 arc minute of visual angle. But what happens if the contrast of the stripes is reduced—that is, if the light stripes are made darker and the dark stripes lighter?

This was the question asked by Otto Schade in 1956, when he was working for the RCA Corporation. Schade showed people sine wave gratings with different spatial frequencies and had them adjust the contrast of the gratings until they could just be detected. **Spatial frequency** refers to the number of times a pattern, such as a sine wave grating, repeats in a given unit of space. For example, if you view your book from about 120 centimeters (about 47 inches) away, the visual angle between each pair of white stripes in **Figure 3.6***b* is about 0.25 degree, so the spatial frequency of this grating is 1/0.25 = 4 **cycles per degree**. Figure 3.6*a* shows a grating with a relatively lower spatial frequency (about 2 cycles per degree), and Figure 3.6*c* illustrates a relatively higher spatial frequency (about

FIGURE 3.5 A Snellen *E*. The letter size is five times the stroke size.

spatial frequency The number of grating cycles in a given unit of space.

cycles per degree The number of pairs of dark and bright bars per degree of visual angle.

FIGURE 3.6 Sine wave gratings illustrating low (*a*), medium (*b*), and high (*c*) spatial frequencies.

(*a*)

(*b*)

(*c*)

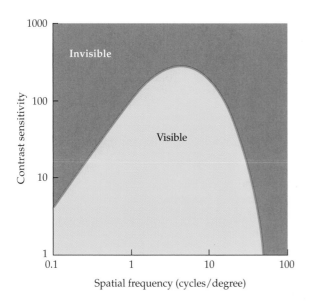

FIGURE 3.7 The contrast sensitivity function (red line): the window of visibility. Any objects whose spatial frequencies and contrasts fall within the yellow region will be visible. Those outside the yellow region are outside the window of visibility. The red line delimits the "threshold" between seeing and not seeing.

8 cycles per degree). **Web Activity 3.3: Gabor Patches** provides additional illustrations of sine wave gratings at different spatial frequencies.

Intuitively, you might think that the wider the stripes (that is, the lower the spatial frequency), the easier it would be to distinguish the light stripes from the dark stripes. But this is not exactly what Schade found. He, and later Fergus Campbell and Dan Green (1965), demonstrated that the human **contrast sensitivity function** (**CSF**) is shaped like an upside-down *U*, as shown in **Figure 3.7**. We obtain the units for the y-axis in this graph by taking the reciprocal of the **contrast threshold**. For example, for a 1-cycle/degree grating to be just distinguishable from uniform gray, the dark stripes must be about 1% darker than the light stripes (that is, if a tiny patch of a light stripe reflects 1000 photons, a patch of a dark stripe should reflect 990 photons). The reciprocal of this threshold is $1/0.01 = 100$, so this is the point plotted on the red CSF line in Figure 3.7 for this spatial frequency.

Note that a contrast of 100% corresponds to a sensitivity value of 1. The CSF reaches this value on the far right side of the curve in Figure 3.7, at about 60 cycles/degree. Sixty cycles/degree corresponds to a cycle width of 1 minute of arc, the resolution limit we measured previously for high-contrast stripes, which, recall, is determined primarily by cone spacing. The falloff in the CSF on the other side of the curve cannot be explained by cone spacing or by limitations in the optics of the eye. Instead, this part of the function must be due to neural factors, which we will discuss later.

You can visualize your own CSF by using **Figure 3.8**. Here we see a sinusoidal grating whose contrast increases continuously from the top of the figure to

contrast sensitivity function (CSF) A function describing how the sensitivity to contrast (defined as the reciprocal of the contrast threshold) depends on the spatial frequency (size) of the stimulus.

contrast threshold The smallest amount of contrast required to detect a pattern.

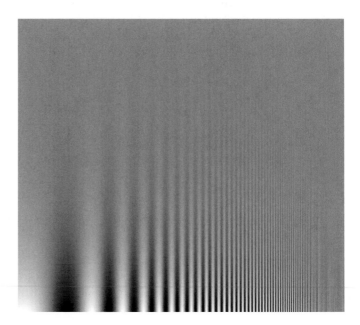

FIGURE 3.8 A grating modulated by contrast (vertically) and by spatial frequency (horizontally). (From Robson and Campbell, 1997; courtesy of Izumi Ohzawa.)

the bottom, and whose spatial frequency increases continuously from the left side of the graph to the right. If you view the figure from a distance of about 2 meters, you will notice the inverted *U* shape where the grating fades from visibility to invisibility. If you bring the book closer to your eye, you should be able to see the stripes on the right side of the figure going farther up, whereas the tops of the stripes on the left side will become less distinct.

Why Sine Wave Gratings?

One answer to this question is that, although "pure" sine wave gratings may be rare in the real world, patterns of stripes with more or less fuzzy boundaries are quite common: think of trees in a forest, books on a bookshelf, and a map of Manhattan (the latter includes a pattern of horizontal stripes superimposed on a pattern of vertical stripes). Furthermore, the edge of any object produces a single stripe, often blurred by a shadow, in the retinal image.

On a larger scale, the visual system appears to break down real-world images into a vast number of components, each of which is, essentially, a sine wave grating with a particular spatial frequency. This method of processing is analogous to the way in which the auditory system deals with sound and is called "Fourier analysis" (see Chapters 1, 7, and 10). We'll return to this idea later in the chapter. For now, rest assured that scientists don't use sine wave gratings just because they're convenient to manipulate in experiments (although they do make very nice stimuli).

phase The relative position of a grating.

Retinal Ganglion Cells and Stripes

In Chapter 2 we learned that retinal ganglion cells respond vigorously to spots of light. As it turns out, each ganglion cell also responds well to certain types of stripes or gratings. **Figure 3.9** shows how an ON retinal ganglion cell responds to gratings of different spatial frequencies. When the spatial frequency of the grating is too low (Figure 3.9*a*), the ganglion cell responds weakly because part of the fat, bright bar of the grating lands in the inhibitory surround, damping the cell's response. Similarly, when the spatial frequency is too high (Figure 3.9*c*), the ganglion cell responds weakly because both dark and bright stripes fall within the receptive-field center, washing out the response. But when the spatial frequency is just right (Figure 3.9*b*), with a bright bar filling the center and dark bars filling the surround, the cell responds vigorously. Thus, retinal ganglion cells are "tuned" to spatial frequency: each cell responds best to a specific spatial frequency that matches its receptive-field size, and it responds less to both higher and lower spatial frequencies.

Christina Enroth-Cugell and John Robson (1984) were the first to record the responses of retinal ganglion cells to sinusoidal gratings. In addition to showing that these cells respond vigorously to gratings of just the right size, these investigators discovered that responses depend on the **phase** of the grating—its position within the receptive field. **Figure 3.10** illustrates how an ON-center retinal ganglion cell might respond to

(*a*) Low frequency yields weak response

(*b*) Medium frequency yields strong response

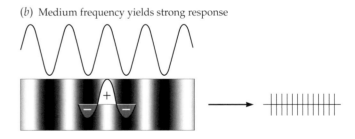

(*c*) High frequency yields weak response

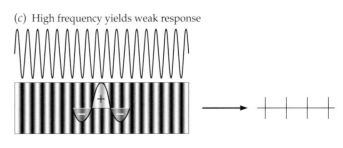

FIGURE 3.9 The response (right) of a ganglion cell to gratings of different spatial frequencies (left): (*a*) low, (*b*) medium, and (*c*) high.

(*a*) 0°— Positive response

(*b*) 90°— No response

(*c*) 180°— Negative response

(*d*) 270°— No response

FIGURE 3.10 The response of a ganglion cell to a grating depends on the phase of the grating. This figure illustrates the response of an ON-center retinal ganglion cell to four different phases of an optimally sized grating.

lateral geniculate nucleus (LGN) A structure in the thalamus, part of the midbrain, that receives input from the retinal ganglion cells and has input and output connections to the visual cortex.

magnocellular layer Either of the bottom two neuron-containing layers of the lateral geniculate nucleus, the cells of which are physically larger than those in the top four layers.

parvocellular layer Any of the top four neuron-containing layers of the lateral geniculate nucleus, the cells of which are physically smaller than those in the bottom two layers.

a grating of just the right spatial frequency (a bar width about the size of the receptive-field center) in four different phases.

When the grating has a light bar filling the receptive-field center and dark bars filling the surround (Figure 3.10*a*), this ON-center cell responds vigorously, increasing its firing rate. If the grating phase is shifted by 90 degrees (Figure 3.10*b*), half the receptive-field center will be filled by a light bar and half by a dark bar, and similarly for the surround. In other words, there will be no net difference between the light intensity in the receptive field's center and its surround. In this case the cell's response rate does not change from its resting rate when the grating is turned on—just what we would predict if the ganglion cell were summing the total amount of light falling on its center and its surround. A second 90-degree shift puts the dark bar in the center and the light bars in the surround, producing a negative response (Figure 3.10*c*) (see Chapter 2); and a third phase shift returns us to the situation after the first shift, with the overall intensities in the center and surround equivalent and the cell therefore blind to the grating (Figure 3.10*d*). (Note that other ganglion cells would respond to the 90-degree and 270-degree phases but not to the 0-degree and 180-degree phases, which is why the visual system as a whole is able to see all four phases equally well.)

The Lateral Geniculate Nucleus

The axons of retinal ganglion cells synapse in the two **lateral geniculate nuclei** (**LGNs**), one in each cerebral hemisphere. These act as relay stations on the way from the retina to the cortex (see Figure 3.1). Figure 3.11 shows that the LGN of primates is a six-layered structure, a bit like a stack of pancakes that has been bent in the middle (*geniculate* means "bent"). The neurons in the bottom two layers are physically larger than those in the top four layers; for this reason, the bottom two are called **magnocellular layers** and the top four **parvocellular layers** (*magno-* and *parvo-* are Latin for "large" and "small," respectively). The two types of layers also differ in another, more important, way: the magnocellular layers receive input from M ganglion cells in the retina, and the parvocellular layers receive input from P ganglion cells. The layers differ in more than the size of the cells. Studies in which magnocellular and parvocellular layers are chemically lesioned indicate

FIGURE 3.11 The primate lateral geniculate nucleus. (From Hubel, 1988.)

that the magnocellular pathway responds to large, fast-moving objects, and the parvocellular pathway is responsible for processing details of stationary targets. This distinction is interesting because it shows that the visual system splits input from the image into different types of information.

Even more splitting takes place *between* the magno- and parvo- layers. There we find the layers consisting of **koniocellular cells** (*konio-* is Greek for "dust"; these little cells were ignored for many years). Each layer seems to be involved in different aspects of processing. For example, one layer is specialized for relaying signals from the S-cones and may be part of a "primordial" blue-yellow pathway (see Chapter 5) (Hendry and Reid, 2000).

The organization of the retinal inputs to the LGN, diagrammed in **Figure 3.12**, provides some important insights into how our visual world is mapped to the brain. First, the left LGN receives projections from the left side of the retina in both eyes, and the right LGN receives projections from the right side of both retinas. Second, each layer of the LGN receives input from one or the other eye. From bottom to top, layers 1, 4, and 6 of the right LGN receive input from the left (**contralateral**) eye, while layers 2, 3, and 5 get their input from the right (**ipsilateral**) eye. The koniocellular layers appear to fall in the spaces between the clearly labeled layers in Figure 3.12 (Casagrande et al., 2007; Szmajda, Grünert, and Martin, 2008).

> **FURTHER DISCUSSION** of koniocellular cells can be found in Chapter 2 on page 44.

Each LGN layer contains a highly organized map of a complete half of the visual field. Figure 3.12 shows schematically how objects in the right visual field (objects to the right of where our gaze is fixated) are mapped onto the different layers of the left LGN (the right side of the world falls on the left side of the retina, whose ganglion cells project to the left LGN). This ordered mapping of the world onto the visual nervous system, known as **topographical mapping**, provides us with a neural basis for knowing where things are in space (we will return to this point a little later).

LGN neurons have concentric receptive fields that are very similar to those of retinal ganglion cells: they respond well to spots and gratings. Given that the LGN cells respond to the same patterns as the ganglion cells that provide their input, you might wonder why the visual system bothers with the LGN. Why don't the ganglion cell axons simply travel directly back to the cerebral cortex? One important reason is that the LGN is not merely a stop on the line from retina to cortex. There are many connections between other parts of the brain and the LGN (Babadi et al., 2010; Dubin and Cleland, 1977). Moreover, there are more feedback connections from the visual cortex to the LGN than from the LGN to the cortex.

It seems that the LGN is a location where various parts of the brain can modulate input from the eyes. For example, the LGN is part of a larger brain structure called the "thalamus" (the medial geniculate nucleus, part of the auditory pathway, is another portion of the thalamus; see Chapter 9). When you go to sleep, the entire thalamus is inhibited by circuitry elsewhere in the brain that works to keep you asleep. Thus, even if your eyelids were open

koniocellular cell A neuron located between the magnocellular and parvocellular layers of the lateral geniculate nucleus. This layer is known as the koniocellular layer.

contralateral Referring to the opposite side of the body (or brain).

ipsilateral Referring to the same side of the body (or brain).

topographical mapping The orderly mapping of the world in the lateral geniculate nucleus and the visual cortex.

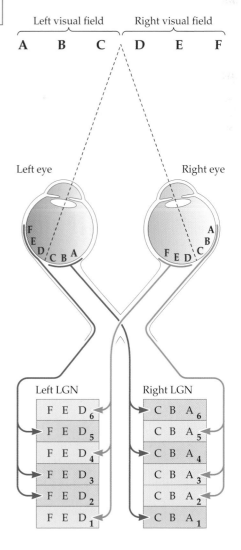

FIGURE 3.12 Input (in this case the letters *ABCDEF*) from the right visual field is mapped in an orderly fashion onto the different layers of the left LGN, and input from the left visual field is mapped to the right LGN. Information from the two eyes is segregated into separate layers. Layers 1 and 2 are the magnocellular layers; layers 3–6 are the parvocellular layers.

1

2/3

4A

4B

4C

5

6

1 mm

while you were sleeping at night, you would not see anything in your dimly lit room. Input would travel from your retinas to your LGNs, but the neural signals would stop there before reaching the cortex, so they would never be registered. The thalamic inhibition is not complete, which is why loud noises (e.g., the alarm clock) or bright lights will be perceived, causing you to wake up.

Striate Cortex

If you place one hand at the back of your head, about an inch or two above the top of your neck, you should be able to feel a small bump known as the "inion." The receiving area for LGN inputs in the cerebral cortex lies below the inion. This area has several names: **primary visual cortex** (**V1**), **area 17**, or **striate cortex** (*striate* means "striped," for the striped pattern V1 takes on following a certain type of staining procedure). By now you're probably getting the idea that layers are an important property of neural structures in the visual pathway. The striate cortex consists of six major layers, some of which have sublayers (**Figure 3.13**). Fibers from the LGN project mainly (but not exclusively) to layer 4, with magnocellular axons coming in to sublayer 4Cα and parvocellular axons projecting to sublayer 4Cβ (Yabuta and Callaway, 1998). (See **Web Essay 3.2: The Whole Brain Atlas**.)

Like the LGN, the striate cortex has a systematic topographical mapping of the visual field. But the striate cortex is not simply a bigger version of the LGN. A major and complex transformation of visual information takes place in the striate cortex. For starters, striate cortex contains on the order of 200 million cells—more than 100 times as many as the LGN has!

Figure 3.14 illustrates two important features of the visual cortex: topography and magnification. First, the fact that the image of the woman's right eyebrow (*her* right; it appears on the left in Figure 3.14) is mapped onto regions corresponding to the numbers 3 and 4 in the striate cortex, tells the visual system that the eyebrow must be in positions 3 and 4 of the visual field. This is topographical mapping, as noted earlier. Second, information is dramatically scaled from different parts of the visual field. Objects imaged on or near the fovea are processed by neurons in a large part of the striate cortex, but objects imaged in the far right or left periphery are allocated only a tiny portion of the striate cortex. This distortion of the visual-field map on the cortex is known as **cortical magnification** because the cortical representation of the fovea is greatly magnified compared to the

primary visual cortex (V1), area 17, or striate cortex The area of the cerebral cortex of the brain that receives direct inputs from the lateral geniculate nucleus, as well as feedback from other brain areas, and is responsible for processing visual information.

cortical magnification The amount of cortical area (usually specified in millimeters) devoted to a specific region (e.g., 1 degree) in the visual field.

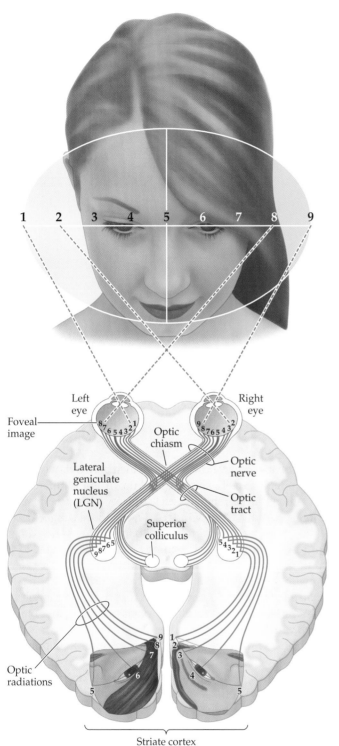

FIGURE 3.14 The mapping of objects in space onto the visual cortex. This figure illustrates both the topographical mapping and the dramatic magnification of the foveal representation in the cortex. (After Frisby, 1980.)

cortical representation of peripheral vision. (See **Web Essay 3.3: Seeing Images on the Cortex.**)

To gain a sense of the extent of this cortical magnification factor, hold your two arms out in front of you, put up your index fingers, hold them about 10 centimeters (4 inches) apart, close your left eye, and fixate your right finger. In this position, your right fingernail, which is taking up about 1 degree of visual angle on the fovea, is being processed by neurons in about 20 millimeters (mm) of striate cortex. Your left fingernail, which is covering the same amount of

(a)

Fovea

2.5 5 10 20 40

(b)

20 40

5 10

2.5

2.5 5 10 20 40
Eccentricity (degrees)

1 cm

FIGURE 3.15 Mapping the visual field onto the cortex, as deduced from studying lesions (*a*) and from functional MRI (*b*). In (*b*), different parts of the visual field are mapped onto the cortex according to the color code provided. Notice that the red area is just the central few degrees, whereas the blue areas cover vast parts of the more peripheral field, from 20 to 40 degrees. (Part *a* from Horton and Hoyt, 1991; *b* from Wandell and Winawer, 2011.)

visual angle but is falling 10 degrees to the left of the fovea, is being processed by only 1.5 mm of cortex.

Topography of the Human Cortex

Much of what we know about cortical topography and magnification comes from anatomical and physiological studies in animals. The earliest studies in humans were based on correlating visual-field defects with cortical lesions. That is, someone with damage to this part of visual cortex would be blind in that part of the visual field. Figure 3.15*a* illustrates how eccentricity (distance from the fovea) maps onto visual cortex, as deduced from studying lesions. However, in the last 20 years or so there have been major advances in our knowledge of human visual cortex—in large part through developments in brain-imaging techniques. If you've ever injured your knee or back, you may be familiar with magnetic resonance imaging (MRI). MRI is very useful for anatomical imaging of soft tissues, including the brain.

MRI lets us see the structure of the brain. *Functional* magnetic resonance imaging (fMRI) is a noninvasive technique for measuring and localizing brain activity. As discussed in Chapter 1, fMRI does not measure neural activity directly. Rather, it measures changes in blood oxygen level that reflect neural activity. Blood oxygen level–dependent (BOLD) signals reflect a range of metabolically demanding neural signals (Wandell and Winawer, 2011). If you compare blood flow when visual stimuli are presented in one portion of the visual field to blood flow when the field is blank, you can find portions of the brain that respond specifically to that stimulation of that portion of the field. In this way it is possible to map the topography of V1 in the living human brain (Figure 3.15*b*). Different parts of the visual field are mapped onto Figure 3.15*b* with a color code. Notice that the red area is just the central few degrees. The blue areas cover vast parts of the more peripheral field, from 20 to 40 degrees. Because of cortical magnification of the central field, these red and blue regions are similar in size. As we move along, we will see that fMRI can be used to localize other visual functions in striate cortex and beyond, in "extrastriate" cortex, the cortex surrounding striate cortex.

FIGURE 3.16 A letter chart in which the letter size increases with eccentricity in proportion to the inverse cortical magnification factor. If you fixate your gaze on the far left side of the figure, all seven letters should be equally easy to see because those on the right, which are in the periphery, are so much larger.

Some Perceptual Consequences of Cortical Magnification

One important consequence of cortical magnification is that visual acuity declines in an orderly fashion with eccentricity (Levi, Klein, and Aitsebaomo, 1985)—a phenomenon demonstrated by Hermann Rudolf Aubert well over a century ago (Aubert, 1886). **Web Activity 3.2: Foveal Acuity** allows you to demonstrate this phenomenon yourself, as does Figure 3.16, in which the letters are scaled in size such that each one covers an approximately equal cortical area.

Why is the foveal representation in the cortex so highly magnified? The visual system must make a trade-off. High resolution requires a great number of resources: a dense array of photoreceptors, one-to-one lines from photoreceptors to retinal ganglion cells, and a large chunk of striate cortex (not to mention the real estate in other areas of cortex necessary to do something with the visual information coming out of V1). To see the entire visual field with such high resolution, we might need eyes and brains too large to fit in our heads! Thus, we have evolved a visual system that provides high resolution in the center and lower resolution in the periphery. If you need to process the details of an object in the corner of your eye, you can simply turn your eye or head so that the object falls on the fovea instead (see Chapter 8 for a discussion of eye movements).

Interestingly, although visual acuity falls off rapidly in peripheral vision, it is not the major obstacle to reading or object recognition in the visual periphery. The real problem in the periphery is known as **visual crowding**—the deleterious effect of clutter on peripheral object recognition (Levi, 2008; Whitney and Levi, 2011). Objects that can be easily identified in isolation seem indistinct and jumbled in clutter (Figure 3.17).

visual crowding The deleterious effect of clutter on peripheral object recognition.

FIGURE 3.17 Visual crowding. (a) Visual crowding occurs in natural scenes. When fixating the bull's-eye near the construction zone, note that it is difficult or impossible to recognize the child on the left-hand side of the road, simply because of the presence of the nearby signs. However, it is relatively easy to recognize the child on the right-hand side. (b) While fixating each cross, it is easy to identify the shape (left cross), line orientation (middle cross), or letter (right cross) above it, but it is difficult or impossible to identify the same shape, line orientation, or letter when it is in the middle of a group below the cross. Crowding impairs the ability to recognize objects, but it does not make them disappear. (From Whitney and Levi, 2011.)

(a)

(b)

Crowding is an essential bottleneck, setting limits on object perception, eye and hand movements, visual search, reading, and perhaps other functions in peripheral vision. Crowding impairs not only the discrimination of object features and contours but the ability to recognize and respond appropriately to objects in clutter. Interestingly, crowded objects don't simply disappear. Rather crowded objects appear "jumbled" (that is, the target and neighboring objects are combined into a texture). Thus, crowding may be a process that simplifies the appearance of the peripheral array by promoting consistent appearance among adjacent objects, at the expense of an ability to pick out individual objects. Luckily, we are able to make eye movements in order to foveate and scrutinize individual objects in clutter.

Receptive Fields in Striate Cortex

In 1958, David Hubel and Torsten Wiesel began work as postdoctoral students in Stephen Kuffler's laboratory. Their goal was to extend Kuffler's ground-breaking work on retinal ganglion cells to the cortex. So they began trying to map the receptive fields of neurons in striate cortex using spots of light, much as Kuffler (1953) had done earlier (see Chapter 2). To their dismay, however, they found that the cat's cortical cells hardly responded at all to the same spots that made its ganglion cells fire like crazy. To project their stimuli onto the retina, Hubel and Wiesel inserted a glass slide with a black spot into a slot in a special ophthalmoscope (that's the instrument the doctor uses when she shines a bright light into your eye in order to see your retina). One day, they had been recording from a neuron without much luck, when suddenly the cell emitted a strong burst of firing as they inserted the glass slide into the slot. Eventually they realized that the response had nothing to do with the spot itself; instead, the cell had been responding to the shadow cast by the edge of the glass slide as it swept across the ophthalmoscope's light path. And the rest, as they say, is history. Hubel related this story when he and Wiesel received the 1981 Nobel Prize in Physiology or Medicine for uncovering many of the remarkable properties of the visual cortex.

Hubel and Wiesel's most fundamental discovery was that the receptive fields of striate cortex neurons are not circular, as they are in the retina and LGN. Rather, they are elongated. As a result, they respond much more vigorously to bars, lines, edges, and gratings than to round spots of light.

Orientation Selectivity

Further investigation by Hubel and Wiesel (1962) uncovered a number of other important properties of the receptive fields of neurons in striate cortex. First, an individual neuron will not respond equivalently to just any old stripe in its receptive field. It responds best when the line or edge is at just the right orientation, and hardly at all when the line is tilted more than 30 degrees away from the optimal orientation (a change equivalent to movement of the minute hand of a clock from 12 to 1). Scientists call this selective responsiveness **orientation tuning**: the cell is tuned to detect lines in a specific orientation in the same way that a piano key is tuned to produce a specific musical note.

A typical orientation tuning function looks like the plot in **Figure 3.18**. The neuron featured here fires vigorously when the line is oriented vertically (at 90 degrees), but the response tapers off rapidly as the line is tilted one way or another, diminishing to close to the cell's resting rate when the line is tilted 30 degrees in either direction. Other cells in striate cortex are selective for 0 degrees (horizontal), 45 degrees, 20 degrees, 62 degrees, and so on, so that the population of neurons as a whole detects all possible orientations.

orientation tuning The tendency of neurons in striate cortex to respond optimally to certain orientations and less to others.

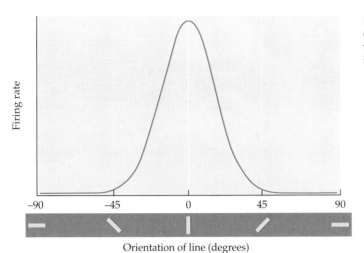

FIGURE 3.18 Orientation tuning function of a cortical cell. The neuron fires vigorously when the line is oriented vertically, but it fires hardly at all when the line orientation is changed by 30 degrees.

However, more cells are responsive to horizontal and vertical orientations than to obliques (De Valois, Yund, and Hepler, 1982; B. Li, Peterson, and Freeman, 2003). This physiological finding meshes well with the psychophysical finding that humans have somewhat lower visual acuity and contrast sensitivity for oblique targets than for horizontal and vertical targets.

How are the circular receptive fields in the LGN transformed into the elongated receptive fields in striate cortex? Hubel and Wiesel suggested a very simple scheme to explain this transformation (**Figure 3.19**). Simply put, their idea was that the concentric LGN cells that feed into a cortical cell are all in a row. Later studies (e.g., J. S. Anderson et al., 2000) have shown that the arrangement of LGN inputs is indeed crucial for establishing the orientation selectivity of striate cortex cells. However, other evidence suggests that neural interactions (e.g., lateral inhibition) within the cortex also play an important role in the dynamics of orientation tuning (Pugh et al., 2000).

Other Receptive-Field Properties

Cortical cells respond not just to bars, lines, and edges. Like retinal ganglion cells, they also respond well to gratings (which are, after all, collections of lines). And like ganglion cells, they respond best to gratings that have just the right spatial frequency to fill the receptive-field center. That is, each striate cortex cell is tuned to a particular spatial frequency, which corresponds to a particular line width. Indeed, cortical cells are much more narrowly tuned (they respond to a smaller range of spatial frequencies) than retinal ganglion cells (De Valois, Albrecht, and Thorell, 1982). These narrow tuning functions mean that each striate cortex neuron functions as a **filter** for the portion of the image that excites the cell. We will return to the idea of striate cortex as a collection of filters later.

Another important discovery made by Hubel and Wiesel was that many cortical cells respond especially well to *moving* lines, bars, edges, and gratings. Moreover, many neurons respond strongly when a line moves in one direction—say, from left to right—but not at all when the same line moves from right to left.

As noted earlier, information from the two eyes is kept separate in the LGN: each LGN cell responds to one eye or the other, but never to both eyes. This arrangement changes dramatically in striate cortex, where a majority of cells can be influenced by input from both the left eye and the right eye. In other words, if a striate cortex neuron responds best to a 5-cycle/degree

filter An acoustic, electrical, electronic, or optical device, instrument, computer program, or neuron that allows the passage of some frequencies or digital elements and blocks the passage of others.

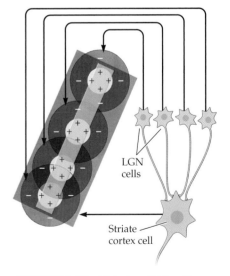

FIGURE 3.19 Hubel and Wiesel's model of how striate cortex cells get their orientation tuning: LGN cells, they hypothesized, were lined up in a row, feeding into the elongated arrangement of the striate cortex receptive fields (left).

ocular dominance The property of the receptive fields of striate cortex neurons by which they demonstrate a preference, responding somewhat more rapidly when a stimulus is presented in one eye than when it is presented in the other.

simple cell A cortical neuron with clearly defined excitatory and inhibitory regions.

complex cell A neuron whose receptive-field characteristics cannot be easily predicted by mapping with spots of light.

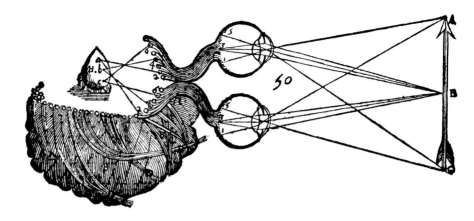

FIGURE 3.20 René Descartes's "fusion center." (From Descartes, 1664.)

grating oriented at 45 degrees, it will respond to such a stimulus whether that stimulus is presented in the right eye or the left eye. However, striate cortex neurons often have a preference, responding somewhat more rapidly when a stimulus is presented in one eye than when it is presented in the other. Hubel and Wiesel called this property of striate receptive fields **ocular dominance**.

Given that we see a single, unified world, intuitively it makes sense that information from the two eyes should be brought together at some point. Until Hubel and Wiesel's discovery, however, there were heated arguments about whether the information converged at all, and if so, whether it was in a specialized "fusion center" in the brain—a notion that dates back to Descartes (1664; see I. P. Howard and Rogers, 2001) (**Figure 3.20**). We'll describe some of these debates in Chapter 6, when we discuss binocular vision.

Simple and Complex Cells

Like precortical neurons, cortical neurons come in a wide variety of types. Hubel and Wiesel characterized neurons as **simple cells** when those neurons had clearly defined excitatory and inhibitory regions. **Figure 3.21** shows two varieties of simple-cell receptive fields and their preferred stimuli. An edge detector (Figure 3.21a) prefers to see light on one side of its receptive field and darkness on the other side. A stripe detector (Figure 3.21b) responds best to a line of light that has a particular width, surrounded on both sides by darkness. If a grating with the appropriate spatial frequency drifts across the receptive field of this cell, the cell's response will be modulated as dark and bright bars drift across the receptive-field center, in exactly the same way the response of the retinal ganglion cell shown in Figure 3.10 is modulated.

Other neurons show responses that cannot be simply predicted from their responses to stationary bars of light. Hubel and Wiesel called these **complex cells**. Like simple cells, each complex cell is tuned to a particular orientation and spatial frequency and shows an ocular preference. However, whereas a simple cell might respond only if a stripe is presented in the center of its receptive field, a complex cell will respond regardless of where the stripe is presented, as long as it is somewhere within the cell's receptive field (**Figure 3.22**). When tested with a drifting grating, the complex cell gives a robust response, with little or none of the modulation shown by simple cells (as well as retinal ganglion and LGN cells). Another way of stating this difference is to say that simple cells are "phase-sensitive," and complex cells are "phase-insensitive."

(a) Edge detector

(b) Stripe detector

FIGURE 3.21 Two flavors of simple cells: (a) an edge detector and (b) a stripe detector.

FIGURE 3.22 A simple cell and a complex cell might both be tuned to the same orientation and stripe width (spatial frequency), but the complex cell will respond to that stripe presented anywhere within its receptive field, whereas the simple cell might respond to the stripe in only one position.

As with all other neurons in the visual system, with the exception of retinal photoreceptors, the receptive fields of complex cells represent a pooling of the responses of several subunits. The subunits give the complex cell its spatial frequency and orientation tuning, but the complex pooling operation makes the complex cell insensitive to the precise position of the stimulus within its receptive field. Hubel and Wiesel hypothesized a hierarchy in which LGN cells fed into simple cells, which in turn provided excitatory inputs to complex cells. However, substantial evidence now suggests that complex cells represent a separate parallel pathway (that is, that both simple and complex cells get direct input from LGN neurons).

Further Complications

Hubel and Wiesel described another property of some cells in striate cortex that they called **end stopping**. When they tested an end-stopped cell with bars of increasing lengths, the response rate first increased as the bar filled up its receptive field, and then decreased markedly as the bar was lengthened further (**Figure 3.23**). Hubel and Wiesel called these cells "hypercomplex" cells, although they now appear to be subclasses of the simple and complex cells already discussed here (that is, there are simple end-stopped cells and complex end-stopped cells). End stopping is thought to play an important role in our ability to detect luminance boundaries and discontinuities.

Recent research has revealed additional idiosyncrasies in the receptive fields of striate cortex neurons. For example, the size of a particular cell's receptive field appears to vary with target contrast; for instance, the cell might respond

end stopping The process by which a cell in the cortex first increases its firing rate as the bar length increases to fill up its receptive field, and then decreases its firing rate as the bar is lengthened further.

FIGURE 3.23 When the stimulus (bar) does not reach the outside edge of the receptive field or it extends beyond the receptive field of an end-stopped cortical neuron, the neuron fires less than when the stimulus is just the right length.

to a smaller portion of the visual field when the grating stimulus has a high contrast as opposed to when the difference between light and dark bars is more subtle (Sceniak et al., 1999). And neurons can be influenced by stimuli that fall outside the classic receptive field, via short- or long-range lateral connections and/or via feedback from neurons in other layers (Zipser, Lamme, and Schiller, 1996).

As is the case for most of the visual system, what we don't know about the workings of striate cortex neurons almost certainly dwarfs what we do know. But to review what we do know, spend some time with **Web Activity 3.4: Striate Receptive Fields**, where you can try your hand at determining the receptive field of an unknown virtual neuron.

Columns and Hypercolumns

As we've discussed, each of the approximately 200 million neurons in striate cortex responds to a distinctive set of stimulus properties: stripes, edges, and/or gratings that are oriented at a particular angle, with a particular width or spatial frequency, possibly moving in a particular direction. Some neurons are simple cells and some are complex cells, and each one is end-stopped or not. Most neurons also respond preferentially to stimuli presented in one eye or another. And each neuron responds only when its preferred stimulus is presented in one particular part of the visual field.

Hubel and Wiesel noticed very early on that these various receptive-field properties are not scattered haphazardly around striate cortex. Once they had figured out what the cells were looking for (stripes rather than spots), they discovered that if they pushed the recording electrode down through the layers of the cortex in a direction perpendicular to the cortical surface, all the cells they encountered showed similar orientation preferences. If they shifted the electrode position over a tiny distance and made another perpendicular penetration, all the cells now responded best to a slightly different orientation, perhaps 10 or 15 degrees from the original orientation. On the basis of these observations, Hubel and Wiesel concluded that neurons with similar orientation preferences are arranged in **columns** that extend vertically through the cortex.

When Hubel and Wiesel made tangential penetrations into striate cortex (inserting an electrode such that it was oriented parallel to the cortical surface, rather than perpendicular), they found a systematic and progressive change in preferred orientation such that essentially all the orientations were encountered in a distance of about 0.5 mm. This finding has been confirmed via alternative physiological techniques. **Figure 3.24***a* shows a small portion of a monkey's striate cortex prepared so that neurons responding to vertically oriented lines are stained black, while other neurons remain white. The distance between the vertical orientation columns revealed by this technique is, sure enough, just about 0.5 mm (LeVay, Hubel, and Wiesel, 1975).

Roughly 25 years ago, it became possible to make detailed maps of the orientation tuning of cells in the cortex using optical imaging. Figure 3.24*c* shows an optical imaging study in which light reflected from the surface of the exposed brain reflects the activity of underlying neurons. In this figure, each color shows a set of neurons, activated by one orientation. You can see the complex, yet orderly organization of orientation tuning in the cortex (Blasdel and Salama, 1986). Recent work (Paik and Ringach, 2011) suggests that this beautiful arrangement arises during early development as a consequence of statistical wiring mechanisms combined with evenly spaced mosaics of ON and OFF retinal ganglion cells.

Orientation is not the only property arranged in columns in the visual cortex. Neurons that share the same eye preference (exhibiting what is referred

column A vertical arrangement of neurons.

(*a*) Orientation columns

(*b*) Ocular dominance columns

(*c*)

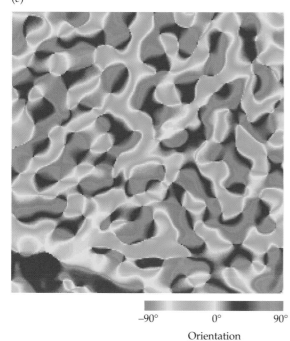

−90°   0°   90°

Orientation

FIGURE 3.24 Orientation (*a*) and ocular dominance (*b*) columns of the striate cortex, revealed by staining. (*c*) Optical imaging of the orientation maps in monkey cortex. (*a* and *b* from Hubel, Wiesel, and Stryker, 1978; *c* from Nauhaus et al., 2008.)

to as "ocular dominance") also have a columnar arrangement (Figure 3.24*b*). Furthermore, single-cell recording experiments, as well as staining experiments, indicate that eye preference switches (you guessed it) every 0.5 mm or so.

Through their studies, Hubel and Wiesel arrived at the model of striate cortical architecture illustrated in **Figure 3.25**. They proposed that a 1-mm block of striate cortex contains "all the machinery necessary to look after everything the visual cortex is responsible for, in a certain small part of the visual world" (Hubel, 1982). Each of these sections of cortex is called a **hypercolumn**. It contains at least two sets of columns, each covering every possible orientation (0–180 degrees), with one set preferring input from the left eye and one set preferring input from the right eye.

Hypercolumns are roughly 1 mm across throughout the striate cortex, but because of the cortical magnification factor discussed earlier, not all hypercolumns see the world at the same level of detail. A hypercolumn in the part of the cortex that represents the fovea may "see" a portion of the visual field that is 0.05 degree

hypercolumn A 1-millimeter block of striate cortex containing two sets of columns, each covering every possible orientation (0–180 degrees), with one set preferring input from the left eye and one set preferring input from the right eye.

FIGURE 3.25 This model of a hypercolumn shows two ocular dominance columns (one for each eye) and many orientation columns, and illustrates the locations of the cytochrome oxidase (CO) blobs. (From Breedlove, Rosenzweig, and Watson, 2007.)

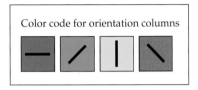

Color code for orientation columns

cytochrome oxidase (CO) An enzyme used to reveal the regular array of "CO blobs," which are spaced about 0.5 millimeter apart in the primary visual cortex.

of visual angle across; a hypercolumn responding to input 10 degrees to the right of the fovea should cover about 14 times as large an area (0.7 degree across).

Orientation and ocular dominance are probably not the only stimulus dimensions that have a systematic columnar arrangement in the visual cortex. For example, another staining technique, which takes advantage of an enzyme called **cytochrome oxidase** (**CO**), has revealed a regular array of "CO blobs" (shown in section in **Figure 3.26**), spaced that magical distance of about 0.5 mm apart (see Figure 3.25). The functional role of these blobs remains unclear, but CO blob columns have been implicated in processing color, with the interblob regions (note the elegant scientific jargon that has developed around this field of study) processing motion and spatial structure (Livingstone and Hubel, 1988). This view is probably too simplistic, but the blob array does suggest some kind of additional organizational layer on top of the orientation and ocular dominance arrays.

FURTHER DISCUSSION of CO blobs, which are also implicated in processing color, can be found in Chapter 5 on pages 132–133.

In sum, the current state of understanding is that striate cortex is concerned with analyzing the orientation, size, shape, speed, and direction of motion of objects in the world, and that it does so using modular groups of neurons—hypercolumns—each of which receives input from and processes a small piece of the visual world. (You can explore these organizational principles interactively in **Web Activity 3.5: Hypercolumns.**) We can think of this arrangement as a big bank of filters. Combining information from multiple hypercolumns is presumably the job of other portions of cortex farther downstream in the visual system. We will consider some of these portions in Chapter 4, when we discuss the representation and recognition of whole objects.

FIGURE 3.26 Cytochrome oxidase (CO) blobs. (From Hubel, 1988.)

Selective Adaptation:
The Psychologist's Electrode

Most of the physiological research reported up to now in this chapter was done using cats, monkeys, or other animals as subjects. Does the human visual system also include neurons selective for orientation, line width, direction of motion, and so on? The difficult thing about answering this question is that we can't normally poke electrodes into a human's brain (which is why Hubel, Wiesel, and their peers had to use cats and monkeys in the first place), so indirect methods of learning about brain function had to be devised. One such method is called **adaptation**, a technique that gives psychologists a noninvasive "electrode" they can use to probe the human brain. Although often attributed to John Frisby (1980), the term was actually coined by Colin Blakemore in the 1970s.

Selective adaptation can provide insights into the properties of cortical neurons, as illustrated in **Figure 3.27**. The green bars in Figure 3.27*a* illustrate

adaptation A reduction in response caused by prior or continuing stimulation.

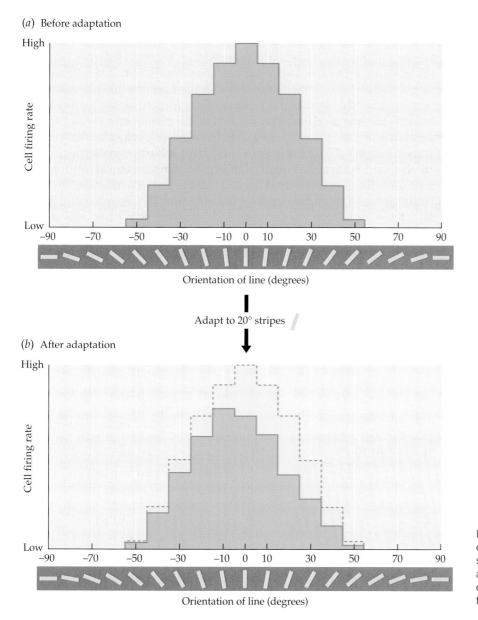

FIGURE 3.27 The psychologist's electrode. This schematic diagram shows how selective adaptation may alter the distribution of neural responses and therefore perception. See the text for explanation.

the normal firing rates of cells tuned to orientations of 0, 10, –10, 20, –20 degrees, and so on, to a vertical grating. By definition, gratings oriented at 0 degrees (vertical) elicit the strongest response from the 0-degree cells, followed closely by the 10-degree and –10-degree cells, followed by the 20-degree and –20-degree cells, and so on (Figure 3.27*a*). Now suppose we expose the visual system that contains these cells to a 20-degree grating for an extended period of time. This adapting stimulus will cause the 20 degree–selective cells to be most active, and the extended activity will fatigue these cells (that is, their maximum firing rate will be reduced for a short period following adaptation). The adaptation procedure will also affect the other cells to some extent: the 10-degree and 30-degree cells will be the next most fatigued, followed by the 0-degree and 40-degree cells, and so on.

Figure 3.27*b* shows what should happen when we present the vertical grating again after adaptation to the 20-degree grating, assuming that our orientation perception is really due to populations of orientation-selective cells like those that Hubel and Wiesel found in the cat cortex. As the dark green bars show, because the 0-degree cells have been fatigued more than the –10-degree cells, the –10-degree cells are now firing fastest. As a result, we should perceive the vertical test stimulus as being oriented 10 degrees to the left.

You can test the validity of this technique yourself using the stimuli in **Figure 3.28**. Start by carefully fixating the black line between the two sets of tilted stripes in Figure 3.28*a* for about a minute. This exercise will result in adaptation to left-tilted stripes in the upper visual field, and right-tilted stripes in the lower field. After about a minute of this adaptation, look quickly to the right at the fixation point between the two sets of vertical stripes in Figure 3.28*b*. The stripes in Figure 3.28*b* should now appear to be tilted slightly from their true vertical orientation (clockwise in the upper panel and counterclockwise in the lower—opposite the orientations in Figure 3.28*a*), just as predicted by the model

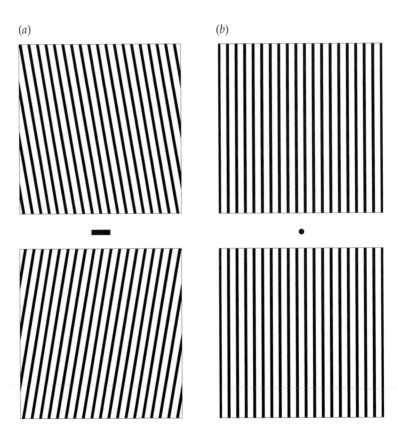

(a)   *(b)*

FIGURE 3.28 Stimuli for demonstrating selective adaptation. See the text for details. (After Frisby, 1980.)

of the human visual system based on the cat research and diagrammed in Figure 3.27. This **tilt aftereffect** strongly supports the idea that the human visual system contains individual neurons selective for different orientations.

Selective adaptation also provides evidence that the human visual system contains neurons selective for spatial frequency. You can check this with the gratings shown in **Figure 3.29**. First, look at Figure 3.29*b* and make a mental note of your contrast sensitivity function (the inverted *U*-shaped area where the gratings fade into the gray background). Now adapt for about 10–20 seconds to the grating in Figure 3.29*a*, and then quickly shift your gaze back to Figure 3.29*b* and make a mental note of your contrast sensitivity function now. After repeating this procedure a few times, the outline of your CSF in Figure 3.29*b* should look something like the red curve in Figure 3.29*c*. It should have a notch (indicating reduced contrast sensitivity) for spatial frequencies that are close to the adapting spatial frequency (Figure 3.29*a*). This demonstration shows that adaptation to the high-contrast top panel is selective—resulting in a loss of sensitivity for spatial frequencies close to the adapting frequency, but not for spatial frequencies that are much higher or lower than the adapting frequency. Note that adaptation to the bottom panel (Figure 3.29*d*) does not result in a similar notch, since spatial-frequency adaptation is orientation-selective. Thus, there is little or no effect on sensitivity to vertical gratings following adaptation to a horizontal grating.

As noted earlier, selective adaptation causes the neurons most sensitive to the adapting stimulus to become fatigued. In this demonstration, neurons sensitive to the spatial frequency of the adapting stimulus have their contrast sensitivity reduced. That is, higher contrast is needed after adaptation for a test grating to be able to stimulate these neurons. Neurons responsive to much higher or much lower spatial frequencies are not fatigued by the adaptation procedure, so contrast sensitivity for these spatial frequencies is not affected.

Figure 3.30*a* shows more precisely how selective adaptation to a 7-cycle/degree grating produces a selective loss of contrast sensitivity at spatial frequencies of about 7 cycles/degree, with little or no loss at, for example, 1 cycle/degree or 15 cycles/degree. After adaptation, the contrast sensitivity function has a "notch," as if the detectors sensitive to spatial frequencies near 7 cycles/degree were selectively destroyed (luckily the effects of spatial-frequency adaptation are reversible!). From these measurements of contrast sensitivity before and after adaptation, we can construct the spatial-frequency tuning function shown in Figure 3.30*b*. This function represents the change in contrast threshold (contrast threshold after adaptation, divided by contrast threshold before adaptation) plotted against the spatial frequency of the test grating. This curve represents the spatial-frequency tuning function for a "channel" that is most sensitive to a grating of 7 cycles/degree. The shape and selectivity of this channel are very similar to the spatial-frequency tuning functions

tilt aftereffect The perceptual illusion of tilt, produced by adaptation to a pattern of a given orientation.

(*a*)

(*b*)

(*c*)

(*d*)

FIGURE 3.29 A demonstration of adaptation that is specific to spatial frequency. (*a*) The adapting grating. (*b*) A grating modulated in contrast (vertically) and spatial frequency (horizontally). This pattern lets you visualize your own contrast sensitivity function (CSF; see also Figure 3.8). Before adaptation, your CSF should have the appearance of an inverted *U*. After adapting to (*a*), it should look something like the red curve in (*c*). The red curve illustrates the effect of adaptation. The notch indicates reduced contrast sensitivity for spatial frequencies that are close to the adapting spatial frequency. Adapting to the horizontal grating in (*d*) results in little or no reduction in sensitivity. (*b* from Robson and Campbell, 1997; courtesy of Izumi Ohzawa.)

(a)

(b)

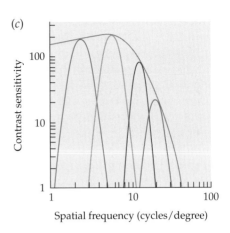

(c)

FIGURE 3.30 Spatial-frequency adaptation. (a) Selective adaptation to a 7-cycle/degree grating produces a selective loss of contrast sensitivity at spatial frequencies of about 7 cycles/degree, leaving a notch (indicated by red line) in the contrast sensitivity function (black line). (b) Threshold elevation (the change in contrast threshold) following adaptation. (c) Physiologically measured spatial-frequency tuning functions for striate cortex neurons in monkeys (colored curves represent different neurons). (b after C. Blakemore and Campbell, 1969; c after Maffei and Fiorentini, 1973.)

for striate cortex neurons of cats and monkeys. Figure 3.30c illustrates that the contrast sensitivity function (gray curve) represents the "upper envelope" of the sensitivities of many spatial-frequency channels, each tuned to a different spatial frequency.

The Site of Selective Adaptation Effects

The adaptation experiments replicated here provide strong evidence that orientation and spatial frequency are coded by neurons somewhere in the human visual system. In cats and monkeys, we know that these neurons are located in striate cortex, not in the retina or LGN. Can we localize the orientation-selective and spatial frequency–selective neurons in humans?

As it turns out, we can do just that with a clever variation on the adaptation experiments. Repeat the orientation (Figure 3.28) and spatial-frequency (Figure 3.29) adaptation demonstrations, but this time view the adapting stimuli with your left eye only (keep your right eye closed during the adaptation period), and then view the test stimuli with your right eye (close your left eye and open your right eye as you shift your gaze to the test stimuli). You should find that the tilt aftereffect and the decreased contrast sensitivity transfer from one eye to the other, although the effect may be somewhat less pronounced than when you did the demonstrations with both eyes open. This transfer of adaptation from the adapted to the nonadapted eye is known as "interocular transfer" (C. Blakemore and Campbell, 1969).

Now recall that information from the two eyes is kept completely separate in the retinas and in the two LGNs; no single neuron receives input from both eyes until the striate cortex. The transfer of adaptation effects from one eye to the other thus implies that selective adaptation occurs in cortical neurons, just as we would predict from animal physiology studies.

Spatial Frequency–Tuned Pattern Analyzers in Human Vision

Selective adaptation to spatial frequency, as well as other evidence, provides strong support for the notion, first suggested by Fergus Campbell and John Robson (1968), that the human contrast sensitivity function actually reflects the sensitivity of multiple individual pattern analyzers. These pattern analyzers are implemented by ensembles of cortical neurons, with each set of cells tuned to a limited range of spatial frequencies and orientations, and they are often referred to as **spatial-frequency channels**. Remember the initially unexplained falloff in the contrast sensitivity function at very low spatial frequencies? Although a number of different explanations have been suggested (e.g., lateral

spatial-frequency channel A pattern analyzer, implemented by an ensemble of cortical neurons, in which each set of neurons is tuned to a limited range of spatial frequencies.

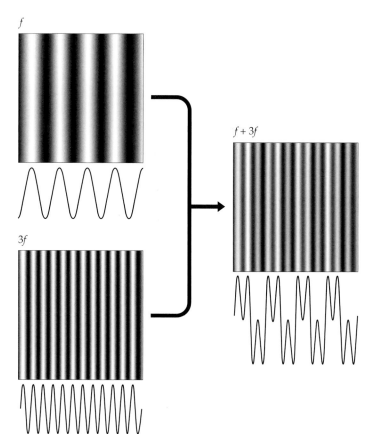

FIGURE 3.31 A compound grating pattern (right), made by the addition of a sine wave of frequency f (top left) to one of frequency $3f$ (bottom left). (After Graham and Nachmias, 1971.)

inhibition), the most likely explanation is that we simply have fewer neurons tuned to low spatial frequencies (De Valois, Albrecht, and Thorell, 1982).

The multiple-spatial-frequency model of vision implies that spatial frequencies that stimulate different pattern analyzers will be detected independently, even if the different frequencies are combined in the same image. Consider the compound grating pattern in **Figure 3.31**, made by adding a sine wave with frequency f to a sine wave with frequency $3f$. Graham and Nachmias (1971) found that the contrast sensitivity for this compound pattern was almost the same as the contrast sensitivity for detecting the individual components of the pattern separately. If the two component sine waves had stimulated a common pattern analyzer, then their effects on the analyzer should have been added, so contrast sensitivity should have been greatly improved. This may sound a bit like the Fourier analysis idea discussed early in this chapter. However, it's now pretty clear that the visual system doesn't carry out an actual Fourier analysis, analyzing the world into very narrow bands of spatial frequencies. Rather, it filters the image into spatially localized receptive fields that have a limited range of spatial frequencies. (Something like a Fourier analysis may be important in quickly appreciating the "gist" of a scene; see Chapter 7.)

Why would the visual system use spatial-frequency filters to analyze images? One important reason may be that different spatial frequencies emphasize different types of information. **Figures** 3.32*b* and *c* show only high-frequency or low-frequency components, respectively, of the face in Figure 3.32*a*. These images show that low frequencies (Figure 3.32*c*) emphasize the broad outlines of the face and high frequencies (Figure 3.32*b*) carry information about fine details. If we want to know how many people are in a scene, it is most efficient to consult our low-frequency channels. But if we want to know about the fine details—for example, whether the people are frowning or smiling—we must rely on our high-frequency channels.

(a)   (b)   (c)

FIGURE 3.32 A complete image (*a*) and simulations of the high-frequency (*b*) and low-frequency (*c*) components of that image. For another example, see Figure 1.18.

It is widely agreed that at near-threshold contrasts, pattern analyzers operating at different scales of analysis are independent. At high contrasts, however, pattern analyzers do interact. You can experience this for yourself in Figure 3.33, where the high spatial frequencies introduced by the small blocks mask the low spatial frequencies that convey an underlying portrait of a famous American. Squinting your eyes will blur the blocks, minimizing the effect of the mask to a point where the face you've seen countless times on the 5-dollar bill will probably show through.

The Development of Spatial Vision

William James (1890) described the infant's world as "a blooming, buzzing confusion." However, studies over the past several decades have shown that the visual system is much more developed at birth than we used to think. One of the difficulties in assessing vision in infants is that we can't simply ask them what they see. Rather, we have to think of tricky ways to coax that information from them. The most widely used method for studying infant vision is based on an observation that Robert Fantz made in the early 1960s. What Fantz noticed is that if infants are shown two scenes, they invariably stare at the more complex scene (the scene with the most contours). So, if an infant is shown two patches, one containing stripes and the other uniform gray, the infant will prefer to look at the stripes. Of course, an infant who couldn't see the stripes would be equally likely to stare at the gray patch as at the striped patch. Thus, preferential looking is one important method used by infant researchers

FIGURE 3.33 Who is hidden behind the high-spatial-frequency mask in this image?

(*a*) Stimulus card

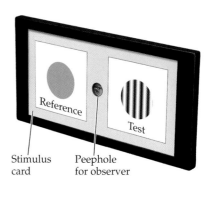

Subject

Stimulus card   Peephole for observer

(*b*)

(*c*) Sweep VEP (grating acuity)

FIGURE 3.34 Assessing vision in infants. (*a*) Forced-choice preferential-looking stimuli (left) and the experimental setup (right). (*b*) Visual evoked potential (VEP) setup. (*c*) Results of a sweep VEP experiment in which the spatial frequency of the stimulus is swept (continuously varied from low to high spatial frequency), illustrating the extrapolated acuity (threshold—in this case, 27.6 cycles/degree). This particular experiment was done at 80% contrast. (Part *c* after Norcia, Tyler, and Hamer, 1990.)

(grown psychologists studying infant vision, not babies in lab coats) to learn what infants can see and respond to behaviorally (**Figure 3.34***a*).

The success of preferential looking depends on the willingness of babies to stare at stimuli near threshold level. An alternative approach, used with considerable success in more recent years, is to measure visually evoked electrical potentials (VEPs)—that is, electrical signals from the brain that are evoked by visual stimuli—by attaching electrodes to the scalp and measuring the changes in electrical activity that are elicited by the changing visual stimulus (Figures 3.34*b* and *c*). Using this technique, we can measure an entire contrast sensitivity function in as little as 10 seconds in a nonverbal infant.

Development of the Contrast Sensitivity Function

The emerging picture suggests that sensitivity to low spatial frequencies develops much more rapidly than sensitivity to high spatial frequencies. Thus, at low spatial frequencies, contrast sensitivity may reach nearly adult levels as early as about 9 weeks of age, whereas sensitivity at higher spatial frequencies continues to develop dramatically (**Figure 3.35**). There remains a substantial difference in the contrast sensitivity of adults and 33-week-olds at high spatial frequencies (Norcia, Tyler, and Hamer, 1990).

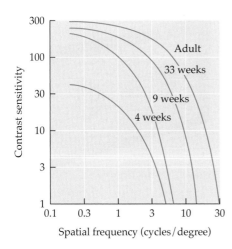

FIGURE 3.35 The development of contrast sensitivity. (After Norcia, Tyler, and Hamer, 1990.)

What limits the development of acuity and contrast sensitivity? The primary postnatal changes in the retina concern differentiation of the macular region (Boothe, Dobson, and Teller, 1985). After birth, foveal receptor density and cone outer segment length both increase, as foveal cones become thinner and more elongated. There is a dramatic migration of ganglion cells and inner nuclear layers from the foveal region as the foveal pit develops during the first 4 months of life, and not until about 4 years of age is the fovea fully adultlike (Yuodelis and Hendrickson, 1986).

From birth to beyond 4 years of age, cone density increases in the central region, because of both the migration of receptors and decreases in their dimensions. Both of these factors result in finer cone sampling (by decreasing the distance between neighboring cones). Alterations in cone spacing and the light-gathering properties of the cones during early development probably contribute a great deal toward the improvements in acuity and contrast sensitivity during the first months of life. The massive migration of retinal cells, and the alterations in the size of retina and eyeball (along with changes in interpupillary distance), may necessitate the plasticity of cortical connections early in life. Interestingly, the peripheral retina appears to develop much more rapidly than the fovea (Yuodelis and Hendrickson, 1986).

The Girl Who Almost Couldn't See Stripes

Normal visual development requires normal visual experience. Abnormal early visual experience can have serious and often permanent consequences for seeing patterns, as illustrated by the story of a girl named Jane. Jane was born with a dense cataract (an opacity of the lens) in her left eye, which prevented clear patterns from forming on her left retina. In addition to causing form deprivation in the left eye, the cataract prevented Jane's two eyes from seeing the same images at the same time.

Studies in cats and monkeys dating back to Hubel and Wiesel in the early 1960s have shown that monocular form deprivation can cause massive changes in cortical physiology that result in a devastating and permanent loss of spatial vision (Wiesel, 1982). Hubel and Wiesel, and many other workers subsequently, demonstrated that there is a critical period of early visual development when normal binocular visual stimulation is required for normal cortical development. In cats and monkeys this critical period covers the first 3–4 months of life; in humans it is extended to something on the order of the first 3–8 years. During the critical period, cortical neurons are still being wired up to their inputs from the two eyes. This is a period of neural plasticity, when abnormal visual experience can alter the normal neural wiring process. If one eye is not receiving normal stimulation, the neurons that should be destined to respond to that eye do not become properly connected. In fact, some evidence suggests that these neurons are actually co-opted by inputs from the other, normally functioning eye.

If cataracts are left untreated during the critical period, the misplaced cortical connections can never be repaired. The result is often **amblyopia** (reduced visual acuity in one eye because of abnormal early visual experience—commonly known as "lazy eye") and an inability to perceive stereopsis (a lack of binocular depth perception; see Chapter 6). Correcting the condition later in life will thus have little effect, because the information from the now-functioning eye can never be properly conveyed to or processed by the cortex.

Luckily for Jane, her pediatrician found the cataract early, and the cataractous lens was surgically replaced by an artificial lens when she was 3 months old. The visual acuity in Jane's left eye just after the contact lens was inserted was 20/1200, about four times worse than the normal value for a 3-month-old.

amblyopia A developmental disorder characterized by reduced spatial vision in an otherwise healthy eye, even with proper correction for refractive error. Also known as *lazy eye*.

But when tested again 1 month later, acuity in her left eye had already begun to catch up with the acuity in her right eye. In fact, a recent study (Maurer et al., 1999) found significant acuity improvements only an hour after corrective measures had been taken.

Not all individuals with congenital cataracts are as lucky as Jane. For example, in much of the third world, because of poverty, children born with congenital cataracts (often in both eyes) go untreated and grow up essentially blind. According to the World Health Organization, India is home to the largest population of blind children in the world. Recently, Pawan Sinha and his collaborators initiated an undertaking (Project Prakash) to perform corrective cataract surgeries for free, and to track how these "blind" children learn to see. These studies are just beginning to provide important new insights into brain plasticity.

Congenital cataracts are not the only cause of amblyopia. Early in life, two other disorders—**strabismus** (in which one eye is turned so that it is receiving a view of the world from an abnormal angle) and **anisometropia** (in which the two eyes have very different refractive errors; e.g., one eye is farsighted and the other not)—may also cause amblyopia. These forms of amblyopia are typically less severe, and often they have a later onset than congenital cataracts. The standard clinical treatment for amblyopia, for over 250 years, has been to patch the good eye and "force" the amblyopic eye to work. This treatment is ordinarily performed only in young children (typically younger than 8 years). However, several recent studies suggest that there may be hope for recovery of vision in older children, and even in adults through "perceptual learning"—repeated practice of a demanding visual task (Levi and Li, 2009).

strabismus A misalignment of the two eyes such that a single object in space is imaged on the fovea of one eye, and on a nonfoveal area of the other (turned) eye.

anisometropia A condition in which the two eyes have different refractive errors (e.g., one eye is farsighted and the other not).

Summary

1. In this chapter we followed the path of image processing from the eyeball to the brain. Neurons in the cerebral cortex translate the array of stars perceived by retinal ganglion cells into the beginnings of forms and patterns. The primary visual cortex is organized into thousands of tiny computers, each responsible for determining the orientation, width, color, and other characteristics of the stripes in one small portion of the visual field. In Chapter 4 we will continue this story by seeing how other parts of the brain combine the outputs from these minicomputers to produce a coherent representation.

2. Perhaps the most important feature of image processing is the remarkable transformation of information from the circular receptive fields of retinal ganglion cells to the elongated receptive fields of the cortex.

3. Cortical neurons are highly selective along a number of dimensions, including stimulus orientation, size, direction of motion, and eye of origin.

4. Neurons with similar preferences are often arranged in columns in primary visual cortex.

5. Selective adaptation provides a powerful, noninvasive tool for learning about stimulus specificity in human vision.

6. The human visual cortex contains pattern analyzers that are specific to spatial frequency and orientation.

7. Normal visual development requires normal visual experience. Abnormal visual experience early in life can cause massive changes in cortical physiology that result in a devastating and permanent loss of spatial vision.

Refer to the
Sensation and Perception
Companion Website
sites.sinauer.com/wolfe3e
for activities, essays, study questions, and other study aids.

CHAPTER 4

Jason Salavon, *Portrait (Rembrandt)*, 2009

Perceiving and Recognizing Objects

We have been traveling up the visual system from the eyes into the brain. By the end of Chapter 3, we had reached primary visual cortex (V1, striate cortex), where we encountered cells that were optimally stimulated by bars and gratings of different orientations. Of course, when you look at the world you do not see an array of bars and gratings; you see coherent objects and extended surfaces. Moreover, you recognize specific objects even if they are odd objects, as in **Figure 4.1**). Chapter 4 continues our journey through the visual system and considers how that visual system manages the task of perceiving and recognizing objects.

What and Where Pathways

To begin, let's extend the visual pathways beyond V1. Recall that cells in V1 are interested in the basic features of the visual image, responding to edges or lines of specific orientation, motion, size, and so forth. These neurons have relatively small and precise receptive fields. That is, a cell will respond to its preferred stimulus only if that stimulus is presented in a very specific location relative to the point where the observer (monkey, cat, human) is fixating its (or his or her) gaze. Beyond V1 is the **extrastriate cortex**, a set of visual areas so called because they lie just outside the primary visual cortex. These areas are named V2, V3, and so on, though they are not a simple chain of processing areas and the naming convention breaks down pretty rapidly. **Figure 4.2** shows the main visual areas of the macaque monkey brain, and **Figure 4.3** shows one wiring diagram of these and a few other visual areas.

First, we might ask what makes a patch of cortex into a visual area in its own right rather than just being part of another larger visual area. A classic, anatomical answer was that there are differences in the structure of the cortex that distinguish some areas (like the stripe in striate cortex). More recently, researchers have found that the visual world is mapped repeatedly in visual cortex. We saw in Chapter 3 that V1 contains a map with a large representation of the fovea and a smaller representation of the more peripheral retina. When researchers find another map of the field, they tend to consider the new map to be evidence for a separate visual area (Wandell and Winawer, 2011). A final criterion is that the cells in an area might all be concerned with one function, and that function is different from what neighboring cells find interesting. Thus, as you might guess, cells in the fusiform face area (FFA) are interested in faces (Kanwisher, McDermott, and Chun, 1997).

extrastriate cortex The region of cortex bordering the primary visual cortex and containing multiple areas involved in visual processing.

FIGURE 4.1 We see a world full of identifiable objects even if we have never seen them in this particular arrangement before.

Why do we have all these areas? The last example, of the FFA, encapsulates the leading theory. The visual system has many different problems to solve—like the problem of face processing—and it appears to have modules that are specialized for working on different problems. One should not take this too far; while there may be areas specialized for faces or motion, you probably do not have separate areas for recognizing tools, vegetables, and so on (Kanwisher, 2010).

We can sketch a broad structure of the visual areas beyond V1. In the extrastriate regions just beyond V1 (like V2), receptive fields begin to show an interest in properties that will be important for object perception, as Figure 4.4 illustrates. A V1 cell tuned for a dark edge on the left side of the receptive field would respond equally in the two situations shown in the figure. A V2 cell might not; it might be concerned with who "owns" the black edge. In Figure 4.4a, the cell "sees" the black edge of the black square. In Figure 4.4b, the black edge is an accident created by the fact that the gray square is occluding the black background. In some sense it is not a real black edge and the V2 cell responds less strongly to it (Craft et al., 2007). We will have more to say about the receptive-field properties of extrastriate cortex after we introduce the broad structure of the visual system.

From the extrastriate regions of the occipital lobe of the brain, visual information moves out along two main pathways (see Figure 4.2). One pathway heads up into the parietal lobe. Visual areas in this pathway seem to be important for processing information relating to the location of objects in space and the actions required to interact with them (moving the hands, the eyes, and so

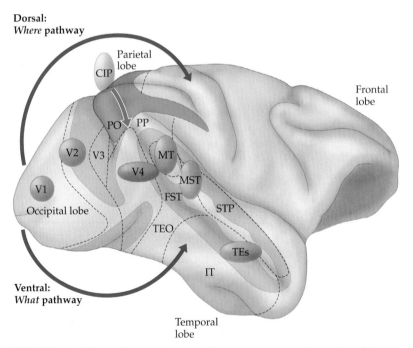

FIGURE 4.2 The main visual areas of the macaque monkey cortex. Humans have comparable visual areas. The drawing of the brain has been distorted to show areas that lie deep in the folds (sulci) of the cortex. Each abbreviation refers to a different visual area, not all of which will be discussed here. Visual cortical processing can be divided into two broad streams. One, heading for the parietal lobe, can be thought of as being interested in *where* things are. The other, heading down into the temporal lobe, is concerned with *what* things are. (After Parker, 2007.)

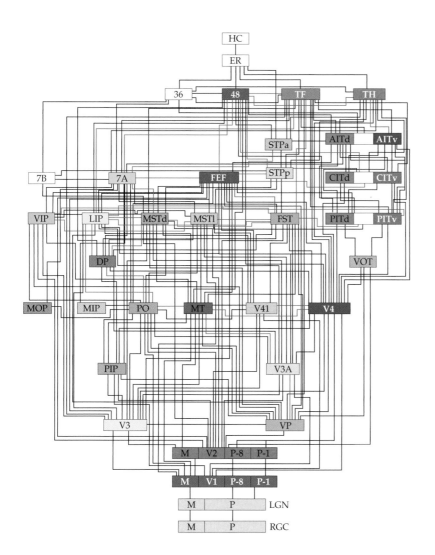

FIGURE 4.3 A partial "wiring" diagram for the main visual areas of the brain. As in Figure 4.2, each abbreviation refers to a different visual area, not all of which will be discussed here. The main message of this figure is that the visual pathways are very complex and that there are a multitude of visual areas. For a bit of orientation, visual information from the eyes enters at the bottom of the diagram, via the retinal ganglion cells (RGC). Feed-forward information generally flows "upward" in this figure. However, visual processing is a two-way street. From the LGN onward, there are both feed-forward and feedback connections between areas.

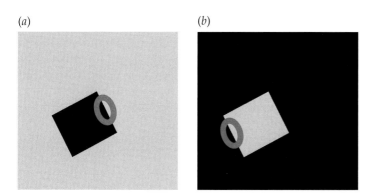

FIGURE 4.4 Notice that the "receptive field" (the red oval) sees the same dark edge in both images. However, a cell in V2 might respond more strongly to the one in (a), where the little square *owns* the edge compared to the case in (b), where the real edge is the edge of a light square, up and to the right of the receptive field.

on). This pathway is sometimes known as the *where* pathway. As we will see in Chapter 7, it plays an important role in the deployment of attention. The other pathway, of more importance to us here in Chapter 4, heads down into the temporal lobe and is known as the *what* pathway. This pathway appears to be the locus for the explicit acts of object recognition that are of particular importance in this chapter (Ungerleider and Mishkin, 1982). As we move down into the temporal lobe, receptive fields get much bigger. As the pathway's name implies, *what* is in view seems more important than where it is. However, though it is a useful organizing principle, one should not become too addicted to this *what* and *where* distinction. For instance, some basic object information is represented in both pathways (Konen and Kastner, 2008), and some *where* information is encoded in the temporal lobe *what* pathway.

Early evidence for a relationship between the temporal lobe and object recognition came from studies in which large sections of the temporal lobe were destroyed (**lesioned**) in monkeys. When Klüver and Bucy (1938, 1939) did this, they found that their monkeys behaved as though they could see but did not know what they were seeing. This deficit, also seen in some human stroke victims, is known as **agnosia**, though Klüver and Bucy called it "psychic blindness." Later work pointed to one part of the temporal lobe, the **inferotemporal (IT) cortex**, as particularly important in the visual problems of these monkeys. In the 1970s, Charlie Gross and his colleagues began to record the activity of single cells in this area. What they found was quite striking. We have seen that neurons in striate cortex are activated by simple stimuli and respond only if their preferred stimuli are presented in very restricted portions of the visual field. In contrast, cells in the IT cortex were discovered to have receptive fields that could spread over half or more of the monkey's field of view. Even more striking were the sorts of stimuli that activated IT cells. The usual spots and lines didn't work well at all, but the silhouette of a monkey hand worked fantastically for some cells. Monkey faces excited other cells (**Figure 4.5**). There was even a cell with a distinct preference for a toilet brush shape (Gross, Rocha-Miranda, and Bender, 1972).

Findings like this led Horace Barlow (1972) and others to suggest a hierarchical model of visual perception in which the small receptive fields and simple features of visual cortex are combined with ever-greater complexity as one moves from striate cortex to IT cortex, eventually culminating in a cell that might fire when you see your grandmother or your *Sensation & Perception* textbook. Indeed, the term *grandmother cell*, coined by Jerry Lettvin, has entered the jargon of the field to stand for any cell that seems to be selectively responsive to one specific object (Barlow, 1995).

We do not know what brain activity actually corresponds to your recognition of your grandmother. It is probably a bit extreme to imagine that this is the work of a single neuron in the IT cortex, and more recent work has cast doubt on the idea that IT cells respond to an object independent of its position in the visual field (DiCarlo and Maunsell, 2003). Nevertheless, it does seem clear that cells in that part of the brain are critically involved in object recognition. The IT cortex maintains close connections with parts of the brain involved in memory formation (notably the hippocampus). This is important because those IT cells need to *learn* their receptive-field properties. The receptive-field properties of primary visual cortex could be written into the genetic code in some manner, but neurons that respond to grandmothers clearly cannot be hardwired, since everyone's grandmother is different. Nikos Logothetis and his coworkers demonstrated that cells in IT cortex have precisely this type of plasticity (Logothetis, Pauls, and Poggio, 1995). After training monkeys to recognize novel objects, these researchers found IT neurons that responded

lesion 1. (n) A region of damaged brain. 2. (v) To destroy a section of the brain.

agnosia A failure to recognize objects in spite of the ability to see them. Agnosia is typically due to brain damage.

inferotemporal (IT) cortex Part of the cerebral cortex in the lower portion of the temporal lobe, important in object recognition.

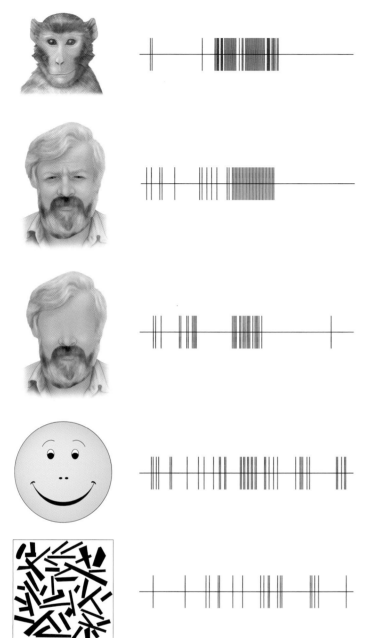

FIGURE 4.5 Cells in the inferotemporal cortex of macaque monkeys are interested in very specific stimuli. In this case, the cell responds vigorously to a monkey face and to some other stimuli that seem related. (After Gross, Rocha-Miranda, and Bender, 1972.)

with high firing rates to those objects, but only when the objects were seen from viewpoints similar to those from which they had been learned.

Human cortex has areas that appear to be the equivalent of monkey IT cortex (the anatomy of human and macaque monkey brains is not identical, so we talk about **homologous regions**). One of the more amazing demonstrations of this fact comes from a 2005 study by Quiroga et al. They made recordings from single cells in the temporal lobe of human observers. Normally we do not put electrodes into the human brain, but these observers were patients being prepared for brain surgery to treat epilepsy. Implanting electrodes was part of the treatment plan, and recording visual responses from these cells involved no extra risk to the patient or interference with treatment. In the experiment, the observer just looked at a collection of images while the activity of a cell

homologous regions Brain regions that appear to have the same function in different species.

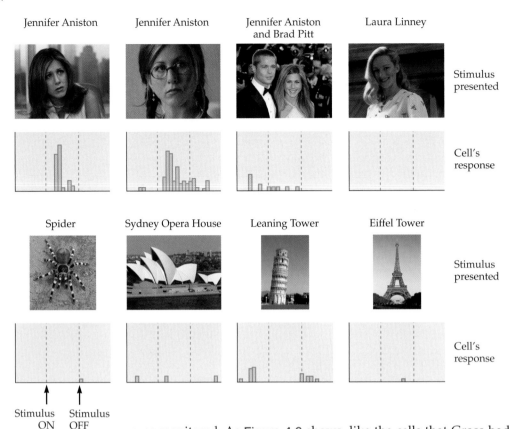

FIGURE 4.6 Results of recording the activity of one cell in the temporal lobe of a human patient. This cell responded to pictures of the actress Jennifer Aniston. The cell did not respond to pictures of anything else, including those of other actresses. (After Quiroga et al., 2005.)

was monitored. As **Figure 4.6** shows, like the cells that Gross had found in monkey IT cortex, some of these cells turned out to have very specific tastes. The cell shown in the figure responded only to the actress Jennifer Aniston, and nothing else presented to the observer. Other cells had preferences for other people, like former President Bill Clinton. One cell responded to the Sydney Opera House; another, to the Eiffel Tower and the Leaning Tower of Pisa but not to other landmarks (Quiroga et al., 2005).

We do not have a lot of systematic data on the responses of single cells in the human visual system. What we do have is evidence from brain lesions caused by strokes or other accidents. Like Klüver and Bucy's monkeys, humans with lesions in the temporal lobe often show symptoms of agnosia, the ability to see without the ability to know what we're seeing. Sometimes these agnosias can be quite specific. Prosopagnosia, an inability to recognize faces, is one example that has received a lot of study and that will be discussed at the end of this chapter (Damasio, Damasio, and Van Hoesen, 1982). There are other interesting subdivisions of agnosia as well, such as the ability to recognize animate objects (e.g., animals) but not inanimate objects (e.g., tools) (Newcombe and de Haan, 1994).

Should all this be taken as clear evidence for something like a grandmother cell model, with one piece of brain holding the "face cells" and others, perhaps, holding "tool cells"? It may not be that simple. Martha Farah (1992) argues that effects that appear to be caused by differences between types of stimuli may reflect *how* an object is being recognized rather than what specific object it is. For example, faces must be processed holistically; that is, the precise relationship of eyes to nose to mouth is critical. Other objects may be quite successfully recognized by their collection of parts (e.g., keyboard + mouse + screen + box = computer, regardless of whether the mouse is 2 inches to the left or 10 inches to the right of the keyboard). It might also be unwise to think of specific cells in this part of the brain as being the neural substrate that recognizes grandma. Those cells might be more of a link between visual processes and stored memories (Quiroga et al., 2008). In our present state of understanding, it seems safe to say that our ability to recognize objects is critically dependent on brain structures in the temporal lobe. Exactly what those structures are doing remains a topic of active research.

Whatever those cells are doing, they're doing it very fast. Electrical activity from the brain can be recorded from electrodes placed on the scalp. If we flash a picture to an observer and ask whether it contains an animal, we can record a signal in the observer that reliably differentiates animal from nonanimal scenes within 150 milliseconds (ms) from the onset of the stimulus (Thorpe, Fize, and Marlot, 1996). That's fast enough to mean that there cannot be a lot of feedback from higher visual or memory processes, suggesting that it must be possible to do some rough object recognition on the basis of the first wave of activity as it moves from retina to striate cortex to extrastriate cortex and beyond. That **feed-forward process** must be able to generate an "animal" signal from a wide range of animals in different positions, sizes, and so on.

To summarize, two pathways emerge from visual cortex. The *where* pathway will be taken up in later chapters. The *what* pathway moves through a succession of stages, building a general representation of your grandmother or the Eiffel Tower out of the very specific, very localized spots, lines, and bars that interest the cells in the retina, lateral geniculate nucleus (LGN), and primary visual cortex. That's a start, but don't be lulled into thinking we fully understand the process of object recognition. It is a really difficult problem, and in the rest of the chapter we will illustrate why this problem is hard and how the visual system attempts to solve different parts of it.

The Problems of Perceiving and Recognizing Objects

Figure 4.7*a* is clearly a picture of a house. The image may contain some other things as well, but the chief object of interest is the house. Figure 4.7*b* is pretty clearly a house as well, though in this case the house is part of a more abstract

feed-forward process A process that carries out a computation (e.g., object recognition) one neural step after another, without need for feedback from a later stage to an earlier stage.

FIGURE 4.7 The problem of object recognition. (*a*) This house and (*b*) Paul Cézanne's Chateau Noir (1902–1905) look completely different, but they are both clearly houses. (*c*) This image is also very different from the image in (*a*), but they are both clearly the same house. (*d*) This image of a red house clearly shows a different house from (*a*) and (*c*).

(*a*)

(*b*)

(*c*)

(*d*)

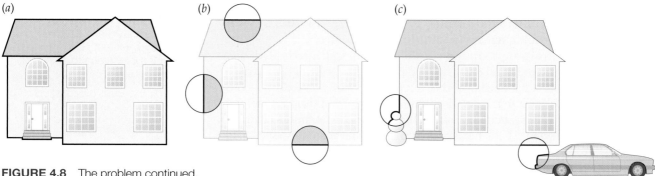

FIGURE 4.8 The problem continued. (a) Another house. (b) Cells in primary visual cortex respond well to the local features (circled) of the house. But how do we go from recognizing a collection of local features to perceiving a house? (c) In this slightly more complicated scene, how do we know which bits belong together?

scene painted by the French artist Paul Cézanne in the early twentieth century. Figures 4.7c and d are two more pictures of houses. It is quite clear that Figure 4.7c is the same house as Figure 4.7a, while Figure 4.7d is not. These seemingly simple acts of object identification require a lot from the *what* pathway, and they constitute the main topic of the rest of this chapter. Like many seemingly simple acts, object perception is actually a collection of complex and remarkable accomplishments.

Consider **Figure 4.8a**. It shows yet another house. How do we recognize it as a house? First we need to gather some basic visual features. The preceding chapters showed us how single cells in the early visual system respond to stimuli such as simple lines. In Figure 4.8b each circle is a cartoon of the receptive field of a simple cortical cell. Those cells in striate cortex will respond well to the high-contrast lines in the outline of the house. That limited receptive field is like a window that allows the cell to "see" only a small part of the world. None of these simple cells see a house. They just collect local features like horizontal, vertical, and oblique lines.

At the very least, the local features will need to be assembled into a house. This process could be imagined as the natural extension of a process we have already discussed. One way to "construct" the lines detected by simple cells is to imagine combining a row of dots detected by retinal ganglion cells. Dots could be grouped together into lines. A pair of lines, each collected by a different cell, could be combined by another cell that would sense a corner. This process could go on and on until we had a house. On closer examination, however, it is clear that this process would not be easy. Consider, for example, Figure 4.8c. Again, simple cells would have no problem detecting the lines and edges in this scene, but how do we know which edges go with which objects? How do we avoid considering the snowman part of the house? The house and snowman make corners, as do the house and its door and steps. The car and house are separate. None of their lines touch. But this is also true of the outline of the house and its windows.

Clearly we must have processes that successfully combine features into objects. That is one of the tasks that defines **middle** (or **midlevel**) **vision** (as opposed to low-level vision, which was the topic of Chapters 2 and 3). The next part of this chapter looks at some of the processes of middle vision. The following part takes the feature combinations given to us by middle-level vision and asks how we come to know what the object is. The act of recognition must involve matching what we perceive now to a memory of something we perceived in the past. How can we do that? For example, how do we know that all of the images in Figures 4.7 and 4.8 show houses? Without having seen these exact objects before, how do we go about placing them in the "house" category? Furthermore, how do we know that Figures 4.7a and 4.7c portray the same house, given that the images delivered to our retinas in the two figures

middle (midlevel) vision A loosely defined stage of visual processing that comes after basic features have been extracted from the image (low-level, or early, vision) and before object recognition and scene understanding (high-level vision).

are radically different? In the final section of this chapter we'll discuss the high-level visual processes that enable us to recognize familiar objects, novel views of familiar objects, and new instances of familiar object categories.

Middle Vision

The goal of middle vision is to organize the elements of a visual scene into groups that we can then recognize as objects. Let's begin with the simplest case of an object isolated on a simple background. Finding the edges of this object will be a good starting place on the road to recognizing the object.

Finding Edges

In Chapter 3 we discussed at length how neurons in striate cortex can detect bits of lines, but how do we decide which bits belong to which objects? We already established that we can't just group all the edges that touch each other into an object. Because objects abut and overlap other objects, simple connectedness will not work. Worse yet, before we can concern ourselves with grouping edges, we need to worry about the quality of the raw edge information. In **Figure 4.9**, part of the house of Figure 4.8 is reduced to a simple, arrow-shaped outline. It is easy to see that arrow. Notice, however, that in some places the object is lighter than the background, while in other places it is darker. This means that, if we trace the edge of the object with a finger, we *must* pass through locations where there is no difference between the luminance of the object and the luminance of the background. In other words, at these points the shape has no edge at all.

Interestingly, this occasional lack of an edge doesn't seem to bother our visual system at all. In fact, it may be hard to see the gap. Asking simple computer graphics software to find the edges in Figure 4.9 would yield something like **Figure 4.10**a. The visual system knows that the gaps are accidents of the lighting and fills in the contour. The computer is not so clever. Figures 4.10b and c show another example. In Figure 4.10c, notice that the edge-finding software finds all sorts of edges. The human visual system, however, is doing something quite different. In the early stages of processing, it is assembling evidence for the presence of significant edges from cells with receptive fields at multiple different scales (see Figure 3.32). All these different bits of information are then combined to make the system's best guess about the presence of a contour.

FIGURE 4.9 In some places this object is darker than the background. In other places it is lighter. If the changes are continuous, it follows that there must be places where the edge of this shape simply disappears, even if you see the edges as continuous.

FIGURE 4.10 Finding edges. (a) The "find edges" function in a popular graphics program finds gaps in the borders of the image in Figure 4.9—gaps that we do not see. (b) When a computer algorithm looks for the edges in this elephant scene, it finds what is shown in (c). You can try various edge-finding algorithms on the "Edge Detector Comparison" web page (http://marathon.csee.usf.edu/edge/edge_detection.html).

(a)

(b)

(c)

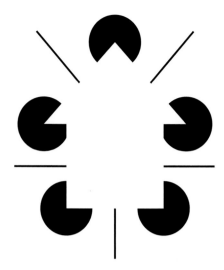

FIGURE 4.11 This "house" outline is constructed from illusory contours. Even though the contour is clearly visible, there is no physical difference between the white background and the white house.

The inferential nature of contour perception can be appreciated in the more extreme demonstration shown in **Figure 4.11**. This an example of a "Kanizsa figure"—named after Gaetano Kanizsa (1913–1993), an Italian psychologist who spent many years investigating such stimuli. Here it is easy to see the arrow outline, even though the vast majority of the shape's lines are missing. Check it yourself. There really is no border between the white figure and the white background. These edges, called **illusory contour**, are perceived because they are the best guess about what is happening in the world at that location. It really does seem likely that a contour is present, even if there is no physical evidence at that location.

RULES OF EVIDENCE Let's consider the sorts of regularities in the stimulus that are taken as evidence for a contour in the world. This tendency of the visual system to make inferential leaps was problematic for one of the earliest group of perceptual psychologists, the **structuralists**. Structuralists such as Wilhelm Wundt (1832–1920) and Edward Bradford Titchener (1867–1927) argued that perceptions are the sum of atoms of sensation—bits of color, orientation, and so forth. In the structuralist view, perception is built up of local sensations the way a crystal might be built up of an array of atoms. An illusory contour challenges this view because an extended edge is seen bridging a gap where no local atom of "edgeness" can be found.

Over time, it became clear that there are many examples where the structuralist argument seems to fail. Inspired by these examples, a second group of psychologists, led by Max Wertheimer (1880–1943), Wolfgang Köhler (1887–1967), and Kurt Koffka (1886–1941), formed the **Gestalt** school. Gestalt theory held that the perceptual whole is more than the sum of its sensory parts. Perhaps the most enduring contribution of this school was to begin the description of a set of organizing principles (sometimes known as **Gestalt grouping rules**) that describe the visual system's interpretation of the raw retinal image. Today we would say that these rules reflect regularities in the world.

For example, in **Figure 4.12a** we have a collection of short line segments. One set of these seems to form a contour. The "rule," cartooned in Figure 4.12*b*, is that we tend to see similarly oriented lines as part of the same contour (D. J. Field, Hayes, and Hess, 1992). Such lines "support" each other in that two visible bits of an edge actually make it easier to perceive a third, colinear segment that lies between them, even if the middle segment is not actually visible (Polat and Sagi, 1993). If a set of such lines forms a closed shape like the roughly circular contour in Figure 4.12*a*, then the short segments support each other even more strongly (Kovacs and Julesz, 1993). The regularity of the world is illustrated in Figure 4.12*c*. W. S. Geisler and Perry (2009) labeled contours in natural scenes. Then they examined pairs of contour pieces and asked, "What is the chance that *this* piece *here* at *this* orientation is part of the same contour as *that* piece *there* at *that* orientation?" These likelihoods are color-coded in the figure, and they show that in the real world, if two contour elements are close to colinear, they are likely to come from the same contour. Sharp turns are much rarer.

The Gestaltists called this the principle of **good continuation**, and they illustrated it with examples like the one shown in **Figure 4.13a**. We tend to see this figure as a pair of intersecting lines (Figure 4.13*b*). There are many other possible organizations (Figure 4.13*c*, for example), but *all else being equal*, the

illusory contour A contour that is perceived even though nothing changes from one side of it to the other in an image.

structuralism A school of thought believing that complex objects or perceptions could be understood by analysis of the components.

Gestalt In German, literally "form." In perception, a school of thought stressing that the perceptual whole could be greater than the apparent sum of the parts.

Gestalt grouping rules A set of rules describing which elements in an image will appear to group together. The original list was assembled by members of the Gestalt school of thought.

good continuation A Gestalt grouping rule stating that two elements will tend to group together if they seem to lie on the same contour.

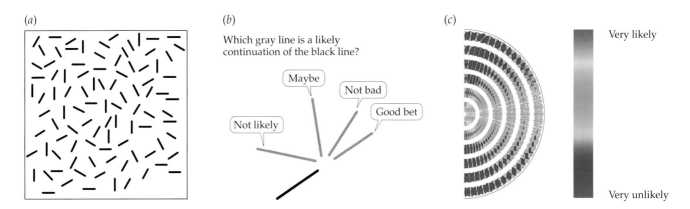

FIGURE 4.12 Contour completion. (*a*) The roughly circular contour seen in the center of this diagram results from the visual system's application of the rule shown in (*b*). (*c*) W. S. Geisler and J. S. Perry actually measured the relationships between nearby line segments in natural scenes. The figure shows the probability that a horizontal line segment would co-occur with other line segments in the image at different distances and orientations. The most likely pairs are colinear or nearly so. (Part *c* after W. S. Geisler and Perry, 2009.)

tendency to see lines continuing in the same direction—in other words, the tendency to group edges that have the same orientation—supports the *X*-like interpretation illustrated in Figure 4.13*b*.

PERCEPTUAL "COMMITTEES"   The "all else being equal" phrase is important. As the Gestalt psychologists knew, and as we will see, a host of rules, principles, and good guesses contribute to our organized perception of the world. These seem to operate on a sort of committee model. Everyone gets together and voices opinions about how the stimulus ought to be understood. Sometimes the opinions collide, and the results in such cases are somewhat unpredictable (in Figure 4.13*c*, for example, color trumps good continuation as an organizing principle). Somehow, though, a consensus view almost always quickly emerges and we settle on a single interpretation of the visual scene. This committee metaphor is very useful and will recur throughout this chapter.

OCCLUSION   If an edge suddenly stops in an image, *why* does that edge stop? One reasonable guess might be that it stops because something else gets in the way, hiding it from our view. So, returning to the Kanizsa figure of Figure 4.11, we can imagine the visual system asking why the vertical line at the bottom of the figure suddenly stops. The answer that the visual system seems to come up with is that there is another contour *occluding* the vertical line, with the occluding edge oriented perpendicularly to the occluded edge.

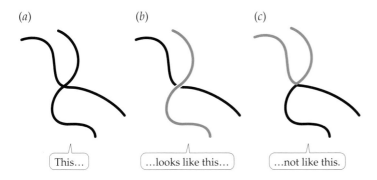

FIGURE 4.13   The Gestalt principle of good continuation. Presented with an image like the one in (*a*), the brain tends to interpret it as a pair of intersecting lines, as in (*b*), rather than reaching any other conclusion, such as that in (*c*).

FIGURE 4.14 The making of illusory contours. The little arrows in (*b*) and (*d*) represent the visual system's best guess about what is going on in (*a*) and (*c*). The illusory disk in (*c*) arises when the visual system combines a whole collection of guesses about the line terminations as shown in (*d*).

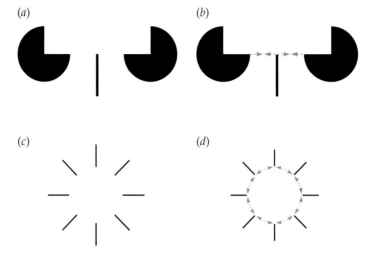

This guess, combined with a guess that the notches in the circles represent contours that can be extended, leads to the inference of an illusory contour (**Figure 4.14***a* and *b*). (Note that we also interpret the notches as places where one object is occluding another.) Figure 4.14*c* shows another example. If each black line generated weak illusory contours at right angles to its endpoint, then this figure would contain a set of roughly colinear line segments (Figure 4.14*d*) that could be grouped together to form a convincing circle in the manner of Figure 4.12*a*. (By the way, illusory contours make excellent doodles when you would rather be doing informal perception experiments than paying attention.)

Texture Segmentation and Grouping

texture segmentation Carving an image into regions of common texture properties.

Connecting short line segments will get us only so far in dividing the raw image into objects. On the left in **Figure 4.15**, you can find a region that differs in the size of its elements. An edge detector like the one described in Figure 4.4 will be oblivious to the difference between the larger-grain and smaller-grain textures. Instead, the region is found by the visual system's sophisticated mechanisms for **texture segmentation** (Beck, 1982; Bergen and Adelson, 1988; Malik and Perona, 1990). On the right-hand side of Figure 4.15, the texture of the water looks different from the texture of the stone surrounding it. Here, rather than deciding which features go together, the visual system may look at the statistics of all the features in one region and find those statistics to be different from the statistics in another region (Alvarez, 2011; Chong and Treisman, 2003). Indeed, the visual system can determine the average of the

FIGURE 4.15 The problem of texture segmentation. How do we distinguish the two halves of the figure? How do we segment out the smaller regions inside each half? On the right, how might we know that the large area is stone, surrounding a smaller area of water?

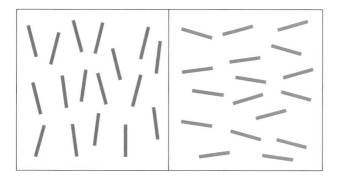

FIGURE 4.16 It is easy to see the approximate average orientation of the lines in the two regions of this figure. The red lines are vertical on average and the blue lines, horizontal. However, you will need to take more trouble to figure out whether there is an individual red line that is perfectly vertical or an individual blue line that is perfectly horizontal. Apparently you can figure out the average orientation without being aware of the orientation of each component line.

features in a region without knowing much about the individual features. In Figure 4.16, for example, it is immediately obvious that the average of the red lines is near vertical, while the blue lines are near horizontal. However, you will have to search to determine whether any individual red line is perfectly vertical or any individual blue line is perfectly horizontal.

Texture segmentation is closely related to the Gestalt grouping principles that we've been discussing. Figure 4.17*a* illustrates two of the strongest principles: similarity and proximity. **Similarity** means that image chunks that are similar to each other will be more likely to group together. Similar in what ways? Texture grouping can be based on similarity in a limited number of features: color, size, orientation, and, as illustrated here, aspects of form. Combinations ("conjunctions") of features do not work well (A. Treisman, 1986b). Thus, in Figure 4.17*b* the texture segmentation is not clear, even though the left side contains orange diamonds and green squares and the right side contains green diamonds and orange squares.

The principle of **proximity** holds that items near each other are more likely to group together than are items more widely separated. Proximity grouping gives Figure 4.17*a* its horizontally striped appearance. The original descriptions of these Gestalt principles did not involve extensive experimentation. Illustrative demonstrations, like those of Figure 4.17, seemed to make the point. Since that early Gestalt work, careful experiments have confirmed and quantified what the early demonstrations illustrated. For example, Kubovy and his colleagues (Kubovy and Cohen, 2001) quite precisely measured the strength of the proximity effect.

similarity A Gestalt grouping rule stating that the tendency of two features to group together will increase as the similarity between them increases.

proximity A Gestalt grouping rule stating that the tendency of two features to group together will increase as the distance between them decreases.

(a)

(b)

FIGURE 4.17 Similarity and proximity. (*a*) Grouping by similarity and by proximity is useful. (*b*) Grouping by a conjunction of color and form does not work.

FIGURE 4.18 Parallelism and symmetry. Which pairs of lines go together?

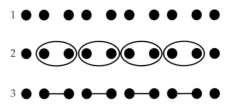

FIGURE 4.19 Proximity grouping (line 1) can be overruled by grouping by common region (line 2) or grouping by connectedness (line 3). (From S. E. Palmer, 1992.)

parallelism A rule for figure-ground assignment stating that parallel contours are likely to belong to the same figure.

symmetry A rule for figure-ground assignment stating that symmetrical regions are more likely to be seen as figure.

Figure 4.18 illustrates two somewhat weaker grouping principles: **parallelism** and **symmetry**. Most people see the *parallel* pair of contours (2 and 3) as a group and the *symmetrical* pair (7 and 8) as another group, and **Figure 4.19** shows the grouping effects of enclosing or connecting items (S. E. Palmer, 1992).

We can't list all the rules (even if we knew them all, which we do not). The visual system's goal here is to decide which bits of the input belong with which other bits of the input. Going back to Figure 4.15, it will be a complicated rule that differentiates the two halves of the figure. On one side is stone; on the other, a collection of ovals. Somehow, grouping and texture segmentation processes will separate the two regions, and you will rapidly be able to identify different collections of features as water or stone, shiny or matte, and so forth (Motoyoshi et al., 2007).

See **Web Activity 4.1: Gestalt Grouping Principles**, for examples of grouping by common fate and synchrony—two principles not covered here (S.-H. Lee and Blake, 1999).

CAMOUFLAGE The same principles that are normally used to help us find objects in the world can be exploited to hide them. The art of camouflage is, to a great extent, the art of getting your features to group with the features of the environment so as to persuade an observer that your features do not form a perceptual group of their own. **Figure 4.20** shows some examples from the animal kingdom. The exercise for you is to determine which principles of grouping are at work hiding the camouflaged animal in each of Figures 4.20*a* and *c*.

(*a*)   (*b*)   (*c*)

FIGURE 4.20 Examples of camouflage. Panel (*b*) shows the hidden animal in (*a*). We leave (*c*) as an exercise for the reader. What Gestalt principles are at work here?

Perceptual Committees Revisited

Now that we've seen some of the problems the visual system has to deal with in parsing an image, let's go back and flesh out the notion of perceptual committees in middle vision. Low-level visual processes deliver fairly straightforward bits of information about a line here and a color there. However, that collection of information needs to be interpreted before we know what we're seeing. Middle vision behaves like a collection of specialists, each with a specific area of expertise and individual opinions about what the input might mean. The goal is to have a single answer emerge out of this diversity of opinions.

The idea of perception by committee has a long history, though the specific metaphor takes different forms at different times. One early version was Oliver Selfridge's (1959) Pandemonium model for letter recognition (a relatively simple subset of the object recognition problem). Selfridge called his committee members "demons." (Indeed, the word *pandemonium*, which we define as "noise and chaos," was originally John Milton's [1608–1674] word for the abode of all demons in *Paradise Lost*.) Selfridge's theologically neutral "feature demons" found vertical lines, acute angles, and so forth. "Cognitive demons," one for each letter, had ideas about the features of their letters. A cognitive demon looked at the work of the feature demons and made noise proportional to the evidence for its letter. A "decision demon" listened to the committee of cognitive demons and identified the letter on the basis of the loudest yell. Figure 4.21 shows a screen shot from **Web Activity 4.2: Pandemonium**. Visit the book's website to experience perception by committee in action.

Of course, no one really thinks that object recognition is accomplished by demons or committees in any literal sense. The physical substrate of a "committee" is probably a massively interconnected set of neurons that takes input and, by virtue of its specific connections, produces an output that can be read as the committee decision by other processes elsewhere (Mozer, 1991). The details of how this might come to pass are beyond the scope of this book. Still, in the next section we will identify some of the working assumptions of these committees.

COMMITTEE RULES: HONOR PHYSICS AND AVOID ACCIDENTS Though we usually come to a single coherent interpretation of the current contents of the sensory world, the decisions made by perceptual committees need not be final. An **ambiguous figure** is a figure that generates two or more plausible interpretations. For example, Figure 4.22*a* shows the famous **Necker cube**. Middle-vision committees of the visual system are willing to entertain either of the two solids shown in Figures 4.22*b* and *c* as interpretations of the wire frame pictured in Figure 4.22*a*. However, the system is unwilling to readily consider any of the infinite number of other possible interpretations of the wire

FIGURE 4.21 The Pandemonium model for recognizing an *A*. See **Web Activity 4.2: Pandemonium** to view this in action.

ambiguous figure A visual stimulus that gives rise to two or more interpretations of its identity or structure.

Necker cube An outline that is perceptually bi-stable. Unlike the situation with most stimuli, two interpretations continually battle for perceptual dominance.

(a)   *(b)*   *(c)*   *(d)*

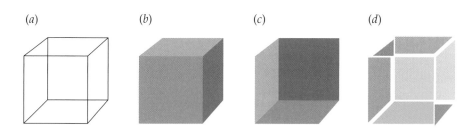

FIGURE 4.22 The wire-frame Necker cube (*a*) can look like either of the solids shown in parts (*b*) or (*c*). It is much less likely to be seen as a collection of flat regions on the page (*d*), even though that's really what it is!

FIGURE 4.23 A classic ambiguous figure gets a new role.

accidental viewpoint A viewing position that produces some regularity in the visual image that is not present in the world (e.g., the sides of two independent objects lining up perfectly).

image—for example, the flat one in Figure 4.22*d*. **Figure 4.23** shows another classic ambiguous figure, now pressed into the service of commerce.

Necker cubes and duck-rabbits are really the exceptions that prove the rule. *Every* image is, in theory, ambiguous, but the perceptual committees almost always agree on a single interpretation. Consider, for example, **Figure 4.24***a*. This pattern might represent the retinal image projected by the scene depicted in Figure 4.24*b*: four surfaces with different shapes, arranged in different orientations, and at different distances. For you to see this as a single shape divided into four square regions, you would have to be viewing the scene from exactly one, very precise location—what object recognition researchers call an **accidental viewpoint**. Any slight shift in viewpoint—say, moving just slightly to the left—would destroy the illusion of the four equidistant square regions. (**Web Activity 4.3: Object Ambiguity** illustrates this situation with an animation that makes the relationship between Figures 4.24*a* and *b* clearer.)

The perceptual committees know about accidental viewpoints. More specifically, they know enough not to bet on them. The chances that Figure 4.24*a* is the two-dimensional representation of the three-dimensional scene in Figure 4.24*b* are so slim that the visual system refuses even to consider this possibility. Nor do the perceptual committees care to assume other unlikely accounts of the perceptual input. Thus, unless it has very good reason to do so, the visual system will not conclude that Figure 4.13 represents the meeting, nose to nose, of four snakes.

A second set of assumptions made by the visual system involves an implicit understanding of some aspects of the physics of the world. For example, returning to the Kanizsa figure (see Figure 4.11), we infer the arrow-shaped object, in part, because of our *implicit* understanding that solid objects block light. This understanding of opacity causes us to infer that the lines disappear because something is blocking our view of them. Calling this understanding "implicit" means that we need not be able to verbalize the rule in order to use it. Monkeys seem to see the subjective contours without benefit of instruction in physics (von der Heydt, Peterhans, and Baumgartner, 1984), and we may assume that similar abilities extend far into the animal kingdom. We and our visual systems "know" this and other physical principles in the same way that a ball "knows" about gravity.

These principles and assumptions may seem so obvious as to be meaningless. But remember that an image has no meaning whatsoever until middle- and high-level visual processes dig into it. One committee uses the knowledge that opaque objects occlude other objects behind them to generate plausible interpretations of image elements like the notched circles and dead-end edges in Figure 4.11. Another committee considers all the possibilities and devalues

FIGURE 4.24 Accidental viewpoint. (*a*) Why do we see these four squares? (*b*) Maybe the eye just happens to be in the right position to see four arbitrary shapes at arbitrary depths line up to form the pattern. That would be quite a coincidence. That would be an accidental viewpoint.

any that involve accidental viewpoints, reducing what is initially a theoretically unsolvable problem (finding the one correct interpretation out of the infinite number of possible ones) to a potentially solvable one. And so we proceed further and further into the visual system, until a single, generally correct interpretation emerges.

FIGURE 4.25 What is figure and what is ground?

Figure and Ground

Armed with this understanding of the ground rules of committee deliberation, we can continue with the effort to go from simple features to recognizable objects. The edge- and region-finding mechanisms, discussed earlier, would divide Figure 4.25 into yellow and red regions without much difficulty. But how should those regions be understood? It is extremely likely that we would interpret the illustration as two red figures on a yellow background. That is, we would infer that the yellow would continue behind the red objects if we could lift them up to check. That need not be the case, however. We could be looking at yellow and red puzzle pieces, cut to fit each other perfectly. Or we could be looking at two yellow objects, a smaller one on the left and a larger one with a squiggly hole on the right, both sitting on top of a red background.

The ability to distinguish figures (objects in the foreground) from ground (surfaces or objects lying behind the figures) is a critical step on the path from image to object recognition. Like the finding of edges and regions, it is a process governed by a collection of principles acting together, as if in another of these perceptual committees, to decide how the visual world should be understood. As before, the governing goal is to determine the most likely reality behind the image on the retina.

Like the grouping principles, the topic of **figure-ground assignment** became important in visual perception because of the work of the Gestalt psychologists. Figure 4.26 shows the classic vase/face figure introduced in the 1920s by the Danish psychologist Edgar Rubin (1886–1951). It must be the best-known illustration from the Gestalt school, and it is analogous to the Necker cube in that it illustrates one of those rare cases in which a perceptual committee has a difficult time reaching consensus. All visual stimuli may be inherently ambiguous, but the processes that determine figure and ground almost always manage to come to a single conclusion, as they do in Figure 4.25. We are surprised when the process fails and delivers two or more interpretations. The surprise we register when the Rubin vase "flips" to a pair of faces reminds us of the perceptual stability that we usually take for granted.

figure-ground assignment The process of determining that some regions of an image belong to a foreground object (figure) and other regions are part of the background (ground).

surroundedness A rule for figure-ground assignment stating that if one region is entirely surrounded by another, it is likely that the surrounded region is the figure.

What principles are at work in the assignment of regions to figure or ground? We can list some of them:

- *Surroundedness*. If one region is entirely surrounded by another, it is likely that the surrounded region is the figure. This **surroundedness** is a factor for the red region on the right in Figure 4.25.
- *Size*. The smaller region is likely to be figure. The cow is smaller than the field in which she stands. These letters that you're reading are smaller than the page.
- *Symmetry*. A symmetrical region is more likely to be seen as figure. How likely is it that the two yellow regions in Figure 4.25 just happen to have the symmetrical contours facing each other over what would be the red gap on the left?

FIGURE 4.26 The Rubin vase/face figure. Do you see a vase or two faces in profile? Notice that the boundary marked by the green line changes its allegiance when the figure flips interpretation. The boundary is "owned" by the figure.

FIGURE 4.27 Why does the beige region appear to be the figure when the beige and green regions are about equal in most respects? Parallel contours are often taken to belong to the figure.

- *Parallelism.* Regions with parallel contours are more likely to be seen as figure (does beige or green "win" as figure in **Figure 4.27**?). Again, how likely is it that two contours would be parallel with one another if they did not belong to the same object?

- *Extremal edges.* Figure-ground calculations are intended to answer the question "Is region A in front of region B?" In the upper left panel of **Figure 4.28**, the edge of the white disk has shading suggesting that the edge is curving away from the viewer and toward the gray texture. The viewer concludes that the disk must be closer and must be the figure. In the upper right panel, the white ring has this "extremal edge" cue, and it becomes the figure. Note that the cue is strong enough to overwhelm cues like surroundedness and size (S. E. Palmer and Ghose, 2008), which seem to flip the figure-ground assignment in the bottom panels of the figure.

- *Relative motion.* How surface details move relative to an edge can also determine which portion of a display is the foreground figure and which is the background (Yonas, Craton, and Thompson, 1987). (See **Web Activity 4.1: Gestalt Grouping Principles.**)

A COMPLICATED BUSINESS Although the assignment of figure and ground is governed by rules, it is not a simple process. Consider, for example, **Figure 4.29**. The surroundedness, size, symmetry, and parallelism rules combine to firmly establish the purple squares as figures on the green background. But what about the circle in the middle of each square? Each one is smaller than the green rectangle and completely surrounded by it. Moreover, each circle is perfectly symmetrical. Yet, of the three, only the center circle is perceived as being a separate object (figure); the circles on the left and right are seen as holes in the green rectangle.

You can (and should) speculate about the factors that determine whether a circle is seen as a hole or a spot (C. Yin, Kellman, and Shipley, 1997). On the right in Figure 4.29, the answer has something to do with the fact that we interpret those three isolated patches of a dollar as one object, occluded by the purple square. Given that theory, the circle must be a hole. Apparently, as part of the journey from image to object, we need to understand something about how one object can occlude another. Indeed, the path to object recognition is not a simple one-way street. Information about object recognition influences

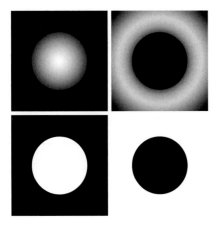

FIGURE 4.28 In the top left panel, the "extremal edge" cue makes the image look like a sphere on a background. The surrounding region in the top right panel looks like a doughnut figure and the hole looks like ground. In the bottom two panels, without the edge cue, the figure-ground relations are reversed. (After S. E. Palmer and Ghose, 2008.)

FIGURE 4.29 Which circles are figures and which are holes?

figure-ground assignment too (Peterson and Skow, 2008). (See **Web Essay 4.1: The Role of Knowledge in Figure-Ground Assignment.**)

Dealing with Occlusion

Objects are rarely kind enough to present themselves to us in splendid isolation on blank backgrounds. In the real world, objects are often partially hidden by other objects. Indeed, three-dimensional objects often hide parts of themselves. We've already discussed how edge-finding processes can fabricate illusory contours on the basis of the physics of occlusion. We will now need yet another committee to connect the visible pieces of occluded objects by inferring the presence of hidden pieces of the object when necessary.

In their quest to understand the rules governing the completion of occluded objects, Philip Kellman and Thomas Shipley (1991) stressed the ways that edges can *relate* across gaps. This concept of **relatability** is illustrated in Figure 4.30. Do the two black line segments in each part look like they belong to the same curve, occluded by the black square? In Figure 4.30*a*, the answer is "yes." In Figure 4.30*b*, the answer is "no." Kellman and his colleagues argue that the critical difference is that the lines in Figure 4.30*a* can be related by a simple curve like an elbow or a bend in the road. The lines in Figure 4.30*b* require a more complex *S* curve to make a smooth connection between them. The visual system is unwilling to propose such an elaborate relationship, so it concludes that the lines are not related at all (that is, they are not parts of the same object). Like the figure-ground rules, this **heuristic** (mental shortcut) is not infallible (after all, some objects really do have *S*-shaped contours). The occlusion committee is apparently willing to accept a few missed completions in order to reduce the vast number of possible completions we would have to consider if we tried to connect every pair of occluded edges. For more on dealing with occlusion, see **Web Essay 4.2: Dynamic Occlusion** and **Web Activity 4.4: Infant Object Perception.**

Additional heuristics emerge when we move from two dimensions to three, as Figure 4.31 shows. Here we see a pair of box-shaped objects, one partially occluding the other. The overlap of the boxes produces a variety of different line junctions, all of which can be classified as *Y*, *T*, or arrow junctions. *T* junctions almost always occur when one surface occludes another; *Y* and arrow junctions almost always correspond to corners and thus don't signal occlusions. These rules fail to hold true only when we're viewing the scene from an accidental viewpoint. Hence, the various junction types are known as **nonaccidental features** (Lowe, 1985), and they provide another potential tool for use by the perceptual committees charged with dividing the scene into objects and deciding what is occluding what.

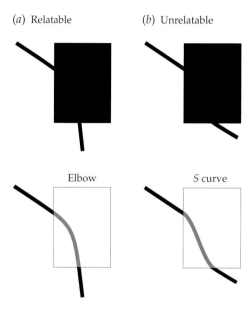

(*a*) Relatable (*b*) Unrelatable

Elbow S curve

FIGURE 4.30 Two edges are relatable if they can be connected with a smooth, convex or concave curve (*a*), but not if the connection requires an *S* curve (*b*). (After Kellman, 1998.)

relatability The degree to which two line segments appear to be part of the same contour.

heuristic A mental shortcut.

nonaccidental feature A feature of an object that is not dependent on the exact (or accidental) viewing position of the observer.

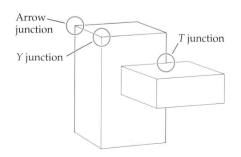

Arrow junction

T junction

Y junction

FIGURE 4.31 Different sorts of line junctions have different meanings. *T* junctions indicate occlusion of one region by another. *Y* and arrow junctions indicate corners.

FIGURE 4.32 Global letters composed of local letters. David Navon argued that perceptual processes work from the global to the local.

Parts and Wholes

global superiority effect The finding in various experiments that the properties of the whole object take precedence over the properties of parts of the object.

Glance quickly at **Figure 4.32** and decide whether you see an *H*. Now glance back and look for a *U*. Which of these tasks took longer? Using stimuli like these, David Navon (1977) found that the big letters interfere with naming of the little letters more than the little letters interfere with recognition of the big letters. This **global superiority effect** is consistent with an implicit assumption we've been making throughout our discussion of middle vision: that the first goal is to carve the retinal image into large-scale objects. But as these stimuli also remind us, most objects are composed of parts, and we can recognize these individual parts as well. Indeed, many recognition models (to be discussed shortly) posit that segmenting an object into its constituent parts is a crucial step in deciding what type of object it is.

One heuristic that might be used by perceptual committees when dividing objects into parts is illustrated in **Figure 4.33**. Don Hoffman and Whitman Richards (1984) noted that when one blob is pushed into another, a pair of concavities is created in the silhouette of the resulting two-part object (Figure 4.33*a*). A process that embodied this bit of physics would conclude that valleys, rather than bumps, should be used to mark part boundaries. Thus, we are inclined to parse the object into two parts as shown in Figure 4.33*b*, not into three parts as in Figure 4.33*c*.

Summarizing Middle Vision

We have gone from the image and its simple features to objects with parts. It now makes sense to talk about recognizing the object, possibly on the basis of these parts. Before moving on, though, it is worth briefly reviewing how we got here. The goals of the middle-vision processes discussed so far in this chapter might be summarized in five principles:

1. *Bring together that which should be brought together.* We have the Gestalt grouping principles (similarity, proximity, parallelism, symmetry, and so forth), and we have the processes that complete contours and objects even when they are partially hidden behind occluders (e.g., the relatability heuristic).

2. *Split asunder that which should be split asunder.* Complementing the grouping principles are the edge-finding processes that divide regions from each other. Figure-ground mechanisms separate objects from the background. Texture segmentation processes divide one region from the next on the basis of image statistics.

FIGURE 4.33 Finding parts from object boundaries. (*a*) When one blob is pushed into another, a pair of concavities is created. We know this (implicitly, of course), and we work backward from this fact to carve this figure into the two parts shown in (*b*) rather than according to a different scheme, such as the one shown in (*c*).

(*a*)   (*b*)   (*c*)

3. *Use what you know.* Two-dimensional edge configurations are taken to indicate three-dimensional corners or occlusion borders, and objects are divided into parts on the basis of an implicit knowledge of the physics of image formation.

4. *Avoid accidents.* Avoid interpretations that require the assumptions of highly specific, accidental combinations of features or accidental viewpoints.

5. *Seek consensus and avoid ambiguity.* Every image is ambiguous. There are always multiple, even infinite physical situations that could generate a given image. Using the first four principles, the "committees" of middle vision must eliminate all but one of the possibilities, thereby resolving the ambiguity and delivering a single solution to the perceptual problem at hand.

From Metaphor to Formal Model

We have been talking about "perceptual committees" in middle vision. While we hope that is a useful way to think about what's going on, it is just a metaphor. There are formal, mathematical ways to model the way in which knowledge about regularities in the world can constrain the interpretation of ambiguous sensory input. One of the most fruitful approaches is known as the **Bayesian approach** (Yuille and Kersten, 2006). Thomas Bayes (1702–1761), an eighteenth-century Presbyterian minister, was the first to describe the relevant mathematics.

Look at **Figure 4.34**. Our visual system looks at the stimulus and makes an observation (call it "O"). Suppose we wanted to make our best guess as to what situation in the real world produced that observation. Let's consider three hypotheses, illustrated in the figure: Hypothesis A says that we're looking at two green rectangles. The light one has a narrow letter *E* on it, and the dark one has a narrow numeral 3. These just happen to precisely line up in order to produce a *B* like the one we observed. Hypothesis B says we're looking at a green square—half light and half dark green—with a *B* on it. Hypothesis C says we're looking at the same green square, but it really has a *C* on it. Of course, an infinity of other hypotheses could be entertained here (it's really a chicken, it's really dinner, and so on), but these three will do as representatives.

Which hypothesis represents the most likely explanation of the observation? We can represent the likelihood of hypothesis A as $P(A \mid O)$, which we would read as the probability of hypothesis A, given observation O. We want to know

Bayesian approach A way of formalizing the idea that our perception is a combination of the current stimulus and our knowledge about the conditions of the world—what is and is not likely to occur. The Bayesian approach is stated mathematically as Bayes' theorem—$P(A \mid O) = P(A) \times P(O \mid A)/P(O)$—which enables us to calculate the probability (P) that the world is in a particular state (A) given a particular observation (O).

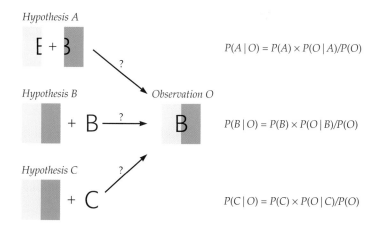

$$P(A \mid O) = P(A) \times P(O \mid A)/P(O)$$

$$P(B \mid O) = P(B) \times P(O \mid B)/P(O)$$

$$P(C \mid O) = P(C) \times P(O \mid C)/P(O)$$

FIGURE 4.34 When the visual system is faced with a stimulus (such as the one on the right of this figure), it tries to figure out the most likely situation in the world that has produced this particular pattern of activity. A few hypotheses are shown on the left. In this case, hypothesis B is much more likely than hypotheses A or C. Bayes' theorem gives a way of formalizing this type of calculation.

which probability is the highest: $P(A\,|\,O)$, $P(B\,|\,O)$, or $P(C\,|\,O)$. Bayes' theorem gives us a way of computing these probabilities. Specifically, the theorem says

$$P(A\,|\,O) = P(A) \times P(O\,|\,A)/P(O)$$

Let's unpack this equation a bit. $P(A)$ is the probability that hypothesis A ever happens. Which hypothesis would we think was correct if we had our eyes closed and never made observation O? We don't know precisely, but given what we know about the world, we can assume that both $P(B)$ and $P(C)$ are likely bigger than $P(A)$, since hypothesis A relies on a very precise and therefore unlikely alignment of a skinny E with a skinny 3. This first term is what is known as the *prior probability*; the probability that a given hypothesis is correct before any observations are made.

The second term, $P(O\,|\,A)$, asks—if a given hypothesis is correct—how likely we were to make the observation O. In Figure 4.34, hypotheses A and B are likely to lead to observations much like O. Hypothesis C is unlikely. (What are the chances that the letter looks like a B but it is really a C?) So, $P(O\,|\,A)$ and $P(O\,|\,B)$ are both larger than $P(O\,|\,C)$.

The third term, $P(O)$, asks—of all possible observations we could possibly have made, anywhere in the world—what's the probability of observing O? This number can be difficult to calculate, but thankfully it's the same for all three hypotheses, so we can ignore the effects of $P(O)$.

What, then, is our best guess about the situation in the real world? Hypotheses B and C have better prior probabilities: $P(B)$ and $P(C)$. Hypotheses A and B have better likelihoods: $P(A\,|\,O)$ and $P(B\,|\,O)$. Overall, the Bayesian approach will tell us that hypothesis B is a better bet than either hypothesis A or hypothesis C (and all those chicken and dinner hypotheses are vastly unlikely).

FURTHER DISCUSSION of the Bayesian approach can be found in Chapter 6 on page 175.

FIGURE 4.35 Response of V4 cells to different shapes. (*a*) Gallant, Braun, and Van Essen (1993) tried this set of stimuli. Warm colors indicate more response from one particular cell. (*b*) Connor and his colleagues presented these shapes to V4 neurons. Darker circles indicate more response. (Part *a* from Gallant, Braun, and Van Essen, 1993; part *b* from Kourtzi and Connor, 2011.)

Object Recognition

With these ideas about middle vision in mind, we can return to Quiroga's discovery of cells that respond to highly specific objects (Quiroga et al., 2005). Traveling the *what* pathway from V1 into the temporal lobe, we can see a progressive change in the responses of cells in different visual areas. In V1, cells respond best to lines and edges in very specific areas of the visual field. In V2, we get early steps from local features to objects. As noted before, these cells have a sensitivity to "border ownership." They are also sensitive to illusory

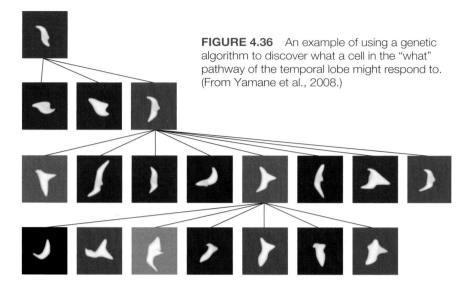

FIGURE 4.36 An example of using a genetic algorithm to discover what a cell in the "what" pathway of the temporal lobe might respond to. (From Yamane et al., 2008.)

contours (Peterhans et al., 1986; von der Heydt, Peterhans, and Baumgartner, 1984). By area V4, cells appear to be interested in much more complex attributes, like those shown in **Figure 4.35**.

No one has ever definitively determined the perfect set of stimuli for V4 cells. Figure 4.35*a* shows some geometric ideas from Gallant, Braun, and Van Essen (1993); Figure 4.35*b* shows a small subset of a collection of bumpy blobs from the Connor lab (Kourtzi and Connor, 2011). The images in Figure 4.35 illustrate a fact about objects: while you can vary orientation or color or other basic features in a systematic way, it is much harder to imagine how you vary object shape. What are the dimensions of shape? We really do not know.

Things get more complex as we move farther into the temporal lobe. **Figure 4.36** shows one approach to finding receptive-field properties when you don't have a clear *a priori* idea about what the features might be (Yamane et al., 2008): Start with a shape. Show it to your neuron (top row). The level of response is color-coded—the redder the better. This shape gets just a little response. Now, make some new shapes that are related to the first one. If one of them generates a larger response (like the third one in the second row), let it produce "children" (shown in the third row). If this "genetic algorithm" is allowed to run for multiple "generations," the shapes will evolve into shapes to which the cells respond more strongly. The winners in this case may not look like anything very recognizable, but they are all elongated things with a sort of spike in the middle. As **Figure 4.37** illustrates, one can imagine that a vast family of shapes like these might be a basis for object perception as letters and syllables can be the basis for words (Ungerleider and Bell, 2011).

We may not know exactly what optimally activates individual cells as we progress down the *what* pathway into the temporal lobe. However, functional imaging studies can show us that different regions of the cortex are activated better by some categories of stimuli than by others. The basic method for

FIGURE 4.37 Neurons might be sensitive to shapes that can be put together into a recognizable object even if no cell's preferred shape looks like anything that we have seen. (After Ungerleider and Bell, 2011.)

FIGURE 4.38 Areas of human cortex specialized for faces (fusiform face area, FFA), places (parahippocampal place area, PPA), body parts (extrastriate body area, EBA), and motion (middle temporal area, MT). (From Spiridon, Fischl, and Kanwisher, 2006.)

■ FFA
■ PPA
■ EBA
■ MT

parahippocampal place area (PPA) A region of extrastriate visual cortex in humans that is specifically and reliably activated more by images of places than by other stimuli.

fusiform face area (FFA) A region of extrastriate visual cortex in humans that is specifically and reliably activated by human faces.

extrastriate body area (EBA) A region of extrastriate visual cortex in humans that is specifically and reliably activated by images of the body other than the face.

middle temporal area (MT) An area of the brain thought to be important in the perception of motion.

naïve template theory The proposal that the visual system recognizes objects by matching the neural representation of the image with a stored representation of the same "shape" in the brain.

showing this distinction is the subtraction method we discussed in Chapter 1. If you show a human observer a series of pictures of spaces like rooms and fields and city streets, lots of pieces of the brain will be activated by these places. Now show the observer other pictures with similar properties that do not happen to be places—maybe scrambled versions of the places, maybe objects or abstract designs. Again, large areas of brain will be active. However, if you subtract the two patterns of activation, there will at least one region, now known as the **parahippocampal place area (PPA)** that is specifically and reliably activated more by places than by other stimuli (Epstein and Kanwisher, 1998). Other well-established specialized areas include the **fusiform face area (FFA)**, mentioned earlier, and the **extrastriate body area (EBA)**. You can see these, laid out over an inflated representation of the human brain (to smooth out the wrinkles), in Figure 4.38. The **middle temporal area (MT)** is specialized for motion (see Chapter 8).

Thus, a network of visual areas gives rise to cells in the temporal lobe with those very specific sensitivities that Quiroga et al. (2005) report. But what is going on when a cell responds to the actress Jennifer Aniston? Could it be that, in listening to a Jennifer Aniston neuron, the researchers were listening in on the act of object recognition? If the image of Jennifer Aniston falls on your retina, you must be able to take that raw image and generate a description that can be matched to a Jennifer Aniston representation in memory. Of course, if you have no idea who Jennifer Aniston is or what she looks like, you won't recognize her. Even so, you will still recognize her as a woman. How?

This is not a trivial problem, and we can quickly dispense with some trivial solutions. You are not matching the "pixels" of the Aniston image with the pixels of an Aniston representation. Figure 4.6 shows that the cell responded to various different images of the actress. Moreover, we know that a detailed, point-by-point representation of objects is not transmitted to the parts of the brain interested in objects. As we've been discussing, the raw image is analyzed by middle-vision processes, and it is the output of those processes that will be available to object recognition processes.

Templates versus Structural Descriptions

The idea that we recognize objects by matching every pixel or even matching every low-level feature of the input to a representation in memory is what might be called **naïve template theory**. It won't work even for simple objects. The basic idea of a template is rather like a lock and key. As we will see in Chapters 14 and 15, locks and keys are quite an apt metaphor in smell and taste, where

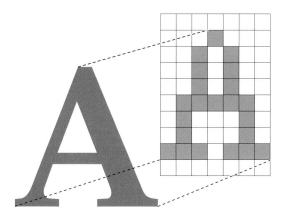

FIGURE 4.39   A basic template.

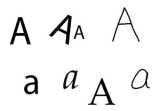

FIGURE 4.40   The problem with templates is that we need a lot of them.

the "key" to be recognized is a molecule like a specific odorant and where that molecular key presents itself in more or less the same shape every time.

Figures 4.39 and 4.40 show that recognizable visual objects like the letter *A* are much less well behaved. Figure 4.39 illustrates the lock-and-key template idea. A letter *A* stimulus falls on an array of spot detectors. If the *A* falls on the filled detectors and not the empty ones, it is identified as an *A*. Therefore, the array of detectors serves as an *A* template. The difficulty with a naïve template model is that too many templates are required. All of the objects in Figure 4.40 are *A*s. If we needed a new template for every letter in every position and orientation, we would run out of brain before we ran out of alphabet. And just think about the problem of building a Jennifer Aniston representation in this way.

One way out of this problem is to notice that all the *A*s—at least all the capital *A*s—share a basic structure. Instead of matching each point in the image to a point in a template, perhaps we perform a more conceptual match. Just about any capital *A* can be described by the relationship of its three lines: the two flanking lines meet, and the third line spans the angle created by those two lines. Now the image of the *A* is being matched to a **structural description** of an *A*, a specification of an object in terms of its parts and the relationships between the parts.

Many versions of structural-description hypotheses have been proposed. A key component of each theory is how object parts are represented in the structural descriptions. Marr and Nishihara (1977) used "generalized cylinders" that could be scaled longer, shorter, fatter, or thinner to represent differently shaped parts. Biederman (1987) proposed a set of **geons** ("geometric ions"); see Figure 4.41 for examples. Geons are specified as collections of nonaccidental features (remember Figure 4.24?), so in theory a visual system should be able to recognize a geon equally accurately and quickly, regardless of how the geon is oriented in space (as long as it's not an accidental view). Geons are featured in Biederman's **recognition-by-components model**, which we'll now describe in a bit more detail.

Just as the finite set of letters in the alphabet can be combined in various ways to produce an infinite number of words, the finite set of geons can be used to construct a very large number of object representations. Attaching a

structural description A description of an object in terms of the nature of its constituent parts and the relationships between those parts.

geon In Biederman's recognition-by-components model, any of the "geometric ions" out of which perceptual objects are built.

recognition-by-components model Biederman's model of object recognition, which holds that objects are recognized by the identities and relationships of their component parts.

FIGURE 4.41   Three of the 36 or so geons in Biederman's "recognition-by-components" theory of object recognition. Each geon is shown in three orientations, illustrating the fact that they are easily recognizable from nearly any viewpoint.

FIGURE 4.42 Combining geons can create a wide variety of object representations. (*a–c*) Three objects "spelled out" by different combinations of the cylinder, noodle, and brick geons. A different view of the coffee mug (*d*) and a different instance of this object class (*e*) would lead to the same structural description as in (*a*).

(*a*)   (*b*)   (*c*)   (*d*)   (*e*)

noodle to the side of a cylinder gives us a coffee mug (**Figure 4.42***a*). Moving the noodle to the top of the cylinder produces a pail (Figure 4.42*b*). Changing the cylinder to a brick gives us an attaché case (Figure 4.42*c*).

Because geons and relationships such as "A is beside B" are designed to be equally recognizable from many different vantage points, structural descriptions composed of these geons and relations should also be **viewpoint-invariant**. Minor shape variations also won't alter the structural descriptions of geons. As noted already, this is the great advantage of structural descriptions over templates: if we can derive the same structural description from any picture of the object (e.g., Figures 4.42*a*, *d*, and *e*), then we need to store only one representation of the object in memory.

Problems with Structural-Description Theories

viewpoint invariance 1. A property of an object that does not change when observer viewpoint changes. 2. A class of theories of object recognition that proposes representations of objects that do not change when viewpoint changes.

We may have made too much progress. Viewpoint invariance is a good thing, but ʇuɐıɹɐʌuı-ʇuıodʍǝıʌ ʎlǝʇǝldɯoɔ ʇou sı uoıʇıuɓoɔǝɹ ʇɔǝɾqo You were probably able to read that last sentence without turning your book upside down, but even Biederman would say that there is something quite clearly viewpoint-dependent about letter recognition and, more generally, object recognition. There are other problems with structural descriptions as well. For example, it is not clear that geons or any of the other "alphabets" proposed by structural-description models are adequate for the language of object recognition. Would the geon description of a cigar box differ from that of a book?

In response to these questions about structural-description models, researchers such as Michael Tarr, Heinrich Bülthoff, and others have returned to template-like representations that they call "views." Support for view-based representations generally comes from experiments that use novel, rather than familiar, objects. For example, Tarr and Pinker (1990) trained observers to recognize letterlike objects. During training, the objects were always shown in the upright orientation. Then, in a "surprise" phase of the experiment, the observers were asked to recognize rotated versions of the objects. The results revealed a linear relationship between orientation shift and the response time to recognize the object. The more the object was rotated, the longer the observers took to name it. This result suggests that the subjects may have stored a template-like representation of the object during the training phase, and then recognized the objects in the surprise phase by mentally rotating the misoriented objects back to the upright views they had stored in memory.

FIGURE 4.43 Recognizing these "greebles" does not seem to be entirely viewpoint-independent, even if they are made up of geonlike shapes. (From Gauthier et al., 1998.)

Biederman and his colleagues protest that these types of stimuli are not well described by geons, but even objects that can be identified on the basis of their geons show a dependence on viewpoint (Hayward and Williams, 2000). Gauthier et al. (1998) made novel objects that they named "greebles" out of geonlike parts (**Figure 4.43**). Recognition of these novel objects also appears to have a viewpoint-dependent component (**Web Activity 4.5: Viewpoint Effects** lets you test yourself in a short experiment using such objects). However, view-based models have their own problems, and the debate between structural-description and view-based theorists has been quite lively (Peterson and Rhodes, 2003).

Multiple Recognition Committees?

If this chapter has had one theme, it is that no step on the road from image to recognition is taken by a single process acting alone. From the grouping of similar pieces of the image to the segregation of figure and ground, every step has been based on consensus—a committee decision. It seems likely that the act of recognition is similar. Indeed, recognition may not be a single act. We can recognize an object in multiple ways, perhaps simultaneously. As an example, Figures 4.44*a* and *b* show two birds. In the terminology of Pierre Jolicoeur and his colleagues (Jolicoeur, Gluck, and Kosslyn, 1984), "bird" is the **entry-level category** for these objects—the first word that comes to mind when we're asked to name them. But these objects are also quite clearly different. At a subordinate level—a more specific level beneath the entry level—Figure 4.44*a* shows a fox sparrow and Figure 4.44*b* shows a cardinal. At a superordinate level—a broader level above the entry level—these two objects, as well as the one in Figure 4.44*c*, are all animals.

We can imagine that each of these acts of recognition ("fox sparrow," "bird," "animal") might rely on different stored representations and different analyses of the visual stimulus. And we can imagine a geon account of "bird," but a geon description of "fox sparrow" would be harder to envision. Subordinate-level recognition seems better suited to a system in which the precise details of a

entry-level category For an object, the label that comes to mind most quickly when we identify it (e.g., "bird"). At the subordinate level, the object might be more specifically named (e.g., "eagle"); at the superordinate level, it might be more generally named (e.g., "animal").

(*a*)

(*b*)

(*c*)

(*d*)

FIGURE 4.44 Two quite different birds (*a* and *b*), a yet more different animal (*c*), and a third "bird" (*d*).

particular view of the object are encoded. Recognizing Figures 4.44*a*,*b*, and *c* as animals seems like quite a different act.

Indeed, a number of studies have shown that it takes considerably longer to recognize objects at the subordinate or superordinate levels than at the entry level. Even more impressively, studies looking at brain recordings provide strong evidence that different parts of the brain are more active when people are engaged in subordinate-level recognition than when they are recognizing objects at the entry level (Palmeri and Gauthier, 2004). There are several more interesting twists. For example, when shown an atypical member of a category, such as the bird in Figure 4.44*d*, people are faster to name the object at a more subordinate level ("ostrich"). And when people become experts at recognizing a certain class of objects, subordinate-level recognition becomes as fast as or faster than entry-level recognition (or, looking at this another way, we might say that the entry level shifts down one level when one becomes an expert). (By the way, bird-watchers and dog show judges seem to be the most extensively studied such experts [Tanaka and Taylor, 1991].) All these results point to the conclusion that the visual system is employing several different object recognition committees, each working with their own sets of tools, at the same time.

Faces: An Illustrative Special Case

Faces are an interesting special case of object recognition. Take, for example, the images in **Figure 4.45**. You should have little difficulty recognizing these as faces, but you will probably have some difficulty quickly identifying which one has been modified. If you turn the faces right side up, however, one of the pictures will look quite strikingly wrong (Thompson, 1980).

This is another demonstration of the point made in the previous section: that different levels of categorization often seem to be subserved by different committees using different types of information. The processes that recognize a face as a face care little about inversion, and they don't seem to be disturbed by distortion of the face. The processes that recognize the face as belonging to a specific individual (in this case, one of the authors of this book) work poorly on inverted faces and are very concerned with the precise configuration of eyes, nose, and mouth. (See **Web Activity 4.6: The Face Inversion Effect**.)

Neuropsychology provides further evidence that the processes can be separated. Damage to specific areas in the temporal lobe of the brain can produce **prosopagnosia**, a disorder in which the patient cannot identify faces. (See **Web Essay 4.3: Face Blindness**.) Though she may be able to recognize an object as a face, she will not know who the person might be. This is not to say

prosopagnosia An inability to recognize faces.

FIGURE 4.45 Which of these two photos has been altered? As you will see, both faces look fine upside down, but one of them looks quite strikingly "wrong" when turned right side up. (After Thompson, 1980.)

that the two levels of face recognition are subserved by completely different systems (Gauthier, Behrmann, and Tarr, 1999). A neuropsychological mark of truly separate brain modules is **double dissociation**. Two functions, such as hearing and sight, are doubly dissociable if one can be damaged without harm to the other and vice versa. Thus, you can be blind and still hear or you can be deaf and still see. In face recognition, it is possible to lose the subordinate ability to recognize specific faces while retaining the ability to recognize an object as a face. It is not clear that the reverse even makes sense. How could you recognize a face as your mother without recognizing it as a face? Interestingly, it is possible to be born with a specific impairment in the ability to recognize faces. The existence of this **congenital prosopagnosia** is a good indication that there is a specific neural module for face recognition (Behrmann and Avidan, 2005). You may think you're suffering from this disorder when you fail to match a name to a face. However, that is a much more common failure of memory. You can recognize the face; you just can't remember the name that goes with it. A prosopagnosic would not know that this particular face was familiar while another one was not.

double dissociation The phenomenon in which one of two functions, such as hearing and sight, can be damaged without harm to the other, and vice versa.

congenital prosopagnosia A form of "face blindness" apparently present from birth, as opposed to "acquired prosopagnosia," which would typically be the result of an injury to the nervous system.

The Pathway Runs in Both Directions: Feedback and Reentrant Processing

We've been discussing object recognition as a progression of steps down the *what* pathway, from V1 into the temporal lobe. It is important to recognize that processing is nothing like a one-way street. All of the connections in Figure 4.3 run both ways. Consider that, as you ascend the *what* pathway, receptive fields get bigger and bigger. The cells care less and less about where an object is in the visual field or how it is oriented. They become increasingly interested in the object's identity as, perhaps, the Eiffel tower. However, you know that the Eiffel tower is right *there* and it has *that* red light in *that* spot. This precision is probably achieved by going back down the pathway, once you have some information about the object, and interrogating earlier visual areas about the details of this instance of the object (Epshtein, Lifshitz, and Ullman, 2008). Indeed, there is evidence that interference with this "reentrant" processing can block conscious awareness of the object (Di Lollo, Enns, and Rensink, 2000). (See **Web Activity 4.7: Object Substitution Masking.**) The act of object recognition should be seen as a conversation among many pieces of the brain rather than as progression from spots and lines to the activation of a grandmother cell in inferotemporal cortex.

Before we leave this topic, it is worth mentioning one very large part of the story that we've omitted up to now. There is good evidence that *attention* to an object is critical in recognition of that object. For example, a specialized piece of the brain might be responsible for our ability to recognize a specific face. If so, that piece of the brain probably requires a single face as its input—two eyes, a nose, and a mouth. If we're looking at a family photo, selective attention processes must come into play, lest we deliver a collection of a brother's eyes, sister's nose, and uncle's mouth to the face processor. Moreover, cells in different parts of the visual system may behave differently before and after attention is directed to an object (Serences and Yantis, 2006). For example, a receptive field might change its size to wrap itself around an attended object (Moran and Desimone, 1985). This makes it part of the network processing that object. The same neuron may be involved in the processing of a different object when attention shifts a moment later. Many of the brain structures critical for the deployment of attention seem to lie in the other main path coming out of the primary visual cortex—the one that goes toward the parietal lobe. This pathway, and the general topic of attention, is taken up in Chapter 7.

Summary

1. A series of extrastriate visual areas continue the work of visual processing. Emerging from V1 (primary visual cortex) are two broad streams of processing: one going into the temporal lobe and the other into the parietal lobe. The temporal pathway seems specifically concerned with *what* a stimulus might be. This chapter follows that pathway. (The parietal *where* pathway will be considered in later chapters.)

2. After early visual processes extract basic features from the visual input, it is the job of middle vision to organize these features into the regions, surfaces, and objects that can, in turn, serve as input to object recognition and scene-understanding processes.

3. Perceptual "committees" serve as an important metaphor in this chapter. The idea is that many semi-independent processes are working on the input at the same time. Different processes may come to different conclusions about the presence of an edge or the relationship between two elements in the input. Under most circumstances, we see the single conclusion that the committees settle on. The math of Bayes' theorem is one way to formalize this process of finding the most likely explanation for input.

4. Multiple processes seek to carve the input into regions and to define the edges of those regions, and many rules are involved in this parsing of the image. For example, image elements are likely to group together if they are similar in color or shape, if they are near each other, or if they are connected. Many of these grouping principles were first articulated by members of the Gestalt school.

5. Other, related processes seek to determine whether a region is part of a foreground figure (like this black *O*) or part of the background (like the white area around the *O*). These rules of grouping and figure-ground assignment are driven by an implicit understanding of the physics of the world. Thus, events that are very unlikely to happen by chance (e.g., two contours parallel to each other) are taken to have meaning. (Those parallel contours are likely to be part of the same figure.)

6. The processes that divide visual input into objects and background have to deal with many complexities. Among these are the fact that parts of objects may be hidden behind other objects (occlusion) and the fact that objects themselves have a structure. Is your nose an object or a part of a larger whole? What about glasses or hair or a wig?

7. Template models of object recognition hold that an object in the world is recognized when its image fits a particular representation in the brain in the way that a key fits a lock. It has always been hard to see how naïve template models could work, because of the astronomical number of templates required: we might need one "lock" for every object in every orientation in every position in the visual field.

8. Structural models propose that objects are recognized by the relationship of parts. Thus, an *H* could be defined as two parallel lines with a perpendicular line joining them between their centers. A cat would be more difficult, but similar in principle. In their pure form, such models are viewpoint-independent. The orientation of the *H* doesn't matter. Object recognition, however, is often viewpoint-dependent, suggesting that the correct model lies between the extremes of naïve template matching and pure structural description.

9. Faces are an interesting special case in which viewpoint is very important. Upright faces are much easier to recognize than inverted faces. Moreover, some regions of the brain seem to be specifically interested in faces. They lie near regions in the temporal lobes that are important for the recognition of other sorts of objects.

10. Recent physiological work showed very specific responses to very specific objects (e.g., the actress Jennifer Aniston) in the human temporal lobe. Other work showed that the first, rough acts of object recognition take place so fast that they must be accomplished by the first, feed-forward sweep of activity from the retina to the higher processing centers of the visual system. However, routine perception of objects requires feedback from higher visual areas to those lying earlier in the pathway.

CHAPTER 5

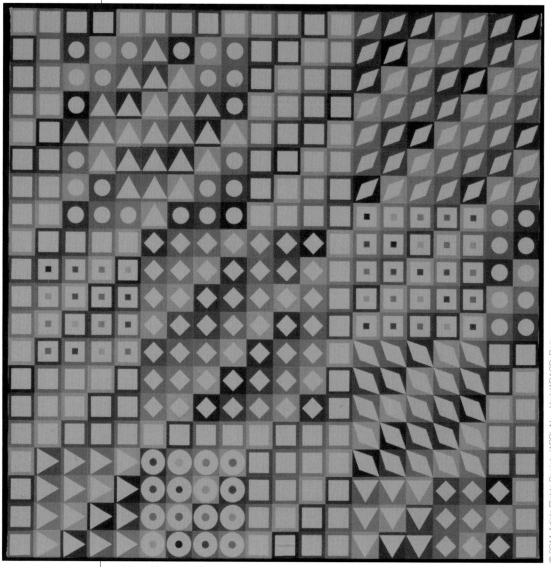

Victor Vasarely, *Folklore*, 1963

The Perception of Color

As you may recall from high school English class, there is a lot of blood in Shakespeare's *Macbeth*. If you didn't read *Macbeth*, take our word for it. The first words out of the lips of King Duncan of Scotland are, "What bloody man is that." Not long after, he is murdered offstage by Macbeth. When Macbeth reenters, he is so covered in blood that he concludes he would stain the ocean red if he tried to wash it off—an exaggeration, of course, but it makes sense because we know and we can see onstage that blood is red. As we will learn in this chapter, however, blood is *not* red. As strange as it may seem, color is not a physical property of things in the world; rather, it is a creation of the mind. Blood looks red because we look at it with our particular visual systems.

Basic Principles of Color Perception

Although color itself is not a physical property of things in the world, it is related to a physical property. As discussed in Chapter 2, humans see a narrow range of the electromagnetic spectrum between the wavelengths of about 400 and 700 nanometers (nm). The apparent color of a bit of the world is correlated with the wavelengths of the light rays reaching the eye from that bit of the world.

Most of the light that we see is reflected light. Typical light sources, like the sun or a lightbulb, emit a broad spectrum of wavelengths that hit surfaces in the world around us. Some wavelengths are absorbed by the surfaces they hit. The more light that is absorbed, the darker the surface will appear. Other wavelengths are reflected, and some of that reflected light reaches the eyes. The color of a surface depends on the mix of wavelengths that reach the eye from the surface (and, as we will see later, from the other surfaces and lights that are present in the scene). In the case of blood, more of the longer-wavelength light (>600 nm) is reflected into the eyes of the observer. Even though (almost) all humans would declare this collection of wavelengths to appear red, it would be a big mistake to think of specific wavelengths of light as being specific colors. As Steven Shevell (2003) puts it, "There is no red in a 700 nm light, just as there is no pain in the hooves of a kicking horse." Like pain, color is the result of the interaction of a physical stimulus with a particular nervous system.

Three Steps to Color Perception

Several problems must be solved in order to go from physical wavelengths to the perception of color. We will organize our discussion around three steps (Stockman and Brainard, 2010):

FIGURE 5.1 The retina contains four types of photo-receptors. These differ in their sensitivity to the wavelengths of light. Three cones are maximally sensitive at short (S), medium (M), and long (L) wavelengths. The single type of rod photoreceptor has its peak sensitivity between those of the S- and M-cones.

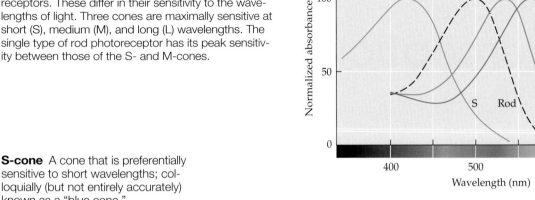

S-cone A cone that is preferentially sensitive to short wavelengths; colloquially (but not entirely accurately) known as a "blue cone."

M-cone A cone that is preferentially sensitive to middle wavelengths; colloquially (but not entirely accurately) known as a "green cone."

L-cone A cone that is preferentially sensitive to long wavelengths; colloquially (but not entirely accurately) known as a "red cone."

photopic Referring to light intensities that are bright enough to stimulate the cone receptors and bright enough to "saturate" the rod receptors (that is, drive them to their maximum responses).

scotopic Referring to light intensities that are bright enough to stimulate the rod receptors but too dim to stimulate the cone receptors.

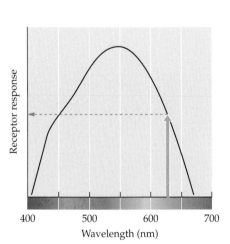

FIGURE 5.2 A single photoreceptor shows different responses to lights of different wavelengths but the same intensity. A 625-nm light of this intensity, indicated by the arrow, produces a response midway between the maximum and minimum responses.

1. *Detection.* Wavelengths must be detected.
2. *Discrimination.* We must be able to tell the difference between one wavelength (or mixture of wavelengths) and another.
3. *Appearance.* We want to assign perceived colors to lights and surfaces in the world. Moreover, we want those perceived colors to go with the object (blood is red) and not to change dramatically as the viewing conditions change (blood should remain red in sun and shadow, for example).

Step 1: Color Detection

Detection was largely covered in Chapter 2. To briefly review, we have three types of cone photoreceptors. These cones differ in the photopigment they carry, and as a result, they differ in their sensitivity to light of different wavelengths. Figure 5.1 shows those sensitivities as a function of wavelength. The three cone types are named for the location of the peak of their sensitivity on the spectrum: The cones that have a peak at about 420 nm are known as short-wavelength cones (**S-cones** for short). The middle-wavelength cones (**M-cones**) peak at about 535 nm, and long-wavelength cones (**L-cones**) peak at about 565 nm. You may be tempted to rename these "blue," "green," and "red" cones, but as we will see, this is a bad idea. L-cones, for example, are not maximally sensitive to red. A wavelength of 565 nm would typically look yellowish. The L-cones are simply more sensitive to long wavelengths than the other cones are. So, it's *S-*, *M-*, and *L-*cones—not *blue*, *green*, and *red* cones.

As mentioned in Chapter 2, S-cones are relatively rare, and they are less sensitive than M- and L-cones. The combination of sensitivities of the three types of cones gives us our overall ability to detect wavelengths from about 400 nm to about 700 nm (Figure 5.1). Remember also that cones work at daylight (**photopic**) light levels. We have one type of rod photoreceptor; it works in dimmer (**scotopic**) light and has a somewhat different sensitivity profile, peaking at about 500 nm.

Step 2: Color Discrimination

The Problem of Univariance

We can detect wavelengths between 400 and 700 nm, but how do we distinguish, for example, lights of 450, 550, and 625 nm? To see how discrimination differs from detection, let's examine the response of a single photoreceptor to a single wavelength of light. Figure 5.2 shows how one kind of human photoreceptor responds to light of a specific wavelength while the intensity of the light is held constant. Because of the properties of the photopigment in the photoreceptor cell, 400-nm light produces only a small response in each cell of this type, 500-nm light produces a greater response, and 550-nm light even more. However, 600-nm light produces less than the maximal response, and 650-nm light produces a minimal response. Light of 625 nm produces a response of moderate strength.

So far, so good. We know that different wavelengths of light give rise to different experiences of color, and the varying responses of this photoreceptor to different wavelengths could provide a basis for color vision. But there is a problem, as illustrated in **Figure 5.3**. Suppose we change the wavelength to 450 nm. Figure 5.3 shows that an equal amount of 450-nm light will produce the same response from this photoreceptor that 625-nm light does. If we were looking at the output of the photoreceptor, we would have no way of distinguishing between the two lights. But when we look with a normal human color vision system, the 625-nm light looks orange and the 450-nm light looks violet.

Actually, the problem is much worse. Remember that Figures 5.2 and 5.3 represent the photoreceptor's response rate when all wavelengths are presented at the same intensity. Under these conditions, the graphs indicate that light at either 450 or 625 nm produces a response lower than the peak response obtained at about 535 nm. If we had a 535-nm light, we could reduce its intensity until it produced exactly the same level of response from our photoreceptor. Indeed, we could take a "white light" or any mix of wavelengths and, by properly adjusting the intensity, get exactly the same response out of the photoreceptor.

Thus, when it comes to seeing color, the output of a single photoreceptor is completely ambiguous. An infinite set of different wavelength-intensity combinations can elicit exactly the same response, so the output of a single photoreceptor cannot by itself tell us anything about the wavelengths stimulating it. This constraint is known as the **problem of univariance** (Rushton, 1972). (See **Web Activity 5.1: The Problem of Univariance**.)

Obviously the human visual system has solved the problem, but not under all circumstances. Univariance explains the lack of color in dimly lit scenes. Remember that there is only one type of rod photoreceptor. All rods contain the same type of photopigment molecule: rhodopsin. Thus, they all have the same sensitivity to wavelength. As a consequence, although it is possible to tell light from dark under scotopic conditions, the problem of univariance makes it impossible to discriminate colors. Our nighttime colorblindness is one hint that color is psychophysical and not physical. The world seen under a bright moon (**Figure 5.4**) has not been physically drained of color. The same mix of wavelengths that produces color perception during the day remains present on that moonlit night, but we fail to see colors under dim illuminants like moonlight because dim light stimulates only the rods, and the output of that single variety of photoreceptor does not permit color vision.

FIGURE 5.3 Lights of 450 and 625 nm each elicit the same response from the photoreceptor whose responses are shown here and in Figure 5.2. This situation illustrates the problem of univariance.

problem of univariance The fact that an infinite set of different wavelength-intensity combinations can elicit exactly the same response from a single type of photoreceptor. One photoreceptor type cannot make color discriminations based on wavelength.

FIGURE 5.4 The moonlit world appears drained of color because we have only one type of rod photoreceptor transducing light under these scotopic conditions. With just one type of photoreceptor, we cannot make discriminations based on wavelength, so we cannot see color.

FIGURE 5.5 The two wavelengths that produce the same response from one type of cone (M) produce different patterns of responses across the three types of cones (S, M, and L).

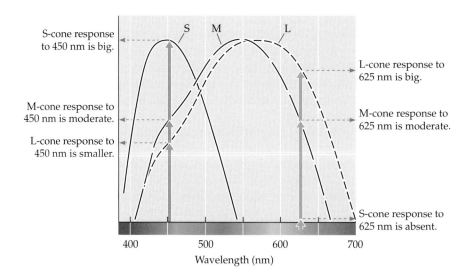

The Trichromatic Solution

We can detect differences between wavelengths or mixtures of wavelengths precisely because we have more than one kind of cone photoreceptor. **Figure 5.5** shows how, with our three cone types, we can tell the difference between lights of different wavelengths. Look at the responses to the two wavelengths that produced the same response from the single cone in Figure 5.3. The two wavelengths of light—450 and 625 nm—still produce the same response from that type of cone, now revealed to be the M-cone. However, these two wavelengths produce different outputs from the L-cones and S-cones. In fact, as you will see if you try **Web Activity 5.2: Trichromacy**, any wavelength from about 420 to 660 nm produces a unique set of three responses from the three cone types. This combined signal, a triplet of numbers for each "pixel" in the visual field, can be used as the basis for color vision. (We can see from about 400 to 700 nm, but the very long and very short wavelengths stimulate only one type of cone.)

In our discussion of the univariance problem, we noted that we can make any wavelength produce the same response as any other from a single cone type by adjusting the intensity of the light. That doesn't happen in the three-cone world of human color vision. A specific light produces a specific set of responses from the three cone types. Suppose that the light produces twice as much M response as S response and twice as much S response as L response. If we increase the intensity of the light, the response sizes will change but the relationships will not. There will still be twice as much M response as S response, and twice as much S response as L response; and those relationships will define our response to the light and, eventually, the color that we see. The idea that ability to discriminate one light from another is defined in our visual system by the relationships among three numbers is the heart of **trichromacy** or, more elaborately, the **trichromatic theory of color vision**.

trichromatic theory of color vision (or trichromacy) The theory that the color of any light is defined in our visual system by the relationships of three numbers—the outputs of three receptor types now known to be the three cones. Also known as the *Young-Helmholtz theory*.

Metamers

The examples presented thus far involve the responses of the visual system to single wavelengths, though you may have noticed that we keep referring to "a wavelength or mixture of wavelengths." Usually, however, we do not see single wavelengths. Almost every light and every surface that we see is emitting or reflecting a wide range of wavelengths. A laser pointer would emit

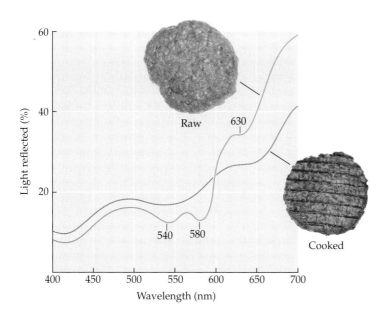

FIGURE 5.6 Objects in the real world reflect light across the spectrum in different amounts. This graph plots the reflectances of raw and cooked hamburger meat. Which one looks redder? Which one reflects more of the long wavelengths?

a very narrow range of wavelengths, but a more normal situation is shown in **Figure 5.6**. It shows the relative amounts of light reflected from raw and cooked hamburger. How can we discriminate the raw from the cooked? When we're studying color vision, this real-world concern gets reduced to a different question: How do our cones respond to combinations of wavelengths of light?

To answer this question, consider what happens if we mix just two wavelengths. For the sake of this example, we will oversimplify by ignoring the S-cones and redrawing the M- and L-cones to make the numbers simpler. Imagine that we shine a wavelength that looks red and a wavelength that looks green onto a white piece of paper so that a mixture of both is reflected back to the eyes (**Figure 5.7a**). Suppose the "green" light alone produces 80 units of activity in the M-cones and 40 in the L-cones (remember, we are ignoring the S-cones for now). In addition, suppose that the "red" light produces 40 units of activity in the M-cones and 80 in the L-cones. If we assume that we can add the cone responses together, then summing the "red" and "green" lights produces a response of 120 units in each cone. The absolute value is not important, because it could change if the intensity of the light changes. What is important is that this red plus this green produce a mixture that excites the L- and M-cones equally.

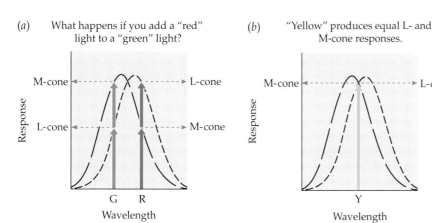

(a) What happens if you add a "red" light to a "green" light?

(b) "Yellow" produces equal L- and M-cone responses.

FIGURE 5.7 The long-wavelength ("red") and shorter-wavelength ("green") lights in part (a), if mixed together, produce the same response from the cones as the medium-wavelength ("yellow") light in part (b). If two sets of lights produce the same responses, they are metamers and must look identical.

metamers Different mixtures of wavelengths that look identical. More generally, any pair of stimuli that are perceived as identical in spite of physical differences.

The key point is that the rest of the nervous system knows *only* what the cones tell it. If the mixture of "red" plus "green" lights produces the same cone output as the single wavelength of "yellow" light (Figure 5.7*b*), then the mixture and the single wavelength *must look identical*. Mixtures of different wavelengths that look identical are called **metamers**. The single wavelength that produces equal M- and L-cone activity will look yellow, and the "red" and "green" lights will mix to produce "yellow."

Two quick warnings:

1. Mixing wavelengths does not change the physical wavelengths. If we mix 500- and 600-nm lights, the physical stimulus contains 500 and 600 nm. It does not contain the average (550 nm). It does not contain the sum (1100 nm) (which we would not be able see anyway). Color mixture is a mental event, not a change in the physics of light.

2. For the mixture of a "red" light and a "green" light to look perfectly yellow, we would have to have just the right red and just the right green. Other mixes might look a bit reddish or a bit greenish.

This example generalizes to *any* mixture of lights. All the light reaching the retina from one patch in the visual field will be converted into three numbers by the three cone types. If those numbers are sufficiently different from the numbers in another patch, you will be able to discriminate those patches. If not, those patches will be metamers. They will look identical, even if the wavelengths are physically different.

The History of Trichromatic Theory

From what you've read so far in this book, you would be forgiven for supposing that clever anatomists and physiologists identified the three cone types and built the trichromatic theory of color vision from there. Indeed, there have been beautiful experiments of this sort: For instance, Schnapf, Kraft, and Baylor (1987) managed to record the activity of single photoreceptors. Nathans, Thomas, and Hogness (1986) found the genes that code for the different photopigments. David Williams and his students even developed a method for photographing and identifying different cone types in the living human eye (see Figure 2.11).

Such research has cemented our understanding of the physical basis of trichromacy, but the basic theory was established by psychophysical experimentation, and theorizing started with Isaac Newton's great discovery that a prism would break up sunlight into the spectrum of hues, and a second prism would put the spectrum back together into white. In 1666, Newton understood that "the rays to speak properly are not coloured. In them is nothing else than a certain Power and Disposition to stir up a Sensation of this or that Colour" (from *Opticks*, published originally in 1704). Newton knew that color is a mental event.

The three-dimensional nature of the experience of color was worked out in the nineteenth century by Thomas Young (1773–1829), and subsequently by Hermann von Helmholtz (1821–1894). In their honor, trichromatic theory is often called the "Young-Helmholtz theory." James Clerk Maxwell (1831–1879) developed a color-matching technique that was central to Helmholtz's work on this topic. (Somehow Maxwell missed having his name attached, or we would have the Young-Maxwell-Helmholtz theory.) Maxwell's color-matching technique is illustrated in **Figure 5.8**. The observer in a modern version of such experiments would try to use different amounts of "primary" colored lights (e.g., the red, green, and blue lights on the right side of the figure) to exactly match another reference color (e.g., the cyan or bluish light on the left side).

Bluish   Blue   Green   Red

FIGURE 5.8 In a modern version of Maxwell's color-matching experiment, a color is presented on the left. On the right, the observer adjusts a mixture of the three lights to match the color on the left.

The central observation from these experiments was that only three mixing lights are needed to match any reference light. Two primaries are not enough. Four are more than are needed. Long before physiology could prove it, these results led Young and Helmholtz to deduce that three different color mechanisms must limit the human experience of color.

A Brief Digression into Lights, Filters, and Finger Paints

The ubiquity of televisions and computer monitors in the twenty-first century may make color mixing and metamers reasonably intuitive. If you've never done so, find a magnifying glass and take a very close look at a yellow patch on your computer screen. You'll find that the patch is actually composed of thousands of intermixed red and green dots. The "red + green = yellow" formula is an example of **additive color mixture** because we are taking one wavelength or set of wavelengths and adding it to another.

For most of us, color mixture begins in kindergarten or earlier, with paints. In that world, red plus green don't make yellow; they make brown. A finger paint, or any other pigment, looks a particular color because it absorbs some wavelengths, subtracting them from white light falling on a surface covered with the pigment. When a toddler smears together red and green, almost all wavelengths are absorbed by one pigment or the other, so we perceive the **subtractive color mixture** as a dark color like brown.

Actually, finger paint mixtures are rather complicated, with some pigment particles sitting next to each other and effectively adding their reflected light together. Other particles occlude each other, and still others are engaged in other complex interactions. Colored filters, like those you might put over stage lights, are a cleaner example of subtractive color mixture. Figure 5.9 shows how a subtractive mixture of blue and yellow filters would produce green. The only

additive color mixture A mixture of lights. If light A and light B are both reflected from a surface to the eye, in the perception of color the effects of those two lights add together.

subtractive color mixture A mixture of pigments. If pigments A and B mix, some of the light shining on the surface will be subtracted by A, and some by B. Only the remainder contributes to the perception of color.

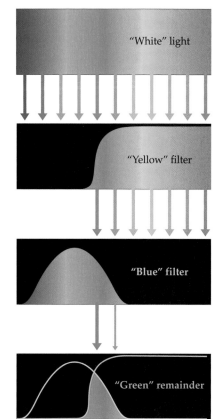

1. Take "white" light that contains a broad mixture of wavelengths.

"White" light

2. Pass it through a filter that absorbs shorter wavelengths. The result will look yellowish.

"Yellow" filter

3. Pass that through a bluish filter that absorbs all but a middle range of wavelengths.

"Blue" filter

4. The wavelengths that make it through both filters will be a mix that looks greenish.

"Green" remainder

FIGURE 5.9 In this example of subtractive color mixture, "white"—broadband—light is passed through two filters. The first one absorbs shorter wavelengths, transmitting a mix of wavelengths that looks yellow. The second absorbs longer wavelengths and the shortest wavelengths, transmitting a mix that looks blue. The wavelengths that can pass through both filters without being subtracted are a middle range of wavelengths that appear green.

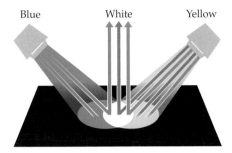

FIGURE 5.10 If we shine "blue" and "yellow" lights on the same patch of paper, the wavelengths will add, producing an additive color mixture. Remember that "yellow" is equivalent to a mix of a long wavelength and a medium wavelength, so blue plus yellow results in a mix of short, medium, and long wavelengths. The mixture looks white (or gray, if it is not the brightest patch in view).

wavelengths passing through both our "yellow" and "blue" filters fall into a middling range that appears green. All the other wavelengths have been subtracted out of the original "white" light. An additive mixture of "blue" and "yellow" lights looks white (**Figure 5.10**) because it includes a mix of wavelengths that stimulate the three cones roughly equally. (See **Web Activity 5.3: Color Mixing**.)

Additive color mixture with paints is possible. Georges Seurat (1859–1891) and other Postimpressionist artists of the late nineteenth century experimented with Pointillism, a style of painting that involved creating many hues by placing small spots of just a few colors in different textures (**Figure 5.11**). Viewing the painting up close, as illustrated in the figure, we see each individual dot of color. Like the red, green, and blue phosphor dots on a computer monitor, the dots in the painting combine additively to produce a wide range of colors. Thus, from a distance the man's face is appropriately skin-colored even if, up close, it is composed of spots of color that would not be found on any normal face.

From Retina to Brain: Repackaging the Information

The cones in the retina are the neural substrate for detection of lights. What is the neural basis for discriminating between lights with different wavelength composition? To tell the difference between different lights, the nervous system will look at differences in the activities of the three cone types. This work begins in the retina. We could send separate L, M, and S signals to the brain, but that approach would be less useful than one might think. For example, the L- and M-cones have very similar sensitivities (see Figure 5.1), so most of the time they are in close agreement: L says, "Lots of light coming from location X." "Yes, lots of light coming from location X," M agrees.

Computing differences between cone responses turns out to be a much more useful way to transmit information to the brain. The nervous system computes two differences: (L − M) and ([L + M] − S). The difference between L and M responses contains considerable information about color. One speculative idea is that (L − M) differences are particularly well suited to appreciating the

FIGURE 5.11 Georges Seurat's painting *La Parade* (1887–88) illustrates the effect of additive color mixture with paints. Seurat used additive color mixture in the manner of a modern computer monitor. Small spots of color blend at a distance to give rise to other colors.

differences between different amounts of blood in skin. Blushing and turning pale are useful signals to observe, and our specific photopigments may be have evolved to help us see those signals (Changizi, Zhang, and Shimojo, 2006). In addition to (L – M), we could create (L – S) and (M – S) signals. However, because L and M are so similar, a single comparison between S and (L + M) can capture almost the same information that would be found in (L – S) and (M – S) signals. Finally, combining L and M signals is a pretty good measure of the intensity of the light (S-cones make a rather small contribution to our perception of brightness). Thus, on theoretical grounds it might be wise to convert the three cone signals into three new signals—(L – M), ([L + M] – S), and (L + M) (Buchsbaum and Gottschalk, 1983; Zaidi, 1997)—and the visual system does something reasonably close to this.

Cone-Opponent Cells in the Retina and LGN

The earliest work on the combination of cone signals was done with fish (Svaetichin and Macnichol, 1959). By the 1960s, Russell De Valois and others had begun to show that these sorts of signals actually exist in the **lateral geniculate nucleus** (**LGN**) of macaque monkeys (De Valois, Abramov, and Jacobs, 1966). As described in Chapter 3, many ganglion cells in the retina and the LGN of the thalamus are maximally stimulated by spots of light. These cells have receptive fields with a characteristic center-surround organization. For example, some cells are excited when a light turns on in the central part of their receptive fields and inhibited when a light turns on in the surround (see Figure 2.14).

A similar antagonistic relationship characterizes color. Some of these retinal and LGN ganglion cells are excited by the L-cone onset in their center and inhibited by M-cone onsets in their surround. These (L – M) cells are one type of **cone-opponent cell**, so named because different sources of chromatic information are pitted against each other. There are also (M – L), ([M + L] – S), and (S – [M + L]) cells—just the sorts of cells we would like to have to support the repackaging of cone signals, described in the previous section. The cells that were excited by light onset could be thought of as (L + M) cells. Thus, we have the three signals that we wanted on theoretical grounds.

Step 3: Color Appearance

The three cones detect a range of wavelengths. Rods make a small, important contribution to color vision, but only in fairly dim light (Stabell and Stabell, 2002). The retina and LGN contain cells that have repackaged that information into cone-opponent difference signals that constrain our ability to see differences between regions. Now is the time to think about what color will be perceived.

Three Numbers, Many Colors

First, it is useful to have a system for talking about all the colors we can see. Because we have exactly three different types of cone photoreceptors, the light reaching any part of the retina will be translated into three responses, one for each local population of cones. After that translation, the rest of the nervous system cannot glean anything more about the physical wavelengths of the light. If the light rays reflecting off two surfaces produce the same set of cone responses, the two surfaces must and will appear to be exactly the same color. They will be metamers, even if their physical characteristics are quite different. Thus, it is possible to produce bloodred color on the page without mimicking the physical properties of blood.

lateral geniculate nucleus (LGN) A structure in the thalamus, part of the midbrain, that receives input from the retinal ganglion cells and has input and output connections to the visual cortex.

cone-opponent cell A cell type—found in the retina, lateral geniculate nucleus, and visual cortex—that, in effect, subtracts one type of cone input from another.

FIGURE 5.12 A color picker may offer several ways to specify a color in a three-dimensional color space. This one, found in Adobe Photoshop, offers two options on the far right. The first (upper) option defines the color space in terms of hue (H), saturation (S), and brightness (B). The second (lower) option uses the parameters red (R), green (G), and blue (B). See the text for details.

color space The three-dimensional space, established because color perception is based on the outputs of three cone types, that describes the set of all colors.

achromatic Referring to any color that lacks a chromatic (hue) component. Black, white, or gray.

Working with just three numbers might not sound very promising, but it has been estimated that, with this system, we can discriminate the surfaces of more than 2 million different colors (Linhares, Pinto, and Nascimento, 2008; Pointer and Attridge, 1998). A lot of these are lightness variations of what we would colloquially consider the same color. Bloodred in dim light, bloodred in brighter light, and so on. But even if we ignore lightness, we can still distinguish about 26,000 colors (Foster, 2011). Unless you're in paint sales, you don't know this many distinctive color *names*, but you could tell two different colors apart even if they were both named "pea green" or "sky blue."

We need some way to talk about all those colors in an orderly way. We can describe each of the colors in the spectrum with a single number—for example, the light's wavelength. Going beyond the spectrum, we have a three-dimensional **color space**. The three dimensions start with the three numbers that come from the outputs of the three cone types. The three-dimensional space is analogous to the height, length, and width of a cube. It doesn't make much sense to talk about height, length, and width in color space, however; we need other terms. There are lots of possibilities. For example, take a look at the color picker in your favorite computer graphics program. The one shown in **Figure 5.12** is borrowed from Photoshop. In the middle is something that looks like the spectrum (but isn't quite, as you'll see shortly). Again, think of that "spectrum" as one of three dimensions. The big square on the left shows two more dimensions, but only for one specific red, picked from that central bar. This color picker offers two different ways to define colors in three dimensions. The controls in the lower right corner of the panel define color space in terms of red, green, and blue dimensions, corresponding to the relative intensities of the glowing red, green, and blue phosphors in a computer monitor. The reddish color marked by the white circle in the large square is the result of setting the "red" signal to 191 and the "green" and "blue" both to 96 on a scale from 0 to 255. If you make R equal to G and B, you will get an **achromatic** color: black if the number is zero, white if it's 255, and an intermediate gray for the numbers in between. If you set R and G to 255, you will see that an additive mixture of red and green appears yellow.

A different set of three numbers defining the color in terms of *hue, saturation,* and *brightness* (*HSB*) is shown above the RGB numbers in Figure 5.12. These dimensions are very different concepts from red, green, and blue, but notice that again the system is three-dimensional. **Hue** is the chromatic aspect of a light. For example, each point on the spectrum defines a different hue. The **saturation** dimension corresponds to the amount of hue present in a light. A pure white light has zero saturation; bloodred is a saturated red. **Brightness** is the perceptual consequence of the physical intensity of a light. The physically intense light of the sun looks brighter than the less intense moon. Our reddish color in Figure 5.12 is 0 (out of 100) in hue, 50% in saturation, and 75% in brightness.

Now we can see that, rather than being the spectrum, the vertical strip in Figure 5.12 represents hue, with saturation running horizontally and brightness running vertically in the big square. If you compare the hue strip in this figure to the light spectrum at the bottom of Figure 5.5, you will notice that some colors—for example, the purplish magentas between red and blue near the top of the hue strip—are not present in the spectrum. These colors are called, logically enough, "nonspectral hues," and they can result only from mixtures of wavelengths, not from single wavelengths. For example, suppose we combined a pure 420-nm light with a pure 680-nm light. As Figure 5.5 shows, this combination would strongly stimulate the L- and S-cones and produce minimal stimulation in the M-cones—a pattern that cannot be produced by any single light wavelength.

Another color space, illustrated in **Figure 5.13**, has dimensions that are somewhat opaquely labeled x, y, and Y. Again, the color space is three-dimensional, as it must be. This picture shows only the x and y dimensions (roughly, but not exactly, red and green). Capital Y is the luminance dimension of this space, so the figure shows all of the colors that we can see at one brightness level. The interesting feature is the smaller triangle. It contains all the colors that can be produced on a standard computer monitor or TV. Notice that many colors

hue The chromatic (colorful) aspect of color (red, blue, green, yellow, and so on).

saturation The chromatic strength of a hue. White has zero saturation, pink is more saturated, and red is fully saturated.

brightness The perceptual consequence of the physical intensity of a light.

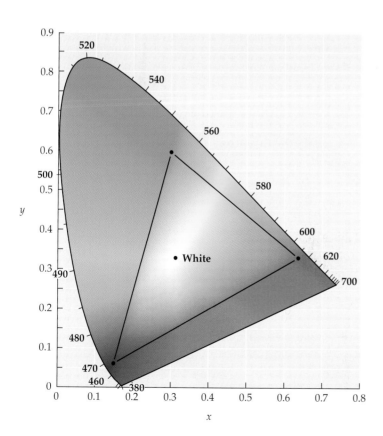

FIGURE 5.13 The curvaceous triangle shown here represents all the colors that can be seen (at one brightness level) by the human visual system. The smaller triangle contains all the colors that can be reproduced by a typical color monitor. Given this limitation, it is amazing that natural scenes on a monitor look as good as they do.

cannot be accurately produced on a monitor. It is a testimony to the flexible powers of the human visual system that a natural scene still looks quite natural when presented in this limited "gamut" of colors.

Opponent Colors

opponent color theory The theory that perception of color is based on the output of three mechanisms, each of them resulting from an opponency between two colors: red-green, blue-yellow, and black-white.

In the nineteenth century, Ewald Hering (1834–1918) described a curious feature of color vision: some combinations of colors are illegal. We can have a bluish green, a reddish yellow (which we would call "orange"), or a bluish red (which we would call "purple"), but reddish green and bluish yellow have never been seen, because they don't exist. Red and green are, in some fashion, opposed to each other, as are blue and yellow (Hering, 1878). Young and Helmholtz were describing a trichromatic theory with three basic colors (red, green, and blue); Hering's **opponent color theory** had four basic colors in two opponent pairs: red versus green, and blue versus yellow. A black-versus-white component formed a third opponent pair, but this "opponency" is a bit different: although you can't have a reddish green, gray can be described as a blackish white.

Figure 5.14 illustrates this idea. The center ring shows the hue dimension of HSB space, wrapped into the color circle that you may remember from grade school. The outer ring offers a cartoon of four color mechanisms in two pairs. The inner patch on the left that looks yellow looks yellow, in opponent color theory, because it stimulates the yellow pole of the yellow-blue opponency and does not stimulate either red or green. Move a bit counterclockwise, and the orange patches add increasing red to the decreasing yellow.

Leo Hurvich and Dorothea Jameson (1957) revived Hering's ideas and developed one way to demonstrate this opponency. The method, called "hue cancellation," is shown in Figure 5.15. In this example, we start with a light that appears to be a yellowish green. We can cancel the yellowness by adding its opponent color, blue (Figure 5.15a). We measure the amount of blue light needed to just remove all traces of yellow. We can do the same for the red-green opponency, adding just the right amount of red to make the patch of color lose all greenness (Figure 5.15b). "But wait," the careful reader protests,

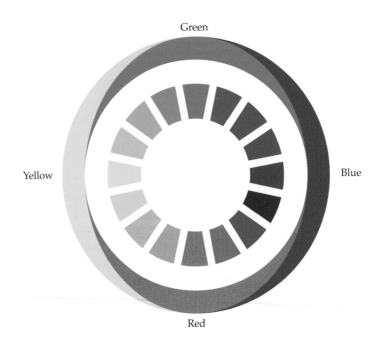

FIGURE 5.14 Hering's idea of opponent colors. Hering noted that all the colors on the "color circle" (the center ring) could be represented by two pairs of opposing colors: blue versus yellow, and red versus green (cartooned in the outer ring). Thus, a color could be a reddish yellow or a bluish green, but not a reddish green or a bluish yellow. (After Stockman and Brainard, 2010.)

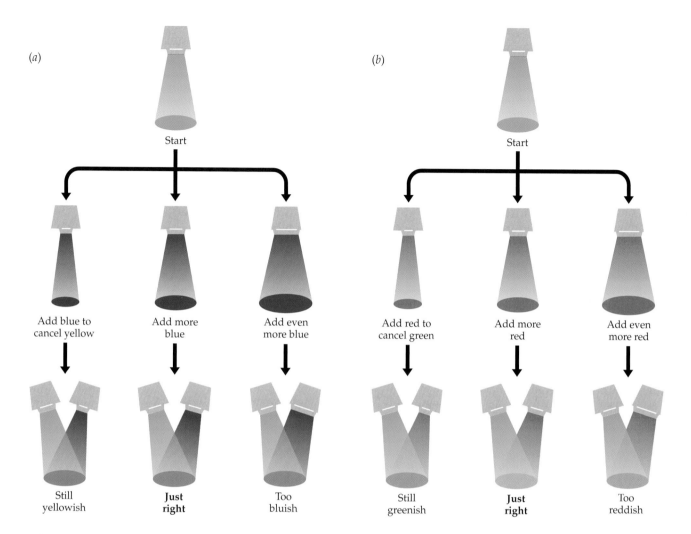

(a) Start

Add blue to cancel yellow

Add more blue

Add even more blue

Still yellowish

Just right

Too bluish

(b) Start

Add red to cancel green

Add more red

Add even more red

Still greenish

Just right

Too reddish

FIGURE 5.15 Hue cancellation experiments start with a color (here, yellowish green) and attempt to determine how much of the opponent color of one of the starting color's components must be added to eliminate any hint of that component from the starting color. In this example, the investigator might ask, *(a)* "How much blue must I add to eliminate any hint of yellow?" or *(b)* "How much red must I add to eliminate any hint of green?" For a reddish starting color, green would be added; for a bluish starting color, yellow would be added.

"earlier you said that red plus green makes yellow. Now it is making a gray or white. What's up?" Here we must plead that color language is a bit crude. Light from the "red" phosphor on a monitor, when added to light from the "green" phosphor, will look yellow, but that's because the "red" phosphor is actually orangish red. To make a pure red, we would need to add a bit of blue to the mix. That red mixed with the right "green" light will appear white.

Hue cancellation can be used for lights across the spectrum, as demonstrated in **Figure 5.16** (these are Dorothea Jameson's data; everyone has slightly different results). If we start at about 400 nm, the lights look reddish blue (or violet) and we need to add some green and some yellow to cancel them. But look what happens at about 470 nm. Here is a light that has no red or green to cancel; it looks perfectly blue. This location on the spectrum is known as "unique blue." Continuing to scan along the spectrum in the figure reveals the locations of the other **unique hues**—hues that can be described with only

unique hue Any of four colors that can be described with only a single color term: red, yellow, green, blue. Other colors (e.g., purple or orange) can be described as compounds (reddish blue, reddish yellow).

FIGURE 5.16 These results from a hue cancellation experiment identify the locations where the hue cancellations cross the neutral midpoint as the locations of the unique blue, green, and yellow hues. "Unique red" is not defined by just one spectral locus. (After Hurvich and Jameson, 1957.)

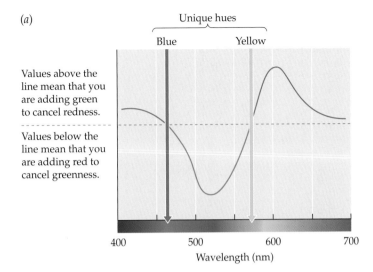

(*a*)

Unique hues

Blue   Yellow

Values above the line mean that you are adding green to cancel redness.

Values below the line mean that you are adding red to cancel greenness.

Wavelength (nm)

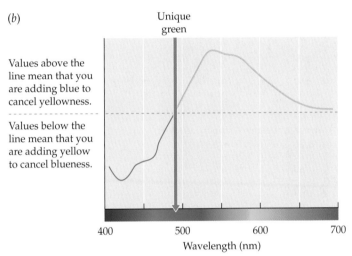

(*b*)

Unique green

Values above the line mean that you are adding blue to cancel yellowness.

Values below the line mean that you are adding yellow to cancel blueness.

Wavelength (nm)

a single color term. Only four hues can be described in this way. As you might guess, they are red, green, yellow, and blue. Only three of them have unique loci on the spectrum. All the very long wavelengths look red (with, maybe, a touch of residual yellow). The two crossings of the red-green function provide the loci of unique blue and unique yellow (Figure 5.16*a*). The point where the blue-yellow function crosses from positive to negative is the locus of "unique green," the green that has no blue or yellow in it (and, of course, no red) (Figure 5.16*b*). There are excellent exemplars of other colors, such as orange or purple, but they are not unique in the same way. Orange, no matter how pure, can still be described as a reddish yellow.

This opponent-process, color appearance story sounds rather similar to the (L − M) and ([L + M] − S) story. However, (L − M) is not the same as red versus green, and ([L + M] − S) is not the same as yellow versus blue. If this were the case, an ([L + M] − S) cell should be a yellow-blue cell, maximally excited by unique yellow and maximally inhibited by unique blue; but a more detailed look reveals that adding and subtracting cone sensitivities to produce those cone-opponent cells results in cells that respond maximally along an axis extending from a purplish hue to a yellowish greenish hue.

The (L − M) cells aren't in quite the right place either. The L-cone end of the axis is near perceptual red, but the M-cone end is a bluish green (Eskew, 2008). Krauskopf, Williams, and Heeley (1982) call these endpoints the "cardinal

(*a*) **Step 1:** Detection (cones)

FIGURE 5.17 Three steps to color perception. (*a*) Detection: Light is differentially absorbed by three photopigments in the cones. (*b*) Discrimination: Differences are taken between cone types, creating cone-opponent mechanisms, important for wavelength discriminations. (*c*) Appearance: Further recombination of the signals creates color-opponent processes that support the color-opponent nature of color appearance. (After Stockman and Brainard, 2010.)

(*b*) **Step 2:** Discrimination

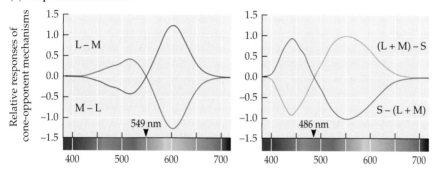

(*c*) **Step 3:** Appearance (opponent colors)

directions" in color space, but they are not perceptual red, green, yellow, and blue. We need another transformation of the color signals in order to make cone-opponent signals into color-opponent signals. The series of transformations that we've been talking about is depicted in **Figure 5.17**. Three cones give rise to cells that take differences between cone types. Further transformations are required to create processes that give rise to properties of color appearance like the unique hues (Stockman and Brainard, 2010).

Color in the Visual Cortex

Cells in the LGN seem to be cone-opponent cells, so the transformations that produce the color-opponent processes that support color appearance are likely to be found in the visual cortex. One useful transformation of the information is shown in **Figure 5.18**. The LGN has opponent cells, and Figure 5.18*a* shows a cartoon of one such cell's receptive field. We will call it R+/G–, indicating that it is excited by redder hues in its center and inhibited by greener hues in its surround. (For present purposes, we will not worry about whether this

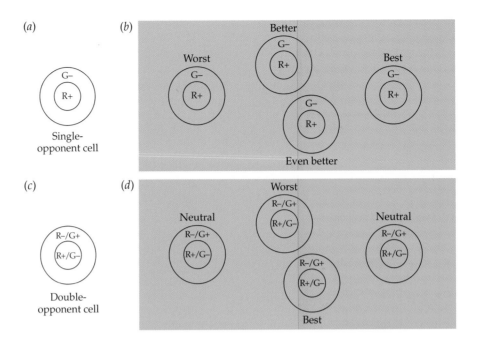

FIGURE 5.18 Color-opponent receptive fields. (*a*) Single-opponent cells get excitatory input from one cone type and inhibitory input from another. (*b*) These cells respond vigorously to regions of the correct color. Here R+/G– prefers the reddish region. (*c*) The center of each double-opponent cell gets excitatory input from one cone type and inhibitory input from another. The pattern is reversed in the surround. (*d*) These cells respond vigorously at an edge between two colors.

cell is *cone*-opponent or *color*-opponent. It is just easier to talk about red and green in this case.)

Figure 5.18*c* shows a **double-opponent cell**. Double-opponent cells are first found in the visual cortex (E. N. Johnson, Hawken, and Shapley, 2001). In the example shown here, the cell is excited by redder hues in its center and by greener hues in the surround, and it is inhibited by redder hues in the surround and by greener hues in the center. To see why this is interesting, look at Figures 5.18*b* and *d*, where we have superimposed these receptive fields across a red/green border. In this context, the cone-opponent cells, described earlier, could be called **single-opponent cells**. A single-opponent cell conveys information about the color of a broad area. In this case, the cell is most excited by red and not green. A double-opponent cell, in contrast, conveys information about chromatic edges. Where does the color change? This information can be useful when you're trying to use color to carve the world into surfaces and objects (see Chapter 4). (See **Web Essay 5.1: Why Use Opponent Processes?**)

Though we know that color information is transformed in the visual cortex, it is not clear how the physiology gives rise to perception (Gegenfurtner, 2003). Perhaps the biggest controversy concerns the possibility of an area (or areas) in the brains of monkeys and humans specialized for color vision. In the 1980s, evidence favored a separate pathway for color. There were "blobs" in V1 where cells did not seem interested in orientation but seemed very interested in color. The blobs sent output to "thin stripe" regions in V2 (Livingstone and Hubel, 1988) and from there to V4, an area that Semir Zeki argued was specialized for color, with cells that responded not to wavelength but to perceived color (Zeki, 1983a, 1983b). However, although these anatomical pathways are there (Federer et al., 2009), it has become less clear that we can separate color processing from

double-opponent cell A cell type, found in the visual cortex, in which one region is excited by one cone type, combination of cones, or color and inhibited by the opponent cones or color (e.g., R+/G–). Another adjacent region would be inhibited by the first input and excited by the second (thus, in this example, R–/G+).

single-opponent cell Another way to refer to cone-opponent cells, in order to differentiate them from double-opponent cells.

other perceptual processes in cortical anatomy (Shapley and Hawken, 2011). Indeed, you may remember from Chapter 4 that V4 is a popular candidate for a "shape" area. This doesn't mean that it is uninterested in color, but merely that it is probably not *only* interested in color.

> **FURTHER DISCUSSION** of the elegantly named "blobs" can be found in Chapter 3 on page 74.

Modern imaging studies show some areas of the human visual cortex that seem particularly interested in color (Grill-Spector and Malach, 2004). Perhaps the best evidence for specialized brain areas for color in humans comes from certain cases of **achromatopsia**, a loss of color vision after brain damage (Zeki, 1990). In achromatopsia, patients may be able to find the boundaries between regions of different colors, but they cannot report what those colors might be. In these patients, vision is largely intact, while the experience of color seems specifically impaired.

Adaptation and Afterimages

You may recall from Chapter 2 that adaptation is one way of dealing with the vast range of light levels in the environment. When you are inside, you may see a black spot on a white piece of paper. When you take that piece of paper outside, you still see a black spot on white paper, even though the light is so much brighter that the black spot outside reflects more light to the eye than does the white paper inside.

> **FURTHER DISCUSSION** of the time course of dark adaptation can be found in Chapter 2 on page 48.

Adaptation can be color-specific, as we see in the phenomenon of negative **afterimages**. If you look at one color for a few seconds, a subsequently viewed achromatic region will appear to take on a color opposite to the original color. We can call the first colored stimulus the **adapting stimulus**. The illusory color that is seen afterward is the **negative afterimage**. (See **Web Activity 5.4: Afterimages**.)

The principle is illustrated in **Figure 5.19**. Figure 5.19*a* consists of a circle of gray spots. Now, stare at the black dot at the center of Figure 5.19*b* and consider what happens as you expose one bit of your retina and visual system to the red dot at the top of Figure 5.19*b*. The L-cones will be more stimulated than the M- or S-cones. L+/M– opponent processes will be stimulated. You will see "red." When you move your eyes back to fixate on the black dot at the center of Figure 5.19*a*, the red is withdrawn from that area of the visual field. The L-cones will be more adapted than M- or S-cones, as will the later processes in the retina and brain that were more stimulated by the red spot. Adapted processes behave as though a bit tired. They respond less vigorously than unadapted processes. The result is a bit like what would happen if you held a pendulum up and released it. The red-green opponent color mechanism swings back toward the **neutral point**, overshoots this point, and slides over to the green side. As a consequence, the gray spot appears greenish until the opponent mechanism settles back to the neutral point.

If you look at the green dot at the bottom of Figure 5.19*b* and then look back at the gray image (Figure 5.19*a*), you will see the result of pushing the red-green mechanism in the other direction. Other colors will produce other results, which you should now be able to predict. In Figures 5.19*c–e*, you can

achromatopsia An inability to perceive colors that is caused by damage to the central nervous system.

afterimage A visual image seen after the stimulus has been removed.

adapting stimulus A stimulus whose removal produces a change in visual perception or sensitivity.

negative afterimage An afterimage whose polarity is the opposite of the original stimulus. Light stimuli produce dark negative afterimages. Colors are complementary; for example, red produces green, and yellow produces blue.

neutral point The point at which an opponent color mechanism is generating no signal. If red-green and blue-yellow mechanisms are at their neutral points, a stimulus will appear achromatic. (The black-white process has no neutral point.)

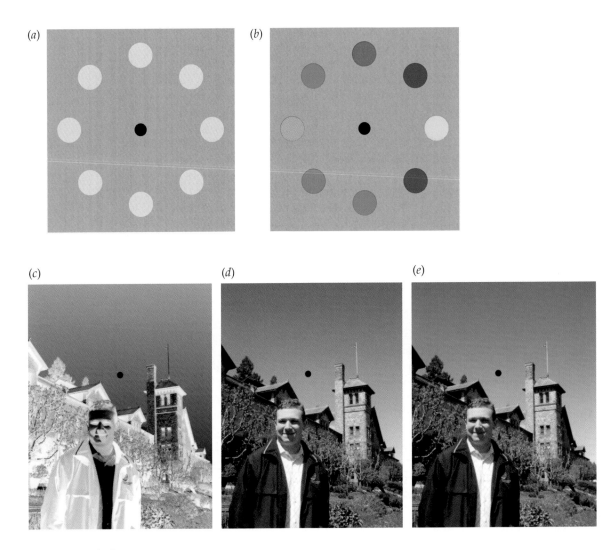

FIGURE 5.19 To understand what negative afterimages are, study the image in part (a) and convince yourself that all the circles are gray. Now stare at the black dot in part (b). After 10 seconds or so, shift your fixation to the black dot in (a). The circles should now look colored. This is a negative afterimage. Why does it happen? (If it didn't happen, try fixating more rigorously. Really look at the black dot.) Now try with a real scene. Fixate the black dot in (c), and then flick your eyes to the same spot in (d). You should see a washed-out version of the colors in (e).

try this with a real scene. If you stare at the black dot in Figure 5.19c and then quickly move your eyes to the same dot in Figure 5.19d, you will see a pale, tinted version of the real photograph (Figure 5.19e, though this effect will be more dramatic if you look at the version in **Web Activity 5.4: Afterimages**). Notice that we are not attributing negative afterimages to *just* the cones or *just* one set of cone- or color-opponent processes. Adaptation occurs at multiple sites in the nervous system.

Does Everyone See Colors the Same Way?

Thus far, with a little caution, we have been talking about color as if we all see colors the same way, but do we? This is one of those questions that everyone asks at one point or another, often as a child. The answer will be "yes," "no," "maybe," or "we just don't know," depending on which version of the question is being asked.

Does Everyone See Colors the Same Way?—Yes

If you declare two lights to be metamerically matched, those around you will generally agree, but there will be some variation between individuals. For example, among different people unique green can vary from at least 495 to 530 nm (Nerger, Volbrecht, and Ayde, 1995). Some of these differences will be due to factors like age, which turns the lens of the eye yellow (J. S. Werner, Peterzell, and Scheetz, 1990). To a first approximation, however, your performance on standard measures of color vision will be the same as others'.

Does Everyone See Colors the Same Way?—No

There is a significant exception to the "yes" answer. Some 8% of the male population and 0.5% of the female population have a form of color vision deficiency commonly known as "color blindness," in which there is a malfunction in one or more of the genes coding the three cone photopigments. It's a "guy thing," because the genes that code for the M- and L-cone photopigments are on the X chromosome (Nathans, 1986). Males have only one copy of the X chromosome, so if one is defective, the male in question will have a problem. Females have two copies and can have normal color vision even if one copy is abnormal (actually, such women can end up with four different cone pigments) (Nagy et al., 1981). The S-cone photopigment is coded elsewhere, so everyone has two copies, and therefore S-cone color deficiencies are rare (Alpern, Kitahara, and Krantz, 1983). (See **Web Essay 5.2: Experiencing Color Blindness**.)

There are a number of different types of color blindness. One determining factor is the type of cone affected. A second factor is the type of defect; either the photopigment for that cone type is "anomalous" (different from the norm) or the cone type is missing altogether. Although we call people who are missing one cone type "color-blind," it is a mistake to think that this means they cannot see colors at all. If you have two cone types rather than three, the normally three-dimensional color space becomes a two-dimensional space. If you have all three cones, you need three primary colors to make a metameric match with an arbitrary patch of color. The world will still be seen in color, but you will have a "flatter" color experience, different from that of people with normal color vision.

Because M- and L-cone defects are the most common, most color-blind individuals have difficulty discriminating lights in the middle- to long-wavelength range. For example, consider the wavelengths 560 and 610 nm. Neither of these lights activates S-cones very much, and the L-cones fire at about the same rate for both. But most of us can distinguish the lights on the basis of the M-cone outputs they elicit, which will be higher for the 560-nm light than for the 610-nm light (you can confirm these assertions by consulting Figure 5.5). English-speaking trichromats would label the colors of these two lights as "green" and "reddish orange," respectively.

Now consider a **deuteranope**, someone who has no M-cones. His photoreceptor output to these two lights will be identical. Following our maxim that the rest of the visual system knows only what the photoreceptors tell it, 560- and 610-nm lights must and will be classified as the same color by our deuteranopic individual.

A **protanope**—someone who has no L-cones—will have a different set of color matches based on the outputs of his two cone types (M and S). And a **tritanope**—with no S-cones—will be different again. Genetic factors can also make people **color-anomalous**. Color-anomalous individuals typically have three cone photopigments, but two of them are so similar that these individuals experience the world in much the same way as individuals with only two cone types.

We actually have some notion of exactly what the world looks like to color-deficient individuals, because there are a few, very rare cases of individuals who are color-blind in only one eye. They can compare what they see with the

deuteranope An individual who suffers from color blindness that is due to the absence of M-cones.

protanope An individual who suffers from color blindness that is due to the absence of L-cones.

tritanope An individual who suffers from color blindness that is due to the absence of S-cones.

color-anomalous A better term for what is usually called "color-blind." Most "color-blind" individuals can still make discriminations based on wavelength. Those discriminations are different from the norm—that is, *anomalous*.

cone monochromat An individual with only one cone type. Cone monochromats are truly color-blind.

rod monochromat An individual with no cones of any type. In addition to being truly color-blind, rod monochromats are badly visually impaired in bright light.

agnosia A failure to recognize objects in spite of the ability to see them. Agnosia is typically due to brain damage.

anomia An inability to name objects in spite of the ability to see and recognize them (as shown by usage). Anomia is typically due to brain damage.

cultural relativism In sensation and perception, the idea that basic perceptual experiences (e.g., color perception) may be determined in part by the cultural environment.

color-blind eye to what they see with the normal eye, enabling us to reconstruct the appearance of the color-blind world (MacLeod and Lennie, 1976).

True color blindness comes in a few, rare forms. It is possible to be a **cone monochromat**, with only one type of cone in the retina. Cone monochromats (who also have rods) live in a one-dimensional color space, seeing the world only in shades of gray. Even more visually crippled is the **rod monochromat**, who is missing cones altogether. Because the rods work well only in dim light and are generally absent in the fovea, these individuals have very poor acuity and serious difficulties seeing under normal daylight conditions, in addition to lacking the ability to discriminate colors.

We already mentioned one other very interesting class of color blindness, coming not from photoreceptor problems but from damage to the visual cortex. Lesions of specific parts of the visual cortex beyond primary visual cortex can cause achromatopsia. An achromatopsic individual sees the world as drained of color, even while showing evidence that wavelength information is processed at earlier stages in the visual pathway. Brain lesions can also produce various forms of color agnosia or anomia (Oxbury, Oxbury, and Humphrey, 1969). In an **agnosia**, the patient can *see* something but fails to know what it is. **Anomia** is an inability to name—in this case, an inability to name colors. A patient with anomia might be able to pick the banana that "looks right" but unable to report that the banana is or should be yellow.

Does Everyone See Colors the Same Way?—Maybe

With the exception of color-deficient individuals, all the readers of this book would agree about the "redness" of a good example of red or the "greenness" of a good green. There might be some disagreement about marginal colors (is that a reddish orange or an orangish red?), but there would be no substantive disagreement about the basics. Does this consensus arise from learned custom or from underlying physiological mechanisms? One way to examine this question is to analyze the color terms used in different languages to see whether most languages honor the same color categories. We are still not quite sure whether this is the case.

We do know that the number of "basic" color terms differs dramatically across cultures. What makes a color term basic? Berlin and Kay (1969) asserted that it must be common (like *red* and not like *beige*), not an object or substance name (excluding *bronze* and *lavender*), and not a compound word (no *blue-green*). This classification is a little subjective (is *beige* that uncommon?), but Berlin and Kay argued that, in English, these rules yield a list of 11 terms: *red*, *green*, *blue*, *yellow*, *black*, *white*, *gray*, *orange*, *purple*, *brown*, and *pink*. Other languages have different numbers of basic terms—some as few as 2 or 3.

At one time it was thought that the differing numbers of basic color terms in different languages meant that color categorization was arbitrary. This notion was called **cultural relativism**, meaning that each group was free to create its own linguistic map of color space. Berlin and Kay's important discovery was that the various maps used in different cultures are actually rather similar (Lindsey and Brown, 2006). After surveying many languages, they found that the 11 basic color terms in English are about as many as any group possesses. Of course, the words themselves differ, but *red* is *rouge* (French) is *adom* (Hebrew). Moreover, languages do not select randomly among the possible color names. If a language has only two basic color terms, speakers of the language divide colors into *light* and *dark*. If a language has three color terms (one chromatic term beyond *light* and *dark*), what do you think the third usually is? If you guessed *red*, you are correct. Next enters *yellow*, then *green* and *blue*.

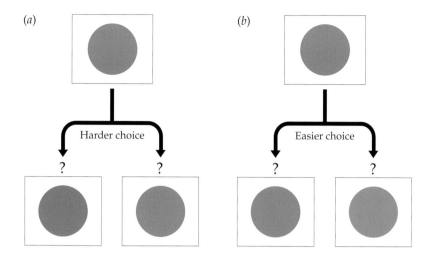

FIGURE 5.20 It is easier to remember which of two colors you have seen if the choices are categorically different. For example, suppose you had to remember the "blue" patch shown at the top of each part of the figure. Picking between two "blues," as in part (a), would be rather hard. The task would be easier if one of the choices were "blue" and the other "green," as in part (b), even if the distance in color space were the same in the two cases.

Of course, these findings raise another interesting question: if a language has only two basic color terms, do its speakers *see* colors differently than we do with our 11 basic terms? Eleanor Rosch (Heider, 1972) studied this question among the Dani of New Guinea, a tribe whose language has only two basic color terms: *mola* for light-warm colors and *mili* for dark-cool colors. Now, it is hard enough to ask your neighbor to define the experience of blue and then to ask if that is the same as your experience of blue. It is much more difficult to ask these questions across a great cultural divide. But there are tricks, as the experiment illustrated in Figure 5.20 demonstrates.

Suppose you are shown a bluish color chip and asked to remember it. Then you are shown two test chips and asked to pick the color you saw before. Obviously, the less similar the two test colors are, the easier this task is. But more important, you will do better if the wrong choice is on the other side of a color categorical boundary. Color boundaries are sharper than you might think. If you show people a collection of colors and ask, "Which are blue and which are green?" people do the task without much difficulty. If you have to remember a color, as in the task shown in Figure 5.20, you are likely to give it a label like "green" or "blue." If the next color has the same label, you are more likely to be confused than if it has a different label.

Rosch found that the Dani's performance on such tasks reflected the same color boundaries, even when their language did not recognize the distinction between the two colors (a Dani might call all the colors in Figure 5.20 *mili* but would still do better with the task in Figure 5.20b). This finding leads to the conclusion that color perception is not especially influenced by culture and language; blue and green are *seen* as categorically different, even if one's language does not employ color terms to express this difference.

In the late 1990s, Debi Roberson went up the Sepik River in New Guinea to study the Berinmo, whose language, like the Dani's, has a limited set of basic color terms. Unlike previously studied groups, the Berinmo have terms that form novel boundaries in color space. For example, their *nol/wor* distinction lies in the middle of colors we categorize as green, and may roughly distinguish live from dead or dying foliage. Moreover, when the Berinmo did the color memory task, they performed better across their *nol/wor* boundary than across the blue/green boundary. English speakers showed the opposite result (Davidoff, Davies, and Roberson, 1999). More recently, similar results have been found in a comparison of English and Russian subjects across the Russian categorical distinction between light blues (*goluboy*) and dark blues (*siniy*) (Winawer et al., 2007). And even more recently, evidence has emerged that learning new color subcategories produces increases in gray matter in parts of the brain implicated in color vision (V. Kwok et al., 2011). So, can language or culture influence color perception? For many years, we thought the answer was "no." Now, thanks to Roberson's work, we are not so sure.

From the Color of Lights to a World of Color

color contrast A color perception effect in which the color of one region induces the opponent color in a neighboring region.

color assimilation A color perception effect in which two colors bleed into each other, each taking on some of the chromatic quality of the other.

All the work of this chapter, up to this point, has concerned the detection, discrimination, and appearance of isolated lights. However, we live in a world where regions of one color abut regions of another, and this proximity changes the appearance of colors, as **Figure 5.21** shows. In **color contrast** effects, the color of one region induces the opponent color in a neighboring region. Thus, in Figure 5.21*a* the yellow surround weakens the yellow of a central square and strengthens the blue. In **color assimilation** effects, two colors bleed into each other, each taking on some of the chromatic quality of the other. So, in Figure 5.21*b* the blue in column 1 looks reddish or purplish in the top image and greenish on the bottom.

Not only can other colors in the scene alter the color of a target region, but scenes can contain colors that cannot exist in isolation. In addition to isolated

(*a*) Color contrast

(*b*) Color assimilation

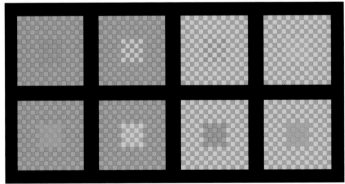

FIGURE 5.21 Color contrast and color assimilation. (*a*) In color contrast, the central square takes on chromatic attributes opposite from the surround, so the green central square looks greener on the red background than on the green background. (*b*) In color assimilation, colors blend together locally. So, in column 2 the yellow squares look a bit reddish in the upper field and a bit greenish in the lower square. (After Stockman and Brainard, 2010.)

or **unrelated colors**, there are **related colors**, colors that can be seen only in the context of other colors (Shevell, 2003). For example, nothing in all of the preceding discussion of color will explain "brown" or "gray," because there is no such thing as an unrelated light that appears brown or gray.

Brown, gray, and a host of other colors exist only as related colors. As we look around, the colors of objects are not determined exclusively by their own reflective properties. The color we see on one object depends in complex ways on the colors of other objects in the vicinity. For example, gray is an achromatic color that is seen when other nearby regions are lighter. Browns are really dark yellows or oranges (depending on the brown). They look brown only if accompanied by other, lighter colors. Seen in isolation, an unrelated "gray" patch will look white and a "brown" patch will look yellow or orange. We can distinguish something on the order of a few thousand unrelated colors. Allowing for context effects is what boosts the number of distinguishable colors to the millions (Shevell, 2003).

Color Constancy

In discussing adaption earlier, we used the example of a black dot and a white background that look black and white, respectively, indoors and out. This is an achromatic example of the more general phenomenon of **color constancy**, the tendency for the colors of objects to appear relatively unchanged in spite of substantial changes in the lighting conditions. The color figures in this book seem to have more or less the same colors wherever you read the book (though there is an entire research area hidden in what we might mean by "more or less"; Foster, 2011).

Figure 5.22 illustrates why color constancy is yet another difficult problem for the visual system to solve. The heart of the problem is that the **illuminant**, the light that illuminates a surface, is not constant. Lighting changes as we go from inside to outside or as the sun moves from the horizon to high in the sky. Figure 5.22*a* shows the **spectral reflectance function** for a surface—the percentage of each wavelength that is reflected from a particular surface. With its preponderance of long and short wavelengths, this surface probably looks purplish. Let's call it "lilac." Figure 5.22*b* shows the **spectral power distribution**—the relative amount of light at different visible wavelengths—of two different types of "daylight": sunlight and skylight. Sunlight is a yellowish light, richer in middle and long wavelengths; skylight is more bluish. Figure 5.22*c* shows that the light reflected to our eyes is the product of the surface and the illumination. For example, a surface might reflect 90% of 650-nm light, but no 650-nm light would reach the eye unless there was some in the original illumination. Figure 5.22*d* shows that those two different products of surface and illumination are converted into two different sets of three numbers by the L-, M- and S-cones (see **Web Essay 5.3: Color Constancy in the Lab**).

Here's the problem. Even though the three numbers from the three cones are different in the two conditions, that lilac surface will look lilac-colored under both illuminants. White paper will look white. A banana will look yellow. This color constancy is good because we want to know the color of the object. We don't really care about the spectral composition of the lights.

The Problem with the Illuminant

Let's think about color constancy as a math problem. In simple terms, we have an illuminant (call it *I*) and a surface (*S*). As shown in Figure 5.22*c*, what we can sense is a result—the product of *I* × *S*—but what we want to know is *S*. It is as if we were given a number (say, 48), told that it is the product of two

unrelated color A color that can be experienced in isolation.

related color A color, such as brown or gray, that is seen only in relation to other colors. For example, a "gray" patch in complete darkness appears white.

color constancy The tendency of a surface to appear the same color under a fairly wide range of illuminants.

illuminant The light that illuminates a surface.

spectral reflectance function The percentage of a particular wavelength that is reflected from a surface.

spectral power distribution The physical energy in a light as a function of wavelength.

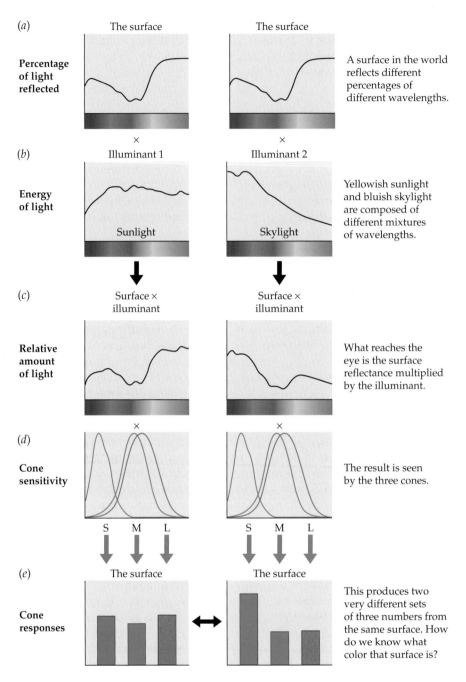

(a)
Percentage of light reflected

The surface   The surface

A surface in the world reflects different percentages of different wavelengths.

×

(b)
Energy of light

Illuminant 1   Illuminant 2

Sunlight   Skylight

Yellowish sunlight and bluish skylight are composed of different mixtures of wavelengths.

(c)
Relative amount of light

Surface × illuminant   Surface × illuminant

What reaches the eye is the surface reflectance multiplied by the illuminant.

×

(d)
Cone sensitivity

S   M   L   S   M   L

The result is seen by the three cones.

(e)
Cone responses

The surface   The surface

This produces two very different sets of three numbers from the same surface. How do we know what color that surface is?

FIGURE 5.22 The same surface (a) illuminated by two different lights (b) will generate two different patterns of activity in the S-, M-, and L-cones (c–e). However, the surface will appear to be the same color under both illuminants. This phenomenon is known as color constancy. (After Smithson, 2005.)

other numbers, and asked to guess what those two numbers might be. The answer could be 12 and 4. Or it could be 16 and 3. Or 6 and 8. Given just the number 48, we cannot solve the problem. Nevertheless, given the result of *I* × *S*, the visual system does a pretty good job of figuring out *S*.

We sometimes talk about "discounting" the illuminant as if our whole goal were to throw away the *I* term and just see the surface color. However, this is not quite right. You can tell the difference between a scene lit by the morning sun as opposed to a scene illuminated by the sun at high noon. Thus, not only can you recover the color of the surface, but you also know something about the illuminant. How do you do this?

Physical Constraints Make Constancy Possible

As noted in the previous section, it is impossible to know which two integers are multiplied to produce 48. However, if you are told that the first number is between 9 and 14, you're saved. The first number must be 12, and the second, then, is 4. In an analogous way, color constancy must be based on some information or assumptions that constrain the possible answers. There are many possible assumptions that could help. Suppose we assumed that, in a complex scene, the brightest region was white (Land and McCann, 1971) or that the average color across the whole scene was gray (Buchsbaum, 1980). We could scale the other colors relative to these white or gray anchors. However, this can't be entirely right. Think what would happen if you were in a dark room with two spots of light on the wall: a red one and a blue one. Under a simple version of a bright-is-white theory, the brighter spot should look white and the other spot would change color. That can't be right (and theorists knew this, so the actual theories are more subtle, but they still do not work perfectly).

There are other possible constraining pieces of information. Assumptions can be made about the illuminant. For instance, natural light sources (and most artificial ones, such as standard lightbulbs) are generally "broadband." That is, they contain many wavelengths, even if some wavelengths are not as intense as others. Furthermore, their spectral composition curves (see Figure 5.22) are usually smooth; spikes at particular wavelengths are uncommon, though this generalization is violated by some artificial light sources. Highly unnatural (e.g., monochromatic) light sources make the world look highly unnatural—a fact exploited in clubs the world over. Indeed, with a monochromatic source, color vision is impossible, though not much broadband light is needed to get color back.

Assumptions can be made about surfaces. Real surfaces also tend to be broadband in their **reflectances** (recall the hamburger distributions of Figure 5.6). It would be very unlikely, for example, to find a surface that reflected 100% of 535-nm light, 0% of 538-nm light, and 100% again of 540-nm light. Even surfaces that are nearly metameric with single wavelengths of light typically reflect a wide range of wavelengths. There are limits on the reflectance of real surfaces. The whitest surface rarely reflects more than 95% of any wavelength, and the blackest rarely reflects less than 5%. The brightest thing in the visual field is likely to be white. A "specular reflection" (like the shiny spot on a billiard ball) has a wavelength composition very similar to that of the illuminant. Any of these facts might help.

Assumptions can be made about the structure of the world. Sharp borders in an image are almost always the result of boundaries between surfaces, not boundaries between light sources. Thus, if you see something that looks pink next to something that looks golden, it is very unlikely to be the result of cleverly placed pink and golden light sources (unless you're in a theater, perhaps). Shadow borders can be an exception to this rule (Adelson, 1993; Cavanagh and Leclerc, 1989). A shadow can produce a sharp edge that is unrelated to any change in the underlying surface. However, the change across a shadow border is typically a change in brightness and not a change in the chromatic

reflectance The percentage of light hitting a surface that is reflected and not absorbed into the surface. Typically reflectance is given as a function of wavelength.

FIGURE 5.23 The visual system "knows" that brightness changes across a shadow boundary but hue does not. As a result, (a) looks like a shadow but (b) does not.

(a) Luminance change without hue change looks like a shadow.

(b) Luminance change *with* hue change looks less like a shadow.

properties of the regions. In **Figure 5.23a**, you can easily imagine that you're looking at three rectangles with a shadow lying across their middles. Not so in Figure 5.23b; though the top and bottom in Figure 5.23b are brighter than the middle, the darker region does not look like a shadow because, for that darkening to be the result of a shadow, the shadow would have to be coincidently aligned with a set of hue changes. Our implicit knowledge of these sorts of constraints helps us sort out the visual world.

Cues like this, perhaps in clever combination, can be used to solve the otherwise unsolvable problem of color constancy (Smithson, 2005). All of these assumptions about the state of the world might sound a lot like the "priors" that are important in Bayesian theories of the sort introduced in Chapter 4. Bayesian ideas have been put to work to explain color constancy (Brainard, 2009; Brainard and Freeman, 1997). The hard part, whether you're working in an explicitly Bayesian framework or not, is to get the prior exactly right (Foster, 2011). What are the precise assumptions that give us our level of color constancy? We are still not sure.

FURTHER DISCUSSION of Bayesian theories in the context of vision can be found in Chapter 4 on pages 105–106.

Nonetheless, we can broadly describe how the visual system might use these assumptions to achieve color constancy. Suppose, for example, that you're standing in a kitchen illuminated by a light source composed primarily of short and middle wavelengths (**Figure 5.24**). None of the surfaces in your visual field will reflect much long-wavelength light, because there isn't much of this light to be reflected. But given the assumption that the illumination is evenly distributed around the room, you will still perceive the strawberries as red because they will be reflecting *more* long-wavelength light than any other surface does.

The subtlety of the visual system's understanding of the physics of light and reflection is evident in an elegant experiment by Bloj, Kersten, and Hurlbert (1999) (**Figure 5.25**). They took a card that was half red and half white (Figure 5.25, step 1) and folded it so that the red region faced the white region (step 2). As a result, some of the light reflected from the red side bounced off the white

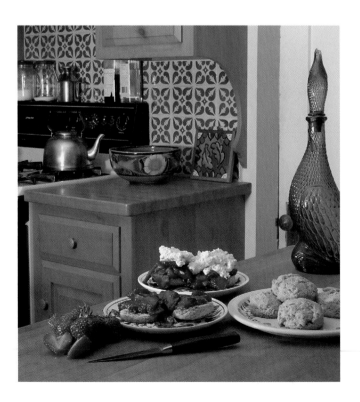

FIGURE 5.24 The strawberries in a complex scene will look red even if there is not much long-wavelength light in the illuminant.

1. Start with a card half red, half white.

2. Fold it so that red faces white.

3. Light reflects from red onto white.

4. The visual system "knows" about the reflection and knows to discount it.

5. Now, fool the visual system into thinking the card is folded like a roof.

6. Without the reflection explanation, the white side now looks quite pink.

FIGURE 5.25 This experiment of Bloj, Kersten, and Hurlbert (1999) shows us how assumptions about the physics of the world influence the psychophysics of color perception.

side and into an observer's eye (step 3). Seen in isolation, that formerly white area would have looked mildly pink. However, the visual system seems to "know" about mutual reflection. Observers saw the white region as white because their visual systems had a way to explain the pinkness as being due to illumination (step 4).

Now comes the clever part. Using an optical trick, Bloj et al., in effect, switched the left and right eyes, making the card look like a roof rather than a corner (step 5). If it were a roof, the red and white areas would not be able to face each other, and consequently, the red area would not be able to reflect onto the white. Because this was a trick, however, all of the actual wavelengths were identical. But the visual system had lost its explanation for the long-wavelength light bouncing off the white region. As a result, the white region now looked quite pink (step 6). If the pinkness could not be attributed to illumination, it had to be attributed to the actual color of the surface.

We dwell on this experiment not because the perception of folded cards is vitally important, but because the experiment, like many others, neatly illustrates that vision is not just a simple translation of the world from photons to neurons. Vision is the nervous system's best guess about what is happening in the world. (See **Web Activity 5.5: Illusions of Lighting** for more on this point.)

Color Vision in Animals

The ability to use wavelength information has evolved several times in several ways during the course of evolution. Evolutionary theory tells us that, for this to be true, color vision must provide an advantage that makes it worth the trouble. An animal can certainly survive without color vision. If we cannot make wavelength discriminations, we can still identify a lion (**Figure 5.26**), and we can still find our way through the forest. Although color vision might make the lion

FIGURE 5.26 A black-and-white lion is still a lion.

(a)

(b)

FIGURE 5.27 Picking a strawberry is easier if you have color vision.

stand out a bit better from the trees, we would be much more impaired if we lacked "orientation vision" or "motion vision." Across the animal kingdom, however, there seem to be at least two realms of behavior where color vision is especially useful: eating and sex.

Having color vision does seem to make it easier to forage for food. Would you rather pick ripe berries with color vision (**Figure 5.27a**) or without (Figure 5.27b)? The colors of wildflowers did not develop to please the aesthetic sense of humans. They are advertisements to bees and other insects offering to trade food for sex (well, at least for pollination). In fact, many flowers have dramatic patterns that we cannot see because they are variations in the reflection of short-wavelength ("ultraviolet") light, which is outside our range. Bees can see these short wavelengths, and it is the bees that flowers are designed to attract (**Figure 5.28**). While we're on the subject, the smell of a flower is also useful way to attract pollinators, and even the shape of specialized leaves can create an auditory beacon to attract echolocating bats (Simon et al., 2011). Other bats make use of the long infrared wavelengths beyond 700 nm. These are vampire bats who use the infrared signal of warmth to find where blood flows near the surface of the skin of its prey. This search for hot spots uses not photoreceptors in the eyes but rather thermoreceptors in the snout, related to those used to feel heat in the skin or the burn of a chili pepper (Gracheva et al., 2011).

FIGURE 5.28 Color vision in different species. (a) These black-eyed Susans are shown as seen with human photoreceptors and color vision. (b) A honeybee can see UV light. In UV, the flower's "black eye" (or maybe the pupil of that eye) is much larger—a better target for the bee. (Courtesy of Tom Eisner.)

(a)

(b)

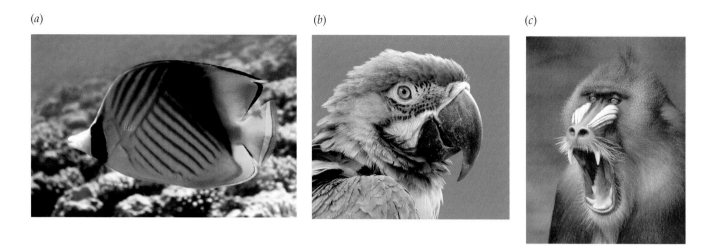

(a)   (b)   (c)

FIGURE 5.29 The colors of animals—from tropical fish (a) to parrots (b) to baboons (c)—are often an advertisement to potential mates.

Colorful displays—from the dramatic patterns on tropical fish (**Figure 5.29**a) to the neck of a parrot (Figure 5.29b) to the face of the baboon (Figure 5.29c)—are all sexual signals. What makes the parrot that has the most colorful neck the most desirable mate for a female parrot? We can't ask her, of course, but a colorful neck might somehow indicate that this parrot's genes are better than his competitors'. A female parrot that sees the world in black and white won't be able to perceive this information and will therefore be at an evolutionary disadvantage. In another example that we mentioned earlier, primate color vision may be particularly well suited to detect the amount of blood in a blushing or blanched cheek (Changizi, Zhang, and Shimojo, 2006).

Color vision is accomplished in different ways in different species. We are trichromats, with three different types of photoreceptors. Dogs appear to be dichromats, with two types of photoreceptors (Neitz, Geist, and Jacobs, 1989). Chickens, surprisingly enough, turn out to be tetrachromats, with four (Okano, Fukada, and Yoshizawa, 1995). There is not much gain in information if the number of photoreceptor types is increased beyond 3 or 4 (Maloney, 1986), which probably explains the lack of octachromats or dodecachromats—individuals with 8 or 12 types of cones, respectively.

Our S-, M-, and L-cones are different because they contain different photopigments (**Figure 5.30**a). It is also possible to use a single photopigment to create more than one functional type of cone. The trick is to put a different filter in front of each type of cone so that some wavelengths are subtracted before light reaches the photoreceptor (Figure 5.30b). A cone with a reddish oil droplet in front of it will respond more vigorously to long-wavelength light than will a cone covered by a greenish droplet. Chicks and other birds have these droplets, as do a variety of reptiles (Govardovskii, 1983).

Even fireflies get into this act in a limited way. Fireflies signal each other with bioluminescence: they make their own light. Different species have different lights, and each species' visual system appears to be tuned to its particular wavelength signature. A combination of a photopigment and a colored filter makes signals of conspecifics (members of the same species) appear brighter than the flashes of other fireflies in the vicinity (Cronin et al., 2000). With this sort of visual system, the firefly will never appreciate the palette of colors in a sunset. But it will be able to locate an appropriate mate, and that, after all, was the pressure shaping the development of this limited sensitivity to wavelength.

Like humans, other animals are interested in the properties of surfaces, not the properties of illuminating lights. Therefore, color constancy is a goal of all animals with dichromatic, trichromatic, or tetrachromatic vision. Researchers have found that animals with quite different color vision systems do, in

(*a*) Different photopigments can tune photoreceptors
to different wavelengths.

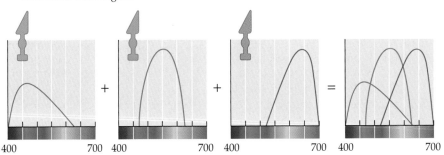

(*b*) Colored oil droplets can also tune photoreceptors
to different wavelengths.

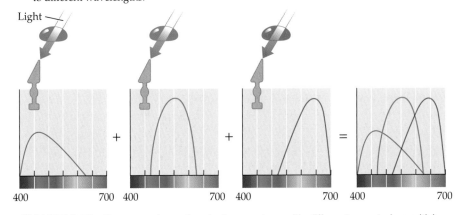

FIGURE 5.30 Two ways to make photoreceptors with different spectral sensitivities. (*a*) Our S-, M-, and L- cones are different because they contain different photopigments. (*b*) Some animals have only one type of photopigment. These animals can have color vision because colored oil droplets sitting on top of photoreceptors create groups of photoreceptors with different sensitivities to wavelength.

fact, show color constancy. Take the honeybee, for example. Annette Werner trained honeybees to land on a region of one color in order to get food, and to ignore two other colors (A. Werner, Menzel, and Wehrhahn, 1988). She could then alter the illuminating light so that the light reflecting off a "bad" color had the same effect on the bee photoreceptors under the new light that the "good" color had had under the old light. Nevertheless, the bees still flew to the good color. We cannot tell what the bees "saw," but they behaved as though the perceived colors stayed constant when the illumination changed. Much the same experiment has been done with goldfish, with much the same result (Dorr and Neumeyer, 1996; Ingle, 1985).

These studies of animals remind us of two important points about color perception. First, if we think about the oil droplets of fireflies, the tetrachromacy of chickens, and so forth, we are reminded that color is a mental experience and not a physical property. These animals can make discriminations according to the wavelength of light, but they live in a different color world than the one we perceive. Second, the experiments on color constancy illustrate that, even though different organisms have different color vision apparatus, all must solve the same basic problems. The physics of the world do not change for different species. If a human needs to ignore the color of the illuminant, so does a bee.

Summary

1. Probably the most important fact to know about color vision is that lights and surfaces look colored because a particular distribution of wavelengths of light is being analyzed by a particular visual system. Color is a mental phenomenon, not a physical phenomenon. Many animal species have some form of color vision. It seems to be important for identifying possible mates, possible rivals, and good things to eat. Color vision has evolved several times in several different ways in the animal kingdom.

2. Rod photoreceptors are sensitive to low (scotopic) light levels. There is only one type of rod photoreceptor; it yields one "number" for each location in the visual field. Rods can support only a one-dimensional representation of color from dark to light. Thus, scotopic vision is achromatic vision.

3. There are three types of cone photoreceptors, each having a different sensitivity to the wavelengths of light. Cones operate at brighter light levels than rods, producing three "numbers" at each location; the pattern of activity over the different cone types defines the color.

4. If two regions of an image produce the same response in the three cone types, they will look identical; that is, they will be metamers. And they will look identical even if the physical wavelengths coming from the two regions are different.

5. In additive color mixture, two or more lights are mixed. Adding a light that looks blue to a light that looks yellow will produce a light that looks white (if we pick the right blue and yellow). In subtractive color mixture, filters, paints, or other pigments that absorb some wavelengths and reflect others are mixed. Mixing a typical blue paint and a typical yellow paint will subtract most long and short wavelengths from the light reflected by the mixture, and the result will look green.

6. Color blindness is typically caused by the congenital absence or abnormality of one cone type—usually the L- or M-cones, usually in males. Most color-blind individuals are not blind to differences in wavelength. Rather, their color perception is based on the outputs of two cone types instead of the normal three.

7. A single type of cone cannot be used, by itself, to discriminate between wavelengths of light. To enable discrimination, information from the three cones is combined to form three cone-opponent processes. Cones sensitive to long wavelengths (L-cones) are pitted against medium-wavelength (M) cones to create an (L – M) process that is *roughly* sensitive to the redness or greenness of a region. (L + M) cones are pitted against short-wavelength (S) cones to create a process *roughly* sensitive to the blueness or yellowness of a region. The third process is sensitive to the overall brightness of a region.

8. Color appearance is arranged around opponent colors: red versus green, and blue versus yellow. This color opponency involves further reprocessing of the cone signals from cone-opponent processes into color-opponent processes.

9. The visual system tries to disentangle the properties of surfaces in the world (e.g., the "red" color of a strawberry) from the properties of the illuminant (e.g., the "golden" light of evening), even though surface and illuminant information are combined in the input to the eyes. Mechanisms of color constancy use implicit knowledge about the world to correct for the influence of different illuminants and to keep that strawberry looking red under a wide range of conditions.

CHAPTER 6

Kurt Wenner, *Dies Irae*, 1985

Space Perception and Binocular Vision

Imagine that you're moving quietly through a meadow, trying to get close enough to a bear cub to get a good picture. Suddenly you discover that Mother Bear is not happy about your photo session. She charges, and you run—back across the field, through a thicket of trees. A quick leap across a stream brings you to a slope that leads down to the road where your partner is waiting in a jeep. You dive into the passenger side and roar off down the track to safety. As the bear lumbers off and your heartbeat returns to normal, your thoughts naturally turn to the acts of visual space perception that you just performed: You picked a path through the three-dimensional world that brought you to safety. You behaved as though you knew where the trees were. You acted as though you understood how far it was across the stream. All in all, you demonstrated a sophisticated grasp of the layout of the physical world around you.

Humans share this sophistication with a large part of the animal kingdom. Faced with the same bear, a rabbit or deer would have shown a similar grasp of the relevant issues in space perception (without the jeep). The ability to perceive and interact with the structure of space is one of the fundamental goals of the visual system. It is also quite a formidable accomplishment, and in this chapter we'll explore how we do it.

As a starting place, let's assume that the external world exists. This is a philosophical position known as **realism**. It is not the only possibility. The **positivists** note that all you really have to go on is the evidence of your senses, so the world could be nothing more than an elaborate hallucination. For less philosophical elaborations of this viewpoint, we could consult the writings of Philip K. Dick and other science fiction authors. In this book, we'll just assume that there is a real world out there to perceive.

The geometry of that real world is **Euclidean** (named in honor of the ancient Greek geometer Euclid, of the third century BCE). This means that parallel lines remain parallel as they are extended in space, that objects maintain the same size and shape as they move around in that space, that the internal angles of a triangle always add to 180 degrees, and so forth. All that stuff you learned in high school math classes is true in the real world.

Euclidean geometry is not the only geometry. Although the real world is Euclidean, the geometry of retinal images of that world is decidedly *non-*Euclidean. The geometry becomes non-Euclidean when the three-dimensional world is projected onto the curved, two-dimensional surface of the retina. Parallel lines in the world do not necessarily remain parallel in the retinal image, as **Figure 6.1** illustrates. The angles of triangles don't always add up to 180 degrees. The retinal area occupied by an object gets smaller as the object moves farther away from the eyeball. What all this means is that if we want to appreciate the Euclidean world, we have to reconstruct it from non-Euclidean input.

realism A philosophical position arguing that there is a real world to sense.

positivism A philosophical position arguing that all we really have to go on is the evidence of the senses, so the world might be nothing more than an elaborate hallucination.

Euclidean Referring to the geometry of the world, so named in honor of Euclid, the ancient Greek geometer of the third century BCE. In Euclidean geometry, parallel lines remain parallel as they are extended in space, objects maintain the same size and shape as they move around in space, the internal angles of a triangle always add to 180 degrees, and so forth.

FIGURE 6.1 The Euclidean geometry of the three-dimensional world (where, for example, parallel lines don't converge) turns into something quite different on the curved, two-dimensional retina.

Retina

Retinal image

More precisely, generally we reconstruct the world from two non-Euclidean inputs: the two distinct retinal images. Close your left eye, stretch your left arm out in front of you, and hold up your left index finger. Then hold up your right index finger about 6 inches in front of your face, so that it appears to be positioned just to the left of the left index finger, as illustrated in Figure 6.2. Now, quickly open your left eye and close your right eye. If you positioned your fingers properly, your right finger will jump to the other side of your left finger. Although this demonstration is designed to exaggerate the different views of your two eyes, the point is a general one: the two retinal images always differ. They differ because the retinas are in slightly different places. Just as you and the person standing next to you see somewhat different views of the world, so do your two eyes. Much of this chapter will be devoted to explaining how the visual system goes to quite elaborate lengths both to exploit and to reconcile these differences.

Why have two eyes at all? Perhaps most fundamentally, having two eyes confers the same evolutionary advantage as having two lungs, two kidneys,

(a)

(b)

Right retinal image

Left retinal image

FIGURE 6.2 The two retinal images of a three-dimensional world are not the same. See the text for details.

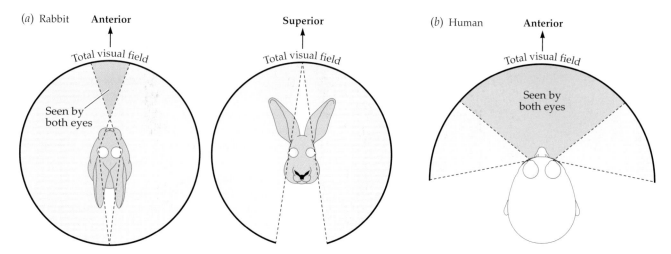

FIGURE 6.3 Visual fields vary, depending on the species. (*a*) A rabbit's visual field is like a planetarium dome (with ears). (*b*) A human visual field is more like a windshield covering a large region in front of the eyes. Light purple indicates the entire visual field; dark purple, the part of the visual field seen by both eyes.

and two brain hemispheres: you can lose one eye and still be able to see. A second advantage to doubling the number of eyes is that they enable you to see more of the world. This explains why it is so hard to sneak up on a rabbit: its visual field actually extends a full 360 degrees (**Figure 6.3***a*), and it can also see straight up (Hughes, 1977).

Our visual field is limited to about 190 degrees from left to right, 110 degrees of which is covered by both eyes (Figure 6.3*b*). The field is more restricted vertically: about 60 degrees up from the center of gaze and 80 degrees down, as was shown in Figure 2.20—limited by the anatomy of cheeks and eyebrows. Overlapping, **binocular** visual fields give predator animals such as humans a better chance to spot small, fast-moving objects in front of them that might provide dinner (e.g., those rabbits, whose dome-shaped visual fields are adapted to avoid being caught). Having two eyes looking for dinner is rather like having two people looking. If each person had a 50% chance of finding the rabbit and the two people were independent, together they would have a 75% chance (Blake, Sloane, and Fox, 1981). In vision, this **binocular summation** principle may have provided the evolutionary pressure that first moved eyes to the front of some birds' and mammals' faces. Under most circumstances, we do not get such a large benefit from binocular summation. The increase from a 50% chance to a 75% chance assumes two completely independent observers, but the two eyes are still embedded in one person. Nevertheless, you will do better at many tasks with two eyes than you would do with just one (R. K. Jones and Lee, 1981).

Once the eyes moved to the front, though, evolution found an additional use for overlapping visual fields. Try this. Take the top off a pen and hold the top in one hand, the pen in the other, both about a foot in front of your face. Now, close one eye and try to quickly put the cap on the pen. Repeat the same task with both eyes open. For most (but not all) people, this task is easier with two eyes than with one. This is a quick demonstration of the usefulness of **binocular disparity**—the differences between the two retinal images of the same world. Disparity is the basis for a vivid perception of the three-dimensionality of the world that is not available with purely **monocular** (one-eyed) vision. The technical term for this binocular perception of depth is **stereopsis**. The geometric and physiological bases for stereopsis are the topic of a large portion of this chapter (I. P. Howard and Rogers, 2001).

When you decide you need a break from reading this chapter, take that break with one eye closed. You should be able to notice the loss of stereopsis

binocular With two eyes.

binocular summation The combination (or "summation") of signals from each eye in ways that make performance on many tasks better with both eyes than with either eye alone.

binocular disparity The differences between the two retinal images of the same scene. Disparity is the basis for stereopsis, a vivid perception of the three-dimensionality of the world that is not available with monocular vision.

monocular With one eye.

stereopsis The ability to use binocular disparity as a cue to depth.

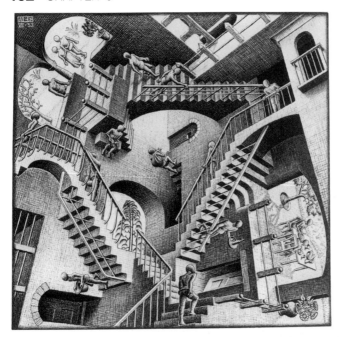

FIGURE 6.4 M. C. Escher, *Relativity*, 1953.

depth cues Information about the third dimension (depth) of visual space. Depth cues may be monocular or binocular.

monocular depth cue A depth cue that is available even when the world is viewed with one eye alone.

binocular depth cue A depth cue that relies on information from both eyes. Stereopsis is the primary example in humans, but convergence and the ability of two eyes to see more of an object than one eye sees are also binocular depth cues.

occlusion A cue to relative depth order in which, for example, one object obstructs the view of part of another object.

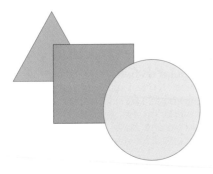

FIGURE 6.5 Occlusion makes it easy to infer relative position in depth.

(and of part of your visual field), but a period of one-eyed visual experience will also make it clear that stereopsis is not a necessary condition for depth perception or space perception. Rabbits do very well with very little binocular vision, and painters and movie directors manage to convey realistic impressions of depth on flat canvases and movie screens. On the other hand, stereopsis does add a richness to perception of the three-dimensional world, as vividly described by Oliver Sacks (2006) in his article about "Stereo Sue," a neuroscientist who regained stereopsis at the age of 48.

Returning from your break, you will find that a description of the set of **monocular depth cues** to three-dimensional space is the first major topic of this chapter. After that, we turn to the more complicated topic of the **binocular depth cue** of stereopsis. Then, in the last section of the chapter, we consider how the various cues are combined to produce a unified perception of space.

Monocular Cues to Three-Dimensional Space

M. C. Escher (1898–1972) titled the drawing in **Figure 6.4** *Relativity*. Escher was a master of the rules that govern our perception of space. Each bit of stairway, each landing, every person—all are drawn using cues that enable us to infer three dimensions from two. But when we try to follow those stairs, we find that Escher's drawing cleverly fails to add up to a coherent representation of a place that could exist. Even when no one is trying to fool us, it is geometrically impossible (not to mention computationally infeasible) for the visual system to create a perfectly faithful reconstruction of Euclidean space, given the non-Euclidean input we receive through our eyes. The best we can do is to use depth cues to infer aspects of the three-dimensional world from our two-dimensional retinal images. On the basis of the retinal images and an implicit understanding of physics and geometry, each cue provides a hint about the likely structure of the space in front of us and the disposition of objects in that space.

Unless we're stuck in an extremely impoverished perceptual environment (say, the Sahara desert during a sandstorm), every view of the world provides multiple depth cues. Usually the cues reinforce each other, combining to produce a convincing and reliable representation of the three-dimensional world. Occasionally, however, the cues are contradictory. Escher could fool us by deliberately manipulating depth cues and other routine visual inferences. He arranges sensible local cues into a globally implausible story. What cues does the visual system use to infer depth relations, and how do we use those cues to create a representation of the three-dimensional world? (See **Web Activity 6.1: Monocular Depth Cues.**)

Occlusion

Some of the cues to the layout of the three-dimensional world were introduced earlier in this book, because hints to the layout of space can also be hints about the structure of objects in that space. **Occlusion** is an example (see the section titled "Finding Edges" in Chapter 4). In Chapter 4, occlusion was a cue to the presence of an otherwise invisible edge. As a depth cue, occlusion gives information about the relative position of objects. Thus, in **Figure 6.5** we are happy to infer a circle in front of a square in front of a triangle. Occlusion is present

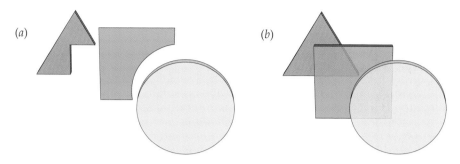

(a)   (b)

FIGURE 6.6 Figure 6.5 could be an "accidental" (unlikely) view of the pieces shown in (a). It is much more likely, however, that it is a generic view of circle, square, and triangle, as shown in (b).

in almost every visual scene (we challenge you to find a situation in normal life where nothing blocks your view of anything else), and many researchers argue that it is the most reliable of all the depth cues. It is wrong only in the case of "accidental viewpoints" (remember those from Chapter 4?). That is, the retinal image shown in Figure 6.5 could be produced by a circle and two oddly shaped puzzle pieces, as shown in **Figure 6.6a**. That scenario would require careful placement of the objects and the viewer. It is much more likely that Figure 6.5 would arise from a more generic view of a circle occluding a square occluding a triangle (Figure 6.6b).

We do not know from the occlusion cue alone whether the red square in Figure 6.5 is in front of a small green triangle, a larger but more distant triangle (maybe a green tree), or an even larger but even more distant green mountain. Occlusion is a **nonmetrical depth cue**; it just gives us the relative orderings of occluders and occludees. A **metrical depth cue** is one that does provide information about distance in the third dimension.

Size and Position Cues

The image on the retina formed by an object out in the world gets smaller as the object gets farther away. (See **Web Activity 3.1: Visual Angle** for a review.) Moreover, your visual system knew this fact of **projective geometry** implicitly before you ever picked up this book and learned it explicitly. Projective geometry describes how the world is *projected* onto a surface. For example, a shadow is a projection of an object onto a surface. An implicit understanding of the rules of projective geometry can be said to undergird many of the depth cues described here. In this case, the visual system knows that, all else being equal, smaller things are farther away. Hence, the plasticine balls in **Figure 6.7** may appear to lie in different depth planes. We can call this depth cue **relative size**.

nonmetrical depth cue A depth cue that provides information about the depth order (relative depth) but not depth magnitude (e.g., his nose is in front of his face).

metrical depth cue A depth cue that provides quantitative information about distance in the third dimension.

projective geometry For purposes of studying perception of the three-dimensional world, the geometry that describes the transformations that occur when the three-dimensional world is *projected* onto a two-dimensional surface. For example, parallel lines do not converge in the real world, but they do in the two-dimensional projection of that world.

relative size A comparison of size between items without knowing the absolute size of either one.

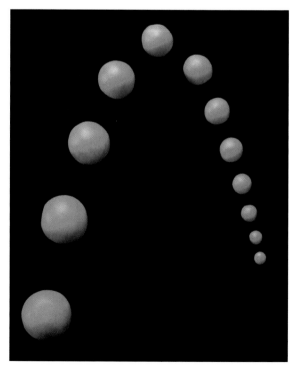

FIGURE 6.7 Even though all of these plasticine balls are resting on the same surface, the small ones appear to be farther away. Some portion of the visual system assumes that all of these items are the same. If one ball projects a smaller image on the retina and if the balls really are the same size, then the smaller one must be farther away. This is the cue of relative size.

FIGURE 6.8 This rabbit texture gradient shows that the size cue is more effective when size changes systematically.

texture gradient A depth cue based on the geometric fact that items of the same size form smaller images when they are farther away. An array of items that change in size smoothly across the image will appear to form a surface tilted in depth.

relative height As a depth cue, the observation that objects at different distances from the viewer on the ground plane will form images at different heights in the retinal image. Objects farther away will be seen as higher in the image.

The impression of three-dimensionality in **Figure 6.8** is more powerful than that in Figure 6.7 because we've added another cue. The critical difference is in the organization of the objects in the two figures. In Figure 6.8, the rabbits form an orderly **texture gradient**, with larger objects in one area and smaller objects in another. Because smaller is interpreted as farther away, this arrangement creates the perception of a ground plane receding into the distance.

In **Figure 6.9**, the rabbits are again arrayed in an orderly texture, but here we get less of a sense of depth. The difference between Figures 6.8 and 6.9 is that the former includes another depth cue that is not present in the latter: **relative height**. Imagine that that you're actually standing in a field of rabbits.

FIGURE 6.9 Organized differently, this illustration of the same rabbits as those shown in Figure 6.8 does not produce the same sense of depth. A size cue is most effective when it is consistent with objects arranged on the ground, not on a wall.

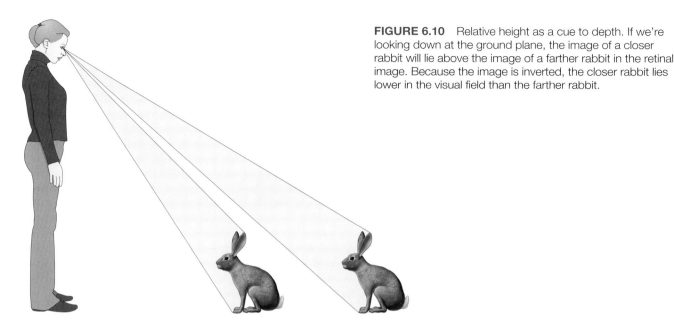

FIGURE 6.10 Relative height as a cue to depth. If we're looking down at the ground plane, the image of a closer rabbit will lie above the image of a farther rabbit in the retinal image. Because the image is inverted, the closer rabbit lies lower in the visual field than the farther rabbit.

Consider the rabbit at your feet (Figure 6.10). It will project its image in your lower visual field. The smaller image of a more distant rabbit will be projected higher in the visual field. Here, then, is another geometric regularity produced by projective geometry that the visual system can exploit: for objects on the ground plane, objects that are more distant will be higher in the visual field.

Texture fields that provide an impression of three-dimensionality are really combinations of relative size and relative height cues. Like the metaphor of perceptual committees in Chapter 4, this is a case in which multiple cues interact to produce a final perception. Figure 6.11 shows how this interaction can give rise to a size illusion. The little rabbits in the top center and lower right of the figure are actually the same physical size on the page, but the one at the bottom looks smaller to most of us than the one at the top. Why? We infer, on the basis of relative height, that the rabbit at the bottom must be

FIGURE 6.11 The two smaller rabbits in the image are the same size. Why don't they look the same size?

(*a*)   (*b*)

FIGURE 6.12 The cue of familiar size. The hand in (*a*) looks closer than the one in (*b*) because we know how big hands should be relative to heads.

closer. If it is closer and it forms an image of the same size as the little rabbit at the top, it follows that the little rabbit at the bottom must be really little.

If we know what size something *ought* to be, that knowledge can be a depth cue in its own right. We infer that the woman in **Figure 6.12***a* is holding her hand out at the end of an outstretched arm. Why do we make this guess? One alternative is that she's holding her hand near her shoulder, as in Figure 6.12*b*. But if that were the case in Figure 6.12*a*, the hand would need to be a *very* big hand. Here, our knowledge of the normal relationship of hand size to head size makes all the difference. This is the depth cue of **familiar size**.

Recall that occlusion is a nonmetrical cue, providing only depth *order*. The relative size and relative height cues, especially taken together, provide some metrical information. This is illustrated in **Figure 6.13**, where the three balls appear to lie at measurable distances from each other. The blue ball seems closer to the red ball than to the green ball in depth, for example. Relative size and height do not tell us the *exact* distance to an object or between objects. These are **relative metrical depth cues**. Familiar size, however, could be an **absolute metrical depth cue**. If your visual system knew the actual size of an object and the visual angle of the object's projection on the retina, it could (at least in theory) calculate the exact distance from object to eye. In practice, however, even if you know that your friend is 5 feet 10 inches tall, the visual system does not seem to know that fact with a precision that would let you know he's standing exactly 12 feet away.

familiar size A depth cue based on knowledge of the typical size of objects like humans or pennies.

relative metrical depth cue A depth cue that could specify, for example, that object A is twice as far away as object B without providing information about the absolute distance to either A or B.

absolute metrical depth cue A depth cue that provides quantifiable information about distance in the third dimension (e.g., his nose sticks out 4 centimeters in front of his face).

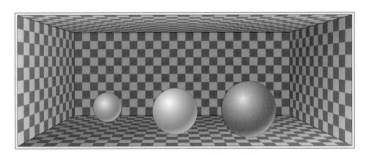

FIGURE 6.13 The metrical cues of relative size and height can give the visual system more information than a nonmetrical cue like occlusion can. Not only does the red sphere in this image appear to be closest and the green sphere farthest away, but also the blue sphere is seen to be closer to the red sphere than it is to the green sphere.

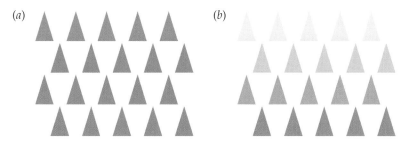

FIGURE 6.14 The triangles seem to recede into depth more in (*b*) than in (*a*). The depth cue here is called "haze" or "aerial perspective."

Aerial Perspective

In addition to its implicit knowledge of geometry and its learned knowledge of familiar size, the visual system "knows" about properties of the atmosphere. The triangles in Figure 6.14*a* give only a faint sense of depth, if any. They are just an array of identical shapes. Adding some grayscale information, however, as in Figure 6.13*b*, provides the impression of something like a mountain range receding in the distance. More specifically, the fainter mountains (triangles) may appear to be farther away than the darker ones. The depth cue at work here relies on an implicit understanding that light is scattered by the atmosphere, and that more light is scattered when we look through more atmosphere. Thus, objects farther away are subject to more scatter and appear fainter and less distinct. This cue is known as **haze** or **aerial perspective**. Figure 6.15 shows a real-world example. Short wavelengths (blue) are scattered more than medium and long wavelengths. This is why the sky looks blue and why objects farther away look not only hazy, but bluish. The real image gives a stronger sense of depth. By now, it should be clear that this effect results from the contribution of other depth cues beyond the blue haze—for instance, occlusion and the known size of boats and swans.

aerial perspective (or haze) A depth cue based on the implicit understanding that light is scattered by the atmosphere. More light is scattered when we look through more atmosphere. Thus, more distant objects are subject to more scatter and appear fainter, bluer, and less distinct.

FIGURE 6.15 A real-world example of aerial perspective. Scattering of light by the atmosphere makes more distant features appear hazy and blue.

FIGURE 6.16 Linear perspective. If we titled this image "Driving across Kansas," you would understand because the converging lines give the impression of parallel lines receding toward the horizon.

linear perspective A depth cue based on the fact that lines that are parallel in the three-dimensional world will appear to converge in a two-dimensional image.

vanishing point The apparent point at which parallel lines receding in depth converge.

pictorial depth cue A cue to distance or depth used by artists to depict three-dimensional depth in two-dimensional pictures.

Linear Perspective

In the six lines shown in **Figure 6.16**, it is not difficult to imagine the view out the windshield of a car moving down a road in a flat landscape. The depth cue in this case—**linear perspective**—is based on the rules that determine how lines in three-dimensional space are projected onto a two-dimensional image. The core piece of projective geometry in this case is that lines that are parallel in the three-dimensional world will appear to converge in the two-dimensional image, except when the parallel lines lie in a plane that is parallel to the plane of the two-dimensional image. For example, if we were standing in front of the closed door in **Figure 6.17a**, the parallel sides of that door would remain parallel in the retinal image. If we opened the door onto a hallway, however, the parallel lines formed by the walls, floor, and ceiling would converge in the two-dimensional retinal image as they receded into the distance in the three-dimensional world (Figure 6.17b). Indeed, if the hall went back far enough, the walls, floor, and ceiling would seem to meet at a point called the **vanishing point**.

Like texture gradients, linear perspective can be seen as a special case of the relative size and height cues. Assuming that the five blue lines in Figure 6.16 are parallel in three dimensions is tantamount to assuming that the distance between the lines remains constant. But the retinal distance between the lines is larger at the bottom of the image and smaller at the top. Therefore, the lines must be farther away at the top of the image than at the bottom. Like the relative size and height cues, linear perspective provides relative, but not absolute, metrical depth information.

Pictorial Depth Cues and Pictures

As a group, the depth cues discussed so far are known as **pictorial depth cues**. These are the cues produced by projection of the three-dimensional world onto the two-dimensional surface of the retina. A realistic picture or photograph is the result of projecting the three-dimensional world onto the two-dimensional surface of film or canvas. When that image is viewed from the correct position, the retinal image (in one eye, at least) formed by the two-dimensional picture will be the same as the retinal image that would have been formed by the three-dimensional world, and hence we see depth in the picture. In theory, this means that a picture should look correct from only one,

(a) *(b)*

FIGURE 6.17 Parallel lines in the image plane, such as those defining the door in (a), remain parallel in the image. But parallel lines in other planes, such as the ground, ceiling, and side walls in the hall in (b), converge as they recede into the distance.

precise viewing position. In fact, pictures look reasonable over quite a range of views. Were this not so, there would be only one good seat in the movie theater.

To correctly interpret the shape of three-dimensional objects from two-dimensional pictures, people take the orientation of the flat surface of the image into account. This allows them to understand that the picture is, in fact, a picture and not the real thing; and at the same time they can calculate an accurate impression of the thing that is portrayed (Vishwanath, Girshik, and Banks, 2005). To illustrate this point, Marty Banks snapped the photo of one of the authors standing alongside a picture of himself that is shown in **Figure 6.18***a*; here the "picture in the picture" appears reasonable. In Figure 6.18*b*, the same picture is shown stripped of its context. Now it appears quite distorted. In Figure 6.18*a*, our visual system can compensate for the perceptual distortion because there is enough context to enable the viewer to attribute the distortion to the slant of the picture surface.

FIGURE 6.18 Picture in a picture. (*a*) One of the authors, Dennis Levi, is seen standing next to a photograph of himself. In this panel the "picture in the picture" appears reasonable. (*b*) The framed picture, isolated without the context. Does the picture appear distorted? (Courtesy of Martin S. Banks.)

The technique known as **anamorphosis**, or **anamorphic projection**, illustrates that the ability to cope with distortion is limited. In anamorphic projection, the rules of linear perspective are pushed to an extreme in which the projection of three dimensions into two creates a picture that is recognizable only from an unusual vantage point (or sometimes with a curved mirror). The results are known as "anamorphic art." In Hans Holbein's sixteenth-century painting *The Ambassadors* (**Figure 6.19***a*), the odd diagonal smear at lower center proves to be a skull when correctly viewed (Figure 6.19*b*). Unlike the successful recovery of the shapes in Figure 6.18, the visual system cannot use knowledge about surface orientation to compensate for the distortion in Figure 6.19. In our own day, the sidewalk chalk artist Kurt Wenner creates amazing anamorphic images that look spectacularly real from

anamorphosis (or anamorphic projection) Use of the rules of linear perspective to create a two-dimensional image so distorted that it looks correct only when viewed from a special angle or with a mirror that counters the distortion.

(*a*)

FIGURE 6.19 In 1533, Hans Holbein painted the double portrait in (*a*) with an odd object at the feet of the two men. Viewed from the correct position (*b*), the object proves to be a skull, making it an example of anamorphic art. No one is sure why Holbein put the anamorphic skull in the picture. Maybe it is intended as a reminder that we all must die, or maybe he included it just to show off his abilities.

(*b*)

(a)

(b)

(c)

FIGURE 6.20 Modern-day anamorphic art. (a) In this photograph, a young woman appears to be sitting in a pit on the sidewalk. But, as shown in (b), this is just a clever bit of anamorphic art by street artist, Kurt Wenner. It is just a flat image that looks three-dimensional when viewed from the correct position. This figure might give you a new way to think about the image that started this chapter. Take a look at a different view of the same drawing in (c).

the right vantage point and spectacularly distorted from elsewhere (**Figure 6.20**). More on the role of pictorial depth cues in art can be found in **Web Essay 6.1: Making the Implicit Explicit**.

Motion Cues

Beyond the pictorial depth cues, a number of additional sources of information are available to our visual system when we view real-world scenes that cannot be reproduced in a static two-dimensional picture. The first nonpictorial depth cue we will discuss is **motion parallax**. To appreciate its power (and to understand why photographs of the forest often don't come out well), the best thing to do is to go outside and lie under a tree. Gaze up into the branches and leaves with one eye covered and your head stationary. You will notice that leaves and branches form a relatively flat texture. You can see all the details,

motion parallax An important depth cue that is based on head movement. The geometric information obtained from an eye in two different positions at two different times is similar to the information from two eyes in different positions in the head at the same time.

FIGURE 6.21 Motion parallax. As you look out the window of a moving train, objects closer to you (the flower in this illustration) shift position more quickly than do objects farther away (the tree) from one moment (*a*) to the next (*b*). This regularity can be exploited as a depth cue.

but you may have trouble deciding whether one little branch lies in front of or behind another. If you open the other eye, stereopsis (introduced earlier and discussed in detail later in the chapter) will allow the branches and leaves to fill out a three-dimensional volume that was lacking before. Close the eye and the volume collapses again. Now, move your head from side to side, and motion parallax will restore the sense of depth.

How does motion provide a cue for depth? Suppose you're sitting on a train, looking out the window at the countryside. At one instant you see the scene sketched in **Figure 6.21***a*. A moment later, the scene has changed to the one in Figure 6.21*b*. Notice that, as your train moved from left to right in the figure, all the objects shifted from right to left. But note that some things shifted more than others. The flower (F) moved almost all the way across your retinal image, the cow (C) moved a much shorter distance, and the tree (T) hardly changed positions at all. The term *parallax* refers to the geometric relationship revealed here: when you change your viewpoint, rolling down the tracks, objects closer to you shift position more than objects farther away. Of course, you don't need to be on a train to experience motion parallax; just moving your head will do. The geometric information obtained from an eye in two different positions at two different times (motion parallax) is similar to the information by two eyes in different positions in the head at the same time (stereopsis) (Durgin et al., 1995; Rogers and Collett, 1989).

Motion parallax provides relative metrical information about how far away objects are; and as the experiment with the tree branches proves, it can provide a compelling sense of depth in some situations in which other cues are not very effective. The downside of motion parallax is that it works only if the head moves (just moving the eyes back and forth won't do, as you can easily prove to yourself). Now you know why a cat might bob her head back and forth as she plans a spectacular leap from the sofa to the table.

FIGURE 6.22 Vergence. (*a*) As we shift focus from a far to a near point, our eyes converge. (*b*) As we go from near to far, the eyes diverge.

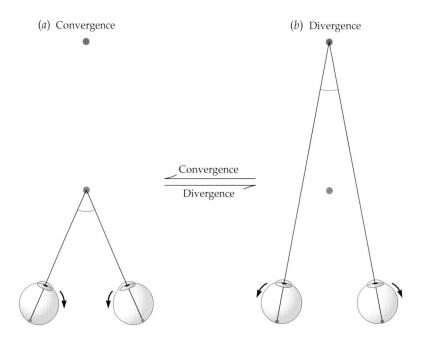

(*a*) Convergence

(*b*) Divergence

Convergence

Divergence

accommodation The process by which the eye changes its focus (in which the lens gets fatter as gaze is directed toward nearer objects).

convergence The ability of the two eyes to turn inward, often used in order to place the two images of a feature in the world on corresponding locations in the two retinal images (typically on the fovea of each eye). Convergence reduces the disparity of that feature to zero (or nearly zero).

divergence The ability of the two eyes to turn outward, often used in order to place the two images of a feature in the world on corresponding locations in the two retinal images (typically on the fovea of each eye). Divergence reduces the disparity of that feature to zero (or nearly zero).

Accommodation and Convergence

Like a camera, the eyes need to be focused to see objects at different distances clearly. As we learned in Chapter 2, the human eye focuses via a process called **accommodation**, in which the lens gets fatter as we direct our gaze toward nearer objects. We also have to point our eyes differently to focus on objects at different distances. As the disembodied eyeballs in **Figure 6.22** move from the red dot to the blue dot, they rotate inward—a process called **convergence** (Figure 6.22*a*); refocusing on the red dot would require rotation outward, which is known as **divergence** (Figure 6.22*b*).

If we could monitor our state of accommodation and/or the extent to which our eyes were converged, we could use this information as a cue to the depth of the object we were trying to bring into focus: the more we have to converge and the more the lens has to bulge in order to focus on the object, the closer it is. When we focus on objects more than about 2–3 meters away, the lens is as thin as it can get and the eyes are diverged about as much as possible, so neither cue provides much useful information. But careful studies have shown that the visual system takes advantage of both cues for objects closer than this limit. Convergence is used more than accommodation (Fisher and Ciuffreda, 1988; Owens, 1987). Moreover, these cues are the only ones besides familiar size that can tell us the *exact* distance to an object. Chameleons, for example, use the absolute metrical depth information from convergence to catch prey insects with their sticky tongues (Harkness, 1977).

Binocular Vision and Stereopsis

As defined earlier, the term *binocular disparity* refers to differences between the images falling on our two retinas, and *stereopsis* refers to the impression of three-dimensionality—of objects "popping out in depth"—that most humans get when they view real-world objects with both eyes. Like the accounts of other depth cues, the story of the route from binocular disparity to stereopsis is a story of the visual system exploiting the regularities of projective geometry to recover the three-dimensional world from its projections—this time, onto a

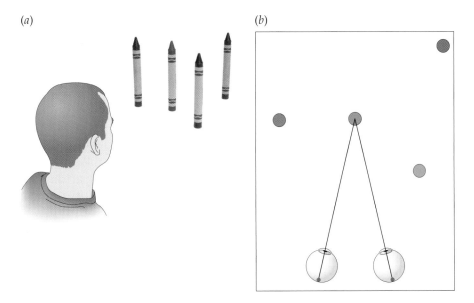

(a)

(b)

FIGURE 6.23 This simple visual scene illustrates how geometric regularities are exploited by the visual system to achieve stereopsis from binocular disparity. (a) The viewer, Bob, is assumed to be fixating his gaze on the red crayon. (b) This top view traces the rays of light bouncing off the red crayon onto Bob's retinas.

pair of two-dimensional surfaces. We will illustrate the translation from disparity to stereopsis using the situation shown in **Figure 6.23***a*, in which the viewer (call him Bob) is facing a scene that includes four colored crayons at different depths. Suppose that Bob is focusing his gaze on the red crayon, as shown in Figure 6.23*b*. The two lines in this figure trace the paths of the light rays that reflect off the red crayon and onto Bob's two retinas. (Bob's experiences with crayon scenes are also demonstrated in **Web Activity 6.2: Binocular Disparity**.)

Because the visual system is designed so that the object of our gaze *always* falls on the fovea, the rays from the red crayon fall on the fovea in each of Bob's eyes. **Figure 6.24** shows the retinal images for the crayons in each eye. The red crayon is in the center of both images. We've added a narrow vertical line behind this crayon in each image to emphasize the fact that this is the location of the fovea.

Now consider the retinal images of the blue crayon. Because the optics of the eye reverse the retinal image, the blue crayon on the right side of the scene falls on the left side of the two retinal images. In our imaginary scene, the blue crayon is placed so that the monocular retinal images of that crayon are formed at the same distance from the fovea in each eye. We say that this crayon's images fall on **corresponding retinal points**. The same can be said of the images of the red crayon, which fall on the two foveas.

In fact, any object lying on the imaginary circle (called the **Vieth-Müller circle**) that runs through the two eyeballs and the object on which Bob is fixated

corresponding retinal points A geometric concept stating that points on the retina of each eye where the monocular retinal images of a single object are formed are at the same distance from the fovea in each eye. The two foveas are also corresponding points.

Vieth-Müller circle The location of objects whose images fall on geometrically corresponding points in the two retinas. If life were simple, this circle would be the horopter, but life is not simple.

Left retinal image

Right retinal image

FIGURE 6.24 The overlapping portions of the images falling on Bob's left and right retinas. Because the retinal image is reversed, the blue and purple crayons on the right side of the scene in Figure 6.23 project to the left side of each retina, whereas the brown crayon on the left side of the scene projects to the right side of each retina. The size differences between the retinal images of the crayons in the two retinas are exaggerated in this figure compared to the differences we would observe if we saw this scene in the real world.

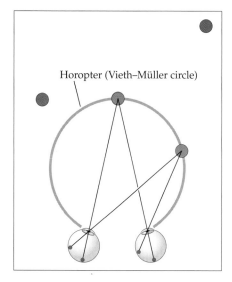

Horopter (Vieth–Müller circle)

FIGURE 6.25 Bob is still gazing at the red crayon. This view from above traces the light rays reflecting from the red and blue crayons onto Bob's retinas. The blue crayon projects to corresponding retinal points—positions that are equidistant from and on the same side of the fovea. The same would be true of any object falling on the gray line shown in the figure. (The horopter and Vieth-Müller circle are not exactly the same, but they would be very similar in this case.)

should project to corresponding retinal points. This imaginary circle is drawn in gray in **Figure 6.25**. Objects that fall on corresponding retinal locations are said to have zero binocular disparity. If the two eyes are looking at one spot (such as the red crayon), then there will be a surface of zero disparity running through that spot. That surface is known as the **horopter**. Any object placed on that imaginary surface in the world will form images on corresponding retinal locations. As it happens, the horopter and the Vieth-Müller circle are not quite the same. If you are *extremely* fond of rather complicated geometry, you may want to pursue this topic in one of the following sources: I. P. Howard and Rogers, 1995 or 2001; or Tyler, 1991. Otherwise, the important point is that there is a surface of zero disparity whose position in the world depends on the current state of convergence of the eyes.

Objects that lie on the horopter are seen as single objects when viewed with both eyes. Objects significantly closer to or farther away from the surface of zero disparity form images on decidedly noncorresponding points in the two eyes, and we see two of each of those objects. This double vision is known as **diplopia**. Objects that are close to the horopter but not quite on it can still be seen as single objects. This region of space in front of and behind the horopter, within which binocular single vision is possible, is known as **Panum's fusional area** (Panum, 1940).

Armed with this terminology, let's return to Bob and his crayons. Consider the retinal images of the brown crayon, lying just off the horopter. As Figure 6.24 and the view from above in **Figure 6.26a** show, rays of light bouncing off this crayon do *not* fall on corresponding retinal points: the crayon's image is farther away from the fovea on the left retina than on the right retina. Relative

horopter The location of objects whose images lie on corresponding points. The surface of zero disparity.

diplopia Double vision. If visible in both eyes, stimuli falling outside of Panum's fusional area will appear diplopic.

Panum's fusional area The region of space, in front of and behind the horopter, within which binocular single vision is possible.

(a)

(b)

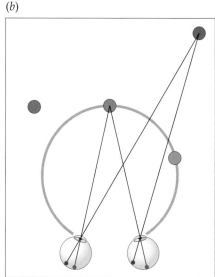

FIGURE 6.26 Light rays projecting from the brown (a) and purple (b) crayons onto Bob's retinas as he continues to gaze at the red crayon.

FIGURE 6.27 Superposition of Bob's left (L) and right (R) retinal images of the crayons in Figure 6.24, showing the relative disparity for each crayon. Size differences are ignored here. The red and blue crayons sit on the horopter and have zero disparity. They form retinal images in corresponding locations. The brown crayon forms images with a small binocular disparity. The purple crayon, farther from the horopter, has larger binocular disparity.

to the horopter, this crayon forms a retinal image with a nonzero binocular disparity. The purple crayon is even farther off the horopter (Figure 6.26*b*); it forms retinal images that are even more disparate (**Figure 6.27**).

The geometric regularity that the visual system uses to extract metrical depth information from binocular disparity should now be growing clear. The larger the disparity, the greater the distance in depth of the object from the horopter.

The direction in depth is given by the *sign* of the disparity, as illustrated in **Figure 6.28**. Suppose that Bob is looking at a red crayon with his eyes converged so that the red crayon falls on the fovea in each eye. A closer, blue crayon will form images on noncorresponding, disparate points. On the left retina, blue will lie to the left of red. Because the image is reversed, this means that, viewed from the left eye, blue is to the right of red. Viewed from the right eye, blue is to the left. Right in left, and left in right. This is known as **crossed disparity** (Figure 6.28*a*), and crossed disparity always means "in front of the horopter." In Figure 6.28*b*, Bob is looking at the blue crayon, and the red is seen to the left with the left eye and to the right with the right. That's **uncrossed disparity**, and uncrossed disparity always means "behind the horopter."

crossed disparity The sign of disparity created by objects in front of the plane of fixation (the horopter). The term *crossed* is used because images of objects located in front of the horopter appear to be displaced to the left in the right eye, and to the right in the left eye.

uncrossed disparity The sign of disparity created by objects behind the plane of fixation (the horopter). The term *uncrossed* is used because images of objects located behind the horopter will appear to be displaced to the right in the right eye, and to the left in the left eye.

(*a*) Crossed disparity

(*b*) Uncrossed disparity

Retina

Bob's view

FIGURE 6.28 Crossed and uncrossed disparity. (*a*) Here Bob is foveating the red crayon. In the Bob's-eye views, the closer, blue object is seen to the right in the left eye and to the left in the right eye. This situation is crossed disparity. (*b*) Here Bob has shifted his gaze and his horopter to the blue crayon. In the Bob's-eye views, the farther, red object is seen to the left in the left eye and to the right in the right eye. This situation is uncrossed disparity.

FIGURE 6.29 Wheatstone's stereoscope. The viewer would bring her nose up the vertical rod at the center of the apparatus so that each eye was looking at the image reflected in one of the two mirrors. (From I. P. Howard and Rogers, 1995.)

Picture panel — Mirrors — Sliding boards

stereoscope A device for simultaneously presenting one image to one eye and another image to the other eye. Stereoscopes can be used to present dichoptic stimuli for stereopsis and binocular rivalry.

FIGURE 6.30 Stereopsis for the masses. (*a*) This Holmes stereoscope—among others—brought stereo photos into many mid-nineteenth-century homes. (*b*) A stereo photo of South African Light Horse, a scouting regiment of the British Army, on Adderly Street, in Cape Town, South Africa, 1900. If you can "free-fuse" (see the next section), you will be able to see this scene jump out in depth.

Stereoscopes and Stereograms

Interestingly, although scientists had studied the geometry of binocular vision for millennia (the geometer Euclid was at it in the third century BCE), not until the nineteenth century was binocular disparity properly recognized as a depth cue. In the 1830s, Sir Charles Wheatstone invented a device called the **stereoscope** (Figure 6.29) that presented one image to one eye and a different image to the other eye. The stereoscope proved that the visual system treats binocular disparity as a depth cue, regardless of whether the disparity is produced by actual or simulated images of a scene.

For the average citizen the stereoscope was not science; it was home entertainment. The Wheatstone stereoscope held two different images in two different places. In the 1850s, however, David Brewster and Oliver Wendell Holmes invented viewers (Figure 6.30*a*) that held a card with a double image like that shown in Figure 6.30*b*. The double images were captured by cameras with two lenses separated by about 2 inches, the distance between the average human's eyes. This arrangement allows stereo cameras to take a pair of pictures that mimic the images produced by the projective geometry of human binocular vision. Photographers traveled the world with these stereo cameras, capturing far-off scenes in a way that enabled a London schoolchild to see, for example, the British Army in Cape Town, South Africa, in a vivid three dimensions. (For a guide to more of these historical images, as well as many other stereograms, see **Web Essay 6.2: Stereo Images on the Web**.)

(*a*)

(*b*)

FIGURE 6.31 Try to converge (cross) or diverge (uncross) your eyes so that you see three (rather than two or four) sets of squares here. If you succeed, you will probably be able to see that the three white squares lie at different depths in the central image.

A stereoscope is very helpful, but you don't actually need one to experience stereopsis. You can teach yourself a technique known as **free fusion**, which John Frisby (1980) called "the poor man's stereoscope." **Figure 6.31** contains two almost identical pictures. If you cross your eyes hard, you should see four sets of squares. This is the phenomenon of double vision (diplopia), described in the previous section. Two of those sets are seen with the left eye and two with the right. The trick is to relax just a bit until you see just three sets of squares. The far-left set is seen only in the left eye; the far-right set, only in the right; but the middle set is the fusion of one set seen by the left eye and another set, seen by the right eye. This fusion of the separate images seen by the two eyes makes stereopsis possible. It is also possible to get there by diverging the eyes, relaxing them until you see three sets of squares.

Achieving the perception of three, instead of four or two, sets of squares in Figure 6.31 is the first step toward free fusion. The second step is to bring the middle set into focus. As noted earlier, convergence and accommodation normally work in lockstep, so crossing your eyes automatically leads your ciliary muscles to make your lenses more spherical. Similar problems (in the opposite direction) will occur if you diverge your eyes. To see the middle set of squares clearly, you have to decouple accommodation and convergence. If you can manage it, then the image will come into focus and the three white squares will appear to lie at different depths in the middle of the three sets of squares that you're seeing. When viewed normally, notice that the white squares in the left and right panels look misaligned in opposite directions. Those are the monocular views. When you free-fuse, the opposite misalignments become the binocular disparity and your visual system converts that disparity into a perception of depth.

The depth that you see depends on whether you converged or diverged your eyes. We described crossing, or converging, the eyes. As noted, it is also possible to free-fuse the images in Figure 6.31 by *diverging* your eyes. Divergence requires focusing on a point beyond the plane of the page, so that the image of the left-hand set of squares falls on the left fovea and the image of the right-hand set falls on the right fovea. Because the images falling on the two retinas in the divergence method are reversed compared to the convergence situation, the disparities are reversed and the perceived depth will be reversed. If you converge, the top square will be the farthest back. If you diverge, it will appear closest to you. Either converging or diverging will produce a clear stereoscopic effect, so give it a try.

Before we go on, we should note that approximately 3–5% of the population lacks stereoscopic depth perception—a condition known as **stereoblindness**.

free fusion The technique of converging (crossing) or diverging the eyes in order to view a stereogram without a stereoscope.

stereoblindness An inability to make use of binocular disparity as a depth cue. This term is typically used to describe individuals with vision in both eyes. Someone who has lost one (or both) eyes is not typically described as "stereoblind."

Stereoblind individuals might be able to achieve the perception of three sets of squares in Figure 6.31, but the little white squares will not pop out in depth. Stereoblindness is usually a secondary effect of childhood visual disorders such as strabismus, in which the two eyes are misaligned. If you had such a visual disorder during childhood and/or you've been diagnosed with stereoblindness, we apologize but you just won't perceive depth in the stereograms presented here and on the website. That said, many people who try and fail to see depth in stereograms have "normal" vision (wearing glasses doesn't count as abnormal). Those people just need practice, so don't give up. **Web Activity 6.3: Stereoscopes and Stereograms** provides more stereograms for practice, and **Web Essay 6.2: Stereo Images on the Web** leads to another website with more tips for free-fusing.

> FURTHER DISCUSSION of strabismus can be found in Chapter 3 on page 83.

Random Dot Stereograms

random dot stereogram (RDS) A stereogram made of a large number (often in the thousands) of randomly placed dots. Random dot stereograms contain no monocular cues to depth. Stimuli visible stereoscopically in random dot stereograms are Cyclopean stimuli.

For 100 years or so after the invention of the stereoscope, it was generally supposed that stereopsis occurred relatively late in the processing of visual stimuli. The idea was that the first step in free-fusing images such as those in **Figure 6.32** would be to analyze the input as a face. We would then use the slight disparities between the left-eye and right-eye images of the nose, eyes, chin, and other objects and parts to enrich the sense that the nose sticks out in front of the face, that the eyes are slightly sunken, and so on.

Bela Julesz, a Hungarian radar engineer who spent most of his career at Bell Labs in New Jersey, thought the conventional wisdom might be backward. He theorized that stereopsis might be used to *discover* objects and surfaces in the world. Why would this be useful? Julesz thought that stereopsis might help reveal camouflaged objects. A mouse might be the same color as its background, but out in the open it would be in front of the background. A cat that could use stereopsis to break the mouse's camouflage would be a more successful hunter. (Cats do have stereopsis, by the way [Blake, 1988; R. Fox and Blake, 1971].) To prove his point, Julesz (1964, 1971) made use of **random dot stereograms** (**RDSs**), an example of which is shown in **Figure 6.33**. If you can free-fuse these images, you will see a pair of squares, one sticking out like a bump, the other looking like a hole in the texture (which one is the bump and which is the hole depends, again, on whether you converge or diverge your eyes).

FIGURE 6.32 A stereo photograph of a woman's face.

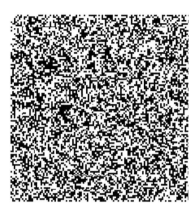

FIGURE 6.33 If you can free-fuse this random dot stereogram, you will see two rectangular regions: one in front of the plane of the page, the other behind the page. Which is which depends on whether you converge or diverge in order to fuse the two squares.

The important point about RDSs is that we cannot see the squares in either of the component images. We cannot see the squares using any monocular depth cues. These are shapes that are defined by binocular disparity alone. Julesz called such stimuli **Cyclopean**, after the one-eyed Cyclops of Homer's *Odyssey*. Wheatstone showed with his stereoscope that binocular disparity is a necessary condition for stereopsis. Julesz demonstrated with the RDS that disparity is *sufficient* for stereopsis. To understand how random dot stereograms are made, visit **Web Activity 6.3: Stereoscopes and Stereograms**, which also explains "magic eye" or "wallpaper" stereograms, known more technically as "autostereograms."

Cyclopean Referring to stimuli that are defined by binocular disparity alone. Named after the one-eyed Cyclops of Homer's *Odyssey*.

Stereo Movies, TV, and Video Games

Whereas the Brewster stereoscope provided home entertainment in Victorian times, in our day 3D movies, TV, and video games are the new stereoscope. Actually, 3D movies have been around for more than 60 years. In general, 3D movies make use of stereoscopic photography (which records the images as seen from two slightly different perspectives) and 3D glasses (which separate the images to the two eyes, so that disparity provides additional cues to depth). Some of the earliest 3D movies used "anaglyphic" glasses, in which one eye had a red lens and the other a blue or green lens, to view the images (Figure 6.34). Images were filtered through separate filters, so that one eye saw

FIGURE 6.34 An audience watching a stereo movie in the 1950s.

one set of images, and the other eye saw the other set. You've probably seen the anaglyphic method in comic books. Later, filmmakers used polarization to separate the images to the two eyes and polarizing glasses to view them. A recent advance on the anaglyphic method is the use of interference filters to present specific wavelengths of red, green, and blue for the right eye, and different wavelengths of red, green, and blue for the left eye. Very expensive goggles that filter out the specific wavelengths enable the filmgoer to see a three-dimensional image and enable the movie theater to charge a few extra dollars per ticket.

Many modern 3D movies, TV, and video games use special glasses that contain liquid crystals (known as LCD shutter glasses) and enable the presentation of images to each eye that are synchronized with the images on the movie, TV, or computer screen. In this method, alternate frames of the movie are presented to different eyes. All of the systems described here have the drawback that they require special glasses or goggles to see in three dimensions. However, certain clever methods do not require glasses. For example, in a method known as lenticular printing, the images are digitally split and interleaved—left, right, left, right, …—at a fixed spacing. A special array of many tiny lenses placed on the screen ensures that the left eye sees only the "left" image and the right eye sees only the "right" image. This setup permits three-dimensional viewing without glasses or other paraphernalia. Nintendo released a small video game console based on this principle in 2011. By the time you read this, some clever inventor may have developed a large-screen system that allows you to see stereoscopic movies or video games with your unaided eyes.

Using Stereopsis

The applications of stereopsis go well beyond entertainment. The military has known for a long time that you can get more information out of aerial surveillance if your view of the ground is stereoscopic. However, if you've ever looked out the window from thousands of feet in the air, you may have noticed the ground looks rather flat. This is yet more geometry. With eyes a few centimeters apart, you don't get adequate disparity from distant targets. What you need are eyes separated by hundreds of feet. This can be done if you have a plane and a special camera. **Figure 6.35** reprints a figure from a 1951 issue of *Popular Mechanics* in which Colonel George W. Goddard showed the public how images taken from two vantage points produced stereo images during the Korean War.

FIGURE 6.35 As this magazine from the 1950s shows, it is possible to make effective stereoscopic images of terrain by taking two aerial pictures from two, quite widely separated viewpoints.

FIGURE 6.36 This stereo mammogram was created by taking X-rays of a woman's breast from two viewpoints. If you can free-fuse, you will see the structures in the image separate in depth, making it easier to decide whether two filaments are part of the same or different structures. (Courtesy of David Getty.)

We can also use stereopsis to have a better look inside the body. Figure 6.36 shows a stereo pair of mammograms, X-rays of the breast used to detect breast cancer. Actually, we've printed the image of the left breast on the left and the right in the figure, with the right breast in the middle. If you free-fuse the images so that you see four breast images, one of the two center images will have the correct disparities (depending on whether you diverge or converge your eyes to free-fuse). The correct one will show the white wire—a marker for the surgeon—on top of the breast. You can see that the breast tissue is characterized by a network of intersecting structures. This is like our earlier example of looking at the little branches of a tree while lying on your back with just one eye open. It can be very hard to tell which linelike structures actually intersect and which ones lie at different depths. This turns out to be important when reading a mammogram. A starlike structure might be a sign of cancer, but not if it is an accidental viewpoint (see Chapter 4) of structures at different depths in the breast forming a suspicious pattern in a two-dimensional projection. Stereopsis can disambiguate this situation. If you can free-fuse these images, you will see the texture in three dimensions, and you will be able to determine how different structures relate to each other in depth. Stereoscopic displays are beginning to be used in radiology (Held and Hui, 2011), and they can reduce the error rate in these important tasks (Getty, D'Orsi, and Pickett, 2008).

correspondence problem In binocular vision, the problem of figuring out which bit of the image in the left eye should be matched with which bit in the right eye. The problem is particularly vexing when the images consist of thousands of similar features, like dots in random dot stereograms.

> FURTHER DISCUSSION of stereo sensation can be found in Chapter 10 (sound localization; pp. 275–280) and Chapter 14 (binaral olfaction; page 412).

Stereoscopic Correspondence

If you successfully free-fused the random dot patterns in Figure 6.33, you solved a truly daunting problem. Even if you didn't, if you have normal binocular vision you are solving the **correspondence problem** all the time. The correspondence problem is the problem of figuring out which bit of the image in the left eye should be matched with which bit in the right eye. Figures 6.37 and 6.38 use an extremely simple situation to illustrate why correspondence is so tricky. There are, of course, just three dots in Figure 6.37. Figure 6.38a traces the paths of rays of light from the printed circles on the page to the images on your retinas. The retinal images of the circles are labeled to make it clear which image on the left retina corresponds to which image on the right retina, but your visual system has no such labels. All it knows about is the retinal images, as shown in Figure

FIGURE 6.37 Is this a simple picture or a complicated computational problem?

(*a*) The actual situation

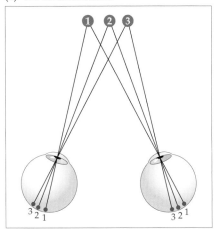

(*b*) What the visual system knows

(*c*) Another plausible interpretation

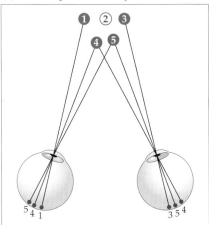

FIGURE 6.38 Interpreting the visual information from the three circles in Figure 6.37.

uniqueness constraint In stereopsis, the observation that a feature in the world is represented exactly once in each retinal image. This constraint simplifies the correspondence problem.

FIGURE 6.39 A low spatial frequency–filtered version of the stereogram in Figure 6.33. Correspondence is much easier to achieve here. If you free-fuse these two images, you will be able to tell roughly where the rectangles lie. The high frequencies in Figure 6.33, however, give more precise information.

6.38*b*. Figure 6.38*c* shows another possible geometric interpretation of the situation: if the left retinal image of circle 2 is matched to the right retinal image of circle 1, and the left retinal image of circle 3 is matched to the right retinal image of circle 2, you will perceive *four* circles, with the inner pair of circles perceived as floating in front of the outer pair. (In fact, you may be able to experience this for yourself if you can cross your eyes correctly.)

With only three elements in the visual scene, it isn't hard to imagine how the visual system might achieve the proper correspondence: first match the two circles whose images fall on the foveas; then match the two images to the left of the foveas with each other; then match the two images to the right of the foveas. Before random dot stereograms, a similar logic seemed reasonable for more complex scenes too. Go back to the face in Figure 6.32. Our visual systems could solve the correspondence problem by first finding the parts of the two faces and then matching nose to nose, mouth to mouth, and so forth. The random dot stereogram in Figure 6.33, however, contains thousands of identical black and white dots falling on each retina. How can we be sure that the dot in the center of the fovea of one eye corresponds to the dot in the center of the other eye? Even if we knew that, could we really match each dot in the right eye with just one dot in the left eye? If there were a little dirt on the page, would the whole process collapse? How in the world does our visual system succeed in making the proper matches?

Matching thousands of left-eye dots to thousands of right-eye dots in Figure 6.33 would require a lot of work for any computational system. However, the problem is simpler if we look at a blurred version of the stereogram. Blurring leaves only the low-spatial-frequency information. **Figure 6.39** shows the low spatial frequencies of the stereogram from Figure 6.33. Now, rather than thousands of dots, we have just a few large blobs. If you free-fuse the images in Figure 6.39, you won't see the rectangles clearly. You may not see them at all; but, as David Marr and Tomaso Poggio (1979) realized, if you match the low-spatial-frequency blobs, you have a good approximation of what goes with what. You can work from there to determine how to match up the high-frequency dots, edges, and so forth.

Marr and Poggio also suggested two additional heuristics for achieving correspondence: the uniqueness and continuity constraints. The **uniqueness constraint** is the reality that a feature in the world is represented exactly once in each retinal image.

Working in the opposite direction, the visual system knows that each monocular image feature (e.g., a nose or a dot) should be paired with exactly one feature in the other image. The **continuity constraint** holds that, except at the edges of objects, neighboring points in the world lie at similar distances from the viewer. Accordingly, disparity should change smoothly at most places in the image. (These constraints are difficult to illustrate on a static page, but **Web Activity 6.4: Stereoscopic Correspondence** provides dynamic explanations.)

The Physiological Basis of Stereopsis

Now that we know something about the theoretical basis of stereopsis, we can ask how it is implemented by the human brain. The most fundamental requirement is that input from the two eyes must converge onto the same cell. As noted in Chapter 3, this convergence does not happen until the striate cortex, where most neurons are binocular (Hubel and Wiesel, 1962). A binocular neuron has two receptive fields, one in each eye. In binocular striate cortex neurons, these two receptive fields are generally very similar in the two eyes, sharing nearly identical orientation and spatial-frequency tuning, as well as the same preferred speed and direction of motion (Hubel and Wiesel, 1973). Thus, these cells are well suited to the task of matching images in the two eyes.

Many binocular neurons respond best when the retinal images are on corresponding points in the two retinas, thereby providing a neural basis for the horopter. However, many other binocular neurons respond best when similar images occupy slightly *different* positions on the retinas of the two eyes (Barlow, Blakemore, and Pettigrew, 1967; Pettigrew, Nikara, and Bishop, 1968). In other words, these neurons are tuned to a particular binocular disparity (diagramed in **Figure 6.40**).

continuity constraint In stereopsis, the observation that, except at the edges of objects, neighboring points in the world lie at similar distances from the viewer. This is one of several constraints that have been proposed to help solve the correspondence problem.

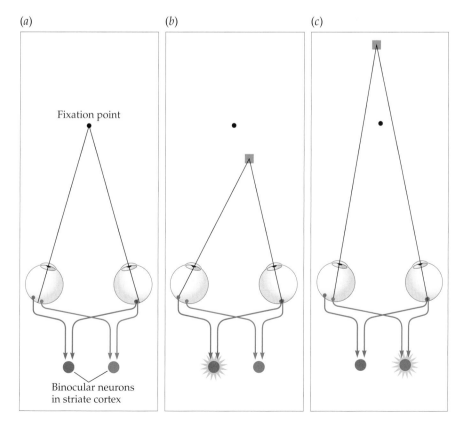

(*a*)   (*b*)   (*c*)

Fixation point

Binocular neurons in striate cortex

FIGURE 6.40 In these simplified diagrams of receptive fields for two binocular disparity–tuned neurons in striate cortex, the red neuron "sees" stimuli falling on the red receptive fields, and the blue neuron responds to stimuli falling on the blue receptive fields (these receptive fields overlap on the right retina). (*a*) The overall picture, showing the fixation point in relation to the two retinas. (*b*) The red neuron responds best to a stimulus closer to and slightly to the right of the fixation point. (*c*) The blue neuron responds best if its preferred stimulus is behind and slightly to the left of fixation.

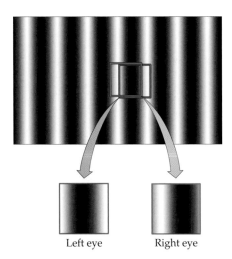

FIGURE 6.41 This figure represents the receptive field of a binocular cell sensitive to the relative phase between the images in the two eyes. See text for details.

Left eye   Right eye

Recall the distinction, from earlier in this chapter, between metrical and nonmetrical depth cues. Stereopsis can be used both metrically and nonmetrically. Nonmetrical stereopsis might just tell you that a feature lies in front of or behind the plane of fixation. Gian Poggio and his colleagues (Poggio and Talbot, 1981) found disparity-tuned neurons of this sort in V2 and some higher cortical areas. Some neurons responded positively to disparities near zero—that is, to images falling on corresponding retinal points. Other neurons were broadly tuned to a range of crossed (near) or uncrossed (far) disparities. On the other hand, stereopsis can also be used in a very precise, metrical manner. Indeed, stereopsis is a "hyperacuity" like Vernier acuity (see **Web Essay 3.1: Hyperacuity**) with thresholds smaller than the size of a cone. Both of these forms of stereopsis have their uses, and fMRI data suggest that the dorsal *where* pathway (see Chapter 4) is most interested in metrical stereopsis, while the ventral *what* pathway makes do with more categorical, near-versus-far information (Preston et al., 2008).

Interestingly, fine-grained metrical stereopsis may not be produced by receptive fields that are just a little displaced from each other in absolute spatial terms. Instead, the receptive fields in the two eyes may differ in "phase." **Figure 6.41** illustrates the concept. Suppose we have two cells, both looking at the same part of the visual field but each sensitive to stimulation of only one eye. The left-eye cell prefers a dark bar, flanked by light regions. This would be an OFF-center, ON-surround cell of the sort described in Chapter 3. The right-eye cell likes an edge, dark on the right. That is a 90-degree phase shift from the preferred stimulus of the left-eye cell. A physical stimulus, in the plane of fixation, would not stimulate both of these cells at the same time. If both cells were optimally stimulated at the same time, the image on the left retina would have to be shifted relative to the image on the right retina. That phase shift corresponds to a binocular disparity and could be used to derive depth from the two retinal images. Ohzawa and Freeman (1986a, 1986b) found cortical cells with receptive fields in the left eye that were phase-shifted inputs from the receptive field in the right eye.

> FURTHER DISCUSSION of phase as it relates to vision can be found in Chapter 3 on page 61. Sensitivity to phase is also important for temporal coding of sound frequency (Chapter 9, page 260).

Combining Depth Cues

If the chapters of this book were novels, this chapter could be said to have the same plot as the discussion of object recognition in Chapter 4, but with different characters. In Chapter 4 we talked about a set of cues that enable us to group local features together into possible objects and then to recognize those objects. We described the process as a sort of committee effort in which different sources of information each contribute their opinions. In this chapter we've covered multiple sources of depth information and they, too, need to be combined. Any or all of these cues might be available to the visual system when we're viewing any visual scene. None of the cues are foolproof, and none work in every possible situation. For example, relative height produces inconsistent or misleading information if we can't see the point at which an object touches the ground. All we really have is a collection of guesses about possible depth relations between different objects in our visual field.

By carefully combining and weighting these guesses, the visual system generally arrives at a coherent, and more or less accurate, representation of three-dimensional space. Helmholtz, writing in the nineteenth century (and translated into English in the twentieth), called this automatic cue combination process "unconscious inference" (Helmholtz, 1924). In recent years, a number of vision researchers have been attempting to put this sort of argument on the more rigorous mathematical footing of the **Bayesian approach** that we introduced in Chapter 4.

The Bayesian Approach Revisited

Recall that the basic insight of Reverend Bayes was that prior knowledge could influence estimates of the probability of a current observation. To review, here is the basic equation:

$$P(A\,|\,O) = P(A) \times P(O\,|\,A)/P(O)$$

Bayes' theorem enables us to calculate $P(A\,|\,O)$, the probability that the world is in state A, given our observation O. This probability can be figured out from $P(A)$, the prior probability of state A, multiplied by $P(O\,|\,A)$ (the probability of *this* observation, given state A), divided by $P(O)$, the probability of collecting observation O.

Let's unpack Bayes' observations with a concrete example. Suppose our visual system is confronted with the retinal image shown in **Figure 6.42**. There are an infinite number of possible ways to produce this retinal image. Actually, this is a bit of a problem for our use of Bayes' theorem. We don't *really* know the prior probabilities (M. Jones and Love, 2011). Still, we can acknowledge that limit and make good use of the basic insight that some hypotheses are more likely than others. Three hypotheses about our pennies are shown in **Figure 6.43**. Maybe the two pennies are the same size, but the one on the left is slightly farther away than the one on the right (Figure 6.43*a*). Maybe the penny on the right is much smaller, but also much closer, than the penny on the left (Figure 6.43*b*). Maybe the two pennies are equidistant, but the penny on the left is smaller and has had a bite taken out of it (Figure 6.43*c*). If you don't

FIGURE 6.42 Retinal image of a simple visual scene.

Bayesian approach A way of formalizing the idea that our perception is a combination of the current stimulus and our knowledge about the conditions of the world—what is and is not likely to occur. The Bayesian approach is stated mathematically as Bayes' theorem—$P(A|O) = P(A) \times P(O|A)/P(O)$—which enables us to calculate the probability (P) that the world is in a particular state (A) given a particular observation (O).

(*a*)   (*b*)   (*c*)

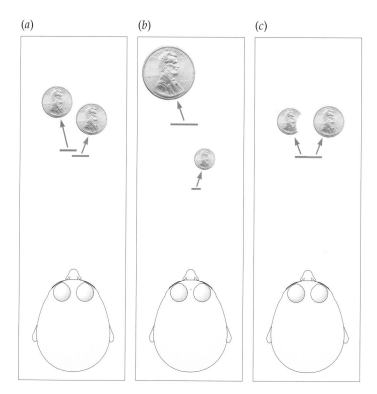

FIGURE 6.43 Three of the infinite number of scenes that could generate the retinal image in Figure 6.42.

ideal observer A theoretical observer with complete access to the best available information and the ability to combine different sources of information in the optimal manner. It can be useful to compare human performance to that of an ideal observer.

think the set of possibilities is infinite, remember that if the size can vary, the distances can vary forever. One penny could be on the moon (it would have to be a really big penny).

How does the visual system decide what we're actually seeing? Which interpretation seems most likely? That is the core of the Bayesian approach (except that it's all automatic; our conscious selves do not get to make the decision). In our experience, all pennies are the same size. This cue of familiar size is one source of prior knowledge in this case. It makes $P(A)$, the *prior probability* of scene A, higher than $P(B)$ or $P(C)$. Furthermore, for the scene in Figure 6.43c to produce the retinal image in Figure 6.42, we would have to be seeing the scene from one of those unusual and unlikely "accidental viewpoints." It is much more likely that the points of contact between penny 1 and penny 2 reflect occlusion. Thus, $P(O\,|\,C)$, the probability of this observation given that C is the true state of the world, is very low. If we were to plug all these probabilities into Bayes' equation, we would find that $P(A\,|\,O)$ is highest. Given the image in Figure 6.42, the most likely answer is the scene depicted in 6.43a.

How precisely can we know the size of a penny? Are they all absolutely identical, or do they vary? If we measured them, there would be some error in the measurement. We simply could not be perfect. That imperfection is a feature of every cue we've discussed here. How precisely can we calculate binocular disparity, for instance? That error puts a limit on reliability of the cue. As an analogy, this is why you were taught about "significant figures" in high school science class. It makes no sense to give your weight as 175.489673969 pounds, because the scale just is not that precise. If we know the quality of each source of information, we can determine the best possible performance of someone using that information. This is known as **ideal observer** analysis (W. S. Geisler, 1989; Hillis et al., 2004).

For the two pennies of Figure 6.42, it is interesting that we and our committees are so willing to come to the quick conclusion that a closer penny is occluding a farther penny. After all, the real answer is that the stimulus is an image on a flat page. There are no pennies and no depth. Moreover, other depth cues, such as stereopsis and convergence, are telling the visual system that the two objects in the scene are equidistant. The unconscious decisions we make involve a complex set of cue combination rules that are only beginning to be worked out. It is not a matter of one cue, one vote. Here, for example, stereopsis information does not contribute to our interpretation of the depth relationships in Figure 6.42. Nevertheless, it probably does provide one of the cues that tell us that this is a flat book illustration.

Illusions and the Construction of Space

If visual perception of the world is a best guess about the causes of visual input, then interesting things should happen when a guess is wrong. In some sense, as with the pennies we just discussed, a guess is wrong whenever we look at a two-dimensional picture and see it as three-dimensional. As noted, however, we are not really fooled into thinking that the picture actually is three-dimensional. It would be more accurate to say that we make a plausible guess about the three-dimensional world that is being represented in the two-dimensional picture.

What about a situation like that shown in **Figure 6.44**? In one of the five pairs of horizontal lines (and only one), the two lines are the same length. Can you pick the correct pair? In fact, it is the second from the left. Odds

FIGURE 6.44 In which image are the two horizontal lines the same length?

FIGURE 6.45 The two people lying across these train tracks are the same size in the image. You can verify this by measuring them. However, if they were really in the three-dimensional world depicted in the image, then the more distant person would need to be much larger in the three-dimensional world in order to produce these images in the two-dimensional figure.

are you picked the third or fourth pair, even though the bottom line in both of those images is physically longer than the top line. This is known as the "Ponzo illusion," named after Mario Ponzo, who described the effect in 1913. What causes this illusion? For many years, a popular family of theories has held that the illusion is a guess gone wrong—a situation in which we overinterpret the depth cues in a two-dimensional image. The basic idea is illustrated in Figure 6.45. Maybe the two tilted lines that induce the illusion in each image of Figure 6.44 are being interpreted by the visual system as linear-perspective cues like the train tracks in **Figure 6.45**. If so, then objects that were the same size in the two-dimensional image would represent objects of different sizes in the three-dimensional world.

Such accounts are very compelling and exist for a wide range of visual illusions (Gillam, 1980). (See **Web Essay 6.3: The Moon Illusion**.) They are consistent with the view that the job of the visual system is to use available cues to make an intelligent guess about the world (Gregory, 1966, 1970). Just because an answer is plausible, however, doesn't mean it's right. In **Figure 6.46a**, line B looks longer than line A. That makes sense if we're interpreting these lines as lines lying at different distances on the wall of the colonnade. As

(a)

(b)

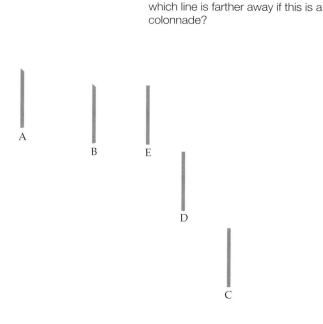

FIGURE 6.46 All of the red lines in this illustration are the same length. Does B look bigger than A? Does D look bigger than C? In each case, which line is farther away if this is a colonnade?

FIGURE 6.47 Despite their appearance, the vertical lines are parallel in (a), as are the horizontal lines in (b).

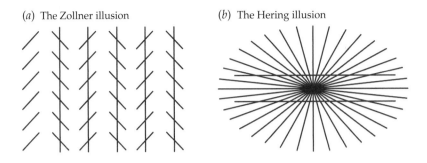

(a) The Zollner illusion

(b) The Hering illusion

in the Ponzo illusion, if line B is farther away than A, then the same image size implies a larger size in the real world. But what about lines C and D? Surely D would be interpreted as farther away than C. Does it look convincingly larger? Figure 6.46b reveals what you probably guessed—that all five of the lines in 6.46a are the same length.

Prinzmetal, Shimamura, and Mikolinski (2001) use a demonstration like this as part of their argument that the Ponzo illusion is not a by-product of depth cues at all. They argued that it reflects a more general aspect of the visual system's response to tilted lines, and is related to illusions like the Zollner and Hering illusions illustrated in **Figure 6.47** (which we will *not* try to explain; see Prinzmetal and Beck, 2001). The point is debatable. After all, line E looks very big down there at the apparent end of the colonnade in Figure 6.46a. Who is right? This note of caution reminds us that even the best theory must always face the next experiment. It will be interesting to see how many of the convincing ideas in this book still seem credible in a generation.

Binocular Rivalry and Suppression

The preceding sections demonstrated that objects in the world often project images on our two retinas that do not overlap (that is, the images fall on non-corresponding retinal points), and that the visual system is physiologically prepared to deal with these discrepancies via disparity-tuned neurons in striate cortex and beyond. But what happens when completely different stimuli are presented to the two eyes? You can answer this question for yourself by fixating on a small object across the room, such as a clock, and moving your hand up so that your fingers occlude the object in the right eye (making sure the left eye still has an unobstructed view). It would seem a bad idea to fuse the fingers and the clock into a single perception of something that does not exist in the world. Accordingly, the visual system chooses instead to *suppress* one image and perceive the other. In the present situation, you probably see the clock as though you were looking through a hole in your hand. (For an even more compelling perception of a hole in your hand, try the demonstration of suppression in **Web Activity 6.2: Binocular Disparity**.)

How does the visual system "decide" what to see? The more interesting of the two stimuli is likely to be dominant. *Interesting* in this case has several meanings. The most important factor is which stimulus is more salient to the early stages of cortical visual processing. High contrast is more salient than low contrast, bright is better than dim, moving objects are more interesting than stationary ones, and so forth (Fahle, 1982). The meaning of the stimulus also has an effect (Yu and Blake, 1992), as does what you're attending to (Ooi and He, 1999).

The competition between the two eyes for control of visual perception, known as **binocular rivalry**, is never completely won by either eye (Alais and

binocular rivalry The competition between the two eyes for control of visual perception, which is evident when completely different stimuli are presented to the two eyes.

FIGURE 6.48 Binocular rivalry. If you free-fuse these two images, you will be able to watch the blue verticals and orange horizontals engage in the perceptual battle known as binocular rivalry.

Blake, 2005; Wheatstone, 1852) or either stimulus (Blake and Logothetis, 2002). If you stare at the combination of the clock and hand long enough, your fingers will eventually conquer the visual territory, only to surrender it back to the clock a moment later. The battle is easier to see if the two combatants are more closely matched. If you free-fuse the two panels of **Figure 6.48**, your visual system will not actually combine the perpendicular stripes in the two center squares. Instead, you will see a battle between the vertically and horizontally striped patches, with regions of dominance growing and shrinking over time as illustrated in **Figure 6.49**.

Binocular rivalry might seem an odd situation that would arise only in a vision lab or a perception course, but a moment's reflection should convince you that the stimuli for rivalry are actually very common. Recall that Panum's fusional area is the region of space surrounding the horopter within which images on the two retinas can be fused. As noted earlier, objects located too far off the horopter—outside Panum's area—are subject to diplopia. In fact, the proportion of the three-dimensional visual world that falls *inside* Panum's area is actually fairly small. Think about two pairs of corresponding points: A_L and A_R, and B_L and B_R (the L and R stand for "left" and "right," respectively). Now imagine that one object falls on two noncorresponding retinal points: A_L and B_R. It follows that *something else* must be forming an image on A_R. There will be noncorresponding images on the corresponding points A_L and A_R (and, similarly, on B_L and B_R). Those are the conditions for rivalry.

The fact that the two eyes are seeing different images brings us to an ancient problem: the problem of binocular single vision. Why, when we see one elephant in one eye and one elephant in the other eye, don't we perceive two elephants? Given what we've learned in this chapter, we're now in a position to answer this question. If the elephant is within Panum's area, we fuse its two images into a single stereoscopic perception. If it is outside Panum's area, we normally suppress one of the copies. Why don't we see the rivalry? In part, because we aren't looking. Our attention and eyes are typically directed toward the foveated object or toward objects falling on roughly corresponding points in each eye. Moreover, acuity is so bad in the periphery of the visual fields that, even when objects are vying for binocular precedence, the rivalry is quite indistinct.

Left eye   Right eye

FIGURE 6.49 If blue vertical bars are shown to one eye while orange horizontal bars are shown to the other, the two stimuli will battle for dominance, with different stimuli dominating at different times in different parts of the visual field.

(a)

(b)

FIGURE 6.50 Binocular rivalry is not just a fight between the two eyes. If you can free-fuse these pairs of images, you will see a typical example of rivalry (a). Different images in each eye struggle for dominance. The chimp and the text struggle for dominance in panel (b) too, but this is pattern rivalry: the two eyes are actually cooperating to put together coherent views of the chimp or the text. (From Kovacs et al., 1996.)

The classic demonstrations of rivalry pit a stimulus in one eye against a stimulus in the other eye. More recently, it has become clear that rivalry is part of a larger effort by the visual system to come up with the most likely version of the world, given the current retinal images (sounds Bayesian again, doesn't it?) (Clifford, 2009). If you can free-fuse **Figure 6.50**, you will see the monkey and the text battle each other in Figure 6.50a. That is just standard binocular rivalry. Interestingly, you will see a similar monkey/text rivalry in Figure 6.50b. In that case the monkey is being put together from bits in the two eyes. Your brain is not trying to pick a winner in a battle between the eyes. It is trying to figure out the world, and if that interesting monkey is seen with one eye in one spot and the other eye in another spot, the brain can put those different bits together into a coherent perception (Blake and Wilson, 2011).

Rivalry is a very useful tool for probing one of the more vexing problems in the neuroscience of perception: what parts of the visual system give rise to the conscious experience of seeing something? For these purposes, the great feature of rivalry is that it dissociates the stimulus on the retina from the stimulus that you see. Now, imagine that you record from single cells somewhere in the monkey visual system (Logothetis and Schall, 1989) or you use functional MRI to look at the working human brain. If you train the monkeys or ask humans to monitor their perception ("Do you see vertical or horizontal?"), you can ask whether the neural signal in a specific part of the visual pathway follows the physical stimulus or the perceived stimulus. It is a complex and evolving story, but one that clearly shows that conscious visual awareness is not something that happens in one discrete step in a chain of visual processing (Tong, Meng, and Blake, 2006).

Development of Binocular Vision and Stereopsis

What is binocular vision like in infants? Babies are born with two eyes, but are they born with stereopsis? If not, how does binocular function develop? In a wonderful conversation about visual development, Davida Teller and Tony Movshon (1986) recalled a lecture by a disillusioned developmental psychologist, John McKee, who argued that the field could be summed up by three laws:

1. As children get older, they get better at things.
2. Whatever it is, girls do it before boys.
3. Everything develops along with everything else.

To these "laws," Teller added a summary statement: "Things start out badly, then they get better; then, after a long time, they get worse again" (Teller and Movshon, 1986).

As it turns out, research over the last 25 years or so has shown that visual development provides support for the first and second "laws," but not for a strict form of the third. The development of binocular vision and stereopsis provides one of the strongest violations of that third law.

Most visual functions indeed start off badly (but not as badly as we used to think) and then improve steadily until they reach adult levels; however, the development of stereopsis is surprising, in that infants are essentially blind to disparity until about 4 months of age. At that point, stereopsis appears quite suddenly—almost out of the blue. Of course, measuring stereopsis (or anything else) in infants is no easy task, but developmental psychologists have been very inventive in designing methods for assessing development.

Despite differences in techniques and procedures, most investigators agree about the onset of stereopsis. **Figure 6.51** summarizes the results of several studies, showing the age at which stereopsis can first be detected. These studies (and others like them) looked for evidence indicating that infants could reliably detect a large binocular disparity (typically on the order of 30–60 arc minutes). The agreement among the studies is remarkable. Infants are essentially stereoblind before 3 months, with most infants showing a sudden onset of stereopsis between 3 and 5 months.

Stereopsis is not an all-or-none phenomenon. Just as an individual's acuity is a measure of his ability to resolve spatial detail, **stereoacuity** is a measure of the smallest binocular disparity that can generate a sensation of depth. Once an infant develops stereopsis, stereoacuity increases rapidly to near adult levels (**Figure 6.52**). Birch and Petrig (1996) found that stereoacuity rose from essentially nothing before 4 months to near adult levels by 6 months! This time course is very different from the time course in the development of simple acuity. Though coarsely present at birth, basic acuity takes years to reach adult levels. The same difference between basic acuity and stereoacuity is seen in monkeys (O'Dell and Boothe, 1997), but the overall rate of development is faster. Interestingly, not only stereoacuity but several other visual functions develop at a rate approximately four times faster than in humans, as if one monkey week were the equivalent of one human month. In keeping with this rule of one human month being equal to one monkey week, stereopsis can be detected in monkeys within the first 3–5 weeks of life, compared to the 3- to 5-month window of onset observed in humans.

How, then, do we explain the sudden emergence of stereopsis in humans at about 4 months? Although newborn infants make convergence eye movements to track a target as it approaches their nose, accurate and consistent convergence probably does not occur until they are 3–4 months old. But we can't conclude that inaccurate convergence prevents stereopsis from developing earlier than 4 months, because convergence need not be very accurate

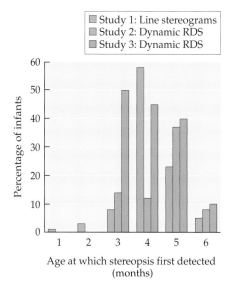

FIGURE 6.51 The onset of stereopsis. This figure shows the percentage of infants demonstrating stereopsis for the first time as a function of their age. In three separate studies (the three different colors), almost all infants showed stereopsis for the first time between 3 and 5 months. (After Birch, 1993.)

stereoacuity A measure of the smallest binocular disparity that can generate a sensation of depth.

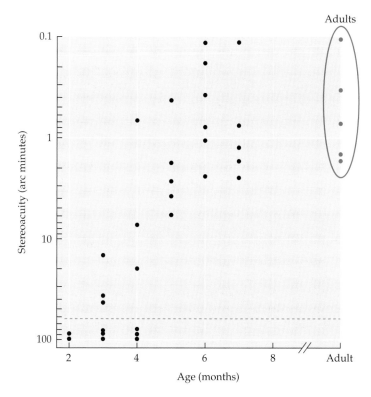

FIGURE 6.52 The development of stereoacuity. Stereoacuity develops to adult levels within the first 6–7 months of life. Data points below the dashed line indicate unmeasurable stereoacuity. (After Birch and Petrig, 1996.)

dichoptic Referring to the presentation of two different stimuli, one to each eye. Different from *binocular* presentation, which could involve both eyes looking at a single stimulus.

in order to detect large disparities. Moreover, several studies used repeating gratings (like striped wallpaper), which would be fused at some disparity even if convergence were inaccurate. Before 4 months, babies don't respond to these stereoscopic stimuli either.

An alternative view is that the failure of stereopsis to develop prior to 4 months might mean that some part of the visual system is immature. Disparity-sensitive neurons in V1 are one plausible candidate for that immature part, but recent anatomical and physiological data suggest that we need to look beyond V1 for an explanation of why infants do not exhibit stereopsis.

Yuzo Chino and his colleagues made the most detailed quantitative study of the binocular responses of V1 neurons of infant monkeys (Chino et al., 1997). They presented a pair of drifting sine wave gratings **dichoptically** (one to each eye). The sine waves were identical in spatial frequency, orientation, contrast, and velocity, and these values were chosen to maximize the cell's response. You will remember, from earlier in this chapter, that a phase difference between the two monocular gratings creates binocular disparity and that some cells in the visual cortex are sensitive to this phase shift. When Chino et al. varied the relative spatial phase of the two drifting sine waves (**Figure 6.53***a*), the response of a binocular neuron waxed and waned (Figure 6.53*b*). The dashed lines in Figure 6.53*b* show the levels of response for each

(*a*)

Left eye

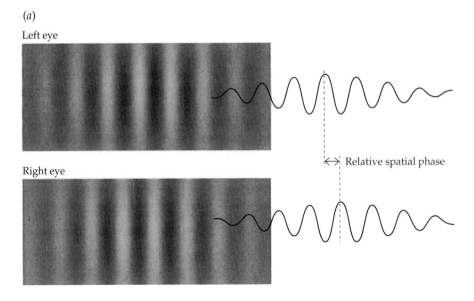

Right eye

Relative spatial phase

(*b*)

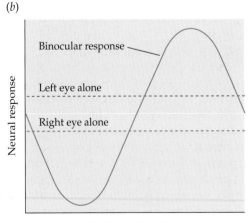

FIGURE 6.53 Interocular phase difference gratings are used to study disparity tuning. (*a*) Two sinusoidal gratings drift differently in each eye, producing a sinusoidal change in spatial phase disparity. (*b*) The response of a binocular neuron. Notice that the binocular response varies with phase, and the monocular responses do not. (After Chino et al., 1997.)

eye, stimulated alone. Notice that for some interocular phase differences, the binocular response was considerably higher than the response through either eye alone. At other interocular phase differences, the binocular response was lower than the response through either eye alone. This sinusoidal binocular phase tuning is the hallmark of this type of binocular neuron in the visual cortex. Using this sensitive method, Chino et al. (1997) found that within the first week of life—well before the onset of stereopsis—infant monkeys had practically the same proportion of phase disparity–sensitive neurons that adults have in primary visual cortex.

In addition, the ocular dominance properties of these infant monkeys were essentially identical to those of adults. Other investigators have also found that ocular dominance columns in the input layers of V1 are essentially adultlike at birth (Horton and Hocking, 1996).

> **FURTHER DISCUSSION** of ocular dominance can be found in Chapter 3 on page 70.

What do these studies tell us about the development of stereopsis? The results suggest that the neural apparatus in V1 of newborns is capable of combining signals from the two eyes and that it is sensitive to interocular disparities. So why are newborns blind to disparity? One possibility is that the extraction of relative disparity, which is needed for stereoacuity, takes place beyond V1, possibly in V2. At this time we do not know much about how V2 neurons in newborns respond to disparity, but emerging evidence suggests that other receptive-field properties mature later in V2 than in V1 (Zhang et al., 2005; Zheng et al., 2007).

Another possibility is that the problem is in V1. Although V1 cells of newborn monkeys are adultlike in their response to interocular phase disparity, these neurons remain immature in several important ways. They do not have adult sensitivity to monocular spatial frequency or direction of motion. Moreover, they are much less responsive overall than are adult neurons (that is, their peak firing rates are considerably lower). In addition, these neurons display more interocular suppression than adult neurons do. Thus, it is also possible that because of the immaturity in V1 neurons, the signals they send to the next stage of processing are too weak or confused to support stereopsis.

Abnormal Visual Experience Can Disrupt Binocular Vision

The presence of all this binocular hardware, even if it is immature, strongly suggests that extensive binocular visual experience is not necessary for binocular connections to form in V1. These connections are present at birth or very shortly thereafter, so we don't need to "learn" or develop binocular vision. However, the normal development of adult binocular vision and stereopsis does require visual experience. In Chapter 3 we learned about Hubel and Wiesel's work on the **critical period**, the period during early visual development when normal binocular visual stimulation is required for normal cortical development. During this period the visual cortex is highly susceptible to any disorder that alters normal binocular visual experience. In cats and monkeys this critical period is approximately the first 3–4 months of life.

We cannot study a child's visual cortex the way we might study a monkey or a cat. How, then, can we estimate the critical period in humans? Some humans are born with two eyes that do not point at the same spot in the world. This not uncommon disorder is known as **strabismus**, as we learned in Chapter 3. The incidence is about 3%. In **esotropia**, one eye is pointed too far toward the nose ("cross-eyed"). In **exotropia**, the deviating eye is pointed too far to the side. There are various ways to treat strabismus. For example, it is possible to

critical period A period of time during development when the organism is particularly susceptible to developmental change. There are critical periods in the development of binocular vision, human language, and so on.

strabismus A misalignment of the two eyes such that a single object in space is imaged on the fovea of one eye, and on a nonfoveal area of the other (turned) eye.

esotropia Strabismus in which one eye deviates inward.

exotropia Strabismus in which one eye deviates outward.

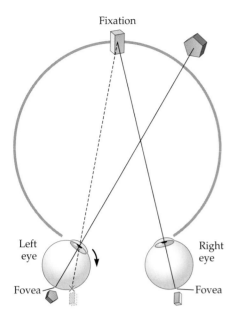

FIGURE 6.54 Left esotropia. The patient wants to fixate on the yellow brick, but the left eye is turned too far toward the nose and, as a result, the left fovea is pointing at a different location (here the purple pentagon), while the image of the yellow brick falls to the right of the left fovea.

tilt aftereffect The perceptual illusion of tilt, produced by adaptation to a pattern of a given orientation.

suppression In vision, the inhibition of an unwanted image. Suppression occurs frequently in persons with strabismus.

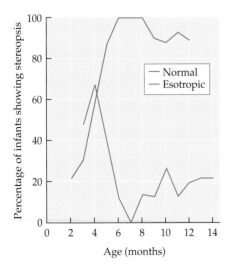

surgically correct the position of the eyes. For the present discussion, however, the important point is that it is possible to test adults who had misaligned eyes at different times and for different durations during childhood.

Recall from Chapter 3 that exposure to lines tilted to one side of vertical will make vertical lines appear tilted to the other side. This is known as the **tilt aftereffect**. One characteristic of the tilt aftereffect is that it shows interocular transfer (transfer of the effect from one eye to the other). If we show the adapting lines to one eye, we can measure an aftereffect through the other eye. This result is generally taken to show that the cells responsible for the effect are binocular; they receive input from both eyes (for some details, see Wolfe and Held, 1981). Individuals who exhibited strabismus during the first 18 months of life do not show normal interocular transfer (Banks, Aslin, and Letson, 1975; Hohmann and Creutzfeldt, 1975). This result provides an indirect estimate of the period during which binocular connections in humans are susceptible to abnormal input.

Let's explore in a bit more detail why strabismus disrupts binocular vision. We will use left esotropia as an example. In left esotropia (**Figure 6.54**), the left eye is turned in. As a consequence, although the object of fixation (the yellow brick in this case) lands on the fovea of the right eye, in the left eye it lands on a region in the "nasal" retina. (The nasal retina is the half of the retina closest to the nose.) This means that the images of the yellow brick are in noncorresponding points in the two eyes. What will the patient see? If an adult becomes esotropic (perhaps because of an injury), she will experience diplopia (double vision), seeing two bricks instead of one. However, people who exhibit strabismus early in life often experience no such problem. Why? Notice that *something* is present at the fovea of the left eye. In Figure 6.54, this something is a purple pentagon. Thus, in strabismus, normally corresponding points in the two eyes receive conflicting information (this situation is known—not unreasonably—as "confusion"). To eliminate diplopia and confusion, the brain **suppresses** one of the two images. It is simply not consciously perceived. In esotropia, the most common pattern is suppression of the input from the eye that is turned in. So, in the example in Figure 6.54, the patient would most likely suppress visual input from the left eye.

Binocular rivalry is a form of suppression, so some suppression is an important part of normal visual experience. Unfortunately, early-onset strabismus can have other, more serious effects on the developing visual nervous system, and on visual performance. For example, strabismus greatly reduces the number of binocular neurons in the visual cortex (Wiesel, 1982). Cells that would normally be driven by both eyes are dominated by only one. You would be correct if you suspected that this situation would disrupt stereopsis. Birch and her colleagues (e.g., Stager and Birch, 1986) followed the development of stereopsis in normal and esotropic infants. **Figure 6.55** illustrates the percentage of infants who showed a measurable ability to perceive stereoscopic depth. The red line shows that by about 6 months of age, almost all normal infants demonstrate stereopsis. In contrast, the esotropes (all of whom were diagnosed with esotropia by 6 months of age) initially demonstrated a normal pattern of stereopsis development. After 4 months, however, very few esotropic infants demonstrated stereopsis.

This result has an interesting parallel in cortical physiology. Chino and his colleagues (Kumagami et al., 2000) made otherwise normal monkeys strabismic.

FIGURE 6.55 Development of stereopsis in normal infants (red line) and in esotropes (blue). Beyond 4 months, very few esotropic infants demonstrated stereopsis. (After Stager and Birch, 1986.)

They found that a brief period of experimental strabismus shortly after the age of onset of stereopsis produced a greater loss of disparity sensitivity and more binocular suppression in V1 neurons than did an earlier episode of strabismus. These physiological and perceptual deficits appear to be permanent and have important implications for the surgical treatment of infantile esotropia. Almost all surgeons agree that treatment should be early, but there has been a lot of debate about just how early. These results suggest that the treatment should take place before the age at which stereopsis normally develops, in order to minimize the damage done by esotropia.

Summary

1. Reconstructing a three-dimensional world from two, non-Euclidean, curved, two-dimensional retinal images is one basic problem faced by the brain.

2. A number of monocular cues provide information about three-dimensional space. These include occlusion, various size and position cues, aerial perspective, linear perspective, motion cues, accommodation, and convergence.

3. Having two eyes is an advantage for a number of reasons, some of which have to do with depth perception. It is important to remember, however, that it is possible to reconstruct the three-dimensional world from a single two-dimensional image. Two eyes have other advantages over just one: expanding the visual field, permitting binocular summation, and providing redundancy if one eye is damaged.

4. Having two laterally separated eyes connected to a single brain also provides us with important information about depth through the geometry of the small differences between the images in each eye. These differences, known as binocular disparities, give rise to stereoscopic depth perception.

5. Random dot stereograms show that we don't need to know what we're seeing before we see it in stereoscopic depth. Binocular disparity alone can support shape perception.

6. Stereopsis has been exploited to add, literally, depth to entertainment—from nineteenth-century photos to twenty-first-century movies. It has also served to enhance the perception of information in military and medical settings.

7. The difficulty of matching an image element in one eye with the correct element in the other eye is known as the correspondence problem. The brain uses several strategies to solve the problem. For example, it reduces the initial complexity of the problem by matching large "blobs" in the low-spatial-frequency information before trying to match every high-frequency detail.

8. Single neurons in the primary visual cortex and beyond have receptive fields that cover a region in three-dimensional space, not just the two-dimensional image plane. Some neurons seem to be concerned with a crude in-front/behind judgment. Other neurons are concerned with more precise, metrical depth perception.

9. When the stimuli on corresponding loci in the two eyes are different, we experience a continual perceptual competition between the two eyes known as binocular rivalry. Rivalry is part of the effort to make the best guess about the current state of the world based on the current state of the input.

10. All of the various monocular and binocular depth cues are combined (unconsciously) according to what prior knowledge tells us about the probability of the current event. Making the wrong guess about the cause of visual input can lead to illusions. Bayes' theorem is the basis of one type of formal understanding of the rules of combination.

11. Stereopsis emerges suddenly at about 4 months of age in humans, and it can be disrupted through abnormal visual experience during a critical period early in life.

Refer to the
Sensation and Perception
Companion Website
sites.sinauer.com/wolfe3e
for activities, essays, study questions, and other study aids.

CHAPTER 7

Victor Bonderoff, *Summer Visitor*, 2006

Attention and Scene Perception

If you're reading this, you are probably a student. If you're a student, you are probably taking more than one course and are therefore very busy. Here's an idea: why not read two books at the same time? One reason this doesn't work is that peripheral visual acuity is limited (as you may recall from Chapter 2): if you're looking at the words on this page, you won't be able to make out the print in another book. This problem can be overcome if the size of the print is increased, as in **Figure 7.1**, but try simultaneously looking at the column of Xs in the figure and reading the two sentences. It should be quite clear that, even with nice large letters, we still cannot read two messages at the same time. Note that we *can* read the words on one side or the other of the Xs while looking at the Xs. We just can't read both sides simultaneously. This is a specific example of a more general problem—that the retinal array contains far more information than we can process. **Figure 7.2** shows another example. We cannot possibly recognize all the objects in this picture at once. That's why "Where's Waldo?" and "I Spy" games are a challenge.

Why can't we process everything at once? Quite literally, we don't have the brains for it. Remember from Chapter 4 that recognizing a single object like an elephant requires a sizable chunk of the brain and its processing power, especially when the elephant could be seen in many different orientations, under different lighting conditions, at different retinal sizes, and so on. Moreover, in order to understand Figure 7.2, we also need to process the relationships between objects—like the fact that the elephant is dousing the yellow car with its trunk. If we do the math for even a fairly small subset of all possible visual stimuli, it turns out that processing everything, everywhere, all at once requires a brain that will not fit in the human head (Tsotsos, 1990).

If it is not possible to process everything all at once, what *should* be processed? This matter can't be left to chance. If we're crossing a road, we need to determine that no car will hit us. Devoting our visual processes exclusively to the doughnut shop on the other side of the street could be dangerous. To deal with this problem, we "pay attention" to some stimuli and not to others. As we will see in this chapter, **attention** is not a single *thing*, and it does not have a single locus in the nervous system (Chun, Golomb, and Turk-Browne, 2011). Rather, *attention* is the name we give to a family of mechanisms that restrict processing in various ways.

Here are some of the distinctions we can make when considering varieties of attention:

- Attention can be internal or external. *External attention* refers to attention to stimuli in the world (our primary concern here), but we should not forget *internal attention*, our ability to attend to one line of thought as opposed to another or to select one response over another.

attention Any of the very large set of selective processes in the brain. To deal with the impossibility of handling all inputs at once, the nervous system has evolved mechanisms that are able to restrict processing to a subset of things, places, ideas, or moments in time.

These	x	Is
letters	x	it
are	x	time
big	x	for
and	x	a
easy	x	quick
to	x	snack
read.	x	yet?

FIGURE 7.1 Even though the letters are big enough to resolve while looking at the *X*s, we simply cannot read the left-hand and right-hand sentences at the same time.

- Attention can be overt or covert. *Overt attention* usually refers to directing a sense organ at a stimulus—fixating the eyes on a single word, for example. If you point your eyes at this page while directing attention to a person of interest off to the left, you are engaging in *covert attention*.
- Reading this text while continuing to be aware of music playing in the room is an example of *divided attention*.
- Watching the pot to note the moment the water begins to boil is *sustained attention*.
- In this chapter we will be most concerned with **selective attention**, the ability to pick one (or a few) out of many stimuli.

These are not mutually exclusive terms. Staring straight ahead while attending only to an interesting person to the exclusion of all else might be described as an act of external, sustained, covert, selective attention.

Although we will focus on visual attention, it is important to remember that attentional mechanisms operate in all of the senses. Getting a shot in the doctor's office may hurt a lot, while an equivalent injury on the playing field may not seem to hurt much at all, because of the different amounts of attention we

FIGURE 7.2 Search for the unicorn in this piece of a "Where's Waldo?" picture. You can searh for Waldo, too, but he is a bit small in this reproduction. (From *Where's Waldo*? © Martin Handford 2005.)

give to each event. We can also use attentional mechanisms to give priority to one sense over others. Right now, you are probably selecting visual stimuli over auditory, even if you have music on in the background. And you didn't even notice the pressure of your posterior on the seat until we mentioned it (sorry for disrupting your attention).

In this chapter, first we discuss evidence that we attend to only one (or perhaps a few) objects at any single moment. We consider attentional selection in space (I am attending to this object and not that object) and selection in time (I was attending to that object, but now I've selected this object). Next we examine the changes that occur in the brain when we attend to one object rather than another, and we will see what happens when the neural substrate of attention is damaged. Having convinced you, we hope, that we can recognize only one object at a time, we will turn to scenes. If we're attending to one object, what does it mean to say that we see a whole scene?

selective attention The form of attention involved when processing is restricted to a subset of the possible stimuli.

reaction time (RT) A measure of the time from the onset of a stimulus to a response.

cue A stimulus that might indicate where (or what) a subsequent stimulus will be. Cues can be valid (giving correct information), invalid (incorrect), or neutral (uninformative).

Selection in Space

To begin, let's consider what it means to "pay attention." A good place to start is with a cueing experiment of the sort pioneered by Michael Posner (1980). Start with the situation shown in **Figure 7.3a**. The subject in the experiment fixates on a central point (*). After a variable delay, a test probe, X, appears in one of the two boxes. All the subject needs to do is hit a response key as fast as possible when the probe appears. The measure of interest is the average **reaction time** (**RT**)—the amount of time that elapses between the point when the probe appears and the point when the subject hits the response key.

Suppose now that the situation is slightly changed: during the waiting period, the subject is given a **cue**, a stimulus that provides a hint about where the target might appear. In Figure 7.3b, the cue is a change in the outline color of one of the two boxes (call this a "peripheral cue"). Because the test probe appears in the cued location, this peripheral cue is said to be a "valid" cue. Given a valid cue, Posner found that RT decreases. Compared to the no-cue control, the subject generally responds faster to the probe, because she is "paying attention" to the correct location. In Figure 7.3c, we have a different kind of cue. The red dot is a "symbolic" cue, but it can also direct attention. Here the rule is "If the cue is green, the probe is likely to be on the left. If the cue is red, the probe is likely to be on the right." In Figure 7.3c, however, the cue is misleading, or "invalid," because the cued location is on the right but the probe appears on the left. RTs are slower here than in the control condition because the subject has been fooled into attending to the wrong location.

We could have valid or invalid instances of either peripheral or symbolic cues. Of course, the experimenter doesn't tell the subject whether a cue will be valid. In a typical experiment, the cue might be valid on 80% of the trials and invalid on the remaining 20%. That would make it in the subject's interest to attend

This cue is valid.

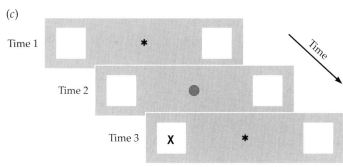

This cue is invalid.

FIGURE 7.3 The Posner cueing paradigm. (*a*) This simple probe detection experiment has two possible probe locations. Here all you have to do is hit one key if the probe appears on the left and another if it appears on the right. (*b*) A valid cue indicates where the target will be. This time the cue is valid; we are telling the truth. (*c*) An invalid cue points to the wrong side. (This is also a different kind of cue—a symbolic cue. Symbolic cues direct attention more slowly.)

FIGURE 7.4 The effect of a cue develops over time. A peripheral cue (like that in Figure 7.3*b*) becomes fully effective 100–150 milliseconds after it appears. A symbolic cue (see Figure 7.3*c*) takes longer to get started and to rise to full effect.

stimulus onset asynchrony (SOA) The time between the onset of one stimulus and the onset of another.

to the cue and would still let the experimenter measure the RTs for plenty of invalid trials.

How long does it take for a cue to redirect our attention? It depends on the nature of the cue. At the beginning of a trial in a Posner cueing experiment, the subject is attending to the fixation point (time 1 in Figure 7.3*b* or *c*). The cue appears at time 2, and the probe appears at time 3. We can measure the timing of the attentional shift by varying the interval between time 2 and time 3. This is called the **stimulus onset asynchrony**, a psychophysical variable that typically goes by its acronym, **SOA**. If the SOA is 0 milliseconds (ms), the cue and probe appear simultaneously. There is no time for the cue to be used to direct attention, and there is no difference between the effects of valid or invalid cues. As the SOA increases to about 150 ms, the magnitude of the cueing effect from a valid peripheral cue increases, as shown by the red line in **Figure 7.4**. After that, the effect of the cue levels off or declines a bit.

Symbolic cues take longer to work, presumably because we need to do some work to interpret the colored dot cue (blue line in Figure 7.4). Interestingly, some rather symbolic cues behave like fast, peripheral cues. For example, we are very quick to deploy our attention to arrow cues and even faster to respond to a pair of eyes looking one direction or another (**Figure 7.5**), as if we were built to get information from the gaze of others (Kuhn and Kingstone, 2009). You can try the cueing experiment in some of its important variations in **Web Activity 7.1: Attentional Cueing**.

The "Spotlight" of Attention

In a cueing experiment, attention starts at the fixation point and somehow ends up at the cued location. But does it actually *move* from one point to the next? Attention could be deployed from spot to spot in a number of ways. It might move in a manner analogous to the movements of our eyes. When we shift our gaze, our point of fixation sweeps across the intervening space (although, as we will see in Chapter 8, "saccadic suppression" keeps us from noticing, and being disturbed by, this movement). Attention might sweep across space in a similar manner, like a spotlight beam (Posner, 1980).

The spotlight metaphor makes good sense and has become, perhaps, the most common way for cognitive psychologists to talk about attention. But there are other possibilities. For example, attention might expand from fixation, growing to fill the whole region from the fixation spot to the cued location, and then shrink to include just the cued location. This would be a version of a zoom lens model of attention (Eriksen and Yeh, 1985). Or, when attention is withdrawn from the fixation spot, it might not move at all. It might simply melt away at that location and then reappear at the cued location (Sperling and Weichselgartner, 1995). It is hard to say for sure which metaphor is "cor-

FIGURE 7.5 Which way does your attention shift when you look at this picture?

rect," because we have no direct way to measure the location and extent of attention. However, the best evidence suggests that attention is not *moving* from point to point in the brain in the way a physical spotlight would move across the world (Cave and Bichot, 1999). Moreover, there is no guarantee that there is just one "spotlight" (see Figure 7.17) (McMains and Somers, 2004), though most of the time visual selective attention is probably directed to one thing in one location.

visual search Search for a target in a display containing distracting elements.

target The goal of a visual search.

distractor In visual search, any stimulus other than the target.

set size The number of items in a visual display.

Visual Search

Cueing experiments provide important insight into the deployment of attention. But the situation is rather artificial, in that all of the experiments involve telling the observer exactly when and where to attend. **Visual search** experiments provide a closer approximation of some of the actions of attention in the real world. In a typical visual search experiment, the observer looks for a **target** item among **distractor** items. Visual searches are ubiquitous in the real world: we look for faces in a crowd, mugs in a cupboard, books on a shelf, and so forth. Some searches are so easy that we hardly think of them as searches (e.g., finding the cold-water tap on a sink). Others, like looking for the unicorn in the "Where's Waldo?" puzzle of Figure 7.2, are much more demanding. Some are, literally, matters of life and death, as when radiologists look for tumors in X-rays or airport security officers look for threats in luggage.

The quest to understand what makes some search tasks easy and others hard has proven to be one of the most productive and interesting lines of cognitive psychology research in the past quarter century. Figure 7.6 shows examples of the simplified visual search tasks often used in the lab. In Figures 7.6*a* and *b*, the target is a red vertical bar. In Figure 7.6*c*, the target is the letter *T* (in any of four possible rotations). Two factors are being varied in this figure: First, the tasks increase in difficulty from Figure 7.6*a* to Figure 7.6*c*. Second, each row of the display shows a different **set size**, the number of items in the display. As a general (and unsurprising) rule, it is harder to find a target as the number of items increases.

To measure the efficiency of a visual search, often we ask how much time is added (on average) for each item added to the display. Observers perform the same type of search over and over while the experimenter measures the RT required for the subject to say "yes" if the target is present or "no" if there is no target in the display. As the task becomes harder, the slope relating RT to set size grows steeper.

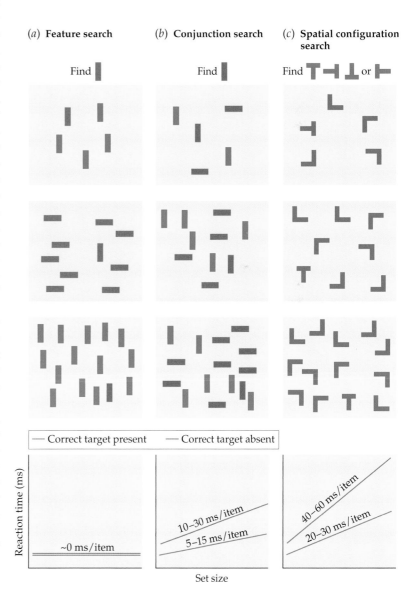

FIGURE 7.6 Laboratory visual search tasks. Each part of the figure shows a different search task, with difficulty increasing from (a) to (c). Each row shows a different number of items (the set size), with difficulty increasing as set size increases. Here we show only examples with the target present. In a typical experiment, a target might be absent in half of the trials. The graphs at the bottom depict typical patterns of results for each type of task. The purple line in each graph represents average reaction times for different set sizes on target-absent trials; the green line shows results for target-present trials.

feature search Search for a target defined by a single attribute, such as a salient color or orientation.

salience The vividness of a stimulus relative to its neighbors.

parallel search A search in which multiple stimuli are processed at the same time.

These slopes are plotted at the bottom of Figure 7.6. Saying "yes," the target is present is faster than saying "no," it is not, because even in the hardest task, a lucky subject might stumble on the presence of the target with her first deployment of attention, but it is not possible to stumble on the *absence* of the target in the same way.

Although all the displays in Figure 7.6 include a target, in a typical experiment the target is present in 50% of the trials and absent in the other 50%. At the end of the experiment, the researcher averages the RTs of all the trials from all the experimental subjects for each set size, for target-present trials and target-absent trials. Schematic results for each task are shown at the bottom of Figure 7.6. In each graph, the lower line represents RTs for target-present trials, and the upper line represents RTs for target-absent trials. You can try a number of different visual search tasks in **Web Activity 7.2: Visual Search**. It's much easier to get a feel for the difficulty of these tasks when you do them yourself.

We can use the term *efficiency* to describe the ease with which we can work our way through a display. It is a way to compare search tasks. If we can direct attention to the target as soon as the display appears, regardless of the set size, then we have an efficient search. If we must examine each item in turn until we find the target, then we have an inefficient search. Different types of search tasks differ in their efficiency.

Feature Searches Are Efficient

The task in Figure 7.6a is called a simple **feature search**. Here the target is defined by the presence of a single feature. Each example contains an item with a unique color or orientation. If the unique item is sufficiently **salient** (that is, if it stands out visually from its neighbors), it really doesn't matter how many distractors there are. The target seems to "pop out" of the display. Apparently we can process the color or orientation of all the items at once (often called a **parallel search**). When we measure the RT, it does not change with the set size. The results will approximate the flat lines plotted at the bottom of Figure 7.6a; more technically, the slope of the function relating RT to set size is about 0 ms per item.

Between one dozen and two dozen basic attributes seem able to support parallel visual search (Wolfe and Horowitz, 2004). These include obvious stimulus properties like color, size, orientation, and motion (A. Treisman, 1986a, 1986b); and some less obvious attributes, like lighting direction (Enns and Rensink, 1990).

In **Figure 7.7a**, look for the bar that is oriented differently in depth. This task is quite easy, even though the orientation of all items in the two-dimensional plane of the page is the same. Notice that the target object in Figure 7.7a is just a 180-degree rotation of the distractor objects. In Figure 7.7b, the target is also a 180-degree rotation of the distractors. You will probably find it harder to locate the target that has light green at the top rather than the bottom. That's interesting because the objects in Figure 7.7a and Figure 7.7b are all composed of elongated white and dark green

FIGURE 7.7 Three-dimensional orientation is a basic feature used in the guidance of search. (*a*) The oddly oriented bar in this image is easy to find, even though all the bars have the same orientation in the two-dimensional image plane. (*b*) To show that the ease of the task in (*a*) had to do with the three-dimensional effects and not just with the relative positions of different regions, the experiment was repeated with apparently two-dimensional items composed of similar parts in similar positions. Now it's harder to find the odd item. (After Enns and Rensink, 1990.)

(*a*)

(*b*)

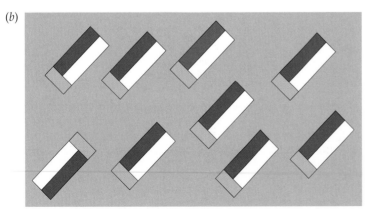

regions with a smaller light green region at one end. The overall shapes and orientations of all objects are about the same. The critical change in Figure 7.7*b* is that the objects no longer look like three-dimensional bricks and no longer differ in their apparent orientation in depth. Without that distinguishing feature, the light-green-on-top target is harder to find.

Many Searches Are Inefficient

When the target and distractors in a visual search task contain the same basic features, as in Figure 7.6*c*, search is inefficient. Here, we are looking for *T*s among *L*s where both targets and distractors are composed of a vertical and a horizontal bar. It is not hard to distinguish a *T* from an *L*, but we need to attend to each item until we stumble on the target. Even if, as in Figure 7.1, the letters are big enough that we don't have to move our eyes to distinguish *T* from *L*, each additional distractor adds about 20–30 ms to a successful search for a target, and about twice that amount of time (40–60 ms) to a search that ends without finding a target. We call this an inefficient search.

Why do we get the particular pattern of results seen in Figure 7.6*c*? One straightforward proposal is that these tasks involve a **serial self-terminating search**, in which items are examined one after another (serially) either until the target is found or until all items have been checked. Consider the case in which a target is present. Sometimes the observer will get lucky and find the target on the first deployment of attention. Sometimes she will be unlucky and have to search all the items before stumbling on the target. On average, she will have to search through about half the items on each trial before the search can be terminated. When no target is present, our observer will always need to search through all the items. There are other accounts that would not involve an exhaustive examination of each item (J. Palmer, 1995). The important point is that some searches are inefficient, meaning that each additional item in the display imposes a significant cost on the searcher.

The inefficient search for a *T* among *L*s is nothing like the hardest search we could devise, of course. For starters, if we need to spend a lot of time with each item, search will be much slower, as it is in the search for a particular Chinese character in **Figure 7.8** (unless, of course, you happen to read Chinese). Other search tasks, like spotting missile sites in satellite images could take days even if, once you found one, the missile site was readily identifiable. The *T*-among-*L*s search is interesting because it is a simpler case where a target can "hide in plain sight." The items are easy to see and very familiar, but search is still inefficient.

Find:

"Grace"

Among:

"Happiness" "Forgiveness" "Flower"

FIGURE 7.8 Search can be much more laborious if you're not familiar with what you're searching for. Here, the search for the Chinese character for "grace" will be much easier if you read Chinese.

FIGURE 7.9 A real-world conjunction search. Find the big, round, red tomatoes among things that might be big or round or red but do not have all three basic features.

guided search Search in which attention can be restricted to a subset of possible items on the basis of information about the target item's basic features (e.g., its color).

conjunction search Search for a target defined by the presence of two or more attributes (e.g., a *red*, *vertical* target among *red* horizontal and blue *vertical* distractors).

In Real-World Searches, Basic Features Guide Visual Search

In the real world, it would be very rare to have a true feature search for the only red item among homogeneous distractors. How often do you have to find the strawberry among the limes? It is probably even rarer to have to search through a scene containing objects that all share the same basic features—perhaps the proverbial needle in the haystack. Usually, those basic features can be used to narrow down the search, even if they cannot eliminate all distractions. This is known as **guided search** (Wolfe, 1994; Wolfe, Cave, and Franzel, 1989). If you're looking for a tomato in **Figure 7.9**, you will be able to find it quite quickly, even though it is not the only red thing or the only round thing or, indeed, the only possessor of any unique feature. Tomatoes are distinguished from most of the distractors by a *conjunction* of several features. If you can guide your attention to red and round and large, you will have eliminated most of the competition.

In the lab, we use **conjunction searches** like those in Figure 7.6b. In a conjunction search, no single feature defines the target. Instead, the target is defined by the conjunction—the co-occurrence—of two or more features. In this case we're looking for the red, vertical items. In terms of efficiency, two-feature conjunction searches tend to lie between the very efficient feature searches and the inefficient serial searches. We can make these conjunctions more complex in an effort to get closer to the real world of cats, vegetables, and so on. So, in **Figure 7.10**, the target is defined in six dimensions: color, shape (straight, curved, jagged), and orientation of the whole object; and the same three characteristics of the part within that object. Each distractor shares two features with the target, but the target is still easy to find because we can guide our attention to the right conjunction of features.

In Real-World Searches, the Real World Guides Visual Search

If feature guidance were the whole solution to finding objects in the real world, then search for a faucet in **Figure 7.11** should be efficient. The searcher would think of the basic features of faucets—shiny, silver, rounded—and then the search for a faucet would be a matter of guiding attention to a complex conjunction like those in Figure 7.10. However, search for arbitrary objects is not efficient (Vickery, King, and Jiang, 2005). Certainly, feature guidance can help—for example, look for the *green* paintbrush in Figure 7.11—but the ease with which we search in the real world must involve more than feature guidance.

Find

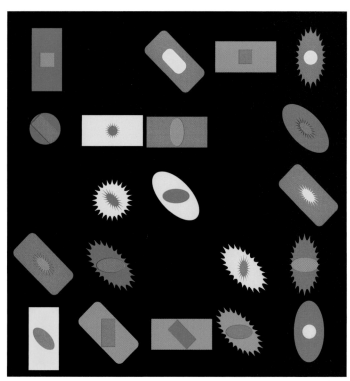

FIGURE 7.10 A six-dimensional conjunction. Suppose the task is to find the yellow, straight, vertical thing with the red, curved, oblique part among distractors, each of which shares two features with the target. The object in the lower right corner matches the target in two dimensions: verticalness of the whole and curvature of the part. The one at lower left matches exactly.

FIGURE 7.11 Search for arbitrary objects is not very efficient. Find the faucet, the violin, or the window.

FIGURE 7.12 Scene-based guidance would help you find the faucet in this scene.

It is quite easy to find the faucet in the kitchen scene in **Figure 7.12**, even though it is less visible than the faucet in Figure 7.11. You are helped by various forms of **scene-based guidance** (Castelhano and Heaven, 2010). Even though you've never seen this kitchen before, you know about kitchens. Kitchens have sinks in typical places. Sinks have faucets in typical places, and there is the faucet. If you were searching for bowls, you would be guided by the knowledge that bowls must rest on surfaces; they do not float. Moreover, you know about the average size of bowls. This knowledge allows you to figure out that only a few objects in this scene are plausibly bowl-sized in the space defined by this picture. In this case, that guidance would speed your conclusion that there are no bowls

We can think of all of these various forms of scene guidance as constituting a Bayesian "prior" that tells you how likely it is that any given object in the scene is the target (Ehinger et al., 2009).

> FURTHER DISCUSSION of the Bayesian approach can be found in Chapters 4 (page 105), 5 (page 142), and 6 (page 175).

This brief introduction to scenes should raise several questions in your mind:

1. How do I know that this is a kitchen before I find the faucet or the sink?
2. How do I know the size of possible bowls before I know if they are bowls?
3. If I know all this, why do I still need to search?

Question 1 will be addressed toward the end of this chapter. We will address questions 2 and 3 now.

The Binding Problem in Visual Search

One way to understand the need for attention and, thus, for search is to consider what is known as the **binding problem** (A. Treisman, 1996; von der Malsburg, 1981), which is this: We might be able to analyze a collection of basic features in a **preattentive stage** of processing, but we won't know how those features are bound together until we attend to the object. Looking back at Figure 7.6c, the problem with Ts and Ls is that they both have vertical and horizontal features. It is the relationship of those features to each other that's

scene-based guidance Information in our understanding of scenes that helps us find specific objects in scenes (e.g., objects do not float in air, faucets are near sinks).

binding problem The challenge of tying different attributes of visual stimuli (e.g., color, orientation, motion), which are handled by different brain circuits, to the appropriate object so that we perceive a unified object (e.g., red, vertical, moving right).

preattentive stage The processing of a stimulus that occurs before selective attention is deployed to that stimulus.

FIGURE 7.13   A conjunction search with a binding problem. In this image it is hard to find the red verticals (there are two of them) because all of the items have the features red and blue and vertical and horizontal.

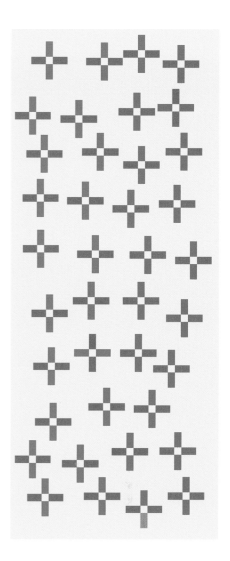

critical. The point is made more forcefully in Figure 7.13. A quick glance tells us that we're looking at *pluses* whose components are red and blue and vertical and horizontal. However, if you need to find the two red-vertical, blue-horizontal items, you will need to search, directing attention to the individual items (Wolfe and Bennett, 1997).

This idea that there is a preattentive stage of basic feature processing followed by a second, attention-demanding stage is the core of Anne Treisman's **feature integration theory** (A. Treisman and Gelade, 1980). The idea of guided search, mentioned earlier, fits into this framework. We can use some preattentive feature information to guide the choice of what should be attended and bound next. If we're searching for a *little, brown* mouse, we should guide our attention to little stuff and brown stuff and not devote attention to shiny, red or large, square things.

If attention is needed to bind features correctly, what happens if we don't have enough time to complete the job? We'll see something, but what? If it works for you, the demonstration in Figure 7.14 (on the next page—but don't look yet) will provide part of the answer. What you must do is look quickly at the figure, and then look away and write down as many of the letters and their colors as you can. Try that now.

If you compare your list to the actual figure, you may find that you matched the wrong color to a letter. For example, you might be quite sure that you saw a green *H*. If so, you have experienced an **illusory conjunction**, a false combination of the features from two or more different objects (A. M. Treisman and Schmidt, 1982). You are unlikely to think that you have seen a blue *H* or a green *T* because neither the color blue nor the letter *T* is present in the figure. We conjoin only those features that are actually in the display. When we can't complete the task of binding, we do the best we can with the information we have.

Returning to those questions about searching in scenes, you have to search because you cannot identify the faucet or the bowl without attention. However, you do know that the scene contains what we could call **proto-objects** (Rensink, 2000). A proto-object is a loose collection of unbound features (size, color, and so forth) that will be a recognizable object, once attended.

Attending in Time: RSVP and the Attentional Blink

So far in this chapter, we've concentrated on attentional selection in space. The *timing* of these acts of selection has been a secondary concern. We learn some interesting new bits of information if we make selection in time our object of study. Imagine the following situation: You're looking at a stream of letters that all appear at the same location in space. Showing the stimuli in this way is known as **rapid serial visual presentation** (**RSVP**). You're trying to decide whether there's an *X* in the stream of letters. How fast can the characters be presented and still permit you to do the task with high accuracy? With fairly large, clearly visible stimuli, we can reliably pick an *X* out of letters when the characters are appearing at a rate of 8–10 items per second. The task does not need to be limited to simple characters. If we're watching a stream of photographs flash by at this rate, we can monitor that stream for the appearance of a picnic photograph. We don't even need to know which particular picnic

feature integration theory Anne Treisman's theory of visual attention, which holds that a limited set of basic features can be processed in parallel preattentively, but that other properties, including the correct binding of features to objects, require attention.

illusory conjunction An erroneous combination of two features in a visual scene—for example, seeing a red *X* when the display contains red letters and *X*s but no red *X*s.

proto-object A loose collection of unbound features (size, color, and so forth) that will be a recognizable object, once attended.

rapid serial visual presentation (RSVP) An experimental procedure in which stimuli appear in a stream at one location (typically the point of fixation) at a rapid rate (typically about eight per second).

FIGURE 7.14 Illusory conjunctions. Look at this figure quickly and then try to recall the colors of the letters. You may know what colors were there and you may remember many of the letters, but you are quite likely to pair a color and a letter incorrectly.

we're looking for. The general idea of "picnic" is adequate for the task (Potter, 1976). You can view scenes in an RSVP sequence yourself in **Web Activity 7.3: The RSVP Paradigm**.

Returning to simple letters, suppose we change the task a bit. Instead of looking for one target in a stream of letters, now we're looking for two. We can call the first T1 (for "target one") and the second T2. For instance, T1 might be a white letter in a stream of black letters, and T2 might be an *X* (**Figure 7.15***a*). The *X* would be present in 50% of the trials. The critical variable is the interval between T1 and T2, and the somewhat surprising result is shown in Figure 7.15*b*. If T2 appears 200–300 ms after T1 and T1 is correctly reported,

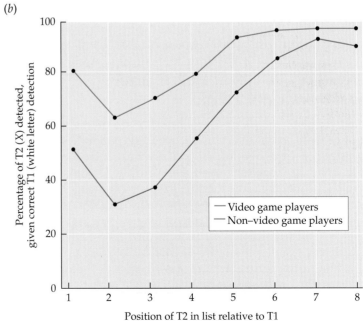

FIGURE 7.15 The attentional blink (AB) in video game and non–video game players. (*a*) In this AB task, observers try to report two targets: a white letter (T1) and an *X* (T2) in the stream after that white letter. Letters appear every 100 ms. T2 can appear in various positions in the list after T1. Here T2 is in position 2. (*b*) If the *X* appears within 500 ms (positions 1–5 after T1), detection is impaired. That impairment is known as the "attentional blink." Video game players show less of a blink.

(a)　(b)　(c)

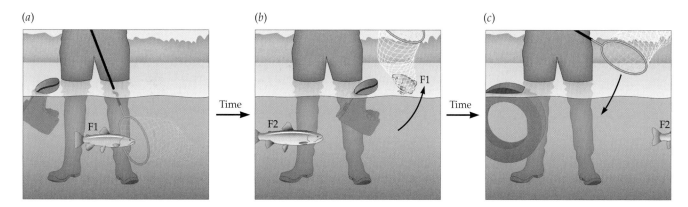

Time　Time

FIGURE 7.16 Marvin Chun's fishing metaphor for attentional blink. (*a*) You can see all the stuff in the river as it drifts by (e.g., the boot and the fish). (*b*) You commit to fishing out fish number 1 (F1). The boot drifts by, and fish 2 (F2) appears. (*c*) Because you're tied up with F1, you will not be able to fish out F2, and that second fish swims by—detected perhaps, but uncollected.

we are very likely to miss T2. (Note that each frame in Figure 7.15*a* and each position on the x-axis in Figure 7.15*b* represents 100 ms of time, since letters appear every 100 ms.) This phenomenon is known as **attentional blink** (Shapiro, 1994); it is as if our ability to visually attend to the characters in the RSVP sequence were temporarily knocked out, even though our eyes remain wide open. You'll find more on this topic in **Web Activity 7.4: The Attentional Blink and Repetition Blindness**.

To show that missing T2 in this scenario is an attentional problem, we can do a control experiment in which subjects report only T2. If subjects are asked to monitor the RSVP stream for the T2 *X*, they pay no particular attention to the now irrelevant white letter, and T2 performance is uniformly good at all delays between T1 and T2.

Somehow the act of attending to T1 makes it very hard to attend to T2 if T2 appears 200–300 ms later in the stream. What is happening? Marvin Chun suggests the following metaphor: Imagine you're fishing with a net in a less-than-pristine stream, with boots and tires and the occasional fish floating or swimming by. You can monitor the stream and identify each item as it passes—boot, tire, boot, fish, boot, and so on. You can also dip your net in and catch a fish (**Figure 7.16***a*). Once you have a fish in the net, however, it takes some time before you can get the net back into the water to catch fish number 2. As a result, you might miss fish 2 if it swims by too soon after you've caught fish 1 (Figure 7.16*b* and *c*) (Chun and Potter, 1995).

Looking back at Figure 7.15, notice that performance is quite good if T2 appears immediately after T1. In Chun's metaphorical account, these are cases in which one scoop nets two fishes. This metaphor illustrates the idea that two processes are at work. Notice the interesting difference between the roles of attention here and in the spatial example of visual search. In search, there is a capacity limit: you just don't seem to be able to recognize more than one object at a time. In the attentional blink, we don't think that the problem is with the size of the metaphorical "net." The problem is that, once attention has dipped that net into the river, there is a temporary inhibition (Olivers and Meeter, 2008) or a temporary loss of control (Di Lollo et al., 2005) that makes it impossible to coordinate a second dip for several hundred milliseconds.

Figure 7.15*b* shows data from two groups of subjects who perform differently on the attentional blink task. Interestingly, the group that shows a smaller attentional blink consists of players of "first-person shooter" video games. Indeed, those gamers seem to do better on a range of attentional tasks (C. S. Green and Bavelier, 2003). Why? It could be that people who choose to play these video games have better attentional resources. Alternatively, the games themselves might enhance attention. To test this idea, Green and Bavelier (2003)

attentional blink The tendency not to perceive or respond to the second of two different target stimuli amid a rapid stream of distracting stimuli if the observer has responded to the first target stimulus within 200–500 milliseconds before the second stimulus is presented.

repetition blindness A failure to detect the second occurrence of an identical letter, word, or picture in a rapidly presented stream of stimuli when the second occurrence falls within 200–500 milliseconds of the first.

conducted a study with two groups of non–video game players. One group got experience with a first-person shooter game, and the other group played Tetris. The first-person shooter group improved on attentional tasks; the Tetris group did not. Of course, this is not an endorsement of violent video games, but it does suggest that attentional abilities can be changed by training and that those first-person shooter video games produce change. In **Web Activity 7.4: The Attentional Blink and Repetition Blindness**, you can experience a related but not identical effect.

Suppose we present an RSVP stream and ask you whether any item is repeated. If the items are reasonably close together, it turns out to be surprisingly difficult to determine whether you've seen one or two of a letter, word, or picture. This deficit is known as **repetition blindness** (Chun, 1997; Kanwisher, 1987). To understand the problem with repetition, it is useful to think back to the recognition demons of the Pandemonium model described in Chapter 4. Suppose we show a stream of words including two instances of the word *cat*. The *cat* demon yells when the first instance of *cat* appears. It is still yelling when the second instance comes along, and subsequent processes, monitoring that demon, cannot tell the difference between one instance and two. If the *cat* instances are sufficiently separated in time, they can be individuated. This effect is so strong that it will cause us to make a meaningful sentence meaningless if the words come fast enough. If we show subjects the sentence "It was time to work because work needed to be done" and ask them to repeat it, they will often say, "It was time to work because needed to be done," losing the second instance of *work*.

The Physiological Basis of Attention

In an oft-quoted passage, William James declared, "Everyone knows what attention is." This great nineteenth-century psychologist went on to say, "It is the taking possession by the mind, in clear and vivid form, of one out of what seem several simultaneously possible objects or trains of thought" (James, 1890, Vol. 1, pp. 403–404). That seems fair enough, but what does it mean for the mind to take possession of a possible object? If we try to get specific, we discover that this attention that everyone "knows" can be rather difficult to pin down. In part, it is difficult to know what attention does because attention performs a variety of tasks, as already discussed. But we also need to deal with the physiological question of what the brain is actually doing when it selects one location in space, or one object, or one moment in time, for further processing (Carrasco, 2011). Let's consider some of the neural possibilities.

Attention Could Enhance Neural Activity

If we are asked to attend to one location in the visual field, as in a Posner cueing task (see Figure 7.3), the neurons that respond to stimuli in that part of the field will become more active. It used to be thought that this response did not apply to striate cortex, the first part of visual cortex to process visual input (see Chapter 3). However, fMRI experiments in humans, as well as electrophysiological studies of monkeys, have shown that even the first stages of cortical processing are influenced by attention (**Figure 7.17**) (Brefczynski and DeYoe, 1999; Gandhi, Heeger, and Boynton, 1998; Haenny and Schiller, 1988; McMains and Somers, 2004).

As we progress further into the visual areas of the cortex, even larger attentional effects are seen (Reynolds and Chelazzi, 2004). In fact, the effects seen at the early stages in the cortex are quite possibly the results of feedback from these later stages of processing (Martinez et al., 1999). That feedback may be a

Subject A

Subject B

FIGURE 7.17 Spotlights of attention in the human brain. This fMRI image of human visual cortex (striate and some extrastriate) shows activity in the brain while subjects paid attention to one stimulus (Att 1) or two stimuli (Att 2). The stimuli were outside the fovea, so the regions of activity don't include the fovea. (From McMains and Somers, 2004.)

FIGURE 7.18 Attentional selection. First, attend to the red items and notice the rough oval that they form. Next, without moving your eyes, switch attention to the blue items or the horizontal items. Different aspects of the picture appear more prominent as you shift the property that you select to attend to.

very important part of visual processing (Ahissar and Hochstein, 2004; Di Lollo, Enns, and Rensink, 2000).

Attention Could Enhance the Processing of a Specific Type of Stimulus

The mechanisms of attention described in the previous section might suffice if we want to keep watch "out of the corner of the eye" by enhancing activity in a specific region of visual cortex. But imagine picking pennies out of a change bowl (a real-world visual search task). Somehow the wish to find pennies makes the pennies more salient. If we switched to quarters, the pennies would recede in salience and the quarters would rise. In this case, we are attending not on the basis of spatial location, but on the basis of a stimulus property.

You can experience this attentional shift in the salience of different stimulus attributes in Figure 7.18. Without moving your eyes, select the red items and notice how an oval emerges with no change in the stimulus. Similarly, you can select the blue items or the horizontal items. Each act of selection seems to alter what you see, even as the stimulus remains physically unchanged.

Attentional selection can also be used to perform one type of specialized processing rather than another. For instance, fMRI has shown that different parts of the human brain are especially important in the processing of faces (the **fusiform face area [FFA]**; Kanwisher, McDermott, and Chun, 1997) and places (the **parahippocampal place area [PPA]**; Epstein et al., 1999) (Figure 7.19). If subjects view an image of a face superimposed on an image of a house (Figure 7.20), the FFA becomes more active when the subject is attending to the face, and the PPA becomes more active when the subject is attending to the house (O'Craven and Kanwisher, 2000).

FURTHER DISCUSSION of FFA and PPA can be found in Chapter 4 on page 108.

Fusiform face area   Parahippocampal place area

Responds strongly
Responds weakly
Doesn't respond

FIGURE 7.19 Functional MRI reveals that different pieces of the cortex are activated by faces and by places. This is true even when both stimuli are present at the same time (as in Figure 7.20) and the observer merely alters his mental set from faces to places. (MRIs courtesy of Nancy Kanwisher.)

fusiform face area (FFA) A region of extrastriate visual cortex in humans that is specifically and reliably activated by human faces.

parahippocampal place area (PPA) A region of extrastriate visual cortex in humans that is specifically and reliably activated more by images of places than by other stimuli.

FIGURE 7.20 These images combine faces and houses. In both cases you can use attention to enhance the perception of one or the other. As you switch your attention from one type of object to the other, you also change the activation of different parts of the brain, as shown in Figure 7.19. (Left image from Downing, Liu, and Kanwisher, 2001.)

response enhancement An effect of attention on the response of a neuron in which the neuron responding to an attended stimulus gives a bigger response.

sharper tuning An effect of attention on the response of a neuron in which the neuron responding to an attended stimulus responds more precisely. For example, a neuron that responds to lines with orientations from −20 degrees to +20 degrees might come to respond to ±10-degree lines.

Attention and Single Cells

On a finer scale, we can ask how attention might change the responses of a single neuron. **Figure 7.21** shows one set of possibilities. Suppose a cell responded to a range of different orientations but was maximally responsive to vertical lines (see Chapter 3). Attention might make the cell more responsive across the board (Figure 7.21*a*). This sort of **response enhancement** has been seen in visual cortex cells, but simple response enhancement seems like a rather indiscriminate change. Alternatively, a cell might become more precisely tuned. In the example in Figure 7.21*b*, **sharper tuning** would mean that attention could make it easier for the neuron to find a weak vertical signal

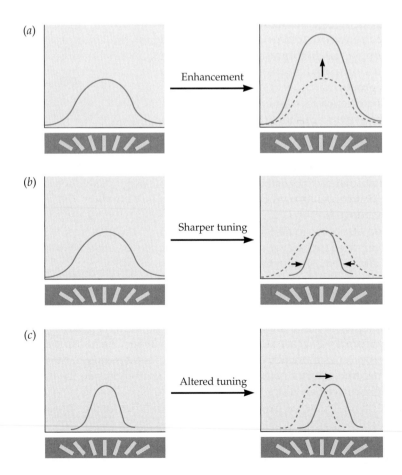

FIGURE 7.21 Three ways that the response of a cell could be changed as a result of attention: (*a*) enhancement, (*b*) sharper tuning, (*c*) altered tuning. In each row, the red line shows the response of a single cell to lines of different orientations, without attention (left column) and with attention (right column).

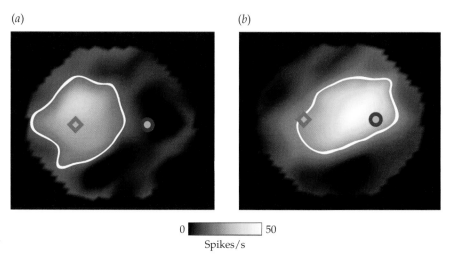

0 50
Spikes/s

FIGURE 7.22 Each of these images is a map of part of the visual field. In this experiment, the investigators flashed little spots of light at different locations and measured the response of one cell. Brighter, whiter locations are areas of greater response. The only difference between (a) and (b) is that in (a) the monkey was attending to the location marked by the diamond, while in (b) it attended to the location of the circle. This change in attention caused the receptive field of the cell to shrink-wrap itself around the attended stimulus location. (From Womelsdorf et al., 2006.)

amid the noise of other orientations (as seems to happen when we attend to the horizontal bars in Figure 7.18). Lu and Dosher (1998) carried out elegant psychophysical experiments showing that attention does make it possible to exclude noise in this way, though some efforts to find physiological evidence for sharper tuning have found only response enhancement (Treue and Trujillo, 1999).

A more radical possibility is that attention changes the preferences of a neuron. As illustrated in Figure 7.21c, a cell that was initially tuned to vertical lines might come to respond better to a different orientation under the influence of attention. The best evidence for a change in the fundamental preferences of a neuron comes from studies of its preferences in space—that is, the size and shape of a neuron's receptive field (Moran and Desimone, 1985). Figure 7.22 shows just such a change in a specific area of monkey cortex. When the monkey attends to one stimulus, the cell's sensitivity is enhanced around that location. When its attention is shifted to another location, the receptive field shifts too (Womelsdorf et al., 2006).

If cells are restricting their processing to the object of attention, then sensitivity to neighboring items might be reduced as resources are withdrawn from them. This prediction is borne out: mapping the effects of attention reveals inhibition surrounding the object of attention (Mounts, 2000).

The three hypotheses about the microcircuitry of attention discussed here are not mutually exclusive. Different neurons perform different parts of the task of attending, and each subtask may require a different type of change in neuronal responses. As a hypothetical example, simple response enhancement from one neuron might be the "command" that causes another neuron to sharpen its tuning and/or to change the shape of its receptive field. In fact, these may not even be different functions, say John Reynolds and David Heeger (2009). Reynolds and Heeger's "normalization" theory says that the current response of a neuron is the product of that neuron's built-in receptive field and the effects of attention. This product must then be "normalized" by neural suppression.

FIGURE 7.23 Five images through the brain of a neglect patient (viewed as though from above). The damage (shown here in yellow) includes the right parietal and frontal lobes. The patient neglects the left side of space. (Image courtesy of Lynn Robertson and Krista Schendel.)

Otherwise the numbers (or the level of excitation of the cell) can get too big. The results of this single process of multiplying and dividing can look like response enhancement, like sharper tuning, or like changes in receptive-field size and shape—all depending on the specific stimuli that are used in the experiment.

Disorders of Visual Attention

What would happen if you could no longer pay attention? A complete inability to attend would be devastating. Because we cannot recognize objects or find what we're looking for without attention, complete inattention would be something near to functional blindness. Brain damage that produces a deficit this severe is very rare. More common is the attentional equivalent of a **visual-field defect**. As you may recall, a person who is unfortunate enough to lose primary visual cortex in the right hemisphere will be blind on the opposite (left) side of visual space. Suppose, however, that the lesion was in the right **parietal lobe**. Patients with this sort of lesion (**Figure 7.23**) have problems directing attention to objects and places on their left. These problems manifest themselves in a curious set of clinical symptoms, including *neglect* and *extinction*.

Neglect

Neglect patients behave as if part of the world were not there. Asked to describe what he is seeing, a patient experiencing neglect of the left visual field will tend to name objects to the right of fixation and ignore objects on the left. A "line cancellation test" is a more systematic way to assess this problem. The patient is given a piece of paper full of lines and asked to draw an intersecting line through each one. A neglect patient might produce something like the drawing in **Figure 7.24**: the lines on one side (the right, in this case) are crossed out, but those on the other side (here, the left) are overlooked. **Figure 7.25** shows what might result if a neglect patient, again experiencing

visual-field defect A portion of the visual field with no vision or with abnormal vision, typically resulting from damage to the visual nervous system.

parietal lobe In each cerebral hemisphere, a lobe that lies toward the top of the brain between the frontal and occipital lobes.

neglect As a neurological symptom, (1) in visual attention the inability to attend to or respond to stimuli in the contralesional visual field (typically, the left field after right parietal damage); (2) ignoring half of the body or half of an object.

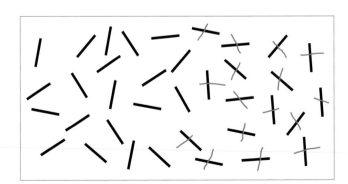

FIGURE 7.24 A neglect patient might produce this sort of result if asked to cross out all the lines on the page.

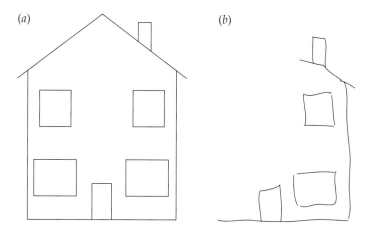

(a) (b)

FIGURE 7.25 In copying a drawing like the one in (a), a neglect patient often omits one side of the object, as in (b).

neglect of the left visual field, were asked to copy a picture. Again, the right side is reproduced fairly faithfully, but the left side is missing. Such a neglect patient might also eat only what's on the right side of his dinner plate or shave only the right side of his face.

It is not always clear whether neglect affects one side of the visual world or one side of objects. Mostly likely, neglect can be either or both. In one elegant illustration of this point, Steve Tipper and Marlene Behrmann (1996) asked neglect patients to detect changes on one or the other side of a barbell. When the barbell had one ball in the left field and one in the right, patients were better on the right. Tipper and Behrmann's clever trick was to rotate the barbell, while the patient was watching, so that the left ball moved into the right field and the right ball moved into the left (Figure 7.26). Now the patients did better than they should have with the piece of the object in the normally neglected, **contralesional field** (the field on the side opposite the lesion). Apparently they were neglecting half of the object, and the neglect somehow moved with the object.

Extinction

The phenomenon of **extinction** is related to neglect; it might even be neglect in a milder form (Driver, 1998). A neurologist might test for neglect by having a patient fixate on her (the neurologist's) nose. She might then hold up a fork in the patient's good (in this case, right) visual field and ask, "What do you see?" "A fork," would come the reply. Next the neurologist might present a spoon in the bad (left) field. A patient with left-visual-field neglect would be nonplussed, but an extinction patient would be able to report the presence of the spoon. If the neurologist were to hold up a fork in one hand and a spoon in the other, however, the extinction patient would report only the object in the good field. The other object would be perceptually "extinguished."

contralesional field The visual field on the side opposite a brain lesion. For example, points to the left of fixation are contralesional to damage in the right hemisphere of the brain.

extinction In visual attention, the inability to perceive a stimulus to one side of the point of fixation (e.g., to the right) in the presence of another stimulus, typically in a comparable position in the other visual field (e.g., on the left side).

Step 1 Step 2 Step 3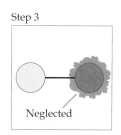

FIGURE 7.26 Tipper and Behrmann's (1996) experiment. Step 1: The patient neglected the left side of the barbell. Step 2: The barbell was rotated through 180 degrees. Step 3: The neglect rotated with the object, indicating that, in this case, the neglect was relative to the object, not to the whole scene.

ipsilesional field The visual field on the same side as a brain lesion.

simultagnosia An inability to perceive more than one object at a time. Simultagnosia is a consequence of bilateral damage to the parietal lobes (Balint syndrome).

In neglect, the patient may be entirely unable to deploy attention to the contralesional side of the world or the object. In extinction, the patient may be able to deploy attention to an object in the contralesional field if it is the only salient object. However, if there is competition from another similar object in the **ipsilesional field** (the same side as the lesion), then the two objects compete for attention and the ipsilesional object wins. Objects are always competing for our attention, but as a general rule it is no great matter for us to redeploy attention from one object to the next. In extinction, the object that is beaten in the competition loses the ability to attract attention far more completely than is the case normally.

Balint Syndrome

What happens if a patient is unfortunate enough to have *bilateral* lesions of the parietal lobes (that is, lesions in both hemispheres)? This condition is rare, but it does happen, and the result can be a disorder known as Balint syndrome (named for the doctor who described it in 1909). The disorder has three major symptoms (Driver, 1998):

1. Spatial localization abilities are greatly reduced. As a result, a patient with Balint syndrome may have a very hard time trying to reach toward an object.

2. Patients with Balint syndrome don't move their eyes very much. They tend to gaze fixedly ahead.

3. Finally, and of most interest for our present purposes, patients with Balint syndrome behave as if they can see only one object at a time. This deficit seems like an extreme form of extinction or neglect, in that attending to one object eliminates everything else. This inability to perceive more than one thing at a time is known as **simultagnosia**. (As noted in earlier chapters, agnosia is a failure to know something. Simultagnosia is a failure to know about more than one object at a time.)

As discussed earlier, even people who are neurologically normal can have trouble binding features together. Remember those pluses in Figure 7.13 that were treated as bundles of red-and-blue-and-vertical-and-horizontal until attention sorted out which color went with which orientation? Remember also the demonstration of illusory conjunction in Figure 7.14, where you may have been convinced that you saw a combination of color and form that was not present? Stacia Friedman-Hill, Lynn Robertson, and Anne Treisman found that binding errors of this sort were much more severe in one patient with Balint syndrome whom they tested (Friedman-Hill, Robertson, and Treisman, 1995). This makes sense if you think about combining simultagnosia with a spatial localization deficit. Not only does a patient with Balint syndrome see only one thing at a time, but the features of that "thing" may have come from several different locations in the world.

Perceiving and Understanding Scenes

Two Pathways to Scene Perception

The work on selective attention indicates that we are able to recognize only one or a very few objects at one time. Still, most of us are not suffering from Balint syndrome. We can "see" more than one object at a time. Moreover, we can use information about the whole scene to guide our attention to a particular object in that scene, such as the faucet in Figure 7.12. Returning to a question we asked before, how do we know that we're looking at a kitchen before we find the faucet or the sink?

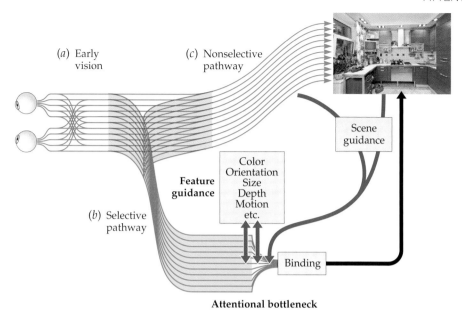

(a) Early vision

(c) Nonselective pathway

Feature guidance

Color
Orientation
Size
Depth
Motion
etc.

Scene guidance

(b) Selective pathway

Binding

Attentional bottleneck

FIGURE 7.27 From the world to our perception of the world. (a) Early stages of the visual system feed two pathways: (b) a selective pathway, with a bottleneck governed by selective attention, and (c) a nonselective pathway that is not subject to this attentional bottleneck. The selective pathway permits the recognition of one or a very few objects at one time. The nonselective pathway contributes information about the distribution of features across the scene, as well as information about the rough "gist" of the scene. (After Wolfe et al., 2011.)

As a framework to think about this and about the perception of scenes, we will use a two-pathway approach that is somewhat similar to the *what* and *where* pathways of Chapter 4 (see Figure 4.2) (Wolfe et al., 2011). Here, the pathways are "selective" and "nonselective." Ron Rensink (2000) originally called this a "triadic" architecture, with early vision as the third part of the triad. Early vision (Figure 7.27a) provides the proto-objects that can be selected and recognized in the selective pathway (Figure 7.27b). We've already discussed that process. Now let's consider what can be done by the nonselective pathway (Figure 7.27c).

The Nonselective Pathway Computes Ensemble Statistics

Look at Figure 7.28. You very rapidly know several things about this school of fish. You know that the school is oriented to the left, perhaps slightly down from horizontal. You know the average size and color of the fish. You also know something about the distribution of orientations, sizes, and colors. That is, you know that a range of fish orientations is present. They are not all pointed in exactly the same direction. To know these things, you are computing **ensemble statistics** (Alvarez, 2011). Ensemble statistics represent knowledge

ensemble statistics The average of and distribution of properties like orientation or color over a set of objects or over a region in a scene.

FIGURE 7.28 Some *fishy* ensemble statistics. In a glance you can tell that these fish are oriented roughly horizontally as a group, even though you cannot tell, in that glance, which specific fishes are oriented exactly horizontally. Similarly, you know in a glance that some fish are more tilted and some are more blue in color. Selective attention is required to determine whether any one fish is both strongly tilted and bluish.

about the properties of a group (ensemble) of objects or, perhaps we should say, an ensemble of proto-objects. Our estimates of these statistics are surprisingly accurate (Chong and Treisman, 2003; Chubb and Landy, 1994).

> **FURTHER DISCUSSION** of our ability to perceive the characteristics of a group of objects can be found in Chapter 4 on page 97 (Figure 4.16).

These are ensemble statistics because we know them without knowing the properties of the individual fish. For example, you would have to search to find a fish that was pointed exactly horizontally, even though that fish's orientation contributes to the estimate of the ensemble orientation. Features are not bound in ensemble statistics. You would have no idea, without attentional scrutiny, whether any of the small fish were bluish fish. You know there are smaller fish and bluer fish, but appreciating conjunctions requires the selective pathway.

The Nonselective Pathway Computes Scene Gist and Layout—Very Quickly

spatial layout The description of the structure of a scene (e.g., enclosed, open, rough, smooth) without reference to the identity of specific objects in the scene.

As was mentioned earlier in our discussion of attending in time, people can monitor a stream of images for one particular image or type of image at rates of one image every 100 ms (see Figure 7.15). In fact, in some cases you don't need as much as 100 ms. Holle Kirchner and Simon Thorpe (2006) presented two side-by-side scenes to observers and found that the observers could reliably move their eyes to fixate the scene with an animal (any animal) in as little as 120 ms. The fact that most of that 120 ms is taken up in generating the eye movement implies that the processing of the scene was really fast. Michelle Greene and Aude Oliva (2009) presented single scenes very fast, followed by masking stimuli. They found that people could differentiate between natural and urban scenes with just 19 ms of exposure to a scene. Global properties that described the **spatial layout** of the scene (e.g., Was it a navigable or non-navigable space?) could be extracted a bit more quickly than could basic categories like "desert" or "lake," but all of these could be appreciated within about 50 ms. It probably takes 20–50 ms to recognize just one object, so observers are certainly not recognizing scenes by recognizing a string of objects and putting them together. What are they doing?

An interesting potential answer comes from the work of Aude Oliva and Antonio Torralba (2001). Consider the very boring "scene" in **Figure 7.29**. It is composed of a vertically oriented, low-spatial-frequency component (a broad, upright sine wave) combined with a diagonally oriented, high-spatial-frequency component (a narrower sine wave that's tilted to the right). As we learned in Chapter 3, *any* image can be broken down like this into its spatial-frequency components, and in fact, the visual system appears to process images in exactly this way, via a set of spatial frequency–tuned channels.

If we further analyze the spatial-frequency components of scenes, we find that certain patterns of frequencies correspond to certain types of scenes. To take a fairly obvious example, wide-open scenes (beaches, prairies, parking lots, and so on) tend to have a lot of strong horizontal components (corresponding to the horizon). Oliva and Torralba called this dimension "openness" and defined a number of other dimensions, including "naturalness" (versus "man-made") and "roughness." They could measure the amount of each of these dimensions by examining the sine waves that made up the stimulus.

When Oliva and Torralba measured the properties of thousands of scenes, they observed something very useful: scenes with the same meaning tended to be neighbors. Suppose we define a simple two-dimensional space using the

FIGURE 7.29 A simple visual "scene" composed of two sinusoidal gratings.

Less perspective depth

Expansion

More perspective depth

Openness

More open ← → Less open

FIGURE 7.30 Spatial layout from global information. In this collection of urban scenes, the x-axis represents openness (from panoramic scenes to vertically structured scenes), and the y-axis represents expansion (capturing a sense of depth from perspective). (Courtesy of Aude Oliva.)

dimensions of openness and expansion. Figure 7.30 graphs a set of man-made scenes using these two dimensions. Look how the scenes organize themselves. The frontal views of buildings fall in the upper right (low openness, low expansion). Highways fall in the lower left (high openness, high expansion). The rules that made this picture don't know about buildings or highways, just sine waves. Nevertheless, scenes with the same "gist" tend to cluster together. Remember that these dimensions are defined on the basis of a spatial-frequency analysis of the entire scene. There would be no need to shift our gaze or even our attentional focus, no need to bind features or recognize objects, no need even for proto-objects.

Oliva and Torralba's work shows how we might achieve a basic understanding of the meaning of a scene very quickly by analyzing the spatial-frequency components of the image. This analysis might tell us that what we're looking at might be a highway, a building, or a farmyard. The selective pathway might contribute the identities and relative locations of a few objects. Now we would have a scene description along the lines of "a farmyard with *this* chicken in *this* pose near *this* cow and *this* tractor." This combination of global and local information might create a representation rich enough to specify a particular scene and to give you the impression of seeing a whole scene.

Memory for Objects and Scenes Is Amazingly Good

The representation of scenes generated by information from the selective and nonselective pathways is very powerful. First, it gives rise to our perception of a world full of coherent objects in a coherent scene, even before we have a chance to attend to most of those objects. Second, it is easily stored in memory. Have a look at **Figure 7.31**. It contains photographs of 16 scenes. Spend about one second on each scene, and then flip the page to view **Figure 7.32**. There you will find another set of 16 scenes. Your job is to determine which 8 of the 16 in Figure 7.32 you saw in Figure 7.31. You probably won't need the answer key (it's in the figure). It is likely that you will correctly classify 14 or more of the images as "old" or "new." That's pretty quick learning of fairly complicated stimuli. Yet it is a mere fraction of what you could do if you had the time and we had the pictures. Roger Shepard (1967) conducted the original version of the test with 612 pictures and found that his observers were 98% correct. They were 90% correct when quizzed a week later. Standing, Conezio, and Haber (1970) got 85% accuracy after showing their observers 2500 pictures for 2 seconds apiece, and Standing (1973) later obtained similar results with 10,000(!) images. In these studies, Standing used a diverse collection of scenes clipped from magazines of the time.

Consider what might happen if we restricted the "scenes" to single objects (an apple, a backpack), and what would happen if we included other examples of these objects in the test set (did I see *that* apple?) or, worse yet, the same object in a different pose (was that backpack lying down before?). Aude Oliva and her students (Brady et al., 2008) tried this with 2500 objects. When asked to pick between an old item and a new one, their observers got 92% correct if the new item was an object of a type that had not been seen before in the experiment. Amazingly, observers were still 88% correct at remembering which example of a category they had seen and 87% correct at remembering which state of a specific object they had seen. If we tried the same experiment with a list of words, the accuracy would be far lower. People are spectacularly good at remembering pictures.

In our discussion of attentional blink earlier in this chapter, we mentioned another set of experiments with pictures, conducted by Molly Potter and her colleagues. They presented pictures of scenes very rapidly and asked observers to say whether, for example, a picnic scene was present in the stream of images (Potter, 1975, 1976). Once again, observers were remarkably good at this task. Helene Intraub (1981) took the paradigm a step further and showed that people could monitor a stream of stimuli for the one that was *not* an animal at rates of eight images per second. That means that every image in the stream could be classified as "animal" or "not animal" after a mere 125 ms of exposure. By the way, at that rate we cannot commit images to memory very effectively, but we do have a pretty clear idea of what we're seeing as it flashes by.

Memory for Objects and Scenes Is Amazingly Bad: Change Blindness

From the findings just described, we could conclude that pictures can be understood very rapidly and that, given enough time—perhaps a second—we can code them into memory in sufficient detail to be able to recognize them days later. But don't endorse that conclusion too quickly. In the 1990s, Ron

FIGURE 7.31 Spend a second or two looking at each of these pictures. Then move on to Figure 7.32.

Rensink and his colleagues introduced a different sort of picture memory experiment (Rensink, O'Regan, and Clark, 1997). They showed observers just one picture at a time. The observers would look at the picture for a while, and then it would vanish for 80 ms and would be replaced with a similar image. The observer's task was to determine what had changed. The two versions

FIGURE 7.32 Without referring back to Figure 7.31, try to identify which of these pictures you already saw. Decide whether each picture is "old" or "new." You can check your answers on the grid to the left. The shaded squares show the locations of old pictures.

of the same image would flip back and forth, with a brief interval between the images in which a blank screen was presented, until the observer spotted the change or time ran out. A static version of the task is illustrated in **Figure 7.33**. Try to find the differences between the two pictures in this figure. The answers are in **Figure 7.34**. You can also try detecting changes in some flicker movies in **Web Activity 7.5: Change Blindness**.

FIGURE 7.33 There are four differences between these two images. Can you find them?

It may have taken you a while to discover all four changes in Figure 7.33. The same thing happened in Rensink's experiment: participants took several seconds on average to find the changes, and some never managed the task at all in the time they were given. This phenomenon is known as **change blindness**. If the blank screen between the two images is removed, the changes are obvious because observers experience a kind of apparent-motion effect (see Chapter 8) when an object changes position, disappears, or changes color. But once we've taken care of that low-level factor by inserting the blank screen, viewers can be quite oblivious to jet engines that vanish from airplanes, branches that jump from tree to tree, and boats that change color.

Actually, we can eliminate the need for a blank screen if the change is made while the eyes are moving. We are virtually blind during an abrupt (saccadic) eye movement. McConkie and Currie (1996) took advantage of this fact to make dramatic changes in a scene while an observer was just looking around. If they made the changes while the eye was in motion, observers often failed to notice.

change blindness The failure to notice a change between two scenes. If the gist, or meaning, of the scene is not altered, quite large changes can pass unnoticed.

FIGURE 7.34 Here are the locations of the differences between the two images in Figure 7.33. When you go back to Figure 7.33 with this information, you will have no trouble seeing what was altered.

FURTHER DISCUSSION of eye movements can be found in Chapter 8 starting on page 235.

It is not immediately obvious how these various facts can all be true of the same visual system. This is a topic of current controversy in the field. How can we remember thousands of objects after a mere second or two of viewing? And if we can do that, how can we fail to notice substantive change in a picture that is right in front of us? Does it make any sense that we remember the picture but seem oblivious to important details?

What Do We Actually See?

In the 1990s, Dan Simons and Dan Levin (1997) conducted a weird experiment on the streets of Ithaca, New York. One experimenter asked an unsuspecting passerby for directions. While the passerby was giving those directions, a couple of other people carried a door down the street and between the passerby and the experimenter. While the door was moving by, the experimenter ducked down, sneaked away, and was replaced by a second experimenter. Then the door was gone down the street, and the critical question was whether the passerby would return to giving instructions. In many cases, the passerby did just that, as if the change in experimenter had gone unnoticed. How could that be? Perhaps this change was undetected because it didn't change the "gist" of the scene. The passerby might think, "I'm giving instructions to a guy. Now there is this weird door. Now I'm giving instructions to a guy again," and simply never register that the *guy* changed. See **Web Activity 7.5: Change Blindness** for another example.

To make this into a more convincing theory, it would help if we really understood what the "gist" of a scene might be. Gist is clearly more than the brief verbal description we might give if asked to describe the gist. Look at **Figure 7.35**. Now look at **Figure 7.36** and decided which one of these two photographs is the same as Figure 7.35. You can probably do this quite easily, even though the gist descriptions of Figures 7.36*a* and *b* would be very

FIGURE 7.35 Look at this picture for a couple of seconds. Describe it to yourself in a sentence. Then go find Figure 7.36.

similar: a skier on a fairly steep slope on a sunny day with mountains in the background. There is something about "gist" that we cannot put into words.

You can experience a much simpler version of change blindness in **Web Activity 7.6: The Attentional Bottleneck**. Participants observed a collection of red and green spots. While they watched, one of the spots suddenly got brighter, and on half the trials the brightened spot also changed color. The change in brightness invariably attracted attention to the critical spot. All the observers had to do was determine whether the spot had changed color when it changed brightness. They performed horribly; they managed to get only 52% correct in a task where they could get 50% correct just by guessing. It seemed that unless the observers happened to be attending to the critical spot *before* the change occurred, they had no idea whether the color had changed (Wolfe, Reinecke, and Brawn, 2006).

This finding is consistent with our change blindness story. The gist of the display did not change when one spot changed, so the change was not detected unless that spot happened to be attended at the time of the change. At any moment, then, we are perceiving the gist of the scene, even if we can't quite verbalize what that gist might be; and we are perceiving the currently attended, bound, and recognized products of the selective pathway. The advantage of this very simple display is that we can estimate how many objects were attended at the moment of the change. The estimate is in the range of zero to four items, indicating, again, that selective attention selects very few objects at any one time.

The problem with this view is that we *think* we see so much more. As we look around the world, we experience a full-color, in-focus, three-dimensional scene filled with clearly identifiable objects. We do not have a perceptual experience of zero to four objects, floating in a sea of ensemble statistics. We know, from the research described in other chapters, that this experience must be a construction of the mind, not an exact copy of the stimulus. We know from Chapter 2 that the world is decently focused only at the fovea and that high-resolution processing occurs only in the central 1 degree or so of the visual field. We will see in Chapter 8 that the scene before us is smeared across the retina three to five times each second as we move our eyes. We know from

(a)

(b)

FIGURE 7.36 Which of these two images is the one you saw in Figure 7.35? You probably know, even though your verbal description of the new image would be very similar to the description you gave for Figure 7.35. Apparently, the "gist" of a scene contains more than is captured by your verbal description

inattentional blindness A failure to notice—or at least to report—a stimulus that would be easily reportable if it were attended.

Chapter 6 that we're actually getting two slightly different copies of the scene from our two retinas, and that both copies are really two-dimensional.

Over and over in this book, we say that a particular aspect of perception is an inference, a guess about the world. Our conscious experience of the world is the mother of all inferences. This realization is hard for us to accept because perception doesn't *feel* like an inference about what is. It feels like it must be showing us what's really out there. It feels like Truth. Phenomena like change blindness are important because they show us the gap between perception and reality. Experiments investigating change blindness show us that we don't see all of what *is* there. Rather, in some spots, we see what *was* there when we last paid attention, and even then we may not remember it perfectly (Irwin, Zacks, and Brown, 1990). In other spots we perceive what we think should be there (see **Web Essay 7.1: Boundary Extension**). Moreover, we may not perceive what we do not expect to see—what does not fit with the current inference. This failure to notice the unexpected leads to the phenomenon of **inattentional blindness**. The great example of inattentional blindness comes from another experiment of Dan Simons, this time in collaboration with Christopher Chabris. They had observers keeping track of ball movements in a basketball passing game. Many of these subjects failed to notice an actor in a gorilla suit who wandered into the middle of the scene, waved, and wandered off (Simons and Chabris, 1999).

Outside the lab, the bottleneck between the world and our perception is not usually much of a problem, because the world is a pretty stable and predictable place—at least on a moment-to-moment basis. If you put your coffee mug down on the desk and turn your attention to the computer screen, the mug will be there when you choose to attend to it again. Only in the lab does the coffee mug vanish during an eye movement. This means that the physical world can serve as an "external memory" that backs up the perceptual world we create in our minds (O'Regan, 1992).

When the world does change, it usually changes in very predictable ways. If we've just driven past Second Avenue and then Third Avenue, we probably don't need to look at the next street sign to know that it says "Fourth." At a rate of about 20 objects per second, we can monitor the relevant items in this relatively stable world and be reasonably sure that we are up-to-date. And if something surprising does occur (a gorilla leaps into the middle of Fourth Avenue, for example), the event will probably be marked by a visual transient that grabs our attention so that we can update our internal representation pretty quickly and maintain our grasp on reality (Yantis, 1993). (See **Web Essay 7.2: Attentional Capture**.)

A certain amount of work needs to be done in order to induce us to miss gorillas. Still, we should not feel too complacent about our inference of the perceptual world. Consider, for example, that eyewitness testimony is based on the assumption that you can report what *was* there, not what you inferred, guessed, hoped, or feared was there. Sadly, if unsurprisingly, we know that eyewitness testimony is subject to the same sorts of effects discussed here and that these factors are probably the cause of errors with real consequences (G. L. Wells and Olson, 2003). We need more data before the courts and the public will understand this problem. As a step in that direction, Chabris and Simons (2011) have extended their work on real-word inattentional blindness to show that people who were given a task of following a jogger down a track could easily fail to notice a very visible apparent beating occurring along their route. The researchers picked this particular scenario because of a real case in which a policeman reported that, as he chased a suspect, he never saw his colleagues beating another man. People didn't believe that he could have been so blind. Now you know that such a scenario is, at least, possible.

Summary

1. Attention is a vital aspect of perception because we cannot process all of the input from our senses. The term *attention* refers to a large set of selective mechanisms that enable us to focus on some stimuli at the expense of others. Though this chapter talked almost exclusively about visual attention, attentional mechanisms exist in all sensory domains.

2. In vision, it is possible to direct attention to one location or one object. If something happens at an attended location, we will be faster to respond to it. It can be useful to refer to the "spotlight" of attention, though deployments of attention differ in important ways from movements of a spotlight.

3. In visual search tasks, observers typically look for a target item among a number of distractor items. If the target is defined by a salient basic feature, such as its color or orientation, search is very efficient and the number of distractors has little influence on the reaction time (the time required to find the target). If no basic feature information can guide the deployment of attention, then search is inefficient, as if each item needed to be examined one after the other. Search can be of intermediate efficiency if some feature information is available (e.g., if we're looking for a red car, we don't need to examine the blue objects in the parking lot).

4. Search for objects in real scenes is guided by the known features of the objects, by the salient features in the scene, and by a variety of scene-based forms of guidance. For example, if you're looking for your can of soda, you will guide your attention to physically plausible locations (horizontal surfaces) and logically sensible places (the desk or counter, probably not the floor).

5. Attention varies over time as well as space. In the attentional blink paradigm, observers search for two items in a rapid stream of stimuli that appear at fixation. Attention to the first target makes it hard to find the second if the second appears within 200–500 ms of the first. When two identical items appear in the stream of stimuli, a different phenomenon, repetition blindness, makes it hard to detect the second instance.

6. The effects of attention manifest themselves in several different ways in the brain. In some cases, attention is marked by a general increase in neural activity. In other cases, attention to a particular attribute tunes cells more sharply for that attribute. And in still other cases, attention to a stimulus or location causes receptive fields to shrink so as to exclude unattended stimuli. All of these effects might be the result of a single, underlying physiological mechanism of attention.

Refer to the
Sensation and Perception
Companion Website
sites.sinauer.com/wolfe3e
for activities, essays, study questions, and other study aids.

7. Damage to the parietal lobe of the brain produces deficits in visual attention. Damage to the right parietal lobe can lead to neglect, a disorder in which it is hard to direct attention into the contralesional (in this case, the left) visual field. Neglect patients may ignore half of an object or half of their own body. Balint syndrome is the result of bilateral damage to the parietal lobe; patients with this disorder may show simultagnosia, an inability to see more than one object at a time.

8. Scene perception involves both selective and nonselective processing. Tasks like visual search make extensive use of selective processing. Nonselective processing allows observers to appreciate the mean and variance of features across many objects (or proto-objects). Thus, you know the average orientation of trees in the woods (vertical) before knowing whether any particular tree is oriented perfectly vertically. Using spatial-frequency information, even without segmenting the scene into regions and objects, the nonselective pathway can provide information about the nature of a scene (e.g., whether it's natural or man-made).

9. Picture memory experiments show that people can remember thousands of images after only a second or two of exposure to each. In contrast, change blindness experiments show that people can miss large changes in scenes if those changes do not markedly alter the meaning of the scene.

10. Our perceptual experience of scenes consists of nonselective processing of the layout and ensemble statistics of the scene, combined with selective processing of a very few objects at each moment. However, the final experience is an inference based on all of the preceding processing, not merely the sum of that processing. Usually this theory is adequate because we can rapidly check the world to determine whether the chair, the book, and the desk are still there. In the lab, however, we can use phenomena like inattentional blindness and change blindness to reveal the limits of our perception, and it is becoming increasingly clear that those limits can have real-world consequences.

CHAPTER 8

Jason Salavon, *The Loop*, 2007

Motion Perception

Take a look at the insect in Figure 8.1. Like any self-respecting ladybug, it flits around from leaf to leaf. At time 1 it is on the lowermost leaf; at time 2 it has moved to the middle leaf. Our visual system distinguishes the bug by a number of features, such as its shape, its location in space, and its color. Previous chapters have established these features as fundamental perceptual dimensions: characteristics of visual stimuli that are directly encoded by neurons fairly early in the visual system.

Is the ladybug's motion also a fundamental perceptual dimension? At first glance, we might think not. After all, motion is really just a change in an object's location over time. If we already have neural mechanisms set up to determine position, why go to the extra expense of adding more low-level machinery to process motion?

Though the added investment might seem unnecessary, consider this question from the position of the primordial vertebrates that "invented" the visual system we eventually inherited. Many bugs move pretty quickly, so if we depend on catching them for our supper, fast detection of their direction of motion will be important to our survival. Similarly, if other animals are trying to catch us for their supper, we need to be adept at detecting the motion of these predators too. In Chapter 6 we saw that motion parallax is an important cue for depth perception. And from a more modern perspective, it would be hard to believe that hockey goalies, baseball batters facing knuckleball pitchers, and boxers trying to avoid being pummeled by their opponents could do their jobs without having a mechanism for very quickly determining the movements of pucks, balls, and fists.

In fact, we've already seen some strong indications that motion is a low-level perceptual phenomenon—in Chapter 3, where we learned that many cells in the primary visual cortex selectively respond to motion in one particular direction. A phenomenon called the "waterfall illusion" provides another piece of evidence that there is something special about motion. Here's how Robert Addams (1834) described this illusion after a visit to the waterfall of Foyers (Figure 8.2a):

> Having steadfastly looked for a few seconds at a particular part of the cascade, admiring the confluence and decussation of the currents forming the liquid drapery of waters, and then suddenly directed my eyes to the left, to observe the face of the sombre age-worn rocks immediately contiguous to the water-fall, I saw the rocky surface as if in motion upwards, and with an apparent velocity equal to that of the descending water, which the moment before had prepared my eyes to behold that singular deception.

The "deception" that Addams described—which had also been noted by Aristotle (384–322 BCE)—was later dubbed the **motion aftereffect (MAE)**.

motion aftereffect (MAE) The illusion of motion of a stationary object that occurs after prolonged exposure to a moving object.

Time 1

Time 2

FIGURE 8.1 Motion is a change in position over time, as the movements of this ladybug demonstrate.

After viewing motion in a constant direction for a sustained period of time (at least 15 seconds or so), we see any stationary objects that we view subsequently (like the rocks around the waterfall) as moving in the opposite direction. This phenomenon may seem a lot like the color aftereffects we studied in Chapter 5, and that's no coincidence. Just as color aftereffects are caused by opponent processes for color vision, MAEs are caused by opponent processes for motion detection. We'll discuss these processes in detail later in the chapter. Let's back up first and take a broader look at how the visual system might go about detecting motion.

The waterfall illusion is just one of many motion illusions. Akiyoshi Kitaoka's art shows other powerful illusions of motion (e.g., *Rollers*; see http://www.ritsumei.ac.jp/~akitaoka/index-e.html). (See also **Web Essay 8.1: Perceiving Motion in Static Images**.) Kitaoka's pictures are stationary on the page, but they can produce a strong illusion of motion if you allow your eyes to drift across them. How does this work? We don't yet have a consensus, but recent work suggests that patterns like Kitaoka's *Rollers* elicit directional responses from neurons in monkey cortex that correspond closely to the directions perceived by humans (Conway et al., 2005).

Computation of Visual Motion

How would you build a motion detector? Because motion involves a change in position over time, a logical place to start is with two adjacent receptors

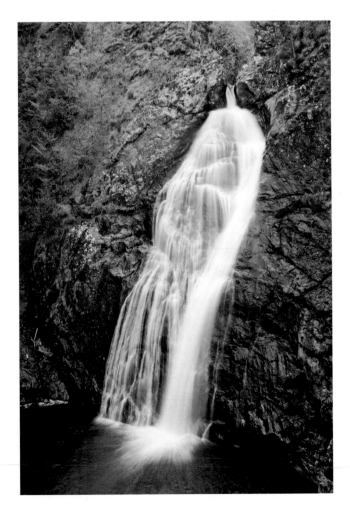

FIGURE 8.2 The lower falls of Foyers.

(call them neurons A and B) separated by a fixed distance. A bug (or a spot of light) moving from left to right would first pass through neuron A's receptive field, and then a short time later it would enter neuron B's receptive field (**Figure 8.3a**). In theory, a third cell that "listens" to neurons A and B should be able to detect this movement.

However, our motion detection cell (call it M) cannot simply add up excitatory inputs from A and B. Given such a neural circuit, M would fire in response to the moving bug, but it would also respond to a large, stationary bug that covered both receptive fields (Figure 8.3b). To solve this problem, we need two additional components in our neural circuit, as shown in Figure 8.3c. The first new cell, labeled "D" in the figure, receives input from neuron A and delays transmission of this input for a short period of time. Cell D also has a fast adaptation rate. That is, it fires when cell A initially detects light, but quickly stops firing if the light remains shining on A's receptive field. Cells B and D are then connected to neuron X, a multiplication cell. This multiplication cell will fire only when both cells B and D are active. By delaying receptor A's response (D) and then multiplying it by receptor B's response (X), we can create a mechanism that is sensitive to motion.

This mechanism would be direction-selective: it would respond well to motion from left to right, but not from right to left. The mechanism would also be tuned to velocity because when the bug is moving at just the right speed, the delayed response from receptor A and the direct response from receptor B occur at the same time and therefore reinforce each other. This simple "bug" motion detector is based on a model developed by Werner Reichardt in the 1950s to explain how flies detect motion (Reichardt, 1986). Almost all models of human motion detection are, at their core, an elaboration of Werner Reichardt's model adapted to the spatial-frequency filtering properties of the human visual system (see Chapter 3).

One elaboration, developed by Barlow and Levick (1965), uses what electrical engineers would call an "AND gate." Cell X fires if and only if *both* its inputs (B and D) are firing simultaneously, and it passes this message on to the motion detection cell M. The AND concept is almost certainly not correct, and a more elaborate version—developed by Adelson and Bergen (1985) and based on linear filters that delay, sum, and then are followed by nonlinearities—seems closer to the "truth." In **Web Activity 8.1: Motion Detection Circuit**, which presents a more elaborate version of this neural circuit, you can interactively move spots of light around and see how it works.

FIGURE 8.3 Constructing a neural circuit for the detection of rightward motion. See the text for details.

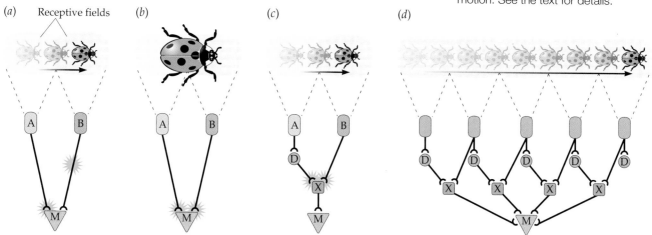

(a) Receptive fields   (b)   (c)   (d)

Now that we've constructed our neural circuit, consider what happens when our bug moves into cell A's receptive field and then into cell B's receptive field. Cell A will activate cell D, which, after a short delay, will communicate its response to cell X. If the bug is flying at just the right speed, it will move into cell B's receptive field just as cell D begins to fire. The signals from B and D will be multiplied by X, and X will drive cell M, the motion detector, to fire. Note that M will not respond to our large sedentary bug, because of the fast adaptation of the D cell. Furthermore, M will respond to motion in only one particular direction (left to right in Figure 8.3). A bug moving from cell B's receptive field into cell A's receptive field would cause B and D to fire in the wrong order, so X would not receive its two inputs simultaneously, and M would not fire. Our motion detector is also velocity-sensitive: if the bug moves too fast or too slow, the outputs from B and D will again be out of sync. A more realistic circuit would include additional receptors to detect longer-range motion, as shown in Figure 8.3d. Here, the M cell fires continually as the bug moves across the fields of the five receptors at the top of the circuit.

Apparent Motion

apparent motion The illusory impression of smooth motion resulting from the rapid alternation of objects that appear in different locations in rapid succession.

One possible objection to this neural circuit is that it does not, in fact, require continuous motion in order to fire. An image of a bug that appears in A's receptive field, then disappears, and then reappears in B's receptive field a short time later will drive M to respond just as strongly as if the image had moved smoothly across the two receptive fields. Although it raises a valid concern, this observation turns out to be a virtue rather than a liability for the Reichardt model, because it provides an excellent explanation for a visual illusion, called apparent motion, that modern humans experience on a daily basis.

Apparent motion was first demonstrated by Sigmund Exner in 1875. Exner set up a contraption that would generate electrical sparks separated from each other by a very short distance in space and a very short period

Frame 1

Frame 2

Frame 3

Frame 4

FIGURE 8.4 Apparent motion on the screen: A series of still images, played one after the other at the correct rate, produces the apparent motion of cartoons (like Daffy Duck impersonating Carmen Miranda in these four stills from the Looney Tunes animation *Yankee Doodle Daffy*).

of time. Even though there were two separate sparks—that is, two different perceptual objects—observers swore that they saw a single spark moving from one position to another. (Apparent motion is demonstrated in **Web Activity 8.2: Types of Motion**.)

We in the twenty-first century experience apparent motion every time we watch television, go to a movie, or use a computer. You are probably aware that an animated cartoon is really a series of still drawings. Objects such as Daffy Duck (**Figure 8.4**) change positions each frame, and when the frames are shown to us at a sufficiently fast speed (e.g., 60 frames per second), we perceive these position changes over time as motion. **Web Activity 8.2: Types of Motion** shows the two frames in Figure 8.1 at a speed that makes it easy to infer motion. Live-action movies and television programs work in exactly the same way, except that the frames are still photographs rather than drawings.

The Correspondence Problem

Although apparent motion turns out to be a win for our motion detection circuit, one of the classic perceptual "problems" that we've discussed over and over in this book remains an issue for the Reichardt model. We can illustrate this problem with the movies diagrammed in **Figure 8.5**. Each movie has two frames that alternate back and forth. The only difference between the two frames is that the only object in the movie, the red square studded with small circles, has been shifted diagonally by a short distance. (These movies are animated in **Web Activity 8.2: Types of Motion**. Viewing the animations as you read this section will make the following discussion much clearer.)

If you view the first version of the movie (depicted in Figure 8.5*a*) on the website (click on "The Correspondence Problem" and select "Movie 1"), you will clearly detect diagonal motion. This scenario appears to present no problem to our motion detector: the square moves down and to the right, and then back up and to the left, and detectors sensitive to these directions pick up and signal this movement. Now consider movie 2 (depicted in Figure 8.5*b*), where we cover most of the square with a black "mask," leaving three of the circles viewable through a small window (in the figure the mask is illustrated as transparent so that you can see what's behind it, but in the movie the mask is opaque). Beneath the mask, the square moves exactly as before, but if you view the movie, you will quite clearly perceive up-and-down, *not* diagonal, motion! (You will need to view the animation to appreciate the difference in the motion perceived in the two movies.)

The larger issue that these movies bring up is called the **correspondence problem** for motion detection. Consider the close-up view of the situation in Figure 8.5*b*, shown in Figure 8.5*c*. Here we superimposed the two frames,

correspondence problem In motion detection, the problem faced by the motion detection system of knowing which feature in frame 2 corresponds to a particular feature in frame 1.

FIGURE 8.5 The correspondence problem. (*a*) The square moves down and to the right. (*b*) For a detector that "sees" just the contents of the white square, the motion is ambiguous. (*c*) What the detector sees is consistent with both motion straight down and motion down and to the right. See **Web Activity 8.2: Types of Motion** for animated versions.

(*a*) (*b*) (*c*)

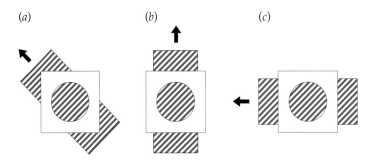

FIGURE 8.6 The aperture problem: The contents of the circle are the same in (*a*), (*b*), and (*c*), even though the physical motion is quite different.

coloring the square and circles blue in their frame 1 positions and green in their frame 2 positions. The difficulty for our motion detection system is this: how does it know which circles in frame 2 correspond to which circles in frame 1? Because we have motion detectors for all directions, one detector will sense the diagonal motion implied by matching the circle labeled "A" in Figure 8.5*c* with the circle labeled "C." But another detector will sense the vertical motion implied by matching circle A with circle B. These detectors compete to determine our overall perception. (You can see some other demonstrations of the correspondence problem in **Web Activity 8.3: Motion Correspondence**.)

> FURTHER DISCUSSION of correspondence as it relates to stereoscopic depth perception can be found in Chapter 6 on page 171.

The Aperture Problem

aperture problem The fact that when a moving object is viewed through an aperture (or a receptive field), the direction of motion of a local feature or part of the object may be ambiguous.

aperture An opening that allows only a partial view of an object.

The **aperture problem** is closely related to the correspondence problem. It gets its name from the fact that a different detector may win this competition when an object is viewed through an aperture than would win if we could see the whole object. Consider the demonstration illustrated in **Figure 8.6** and web movie 2 ("The Aperture Problem"). Here the object is a grating moving behind a window, which is referred to as the **aperture**. The motion direction of the grating is ambiguous—the grating could be moving up and to the left (perpendicular to the stripes, but diagonally overall) (Figure 8.6*a*), but it could also be moving just up (Figure 8.6*b*) or just to the left (Figure 8.6*c*). The motion component parallel to the line cannot be inferred from the visual input. This means that a variety of contours of different orientations moving at different speeds can cause identical responses in a motion-sensitive neuron in the visual system. Without the aperture, there's no ambiguity and no problem. But when we view the grating through the aperture, the system appears to impose some kind of shortest-distance constraint, and thus the vertical-motion detector wins.

At this point you may be thinking it's rather silly to claim that an artificial situation such as the one we've set up here poses a broad challenge to the visual system. After all, how often is our view of a moving object limited to a small window as in the examples presented here? To understand the broader implications of the correspondence and aperture problems, consider the fact that every neuron in V1 (the primary visual cortex) has a limited receptive field. In other words, *every V1 cell sees the world through a small aperture*. Therefore, as **Figure 8.7** illustrates, none of the V1 cells (represented in the figure as gray triangles) can tell with certainty which visual elements correspond to one another when an object moves, even when no mask is present.

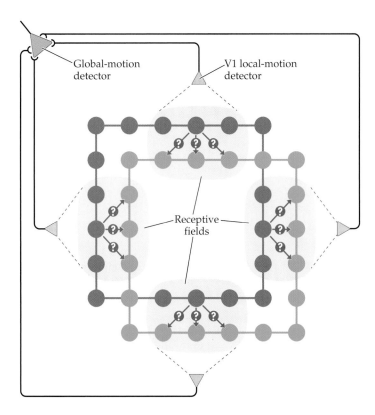

FIGURE 8.7 Building a global-motion detector. See the text for details.

The solution to this problem is to have another set of neurons listen to the V1 neurons and integrate the potentially conflicting signals. As Figure 8.7 shows, only one direction—down and to the right—is consistent with what all four V1 cells are seeing here, and this is the direction we perceive when we see the object as a whole. If the neuron represented by the orange triangle in the figure has access to all the V1 cells detecting local-motion directions, it will be in a position to compare their outputs and find this common denominator. Of course, we haven't specified *how* this global-motion detector performs this comparison, but that question would lead us beyond the scope of this book.

Detection of Global Motion in Area MT

Though a discussion of how global-motion detectors work would be too broad for this text, we can say something about *where* the global-motion detectors are. We saw in Chapter 3 that lesions to the magnocellular layers of the lateral geniculate nucleus (LGN) impair the perception of large, rapidly moving objects. Information from magnocellular neurons feeds into V1 and is then passed on to (among other places) the **middle temporal area** of the cortex, an area commonly referred to as **MT** (Figure 8.8*a*) in nonhuman primates. The human equivalent of MT, has been localized using functional MRI (fMRI), and variously labeled as MT+ or V5. Recent work suggests that this motion-sensitive area may have at least two separate maps located on the lateral surface at the temporal-occipital (TO) boundary (labeled TO-1 and TO-2 in Figure 8.8*b* and *c*). The vast majority of neurons in the MT are selective for motion in one particular direction, but they show little selectivity for form or color. But do these MT cells correspond to the orange neuron in Figure 8.7, which responds to large-scale motion of whole objects, or are they the low-level motion detectors represented by the gray triangles in Figure 8.7?

middle temporal area (MT) An area of the brain thought to be important in the perception of motion.

FIGURE 8.8 Motion-sensitive areas in the brain. (*a*) The middle temporal area (MT; orange area) and other regions of the cortex involved in motion perception. (*b,c*) Motion-sensitive areas in the human cortex revealed by functional MRI on the lateral surface at the temporal-occipital (TO) boundary (TO-1 and TO-2). The inset at the right shows the motion-selective MT. The black rectangle indicates the region of posterior temporal-occipital cortex that is shown in a more detailed view in the left panels. (*b*) Angle maps. The most effective stimulus angle is the stimulus angle or tilt that drives the response most strongly. For example, areas colored yellow respond best to stimuli oriented between 12:00 and 1:00 (see key). (*c*) Eccentricity maps. The key shows the relationship between color and most effective eccentricity for a motion at a 12° angle. For example, areas colored red respond best to the stimulus if it is near the center of the visual field; areas colored purple are most sensitive to motion in the periphery. Other visual areas shown in these maps are V1, V2, V3, and the lateral occipital (LO) areas (LO-1 and LO-2). (Parts *b* and *c* from Amano, Wandell, and Dumoulin, 2009.)

(*a*)

Central sulcus
Postcentral sulcus
Motion-processing parietal cortex
Lingual gyrus (V3)
Primary visual cortex (V1)
Middle temporal and middle superior temporal areas (V5)

Lateral fissure   Superior temporal sulcus

(*b*) Angle maps

(*c*) Eccentricity maps

To find out, Newsome and Pare (1988) trained a group of monkeys to respond to correlated dot motion displays (**Figure 8.9**). In Figure 8.9*a*, all the dots (100%) are moving to the right. In Figure 8.9*b*, 50% of the dots have correlated motion (that is, they are moving in the same direction), while the motion of the rest of the dots is uncorrelated (these dots are moving in random directions). In Figure 8.9*c*, only 20% of the dots have correlated motion. Just as in the aperture problem demonstration, no single dot in these displays is sufficient to determine the overall direction of correlated motion. So, to detect the correlated direction a neuron must integrate information from many local-motion detectors. (Note that in the actual stimuli, all dots are the same color and no arrows are present. You can get a much better feel for what Newsome and Pare's monkeys were experiencing by visiting the "Correlated Dot Motion" section of **Web Activity 8.2: Types of Motion**).

Once they were fully trained, the monkeys in Newsome and Pare's study could recognize the correlated-motion direction when only 2–3% of the dots

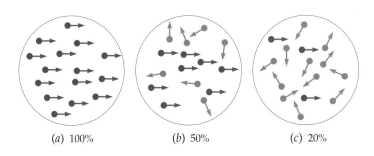

(a) 100%   (b) 50%   (c) 20%

FIGURE 8.9 The Newsome and Pare paradigm. The observer's task is to identify the direction of motion of the correlated dots, shown in purple here. (In the actual stimuli the dots are not colored and there are no arrows.)

were moving in this direction. The researchers then lesioned the monkeys' MT areas. Following the surgery, the monkeys needed about ten times as many correlated dots in order to correctly identify the direction of motion. However, the monkeys' ability to discriminate the orientation of stationary patterns was generally unimpaired. Interestingly, the monkeys' performance in the correlated-dot-motion task improved markedly during the weeks following the lesion, presumably because they learned to use other brain areas to discriminate motion.

Lesion studies have been central to our understanding of the specificity of brain areas. However, such studies are often less than completely compelling, because lesions (even nice "clean" chemical lesions, like those used by Newsome and Pare) may be incomplete or may influence other structures. To test the involvement of MT neurons in global-motion perception more directly, Newsome et al. (Salzman, Britten, and Newsome, 1990) trained a new group of monkeys to discriminate correlated-motion directions, and then poked around in the monkeys' MT areas to find groups of neurons that responded to one particular direction. Once they had found a group of neurons that responded, for example, to rightward motion, they showed the monkey a new set of stimuli and electrically stimulated the identified MT neurons. Remarkably, the monkeys showed a strong tendency to report motion in the stimulated neurons' preferred direction, even when the dots they were seeing were actually moving in the opposite direction! These results make a very strong case that the MT is the site of global-motion detection neurons in the visual system.

Motion Aftereffects Revisited

We know that the monkey brain is very similar to the human brain, but it is always nice to establish converging evidence suggesting that results from monkey labs apply to human vision as well. In the case of motion perception, researchers have looked for this evidence using the motion aftereffect (MAE). As noted earlier, the existence of the MAE implies an opponent-process system much like the one that plays a role in color vision (discussed in Chapter 5). When we view a stationary object, the responses of neurons tuned to different directions of motion are normally balanced. That is, neurons sensitive to upward motion fire at the same rate as neurons sensitive to downward motion, so the signals cancel out and no motion is perceived. But when we look at a waterfall for a prolonged period, the detectors sensitive to downward motion become fatigued. When we then switch our gaze to a stationary object, such as the rocks next to the waterfall, the neurons sensitive to upward motion fire faster than the tuckered-out downward-sensitive neurons, and we therefore perceive the rocks as drifting up.

You might wonder why *any* motion detectors would fire in response to a stationary rock, but as we will see in a bit, our eyes are constantly drifting around, so there is always a small amount of retinal motion to stimulate motion detectors at least slightly. You might also wonder what happens when

interocular transfer The transfer of an effect (such as adaptation) from one eye to the other.

first-order motion The motion of an object that is defined by changes in luminance.

luminance-defined object An object that is delineated by changes in reflected light.

second-order motion The motion of an object that is defined by changes in contrast or texture, but not by luminance.

texture-defined (contrast-defined) object An object that is defined by changes in contrast, or texture, but not by luminance.

we adapt to downward motion and then see something moving horizontally. Make a prediction, and then test your hypothesis using **Web Activity 8.4: Motion Aftereffects**.

Here's another experiment to try with this activity: adapt for 15 seconds or so to rightward motion with your right eye open but your left eye closed, and then quickly switch eyes, closing your right eye and opening your left. You should experience an aftereffect that is only slightly reduced in magnitude compared to the aftereffect you get with both eyes open the whole time. What does this **interocular transfer** tell us about the locus of the MAE in the visual system? Could motion aftereffects be subserved by neurons in the retinas? What about neurons in the LGN?

The fact that a strong MAE is obtained when one eye is adapted and the other tested means that the effect must be reflecting the activities of neurons in a part of the visual system where information collected from the two eyes is combined (Raymond, 1993). As we learned in Chapter 3, input from both eyes is not combined until cortical area V1, where neurons show a preference for input from one eye or another but respond to some extent to stimuli in both eyes. Recent advances in functional imaging techniques may make it possible to locate the site of motion aftereffects even more precisely. The emerging evidence suggests that the MAE in humans is caused by the same brain region shown to be responsible for global-motion detection in monkeys: cortical area MT. For example, David Heeger and colleagues (Huk, Ress, and Heeger, 2001), after controlling for the important effects of attention, demonstrated that the direction-selective adaptation produced a selective imbalance in the fMRI signal in human MT, providing evidence that MAEs are due to a population imbalance in area MT.

> **FURTHER DISCUSSION** of the role of the striate cortex (V1) in combining input from both eyes can be found in Chapter 3 on pages 69–70.

Up to this point our discussion has focused on **first-order motion**—the change in position of **luminance-defined objects** over time. In the next section we describe another interesting motion phenomenon: **second-order motion**, in which **texture-defined objects** (also called **contrast-defined objects**) change position over time.

Second-Order Motion

Second-order motion, illustrated in **Figure 8.10**, is an interesting phenomenon. The three frames in the figure look like collections of random black and white dots, which is what they are. But if you go to the website and look at the sequence of frames played as a movie, you will clearly perceive a set of leftward-moving stripes. (**Web Activity 8.2: Types of Motion** includes some

Frame 1   Frame 2   Frame 3

FIGURE 8.10 Second-order motion. If you try **Web Activity 8.2: Types of Motion** you will quite clearly see stripes moving from right to left across the field of dots even though you cannot see the stripes in these static images. See the text for details.

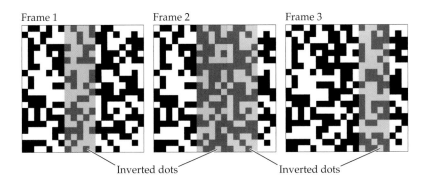

Frame 1   Frame 2   Frame 3

Inverted dots   Inverted dots

FIGURE 8.11 Close-ups of one section of the frames in Figure 8.10, illustrating the changes from frame to frame.

additional frames that lead to the perception of an infinite loop in which the stripes move leftward off the edge of the movie and reappear on the right side.)

This movie is constructed from a combination of two patterns: a random collection of small white and black dots, and a series of wide white and black stripes. The patterns are overlaid and combined in such a way that dots covered by white bars are inverted (black dots turn white and vice versa), and dots covered by black bars are left alone. The frames of the movie are made by the process of shifting the bars to the left while the dots remain stationary. The resulting perception of movement is called "second-order motion."

As in first-order apparent-motion displays, nothing actually moves in second-order motion. Even more incredibly, there is nothing *to* move in second-order motion. As Figure 8.11 shows, the only thing that changes in our second-order-motion movie is that strips of dots are inverted from one frame to another: from frame 1 to frame 2 the dots in the orange strip are inverted; then from frame 2 to frame 3 the dots in the blue strip are inverted. Just as random dot stereograms prove that matching discrete objects across the two eyes is not necessary for stereoscopic depth perception (see Chapter 6), second-order motion proves that matching discrete objects across movie frames is not necessary for motion perception.

Several lines of evidence suggest that the visual system includes specialized mechanisms for second-order motion. For example, Lucia Vaina et al. (Vaina and Cowey, 1996; Vaina et al., 1998) described one neurological patient who suffered brain damage that impaired the perception of first-order motion but not of second-order motion. A second patient showed the opposite pattern: impaired second-order but spared first-order motion perception. These two patients had lesions in different brain areas, and together they demonstrate a "double dissociation" of function, which would not be possible if there were a single motion mechanism. Tim Ledgeway demonstrated a motion aftereffect for second-order motion and found that the second-order MAE transfers even more completely between eyes than does the first-order MAE (Ledgeway, 1994; Ledgeway and Smith, 1994).

Why did we evolve a motion detection system for something as esoteric as second-order motion? It turns out that second-order–like motion does occur in the real world, especially when an object is effectively camouflaged. This chapter's home page on the website shows a situation in which something like second-order motion makes an otherwise invisible object spring to life. (See **Web Essay 8.2: Beyond Second-Order Motion**.)

Using Motion Information

Now that we know something about how the motion perception system works under the hood, let's consider some ways we might use motion information to interpret the world around us.

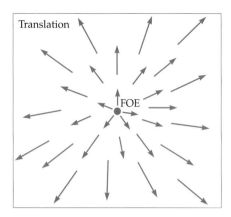

Translation

FOE

FIGURE 8.12 The optic flow field produced by movement forward in space. FOE = focus of expansion. (After W. H. Warren and Saunders, 1995.)

optic array The collection of light rays that interact with objects in the world that are in front of a viewer. Term coined by J. J. Gibson.

optic flow The changing angular positions of points in a perspective image that we experience as we move through the world.

focus of expansion The point in the center of the horizon from which, when we're in motion (e.g., driving on the highway), all points in the perspective image seem to emanate. The focus of expansion is one aspect of optic flow.

Going with the Flow: Using Motion Information to Navigate

For sighted people, getting around is easy. Our vision effortlessly guides our motion through space, whether we're walking or driving, so that we usually reach a destination quite safely and efficiently. Indeed, safe navigation is one of the primary functions of the visual system. What information does the visual system use to help us navigate our way across a busy intersection? Or consider the challenge that confronts a pilot landing an airplane at high speed. In an attempt to improve World War II pilots' performance in such situations, J. J. Gibson (1957), who was working for the US Army at the time, developed an influential theory about the **optic array**, the collection of light rays that interact with objects in the world in front of a viewer. Some of these rays strike our retinas, enabling us to see. Gibson argued that when we move through our environment, we experience patterns of **optic flow** that our visual systems use to determine where we're going.

Consider a pilot coming in to land her plane. As the plane approaches the ground, the optic array will expand outward, in a pattern known as "radial expansion" (**Figure 8.12**). The pilot's heading—the specific point at which she is aiming her plane—will always be the center, or **focus of expansion**, of the optic array. As indicated in the figure, the focus of expansion is the one place in the visual field that will be stationary, so if the pilot's visual system can locate this stationary point, it can determine the heading. (For a relevant demonstration, see **Web Activity 8.2: Types of Motion.**)

Gibson was able to derive a number of optic flow heuristics that the visual system might use to navigate around the world. At the most basic level, the mere presence of optic flow indicates locomotion, and a lack of flow is a signal that you are stationary. If you have ever left your car in neutral with the brake off at the top of a hill, you may have experienced a situation in which optic flow alone tells you that you are in (unintentional) motion. Outflow (flow toward the periphery, as depicted in Figure 8.12) indicates that you are approaching a particular destination; inflow indicates retreat (assuming that your head is facing forward; you will also experience outflow when you look over your shoulder as you walk forward). And as mentioned already, the focus of expansion, or "focus of constriction" if you're driving in reverse, tells you where you're going to or coming from.

Are humans actually able to make use of optic flow information? Laboratories like Bill Warren's have used elaborate computer-generated displays of moving dots and lines to simulate optic flow information, and they have made a good deal of progress in understanding both the utility and complexity of optic flow information. For example, Warren et al. (W. H. Warren, Morris, and Kalish, 1988) demonstrated that humans could estimate their direction of heading to within about 1 or 2 degrees, using as their sole guide the pattern of optic flow simulated by the moving dots, even when the display contained only a very small number of dots.

Of course, the nice clean optic flow pattern diagrammed in Figure 8.12 occurs only if the head and eyes remain fixed and pointed straight ahead. As soon as gaze shifts to one side, a new "radial" component is introduced to the optic flow. However, Warren showed that observers were able to discount these radial components, both when the observers moved their own eyes and when the computer-generated display mimicked the radial flow caused by an eye movement (W. H. Warren and Hannon, 1990). If the radial shift is relatively slow, observers can compensate for simulated eye movements just as readily as they do for real eye movements; but with faster simulated eye movement speeds, performance breaks down (Royden, Banks, and Crowell, 1992). This result implies that the visual system can make use of the copies of eye muscle signals when it is processing optic flow information. We'll discuss this notion later, in the section titled "Saccadic Suppression and the Comparator."

Something in the Way You Move: Using Motion Information to Identify Objects

The fact that we use motion information to guide us as we move through our environment is not all that surprising. What may be less obvious is that motion can also help inform us about the nature of objects. More than 30 years ago, Gunnar Johansson (1975) recognized that there might be something special about the motion of animals and people—**biological motion**—that helps us identify both the moving object and its actions.

Consider the tennis player in **Figure 8.13***a*. It's clear from the contours of her body that she's just smashed an innocent little tennis ball in the direction of her opponent. Figure 8.13*b* shows the same tennis player in the dark. All we can see are the little lights attached to her ankles, knees, hips, elbows, wrists, and shoulders. There's not very much in the static pattern of the lights to inform us that the contour is a human (let alone a woman), or that she/ it is engaged in athletic activity. What Johansson discovered, though, is that when the lights move, their motion gives the viewer an immediate and very compelling impression of a live human in action. Once again, you really need to see this to appreciate it, so watch the classic "dot walker" movie in **Web Activity 8.2: Types of Motion**.

There is even evidence that observers can use biological motion to identify whether a set of moving lights is attached to a male or female walker. How do they do that? As we walk, when the right leg is in front of the left leg, the right shoulder is behind, and vice versa. If we draw one line connecting the left shoulder with the right hip and another connecting the right shoulder with the left hip, the intersection of the two lines is the center of the walker's motion. Because males typically have broader shoulders and narrower hips than females, the average male's center of motion is higher than that of females. James Cutting et al. (Barclay, Cutting, and Kozlowski, 1978) suggested that observers use estimates of the center of motion as a cue to the walker's gender. Other studies (e.g., Mather and Murdoch, 1994) suggest that, in certain views, the amount of body sway might provide an even more salient gender cue;

biological motion The pattern of movement of living beings (humans and animals).

FIGURE 8.13 Biological motion can be seen compellingly when lights attached to a moving human are viewed in total darkness. You can experience biological motion in **Web Activity 8.2: Types of Motion**.

(a)

(b)

FIGURE 8.14 This batsman has just been hit by a very hard cricket ball.

and other work (Neri, Morrone, and Burr, 1998) shows that the mechanisms that analyze biological motion obey different rules for integrating motion over space and time than do mechanisms for other forms of complex motion.

Biological motion appears to play an important role in how we understand human actions. Recent studies of biological motion with two "actors" either dancing or fighting show that we are much more efficient in discriminating biological motion of a human when two humans are acting in synchrony (e.g., fighting or dancing) than when they are out of sync. This finding suggests that when we watch two people interacting, knowing what one is doing helps us understand the actions of the other. We can think of this phenomenon as proof of the old adage that "it takes two to tango" (Neri, Luu, and Levi, 2006).

Avoiding Imminent Collision: The Tao of Tau

In cricket, as in so much of life, the object is to keep your eye on the ball and to stay out of trouble. Indeed, much of our visual apparatus may be designed to do just that. The batsman shown in Figure 8.14 evidently did not keep his eye on the ball. Luckily, accidents like this are not too common, because cricketers are extremely good at judging precisely when a tiny ball, hurtling toward them at speeds approaching 100 miles per hour, is about to collide with their head (Regan, 1991). What visual information do we use to avoid imminent collisions, or to achieve collision when catching or batting a ball? To rephrase somewhat more precisely, how do we estimate the **time to collision** (**TTC**) of an approaching object?

Consider a small, red cricket ball, thrown by a large, rather angry-looking man (on the other team), that bounces off the ground about 10 feet way from you. At this distance, if the ball hurtles toward the bridge of your nose at a constant rate of 50 feet per second, it will collide with your face in 0.20 second (TTC = distance/rate = 10/50). The most direct way to estimate TTC would therefore be to estimate the distance and speed of the ball. However, determining absolute distances in depth is a tricky proposition, as we saw in Chapter 6, and humans are far better at judging TTC than would be predicted on the basis of their ability to judge distance.

In an attempt to reconcile this apparent discrepancy, D. N. Lee (1976) and others have pointed out that there is an alternative source of information in the optic flow that could signal TTC without absolute distances or rates having to be estimated. Lee called this information source **tau** (**τ**). Here's how tau works. As it approaches your nose, the image of the ball on your retina will grow larger (if you don't believe this, have someone throw a ball—preferably a soft one—at your face and see for yourself). The ratio of the retinal image size at any moment to the rate at which the image is expanding is tau, and TTC is proportional to tau. The great advantage of using tau to estimate TTC is that it relies solely on information available directly from the retinal image; all you need to do is track the visual angle subtended by the cricket ball as it approaches your eye.

Do we actually make use of tau? The jury is still out. It is clear that estimating the time to imminent collision is critically important to animals and humans, and almost every species tested will attempt to avoid a simulated collision. There is also evidence that certain neurons in the visual systems of pigeons and locusts respond to objects on a collision course with them and can signal a particular time to collision (Rind and Simmons, 1999; Wang and Frost, 1992). However, Tresilian (1999) concluded that tau is just one of a number of different sources of visual information that can be used to judge the time to collision.

time to collision (TTC) The time required for a moving object (such as a cricket ball) to hit a stationary object (such as a batsman's head). TTC = distance/rate.

tau (τ) Information in the optic flow that could signal time to collision (TTC) without the necessity of estimating either absolute distances or rates. The ratio of the retinal image size at any moment to the rate at which the image is expanding is tau, and TTC is proportional to tau.

Eye Movements

Place a blank piece of paper on the desk in front of you and draw a small black dot right in the center of the paper. Close your left eye and focus your right eye's gaze on the dot; then position a pencil so that it is near the bottom right corner of the paper. Keeping your eye trained on the dot, move the pencil slowly across the sheet to the left side, as shown in **Figure 8.15a**. What did you perceive? The image of the pencil just swept across your retina from right to left, so assuming that your rightward-motion detectors are functioning correctly, you should have perceived movement in this direction. (You may have thought that the word *rightward* in the previous sentence was a typo, but technically the image sweeps across the retina in the opposite direction from the actual movement, since the right side of the world projects to the left side of the retina and vice versa. To avoid confusion, we'll ignore this inconvenient bit of physics for now and pretend that images move on the retina in the same direction that the objects in the world are moving. **Web Activity 8.5: Eye Movements** provides illustrations of these phenomena that honor physics.)

Now try a slightly different demonstration. Start with the pencil near the bottom left corner of the paper, fixate the eraser, and track it with your eye as you move it back across the sheet of paper to the right corner (Figure 8.15b). Congratulations! You have just executed a type of eye movement called **smooth pursuit**, which kept the image of the pencil stationary on the retina while it was in motion. But think about what happened to the image of the dot just above your finger. When the pencil was on the left side of the page, the dot was to the right of your fixation point. As you tracked the pencil, the dot shifted to the center of your retina, and then it slid to the left of fixation once the pencil reached the right side of the paper. However, you should *not* have perceived the dot to be moving in this case, even though the image of the dot made essentially the same journey across your retina as the image of the pencil did in Figure 8.15a.

We hope you've convinced yourself that the retinal image movement of the pencil when you keep your gaze centered on the dot (see Figure 8.15a) is essentially the same as the retinal image movement of the dot when you keep your gaze centered on the pencil (see Figure 8.15b). The question is, Why do we perceive the pencil to be in motion in the first case, but perceive the dot to be stationary in the second case? The reason is that in one case there's an eye movement. Think about how the visual system might accomplish this balancing act while we back up and describe eye movements in a bit more

smooth pursuit A type of voluntary eye movement in which the eyes move smoothly to follow a moving object.

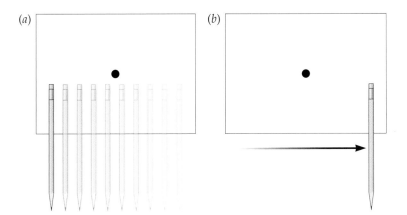

FIGURE 8.15 Studying eye movements. (a) Fixating our gaze on the dot while the pencil moves to the left causes the pencil to generate motion across the retina, and we perceive the pencil to be moving in this direction. (b) Fixating our gaze on the pencil while it moves to the right causes the dot to generate motion in the same direction across the retina, but we do not perceive the dot to move.

detail. (By the way, you may want to save the piece of paper with the dot for another exercise later in this chapter.)

Physiology and Types of Eye Movements

superior colliculus A structure in the midbrain that is important in initiating and guiding eye movements.

As **Figure 8.16***a* shows, six muscles are attached to each eye, arranged in three pairs. These muscles are controlled by an extensive network of structures in the brain. One way to get some inkling of the role of these brain structures is to stimulate them with small electrical signals and observe the movements of the eyes. For example, if a cell in the midbrain (**superior colliculus**) of a monkey is stimulated, the monkey's eyes will move by a specific amount in a specific direction (Figure 8.16*b*). Every time that cell is stimulated, the same eye movement will result. Stimulating a neighboring cell will produce a different eye movement (Stryker and Schiller, 1975). (The superior colliculus also gets some input directly from retinal ganglion cells; this input presumably helps with the planning of eye movements.) By contrast, in response to stimulation of some of the cells in the frontal eye fields (Figure 18.16*b*) (and, indeed, certain superior colliculus cells too), the monkey will move its eyes to fixate a specific spot in space. Depending on where the eyes start, this adjustment may require an eye movement up, down, left, or right. In this case, it is the destination and not the movement that is coded (Mays and Sparks, 1980; Schiller and Sandell, 1983).

(*a*)

(*b*)

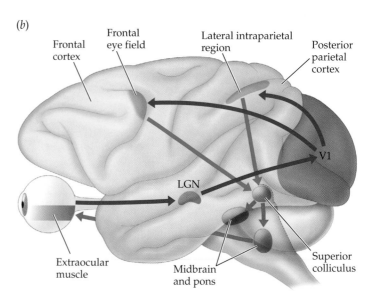

FIGURE 8.16 Muscles of the eye. (*a*) Six muscles—arranged in three pairs (superior and inferior oblique, superior and inferior rectus, and medial and lateral rectus)—are attached to each eye. (*b*) Brain circuits for visually guided saccades. (Part *b* after Wurtz, 2008.)

This description merely scratches the surface of a motor system that is not only very complex, but very active. For example, even when we try to hold our eyes completely stationary, they continue to execute small but important movements. Specifically, there are involuntary eye drifts and small jerks (**microsaccades**); if the eye muscles are temporarily paralyzed—say, as a result of taking curare (it's amazing what some people will subject themselves to in the name of science!) (Matin et al., 1982)—the entire visual world gradually fades from view. Of course, in normal viewing, image velocities are fast enough to prevent fading without the need for microsaccades (Kowler and Collewijn, 2010). So what are microsaccades good for? Recent work suggests that they may be important for very fine spatial judgments, such as threading a needle, by precisely moving the eye to nearby regions of interest (Ko, Poletti, and Rucci, 2010).

In addition to involuntary eye movements, there are three types of voluntary eye movements. Most obvious, perhaps, are the previously discussed smooth-pursuit movements that we make when tracking a moving object. **Vergence** eye movements occur when we rotate our eyes inward (converging the eyes) or outward (diverging the eyes) to focus on a near or far object. The third type of voluntary movement is the **saccade**: a fast jump (up to 1000 degrees per second) (Bahill and Stark, 1979) of the eye that shifts our fixation point from one spot to another. We can decide to make a saccade deliberately, but whether we're thinking about it or not, we will make three or four saccades every second of every minute of every waking hour of the day. That's something like 3 saccades × 60 seconds × 60 minutes × 16 hours = 172,800 saccades per day—and that doesn't include the saccades we make during our dreams in rapid-eye-movement (REM) sleep (Maquet et al., 1996).

When we view a scene, our saccades are not random. We tend to fixate the "interesting" places in the image. Thus, the eyes are more likely to make saccades in response to contours than to broad featureless areas of an image (**Figure 8.17**). Interest also has a richer semantic meaning: We make eye movements that are based on the content of a scene and on our specific interests in that scene (Yarbus, 1967). Our pattern of eye movements as we enter the cafeteria will be different if we're looking for lunch than if we're looking for love.

There are also **reflexive eye movements**—for example, when the eyes move to compensate for head and body movement while maintaining fixation on a particular target. These are known as vestibular eye movements and operate via the vestibulo-ocular reflex (VOR) (see Chapter 12). In optokinetic nystag-

microsaccade An involuntary, small, jerklike eye movement.

vergence A type of eye movement in which the two eyes move in opposite directions; for example, both eyes turn toward the nose (convergence) or away from the nose (divergence).

saccade A type of eye movement, made both voluntarily and involuntarily, in which the eyes rapidly change fixation from one object or location to another.

reflexive eye movement A movement of the eye that is automatic and involuntary.

FIGURE 8.17 A classic scan path (right) showing the pattern of eye movements during inspection of the picture of the girl on the left. (From Yarbus, 1967.)

mus (OKN)—another reflexive eye movement—the eyes will involuntarily track a continually moving object. OKN is characterized by the eyes moving smoothly in one direction (e.g., right) in pursuit of an object moving in that same direction, and then snapping back. The presence of OKN in response to moving stripes has often been used as a measure of visual acuity in infants.

Eye Movements and Reading

If you are reading this chapter, then your eyes are doing a lot of moving! Reading English involves fixating for roughly a quarter of a second, and then making a saccade of about 7–9 letter spaces—over and over again. We make saccades in order to bring the text into our fovea, because print that's too far from our fixation cannot be read, in part because of visual crowding (see Chapter 3 and Levi, 2008). Interestingly, readers of English are able to gain information from up to 15 characters to the right of fixation, but only 3–4 characters to the left. Thus, the perceptual span is asymmetrical. Readers of Hebrew (which is read from left to right) have the reverse asymmetry. Readers of both Hebrew and English can switch this asymmetry depending on which language they're reading (Rayner, 1978), so the asymmetry is attentional, not a product of limitations imposed by the visual system.

As we discuss next, there is no information processing during saccades, so while we're reading, all of the information processing must take place during the fixations. Interestingly, such processing occurs during only a small fraction of each fixation. "Disappearing text" experiments (in which the words actually disappear off of the computer screen while participants are reading) reveal that if a word remains on the screen for only 50 milliseconds after it is first fixated, reading proceeds normally (Rayner et al., 2003). There are many other interesting aspects of eye movements in scene perception and in visual search and attention (see Chapter 7).

Saccadic Suppression and the Comparator

Now let's return to the tricky problem of discriminating motion across the retina that is due to eye movements versus object movements. Let's do one more demonstration using that white piece of paper with the dot in the middle. Close your left eye again and gaze just to the left of the dot; then execute some saccades, shifting your eyes back and forth to the right and then to the left of the dot. The dot will be moving across your retina, but you should not experience any perception of movement. Now, with your left eye still closed, fixate the dot, place your right index finger on the right side of your right eye socket, and gently "jiggle" your eyeball. *Now* the dot (as well as the paper and the desk the paper is sitting on) *should* appear to move back and forth! What's going on here?

Part of the answer is thought to be **saccadic suppression**. When we make a saccade, the visual system essentially shuts down for the duration of the eye movement (visual activity is suspended in a similar way when we blink). To be a bit more precise, the visual system does not shut down altogether. Saccadic suppression acts mainly to suppress information carried by the magnocellular pathway.

To observe saccadic suppression, you need to find a mirror. As you look at yourself in the mirror, fixate first one eye and then the other. You will notice that you do not see the saccadic eye movements that you must be making. If you're concerned that the saccades might be too small to see, find a friend to help you. Have this person stand in front of you and move his or her fixation

saccadic suppression The reduction of visual sensitivity that occurs when we make saccadic eye movements. Saccadic suppression eliminates the smear from retinal image motion during an eye movement.

from one of your eyes to the other. You will have no trouble seeing your friend's saccades, even though you are quite blind to your own.

Although saccadic suppression eliminates the smear of the moving world during a saccade, it seems as if we should still be disturbed by the sudden displacement of the objects in front of us. In any case, no suppression takes place when we execute smooth-pursuit eye movements, as in the earlier exercise with the pencil. Although many scientists believe suppression to be an active process, others argue that saccadic suppression is little more than masking and that the magnocellular pathway is not suppressed during saccades (Castet, Jeanjean, and Masson, 2001).

By sending out two copies of each order to move the eyes, the motor system is thought to solve the "problem" of why an object in motion may appear stationary. One copy goes to the eye muscles; another (often referred to as the "efference copy") goes to an area of the visual system that has been dubbed the **comparator** (Figure 8.18). The comparator can then compensate for the image changes caused by the eye movement, inhibiting any attempts by other parts of the visual system to interpret the changes as object motion. When we jiggle the eyeball with a finger, no signal is sent from the eye muscles to the comparator (the eye muscles are not what move the eye), so the visual input is interpreted as our world being rocked. (For interactive demonstrations of the similarities and differences between eye movements and object movements, see **Web Activity 8.5: Eye Movements**.) While a lot of work has been dedicated to the analysis of extraretinal signals during smooth pursuit, visual stability during saccades remains a matter of active research (Cavanagh et al., 2010; Poletti, Listorti, and Rucci, 2010), and attention seems to play an important role.

comparator An area of the visual system that receives one copy of the command issued by the motor system when the eyes move (the other copy goes to the eye muscles). The comparator compares the image motion signal with the eye motion signal and can compensate for the image changes caused by the eye movement.

Development of Motion Perception

Sensitivity to visual motion does not develop all at once. Some aspects of motion perception are already evident at birth. For example, reflexive eye

FIGURE 8.18 The comparator. The brain sends two copies (red lines) of each command to move the eyes. One copy (the motor signal) goes directly to the extraocular muscles; the other (known as the efference copy or "corollary discharge signal") goes to the comparator, which compares the image motion signal with the eye motion signal and can compensate for image changes produced by the eye movement.

movements to moving targets (OKN) are present in newborns (as long as the targets are sufficiently large), and physiological studies show that neurons in V1 have adultlike sensitivity to visual direction. On the other hand, sensitivity to global motion, which is thought to reflect processing in the MT, appears to develop more slowly, reaching maturity at about 3–4 years of age, while sensitivity to motion-defined form and biological motion takes even longer (Freire et al., 2006; Parrish et al., 2005).

The Man Who Couldn't See Motion

akinetopsia A rare neuropsychological disorder in which the affected individual has no perception of motion.

Recall what it's like to experience a motion aftereffect. You stare at a waterfall and then shift your gaze to the cliff next to the falls. You know that the rocks are not moving, and you can see that they aren't actually going anywhere, yet you still experience an otherworldly sense of "disembodied" motion. (Review the phenomenon in **Web Activity 8.4: Motion Aftereffects**, if you haven't tried it for a while.)

Now imagine the opposite experience: objects change position, and you are fully aware of these location shifts but you experience *no* perception of motion. As bizarre as it seems, this is exactly what happens in a rare neuropsychological disorder known as **akinetopsia**, described in the following case report (Horton and Trobe, 1999):

> A 47-year-old man reported seeing streams of multiple, frozen images trailing in the wake of moving objects. As soon as motion ceased, the images collapsed into each other. He compared his vision to a scene lit by a flashing strobe, except that stationary elements were perceived normally. In fact, if nothing was in motion and he held perfectly still, his vision was entirely normal. The moment anything moved, however, it left a stream of static copies in its path. For example, while out for an evening stroll, he saw a pack of identical dogs lined up behind his West Highland terrier. Driving was impossible because he was confused by multiple snapshots of cars, streets, and signs. Moving lights were followed by a long comet trail.

Another patient reported that when she watched her own arm moving, "passage of the limb would be reduplicated by multiple, fuzzy images, the way a cartoonist might draw motion."

Not surprisingly, akinetopsia appears to be caused by disruptions to cortical area MT. For the two patients described here, the disruptions were side effects of a prescription antidepressant drug, and their motion perception problems disappeared once they were taken off the drug. In other cases, akinetopsia is brought on by direct trauma to area MT that is due to stroke or elective brain surgery (e.g., surgery to alleviate epileptic seizures). Patients in the latter category sometimes regain normal motion perception abilities several weeks after surgery, indicating that, as in Newsome's monkeys, the human brain can sometimes rearrange its connections so that different areas take over the MT's motion-processing functions.

Summary

1. Like color or orientation, motion is a primary perceptual dimension that is coded at various levels in the brain. Motion information is used to determine where objects are going and when they're likely to get there, and to help us move through our environment without being hit in the head by flying objects.

2. We can build a simple motion-detecting circuit by using linear filters that delay and sum information (and are followed by nonlinearities).

3. V1 neurons view the world through a small window, leading to the well-known aperture problem (that is, a V1 neuron is unable to tell which elements correspond with one another when an object moves through its receptive field).

4. Strong physiological and behavioral evidence suggests that the middle temporal area (MT) is involved in the perception of global motion.

5. Aftereffects for motion, like those for orientation or color, can provide important insights into the underlying mechanisms of perception in humans.

6. Luminance-defined (first-order) motion and contrast- or texture-defined (second-order) motion appear to be analyzed by separate systems.

7. The brain has to figure out which retinal motion arises in the world, and which arises because of eye movements. Moreover, the brain must suppress the motion signals generated by our eye movements, or the world will be pretty "smeared."

8. Motion information is critically important to us for navigating around our world, avoiding imminent collision, and recognizing the movement of animals and people.

Refer to the
Sensation and Perception
Companion Website
sites.sinauer.com/wolfe3e
for activities, essays, study
questions, and other study aids.

CHAPTER 9

Bruno Mallart, *Mobile World Congress*, 2010

Hearing: Physiology and Psychoacoustics

I t is often said that humans are visual animals. We are reminded of the importance of vision in our lives whenever we close our eyes or awaken in the night, because so much of what we sense and know about our environment is suddenly gone. In contrast, most people never get such reminders of the importance of hearing. Our ears are always open, and we can hear perfectly well in the dark. When we enter a theater just before the movie starts, we don't need to wait half an hour to be able to hear the soft strains of the opening theme. We can hear things when our nose is not pointed at the source of the sound, and we can even hear around obstacles and corners. For better or worse, we can often hear through barriers that light cannot penetrate. For all these reasons, it is easy to take hearing for granted.

Try to imagine a world, though, where nothing makes a sound. You cannot hear a train coming, and the blast of its air horn silently escapes into the night. At a concert, musicians move deftly as the audience stands or jumps or claps, but the enthusiasm of both performers and spectators is only a curiosity. A person cries out, and you don't help because you cannot hear the cry. You cannot talk on the phone. Deafness deprives you of the most fundamental of human abilities: communication through speech. Without hearing, the world is a more dangerous place in which you are relatively isolated by day and nearly totally isolated by night. At night your sense of vision, which helps compensate for hearing loss when it's light out, is compromised by darkness. (See **Web Activity 9.1: What We Hear**.)

The Function of Hearing

For the next three chapters, you will be hearing all about hearing. In this chapter we cover the basics: the nature of sound, the anatomy and physiology of the auditory system, and how we perceive the two fundamental sound qualities: loudness and pitch. We conclude this chapter by looking at some of the ways in which hearing can be impaired and what we can do to ameliorate these impairments. In Chapter 10 we will move on to discuss some of the ways we use acoustic information to learn about our environment. Then, in Chapter 11, we will cover the higher-level auditory functions that come into play when we're listening to speech and music.

Many fundamental principles apply to vision, hearing, and all the other senses. However, each sense developed at different periods in our evolutionary history and in response to different environmental challenges. So although you should find that much of what you've learned thus far will prove helpful for understanding hearing, you should also come to appreciate that biology has provided some very different (and very clever) solutions to the challenges of sensing and interpreting sound.

(a)

Concentric waves

Speaker

(b)

Sinusoidal wave

Normal atmospheric pressure

Air pressure

Distance ⟶

FIGURE 9.1 The pattern of pressure fluctuations of a sound stays the same as the sound wave moves away from the source (a), but the amount of pressure change decreases with increasing distance (b).

amplitude or intensity The magnitude of displacement (increase or decrease) of a sound pressure wave. Amplitude is perceived as *loudness*.

frequency For sound, the number of times per second that a pattern of pressure change repeats. Frequency is perceived as *pitch*.

hertz (Hz) A unit of measure for frequency. One hertz equals one cycle per second.

What Is Sound?

Sounds are created when objects vibrate. The vibrations of an object (the sound source) cause molecules in the object's surrounding medium (for humans, usually the Earth's atmosphere) to vibrate as well, and this vibration in turn causes pressure changes in the medium (**Figure 9.1**). These pressure changes are best described as waves, and they are similar to the waves on a pond that are caused when we drop a rock into the water. The water molecules displaced by the rock do not themselves travel very far, but the *pattern* of displacement will move outward from the source until something (the shore, a boat, a swimming duck, or anything else) gets in the way. Although the patterns of pond and sound waves do not change as they spread out, the initial amount of pressure change is dispersed over a larger and larger area as the wave moves away, so the wave becomes less prominent as it moves farther from its source.

Sound waves travel at a particular speed depending on the medium, moving faster through denser substances. For example, the speed of sound through air is about 340 meters per second, depending on the humidity level (sounds travel a bit faster on muggy days), but the speed of sound through water is about 1500 meters per second. Light waves move through air almost a million times faster than sound waves do, accounting for the lag time between seeing lightning and hearing thunder—about 1 second per mile.

Basic Qualities of Sound Waves: Frequency and Amplitude

As we've seen, the sound waves that we hear are simply fluctuations in air pressure across time. The magnitude of the pressure change in a sound wave—the difference between the highest pressure area and the lowest pressure area—is called the **amplitude**, or **intensity**, of the wave (**Figure 9.2**). Pressure fluctuations may be very close together or spread apart over longer periods. For light waves, we usually describe the pattern of fluctuations by measuring the distance between peaks in the waves—that is, the "wavelength." Although sound waves also have wavelengths, we more typically describe their patterns by noting how quickly the pressure fluctuates; this rate of fluctuation is known as the **frequency** of the wave (see Figure 9.2). To see an example of frequency, dangle a thread in front of a stereo. As the speaker creates fluctuations in air pressure, the thread will wave back and forth. The speed of this waving is the thread's frequency. Sound wave frequencies are measured in **hertz (Hz)**, where 1 Hz equals 1 cycle per second. For example, the pressure in a 500-Hz

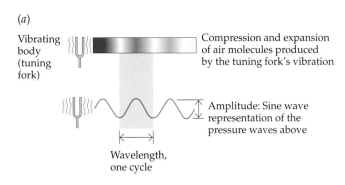

(a)

Vibrating body (tuning fork)

Compression and expansion of air molecules produced by the tuning fork's vibration

Amplitude: Sine wave representation of the pressure waves above

Wavelength, one cycle

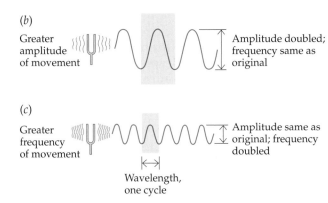

(b)

Greater amplitude of movement

Amplitude doubled; frequency same as original

(c)

Greater frequency of movement

Amplitude same as original; frequency doubled

Wavelength, one cycle

FIGURE 9.2 Amplitude and frequency. (a) Sound waves are described by the frequency and amplitude of pressure fluctuations. Changes in amplitude (b) and frequency (c) are shown for sine waves, the simplest kind of sound wave.

FIGURE 9.3 Humans can hear frequencies that range from about 20 to 20,000 Hz across a very wide range of intensities, or sound pressure levels (dB SPL, where dB = decibels).

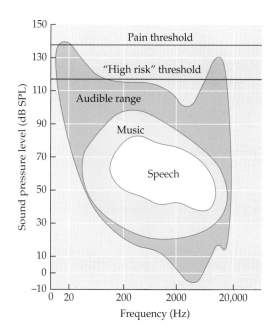

wave goes from its highest point down to its lowest point and back up to its highest point 500 times every second.

Just as the amplitude and wavelength of light waves correspond to perceptual qualities in vision (brightness and color, respectively), the amplitude and frequency of sound waves are highly correlated with auditory characteristics. Amplitude is associated with the perceptual quality of **loudness**: the more intense a sound wave is, the louder it will sound. Frequency is associated with **pitch**: low-frequency sounds correspond to low pitches (e.g., low notes played by a tuba), and high-frequency sounds corresponding to high pitches (e.g., the high notes from a piccolo). We will have much more to say about the relationships between amplitude and loudness and between frequency and pitch later in this chapter.

In Chapter 2 you learned that visible light makes up only a small portion of the much broader range of electromagnetic energy; similarly, human hearing uses a limited range of the frequencies present in environmental sounds. If you are relatively young and you've been careful about your exposure to loud sounds, you may be able to detect sounds that vary from about 20 to 20,000 Hz (**Figure 9.3**). Some animals hear sounds that have lower and higher frequencies than those heard by humans. Elephants hear vibrations at very low frequencies that help them detect the presence of large animals, such as other elephants. Dogs can be called with whistles that emit sounds at frequencies too high for humans to hear, and the sonar systems used by some bats use sound frequencies above 60,000 Hz.

Humans hear across a very wide range of sound intensities. The ratio between the faintest sound humans can detect and the loudest sounds that do not cause serious damage to human ears is more than one to a million. To describe differences in amplitude across such a broad range, sound levels are measured on a logarithmic scale using units called **decibels** (**dB**). Decibels define the difference between two sounds in terms of the ratio between sound pressures. Each 10:1 sound pressure ratio is equal to 20 decibels (dB), so a 100:1 ratio is equal to 40 decibels. The equation for defining decibels is

$$dB = 20 \log(p/p_0)$$

The variable p corresponds to the pressure (intensity) of the sound being described. The constant term p_0 is a reference pressure and is typically defined in auditory research contexts to be 0.0002 dyne per square centimeter (dyne/cm^2), and levels are defined as dB SPL (sound pressure level). This level (0.0002 dyne/cm^2) is close to the minimum pressure that can be detected at frequencies for which hearing is most sensitive, and decibel values greater than zero describe the ratio between a sound being measured and 0.0002 dyne/cm^2. The range of human hearing extends from 0 to over 120 dB SPL, and as shown in **Table 9.1**, this decibel range corresponds to a ratio of greater than 1,000,000:1.

Using a reference value such as p_0 is common to many measuring systems. For example, 0°C is defined as the temperature at

loudness The psychological aspect of sound related to perceived intensity (amplitude).

pitch The psychological aspect of sound related mainly to perceived frequency.

decibel (dB) A unit of measure for the physical intensity of sound. Decibels define the difference between two sounds as the ratio between two sound pressures. Each 10:1 sound pressure ratio equals 20 dB, and a 100:1 ratio equals 40 dB.

TABLE 9.1 *Decibel levels that correspond to different sound pressure ratios*

Ratio	dB
1	0.0
2	6.0
4	12.0
8	18.0
10	20.0
20	26.0
50	34.0
100	40.0
1000	60.0
10,000	80.0
100,000	100.0
1,000,000	120.0

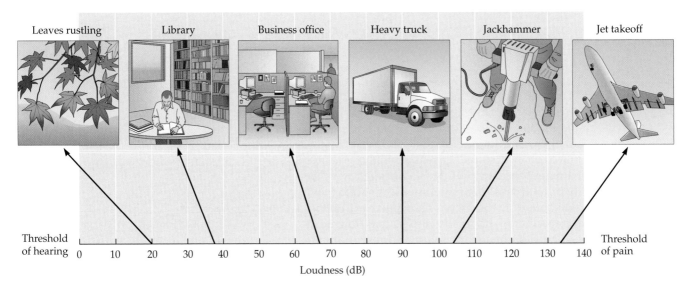

Leaves rustling Library Business office Heavy truck Jackhammer Jet takeoff

Threshold of hearing

0 10 20 30 40 50 60 70 80 90 100 110 120 130 140

Threshold of pain

Loudness (dB)

FIGURE 9.4 Sounds that we hear in our daily environments vary greatly in intensity.

which water freezes, and 100°C is the temperature at which water boils. If the pressure of the sound that you're measuring (p) is equal to 0.0002 dyne/cm², then dB = 20 log(1). Because the log of 1 is zero, a sound pressure that low would be equal to 0 dB SPL. Sounds with amplitudes even smaller than p_0 have negative decibel levels, just as substances colder than the freezing point of water have negative centigrade temperatures.

An important thing to remember about logarithmic scales such as decibels is that relatively small decibel changes can correspond to large physical changes. For example, an increase of 6 dB corresponds to a doubling of the amount of pressure. **Figure 9.4** shows the decibel levels of some common sound sources.

Sine Waves and Complex Sounds

In Chapter 1 you were introduced to one of the simplest kinds of sounds: a **sine wave**, which is often called a **pure tone**. All sounds, even as complex as the sounds produced by musical instruments, human speech, and city traffic, can be described as a combination of sine waves. (See **Web Activity 1.2: Fourier Analysis**.)

Complex sounds are best described in a **spectrum** (plural *spectra*) that displays how much energy, or amplitude, is present at multiple frequencies, as shown in **Figure 9.5**. Sounds with **harmonic spectra**, illustrated in **Figure 9.6**, are typically caused by a simple vibrating source, such as the string of a guitar or the reed of a saxophone. Each frequency component in such a sound is called a "harmonic." The first harmonic, called the **fundamental frequency**, is the lowest-frequency component of the sound. All the other harmonics have frequencies that are integer multiples of the fundamental.

The shape of the spectrum is one of the most important qualities that distinguish different sounds. The properties of sound sources determine the spectral shapes of sounds; thus these shapes can help us identify sound sources. For example, Figure 9.6 illustrates spectra from three musical instruments. Each instrument is producing a tone with the same fundamental frequency (262 Hz, which corresponds to the note C_4, or middle C) and the same harmonics (524 Hz, 786 Hz, 1048 Hz, and so on). However, the shapes of the spectra (the pattern of amplitudes for each harmonic) vary. **Timbre** (pronounced "tamber," like "amber") is a term used to describe the quality of a sound that depends, in part, on the relative energy levels of harmonic components.

sine wave or pure tone A waveform for which variation as a function of time is a sine function.

spectrum A representation of the relative energy (intensity) present at each frequency.

harmonic spectrum The spectrum of a complex sound in which energy is at integer multiples of the fundamental frequency.

fundamental frequency The lowest-frequency component of a complex periodic sound.

timbre The psychological sensation by which a listener can judge that two sounds with the same loudness and pitch are dissimilar. Timbre quality is conveyed by harmonics and other high frequencies.

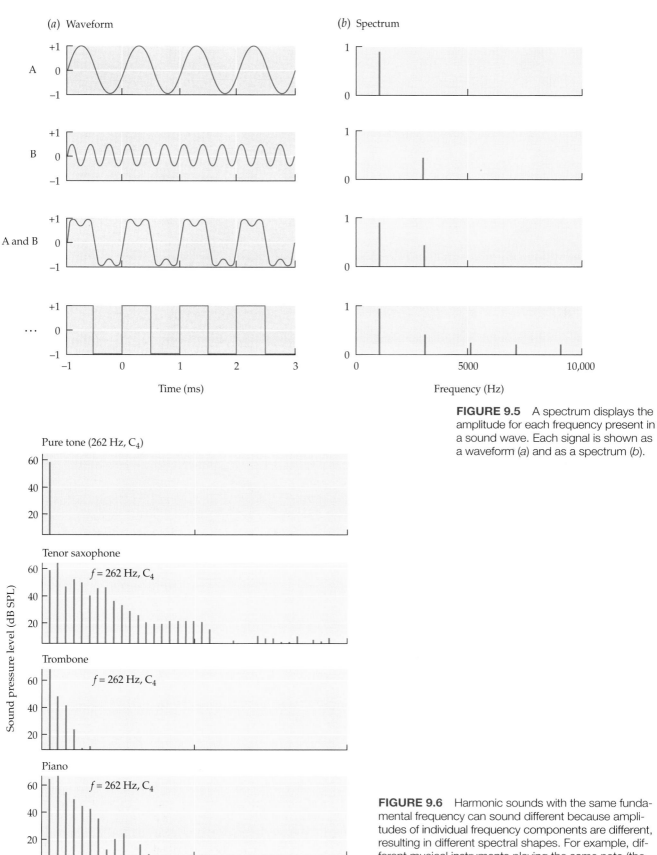

FIGURE 9.5 A spectrum displays the amplitude for each frequency present in a sound wave. Each signal is shown as a waveform (a) and as a spectrum (b).

FIGURE 9.6 Harmonic sounds with the same fundamental frequency can sound different because amplitudes of individual frequency components are different, resulting in different spectral shapes. For example, different musical instruments playing the same note (the same fundamental frequency, abbreviated f) sound different. C_4 = middle C.

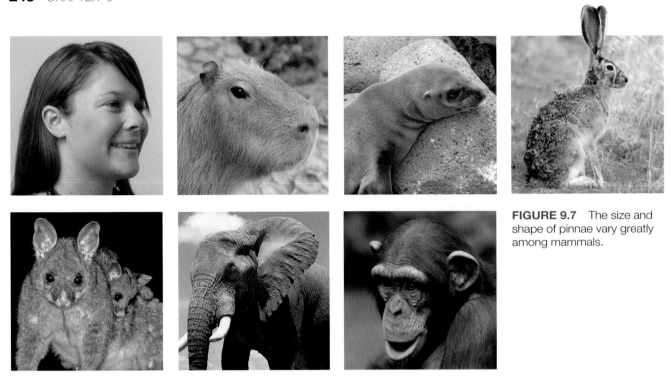

FIGURE 9.7 The size and shape of pinnae vary greatly among mammals.

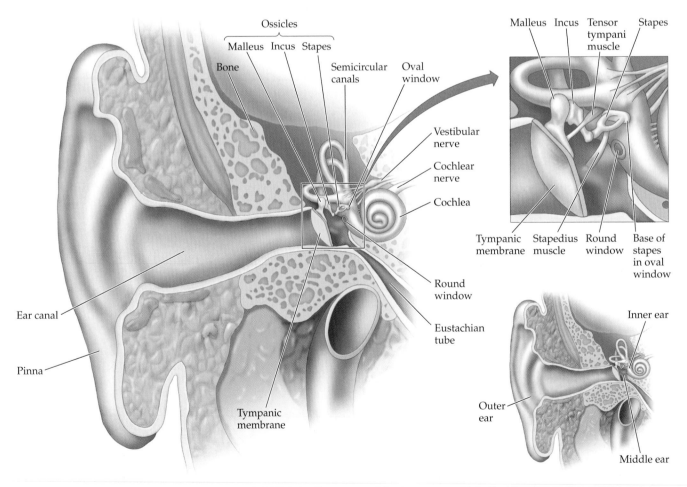

FIGURE 9.8 Structures of the human ear. Note that the tympanic membrane has about 18 times as much surface area as the oval window beneath the stapes.

We will return to harmonics, timbre, and other aspects of complex sounds in Chapter 11. In this chapter we'll stick mainly to the story of how the auditory system processes simple sounds such as sine wave tones.

Basic Structure of the Mammalian Auditory System

Now that you know what sound is, we can examine how sounds are detected and recognized by the auditory system. The sense of hearing has evolved over millions of years to be able to do some pretty amazing things. We are about to describe quite a few anatomical structures that are essential for understanding how sequences of tiny air pressure changes are turned into meaningful sound perception. The discussion may occasionally be a bit confusing, but if you consult the figures and **Web Activity 9.2: Structure of the Auditory System** often, you will soon know the parts and how they fit together.

Outer Ear

Sounds are first collected from the environment by the **pinna** (plural *pinnae*), the curly structure on the side of the head that we typically call an ear. Only mammals have pinnae, which vary wildly in shape and size across species and vary somewhat less dramatically across individuals within species (**Figure 9.7**). As we will see in Chapter 10, the particular shapes of the pinnae play an important role in our ability to localize sound sources.

Sound waves are funneled by the pinna into and through the **ear canal**, which extends about 25 millimeters (mm) into the head (**Figure 9.8**). The length and shape of the ear canal enhance sound frequencies between about 2000 and 6000 Hz, but the main purpose of the canal is to protect the structure at its end, the **tympanic membrane** (eardrum), from damage. The tympanic membrane is a thin sheet of skin that moves in and out in response to the pressure changes of sound waves.

It is a common myth that puncturing your eardrum will leave you deaf. While a ruptured eardrum can be excruciating, in most cases a damaged tympanic membrane will heal itself, just as other parts of the skin do. However, it is possible to damage the tympanic membrane beyond repair, so it's a good idea to follow your mother's advice and refrain from sticking things in your ear.

Middle Ear

Together, the pinna and ear canal make up a division of the auditory system called the **outer ear** (see Figure 9.8). The tympanic membrane is the border between the outer ear and the **middle ear**, which consists of three tiny bones, the **ossicles**, that amplify sound waves. The first ossicle, the **malleus**, is connected to the tympanic membrane on one side and to the second ossicle, the **incus**, on the other. The incus is connected in turn to the third ossicle, the **stapes**, which transmits the vibrations of sound waves to the **oval window**, another membrane, which forms the border between the middle ear and the **inner ear**.

The ossicles are the smallest bones in the human body, and they amplify sound vibrations in two ways. First, the joints between the bones are hinged in a way that makes them work like levers: a modest amount of energy on one side of the fulcrum (joint) becomes larger on the other. This lever action increases the amount of pressure change by about a third. The second way the ossicles increase the energy transmitted to the inner ear is by concentrating energy from a larger to a smaller surface area: the tympanic membrane, which

pinna The outer, funnel-like part of the ear.

ear canal The canal that conducts sound vibrations from the pinna to the tympanic membrane and prevents damage to the tympanic membrane.

tympanic membrane The eardrum; a thin sheet of skin at the end of the outer ear canal. The tympanic membrane vibrates in response to sound.

outer ear The external sound-gathering portion of the ear, consisting of the pinna and the ear canal.

middle ear An air-filled chamber containing the middle bones, or ossicles. The middle ear conveys and amplifies vibration from the tympanic membrane to the oval window.

ossicle Any of three tiny bones of the middle ear: malleus, incus, and stapes.

malleus One of the three ossicles. The malleus receives vibration from the tympanic membrane and is attached to the incus.

incus The middle of the three ossicles, connecting the malleus and the stapes.

stapes One of the three ossicles. Connected to the incus on one end, the stapes presses against the oval window of the cochlea on the other end.

oval window The flexible opening to the cochlea through which the stapes transmits vibration to the fluid inside.

inner ear A hollow cavity in the temporal bone of the skull, and the structures within this cavity: the cochlea and the semicircular canals of the vestibular system.

tensor tympani The muscle attached to the malleus; tensing the tensor tympani decreases vibration.

stapedius The muscle attached to the stapes; tensing the stapedius decreases vibration.

acoustic reflex A reflex that protects the ear from intense sounds, via contraction of the stapedius and tensor tympani muscles.

cochlea A spiral structure of the inner ear containing the organ of Corti.

tympanic canal One of three fluid-filled passages in the cochlea. The tympanic canal extends from the round window at the base of the cochlea to the helicotrema at the apex. Also called *scala tympani*.

vestibular canal One of three fluid-filled passages in the cochlea. The vestibular canal extends from the oval window at the base of the cochlea to the helicotrema at the apex. Also called *scala vestibuli*.

middle canal One of three fluid-filled passages in the cochlea. The middle canal is sandwiched between the tympanic and vestibular canals and contains the cochlear partition. Also called *scala media*.

helicotrema The opening that connects the tympanic and vestibular canals at the apex of the cochlea.

Reissner's membrane A thin sheath of tissue separating the vestibular and middle canals in the cochlea.

basilar membrane A plate of fibers that forms the base of the cochlear partition and separates the middle and tympanic canals in the cochlea.

moves the malleus, is about 18 times as large as the oval window, which is moved by the stapes (see Figure 9.8). Therefore, pressure on the oval window is magnified 18 times relative to the pressure on the tympanic membrane. This is the same principle that makes snowshoes effective for keeping feet from sinking in the snow and makes stiletto heels a danger to wood floors (think of the tympanic membrane as the heel of the foot and the oval window as the tip of the stiletto).

Amplification provided by the ossicles is essential to our ability to hear faint sounds because the inner ear, as we will see in a moment, is made up of a collection of fluid-filled chambers. Because it takes more energy to move liquid than it does to move air, this fluid creates an impedance mismatch: if sound waves were transmitted to the oval window directly, many would simply bounce back without moving the oval window at all.

The ossicles play an important role for loud sounds too. The middle ear has two muscles: the **tensor tympani** (attached to the malleus) and the **stapedius** (attached to the stapes) (see Figure 9.8). As might be expected, given that the ossicles are the smallest bones in the body, the tensor tympani and the stapedius are the smallest muscles in the body. Their main purpose is to tense when sounds are very loud, restricting the movement of the ossicles and thus muffling pressure changes that might be large enough to damage the delicate structures in the inner ear. Unfortunately, this **acoustic reflex** follows the onset of loud sounds by about one-fifth of a second. So although it helps in environments that are loud for sustained periods, the acoustic reflex cannot protect against abrupt loud sounds, such as the firing of a gun. The muscles of the middle ear can also be tensed during swallowing, talking, and general body movement, helping to keep the auditory system from being overwhelmed by sounds generated by our own bodies.

Inner Ear

The inner ear is an impressive feat of evolution. It is here that the fine changes in sound pressure available in the environment are translated into neural signals that inform the listener about the world. The function of the inner ear with respect to sound waves in hearing is thus roughly analogous to that of the retina with respect to light waves in vision: it translates the information carried by the waves into neural signals.

COCHLEAR CANALS AND MEMBRANES The major structure of the inner ear is the **cochlea** (from the Greek *kochlos*, "snail"), a tiny coiled structure embedded in the temporal bone of the skull (see Figure 9.8). Rolled up, the cochlea is the size of a baby pea, about 4 mm in diameter in humans. Uncoiled, it would be a tube about 35 mm long. The cochlea is filled with watery fluids in three parallel canals (**Figure 9.9**): the **tympanic canal** (or *scala tympani*), the **vestibular canal** (or *scala vestibuli*), and the **middle canal** (or *scala media*). The tympanic and vestibular canals are connected by a small opening, the **helico-trema**, and these two canals are effectively wrapped around the middle canal. Think of the tympanic and vestibular canals as one long skinny balloon (the kind clowns use to make hats and animals), blown up and folded back on itself. The middle canal is another long balloon that is squeezed, lengthwise, between the two halves of the first balloon.

The three canals of the cochlea are separated by two membranes (see Figure 9.9): **Reissner's membrane**, between the vestibular canal and the middle canal; and the **basilar membrane**, between the middle canal and the tympanic canal. Strictly speaking, the basilar membrane is not really a membrane, because it is not a thin, pliable sheet like the tympanic membrane, the oval window, or Reissner's membrane. Rather, it is a plate made up of fibers that have some stiffness. The basilar membrane forms the base of the **cochlear partition**, a complex structure through which sound waves are transduced into neural signals.

Vibrations transmitted through the tympanic membrane and middle-ear bones cause the stapes to push and pull the flexible oval window in and out of the vestibular canal at the base of the cochlea. This movement of the oval window causes waves of pressure changes, called "traveling waves," to flow through the fluid in the vestibular canal, in much the same way that the membrane of a loudspeaker initiates sound waves in the air. Because the cochlea is a closed system, however, the pressure changes cannot spread out in all directions, as they do in the atmosphere. Instead, a displacement, or "bulge," forms in the vestibular canal and travels from the base of the cochlea down to the apex. By the time the traveling wave reaches the apex, its displacement has mostly dissipated (see Figure 9.12). If sounds are extremely intense, any pressure that

cochlear partition The combined basilar membrane, tectorial membrane, and organ of Corti, which are together responsible for the transduction of sound waves into neural signals.

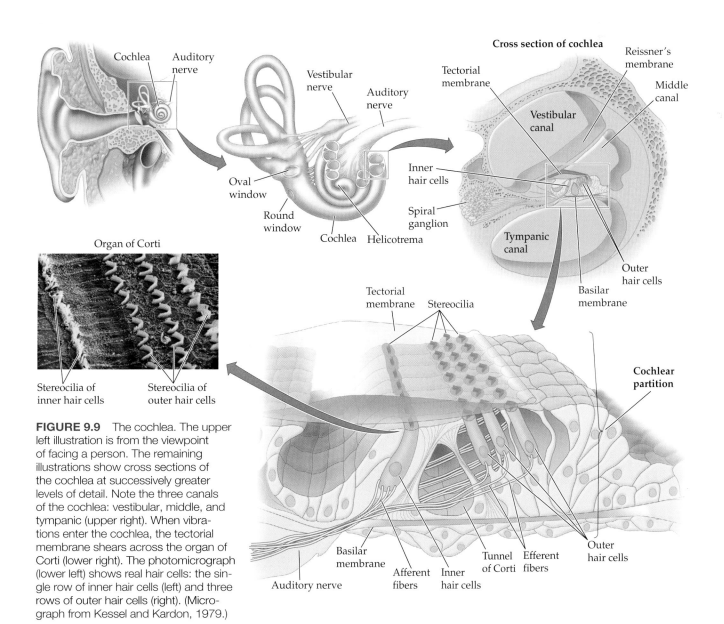

FIGURE 9.9 The cochlea. The upper left illustration is from the viewpoint of facing a person. The remaining illustrations show cross sections of the cochlea at successively greater levels of detail. Note the three canals of the cochlea: vestibular, middle, and tympanic (upper right). When vibrations enter the cochlea, the tectorial membrane shears across the organ of Corti (lower right). The photomicrograph (lower left) shows real hair cells: the single row of inner hair cells (left) and three rows of outer hair cells (right). (Micrograph from Kessel and Kardon, 1979.)

round window A soft area of tissue at the base of the tympanic canal that releases excess pressure remaining from extremely intense sounds.

organ of Corti A structure on the basilar membrane of the cochlea that is composed of hair cells and dendrites of auditory nerve fibers.

hair cell Any cell that has stereocilia for transducing mechanical movement in the inner ear into neural activity sent to the brain; some hair cells also receive inputs from the brain.

auditory nerve fiber A collection of neurons that convey information from hair cells in the cochlea to (afferent) and from (efferent) the brain stem.

stereocilium Any of the hairlike extensions on the tips of hair cells in the cochlea that, when flexed, initiate the release of neurotransmitters.

tectorial membrane A gelatinous structure, attached on one end, that extends into the middle canal of the ear, floating above inner hair cells and touching outer hair cells.

remains is transmitted through the helicotrema and back to the cochlear base through the tympanic canal, where it is absorbed by stretching yet another membrane, called the **round window** (see Figure 9.9).

Because the vestibular and tympanic canals are wrapped tightly around the middle canal, when the vestibular canal bulges out it puts pressure on the middle canal. This pressure has the effect of displacing the cochlear partition (which, recall, lies at the bottom of the middle canal), moving the partition down as the vestibular-canal bulge comes through, and back up as the bulge passes by.

THE ORGAN OF CORTI Movements of the cochlear partition are translated into neural signals by structures in the **organ of Corti**, which extends along the top of the basilar membrane (see Figure 9.9). The organ of Corti is made up of specialized neurons called **hair cells**, dendrites of **auditory nerve fibers** that terminate at the base of hair cells, and a scaffold of supporting cells. Hair cells in each human ear are arranged in four rows that run down the length of the basilar membrane: one row of about 3500 inner hair cells and three rows with a total of about 10,500 outer hair cells.

Inner and outer hair cells provide the foundations for minuscule hairlike bristles called **stereocilia** (singular *stereocilium*). On an inner hair cell, stereocilia are arranged as if posing for a group photo, in several nearly straight rows with the shorter stereocilia in front and the taller ones peering over their shoulders in the back. On an outer hair cell, stereocilia stand in rows that form the shape of a *V* or *W* (see Figure 9.9).

The **tectorial membrane** extends atop the organ of Corti. Like the basilar membrane, it isn't really a membrane. Rather, it is a gelatinous flap that is attached on one end and floats above the outer hair cells on the other end. Taller stereocilia of outer hair cells are embedded in the tectorial membrane, and the cilia of inner hair cells are nestled against it. Because the tectorial membrane is attached on only one end, it shears across the width of the cochlear partition whenever the partition moves up and down. This shearing motion in turn causes the stereocilia of both inner and outer hair cells to bend back and forth (Figure 9.10).

INNER AND OUTER HAIR CELLS Like photoreceptors in the retina, hair cells are specialized neurons that transduce one kind of energy (in this case, sound

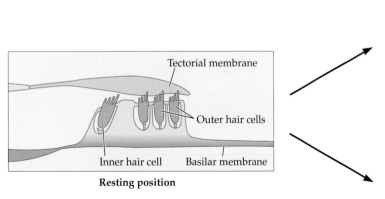

FIGURE 9.10 When vibration causes a displacement along the cochlear partition, the tectorial membrane and hair cells move in opposite directions (shear), and the deflection of stereocilia during this action results in the release of neurotransmitters.

pressure) into another form of energy (neural firing). Deflection of a hair cell's stereocilia causes a change in voltage potential that initiates the release of neurotransmitters, which in turn encourages firing by auditory nerve fibers that have dendritic synapses on hair cells. However, it is the differences between photoreceptors and hair cells that are the most interesting.

tip link A tiny filament that stretches from the tip of a stereocilium to the side of its neighbor.

> **FURTHER DISCUSSION** of hair cells in the context of sensing head movements can be found in Chapter 12 on pages 337–338.

While the retina has almost 100 million photoreceptors, the cochlea has only about 14,000 hair cells. And the stereocilia of hair cells blow away the competition when it comes to speed and sensitivity. As we'll see in Chapter 10, hair cells must be capable of responding so fast that we can detect time differences of as little as 10 millionths of a second—10 microseconds (μs)—in order to know the direction from which a sound arrives. In contrast, when we watch a movie, pictures shown at 24 frames per second appear continuous to the visual system. Hair cells are not only extremely fast, but also extremely sensitive. It may take 30 minutes for our eyes to fully adjust to a dark theater, but our ears are always ready for the slightest sound.

Recall that the shortest stereocilia are in front of slightly taller stereocilia that are in front of still-taller stereocilia (Figure 9.11). Each stereocilium is connected to its taller neighbor by a tiny filament called a **tip link**, so the stereocilia connected by tip links bend together as a set when deflected by the shearing motion of the tectorial membrane. When a stereocilium deflects, the tip link pulls on the taller stereocilium in a way that opens an ion pore somewhat like opening a gate for just a tiny fraction of a second. This action permits potassium ions (K+) to flow rapidly into the hair cell, causing rapid depolarization (see

FIGURE 9.11 Stereocilia regulate the flow of ions into and out of hair cells. (a) This photomicrograph shows the threadlike tip links that connect the tip of each stereocilium to its taller neighbor. (b, c) Bending the stereocilia atop a hair cell opens the ion pores, permitting a rapid influx of potassium ions (K+) into the hair cell. The resulting depolarization opens channels that allow calcium ions (Ca2+) to enter the base of the hair cell, causing the release of neurotransmitter into the synapse between the hair cell and an afferent auditory nerve fiber.

(a)

(b)

(c)
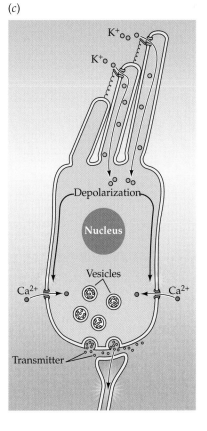

Figures 9.11*b* and *c*). In turn, depolarization leads to a rapid influx of calcium ions (Ca^{2+}) and initiation of the release of neurotransmitters from the base of the hair cell to stimulate dendrites of the auditory nerve (Fettiplace and Hackney, 2006; Hudspeth, 1997).

The opening of ion pores that results from the direct connection between stereocilia via tip links is the only known example of mechanoelectrical transduction (MET), which is responsible for both the extreme speed and the sensitivity of hair cells. Unlike the case in vision, depolarization in hearing does not await a cascade of biochemical processes such as those in photoactivation. MET is also extremely sensitive: ion pores open when deflection is as little as 1 nanometer (nm), roughly the diameter of a single atom. This deflection is equivalent to only half an inch of movement at the top of the 324-meter (1063-foot) Eiffel Tower as it sways (Goldberg, 2008).

The firing of the auditory nerve fibers finally completes the process of translating sound waves into patterns of neural activity.

Here's a brief summary of the whole process: An air pressure wave is funneled by the pinna through the auditory canal to the tympanic membrane, which vibrates back and forth in time with the sound wave. The tympanic membrane moves the malleus, which moves the incus, which moves the stapes, which pushes and pulls on the oval window. The movement of the oval window causes pressure bulges to move down the length of the vestibular canal, and these bulges in the vestibular canal displace the middle canal up and down. This up-and-down motion forces the tectorial membrane to shear across the organ of Corti, moving the stereocilia atop hair cells back and forth. The flexing of the stereocilia initiates rapid depolarization that results in the release of neurotransmitters into synapses between the hair cells and dendrites of auditory nerve fibers. These neurotransmitters initiate action potentials in the auditory nerve fibers that are carried to the brain. And that's all there is to it!

CODING OF AMPLITUDE AND FREQUENCY IN THE COCHLEA   Now let's return to the bulging vestibular canal and undulating middle canal to see how the two fundamental characteristics of sound waves—amplitude and frequency—are encoded by the cochlea.

As the amplitude of a sound wave increases, the tympanic membrane and oval window move farther in and out with each pressure fluctuation. The result is that the bulge in the vestibular canal becomes bigger, which causes the cochlear partition to move farther up and down, which causes the tectorial membrane to shear across the organ of Corti more forcefully, which causes the hair cells to bend farther back and forth, which causes more neurotransmitters to be released, which causes the auditory nerve fibers to fire action potentials more quickly. Thus, sound wave amplitude is conveyed in much the same way as light wave amplitude: the larger the amplitude, the higher the firing rate of the neurons that communicate with the brain. (We will discuss some complications of this simple explanation later in the chapter.)

Coding for frequency is a bit trickier. Earlier we said that the cochlear partition is displaced up and down in a pattern reflecting the pattern (frequency) of the sound wave. This statement is true as far as it goes, but it does not tell the whole story, because *different parts of the cochlear partition are displaced to different degrees by different sound wave frequencies*. High frequencies cause displacements closer to the oval window, near the base of the cochlea; lower frequencies cause displacements nearer the apex. In other words, different places on the cochlea are "tuned" to different frequencies. This tuning is known as the **place code** for sound frequency.

Cochlear tuning to frequency is caused, in large part, by the way the structure of the basilar membrane changes along the length of the cochlea (**Figure 9.12**).

place code Tuning of different parts of the cochlea to different frequencies, in which information about the particular frequency of an incoming sound wave is coded by the place along the cochlear partition that has the greatest mechanical displacement.

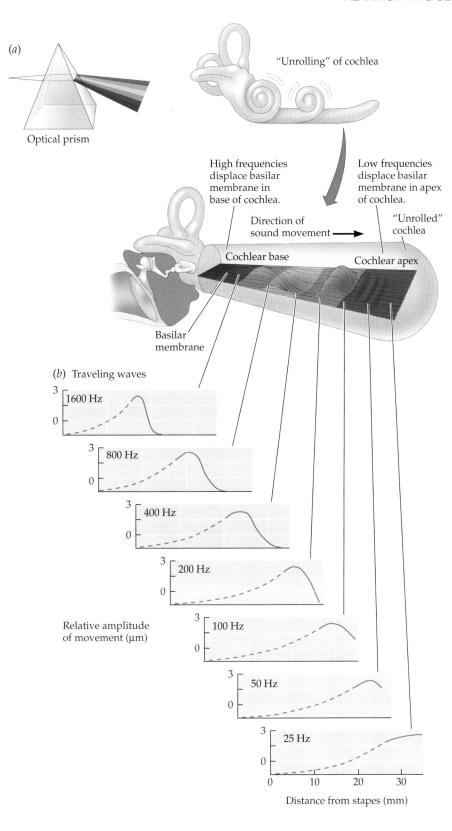

(a) Optical prism

"Unrolling" of cochlea

High frequencies displace basilar membrane in base of cochlea.

Low frequencies displace basilar membrane in apex of cochlea.

Direction of sound movement →

"Unrolled" cochlea

Cochlear base

Cochlear apex

Basilar membrane

(b) Traveling waves

1600 Hz

800 Hz

400 Hz

200 Hz

Relative amplitude of movement (μm)

100 Hz

50 Hz

25 Hz

Distance from stapes (mm)

FIGURE 9.12 The cochlea is like an acoustic prism in that its sensitivity spreads across different sound frequencies along its length. The narrower end of the basilar membrane toward the base is stiffer and most sensitive to higher frequencies. The wider, more flexible end toward the apex is most sensitive to lower frequencies. Here the cochlea is illustrated as if it were uncoiled (a), and the shapes of the traveling waves for different frequencies of vibration are shown (b).

The cochlea as a whole narrows from base to apex, but the basilar membrane actually widens toward the apex. In addition, the basilar membrane is thick at the base and becomes thinner as it widens. As a result, the cochlea separates frequencies along its length like an acoustic prism. Higher frequencies bend the narrower, stiffer regions of the basilar membrane near the base more, and

afferent fiber A neuron that carries sensory information to the central nervous system.

efferent fiber A neuron that carries information from the central nervous system to the periphery.

threshold tuning curve A graph plotting the thresholds of a neuron or fiber in response to sine waves with varying frequencies at the lowest intensity that will give rise to a response.

characteristic frequency (CF) The frequency to which a particular auditory nerve fiber is most sensitive.

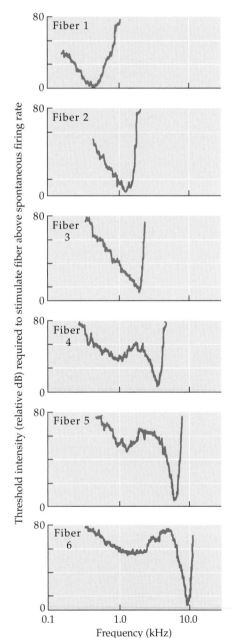

lower frequencies cause greater displacements in the wider, more flexible regions near the apex.

In addition to this passive, structural way of being tuned to frequency, active processes sharpen the tuning. Remember that there are two different types of hair cells: inner and outer. Over 90% of the **afferent fibers** in the auditory nerve—fibers that take information *to* the brain—synapse on the 3500 inner hair cells (10–30 auditory nerve fibers listen to each inner hair cell). If the inner hair cells are conveying almost all the information about sound waves to the brain, then what do the 10,500 outer hair cells do? It turns out that most of the nerve fibers that synapse with the outer hair cells are **efferent fibers**, conveying information *from* the brain. When these efferent fibers become active, outer hair cells with which they synapse become physically longer, making the nearby cochlear partition stiffer (Fettiplace and Hackney, 2006). By making some parts of the cochlear partition stiffer than other parts, the outer hair cells make the cochlea more sensitive and more sharply tuned to particular frequencies.

The Auditory Nerve

Now that we've covered the mechanics of how the auditory system translates air pressure changes into auditory nerve firing, let's discuss what we know about the characteristics of these auditory nerve (AN) fibers. More specifically, we'll consider the quality of the information conveyed by afferent AN fibers from the cochlea to the brain.

Remember that sounds with different frequencies displace different regions of the cochlear partition, and inner hair cells, on which most afferent AN fibers synapse, extend along a line traveling the length of the cochlear partition. Put these two pieces of information together, and we can infer that the responses of individual AN fibers to different frequencies should be related to their place along the cochlear partition. Sure enough, when scientists record from individual AN fibers in animals, they find that different fibers selectively respond to different sound frequencies.

This frequency selectivity is clearest when sounds are very faint: at very low intensity levels (even less than 0 dB), an AN fiber will increase firing to only a very restricted range of frequencies. **Figure 9.13** shows **threshold tuning curves** for several AN fibers. To graph these curves, researchers insert an electrode very close to a single AN fiber, and then they measure how intense the sine waves of different frequencies must be for the neuron to fire faster than its normal, spontaneous firing rate. The frequency that increases the neuron's firing rate at the lowest intensity (the lowest point on the threshold tuning curve) is called the neuron's **characteristic frequency (CF)**.

Up to this point, the way the ear transduces acoustic energy at different frequencies into a pattern of neural responses seems fairly straightforward. A low-intensity sine wave tone with a certain frequency will cause certain AN fibers to increase their firing rates, while other AN fibers continue to fire at their spontaneous rates. As long as the brain knows which AN fibers have which characteristic frequencies, the brain can interpret the pattern of firing rates across all the AN fibers to determine the frequency of any tone (as long as it is within the range of frequencies picked up by the human cochlea).

FIGURE 9.13 Threshold tuning curves for six auditory nerve fibers, each tuned to a different frequency. Curves define the lowest intensity necessary for the neuron to fire above its spontaneous rate at each frequency. The characteristic frequency for each of these six nerve fibers is at the lowest point of the tuning curve.

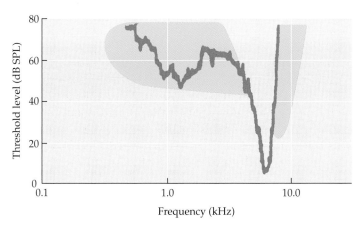

FIGURE 9.14   Two-tone suppression. The threshold tuning curve (dark red) plots the responses of one auditory nerve fiber with a characteristic frequency of 8000 Hz. Whenever a second tone is played at the frequencies and levels within the light red areas to each side, the response of this AN fiber to an 8000-Hz tone is reduced (suppressed).

Unfortunately, it's not quite this simple. Almost all sounds in the environment are more complex than single sine waves, and most sounds we hear are also much louder than the very quiet sound waves used to measure threshold tuning curves. So although the previous paragraph captures the gist of how AN fibers code for sound frequencies, we have to do a bit more work to understand how higher-intensity, complex sounds are encoded in the auditory nerve. We will consider two of the specific complications we have to deal with; then we'll look at one additional mechanism that the auditory system uses to convey low-frequency components of sound waves.

TWO-TONE SUPPRESSION   The rate at which an AN fiber responds changes when energy is introduced at nearby frequencies. In particular, when a second tone of a slightly different frequency is added, the rate of neural firing for the first tone actually decreases—a phenomenon called **two-tone suppression**. As **Figure 9.14** shows, suppression effects are particularly pronounced when the second (suppressor) tone has a lower frequency than the first tone. In other words, if we're recording from an AN fiber whose CF is 8000 Hz and we use an 8000-Hz test tone, a 1000-Hz suppressor tone has a greater effect on the neuron's firing rate than a 15,000-Hz suppressor tone has.

The suppression effect appears to be caused by mechanical changes to the basilar membrane (Rhode and Cooper, 1993). The important point for our purposes is that understanding the response of the whole auditory nerve to complex sounds (that is, frequency combinations) is more complicated than simply adding up the responses of individual AN fibers to individual pure tones.

RATE SATURATION   The sounds that matter most to listeners—most conversational speech, for example—are usually heard at intensities that greatly exceed the threshold for just detecting sounds. Are AN fibers as selective for their characteristic frequencies at levels well above threshold as they are for the barely audible sounds used to chart threshold tuning curves?

To answer this question, we can look at **isointensity curves**, which we chart by measuring an AN fiber's firing rate to a wide range of frequencies, all presented at the same intensity level. **Figure 9.15** shows a family of isointensity curves for one AN fiber with a CF of 2000 Hz. The bottom curve

two-tone suppression   A decrease in the firing rate of one auditory nerve fiber due to one tone, when a second tone is presented at the same time.

isointensity curve   A map plotting the firing rate of an auditory nerve fiber against varying frequencies at a steady intensity.

FIGURE 9.15 Isointensity functions for one AN fiber with a characteristic frequency of 2000 Hz. Tones of varying frequencies are presented at 20, 40, 60, and 80 dB. The neuron fires vigorously to a wider range of frequencies (mostly lower) when intensity is increased. Note that the 20-dB curve resembles an upside-down threshold tuning curve (compare to Figure 9.13) because 20 dB is almost as low as the intensities at which thresholds are measured.

shows the average firing rate (number of action potentials per second) of the neuron in response to 20-dB tones with frequencies between 50 and 3300 Hz. The other curves track firing rates for 40-dB, 60-dB, and 80-dB tones over the same frequency range (for higher frequencies, the neuron always fires at its spontaneous rate).

We learn from these curves that for relatively quiet, 20-dB sounds (this is about the sound level of leaves rustling in the wind), the neuron is still quite selectively tuned, firing much faster in response to its CF (2000 Hz) than to neighboring frequencies. At 80 dB, however, the neuron appears to fire at about the same rate for any frequency in the range of 800–2500 Hz. In other words, frequencies such as 1000 Hz, to which the AN fiber had almost no response at low intensity levels, evoke quite substantial responses when intensity is increased.

The phenomenon behind this broadening of frequency selectivity is called **rate saturation**. Remember that AN fibers fire in response to the bending of stereocilia on hair cells, and that, in general, the farther they bend, the faster the firing rate is. For a 20-dB tone at 1000 Hz, the stereocilia on the hair cell feeding the AN fiber featured in Figure 9.15 will not bend at all, so the fiber's firing rate remains at its resting level. The firing rate rises above this resting level when the frequency of the 20-dB tone is increased to 1700 Hz, and it reaches its highest level at the AN fiber's characteristic frequency, 2000 Hz.

When the intensity is increased to 40 dB, however, the bulge in the vestibular canal is so large that stereocilia start bending even to a 1000-Hz tone (see Figure 9.15). If we increase the frequency to 1250 Hz, the firing rate increases, and it increases even more at 1500 Hz. The problem is that at about 1500 Hz, the fiber's firing rate maxes out (saturates). The stereocilia are bending as much as they can at this point, so increasing the frequency of the tone has no additional effect on the AN fiber's firing rate until we increase the frequency above the

rate saturation The point at which a nerve fiber is firing as rapidly as possible and further stimulation is incapable of increasing the firing rate.

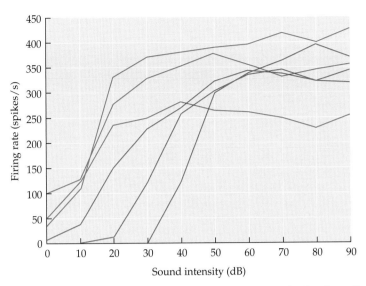

FIGURE 9.16 Firing rate plotted against sound intensity for six auditory nerve fibers: three low-spontaneous (red) and three high-spontaneous (blue). Firing rates for all six neurons increase with increasing sound level. Low-spontaneous neurons require higher-intensity sounds before they begin to fire, and they continue to increase firing rate to higher sound levels.

fiber's CF and the firing rate starts dropping again. For 80-dB tones, the fiber maxes out at even lower and higher frequencies relative to the CF of 2000 Hz.

For moderately intense tones, then, the brain cannot rely on a single AN fiber to determine the frequency of the tone. For example, we can't use the rule "if an AN fiber with a characteristic frequency of 2000 Hz is firing very fast, the sound must be 2000 Hz" because, as Figure 9.15 illustrates, this neuron will fire at its maximum rate to a 1000-Hz tone if the sound wave has a large-enough amplitude.

One way the auditory system gets around this problem is to use AN fibers with different spontaneous firing rates. **Figure 9.16** shows **rate-intensity functions** for six fibers, all of which listen to the same hair cell (remember that dendrites from 10–30 auditory neurons synapse with each inner hair cell). To plot these curves, the intensity level of a tone at the AN fiber's CF is slowly raised from 0 dB up to 90 dB. As you can see, the resting rates of some fibers (whose functions are plotted in red) are less than 10 spikes per second. These neurons are **low-spontaneous fibers**. The blue lines plot firing rates for **high-spontaneous fibers**, which fire 30 or more times per second, even in silence. **Mid-spontaneous fibers** have resting rates between these levels.

High-spontaneous AN fibers are somewhat analogous to rods in the retina: they are especially sensitive to low levels of sound, responding at rates above resting level even when decibel levels are quite low. The trade-off is that the firing rates of these fibers quickly reach saturation, so their frequency selectivity is relatively poor when intensity is relatively high. Low-spontaneous fibers are more like cones, requiring more energy (higher-intensity sound waves) to start responding, but retaining their frequency selectivity over a broader range of intensity.

In addition to deploying different AN fibers with different spontaneous rates, the auditory system accurately determines the frequency of incoming sound waves by integrating the information across a broad range of AN fibers, and using the *pattern* of firing rates across all these fibers. Remember that in the visual system, we use the pattern of firing across our three types of cones to

rate-intensity function A graph plotting the firing rate of an auditory nerve fiber in response to a sound of constant frequency at increasing intensities.

low-spontaneous fiber An auditory nerve fiber that has a low rate (less than 10 spikes per second) of spontaneous firing; low-spontaneous fibers require relatively intense sound before they will fire at higher rates.

high-spontaneous fiber An auditory nerve fiber that has a high rate (more than 30 spikes per second) of spontaneous firing; high-spontaneous fibers increase their firing rate in response to relatively low levels of sound.

mid-spontaneous fiber An auditory nerve fiber that has a medium rate (10–30 spikes per second) of spontaneous firing. The characteristics of mid-spontaneous fibers are intermediate between low- and high-spontaneous fibers.

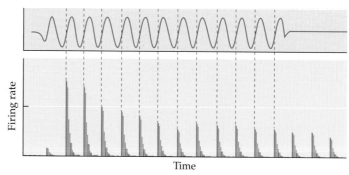

FIGURE 9.17 Phase locking. The histogram (bottom) shows neural spikes for an AN fiber in response to the same low-frequency sine wave (top) being played many times. Note that the neuron is most likely to fire at one particular phase of each cycle of the sine wave. This phase locking provides a temporal code to sound frequency.

phase locking Firing of a single neuron at one distinct point in the period (cycle) of a sound wave at a given frequency. (The neuron need not fire on every cycle, but each firing will occur at the same point in the cycle.)

temporal code Tuning of different parts of the cochlea to different frequencies, in which information about the particular frequency of an incoming sound wave is coded by the timing of neural firing as it relates to the period of the sound.

volley principle The idea that multiple neurons can provide a temporal code for frequency if each neuron fires at a distinct point in the period of a sound wave but does not fire on every period.

calculate the wavelength of light. The auditory system uses the same principle, but it has some 14,000 AN fibers in each ear to discern acoustic frequency. Consequently, the frequency sensitivity of the human auditory system as a whole is exquisite across a wide range of intensity levels, despite the coarse selectivity of individual AN fibers.

THE TEMPORAL CODE FOR SOUND FREQUENCY In addition to the cochlear place code, the auditory system has another way to encode frequency. As **Figure 9.17** illustrates, many AN fibers tend to fire action potentials at one particular point in the phase of a sound wave—a phenomenon called **phase locking**. Phase locking may occur because AN fibers fire when the stereocilia of hair cells move in one direction (e.g., as the basilar membrane moves up toward the tectorial membrane) but do not fire when the stereocilia move in the other direction. Recall from our discussion of mechanoelectrical transduction in stereocilia that the encoding of time is extremely accurate.

The existence of phase locking means that the firing pattern of an AN fiber carries a **temporal code** for the sound wave frequency. For example, if the AN fiber fires an action potential 100 times per second, then downstream neurons listening to the AN fiber can infer that the sound wave includes a frequency component of 100 Hz.

As measured in the auditory nerve, temporal coding becomes inconsistent for frequencies higher than 1000 Hz and is virtually absent above 4000 or 5000 Hz. In large part, this inconsistency is due to the refractory period of the AN fiber. For high frequencies, the fibers simply cannot produce action potentials quickly enough to fire on every cycle of the sound. However, multiple neurons could, in principle, encode higher frequencies as a group. For example, four neurons could each fire only once every fourth cycle of a 2000-Hz sound. If the four neurons "took turns," each would have to fire only 500 times per second to fully encode the 2000-Hz sound in their combined temporal pattern. This idea has a long history (Wever, 1949), and it is referred to as the **volley principle** (Figure 9.18). According to this hypothesis, neurons sustain a temporal pattern of firing much like the pattern of Revolutionary War–era soldiers firing guns from the front line of a formation while the second and third lines took time to reload.

Interestingly, even AN fibers with relatively high-frequency CFs encode lower-frequency energy in the temporal pattern of their responses. For example, if you are listening to a fairly loud sound that is a combination of 200- and

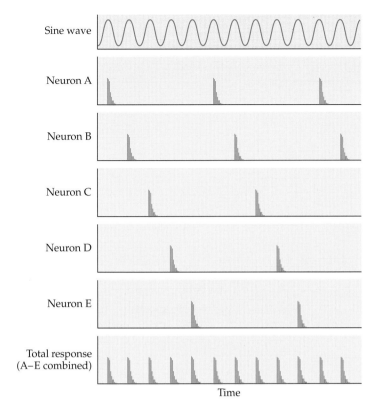

FIGURE 9.18 The volley principle. Even if one neuron cannot fire in response to every cycle of a higher-frequency tone, multiple AN fibers together can provide a temporal code for frequency if different neurons (A, B, C, D, E) each fire at different periods of the sine wave.

8000-Hz sine wave tones, a neuron near the base of the cochlea that becomes wildly excited by the 8000-Hz component of the sound will also tend to be phase-locked to the 200-Hz component. This neuron thus carries information about both the high-frequency component (via place coding, because the brain knows the neuron's CF) and the low-frequency component (via temporal coding).

Auditory Brain Structures

The nerve fibers that make up the auditory nerve share cranial nerve VIII with nerve fibers for the vestibular system (which is discussed in Chapter 12); this is why cranial nerve VIII is known not only as the auditory nerve, but also as the "vestibulocochlear nerve." All AN fibers initially synapse in the **cochlear nucleus**, which consists of three subnuclei (Figure 9.19). The cochlear nucleus contains many different types of specialized neurons. Some of these are especially sensitive to just the onsets of sound at particular frequencies. Some are sensitive to the coincidence of onsets across many frequencies (that is, they fire when multiple frequencies are initially heard, but stop firing if the sound continues playing). Some cochlear nucleus neurons use lateral inhibition to sharpen the tuning to one frequency by suppressing nearby frequencies—a mechanism reminiscent of that used by retinal ganglion cells to respond to spots of light instead of broad fields of light. Others respond in exactly the same way as the AN fibers that feed them. Some neurons appear to serve as little more than quick relays from the cochlea to the **superior olive**, another brain stem nucleus.

cochlear nucleus The first brain stem nucleus at which afferent auditory nerve fibers synapse.

superior olive An early brain stem region in the auditory pathway where inputs from both ears converge.

FIGURE 9.19 Pathways in the auditory system. Not all pathways are shown in this schematic. Although there are two parallel pathways, information from both ears comes together very early in the auditory system, at the superior olives.

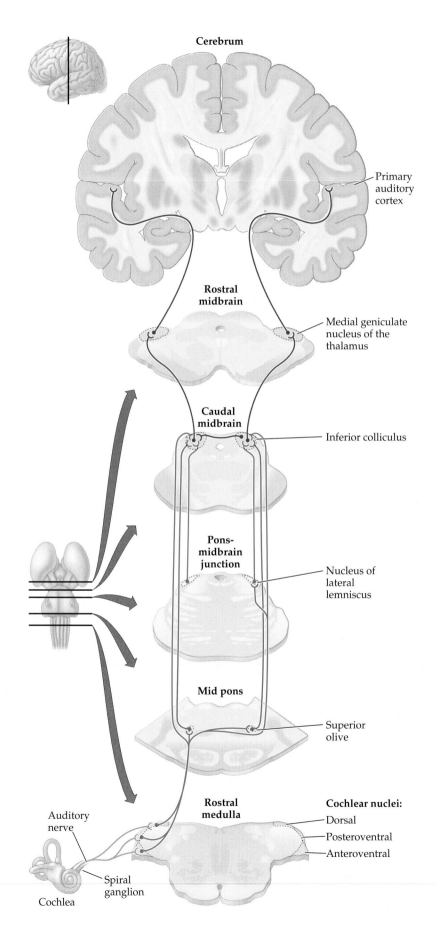

Cerebrum

Primary auditory cortex

Rostral midbrain

Medial geniculate nucleus of the thalamus

Caudal midbrain

Inferior colliculus

Pons-midbrain junction

Nucleus of lateral lemniscus

Mid pons

Superior olive

Rostral medulla

Cochlear nuclei:
Dorsal
Posteroventral
Anteroventral

Auditory nerve

Spiral ganglion

Cochlea

As Figure 9.19 shows, some of the neurons that project from the cochlear nuclei to the superior olives cross over to the opposite side of the brain. Thus, unlike the visual system, where inputs from each visual field remain separate until they have extended a fair distance in the visual cortex, signals from both cochleas reach both sides of the brain after only a single synapse. As we will see in Chapter 10, this direct relay of information from both ears is essential to using tiny timing differences between the two ears to detect the source of a sound.

Neurons from the cochlear nucleus and superior olive travel up the brain stem to the **inferior colliculus**. Most (but not all) of the input to each inferior colliculus comes from the opposite (contralateral) ear; that is, the left inferior colliculus listens primarily to the right ear, and vice versa.

The **medial geniculate nucleus** of the thalamus is the last stop in the auditory pathway before the cerebral cortex. As is the case in the lateral geniculate of the visual system, many more neurons project from the cortex to the medial geniculate (efferent) than project from the medial geniculate to the cortex (afferent). These efferent connections, some of which presumably convey information back to lower stages of the auditory system, provide further anatomical evidence that sensory systems are two-way streets, in which feedback from the brain is tightly integrated with sensory information flowing up to the brain.

All structures of the auditory system, beginning with the basilar membrane and continuing through the cochlear nucleus, superior olive, inferior colliculus, and medial geniculate, show a consistent organizational pattern in which neurons are aligned respective to the frequencies to which they are most sensitive. That is, neurons most responsive to low-frequency energy lie on one edge of each structure, neurons responding to high frequencies lie on the other edge, and neurons responding to other frequencies are spread out in an orderly fashion in between. The pervasiveness of this **tonotopic organization** pattern reflects both the early mechanical properties of transduction and the importance of the frequency composition of sounds for auditory perception.

Tonotopic organization is maintained in the **primary auditory cortex**, which is referred to as **A1**, just as primary visual cortex is called V1. Neurons from A1 project to the surrounding **belt area** of cortex, and neurons from this belt synapse with neurons in the adjacent **parabelt area** (Figure 9.20). Just about any sound will cause activation in some part of A1. In the belt and parabelt areas, referred to as "secondary" or "associational" auditory areas, simple sounds such as sine waves and white noise elicit less activity, particularly if the stimuli don't change much over time. Thus we see that, as in other sensory systems, processing proceeds from simpler to more complex stimuli as we move farther along the auditory pathway. We also find greater evidence of cross-modal processing (e.g., combining acoustic and optic information), particularly in parabelt areas.

Comparing the overall structure of the auditory and visual systems shows that a relatively large proportion of the processing in the auditory system is done before A1. By contrast, you learned in Chapter 3 that the majority of the most important visual processing occurs in cortical areas V1 and beyond. This difference may be a by-product of the evolutionary history of the two senses. The earliest mammals were small animals that were probably prey

inferior colliculus A midbrain nucleus in the auditory pathway.

medial geniculate nucleus The part of the thalamus that relays auditory signals to the temporal cortex and receives input from the auditory cortex.

tonotopic organization An arrangement in which neurons that respond to different frequencies are organized anatomically in order of frequency.

primary auditory cortex (A1) The first area within the temporal lobes of the brain responsible for processing acoustic information.

belt area A region of cortex, directly adjacent to the primary auditory cortex (A1), with inputs from A1, where neurons respond to more complex characteristics of sounds.

parabelt area A region of cortex, lateral and adjacent to the belt area, where neurons respond to more complex characteristics of sounds, as well as to input from other senses.

FIGURE 9.20 The first stages of auditory processing begin in the temporal lobe in areas within the Sylvian fissure. The top picture is from the side of the brain, and the lower two pictures are looking down at the brain with the parietal cortex cut away. Primary auditory cortex (A1) is in the center. It is surrounded by belt regions, and parabelt regions extend past the belt to the front and side. (From Brugge and Howard, 2002.)

favored by dinosaurs and early birds. They were also nocturnal, so hearing, smell, and touch were their primary senses. Survival may have required these mammals to become proficient listeners with primarily brain stem processes to rely on, because the stem was just about all there was to the brain in those days. The shift of some mammals to a diurnal lifestyle coincided evolutionarily with an enormous expansion of the cortex, so it makes sense that the new visual capabilities that arose later in mammals developed largely in the cortex. Interestingly, one auditory capability that we know to be a very recent evolutionary advance—speech processing—is subserved almost entirely by cortical areas. We will return to the role of the cortex in auditory processing when we discuss speech and music perception in Chapter 11.

Basic Operating Characteristics of the Auditory System

Up to this point we have discussed the anatomy of the auditory system and the physiology of how the system encodes the two basic physical attributes of sound waves: amplitude (intensity) and frequency. As we've seen, these issues are investigated by direct observation of the anatomical structures: scientists examine basilar membranes, record from auditory nerve fibers, dissect various brain structures, and so on.

We turn now to the findings of researchers who have approached the auditory system from a different perspective. Instead of playing a sound and trying to determine how one particular neuron responds, we can instead play the sound and ask actual human listeners—each of whom is the sum total of a great many neurons—what they hear. When human listeners are asked to report their auditory sensations, their answers are due partly to the acoustic properties of the sound signal and partly to their own psychological characteristics. This method of investigation is thus called **psychoacoustics**.

Scientists who study psychoacoustics (psychoacousticians) are always careful to distinguish between the physical characteristics of sounds and the impressions of these sounds for listeners. As we noted earlier, whereas frequency, measured in hertz, is a physical description of the spectral composition of a sound, the subjective attribute of frequency for listeners is *pitch*. Sounds are measured with respect to frequency, but listeners hear pitch. Similarly, the intensity of sound is measured as sound pressure in decibels, but listeners hear *loudness*. If the auditory system operated exactly the same as electronic measuring devices, we could treat the terms *frequency* and *pitch* and the terms *intensity* and *loudness* interchangeably. As we will see, however, biological auditory systems do not work exactly as electronic measuring devices work. For example, one sound wave may be heard as quite a bit louder than another, even though the two waves have exactly the same amplitude. Careful study of the differences between the responses of mechanical listening devices (sound-level meters and spectrum analyzers) and biological listening devices (human beings) provides great insight into how the human auditory system works.

Intensity and Loudness

The bottom curve in **Figure 9.21** shows the human **audibility threshold**, which graphs the lowest sound pressure level that can be reliably detected across the frequency range of human hearing (20–20,000 Hz). Note that the best (lowest) absolute thresholds for human hearing are between 2000 and 6000 Hz (2–6 kilohertz [kHz]; remember that these frequencies are enhanced by the physical properties of the auditory canal). Thresholds rise on both sides of this range,

psychoacoustics The study of the psychological correlates of the physical dimensions of acoustics; a branch of psychophysics.

audibility threshold The lowest sound pressure level that can be reliably detected at a given frequency.

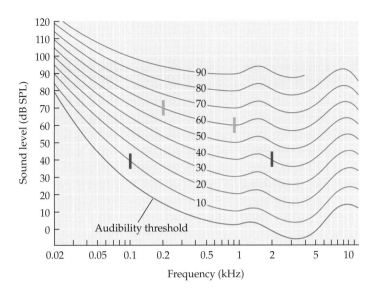

FIGURE 9.21 The lowest curve (red) illustrates the threshold for hearing sounds at varying frequencies. The curves labeled "10," "20," "30," and so on are equal-loudness curves. For a single contour, tones of different frequencies have different physical intensities, but they sound equally loud. (After Suzuki and Takeshima, 2004.)

meaning that higher- and lower-frequency sound waves must have larger amplitudes in order to be heard.

The other lines in Figure 9.21 are **equal-loudness curves** (Suzuki and Takeshima, 2004). We obtain these curves by asking listeners to equate the loudness of sounds with different frequencies. The starting point for each curve is always 1000 Hz, so the curve marked "40" tracks the amplitude necessary to make tones at other frequencies sound exactly as loud as a 1000-Hz, 40-dB tone; the curve marked "60" represents the decibel levels necessary to match a 1000-Hz, 60-dB tone; and so on. As the figure shows, the same pattern of frequency-dependent sensitivity that we see in the audibility threshold curve extends to sounds above threshold. (See **Web Activity 9.3: Equal-Loudness Curves.**)

The two orange tick marks in Figure 9.21 indicate that a 200-Hz tone presented at 70 dB sounds about as loud as a 900-Hz tone presented at 60 dB (that is, both points fall on the equal-loudness curve marked "60"), whereas a 2000-Hz tone presented at 40 dB sounds much louder than a 100-Hz tone presented at the same level (purple tick marks). These observations demonstrate the inequality of sound pressure level and loudness: equal-amplitude sounds can be perceived as softer or louder than each other, depending on the frequencies of the sound waves.

Another way to track the relationship between amplitude and loudness is to pick one frequency, steadily raise the intensity of the sound, and ask a listener to judge how the loudness increases. Experiments of this type show, once again, that the relationship between intensity and loudness is far from perfect. Doubling the perceived loudness of a sound requires more than a doubling in the amount of acoustic energy present in a sound wave, especially above 40 dB. The same kind of relationship holds in vision: the number of photons must be more than doubled to double the perceived brightness of a light.

The loudness of a sound also depends on its duration: within limits, longer sounds are heard as being louder. Again, the same thing happens in vision: flashes of light appear brighter when they last longer. The reason for this general phenomenon is that the perception of loudness or brightness depends on the summation of energy over a brief, but noticeable, period of time—a process called **temporal integration**. For hearing, temporal integration occurs over an interval of 100–200 milliseconds (ms). So if a sound is presented for less than 100 ms, it will be perceived as softer than the same amplitude

equal-loudness curve A graph plotting sound pressure level (dB SPL) against the frequency for which a listener perceives constant loudness.

temporal integration The process by which a sound at a constant level is perceived as being louder when it is of greater duration. The term also applies to perceived brightness, which depends on the duration of light.

and frequency presented for 300 ms. However, there will be little difference in loudness perception if the duration of the sound is increased from 300 to 1000 ms or longer.

In addition to studying absolute loudness judgments, psychoacousticians are interested in how proficient humans are at discriminating between the loudness levels of two sounds. There are several different ways to measure the smallest differences in intensity that can be detected, and many measures show sensitivity to changes of less than 1 dB. This ability is quite impressive, given the wide range of sound intensities (from 0 dB to about 100 dB) that humans can perceive and the fact that, unlike the visual system, the auditory system is always sensitive to this entire range (remember that, to achieve maximum visual sensitivity, we need time to adapt to lower or higher ambient light levels). Although the ability to discriminate between subtle loudness differences might not seem all that important to survival, we will see in Chapter 10 how the auditory system uses differences between the intensity levels of sounds reaching the left and right ears to determine *where* sound sources are located.

For a time, it was difficult to understand how listeners could be sensitive to such small differences in loudness over such a large range. As we noted earlier, sound wave intensity is generally signaled by the firing rate of auditory nerve fibers: larger intensities (loud sounds) correspond to higher firing rates, and smaller intensities (quiet sounds) correspond to lower firing rates. When researchers recorded from individual AN fibers, however, they found that the difference between the intensity at which a neuron just starts firing and the intensity at which the neuron's firing rate saturates is typically less than 30 dB—a much smaller window than the 100-dB range over which humans can detect loudness differences.

The auditory system has a number of ways to get around this limitation. Perhaps most important, intensity thresholds vary from one AN fiber to the next. For example, one fiber might selectively respond to the range of amplitudes between 0 and 25 dB, another might span the range of 15–40 dB, a third might cover 38–65 dB, and so on (see Figure 9.16). A population of neurons with different thresholds can then encode a much broader range of intensities than is possible with any single neuron. In addition, remember that neurons become responsive to a broader range of frequencies when intensity is higher. One result is that, as sounds become more intense, many more AN fibers become excited.

Frequency and Pitch

The tonotopic organization of the auditory system, from basilar membrane to primary auditory cortex, is a very big hint that frequency composition is a fundamental determinant of how we hear sounds. More than anything else, psychoacousticians have studied how listeners perceive pitch, the psychological counterpart to frequency. As is the case with intensity and loudness, the frequency of a sound is related to, but not perfectly correlated with, the perceived pitch of the sound. For any given frequency increase (for example, an increase of 50 Hz), listeners will perceive a greater rise in pitch for lower frequencies than they do for higher frequencies. Consequently, listeners perceive a greater pitch difference when a tone shifts from 500 to 1000 Hz than when a tone shifts from 5000 to 5500 Hz.

Research done using pure tones (sounds composed of a single sine wave) indicates that humans are remarkably good at detecting very small differences in frequency. For example, listeners can discriminate between tones of 999 and 1000 Hz—a difference of only one-tenth of 1%! Pitch discrimination at the lower and higher ends of the auditory system's frequency range is not quite as good, but it is still impressive. Part of the reason that discriminability decreases for high pitches appears to be that the temporal code for frequencies starts breaking down above 1000 Hz and is relatively nonfunctional above 5000 Hz. Performance thus suffers because the auditory system has to rely exclusively on place coding (the pattern of AN fiber responses from different parts of the cochlea).

Psychoacousticians have also used **masking** experiments to investigate frequency selectivity. In the research described in the previous paragraph, listeners never hear more than one sound frequency at a time. In a masking experiment, multiple frequencies are combined, and we see how well listeners can pick out certain components. That is, we look at how effective one sound—the masker—is at hiding another sound. We already discussed a phenomenon of two-tone suppression, in which an auditory nerve's response to one frequency can be disrupted by a second frequency. If place coding underlies pitch perception, we should expect to see the same kind of phenomenon in masking experiments.

In the classic approach to measuring frequency selectivity using masking, a single sine wave tone is placed in the middle of a band of acoustic noise (Fletcher, 1940). **White noise** is a signal that includes equal energy of every frequency in the human auditory range (20–20,000 Hz), just as white light includes light rays of all frequencies in the visible spectrum. A more limited band of noise might include all frequencies in the range of 500–1500 Hz; an even smaller band could span 500–510 Hz.

In a typical experiment, we might start with a 2000-Hz sine wave test tone presented along with a very narrow band of noise—say, 1975–2025 Hz (see Figure 9.22). We would then adjust the intensity of the test tone until listeners could just hear it over the noise. Next we would increase the bandwidth of the noise, perhaps from 50 to 100 Hz, so that now the noise would include frequencies between 1950 and 2050 Hz. As we might expect, the listener would need to increase the intensity of the test tone to be able to hear it over this broader range of noise frequencies.

If we keep widening the bandwidth, however, we will eventually reach a point at which adding more energy to the noise stops affecting the detectability of the test tone. The size of the noise band at this point is called the **critical bandwidth** (Figure 9.22a). For the experimental data plotted in Figure 9.22b, the critical bandwidth is 400 Hz. In this case, to pick out a 2000-Hz tone from the background noise, listeners must increase the intensity of the tone when the bandwidth is widened from 50 to 100 Hz and from 200 to 400 Hz, but going from a 400-Hz noise band to an 800-Hz band does *not* require the listener to make the test tone any louder. In fact, the 400-Hz noise band is just as effective a masker as white noise covering the entire spectrum of human hearing.

Results from the masking paradigm have helped cement the role of place coding in pitch perception by revealing similarities between perceptual effects and physiological findings. First of all, the width of the critical bandwidth

masking Using a second sound, frequently noise, to make the detection of another sound more difficult.

white noise Noise consisting of all audible frequencies in equal amounts. White noise in hearing is analogous to white light in vision, for which all wavelengths are present.

critical bandwidth The range of frequencies conveyed within a channel in the auditory system.

FIGURE 9.22 Critical bandwidth and masking. (*a*) To measure the width of a critical band, subjects listen for a tone in the center of a band of noise of constant intensity. It is harder to detect the tone as the band of noise widens up to a point, when further widening has no effect on detecting the tone. This point defines the critical bandwidth. (*b*) For this plot of bandwidth data, a 2000-Hz tone was used (Schoonevelt and Moore, 1989). The bandwidth of the noise had no effect on detection of the tone when it exceeded 400 Hz, so 400 Hz is the width of the critical band at 2000 Hz.

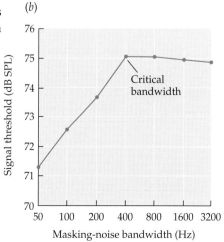

(*a*)

Critical bandwidth

Noise   Tone

Frequency (kHz)

(*b*)

Signal threshold (dB SPL)

Critical bandwidth

Masking-noise bandwidth (Hz)

changes depending on the frequency of the test tone, and these widths correspond to the physical spacing of frequencies along the basilar membrane. For example, we know that a greater proportion of the basilar membrane vibrates in response to low frequencies, and that higher-frequency ranges vibrate smaller portions of the membrane. Correspondingly, masking studies show that the critical bandwidths for low frequencies are smaller than the critical bandwidths for high frequencies, because the spacing between low frequencies is larger on the basilar membrane.

Another important finding is that masking effects are asymmetrical. More specifically, for a mask whose bandwidth is below the critical bandwidth of a test tone, the mask is more effective if it is centered on a frequency *below* the test tone's frequency—a phenomenon called the "upward spread of masking." This phenomenon may seem counterintuitive, but a look back at Figure 9.12 shows how displacement of the basilar membrane (the traveling wave) extends from the high-frequency base to the low-frequency apex. Displacement for low-frequency energy sounds toward the apex leaves a trail of displacement across high-frequency regions toward the base. In addition, two-tone suppression experiments indicate that suppression is greater if the suppressor tone is slightly below an AN fiber's characteristic frequency than if the suppressor tone is slightly above the fiber's characteristic frequency (see Figure 9.14).

Hearing Loss

Roughly 30 million Americans suffer some form of hearing impairment. When we talk about hearing loss, we typically do not mean the total loss of all hearing (deafness), but rather the elevation of sound thresholds. For example, frequencies that used to be audible at 20 dB may become inaudible unless they are presented at 40 or 60 dB. Of course, in the end we do not just need to detect sounds; the term *hearing* really refers to using spectral and temporal differences between sounds in order to learn something about events going on in the environment. As we will see, common forms of hearing loss affect the ability to interpret sounds, even when the sounds are loud enough to be detectable.

Hearing can be impaired by damage to any of the structures along the chain of auditory processing from the outer ear all the way up to the auditory cortex. The simplest way to introduce some hearing loss is to obstruct the ear canal, thus inhibiting the ability of sound waves to exert pressure on the tympanic membrane. Many people do this on purpose by wearing earplugs. A less intentional hearing loss can be created by the excessive buildup of earwax (cerumen) in the ear canal. This problem is easy to remedy, as long as the effort to clear out the ear canal does not damage the tympanic membrane.

Another type of hearing impairment, called **conductive hearing loss**, occurs when the middle-ear bones lose (or are impaired in) their ability to freely convey (conduct) vibrations from the tympanic membrane to the oval window. Such impairment occurs most often when the middle ear fills with mucus during ear infections—a condition known as **otitis media**. The oval window usually still vibrates under these conditions; but without the amplifying power of the ossicles, hearing thresholds can be raised by as much as 50 dB (that is, sounds need to be 50 dB louder in order to be heard). Thankfully, for the millions of young children who suffer ear infections, normal hearing returns after mucus is absorbed back into surrounding tissues; however, this reabsorption can take up to several months. A more serious type of conductive loss, **otosclerosis**, is caused by abnormal growth of the middle-ear bones, most typically around the oval window next to the stapes. Surgery can free the stapes from these bone growths and improve hearing.

conductive hearing loss Hearing loss caused by problems with the bones of the middle ear.

otitis media Inflammation of the middle ear, commonly in children as a result of infection.

otosclerosis Abnormal growth of the middle-ear bones that causes hearing loss.

By far the most common, and most serious, form of auditory impairment is **sensorineural hearing loss**, which most commonly occurs inside the cochlea, and sometimes as a result of damage to the auditory nerve. Most often, sensorineural hearing loss occurs when hair cells are injured. For example, certain antibiotics and cancer drugs are **ototoxic**, meaning that they kill hair cells directly. In part, the reason for this effect is that ion pores on stereocilia that have been opened through mechanoelectrical transduction (MET) are not especially selective about what they permit to flow into the hair cell. Physicians are well aware of these dangers and typically avoid using such drugs, but sometimes a patient faces the decision of life with deafness versus no life at all.

A more common cause of hearing loss is damage to the hair cells by excessive exposure to noise. Those exquisitely fast and sensitive hair cells are also very vulnerable to damage from excessive sound levels. It is fairly well known that shooting a gun without ear protection can cause hearing loss. Extended exposure to loud sounds such as the noise of factory equipment also causes hearing loss. It is no coincidence that so many aging rock stars and race car drivers wear hearing aids. (It is ironic, but wise, that many heavy-metal music fans now wear ear protection at concerts.) And evidence suggests that cumulative exposure to even everyday noises present in the environments of industrialized countries can cause hearing loss. In one study (Goycoolea et al., 1986), middle-aged and elderly residents of Easter Island who stayed almost exclusively on their quiet island their whole lives were compared to other Easter Islanders, who made more frequent trips to the noisier outside world. As **Figure 9.23a** shows, the more time people spent off the island, the more hearing loss they experienced.

Hearing loss is a natural consequence of aging for many people, and it is difficult to separate a person's age from the amount of exposure to noise. Typically, age-related hearing loss first affects the perception of high frequencies (Figure 9.23b). The 20- to 20,000-Hz frequency range for human hearing really applies only to young people; by the time most of us reach college age, we may have already lost the ability to hear frequencies above 15,000 Hz. The decrease in the ability to hear higher-frequency sounds continues throughout life, with the highest audible frequency becoming lower and lower as we grow older. Fortunately, many of the auditory stimuli that people care most about, including speech and music, are composed predominantly of lower frequencies.

The earliest devices for helping people with hearing loss were simple horns. The small end of the horn would be held at the entry to the ear canal, and the wide end would be used to funnel more acoustic energy toward the listener's

sensorineural hearing loss Hearing loss due to defects in the cochlea or auditory nerve.

ototoxic Producing adverse effects on cochlear or vestibular organs or nerves.

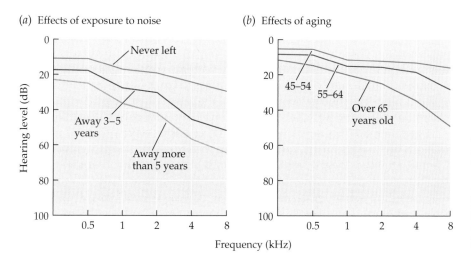

(*a*) Effects of exposure to noise

(*b*) Effects of aging

FIGURE 9.23 Environmental noise affects hearing. (*a*) The more people are exposed to noise in their environment, the more their hearing deteriorates. Easter Island residents who spent more years off of the relatively quiet island had relatively worse hearing. (*b*) Hearing becomes less sensitive with age, particularly for high frequencies. (After Goycoolea et al., 1986.)

FIGURE 9.24 When hearing thresholds are increased by impairment, it takes more energy to hear a sound, but loudness increases faster than it does with healthy ears. When a hearing aid is used to increase the intensity of sounds, all variation in sound levels must be compressed into a smaller range of intensity because very loud sounds can be just as painful for listeners with hearing impairment as they are for listeners with healthy hearing. (After C. D. Geisler, 1998.)

ear. Although effective, these horns were obviously somewhat cumbersome. Electronic hearing aids are much more convenient, but they must be designed to do more than simply amplify all sounds, because extremely loud sounds (above 100 dB) are just as annoying (or painful) for impaired listeners as they are for listeners with normal hearing. For a person who cannot hear sounds until they are at least 70 dB intense, compared to about 0 dB for healthy hearing, sounds that could normally vary between 0 and 100 dB must be squeezed between 70 and 100 dB (**Figure 9.24**). Nearly all modern hearing aids use some means to amplify the signal while also compressing intensity differences to keep the highest intensities within a comfortable listening level. Hearing aids can also be tuned to provide the greatest amplification only for frequencies in the region of greatest loss (for most people, higher frequencies will need to be amplified more).

One advantage of the old horns over electronic hearing aids was that they permitted listeners to direct their hearing toward the sound source they were most interested in. We may think about hearing aids as amplifying the voice to which one is listening, but they also amplify all the other sounds in the environment. The background noise in a car, or even the sound of a refrigerator, can become loud enough to compete with the sound of a person's voice. When the entire range of hearing is compressed from 100 dB to only 30 dB, a 10-dB difference between the rumbling of the car's engine and the voice of the person in the passenger seat becomes compressed into only a 3-dB difference.

Hearing aids are gradually improving, and they have provided relief to millions of Americans, including former presidents Ronald Reagan and Bill Clinton. However, despite researchers' many clever innovations for improving the signal that arrives at the tympanic membrane, damage to the mechanisms that transduce sound waves into neural signals is proving difficult or impossible to overcome completely. By analogy to vision, the best eyeglasses, contact lenses, or even laser surgery cannot change an image enough to overcome retinal

(a)

(b) Microphone and transmitter

Receiver

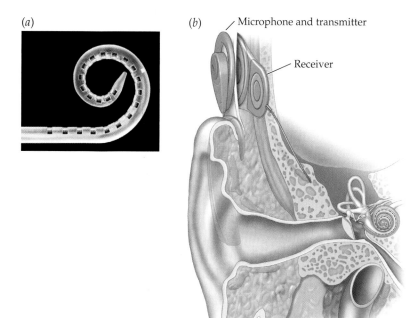

FIGURE 9.25 Cochlear implants give some people who are deaf the ability to hear. (*a*) The cochlear implant electrode array. The flexible array of electrodes is inserted through the round window as far as possible toward the apex of the cochlea. (*b*) The electrode array is connected to a small receiver beneath the scalp, and a small microphone and transmitter are placed over the receiver on the outside of the head.

degeneration. Similarly, hearing aids cannot change sounds enough to overcome the loss of hair cells. The best advice is to never need a hearing aid. Protect your hair cells by avoiding exposure to loud sounds and by using hearing protection such as earplugs or muffs when necessary. If someone else can sing along to the song you're listening to on your personal media player, turn it down!

Modern medical science and engineering are providing some degree of hearing to thousands of people who are deaf. Cochlear prosthetics, more commonly known as cochlear implants (**Figure 9.25***a*), are tiny flexible coils with about two dozen miniature electrode contacts along their length. Surgeons delicately thread these electrode arrays through the round window as far toward the apex of the cochlea as possible. The electrode array is connected to a tiny radio receiver under the scalp, and signals are transmitted from a small microphone device on the outside of the head behind the ear (Figure 9.25*b*). Signals coming in from the microphone activate the miniature electrodes at appropriate positions along the cochlear implant, which in turn stimulates associated auditory nerve fibers.

Although cochlear implants are a modern medical miracle, they cannot provide hearing that approaches what nature provides. But it is not surprising that a handful of electrodes cannot replace the function of 14,000 hair cells. Some people benefit more than others from implants, and many adults with electrical hearing converse flawlessly over the phone. Young children, receiving implants as young as age 1 or 2, do best of all because young brains are particularly plastic. Children's brain circuitry develops to get the most information possible from their electronic ears.

Refer to the
Sensation and Perception
Companion Website
sites.sinauer.com/wolfe3e
for activities, essays, study
questions, and other study aids.

Summary

1. Sounds are fluctuations of pressure. Sound waves are defined by the frequency, intensity (amplitude), and phase of fluctuations. Sound frequency and intensity correspond to our perceptions of pitch and loudness, respectively.

2. Sound is funneled into the ear by the outer ear, made more intense by the middle ear, and transformed into neural signals by the inner ear.

3. In the inner ear, cilia on the tops of inner hair cells are flexed by pressure fluctuations in ways that provide information about frequency and intensity to the auditory nerve and the brain. Auditory nerve fibers convey information through both the rate and the timing patterns with which they fire.

4. Different characteristics of sounds are processed at multiple places in the brain stem before information reaches the cortex. Information from both ears is brought together very early in the chain of processing. At each stage of auditory processing, including primary auditory cortex, neurons are organized in relation to the frequencies of sounds (tonotopically).

5. Humans and other mammals can hear sounds across an enormous range of intensities. Not all sound frequencies are heard as being equally loud, however. Hearing across such a wide range of intensities is accomplished by the use of many auditory neurons. Different neurons respond to different levels of intensity. In addition, more neurons overall respond when sounds are more intense.

6. Series of channels (or filters) process sounds within bands of frequency. Depending on frequency, these channels vary in how wide (how many frequencies) or narrow they are. Consequently, it is easier to detect differences between some frequencies than between others. When energy from multiple frequencies is present, lower-frequency energy makes it relatively more difficult to hear higher frequencies.

7. Hearing loss is caused by damage to the bones of the middle ear, to the hair cells in the cochlea, or to the neurons in the auditory nerve. Although hearing aids are helpful to listeners with hearing impairment, they cannot restore hearing as well as glasses can improve vision.

CHAPTER 10

Victor Bonderoff, *Listening to Me*, 2008

Hearing in the Environment

The auditory system's ability to transform tiny air pressure changes into a rich perceptual world is quite amazing. From the funneling of sound waves by the pinnae, to the mechanics of middle-ear bones, to the tiny perturbations of the basilar partition and hair cells, to the sophisticated neural encoding in the brain stem and cerebral cortex—some remarkable mechanisms have evolved to interpret acoustic information about the world around us.

Research revealing these inner workings of the auditory system, described in the previous chapter, typically uses very simple stimuli under constrained situations—often isolated pure tones heard through headphones by listeners sitting in an otherwise perfectly quiet laboratory. Although this research is invaluable for understanding how the auditory system functions, this is obviously not the way we experience auditory stimuli in our daily lives. In this chapter we get "outside the head" to investigate how hearing helps us learn about the real-world environment.

We start by looking at how it is possible to determine the location of a sound source. As we will see, in many respects sound localization parallels visual depth perception, described in Chapter 6. We then turn from *where* to *what*, describing some important perceptual aspects of complex sounds, which are composed of simpler sounds in much the same way that visual representations of objects are built up from simple features (see Chapter 4). The third part of the chapter deals with auditory scene analysis, where we will see how some sounds group together, while separating from others, in ways that resemble the Gestalt principles introduced in Chapter 4. In the final section of the chapter, we consider the auditory analog of visual object occlusion (see Chapter 6), and we see how the auditory system seamlessly fills in gaps to form a complete and coherent "picture" of our auditory environment.

Sound Localization

Suppose you were out camping in your local state park one mild summer night, enjoying the last embers of your campfire, when suddenly an owl began hooting somewhere in front of you. You would instantly know whether the owl was perched to the left, to the right, or directly behind the fire pit. Moreover, if you were willing to leave the comfort of the fire, and if the owl were cooperative enough to sit still and keep hooting, you could easily walk to the exact source of the sound, even though you wouldn't be able to see the owl until you were very close to it.

When you think about it a bit, you will realize that this feat of auditory localization is quite different from determining the location of a visual object. If you could see the owl in front of you, you would know that it was to the left or the right of your fovea because its image would appear on the right or left

FIGURE 10.1 The position of the owl is easily encoded by the visual system because the owl's image falls on different parts of the retina (and thus activates different receptors) depending on whether it is to the left (A) or to the right (B) of the observer. In the auditory system, however, the same receptors are activated regardless of the owl's position.

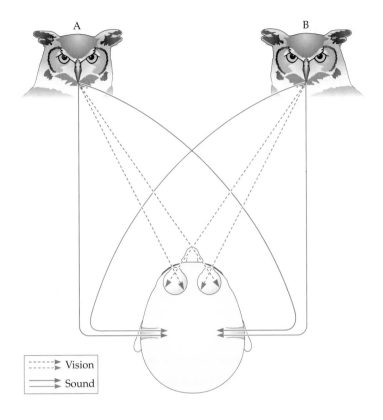

side of your retina (**Figure 10.1**). But the owl's hoots enter your ears in exactly the same place (funneled through the pinnae into the middle and inner ear) regardless of where the owl is.

You may recall that we face a similar dilemma when trying to determine how far away a visual object is. For example, if you hold your right and left index fingers in front of your face, with your right finger closer than your left, the location of the two images on your retinas will not tell you anything about which finger is closer to you. As we saw in Chapter 6, visual depth perception involves processing and integrating a set of "cues"—stimulus aspects that provide indirect evidence about how far away an object is. The auditory system uses a similar approach to determine the location in space from which a sound is coming. (See **Web Activity 10.1: Auditory Localization Cues**.)

Just as having two eyes turned out to be one of the keys to determining visual depth relations, having two ears is crucial for determining auditory locations. For most positions in space, the sound source will be closer to one ear than to the other. Thus, there are two potential types of information for determining the source of a sound (**Figure 10.2**). First, even though sound travels fast, the pressure wave will not arrive at both ears at the same time. Sounds arrive sooner, albeit very slightly, at the ear closer to the source. Second, the intensity of a sound is greater at the ear closer to the source. These are our first two auditory localization cues.

Interaural Time Difference

interaural time difference (ITD) The difference in time between a sound arriving at one ear versus the other.

Let's first consider what we can learn from the **interaural time difference**, or **ITD**. If the source is to the left, the sound will reach the left ear first. If it's to the right, it will reach the right ear first. Thus, we can tell whether a sound is coming from our right or left by determining which ear receives the sound

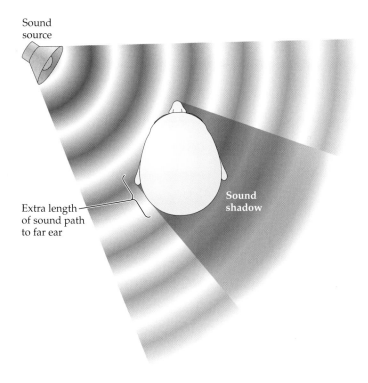

FIGURE 10.2 The two ears receive slightly different inputs when the sound source is located to one side or the other. For frequencies greater than 1000 hertz, the head blocks some of the energy from reaching the opposite ear.

first (Figure 10.3). The term that is used to describe locations on an imaginary circle extending around us—front, back, left, and right—in a horizontal plane is **azimuth**.

A more detailed analysis of the ITD can tell us even more. See if you can answer the following questions: Where would a sound source need to be located to produce the maximum possible ITD? What location would lead to

azimuth The angle of a sound source on the horizontal plane relative to a point in the center of the head between the ears. Azimuth is measured in degrees, with 0 degrees being straight ahead. The angle increases clockwise toward the right, with 180 degrees being directly behind.

FIGURE 10.3 Interaural time differences for sound sources varying in azimuth from directly in front of listeners (0 degrees) to directly behind (180 degrees). How much variation there is in the time it takes for a sound to reach each ear depends on where a sound comes from in space. (Data from Fedderson et al., 1957.)

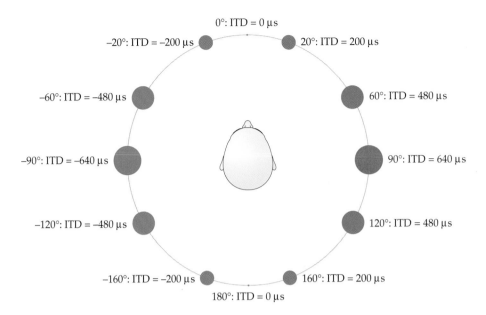

FIGURE 10.4 Interaural time differences for different positions around the head. Blue indicates locations from which sound reaches the left ear first; red indicates locations from which sound reaches the right ear first. (Data from Fedderson et al., 1957.)

the minimum possible ITD, and what would the ITD be in this case? Finally, what would happen at intermediate locations? **Figure 10.4** illustrates the answers to these questions. The ITDs for sounds coming from various angles are represented by colored circles. Red circles indicate positions from which a sound will reach the right ear before the left ear; blue circles show positions from which a sound will reach the left ear first. The size and brightness of each circle represent the magnitude of the ITD.

As Figure 10.4 shows, ITDs are largest, about 640 microseconds (millionths of a second, abbreviated µs) when sounds come directly from the left or directly from the right, although this value varies somewhat depending on the size of your head. A sound coming from directly in front of or directly behind the listener produces an ITD of 0; the sound reaches both ears simultaneously. For intermediate locations, the ITD will be somewhere between these two values. Thus, a sound source located at an angle of 60 degrees will always produce an ITD of 480 µs, and a sound coming from –20 degrees will always produce an ITD of –200 µs. That might not seem like much of a time difference, but studies have shown that listeners can detect interaural delays of as little as 10 µs (Klumpp and Eady, 1956), which is good enough to detect the angle of a sound source to within 1 degree.

THE PHYSIOLOGY OF ITDs The portion of the auditory system responsible for calculating ITDs obviously needs to receive input from both ears. As we saw in Chapter 9, binaural input enters almost every stage of the auditory nervous system after the auditory nerve. As information moves upward through the system, however, with every additional synapse the timing between the two ears is likely to become less precise. The **medial superior olives (MSOs)** are the first places in the auditory system where inputs from both ears converge (**Figure 10.5**), so this is a natural place to look for ITD detectors. Sure enough, T. C. Yin and Chan (1990) found neurons in the MSOs whose firing rates increase in response to very brief time differences between inputs from the two ears of cats.

medial superior olive (MSO) A relay station in the brain stem where inputs from both ears contribute to detection of the interaural time difference.

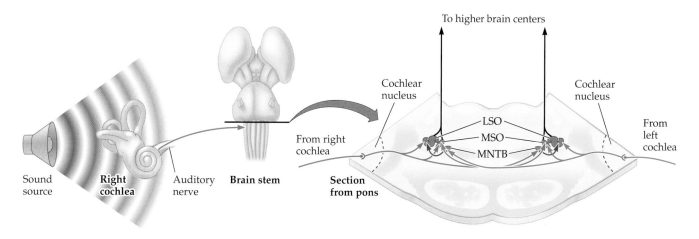

FIGURE 10.5 After only a single synapse in the cochlear nucleus, information from each ear travels to both the medial superior olive (MSO) and the lateral superior olive (LSO) on each side of the brain stem. MNTB = medial nucleus of the trapezoid body.

ITD detectors form their connections from inputs coming in from the two ears during the first few months of life (Brand et al., 2002; Kapfer et al., 2002), and developing the ability to use ITDs to localize sounds depends critically on having experience with separate sounds coming from different places in space (Seidl and Grothe, 2005). The developmental sequence is similar to the one for the formation of binocular neurons in the visual cortex, and it probably has a similar cause. The interpretation of ITDs (e.g., associating a given ITD with a given angle, as shown in Figure 10.4) is critically dependent on the size of the head. If babies came out of the womb with their ITD interpretation mechanisms prewired to the size of their infant heads, their sound localization abilities would steadily decline as their ears moved farther and farther apart as a result of the growth of their heads during childhood and adolescence (H. G. Jones et al., 2011).

Interaural Level Difference

The second cue to sound localization is called the **interaural level difference**, or **ILD**, in sound intensity. Sounds are more intense at the ear closer to the sound source because the head partially blocks the sound pressure wave from reaching the opposite ear (see Figure 10.2). The properties of the ILD relevant for auditory localization are similar to those of the ITD:

interaural level difference (ILD)
The difference in level (intensity) between a sound arriving at one ear versus the other.

- Sounds are more intense at the ear that is closer to the sound source, and less intense at the ear farther away from the source.
- The ILD is largest at 90 and –90 degrees, and it is nonexistent at 0 degrees (directly in front) and 180 degrees (directly behind).
- Between these two extremes, the ILD generally correlates with the angle of the sound source, but because of the irregular shape of the head, the correlation is not quite as precise as it is with ITDs.

Although the general relationship between ILD and sound source angle is almost identical to the relationship between ITD and angle, there is an important difference between the two cues: the head blocks high-frequency sounds much more effectively than it does low-frequency sounds. This is because the long wavelengths of low-frequency sounds "bend around" the head in much the same way that a large ocean wave crashes over a piling near the shore.

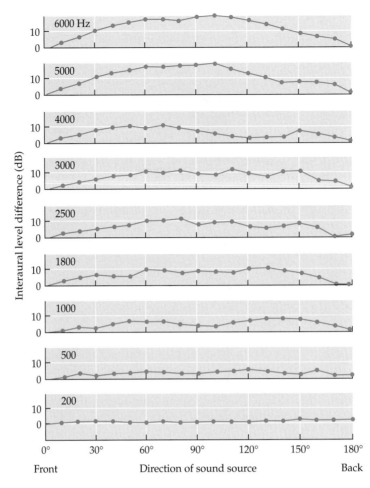

FIGURE 10.6 Interaural level (intensity) differences (ILDs) for tones of different frequencies presented at different positions around the head. Note that the biggest differences are for frequencies greater than 1000 Hz, at which point the head creates a shadow. The curves are not symmetrical toward the front and back, because of filtering characteristics of the pinnae. (Data from Fedderson et al., 1957.)

Thus, as shown in Figure 10.6, ILDs are greatest for high-frequency tones, and the ILD cue provides the best information about sound source location. ILDs are greatly reduced for low frequencies, becoming almost nonexistent below 1000 hertz (Hz). This inability to localize low frequencies is the reason it does not matter where in a room you place the subwoofer of your stereo system.

lateral superior olive (LSO) A relay station in the brain stem where inputs from both ears contribute to detection of the interaural level difference.

THE PHYSIOLOGY OF ILDs Neurons that are sensitive to intensity differences between the two ears can be found in the **lateral superior olives** (**LSOs**), which receive both excitatory and inhibitory inputs. Excitatory connections to the LSOs come from the ipsilateral ear (that is, excitatory connections to the left LSO originate in the left cochlea, and excitatory connections to the right LSO come from the right cochlea). Inhibitory inputs come from the contralateral ear (the ear on the opposite side of the head) via the medial nucleus of the trapezoid body (MNTB) (see Figure 10.5).

What makes neurons in the LSOs so sensitive to differences in intensity across the two ears is the competition between excitatory inputs from one ear (ipsilateral) and inhibitory inputs from the other ear (contralateral). When the sound is more intense at one ear, connections from that ear are better both at exciting LSO neurons on that side and at inhibiting LSO neurons on the other side.

Cones of Confusion

If you examine Figures 10.4 and 10.6 for a bit, you should see a potential problem with using ITDs and ILDs for sound localization: An ITD of –480 μs arises from a sound source that is located at either an angle of –60 degrees from the line of sight (ten o'clock in Figure 10.4) or an angle of –120 degrees (eight o'clock). Adding information from intensity differences does not help us here, because the ILDs for these two angles are also identical. If we also consider the elevation of a sound source (how far above or below our head the sound source is—a factor we've been ignoring up to now), we find that a given ITD or ILD could arise from any point on the surface of a **cone of confusion** that extends perpendicularly from the left or right ear (Figure 10.7).

Although many books speak of a single cone of confusion, actually an infinite number of cones are nested inside one another. In fact, the widest "cone" is really a circle extending from directly in front of you, up to directly over your head, back to directly behind your head, and continuing to directly below you. As strange as it may seem, this widest cone is the most confusing of the cones. Cones of confusion are real perceptual phenomena, not just theoretical problems for the auditory system. In the real world, however, our heads are

cone of confusion A region of positions in space where all sounds produce the same time and level (intensity) differences (ITDs and ILDs).

(a)

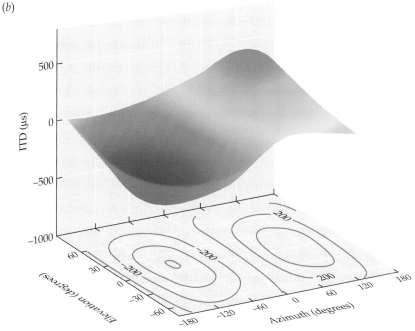

(b)

FIGURE 10.7 Elevation adds another dimension to sound localization. (a) Cones of confusion. (b) Interaural time differences (ITDs) are plotted here across azimuth and elevation. A sound with zero azimuth and elevation is directly in front of a listener's head. All of the locations in space that share the same color provide exactly the same ITDs. Red contours plotted beneath the colored surface illustrate how all the locations on the red line give rise to the same ITD. (Part b after Wightman and Kistler, 1998.)

(a)

(b)

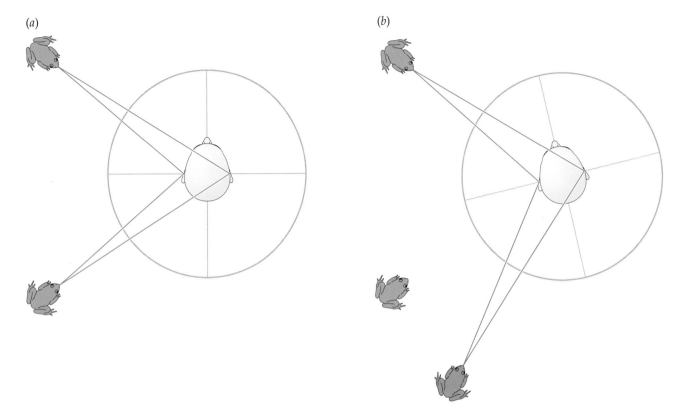

FIGURE 10.8 Evaluating ITDs and ILDs from two different head positions helps in sound localization. (a) At first, a sound source coming from the blue frog will lead to an ITD and an ILD that would also be consistent with a sound coming from the green frog. (b) If the listener's head is rotated slightly counterclockwise, the ITD/ILD will no longer be consistent with the location of the green frog. There will still be an ambiguity, however. Now the ITD/ILD will be consistent with the red frog as well as the blue frog. But only the blue location is consistent with both the first and the second sets of ITDs and ILDs.

not held in a fixed position. As soon as you move your head, the ITD and ILD of a sound source shift, and only one spatial location will be consistent with the ITDs and ILDs perceived at both head positions (**Figure 10.8**).

Pinna and Head Cues

Another reason why cones of confusion are not major practical problems for the auditory system is that time and intensity differences are not the only cues for pinpointing the location of sound sources. Take a look at one of your pinnae (or, more realistically, take a look at a friend's pinna). You'll see that the shape of the pinna is quite complex, with lots of idiosyncratic nooks and crannies (**Figure 10.9**). Remember that the pinnae funnel sound energy into the ear canal. But because of their complex shapes, the pinnae funnel certain sound frequencies more efficiently than others. In addition, the size and shape of the rest of the body, especially the upper torso, affect which frequencies reach the ear most easily. Because of these two effects, the intensity of each frequency varies slightly according to the direction of the sound. This variation provides us with another auditory localization cue.

Here's a simple example to illustrate how the effects of pinna and upper body shapes are measured. Suppose you're in an anechoic room, a room in

FIGURE 10.9 Pinna shapes vary quite a lot between people. Listeners learn how their personal pinnae affect how they hear sounds from different places in the environment.

which the walls are padded so that very little sound enters from the outside and very little sound reverberates off the walls. The room is full of speakers at many locations—up, down, and all around you. Tiny microphones are inserted inside your auditory canals, right next to your eardrums. These microphones can measure just how much energy from different frequencies actually reaches your eardrums from different locations around you. Figure 10.10 shows the measurements at the eardrum in an experimental setup like the one just described—in this case for sounds played over a speaker 30 degrees to the left of a listener and 12 degrees up from the listener's head. Although energy at all frequencies was equally intense coming from the speaker, you can see that energy at all frequencies is not equally intense at the eardrum. Some frequencies (e.g., 5000 Hz) have higher intensity when they arrive at the eardrum; others (e.g., 800 Hz) have less intensity.

These changing "spectral shapes" across changes in elevation provide cues to auditory localization. Figure 10.6 showed how the relative intensities of different frequencies change depending on azimuth, and illustrated that those curves are not symmetrical toward the front and back, because of

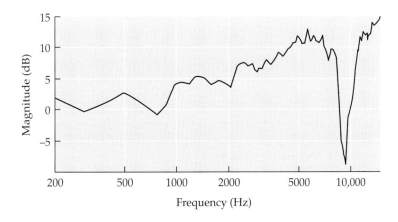

FIGURE 10.10 Directional transfer functions (DTFs). Differences in intensity at the eardrum for sounds of varying frequency are plotted in this DTF for a single point in space. (From Kistler and Wightman, 1992.)

FIGURE 10.11 The effect of elevation on DTFs. The series of DTFs plotted here is for the same azimuth, but at different elevations. (From Wightman and Jenison, 1995.)

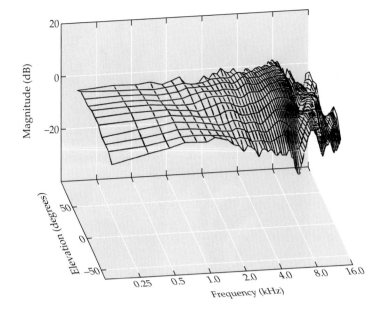

filtering characteristics of the pinnae. For the final piece of the puzzle, look at Figure 10.11, which shows the sound recorded by in-ear microphones when the speaker is moved up and down in elevation. As you can see, the relative intensities of different frequencies continuously change with changes in elevation as well as azimuth. The sum total of these intensity shifts can be measured and combined to determine the **directional transfer function** (usually referred to by its acronym, **DTF**) for an individual.

The importance of the DTF in sound localization is easily understood if we consider the difference between hearing a concert live versus listening to music through a set of headphones. In person, we perceive the sound of the French horns as coming from one side of the orchestra and the sound of the flutes as coming from the other side. But when we wear headphones (especially the type inserted directly inside the auditory canals), sounds are delivered directly to the eardrums, bypassing the pinnae. Auditory engineers can use multiple microphones to simulate the ITDs and ILDs that result from the musicians' different locations (the Beatles were early users of this type of technology), but the DTFs are not so easily simulated. As a result, you may be able to get some sense of direction when listening to a concert through headphones, but the sounds will seem to come from inside your skull, rather than from out in the world. The situation is akin to that of visual depth perception. Pictorial cues can give a limited sense of depth, but to get a true perception of three-dimensionality, we really need binocular-disparity information that we normally get only when we're seeing real objects.

Actually, just as stereoscopes can be designed to simulate binocular disparity, it is possible to simulate DTFs. Instead of using two camera lenses in place of two eyes, two microphones are placed near the eardrums as described earlier. Then the sound source, such as a concert, is recorded from these two microphones. If this special stereo recording, called a "binaural recording," is played over headphones, the listener experiences the sounds as if they were back out in the world where they belong. Unfortunately, however, every set of pinnae is different (see Figure 10.9), so for this simulation to work, all listeners need their own individual recordings.

Just as heads (and their corresponding ITDs and ILDs) grow to be larger, ears grow and change during development and are often subject to mutilations of varying degrees (e.g., piercings). Research suggests that listeners learn about

directional transfer function (DTF) A measure that describes how the pinna, ear canal, head, and torso change the intensity of sounds with different frequencies that arrive at each ear from different locations in space (azimuth and elevation).

the way DTFs relate to places in the environment through their extensive experience listening to sounds, while other sources of information, such as vision, provide feedback about location (Wightman and Kistler, 1998). This learning through experience suggests that children may update the way they use DTF information during development, and it appears that such learning can continue into adulthood. Hofman, Van Riswick, and Van Opsal (1998) inserted plastic molds into folds of adults' pinnae. As expected, listeners immediately became much poorer at localizing sounds. But after 6 weeks of living with these molds in their ears, the subjects' localization abilities had greatly improved. Somewhat surprisingly, these listeners also remained quite good at localizing with their "old ears" when the molds were removed. It would be interesting to know how well Leonard Nimoy (who played Spock in the original *Star Trek* series) could localize sounds with his Vulcan ear molds. The experience of listeners in this study suggests that switching between human and Vulcan pinnae every day may have become just a normal part of Nimoy's auditory life.

Auditory Distance Perception

How do listeners know how far away a sound is? Although it is important to know what direction a sound is coming from, none of the cues we've discussed so far (ITD, ILD, DTF) provide much information concerning the distance between a listener and a sound source that is much more than an arm's length away.

The simplest cue for judging the distance of a sound source is the *relative intensity* of the sound: Because sounds become less intense with greater distance, listeners have little difficulty perceiving the relative distances of two identical sound sources—for example, a pair of croaking bullfrogs (the louder croaks must be coming from the closer frog). Unfortunately, this cue suffers from the same problem as relative size in depth perception. Interpreting the cue requires one to make assumptions about the sound sources that may turn out to be false (e.g., the softer-sounding frog might be very close, but its croaks muffled by surrounding vegetation).

Furthermore, the effectiveness of relative intensity decreases substantially as distance increases, because sound intensity decreases according to the **inverse-square law**. When sound sources are close to the listener, a small difference in distance can produce a relatively large intensity difference. For example, a sound that is 1 meter away is 6 decibels (dB) more intense than a sound that is 2 meters away. But the same 1-meter difference between sound sources 39 and 40 meters away produces an intensity change of only a fraction of 1 dB. As one might expect from these facts, listeners are fairly good at using intensity differences to determine distance when sounds are presented within 1 meter of the head (Brungart, Durlach, and Rabinowitz, 1999), but listeners tend to consistently underestimate the distance to sound sources farther away, and the amount of underestimation is larger for greater distances (Zahorik, 2002).

Intensity works best as a distance cue when the sound source or the listener is moving. If a croaking frog starts hopping toward you, you will know it because its croaks will become louder and louder. Listeners also get some information about how far away a source is when they move through the environment. This is because, in a manner akin to motion parallax in the perception of visual depth, sounds that are farther away do not seem to change direction in relation to the listener as much as nearer sounds do.

Another possible cue for auditory distance is the *spectral composition* of sounds. The sound-absorbing qualities of air dampen high frequencies more than low frequencies, so when sound sources are far away, higher frequencies decrease in energy more than lower frequencies as the sound waves travel

inverse-square law A principle stating that as distance from a source increases, intensity initially decreases much faster than distance increases, such that the decrease in intensity is equal to the increase in distance squared. This general law also applies to optics and other forms of energy.

FIGURE 10.12 The relative amounts of direct and reverberant energy coming from the listener's neighbor and the singer will inform the listener about the relative distances of the two sound sources.

from the source to the ear. Thus, the farther away a sound source is, the "muddier" it sounds. This change in spectral composition is noticeable only for fairly large distances, greater than 1000 meters. You experience the change in spectral composition when you hear thunder from near your window or from far away. Nearby, you hear a loud "crack," but farther away the sound is more like a "boom." Note that this auditory cue is analogous to the visual depth cue of aerial perspective (see Chapter 6; more distant objects look more blurry).

A final distance cue stems from the fact that, in most environments, the sound that arrives at the ear is some combination of direct energy (which arrives directly from the source) and reverberant energy (which has bounced off surfaces in the environment). The *relative amounts of direct versus reverberant energy* inform the listener about distance because when a sound source is close to a listener, most of the energy reaching the ear is direct, whereas reverberant energy provides a greater proportion of the total when the sound source is farther away. Suppose you're attending a concert. The intensities of the musician's song and your neighbor's whispered comments might be identical, but the singer's voice will take time to bounce off the concert hall's walls before reaching your ear, whereas you will hear only the direct energy from the whispers (Figure 10.12). (See **Web Essay 10.1: Reverberations and the Precedence Effect**.)

Complex Sounds

Simple sounds like sine waves and bands of noise are very useful for exploring the fundamental operating characteristics of auditory systems, just as sinusoidal contrast gratings and single-wavelength light sources are crucial tools for vision researchers. But pure sine wave tones, like pure single-wavelength light sources, are rare in the real auditory world, where objects and events that

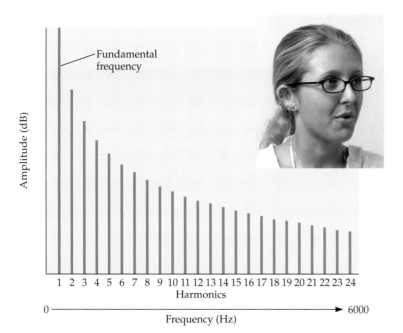

FIGURE 10.13 Many environmental sounds, including voices, are harmonic. The lowest frequency of a harmonic sound is the fundamental frequency, and there are peaks of energy at integer multiples of the fundamental.

matter to listeners are more complex, more interesting, and therefore more challenging for researchers to study.

Harmonics

Many environmental sounds, including the human voice and musical instruments, have harmonic structure (Figure 10.13). In fact, harmonic sounds are among the most common types of sounds in the environment. The lowest frequency of a harmonic spectrum is the **fundamental frequency**. With natural vibratory sources (as opposed to pure tones produced in the laboratory), there is also energy at frequencies that are integer multiples of the fundamental frequency. For example, a female speaker may produce a vowel sound with a fundamental frequency of 250 Hz. The vocal cords will produce the greatest energy at 250 Hz, less at 500 Hz, less still at 750 Hz, even less at 1000 Hz, and so on. In this case, 500 Hz is the second harmonic, 750 is the third, and 1000 is the fourth. For harmonic complexes, the perceived pitch of the complex is determined by the fundamental frequency, and the harmonics (often called "overtones" by musicians) add to the perceived richness of the sound.

The auditory system is acutely sensitive to the natural relationships between harmonics. In fact, if the first harmonic (fundamental frequency) is removed from a series of harmonics as shown in Figure 10.14, and only the others (second, third, fourth, and so on) are presented, the pitch that listeners hear corresponds to the fundamental frequency—even though it is not part of the sound! Listeners hear the *missing fundamental*. (See **Web Activity 10.2: The Missing-Fundamental Effect**.) It is not even necessary to have all the other harmonics present in order to hear the missing fundamental; just a few will do.

fundamental frequency The lowest-frequency component of a complex periodic sound.

FIGURE 10.14 If the fundamental (lowest frequency) of a harmonic sound is removed, listeners still hear the pitch of this "missing fundamental."

FIGURE 10.15 When only three harmonics of the same fundamental frequency are presented (*b–d*), listeners still hear the pitch of the missing fundamental frequency (*a*) because the harmonics share a common energy fluctuation every 4 ms, the period of a 250-Hz signal (*e*).

The most straightforward explanations of the missing-fundamental effect involve the temporal code for pitch discussed in Chapter 9. One thing that all harmonics of a fundamental have in common is fluctuations in sound pressure at regular intervals corresponding to the fundamental frequency. For example, the waveform for a 500-Hz tone has a peak every 2.0 milliseconds (ms) (**Figure 10.15***b*). The waveforms for 750- and 1000-Hz tones have peaks every 1.3 and 1.0 ms, respectively (Figures 10.15*c* and *d*). As shown in Figure 10.15*e*, these three waveforms come into alignment every 4 ms, which, conveniently, happens to be the period of the fundamental frequency for these three harmonics: 250 Hz. Indeed, *every* harmonic of 250 Hz will have an energy peak every 4 ms. Researchers have shown that some neurons in the auditory nerve and cochlear nucleus will fire action potentials every 4 ms to the collection of waves shown in Figure 10.15*e*, providing an elegant mechanism to explain why listeners perceive the pitch of this complex tone to be 250 Hz, even though the tone has no 250-Hz component.

Timbre

Loudness and pitch are relatively easy to describe because they correspond fairly well to simple acoustic dimensions (amplitude and frequency, respectively). But the richness of complex sounds like those found in our world depends on more than simple sensations of loudness and pitch. For example, a trombone and a tenor saxophone might play the same note (that is, a note with exactly the same fundamental frequency) at exactly the same loudness (the sound waves have identical intensities), but we would have no trouble discerning that two different instruments were being played. The perceptual

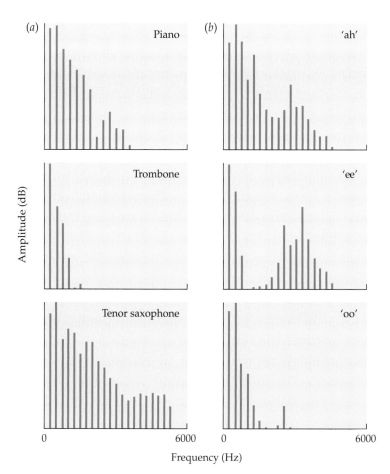

FIGURE 10.16 Timbre. (*a*) Three different musical instruments playing the same note (middle C, 262 Hz) sound different because they have different spectral shapes. (*b*) Three vowels produced by the same female talker, also with a fundamental frequency of 262 Hz, sound very different to listeners.

quality that differs between these two musical instruments, as well as between vowel sounds such as those in the words *hot*, *heat*, and *hoot*, is known as **timbre**. (See **Web Activity 10.3: Timbre**.)

What exactly is timbre? You won't find an answer to this question in the dictionary, because the official definition of *timbre* is "the quality that makes listeners hear two different sounds even though both sounds have the same pitch and loudness" (American Standards Association, 1960). However, differences in timbre between musical instruments or vowel sounds can be estimated closely by comparison of the extent to which the overall spectra of two sounds overlap (Plomp, 1976). Perception of visual color depends on the relative levels of energy at different wavelengths (see Chapter 5), and very similarly, perception of timbre is related to the relative energy of different acoustic spectral components (**Figure 10.16**). For example, the trombone and tenor saxophone notes whose spectra are plotted in Figure 10.16*a* share the same fundamental frequency (middle C, 262 Hz). However, note that the trombone's third (786-Hz) component is stronger than its fourth (1048-Hz) component, whereas for the saxophone, the relationship between the energies of these two components is reversed.

Auditory "Color" Constancy

Perception of timbre depends on the environment in which a sound is heard. For example, higher frequencies tend to be reinforced by hard surfaces such as tile floors and concrete walls, but they are dampened by soft surfaces such as thick carpet and curtains. This is much like the problem of color constancy

timbre The psychological sensation by which a listener can judge that two sounds with the same loudness and pitch are dissimilar. Timbre quality is conveyed by harmonics and other high frequencies.

that you learned about in Chapter 5. In vision, the goal is to perceive the same colors even though the spectrum of illumination can be quite different depending on the type of lighting (e.g., sunlight, incandescent, and so on). In hearing, surfaces in the environment reflect and absorb energy at different frequencies in ways that change the spectral shape that finally arrives at your ears.

Kiefte and Kluender (2008) used the different spectral shapes of the vowel sounds 'ee' and 'oo' to learn how hearing calibrates for changes in the listening environment. They took advantage of the fact that the spectra for 'ee' and 'oo' differ in two important ways (Figure 10.17*a*). The vowel sound 'ee' has a relatively flat spectrum with almost as much energy in high frequencies as in low frequencies (upper left). In contrast, energy in 'oo' is dominated by low frequencies that have less and less energy as frequency increases (lower right). We can say that the "tilt" of the 'ee' spectrum is much flatter than the tilt of 'oo.' The sounds 'ee' and 'oo' differ also in where peaks are present in

FIGURE 10.17 Listeners use both spectral tilt and the frequencies of spectral peaks to identify vowels. (*a*) Spectra of natural 'ee' and 'oo' are shown in the upper left and lower right, respectively. The vowel 'ee' has a relatively flat spectrum, and 'oo' has a tilted spectrum, such that there is much less energy at higher frequencies. The second spectral peak is lower in frequency for 'oo' (red circle) than for 'ee' (blue circle). Experimentally manipulated vowel sounds are also shown with the tilt of 'ee' and second peak of 'oo' in the upper right, and the tilt of 'oo' and second peak of 'ee' in the lower left. (*b*) Listeners use both tilt and frequency of the second peak to identify vowels. Lighter areas correspond to sounds that subjects hear as 'ee'; darker areas represent sounds that listeners hear as 'oo.' (*c*) Upon hearing a vowel after a sentence that has the same tilt as the vowel, listeners use only the frequency of the second peak to identify the vowel. In this case, the 'oo' tilt / 'ee' peak hybrid vowel is perceived as 'ee' (and vice versa for the 'ee' tilt / 'oo' peak hybrid). (*d*) However, when the preceding sentence includes a peak at the same frequency as the second peak in the vowel, listeners use mostly tilt to identify the vowel. Consequently, the tilt component of the hybrid vowels determines how they are perceived.

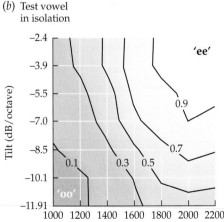

(*b*) Test vowel in isolation

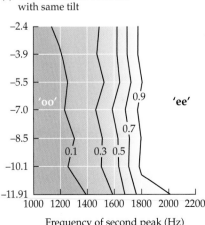

(*c*) Test vowel after sentence with same tilt

Frequency of second peak (Hz)

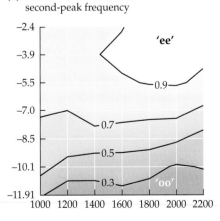

(*d*) Test vowel after sentence with same second-peak frequency their spectra. The second peak in the 'ee' spectrum (blue circle) is at a higher frequency than the second peak in the 'oo' spectrum (red circle). Listeners use both tilt and the frequency of this second peak to tell 'ee' from 'oo' (Figure 10.17*b*) (Kiefte and Kluender, 2005).

To learn how the auditory system adjusts for listening context, Kiefte and Kluender (2008) created stimuli that enabled them to separately measure the contributions of tilt and frequency of the second peak when perceiving these vowels. Then they had listeners identify vowels following a sentence like "you will now hear the vowel," but with an interesting twist. They created some sentences so that the overall tilt of the sentence was the same as the tilt of the following vowel, either 'ee'-like or 'oo'-like. To other sentences they added a peak in the spectrum all the way through the sentence at the same frequency as the second peak in the vowel ('ee' or 'oo') that listeners would identify. Listeners heard the very same vowels in dramatically different ways depending on which type of manipulated sentence preceded the vowels. When tilt stayed the same for both the preceding sentence and the vowel, listeners used only the frequency of the second peak to identify the vowel (Figure 10.17*c*). When the second peak was present all the way through the preceding sentence, listeners relied mostly on tilt to identify the vowel (Figure 10.17*d*).

Listeners calibrate for reliable spectral characteristics of a listening context much as observers calibrate for the spectral composition of illuminating light when perceiving color (Stilp et al., 2010). When the brain interprets spectral tilt as a consequence of the environment in which a sound is heard (concrete versus curtains), listeners ignore tilt and use only the second peak. Conversely, when there seems to always be energy around the second peak in a listening environment, listeners use only tilt to decide which vowel they heard.

attack The part of a sound during which amplitude increases (onset).

decay The part of a sound during which amplitude decreases (offset).

Attack and Decay

Another very important quality of a complex sound is the way it begins (the **attack** of the sound) and ends (the sound's **decay**) (**Figure 10.18**). Our auditory systems are very sensitive to attack and decay characteristics. For example, as you will learn in Chapter 11, important contrasts between speech sounds in the words *bill* and *will* or the words *cheat* and *sheet* relate to differences in how quickly sound energy increases at the onset (the rate of attack).

The same musical instrument can have quite different attacks, from the rapid onset of a plucked violin string to the gradual onset of a bowed string (Figures 10.18*a* and *b*). How quickly a sound decays depends on how long it takes for the vibrating object creating the sound (e.g., the violin string) to dissipate

FIGURE 10.18 We use the onsets of sounds (attacks) to identify them. The attack is quite different when a violin string is plucked (*a*) versus bowed (*b*). Similarly, different speech sounds, such as 'ba' (*c*) and 'wa' (*d*), have different attacks.

(*a*) Violin (pluck)

(*b*) Violin (bow)

(*c*) Speech ('ba')

(*d*) Speech ('wa')

energy and stop moving. One of the more challenging aspects of designing music synthesizers that could mimic real musical instruments was learning how to mimic the attacks and decays of the instruments.

To appreciate the importance of attack and decay in sound quality, explore **Web Activity 10.3: Timbre**, where you will first hear a normal piano recording. The sound of a piano note is caused by a small hammer hitting a string. The amplitude of the resulting sound increases very quickly before more gradually dissipating. If a recording of a piano note is played backward, the sound no longer even remotely resembles that of a piano. Instead, the backward piano note sounds more like the same note played on an accordion.

Auditory Scene Analysis

The acoustic environment can be a busy place. In most natural situations, the sound source that one is listening to is not the only source present. Consider, for example, conversing with a friend at a party where many other people are talking, music is playing, chips are being munched, the door is being opened and closed, and so on. Now consider simpler environments, such as those you choose for studying. To read this chapter, you probably chose the spot where you are right now because it was relatively quiet, but stop and listen carefully. Is a heater, air conditioner, computer, refrigerator, or some combination of these devices humming in the background? Can you hear people talking somewhere in the vicinity? Are chair legs sliding across floors? Places with only a single sound source are very uncommon. Indeed, there are few truly quiet places outside the laboratories of hearing scientists and the testing chambers of audiologists.

Environments with multiple sound sources are the rule, not the exception. How does the auditory system sort out these sources? Note that the visual system also has to contend with a busy world, but eyes can be directed to any part of the scene that is of interest to the visual system. Moreover, the rods and cones on the right side of the retina always see the objects on the left, politely leaving the receptors on the other side of the retina to collect data about objects on the right. For an auditory scene, the situation is greatly complicated by the fact that all the sound waves from all the sound sources in the environment are summed together in a single complex sound wave (Figure 10.19). You can move your ears around all you want, but everyone's voice at the party still has to be picked up by the same two sets of cochlear hair cells. Separating different sounds from one another is like living in a world in which everything is made of glass: it is difficult to distinguish separate objects, because they all merge into a single combination of shapes, as Figure 10.19*e* illustrates.

Somehow, however, the auditory system contends quite well with the situation: our perception is typically of a world with easily separable sounds. We can understand the conversation of a dance partner at a party, and we can pick out a favorite instrument in the band. This distinction of auditory events or objects in the broader auditory environment is commonly referred to as **source segregation** or **auditory scene analysis**.

Spatial, Spectral, and Temporal Segregation

The auditory system uses a number of strategies to segregate sound sources. One of the most obvious strategies is *spatial separation* between sounds. Sounds that emanate from the same location in space can typically be treated as if they arose from the same source. Moreover, in a natural environment in which sound sources move, a sound that is perceived to move in space can more

source segregation or auditory scene analysis Processing an auditory scene consisting of multiple sound sources into separate sound images.

(a) Frog

(b) Bird

(c) Splash

(d) Frog + bird + splash

(e)

FIGURE 10.19 Separating sounds from one another is like living in a visual world made of glass, because all the waveforms from all the sounds around us are summed into a single waveform arriving at the ears. Here the sounds are a frog, a bird, and a splash, shown both separately (a–c) and as they occur together at the ear (d). In this way, sounds are transparent like the glassware in (e).

easily be separated from background sounds that are relatively stationary. Listeners move too, so if a sound stays in the same place relative to the path of a listener, it will be easier for that sound to be sorted out from other sounds.

In addition to location, sounds can be segregated on the basis of their spectral or temporal qualities. For example, sounds with the same or similar pitch are more likely to be treated as coming from the same source and to be segregated from other sounds. Sounds that are perceived to emanate from the same source are often described as being part of the same *auditory stream*, and dividing the auditory world into separate auditory objects is known as **auditory stream segregation**.

A very simple example of auditory stream segregation involves two tones with similar frequencies that are alternated (see Figure 10.20a and **Web Activity 10.4: Auditory Stream Segregation**). This sequence sounds like a single coherent stream of tones that warble up and down in frequency. But if the alternating tones are markedly different in frequency (Figure 10.20b), two streams of tones are heard—one higher in pitch than the other (G. A. Miller and Heise, 1950).

auditory stream segregation The perceptual organization of a complex acoustic signal into separate auditory events for which each stream is heard as a separate event.

(a)　　　　(b)

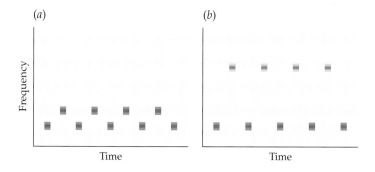

FIGURE 10.20 When tones that are close in frequency occur in rapid succession, they are heard as a single warbling stream (a), but when successive, rapidly alternating tones have very different frequencies, they are heard as two separate streams (b).

FIGURE 10.21 This musical sequence from J. S. Bach's "Toccata and Fugue in D Minor" utilizes the stream segregation principles "discovered" by auditory researchers in the twentieth century. When played in rapid succession, the higher notes (red) are heard as one melody separate from the lower notes (blue).

Auditory stream segregation is a powerful perceptual phenomenon that is not limited to simple tones in the laboratory. Before stream segregation was "discovered" by auditory scientists, the composer Johann Sebastian Bach exploited these auditory effects in his compositions (Figure 10.21). The same instrument, such as a pipe organ, would rapidly play interleaved sequences of low and high notes. Even though the musician played a sequence in the order H1-L1-H2-L2-H3-L3, listeners heard two melodies—one high (H1-H2-H3) and one low (L1-L2-L3). (See **Web Activity 10.4: Auditory Stream Segregation**.) This bit of knowledge about auditory perception was known not only to Bach, but also to other Baroque composers of the seventeenth and early eighteenth centuries.

When thinking about auditory scene analysis, it is sometimes useful to describe effects using Gestalt principles such as those elucidated for vision in Chapter 4. The examples of auditory stream segregation presented in this section can be described as applications of the Gestalt principle of *similarity* (see Figure 4.17*a*): sounds that are similar to each other tend to be grouped together into streams.

Grouping by Timbre

When a sequence of tones that have increasing and decreasing frequencies is presented (Figure 10.22*a*), tones that deviate from the rising/falling pattern are heard to "pop out" of the sequence (Heise and Miller, 1951). What happens when two patterns overlap in frequency—one increasing and then decreasing in frequency, and one decreasing and then increasing in frequency (Figures 10.22*b* and *c*)? If the tones are simple sine waves, two streams of sound are heard without overlapping pitches (Figure 10.22*b*); one stream includes all the high tones and one includes all the low tones. However, if harmonics are

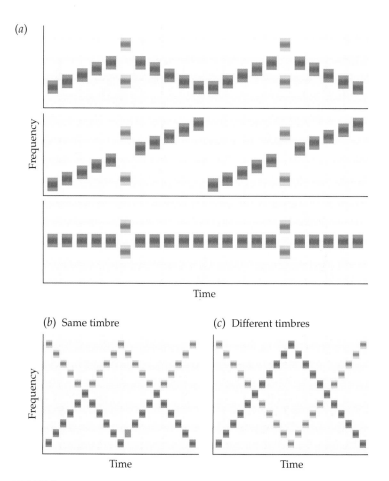

FIGURE 10.22 Timbre affects how sounds are grouped. (*a*) Individual tones (green) "pop out" of a stream if they do not fit the patterns of rising or falling frequency for the other tones (red). (*b*, *c*) Sounds that share the same timbre group together. When sounds in a succession all share the same timbre (*b*), they are heard as streams according to similar frequency. But if sounds have different timbres (*c*), they will separate according to timbre, even if their frequencies cross another pattern with a different timbre.

added to one of the sequences, thus creating a richer timbre, two overlapping patterns are heard as distinct (Figure 10.22*c*) (van Noorden, 1975).

Auditory stream segregation based on groups of notes with similar timbres can be seen as another example of the principle of similarity at work. As Figure 10.16 illustrated, timbres are very different for pianos, trombones, and saxophones. Grouping by timbre is particularly robust because sounds with similar timbre usually arise from the same sound source. This principle is the reason why listeners are able to pick out the melody played on a single instrument—a trombone, for example—even when another instrument, such as a saxophone, plays a different or even opposite sequence of notes (Wessel, 1979).

Neural processes that give rise to stream segregation can be found throughout the auditory system, from the first stages of auditory processing to the primary auditory cortex (A1) to secondary areas of the auditory cortex, such as the belt and parabelt areas (J. S. Snyder and Alain, 2007). The brain stem shows neural evidence of stream segregation based on simple cues such as frequencies of tones, but segregation based on more sophisticated perceptual properties of sounds is more likely to take place in the cortex.

Grouping by Onset

In addition to timbre, sound components that begin at the same time, or nearly the same time, such as the harmonics of a music or speech sound, will also tend to be heard as coming from the same sound source. One way this phenomenon helps us is by grouping different harmonics into a single complex sound. Frequency components with different onset times are less likely to be grouped. For example, if a single harmonic of a vowel sound begins before the rest of the harmonics of the vowel, that lone harmonic is less likely to be perceived as part of the vowel than if the onsets are simultaneous (C. J. Darwin, 1984).

R. A. Rasch (1978) showed that it is much easier to distinguish two notes from one another when the onset of one precedes the onset of the other by at least three-hundredths of a second (30 ms). He noted that musicians playing together in an ensemble such as a string quartet do not begin playing notes at exactly the same time, even when the musical score instructs them to do so. Instead, they begin notes slightly before or after one another, and this staggered start probably helps listeners pick out the individual instruments in the group. Part of the signature style of the Rolling Stones was to carry this practice to an extreme. Members of the group would begin the same beat with such widely varying onsets that it was sometimes unclear whether they were playing together or not.

Grouping of sounds with common onsets is consistent with the Gestalt law of *common fate*. Consider the consequences of dropping a bottle on a hard surface and listening for whether the bottle breaks. When any object bounces, each bounce results in a set of overtones that relate to the size, shape, and material of the object. If the dropped bottle does not break (**Figure 10.23***a*), this pattern of overtones repeats as a group, and the intensity of the sounds decreases with every additional bounce. But when the bottle breaks upon landing (Figure 10.23*b*), individual shards of the bottle have different spectral compositions, each shard

(*a*) Bouncing

(*b*) Breaking

Loud

Intensity

Silent

FIGURE 10.23 Spectrograms of a bottle bouncing (*a*) or breaking (*b*). When the bottle breaks, there are multiple patterns of onsets for multiple pieces of glass. Listeners can use patterns of onsets to accurately determine whether or not the bottle broke.

being its own resonator. Onsets of the overtones for different shards will differ because the pieces bounce independently until they bounce no more. Thus, even when the initial burst of noise is removed from the sound of the bouncing and breaking bottles, listeners can use patterns of onsets to accurately determine whether the bottle broke (W. H. Warren and Verbrugge, 1984).

When Sounds Become Familiar

In addition to the simple Gestalt principles that we've already discussed, listeners make use of experience and familiarity to separate different sound sources. When you know what you're listening for, it's easier to pick out sounds from a background of other sounds. An obvious example is how quickly you recognize someone saying your name even though there are many other sounds, including other voices, in the room.

You might be surprised to learn how quickly you can come to recognize a completely new sound once you've heard it a few times. Sounds in the environment, such as bird calls, often occur more than once. To test how much experience listeners need in order to benefit from familiarity, McDermott, Wroblewski, and Oxenham (2011) created complex novel sounds by combining natural sound characteristics in ways that listeners had never heard before. They repeatedly played these sounds (the "targets") at the same time and intensity as a background of other novel sounds ("distractors") that did not repeat, as shown in Figure 10.24. Although a single instance of a sound and its background was impossible to segregate, listeners could nonetheless segregate and identify the sound when it repeated. Listeners needed only a few repetitions to perform well above chance, even though they had never heard the complex sounds before they came to the laboratory.

(a)

(b)

FIGURE 10.24 (a) The listener's task was to identify a novel complex sound (the target) when the target and another complex sound (a distractor) overlapped in one combined sound (a mixture). (b) A new target (represented by the red bars under the graph) was repeatedly played at the same time as different distractors (the non-red bars). After just a few repeats, listeners became familiar enough with the repeated target that they could pick it out from other sounds in the background.

Continuity and Restoration Effects

As already discussed, the sound we're trying to listen to at any given time is usually not the only sound in the environment. In addition to dealing with overlapping auditory streams, we also often have to deal with the total masking of one sound source by another for brief periods. Suppose you're listening on your cell phone as a friend gives you directions to the restaurant where you're to meet for lunch. A car may honk, a baby may cry, or your cell phone may produce a short burst of static, but if you're paying attention and the interruption is not too long, you will probably be able to "hear through" the interruption. This effect is consistent with the Gestalt principle of *good continuation* (see Figure 4.13): the continuous auditory stream is heard to continue behind the masking sound. Auditory researchers have labeled these phenomena "continuity effects" or "perceptual restoration effects"—the latter label arising because the auditory system appears to restore the portion of the continuous stream that was blocked out by the interrupting sound (R. M. Warren, 1984). In this sense, auditory restoration is analogous to the visual system's filling in the portions of a background object that is sitting behind an occluding object.

Continuity effects have been demonstrated in the laboratory with a wide variety of target sounds and interrupting sounds. The simplest version of such an experiment is to delete portions of a pure tone and replace them with noise (Figure 10.25*a*). The tone will sound continuous if the noise is intense enough to have masked the tone, had it been present (R. M. Warren, 1984).

How do we know that listeners really hear a sound as continuous in experiments such as this? One of the best ways to determine what people really perceive is to use a signal detection task. Kluender and Jenison (1992) used signal detection methodology with a slightly more complex version of the continuity effect (Figure 10.25*b*). In their experiments, listeners heard tone *glides*, in which a sine wave tone varies continuously in frequency over time (the resulting sound is similar to that of a slide whistle). When intense noise is superimposed over part of the glide, listeners report hearing the glide continue behind the noise. (See **Web Activity 10.5: Continuity and Restoration Effects**.) Kluender and Jenison created stimuli in which the middle portion of the glide either was present with the noise or was completely removed. In trials in which the noise was shortest and most intense, the signal detection

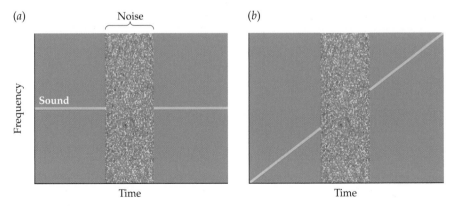

FIGURE 10.25 When a sound is deleted and replaced with a loud noise, listeners will hear the sound as if it continues through the noise. This is true when a tone maintains the same frequency (*a*) and when the tone steadily increases or decreases in frequency (a glide) (*b*).

measure of discriminability (d') dropped to 0. For these trials, perceptual restoration was complete: listeners had no idea whether or not the glide was actually present with the noise.

The compelling nature of perceptual restoration suggests that at some point the restored missing sounds are encoded in the brain as if they were actually present in the signal. Imaging studies of humans, who can report when they do and do not hear the tone through the noise, show metabolic activity in the primary auditory cortex (A1) that is consistent with what listeners report hearing, whether or not the tone is present (Riecke et al., 2007, 2009). Macaque monkeys also hear tones being restored even when interrupted by noise (Petkov, O'Connor, and Sutter, 2003), and neurons in A1 of monkeys show the same responses to real and restored tones (Petkov, O'Connor, and Sutter, 2007). These data from the auditory cortex cannot tell us whether the glides were restored in the cortex or at a point earlier in auditory processing. However, they make it easier to understand why perceptually restored sounds really sound present.

Restoration of Complex Sounds

Complex sounds such as music and speech can also be perceptually restored. When DeWitt and Samuel (1990) played familiar melodies with notes excised and replaced by noise, listeners perceived the missing notes as having been present. Restoration was so complete that listeners could not report which notes had been removed and replaced with noise. The researchers also tested whether familiarity of the melodies mattered. Just as you might expect, listeners were much less likely to "hear" a missing note in an unfamiliar melody.

Just in case you think only human listeners would care about melodies, listen up. Seeba and Klump (2009) trained European starlings (**Figure 10.26**) to peck when they heard a difference between two parts of starling song, called motifs. When starlings heard motifs with short snippets filled with noise or with silence, they were more likely to peck as if there was a difference between an intact and an interrupted motif when silence filled the gap. This observation suggests that the starlings restored the missing bits of motifs when noise was inserted into the gap. Not all starling songs are equal, however. In the same set of experiments, the researchers used bits of song that were either familiar to the starling in the experiment (the bird's own song or the song of its cagemates) or unfamiliar (from starlings the subject had never heard). Just like humans listening to familiar and unfamiliar melodies, starlings are more likely to restore missing bits of a familiar song.

Perceptual restoration in speech is even more compelling than restoration of music. R. M. Warren and Obusek (1971) played the sentence "the state governors met with their respective legi*latures convening in the capital city" with the first *s* in *legislatures* removed and replaced by silence, a cough, a burst of noise, or any of a few other sounds. Despite the missing *s*, listeners heard the sentence as if it were intact and complete. Even when listeners were explicitly warned that a small part of the sentence had been removed and replaced with silence or another sound, they were unable to accurately report where the sentence had been changed, except when the missing *s* was replaced with silence.

Listening to familiar melodies and to real speech sentences, as opposed to simple sounds such as sine waves and tonal glides, permits listeners to use more than just auditory processing to fill in missing information. Clearly, these "higher-order" sources of information are used for listening to sources in the face of other acoustic clutter. In a particularly compelling example, listeners

FIGURE 10.26 European starlings perceptually restore bits of starling songs, and they are more likely to restore song parts when they are familiar with the starling that produced them.

FIGURE 10.27 Adding noise improves comprehension. (*a*) Spectrogram of the sentence "the mailman brought a letter." (*b*) Listeners have great difficulty understanding the sentence when intervals are removed and replaced with silence. (*c*) When the same intervals are replaced by noise, however, it becomes easier to understand the sentence, because of perceptual restoration. (After Bashford and Warren, 1987.)

restored a missing sound on the basis of linguistic information that followed the deletion (R. M. Warren and Sherman, 1974). For example, Warren and Sherman played utterances such as "The *eel fell off the car" and "The *eel fell off the table" (the asterisk represents a patch of noise). Listeners were much more likely to report hearing "wheel" in the former utterance and "meal" in the latter, even though the context information came well after the missing phoneme in the sentences. (See **Web Activity 10.5: Continuity and Restoration Effects**.) As this result hints, meaningful sentences actually become more intelligible when gaps are filled with intense noise than when gaps are left silent (Figure 10.27). Think about this: adding noise improves comprehension!

Summary

1. Listeners use small differences, in time and intensity, across the two ears to learn the direction in the horizontal plane (azimuth) from which a sound comes.

2. Time and intensity differences across the two ears are not sufficient to fully indicate the location from which a sound comes. In particular, time and intensity differences are not sufficient to indicate whether sounds come from the front or the back, or from higher or lower (elevation).

3. The pinna, ear canal, head, and torso alter the intensities of different frequencies for sounds coming from different places in space, and listeners use these changes in intensity across frequency to identify the location from which a sound comes.

4. Perception of auditory distance is similar to perception of visual depth because no single characteristic of the signal can inform a listener about how distant a sound source is. Listeners must combine intensity, spectral composition, and relative amounts of direct and reflected energy of sounds to estimate distance to a sound source.

5. Many natural sounds, including musical instruments and human speech, have rich harmonic structure with energy at integer multiples of the fundamental frequency, and listeners are especially good at perceiving the pitch of harmonic sounds.

6. Important perceptual qualities of complex sounds are timbre (conveyed by the relative amounts of energy at different frequencies) and the onset and offset properties of attack and decay, respectively.

7. Because all the sounds in the environment are summed into a single waveform that reaches each ear, a major challenge for hearing is to separate sound sources in the combined signal. This general process is known as auditory scene analysis. Sound source segregation succeeds by using multiple characteristics of sounds, including spatial location, similarity in frequency and timbre, onset properties, and familiarity.

8. In everyday environments, sounds to which a person is listening often are interrupted by other, louder sounds. Perceptual restoration is a process by which missing or degraded acoustic signals are perceptually replaced.

CHAPTER 11

Marcus van Soest, *Doggie Pim goes Doggie Jazz*, 2002

Music and Speech Perception

Sounds from musical instruments and human vocal tracts obey the same laws of physical acoustics as all other sounds. Guitar strings and human vocal folds are vibratory structures, with similarities to rubber bands and suspension bridges. Trombones and vocal tracts act as resonators following the same laws as empty bottles and hollow logs. In this sense, spoken words and musical notes are nothing more than very familiar, complex sounds.

In other ways, however, music and speech can be distinguished from most other environmental sounds. Much like visual art such as paintings and sculpture, music and speech are created with perceivers in mind. Both music and speech serve to communicate, and both can convey emotion and deeper meanings. In song, music and speech conspire to move the listener. Although dogs, birds, and whales share acoustic messages and even sing to one another, there is no question that the depth and breadth of human communication by music and language has no rival in the acoustic world. In this chapter we explore these communicative aspects of hearing: music and speech.

Music

People have been using music as a way to express themselves and influence the thoughts and emotions of others for a very long time. The oldest discovered musical instruments—flutes carved from vulture bones—are at least 30,000 years old (Conard, Malina, and Münzel, 2009). You probably know of the great ancient Greek scholar Pythagoras (c.580–c.500 BCE) from the Pythagorean theorem in high school geometry. To say that Pythagoras was obsessed with numbers would be an understatement. And the numbers that he and his followers cared about most were those found in musical scales. They were convinced that the musical intervals they found most pleasing should provide the greatest insights not only to mathematics, but to the universe as a whole. Although music may not actually explain the known universe, we all appreciate how important music is to culture and, perhaps, to personal cultural identity.

Music and Emotion

Listening to music affects people's moods (Eich, 1995; Pignatiello, Camp, and Rasar, 1986) and emotions (Sloboda, 1999). When listeners hear pleasant-sounding chords preceding a word, they are faster to respond that a word such as *charm* is positive, and they are slower to respond that a word such as *evil* is negative (Sollberger, Reber, and Eckstein, 2003). Given the powerful effects of music on mood and emotion, some clinical psychologists practice music

An ear can break a human heart
As quickly as a spear
We wish the ear had not a heart
So dangerously near

— Emily Dickinson,
"The Saddest Noise,
the Sweetest Noise"

pitch The psychological aspect of sound related mainly to perceived frequency.

therapy, through which people sing, listen, play, and move to music in efforts to improve mental and physical health.

Music has been shown to have deep physiological effects. Music can promote positive emotions, reduce pain, alleviate stress, and may even improve resistance to disease (Gangrade, 2011; Roy, Peretz, and Rainville, 2007). High levels of the neurotransmitter serotonin (which is targeted by many antidepressant drugs, such as Prozac) are responsible for negative aspects of emotion and mood. When people must listen to disagreeable music, their levels of serotonin actually rise (Evers and Suhr, 2000). When people listen to highly pleasurable music, they experience changes in heart rate, muscle electrical activity, and respiration; and blood flow increases in brain regions that are thought to be involved in reward and motivation (Blood and Zatorre, 2001). Music is a powerful human invention indeed.

Musical Notes

From Chapter 9 you know that one of the most important characteristics of any acoustic signal is frequency. You also know that brain structures for processing sounds are tonotopically organized to correspond to frequency. The psychological quality of perceived frequency is **pitch**. When you imagined pitch while reading Chapter 9, you probably imagined musical pitch. Figure 11.1 illustrates the extent of the frequency range of musical sounds in relation to human hearing.

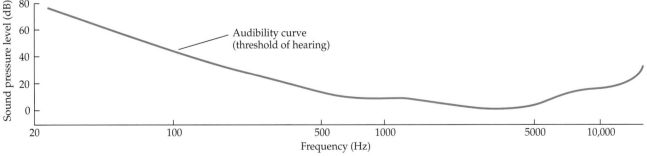

FIGURE 11.1 The sounds of music extend across a frequency range from about 25 to 4200 hertz (Hz).

TONE HEIGHT AND TONE CHROMA   Musical pitch is one of the characteristics of musical notes, the sounds that constitute melodies. A very important concept in understanding musical pitch is the **octave**. When we described pitch (or psychoacoustic pitch) in Chapter 9, it seemed clear that the nearer any two sounds were in frequency, the nearer they were in pitch. Here's where octaves come in. When one of two periodic sounds is double the frequency of the other, those two sounds are one octave apart. For example, middle C (C_4) has a fundamental frequency of 261.6 hertz (Hz). Notes that are one octave below and above middle C are 130.8 Hz (C_3) and 523.2 Hz (C_5), respectively. Not only do these three sounds have the same names on the musical scale (C), but they also sound similar. In fact, C_3 (130.8 Hz) sounds more similar to middle C (C_4, 261.6 Hz) than to a sound with a closer frequency—for example, E_3 (164.8 Hz)! Clearly there is more to musical pitch than just frequency.

The preceding example illustrates the concept of "just intonation," in which frequencies of sounds are in simple ratios with one another (e.g., 2:1 for an octave). But in typical Western music, the frequencies of notes are adjusted slightly from simple ratios so that combinations of notes will sound equally good when played in higher or lower frequency ranges (keys). The set of notes (scale) used commonly in Western music is called "equal temperament."

Because of octave relations, musical pitch is typically described as having two dimensions. The first is **tone height**, which relates to frequency in a fairly straightforward way. The second dimension, related to the octave, is **tone chroma** (*chroma* is the Greek word for "color"). We can visualize musical pitch as a helix. Frequency and tone height increase with increasing height on the helix, as shown in Figure 11.2. The circular laps around the helix correspond to changes in tone chroma. At the same point along each lap around the helix, a sound lies on a vertical line, and all sounds along that line share the same tone chroma and are separated by octaves. (See **Web Activity 11.1: Notes, Chords, and Octaves**.)

In your early years of schooling, you probably learned to sing the notes of the musical scale: do, re, mi, fa, sol, la, ti, do. Perhaps you even tested how many times you could sing the scale at increasingly higher pitches. In that case you were actually singing your way up the musical helix. Your pitch traveled a full turn upward with each repetition of a particular note—for example, do or re.

In Chapter 9 you learned that both a place code and a temporal code can be used in the perception of pitch. Neurons in the auditory nerve signal frequency both by their location in the cochlea (place) and by the timing of their firing (temporal). For frequencies greater than 5000 Hz, temporal coding does not contribute to the perception of pitch, and pitch discrimination becomes appreciably worse because only place coding can be used. Most musical instruments generally produce notes that are below 4000 Hz. Could tone chroma somehow be related to the temporal encoding of pitch (Moore, 2003)? We do not know. We do know that a sequence of pure tones with frequencies greater than 5000 Hz does not convey a melody very well (Attneave and Olson, 1971), and listeners have great difficulty perceiving octave relationships between tones when one or both tones have a frequency greater than 5000 Hz (Ward, 1954).

CHORDS   Music is further defined by richer, complex sounds called **chords**, which are created when three or more notes are played simultaneously. (The simultaneous playing of two notes is called a "dyad.") The major distinction between chords is whether they are *consonant* or *dissonant*. Perceived to be

octave The interval between two sound frequencies having a ratio of 2:1.

tone height A sound quality corresponding to the level of pitch. Tone height is monotonically related to frequency.

tone chroma A sound quality shared by tones that have the same octave interval.

chord A combination of three or more musical notes with different pitches played simultaneously.

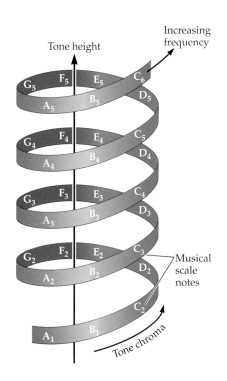

FIGURE 11.2   This helix illustrates the two characteristics of musical pitch: tone height and tone chroma.

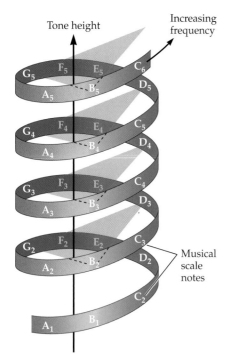

Tone height

Increasing frequency

Musical scale notes

FIGURE 11.3 Chords are made up of three or more notes and can be played with different tone heights while their chromatic relationships are maintained. Here, the G-major chord is shown being played at different heights (purple triangles).

most pleasing, consonant chords are combinations of notes in which the ratios between the note frequencies are simple. This is why Pythagoras was so taken by the relationship between pleasantness and mathematics. You already know one of the consonant relationships, the octave, in which the frequencies of the two notes are in the simple ratio of 2:1. Other major consonant intervals are the perfect fifth (3:2) and the perfect fourth (4:3). Dissonant intervals are defined by less elegant ratios. For example, the minor second (16:15) and the augmented fourth (45:32) do not sound very pleasing. Indeed, during the Middle Ages the augmented fourth was called the "devil in music" (Seay, 1975).

Because chords are defined by the ratios of the note frequencies combined to produce them, they are named the same no matter what octave they're played in. For example, the G-major chord consists of G, B, and D, and it can be played as $G_2 + B_2 + D_3, G_4 + B_4 + D_5, G_6 + B_6 + D_7$, or in any other octave, provided the ratios remain the same. Note that in the musical helix in **Figure 11.3**, the relationships between the notes of the chord on the helix stay the same, as in Figure 11.2; the only thing that changes is the pattern's height.

CULTURAL DIFFERENCES   Musical scales and intervals vary widely across cultures. Although potent relationships between notes such as octaves are relatively universal, different musical traditions use different numbers of notes and spaces between notes within an octave. All of our discussion has concerned the heptatonic (seven-note) scale. Another common scale, pentatonic, has five notes per octave, and you've heard this scale in gospel, jazz, rock, and blues music, among other North American genres. The pentatonic scale is traditional in many other parts of the world, especially Asia.

You may be aware that Asian languages such as Mandarin (China), Thai, and Vietnamese are tone languages, giving a singsongy impression to some English listeners. Speakers of tone languages use changes in voice pitch (fundamental frequency) to distinguish different words in their language. For example, the Mandarin word *ma* means "horse" or "mother" depending on how voice pitch rises or falls.

It appears that language may affect the types of musical scales people use. Changes in pitch direction are larger and more frequent in spoken tone languages such as Mandarin, Thai, and Vietnamese when compared to English, French, and German. Parallel acoustic differences are found between the pentatonic music of China, Thailand, and Vietnam and the heptatonic music of Western cultures. Pitch changes in Asian music are larger and occur more often (Han et al., 2011).

In scales in which octaves contain fewer notes, the notes may be more loosely tuned than are notes in the heptatonic Western scale, so a wider range of pitches could qualify for a given note. For example, the Javanese *sléndro* and *pélog* scales have fewer than seven notes within an octave, and there is greater variation in a note's acceptable frequencies.

Because people around the world have very different listening experiences, you might expect them to hear musical notes in different ways. Indeed, when Javanese and Western musicians hear intervals between notes, their estimates of the intervals vary according to how well those notes correspond to Javanese versus Western scales, respectively (Perlman and Krumhansl, 1996). Furthermore, infants seem equipped to learn whatever scale is used in their environment. Lynch and Eilers (1990) tested the degree to which 6-month-old infants noticed inappropriate notes within both the traditional Western scale and the Javanese *pélog* scale. The infants appeared to be equally good at detecting such "mistakes" within both Western and Javanese scales, but adults from Florida were reliably better at detecting deviations from the Western scale.

FIGURE 11.4 The pattern of increasing and decreasing pitches can remain the same, but the melody will change if notes have different durations. Here, three series of notes with the same melody contour are shown with notes that differ only in duration.

Making Music

Notes or chords can form a **melody**, a sequence of sounds perceived as a single coherent structure. The notes of a familiar melody, such as "Twinkle, Twinkle, Little Star" (a.k.a. "Now I Know My ABCs," "Baa Baa Black Sheep," and Variation K.265 [300e] by Wolfgang Amadeus Mozart), "belong together" perceptually because they form this melody. Note that a melody is defined by its contour—the pattern of rises and declines in pitch—rather than by an exact sequence of sound frequencies (Handel, 1989).

You've already learned one simple way in which melody is not a sequence of specific sounds: shift every note of a melody by one octave and the resulting melody is the same. When you sing with other people possessing higher or lower voices, they sing the same melody at very different pitches. Even within a single octave, the same melody can be heard from different notes if the steps between notes stay the same.

In addition to varying in pitch, notes and chords vary in duration. The average duration of a set of notes in a melody defines the music's **tempo**. Any melody can be played at either a fast or a slow tempo. But the relative durations within a sequence of notes are a critical part of the melodies themselves. If the notes of a given sequence are played with different relative durations, we will hear completely different melodies (**Figure 11.4**).

RHYTHM In addition to varying in speed, music varies in rhythm. The fact that music has rhythm should go without saying. After all, how else would we dance to it? Less obvious, perhaps, is that many—or even most—activities have rhythm. Walking and galloping have rhythm. So do finger tapping, waving, and swimming. Perhaps it is the very commonness of rhythm that causes us to hear nearly all sounds as rhythmic, even when they're not!

Over a century ago, Thaddeus Bolton (1894) conducted experiments in which he played a sequence of identical sounds perfectly spaced in time; they had no rhythm. Nevertheless, his listeners readily reported that the sounds occurred in groups of two, three, or four. Moreover, they reported hearing the first sound of a group as "accented," or "stressed," while the remaining sounds were unaccented, or unstressed. You've probably had a similar experience while riding in a train or car. Even though a train travels over junctions in the rails

melody A sequence of notes or chords perceived as a single coherent structure.

tempo The perceived speed of the presentation of sounds.

FIGURE 11.5 When two rhythms are played together and one rhythm (in this case Aaa) is dominant, listeners tend to perceive the timing of beats in the non-dominant rhythm (Bbbb) adjusted to conform with the dominant rhythm.

A̲a a A a a A a a A a a A̲a a A a a A a a A a a A̲a a

B̲b b b B b b b B b b b B̲b b b B b b b B b b b B̲b b b

←   →   ←   →

at nearly equal intervals, you hear the sound as "CLICK click CLICK click." When you ride in a car at a steady speed, you hear "THUMP thump THUMP thump" as your tires roll over cracks in a concrete road.

As Bolton's studies show, listeners are predisposed to grouping sounds into rhythmic patterns. Several qualities contribute to whether sounds will be heard as accented (stressed) or unaccented (unstressed). Sounds that are longer, louder, and higher in pitch all are more likely to be heard as leading their group (Woodrow, 1909). The timing relationship between one sound and the others in a sequence also helps determine accent. For example, we are more likely to hear a series of three sounds as "Aaa Aaa Aaa" than as "aAa aAa aAa."

Listeners prefer, or at least expect, sequences of notes to be fairly regular, and this tendency provides opportunities for composers to get creative with their beats. One way to be creative in deviating from a bland succession of regular beats is to introduce **syncopation**. Syncopation is any deviation from a regular rhythm, for example, by accenting a note that is expected to be unaccented or not playing a note (rest) when a note is expected. Syncopation has been used for centuries and can be found in compositions by all the great composers, including Bach, Beethoven, and Mozart. Typical college students may be more familiar with syncopation from jazz, reggae, and ska.

One particularly interesting example of syncopation is syncopated auditory polyrhythms. When two different rhythms are overlapped, they can collide in interesting ways. For example, if one rhythm is based on 3 beats (AaaAaaAaaAaa) and the other on 4 (BbbbBbbbBbbb), the first accented sound for both rhythms will coincide only once every 12 beats. Across the 11 intervening beats, the two rhythms will be out of sync. When we listen to syncopated polyrhythms, one of the two rhythms becomes the dominant or controlling rhythm, and the other rhythm tends to be perceptually adjusted to accommodate the first (Figure 11.5). In particular, the accented beat of the subordinate rhythm shifts in time (Handel and Oshinsky, 1981). Thus, syncopation is the perception that beats in the subordinate rhythm have actually traveled backward or forward in time!

These findings reveal that rhythm is, in large part, psychological. We can produce sequences of sounds that are rhythmic and are perceived as such. But we also hear rhythm when it does not exist, and notes effectively travel in time to maintain the perception of consistent rhythm.

MELODY DEVELOPMENT   Like rhythm, melody is essentially a psychological entity (Handel, 1989). There is nothing about the particular sequence of notes in "Twinkle, Twinkle, Little Star" that makes them a melody. Rather, it is our experience with a particular sequence of notes or with similar sequences that helps us perceive coherence.

Studies of 8-month-old listeners reveal that learning of melodies begins quite early in life. Saffran et al. (1999) created six simple and deliberately novel "melodies" composed of sequences of three tones. Infants sat on a parent's lap while hearing only 3 minutes of continuous random repetitions of the melodies. Next, infants heard both the original melodies and series of new three-tone sequences. These new sequences contained the same notes as the originals, but

syncopation Any deviation from a regular rhythm.

one part of the sequence was taken from one melody and another part from another melody. Because the infants responded differently to the new melodies, we can deduce that they had learned something about the original melodies.

This ability to learn new melodies is not limited to simple sequences of tones. In a study with 7-month-old infants, parents played a recording of two Mozart sonata movements to their infants every day for 2 weeks (Saffran, Loman, and Robertson, 2000). After another 2 weeks had passed, the infants were tested in a laboratory to see whether they remembered the movements. Infant listeners responded differently to the original movements than to similar Mozart movements introduced to them for the first time in the laboratory.

Speech

Most people who listen to speech also produce speech. Talkers speak so that they can be understood, and the relationship between the production and perception of speech is an especially intimate one. Therefore, it is important to know some things about speech production before trying to understand speech perception.

Humans are capable of producing an incredible range of distinct speech sounds (the 5000 or so languages across the world use over 850 different speech sounds) (Maddieson, 1984). If you've ever heard Kenny Muhammad, the "Human Orchestra," you've experienced the unrivaled versatility of human sound production. This flexibility arises from the unique structure of the human **vocal tract** (Figure 11.6) (Lieberman, 1984). Unlike that of other animals, the human larynx is positioned quite low in the throat. One notorious disadvantage of such a low larynx is that humans choke on food more easily

vocal tract The airway above the larynx used for the production of speech. The vocal tract includes the oral tract and nasal tract.

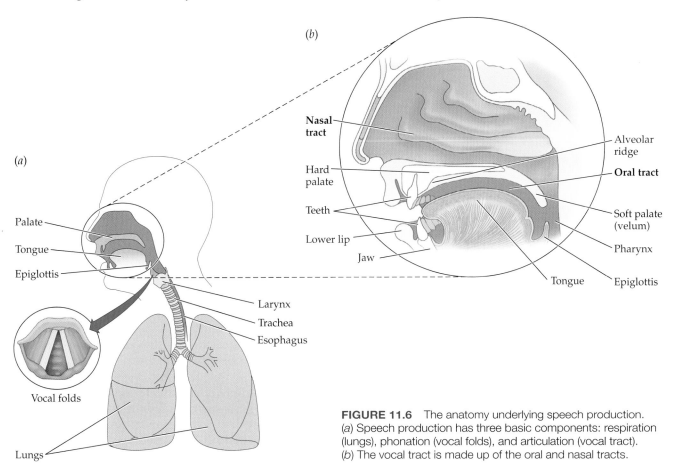

FIGURE 11.6 The anatomy underlying speech production. (a) Speech production has three basic components: respiration (lungs), phonation (vocal folds), and articulation (vocal tract). (b) The vocal tract is made up of the oral and nasal tracts.

than any other animal does. Another disadvantage is that, beyond infancy, we cannot swallow and breathe at the same time. The fact that these life-threatening anatomical liabilities were evolutionarily trumped by the survival advantage of oral communication is a testament to the importance of language to human life.

Speech Production

The production of speech has three basic components: respiration (lungs), phonation (vocal cords), and articulation (vocal tract) (see Figure 11.6). Speaking fluently requires an impressive degree of coordination among these components.

phonation The process through which vocal folds are made to vibrate when air pushes out of the lungs.

articulation The act or manner of producing a speech sound using the vocal tract.

formant A resonance of the vocal tract. Formants are specified by their center frequency and are denoted by integers that increase with relative frequency.

RESPIRATION AND PHONATION   To initiate a speech sound, the diaphragm pushes air out of the lungs, through the trachea, and up to the larynx. At the larynx, air must pass through the two vocal folds, which are made up of muscle tissue that can be adjusted to vary how freely air passes through the opening between them. These adjustments are described as types of **phonation**.

The rate at which vocal folds vibrate depends on their stiffness and mass. Consider guitar strings as an analogy. Just like guitar strings, vocal folds become stiffer and vibrate faster as their tension increases, creating sounds with higher pitch. The pitch of a guitar string also depends on its thickness or mass. Thinner guitar strings vibrate more quickly and create higher-pitched sounds. Similarly, children, who have relatively small vocal folds, have high-pitched voices. Adult men generally have lower-pitched voices than women have because one of the effects of testosterone during puberty is to increase the mass of the vocal folds. By varying the tension of vocal folds (stiffness) and the pressure of airflow from the lungs, individual talkers can vary the fundamental frequency of voiced sounds.

If we were to measure the sound right after the larynx, we would see that vibration of the vocal folds creates a harmonic spectrum as described in Chapter 10 and illustrated in **Figure 11.7a**. If we could listen to just this part of speech, it would sound like a buzz. The first harmonic corresponds to the actual rate of physical vibration of the vocal folds—the fundamental frequency. Talkers can make interesting modifications in the way their vocal folds vibrate—creating breathy or creaky voices, for example—and singers can vary vocal-fold tension and air pressure to sing notes with widely varying frequencies. However, the really extraordinary part of producing speech sounds occurs above the larynx and vocal folds.

ARTICULATION   The area above the larynx—the oral tract and nasal tract combined—is referred to as the "vocal tract" (see Figure 11.6b). Humans have an unrivaled ability to change the shape of the vocal tract by manipulating the jaw, lips, tongue body, tongue tip, velum (soft palate), and other vocal-tract structures. These manipulations are referred to as **articulation**. As you will recall from Chapter 9, changing the size and shape of the space through which sound passes increases and decreases energy at different frequencies. We call these effects "resonance characteristics," and the spectra of speech sounds are shaped by the way people configure their tracts as resonators. Figure 11.7b illustrates the filtering effects of the vocal tract for the vowel sound 'ah,' as in *father*. Figure 11.7c portrays the net result of passing the periodic energy from the larynx through the vocal tract.

Peaks in the speech spectrum are referred to as **formants**, and formants are labeled by number, from lowest frequency to highest (F_1, F_2, F_3, and so on). These concentrations in energy occur at different frequencies, depending on the length of the vocal tract. For shorter vocal tracts (in children and short adults), formants are at higher frequencies than for longer vocal tracts. Because

(*a*) Harmonic spectrum

(*b*) Filter function

(*c*) Vowel output

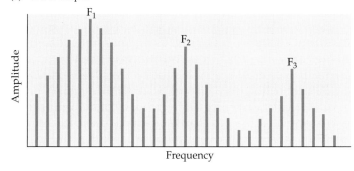

FIGURE 11.7 The spectrum of sound coming from the vocal folds is a harmonic spectrum (*a*). After passing through the vocal tract, which has resonances based on the vocal tract's shape at the time (*b*), there are peaks (formants) and troughs of energy at different frequencies in the sounds that come out of the mouth (*c*).

absolute frequencies change depending on who's talking, listeners must use the relationships between formant peaks to perceive speech sounds. Only the first three formants are depicted in Figure 11.7*c*. For the most part, we can distinguish almost all speech sounds on the basis of energy in the region of these lowest three formants. However, additional formants do exist, at higher frequencies with lower amplitudes.

In the previous two chapters, most of the sounds that we discussed had constant frequency spectra. That is, if a sound started with a 50-decibel (dB), 100-Hz component and a 60-dB, 200-Hz component, these frequencies continued at these amplitudes for the duration of the sound. One of the most distinctive characteristics of speech sounds is that their spectra change over time. To represent this third dimension (time) in addition to the dimensions of frequency and amplitude represented in frequency spectrum graphs of static sounds, auditory researchers use a type of display called a **spectrogram**. In a sound spectrogram, frequency is represented on the y-axis, time is tracked on the x-

spectrogram In sound analysis, a three-dimensional display that plots time on the horizontal axis, frequency on the vertical axis, and amplitude (intensity) on a color or gray scale.

(a)

(b)

FIGURE 11.8 For sounds that do not vary over time, frequency spectra can be represented by graphs that plot amplitude on the y-axis and frequency on the x-axis (*a*). To graphically show sounds whose spectra change over time, we rotate the graph so that frequency is plotted on the y-axis (*b*); and then we plot time on the x-axis (*c*), with the amplitude of each frequency during each time slice represented by color (redder showing greater intensity). The spectrogram in part (*c*) shows the acoustic signal produced by a male uttering the sentence, "We were away a year ago."

(c)

axis, and amplitude is indicated by the color of any point on the graph (**Figure 11.8**). Formants show up clearly in spectrograms as bands of acoustic energy that undulate up and down, depending on the speech sounds being produced.

CLASSIFYING SPEECH SOUNDS   Speech sounds are most often described in terms of articulation. This is because, in the early days of studying speech, people did not have electronic recording or the ability to analyze sounds. Instead, they paid close attention to their own vocal tracts and described speech sounds in terms of the articulations necessary to produce them. You will get the most out of the following discussion if you "sing along" just as these early speech researchers did, producing the speech sounds yourself and feeling the various articulatory maneuvers necessary to speak them.

Vowel sounds are all made with a relatively open vocal tract, and they vary mostly in how high or low and how far forward or back the tongue is placed in the oral tract, along with whether or not the lips are rounded. We produce the 'ee' sound in the word *beet* by placing the tongue up and forward, the 'aw' in *bought* by moving the tongue down and back, and the 'oo' in *boot* by moving the tongue up and back while rounding the lips (**Figure 11.9**).

We produce consonants by obstructing the vocal tract in some way, and each consonant sound can be classified according to three articulatory dimensions:

1. *Place of articulation* (see Figure 11.6*b*). Airflow can be obstructed
   • At the lips (bilabial speech sounds: 'b,' 'p,' 'm')
   • At the alveolar ridge just behind the teeth (alveolar speech sounds: 'd,' 't,' 'n')
   • At the soft palate (velar speech sounds: 'g,' 'k,' 'ng')

2. *Manner of articulation.* Airflow can be
   • Totally obstructed (stops: 'b,' 'd,' 'g,' 'p,' 't,' 'k') (see Figure 11.10)
   • Partially obstructed (fricatives: 's,' 'z,' 'f,' 'v,' 'th,' 'sh')
   • Only slightly obstructed (laterals: 'l,' 'r'; and glides: 'w,' 'y')
   • First blocked, and then allowed to sneak through (affricates: 'ch,' 'j')
   • Blocked at first from going through the mouth, but allowed to go through the nasal passage (nasals: 'n,' 'm,' 'ng')

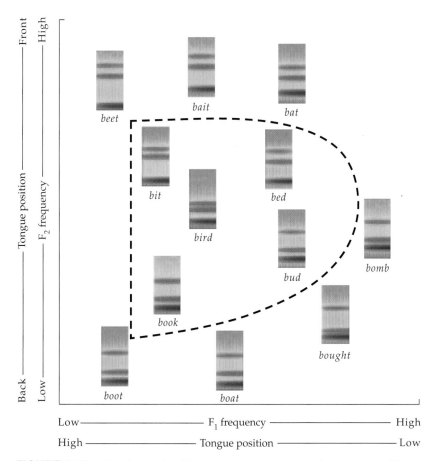

FIGURE 11.9 Vowel sounds of English, showing how the frequencies of the first (F_1) and second (F_2) formants relate to how high or low (F_1) and how far forward or back (F_2) the tongue is. The dashed line illustrates limits on how far the tongue moves when vowels are produced. For example, the vowels 'ee' and 'oo' are produced with the tongue very high in the mouth. In the case of 'ee,' the tongue is far forward; but for 'oo,' the tongue is far back.

3. *Voicing* (**Figure 11.10**). The vocal cords may be
   - Vibrating (voiced consonants: 'b,' 'm,' 'z,' 'l,' 'r'; put your finger on your larynx as you say these consonants out loud and you will feel the vocal cords vibrating)
   - Not vibrating (voiceless consonants: 'p,' 's,' 'ch')

These speech sounds from English are only a small sample of the sounds used by languages around the world. Most languages use fewer consonants and vowels than are used in English. Some sounds are quite common across languages, and others, such as English 'th' and 'r,' are fairly uncommon around the world. When many or most languages include particular speech sounds, often the reason is that the differences between them are particularly easy to perceive. Humans must com-

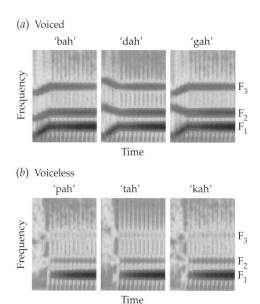

FIGURE 11.10 English stop consonants may be (a) voiced, as in 'bah,' 'dah,' and 'gah'; or (b) voiceless, as in 'pah,' 'tah,' and 'kah.' The main articulatory difference between voiced and voiceless stop consonants is that, for the latter, talkers delay vibration of the vocal folds by about one-twentieth of a second after opening the vocal tract to begin the sound.

FIGURE 11.11 Because the speech signal has so many redundant acoustic characteristics, listeners can understand speech when all energy either below or above 1800 Hz is removed. The green line shows performance when energy above different frequencies (high pass) is available to listeners, and the red line shows performance when energy below different frequencies (low pass) is present. The red curve shows intelligibility when the cutoff is above the given *x* value, and the green curve shows intelligibility when the cutoff is below the given *x* value. Notice that intelligibility is excellent when all energy is removed below about 1500 Hz (green), and when all energy is removed above about 2000 Hz (red). (After Fletcher and Galt, 1950.)

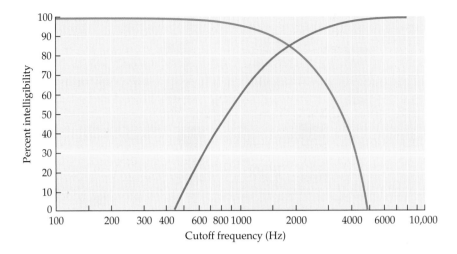

municate in difficult environments where the listener is far away or there are many competing sounds. To be effective, speech sound repertoires of languages have developed over generations of individuals to include only sounds that are relatively easy to tell apart.

In addition to using relatively easily distinguishable sounds, another reason speech communicates well is that all distinctions between vowels and consonants are signaled with multiple differences between sounds. Because more than one acoustic property can be used to tell two sounds apart, distinctions are signaled redundantly, and this redundancy helps listeners. The speech signal is so redundant that if we remove all energy below 1800 Hz, listeners will still perceive speech nearly perfectly, and the same is true if we remove all energy above 1800 Hz (Figure 11.11).

Speech Perception

Speech production is very fast. In casual conversation we produce about 10–15 consonants and vowels per second, and if we're in a hurry we can double this rate. To achieve this acoustic feat, our articulators (tongue, lips, jaw, and so on) must do many different things very quickly. However, articulators can move only so fast, and mass and inertia keep articulators from getting all the way to the position for the next consonant or vowel. Experienced talkers also adjust their production in anticipation of where articulators need to be next. In these ways, production of one speech sound overlaps production of the next. This overlap of articulation in space and time is called **coarticulation**. As we turn from speech production to speech perception, we will find that, although coarticulation does not cause much trouble for listeners understanding speech, it has made it harder for speech perception researchers to explain how we do it.

coarticulation The phenomenon in speech whereby attributes of successive speech units overlap in articulatory or acoustic patterns.

COARTICULATION AND LACK OF INVARIANCE   To get a better sense of what coarticulation is, say the word *moody* a few times, and note the activity of your tongue as you form the 'd' sound. You will find that it starts in the back of your mouth, where it must be to form the 'oo' vowel sound, then it touches the alveolar ridge just behind the teeth to form the 'd,' and finally it ends up toward the front of the mouth to form the 'ee.' Now say the nonsense word *eedoom*. Reversing the vowel sounds means sending the tongue on the opposite journey, from front to alveolar ridge to back. As a result of the very different path taken by the tongue in these two utterances, the acoustic qualities of the 'd' in the two utterances are quite different.

This context sensitivity is a signature property of speech. One might expect context sensitivity to cause a significant problem for speech perceivers, because it means there are no "invariants" that we can count on to uniquely identify different speech sounds. For the earlier examples 'b,' 'd,' and 'g' (see Figure 11.10*a*), notice that the shape of the first formant (F_1) is pretty much the same for all three consonants when they precede the same vowel. F_1 is helpful in telling 'b,' 'd,' and 'g' apart from other speech sounds, but it does not help much in telling these sounds apart from one another. An F_1 like that shown in **Figure 11.12** is necessary for a sound to be 'b,' but it is not sufficient to inform the listener that the sound is 'b,' and not 'd' or 'g.' F_2 is very important for telling 'b' from 'd' from 'g,' but what F_2 tells the listener depends on the quality of F_3 and the nature of the following vowel.

Explaining how listeners understand speech despite all this variation has been one of the most significant challenges for speech researchers. Context sensitivity due to coarticulation also presents one of the greatest difficulties in developing computer recognition of speech. We cannot program or train a computer to recognize a speech sound—consonant or vowel—without also taking into consideration which speech sounds precede and follow that sound. And we cannot identify those preceding and following sounds without also taking into consideration which sounds precede and follow them, and so on. You can see that the problem quickly becomes very difficult, and it may not surprise you that the most advanced computer speech recognition systems cannot recognize speech much better than a 2-year-old child can.

CATEGORICAL PERCEPTION How do the 2-year-olds do it? *Something* in the acoustic signal must lead them to perceive the 'd' in *deem, doom,* and *dam* as the same consonant. Almost 50 years ago, researchers invented machines that could produce speechlike sounds and started testing listeners to try to determine exactly what the acoustic cues were that enabled them to distinguish different speech sounds. They found, for example, that by varying the transitions of F_2 and F_3, they could produce sounds that listeners reliably reported hearing as 'bah,' 'dah,' or 'gah' (Figure 11.13). (See **Web Activity 11.2: Categorical Perception.**)

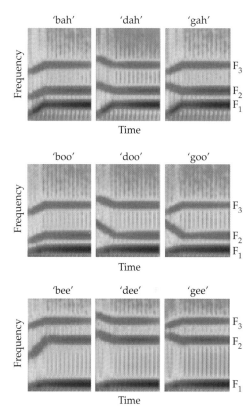

FIGURE 11.12 Spectrograms of 'd' sounds (center column), along with stop-consonant cousins 'b' (left) and 'g' (right). Changes in formants across time (formant transitions) for these sounds differ dramatically depending on the following vowels: 'ah' (top row), 'oo' (middle), and 'ee' (bottom).

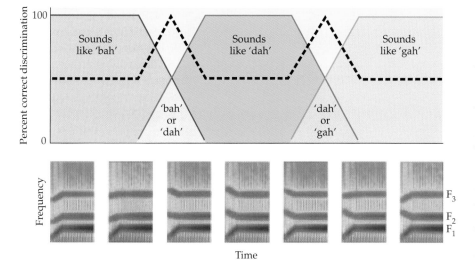

FIGURE 11.13 The sound spectrograms at the bottom of this figure indicate auditory stimuli that change smoothly from a clear 'bah' on the left through 'dah' to a clear 'gah' on the right. Perception, however, does not change smoothly. All the sounds on the left sound like a 'bah' (blue curve) until we reach a sharp 'bah'-'dah' border. Listeners are much better at discriminating a 'bah' from a 'dah' than at discriminating two 'bah's or two 'gah's. The dashed black line indicates discrimination performance. The same is true for 'dah' (red curve) and 'gah' (green curve).

categorical perception For speech as well as other complex sounds and images, the phenomenon by which the discrimination of items is no better than the ability to label items.

These researchers knew that making small, incremental changes to simple acoustic stimuli such as pure tones leads to gradual changes in people's perception of these stimuli. For example, tones would sound just a little higher in pitch with each small step in frequency. Surprisingly, speech sounds were not perceived in this way. When researchers started with a synthesized 'bah' and gradually varied the formant transitions moving toward 'dah' and then 'gah,' listeners' responses did not gradually change from 'bah' to 'bah'-ish 'dah' to 'dah' to 'dah'-ish 'gah' to 'gah.' Instead, listeners identified these sounds as changing abruptly from one consonant to another.

Furthermore, listeners appeared incapable of hearing that anything was different when two sounds were labeled as the same consonant. When researchers played pairs of synthesized speech sounds and asked listeners to tell them apart, they could easily detect small differences between two sounds if one was 'bah' and the other was 'dah.' But if both sounds were 'bah' or both were 'dah,' performance dropped to chance levels (dashed line in Figure 11.13), even though the differences in formant transitions in the first and second pairs of stimuli were equally large.

This pattern of results has come to be called **categorical perception**. As illustrated in Figure 11.13, three qualities define categorical perception. The first two were just described: a sharp labeling (identification) function and discontinuous discrimination performance. The third definitional quality of categorical perception follows from the first two: researchers can predict discrimination performance on the basis of labeling data. In short, listeners report hearing differences between sounds only when those differences would change the label of the sound, so the ability to discriminate sounds can be predicted by how listeners label the sounds.

> **FURTHER DISCUSSION** of a visual phenomemon similar to catergortical perception can be found in Chapter 5 on page 137.

HOW SPECIAL IS SPEECH?   Categorical perception of speech sounds is not limited to the 'bah'/'dah'/'gah' dimension; it has been shown for many different contrasts between sounds in English, as well as other languages. These findings, along with the failure to find invariants that distinguish speech sounds from each other, led many speech researchers to suspect that humans had evolved special mechanisms just for perceiving speech. One very influential version of the "speech is special" idea, called the "motor theory" of speech perception (Liberman and Mattingly, 1985; Liberman et al., 1967), holds that processes used to produce speech sounds can somehow be run in reverse to understand the acoustic speech signal. Attempts have even been made to develop computer speech recognition by calculating back from the speech signal to articulations (**Figure 11.14**).

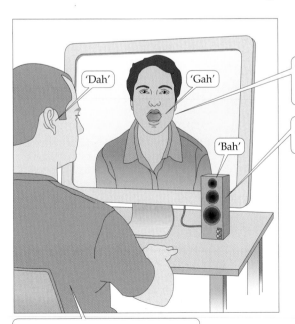

1. A videotape shows a person repeating the sound 'gah.'

2. An audio track plays the sound 'bah.'

'Dah' 'Gah' 'Bah'

3. The subject hears the sound 'dah.'

FIGURE 11.14 The motor theory was bolstered by, among other things, a somewhat peculiar finding by McGurk and MacDonald (1976). Experimental subjects were shown a video of a person saying the syllable 'gah' over and over. The audio track, however, was playing the sound 'bah' repeatedly. Incredibly, subjects consistently reported hearing a third syllable, 'dah,' even if they knew how they were being fooled (because they heard 'bah' when they closed their eyes). (This effect really has to be experienced to be believed; try it now in **Web Activity 11.3: The McGurk Effect**.)

(a)

(b)

FIGURE 11.15 Speech perception by nonhumans. (a) Japanese quail can learn to tell 'd' from 'b' and 'g' preceding different vowels just as humans do. (b) Chinchillas have shown categorical perception of sounds varying from 'dah' to 'tah.' (Part a courtesy of Keith R. Kluender; b courtesy of Annie Huyler, Pioneer Valley Chinchillas.)

Over time, however, a number of problems with the motor theory have cropped up. First, it turns out that speech production is at least as complex as speech perception, if not more so. Every aspect of the acoustic signal relates to a particular aspect of the vocal tract. So if the acoustic signal is complex, this complexity must be the result of complexity in production. Trying to explain speech perception by reference to production is at least as difficult as explaining speech perception on the basis of acoustics alone.

A second reason to doubt that processes for perceiving speech are unique to humans is that numerous demonstrations have shown that nonhuman animals can learn to respond to speech signals in much the same way that human listeners do (Kluender, Lotto, and Holt, 2005; Kluender et al., 1998). For example, Japanese quail (Figure 11.15a) can be taught to tell 'd' from 'b' and 'g' across the same sort of acoustic variation depicted in Figure 11.12 (Kluender, Diehl, and Killeen, 1987). Chinchillas (Figure 11.15b) have also shown classic categorical-perception effects (Kuhl, 1981; Kuhl and Miller, 1978).

Furthermore, we now know that categorical perception, one of the definitional characteristics of speech that was thought to be so unusual as to require a special processing mechanism, is not at all limited to speech sounds. Other types of auditory stimuli, such as musical intervals (Smith et al., 1994), are also perceived categorically, as are visual stimuli such as familiar objects (Newell and Bülthoff, 2002), human faces (Levin and Beale, 2000), and facial expressions (De Gelder, Teunisse, and Benson, 1997). People even perceive differences between familiar animals categorically (R. Campbell et al., 1997) (Figure 11.16), and monkeys perceive images of cats versus dogs categorically (Freedman et al., 2001).

COARTICULATION AND SPECTRAL CONTRAST Contemporary research has turned increasingly to investigating how speech perception is explained by general ways that hearing, and perception more broadly, works. For example,

FIGURE 11.16 People categorically perceive changes between images of familiar animals such as monkeys and cows. The labels that observers use shift abruptly between "monkey" and "cow" when they identify images like those in the series shown here. Observers also are better at discriminating two images when they label one as "monkey" and one as "cow." (After R. Campbell et al., 1997.)

'eebah'   'oobah'

Frequency

Time

'eedah'   'oodah'

Frequency

Time

F_3

F_2
F_1

F_3

F_2
F_1

FIGURE 11.17 Because of coarticulation, consonant sounds such as 'bah' and 'dah' are acoustically very different, depending on the preceding vowel. Here, 'bah' is shown following 'ee' (top left) and 'oo' (top right), and 'dah' is shown following the same vowels (bottom). Note that F_2 in 'eebah' (top left) is acoustically identical to F_2 in 'oodah' (bottom right) (marked with ellipses). Listeners hear the same consonant sound as 'b' following 'ee' and as 'd' following 'oo' because of the contrast between the spectrum of 'ee' and 'oo' and the spectrum of the following consonant.

the perception of coarticulated speech appears to be at least partially explained by some fundamental principles of perception that you've already read about. Let's turn again to our example of stop consonants such as 'b' and 'd.' Two of the acoustic features that contribute to the perception of 'b,' as contrasted with the perception of 'd,' are the onset frequency and trajectory of the second formant (F_2). Because of coarticulation, production of one speech sound always affects production of the next sound; formants for one sound always are more like (assimilate to) the sounds that precede and follow. The onset of F_2 varies depending on whether 'bah' or 'dah' follows vowels such as 'ee' (higher) or 'oo' (lower).

Perception of the syllables 'bah' and 'dah' works in a way that nicely fits the facts of coarticulation. The very same F_2 onset is heard as 'dah' following 'oo' and as 'bah' following 'ee' (**Figure 11.17**). Why does perception work this way? Because coarticulation always causes a speech sound to become more like the previous speech sound, auditory processes that enhance the contrast between successive sounds undo this assimilation. Listeners are more likely to perceive 'bah' (low F_2) when preceded by the vowel sound 'ee' (high F_2), and to perceive 'dah' (high F_2) when preceded by 'oo' (low F_2). Preceding sounds do not even have to be speech sounds. If, instead of playing 'ee' and 'oo' before syllables varying from 'bah' to 'dah,' we present only a single small band of energy at the frequencies where F_2 would be in 'ee' or 'oo,' perception of the following syllable changes just as it does with the full 'ee' or 'oo' vowel sound (Coady, Kluender, and Rhode, 2003). The onset of F_2 for 'bah' and 'dah' is perceived relative to whether the preceding energy is lower or higher in frequency. We perceive syllables such as 'bah' and 'dah' in terms of the relative change in the spectrum—how the onsets contrast with the energy that precedes them.

You've encountered contrast effects several times before in this book—for example, lightness contrast in Chapter 2. Remember that melodies are defined by *changes* between adjacent notes, and not by the exact notes in particular. While learning about vision, you saw many examples of contrast. Contrast plays a large role in the perception of lightness, color, and size, as well as line orientation, position, curvature, depth, and spatial frequency. Here, spectral contrast helps listeners perceive speech, despite the lack of acoustic invariance due to coarticulation.

USING MULTIPLE ACOUSTIC CUES What do speech sounds, musical intervals, and faces all have in common? They are all stimuli that people have a great deal of experience perceiving. We spend a large chunk of our waking lives listening to speech and identifying people by their faces. Another thing that makes distinguishing between individual speech sounds and individual faces similar is that many small differences must be used together in order to discriminate different speech sounds and different faces (e.g., small changes in formant transitions and small changes in nose shape). At the same time, other stimulus differences must be ignored so that multiple instances of the same speech sound or multiple images of the same face can be classified properly (e.g., acoustic variation introduced when different speakers utter the same speech sound, or image variation introduced when a face is viewed from different angles).

To the extent that perception depends heavily on experience, speech is special because (1) humans have evolved unique anatomical machinery for producing it and (2) we spend a great deal of time practicing the perception of speech. The fact that there are no acoustic invariants for distinguishing speech sounds is really no different from many comparable situations in visual perception. For example, we saw in Chapter 6 that one particular cue for depth perception may fail us, but by taking multiple cues into account, we rarely make large mistakes when calculating distance relations. The comparison with face recognition may be even more apt. Bob's nose may be quite similar to Ken's nose, Bob's eyes may be exactly as far apart as Paul's eyes, and Bob's mouth may be shaped just like Tom's mouth. But given enough experience with all four faces (and enough experience with face recognition in general), we can use the pattern of facial features to pick Bob out from a lineup every time—even if he's covering his mouth with his hand. Turning to speech perception, utterances of the syllables 'aba' and 'apa' can be distinguished from each other by at least 16 different characteristics of the acoustic signal (Figure 11.18) (Lisker, 1978). Listeners can make use of their experience with the co-occurrence of these multiple acoustic differences to understand speech.

To sum up, we don't need individual acoustic invariants to distinguish speech sounds; we just need to be as good at pattern recognition for sounds as we are for visual images. And one of the things that the billions of neurons in the brain do best is integrating multiple sources of information to recognize patterns (Kluender and Alexander, 2008). Computer simulations of neural connectivity (neural network models) designed to mimic the use of multiple attributes and associations between attributes are among the most successful artificial pattern recognizers yet invented by humankind. Interestingly, many neural network models (e.g., those developed by J. A. Anderson et al. [1977] or by Damper and Harnad [2000]) also show categorical-perception effects when the models are trained on enough examples.

FIGURE 11.18 The simple distinction between 'aba' (left) and 'apa' (right) includes at least 16 acoustic differences. Some differences that are easy to see include duration of the first vowel, duration of the interval between syllables, and the presence of low-frequency energy in the middle of 'aba.'

Learning to Listen

In our discussion of vision earlier in the book, we saw that experience is incredibly important for visual perception, particularly the higher-level perception of objects and events in the world. Experience is every bit as important for auditory perception, especially for the perception of speech. And unlike vision, experience with speech begins very early in development. In fact, babies gain significant experience with speech even before they're born!

Measurements of heart rate as an indicator of the ability to notice change between speech sounds have revealed that late-term fetuses can discriminate between different vowel sounds (Lecanuet et al., 1986). Prenatal experience with speech sounds appears to have considerable influence on subsequent perception. For one thing, newborns prefer hearing their mother's voice over other women's voices (DeCasper and Fifer, 1980). When 4-day-old infants in Paris were tested, they preferred hearing French instead of Russian (Mehler et al., 1988). Perhaps most amazingly, newborns prefer hearing particular children's stories that were read aloud by their mothers during the third trimester of pregnancy (DeCasper and Spence, 1986).

BECOMING A NATIVE LISTENER   As we have seen, speech sounds can differ in many ways. Acoustic differences that matter critically for one language may be irrelevant or even distracting in another language. For example, the English language makes use of the distinction between the sounds 'r' and 'l,' whereas these two sounds are both very similar to only one sound (called a "flap") in Japanese. As another example, Spanish is one of many languages that uses only the five vowel sounds 'ee' (as in *beet*), 'oo' (as in *boot*), 'ah' (as in *bomb*), 'ay' (as in *bake*), and 'oh' (as in *boat*), whereas English employs numerous other vowel sounds.

FIGURE 11.19 How we hear speech sounds depends on our experience with the speech sounds of our first language. Because of experience with one language, it is often difficult to perceive and produce distinctions in a new language. For example, most Japanese people learning English as a second language have trouble distinguishing between 'l' and 'r,' both when they listen and when they speak.

As anyone who has spoken to a native Japanese speaker in English knows, the 'r'/'l' distinction is very difficult for Japanese people to pick up when they learn English as a second language (Figure 11.19). Because the difference between 'l' and 'r' is irrelevant to native Japanese speakers when they're learning their native language, it is adaptive for them to learn to ignore it, thus allowing them to focus on speech sound distinctions that are important in Japanese. When people have spent most of their lives listening to Japanese and not hearing the difference between 'r' and 'l,' we are not surprised that they have difficulty learning to produce the 'r' and 'l,' because the two sound much the same to a Japanese person. By the same token, a native Spanish speaker who complains that your dog just "beat him" is probably not claiming that Rover threw a punch; rather, the difference between 'ee' and 'ih' is less perceptible to the Spanish speaker because both of these English sounds are similar to the Spanish 'ee.'

Interestingly, studies show that infants begin filtering out irrelevant acoustic differences long before they begin to utter speech sounds (even before their babbling stage). One study found that by 6 months of age, infants from Seattle were more likely to notice acoustic differences that distinguish two English vowels than to notice equivalent differences between Swedish vowels, and infants from Stockholm were more likely to notice the difference between two Swedish vowels than between two English vowels (Kuhl et al., 1992). Tuning of perception for consonants appears to take a bit longer to develop, but by the time infants are 1 year old, they have also begun to ignore, just as their parents do, consonant distinctions not used in their native language (Figure 11.20).

Of course, it is possible, with much training, to learn to perceive and produce speech sound distinctions that you've spent most of your life ignoring. As you might expect, the longer a person uses only her first language, the longer it takes to learn to produce and perceive sounds from a second language (Flege, Bohn, and Jang, 1997; Imai, Flege, and Wayland, 2002). Many studies have been aimed at determining what makes new distinctions hard or easy for second-language learners to pick up. Learning is most difficult when both of the sounds in the second language are similar to a single sound in the first language (e.g., 'r' and 'l' for Japanese speakers learning English). Learning is easier if the two new sounds are both unlike any sound in the native language. For example, native English listeners have no problems distinguishing click sounds from Zulu because Zulu clicks are so unlike any English sounds. Learning also is easier if two new sounds from a new language differ in the same way that two sounds from the first language differ.

Picking up the distinctions in a second language is easiest if the second language is learned at the same time as the first. This is why language immersion programs are becoming popular in preschool and elementary curriculums of multicultural countries such as the United States. The downside to this strategy is that kids learning multiple languages at the same time usually take a little longer to master each of the languages when compared to children learning only a single language (Bialystok and Hakuta, 1994). This is a natural consequence of having to learn not one but two sets of rules about when to ignore and when to pay attention to speech sound differences (as well as learning two vocabularies, two sets of grammatical rules, and so on).

LEARNING WORDS   Thus far in this chapter, we've learned many things about the nature and complexity of speech sounds, and about how listeners perceive consonants and vowels. But the whole point of producing and perceiving these speech sounds is to put them together to form words, which are the units of language that convey meaning. How do novice language learners (infants) make the leap from streams of meaningless speech sounds to the meaningful groups of speech sounds that we call words?

First, let's state the obvious. Just like strings of musical notes, no string of speech sounds is inherently meaningful. The string 'd'-'aw'-'g' becomes meaningful to English-speaking infants, but to French-speaking, Spanish-speaking, and German-speaking infants this string remains completely meaningless because their parents refer to their furry house companion as *chien, perro,* and *Hund,* respectively. Infants in different places in the world must learn the words that are specific to their native language.

We've already seen how a series of consonants and vowels within a single word tend to "run into" one another because of coarticulation. It turns out the situation is not much better for a series of words forming a sentence. This fact is easily seen in **Figure 11.21**: without the letters at the bottom of the figure, you would have no idea where the spoken word "where" ends and "are" begins.

Interestingly, our perception usually seems at odds with this acoustic reality. When we listen to someone talk to us in our native language, individual words seem to stand out quite clearly as separate entities. But listening to someone speak in a different language is often a very different experience. Listen to the Chinese and Arabic speakers in **Web Activity 11.4: Word Breaks.** Unless you have experience with these languages, it probably sounds as if they include lots

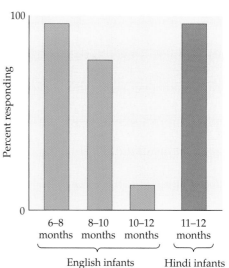

FIGURE 11.20   Hindi has a dental stop consonant produced with the tongue tip touching the teeth and a retroflex stop consonant that requires the tongue to bend up and back in the mouth. Adult speakers of English hear both of these sounds as 't' because they are similar to the English 't.' When Werker and Tees (1984) tested infants from English-speaking families in Vancouver, the youngest (6–8 months old) reliably responded to the difference between these two Hindi sounds. By age 1 year, however, the infants were mimicking their parents' behavior by ignoring the distinction between the two sounds.

Wherearethe s i l en c es be t w een wo rd s ?

FIGURE 11.21   In this sentence—"Where are the silences between words?"—we can see that there are no breaks between the sounds of one spoken word and the sounds of the next. Infants can use their experience with particular sequences of speech sounds to learn about boundaries between words.

of really long words—some as long as whole English sentences. It may also seem as if people in these cultures speak much faster than English speakers do. Native Chinese and Arabic speakers probably say the same things about the English language and English speakers. This is the situation faced by infants the world over.

To study how infants learn words from the continuous streams of speech that they encounter in their environment, Saffran, Aslin, and Newport (1996) invented a novel language. The words of this new language all had three syllables—for example, *tokibu, gopila, gikoba,* and *tipolu*. Next they created randomized sequences of these novel words, with words running together just as they do in fluently produced sentences (**Figure 11.22**). A sample sequence would be "*gopilatipolutokibugikobatokibugopilatipolugikobagopilatipolutokibugikoba.*" Eight-month-old infants listened to a 2-minute sequence such as this while sitting on a parent's lap. After this brief period of learning, infants heard either

(*a*)

tokibugopilagikobatipolutokibu
gopilatipolutokibugikobagopila
gikobatokibugopilatipolugikoba
tipolugikobatipolugopilatipolu
tokibugopilatipolutokibugopila
tipolutokibugopilagikobatipolu
tokibugopilagikobatipolugikoba
tipolugikobatipolutokibugikoba
gopilatipolugikobatokibugopila

(*b*)

tokibugopilagikobatipolutokibu
gopilatipolutokibugikobagopila
gikobatokibugopilatipolugikoba
tipolugikobatipolugopilatipolu
tokibugopilatipolutokibugopila
tipolutokibugopilagikobatipolu
tokibugopilagikobatipolugikoba
tipolugikobatipolutokibugikoba
gopilatipolugikobatokibugopila

FIGURE 11.22 Eight-month-old infants can learn to pick out words from streams of continuous speech based on the extent to which successive syllables are predictable or unpredictable. While sitting on a parent's lap, infants heard 2-minute sequences of syllables (*a*). In the second part of the experiment, infants were familiar with 3-syllable sequences (*tokibu, gopila, gikoba, tipolu*) that they heard before (*b*), but they noticed that they had never heard other syllable combinations (*poluto, bugopi, kobati,* etc.).

"*tokibu*" (one of the novel words) or "*poluto*" (a new combination of the same syllables used to produce the "real" novel words). The infants listened longer to the nonwords than to the words, indicating that after just 2 minutes of exposure, they had already begun to learn the words in this new "language." How did they do it?

Saffran and her colleagues suggest that the infants in their study learned the words by being sensitive to the statistics of the sequences of sounds that they had heard in the first part of the experiment. In the real world of language, words are simply sequences of speech sounds that tend to occur together. Other sequences occur together less often. For example, think about the sequence 'p'-'r'-'ih'-'t'-'ee'-'b'-'ay'-'b'-'ee.' An infant will hear the sounds making up the word *pretty* in many different contexts ("pretty dress," "pretty good," and so on) and the sounds making up the word *baby* in other contexts (e.g., "good baby," "baby doll"). In contrast, the sequence 'tyba' will almost never be heard in any other context, because no English words have this sequence of syllables. Saffran (2001, 2002) suggests that infants learn to pick words out of the speech stream by accumulating experience with sounds that tend to occur together; these are words (at least to babies). For example, infants eventually split the "word" *allgone* into two as they acquire more linguistic experience. When sounds that are rarely heard together occur in combination, that's a sign that there is a break between two words.

Speech in the Brain

Our earliest understanding of the role of cerebral cortex for the perception of speech and music was gained through unfortunate "natural" experiments in which people had lost their ability to understand speech following stroke or other brain injuries. However, it is difficult to draw strong conclusions about brain processes from brain injuries. Brain damage from stroke follows patterns of blood vessels, not brain function. Damage from stroke might cover just part of a particular brain function, leaving some of the function undamaged; or damage could cover a wide region that includes some or all of a particular brain function, as well as all or part of other functions. Performance following brain damage, along with later experimental findings, has taught us that different hemispheres of the brain are better at doing some types of tasks. For most people, the left hemisphere is dominant for language processing. The development of techniques for brain imaging such as positron emission tomography (PET) and functional magnetic resonance imaging (fMRI), described in Chapter 1, has made it possible for us to learn more about how speech is processed in the brain.

As we would expect on the basis of what we learned in Chapter 9, hearing sounds of any kind activates the primary auditory cortex (A1). Further, we learned that the processing of complex sounds relies on additional areas of cortex adjacent to A1. These nearby areas of auditory cortex, called belt and parabelt areas, as shown in Figure 9.20, often are referred to as "secondary" or "association" areas. As one might expect, we see these areas activated when listeners hear speech and music. In addition, at these relatively early levels of cortical processing, activity in response to music, speech, and other complex sounds is relatively balanced across the two hemispheres (Binder, 2000).

Because we know that language is typically lateralized to one hemisphere—usually the left side for right-handed people—processing of speech should become more lateralized at some point because perceiving speech is part of understanding language. One challenge for researchers is to create stimuli that have all the complex properties of speech without being heard as speech. We already learned that listeners are very good at understanding even severely

FIGURE 11.23 Cortical responses to acoustic complexity, versus responses to speech. (*a*) This spectrogram represents an intact intelligible sentence with natural changes in frequency and amplitude. (*b–e*) In these spectrograms, the same sentence is now unintelligible because either frequency changes were removed (*b*) or amplitude changes were removed (*c*). The spectrogram in (*d*) has amplitude changes from (*e*) and frequency changes from (*a*). While (*d*) is equal to (*a*) in acoustic complexity, it is unintelligible because of the mismatch between changes in amplitude and frequency.

(*a*)
"The wife helped her husband."   Frequency changes
Amplitude changes

(*b*)
No frequency changes
Amplitude changes

(*c*)
Frequency changes
No amplitude changes

(*d*)
Hybrid
Frequency changes
Wrong amplitude changes

(*e*)
"The machine was quite noisy."   Different sentence

distorted speech, so this capability makes it pretty difficult to construct stimuli that are complex like speech without being heard as speech.

Rosen et al. (2011) developed a particularly clever way to tease apart cortical responses to acoustic complexity from responses to speech per se. As **Figure 11.23** shows, they began with complete sentences that included natural changes in both amplitude and frequency (Figure 11.23*a*), and they replaced voicing vibration with noise. Although using noise made the sentences sound whispered, they were perfectly intelligible. Next the researchers took away changes in frequency, leaving behind only changes in amplitude (Figure 11.23*b*); and they took away changes in amplitude, leaving only changes in frequency (Figure 11.23*c*). Finally, to match the amount of acoustic complexity, they created hybrid "sentences" by adding the amplitude changes of one sentence (Figure 11.23*e*) to the frequency changes in another (Figure 11.23*a*). These hybrids (Figure 11.23*d*) were just as complex as the sentence in Figure 11.23*a*, but they were completely unintelligible. The researchers played these four types of sentences (Figure 11.23*a–d*) to listeners while their brains were being scanned using PET.

As **Figure 11.24** illustrates, neural activity in response to unintelligible hybrid "sentences" (see Figure 11.23*d*) was found bilaterally, with a little

FIGURE 11.24 Substantial neural activity was observed in both left and right superior temporal lobes (red) when listeners heard unintelligible hybrid sentences such as the one shown in Figure 11.23*d*, for which amplitude and frequency changes came from different sentences. An increase in activity only in the language-dominant left anterior superior temporal lobe (purple) was evident when the sentences were intelligible (see Figure 11.23*a*), with matching amplitude and frequency changes.

more activity in the right temporal lobe. Responses in the left temporal lobe became dominant only when sentences were intelligible because amplitude and frequency changes coincided properly (see Figure 11.23*a*). From these findings, it appears that language-dominant hemisphere responses depend on listeners using speech for linguistic understanding, and not from acoustic complexity alone.

A great deal of research is being conducted to further our understanding of how speech is processed in the brain on its way to becoming part of words and sentences. For now, the evidence suggests that as sounds become more complex, they are processed in more anterior and ventral regions of the superior temporal cortex farther away from A1 (Patterson and Johnsrude, 2008; Uppenkamp et al., 2006). When speech sounds become more clearly a part of language, they are processed more anteriorly (forward) in the left temporal lobe. This much appears true; however, this back-to-front path may not be all there is to speech perception in the brain. Other brain regions are likely involved.

What could we learn if we could actually place electrodes right on top of the brain? Prior to performing brain surgery to remove a tumor or to reduce effects of very severe epilepsy, neurosurgeons often place electrodes directly on the surface of the brain to identify regions of neural activity. **Figure 11.25** illustrates an electrode grid placed over a region of left superior posterior temporal lobe. Chang et al. (2010) played a series of synthesized syllables varying incrementally from 'bah' to 'dah' to 'gah,' much like those in Figure 11.13, to patients who were awaiting surgery. The researchers found that, across populations of thousands of neurons recorded by their surface electrodes, neural responses were much like listening data for the same syllables. Neural responses were very similar for pairs of stimuli that listeners would label both as 'bah' or 'dah' or 'gah,' and responses were quite distinct for pairs of

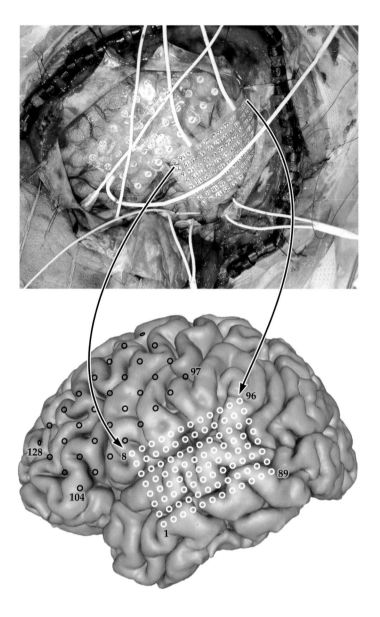

FIGURE 11.25 Prior to performing brain surgery to remove a tumor or to reduce effects of very severe epilepsy, neurosurgeons often place electrodes directly on the surface of the brain to identify regions of neural activity. Before surgery, researchers can take advantage of these electrodes to record responses to experimental materials. (Courtesy of Rick L. Jenison and Richard A. Reale.)

syllables that were acoustically separated by the same extent but were labeled as 'bah' and 'dah' or as 'dah' and 'gah.' This experiment included recordings only from the language-dominant side of each patient's brain, and it did not include other areas of the temporal lobes. It does, however, demonstrate sensitivity to linguistically significant differences between speech sounds in the posterior superior temporal lobe.

As with perception in general, cortical organization depends critically on experience, and the perception of speech sounds is tremendously experience-dependent. Because we know that English and Hindi speakers hear sounds like 'd' differently, we know that the way listeners discriminate 'bah' and 'dah' depends on experience. Chang et al. (2010) may have revealed a place in the left temporal lobe where experience with English 'b' and 'd' shapes neural activity.

Cortical processes related to speech perception could be distinguished from brain processes that contribute to the perception of other complex sounds in two other ways. Listeners have a wealth of experience simultaneously hearing speech and viewing talkers' faces, and the McGurk effect (see Figure 11.14) is evidence of the profound effects that visual cues can have on the way speech sounds are perceived. Reale et al. (2007) also used grids of electrodes on the surface of posterior temporal cortex (see Figure 11.25) in their experiments investigating cortical processing of audio and visual speech. They found that neural responses to auditory speech stimuli in the language-dominant hemisphere were influenced substantially by simultaneous viewing of the lower half of the face of a person either producing audible speech or carrying out a meaningless mouth motion.

Because visual information combines with auditory experience when we're perceiving speech, you may wonder what happens for people who are deaf. Zatorre (2001) studied a group of people with cochlear implants who previously had been deaf. These listeners exhibited increased brain activity in the visual cortex when listening to speech. Zatorre hypothesized that this activation of visual areas of the brain is the result of increased experience and ability with lip-reading for these previously deaf individuals.

Finally, whenever people talk, they both hear the sounds they're producing and experience the movements of speech production in their own vocal tracts. One thing to learn from future studies of brain activity is how these processes of hearing and speaking interact. People have a lot of experience with the simultaneous activities of producing and perceiving their own speech, so one might expect to find brain regions where these related activities combine. (See **Web Essay 11.1: Studying Brain Areas for Language Processing.**)

Summary

1. Musical pitch has two dimensions: tone height and tone chroma. Musical notes are combined to form chords. Notes and chords vary in duration and are combined to form melodies.

2. Melodies are learned psychological entities defined by patterns of rising and falling musical pitches, with different durations and rhythms.

3. Rhythm is important to music, and to auditory perception more broadly. The process of perceiving sound sequences is biased to hear rhythm.

4. Humans evolved to be able to produce an extremely wide variety of sounds that can be used by languages. The production of speech sounds has three basic components: respiration, phonation, and articulation. Speech sounds vary in many dimensions, including intensity, duration, periodicity, and noisiness.

5. In terms of articulation and acoustics, speech sounds vary according to other speech sounds that precede and follow (coarticulation). Because of coarticulation, listeners cannot use any single acoustic feature to identify a vowel or consonant. Instead, listeners must use multiple properties of the speech signal.

6. In general, listeners discriminate speech sounds only as well as they can label them. This is categorical perception, which also has been shown for the perception of many other complex familiar auditory and visual stimuli.

7. How people perceive speech depends very much on their experience with speech sounds within a language. This experience includes learning which of the many acoustic features in speech tend to co-occur. Because of the role of experience in how we hear speech, it is often difficult to perceive and produce new speech sounds from a second language following experience with a first language.

8. One of the ways that infants learn words is to use their experience with the co-occurrence of speech sounds.

9. Speech sounds are processed in both hemispheres of the brain much like other complex sounds, until they become part of the linguistic message. Then, speech is further processed in anterior and ventral regions, mostly in the left superior temporal cortex, but also in superior posterior temporal cortex.

Refer to the
Sensation and Perception
Companion Website
sites.sinauer.com/wolfe3e
for activities, essays, study questions, and other study aids.

CHAPTER 12

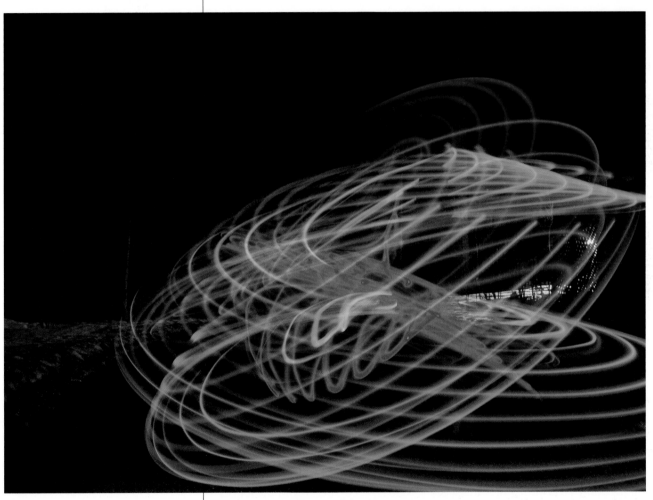

Megan E. LaBonte, *Circle of Light*, 2011

Spatial Orientation and the Vestibular System

Remember when you were a child and you used to spin around until you were dizzy and couldn't walk straight? Perhaps you even lost your balance and fell. Why were you dizzy? The sensations did not arise from one of the five senses that Aristotle recognized—vision, hearing, touch, taste, or smell. Your dizziness arose from contributions of the vestibular system to your sense of spatial orientation.

The **vestibular organs**—sometimes collectively called the vestibular labyrinth or vestibular system—are a set of specialized sense organs located in the inner ear right next to the cochlea. Vestibular organs sense motion of the head, as well as the orientation of gravity, and make a predominant contribution to our sense of tilt and our sense of self-motion. Taken together, the senses of tilt and self-motion constitute our sense of **spatial orientation**.

> FURTHER DISCUSSION of the cochlea can be found in Chapter 9 on page 250.

You may be asking, "Wait a minute, why didn't I learn about the vestibular system and spatial orientation when I first learned about the five senses?" Good question. Perhaps you should have. The vestibular "sixth sense" provides fundamental contributions that are often overlooked. For example, the vestibular system contributes to clear vision when we move and helps us maintain balance when we stand. And it is so crucial that some patients even report cognitive deficits when it fails. Yet despite these essential contributions, the vestibular system toils in anonymity. Much of the time we remain unaware of it until it stops working properly.

The fundamental nature of the vestibular system is emphasized by the fact that the vestibular organs appeared very early in evolutionary history and have remained relatively unchanged. The vertebrate fossil record shows the presence of distinct vestibular organs in fish at least 400 million years ago. The system is not only ancient but largely automatic: vestibular perception is often relegated to the attentional background, and many responses evoked by the vestibular system are reflexive. Though we are all aware of the normal function of our eyes and ears, only when we experience problems such as **dizziness**, **vertigo**, **spatial disorientation**, **imbalance**, blurred vision, and/or illusory self-motion are we likely to become acutely aware of our vestibular sensation.

Obviously, we can no longer ask Aristotle—who is credited with first cataloging our sensory systems—why he did not include spatial orientation or our vestibular sense among the specialized sensory systems, but we can speculate. It certainly is not because vertigo was unknown, since Aristotle himself described the vertiginous effects of alcohol. One explanation may be that it was not until the nineteenth century that scientists understood

vestibular organs The set of five organs—three semicircular canals and two otolith organs—located in each inner ear that sense head motion and head orientation with respect to gravity. These organs are also sometimes called the *vestibular system* or the *vestibular labyrinth*, but the name *vestibular system* is often used more generally to refer to the vestibular organs and their neural pathways.

spatial orientation A sense consisting of three interacting sensory modalities: the senses of linear motion, angular motion, and tilt.

dizziness A commonly used lay term that nonspecifically indicates any form of perceived spatial disorientation, with or without instability.

vertigo A sensation of rotation or spinning. The term is sometimes used erroneously to mean any form of dizziness.

spatial disorientation Any impairment of spatial orientation. More specifically, any impairment of our sense of linear motion, angular motion, or tilt.

imbalance Lack of balance; unsteadiness; nearly falling over.

(a)

Subject's view

(b)

Subject's view

(c)

Subject's view

TEXT

FIGURE 12.1 Demonstration of the vestibulo-ocular reflex. (a) As your fingertip moves faster and faster in front of your face, the fingertip begins to blur. (b) When you shake your head back and forth as if to say "no," the fingertip remains clearer. (c) Text also remains clearer during head shaking.

that the vestibular system is a specialized set of sense organs. Until then, the vestibular system had been considered an entrance to the cochlea. In fact, the name *vestibular* records this error for posterity because *vestibule* means "entrance." But this explanation is not entirely satisfactory, since Aristotle had cataloged other senses without detailed anatomical or physiological knowledge. (See Wade [2000] for a historical review of vestibular research prior to the nineteenth century.)

Another explanation may be the inconspicuous nature of our vestibular sense. In fact, as we'll see, many responses evoked by the vestibular system are reflexive. For example, the vestibular system helps us see clearly by reflexively rotating the eyeballs in the sockets to compensate for head rotation—thereby helping to keep visual images stable on the retina. To demonstrate this to yourself, move your hand a few inches back and forth in front of your face (**Figure 12.1a**). Start slowly and then speed up the movement. Focus on a fingertip and notice that it starts to appear more and more blurry as your hand moves at a higher frequency. This exercise demonstrates the limits of smooth pursuit, a form of visual tracking that you learned about in Chapter 8. Now hold your hand in front of your face and shake your head from side to side as if to say "no" (Figure 12.1b). Again, start slowly and gradually increase the speed. At higher frequencies of motion, you should notice that each fingertip stays in focus more readily when you move your head than when you move your hand. You can compensate for head movement more readily than hand movement because of a vestibulo-ocular reflex that we will discuss in more detail later in this chapter.

Before we move on, there's one more lesson to draw from this example. Rotate your head back and forth while you read this text (Figure 12.1c). Until now, because you were asked to attend to vision, you probably were focused on visual perception and didn't explicitly perceive your head rotation. In fact, your head often moves around, but you do not typically perceive your head motion, because the vestibular system usually performs its job automatically—with little, if any, conscious awareness. But now that we've called your attention to it, as you continue to shake your head you can perceive your head rotating, can't you? Thus, it is not that you are unable to perceive vestibular stimulation, but rather that, under normal circumstances, vestibular stimulation is relegated to the attentional background (discussed in Chapter 7).

Modalities and Qualities of Spatial Orientation

Our sense of spatial orientation is based on three *sensory modalities*: the senses of **angular motion**, **linear motion**, and **tilt**. Why do we call these "modalities," as though they were different senses? Vision and hearing are different modalities, but we would say that color and brightness are different qualities, not different modalities. The key lies in the energy **transduced**. Color and brightness are different interpretations of the same light—hence, *qualities*. Seeing and hearing involve different types of stimulation energy—light and pressure waves, respectively. Perceiving angular motion, linear motion, and tilt requires that three different types of stimulation energy—angular acceleration, linear acceleration, and gravity, respectively—be sensed.

Sensing Angular Motion, Linear Motion, and Tilt

These three stimulation energies are sensed by two types of vestibular sense organs: the semicircular canals and the otolith organs. The **semicircular canals** sense **angular acceleration**, which is a change in angular velocity; this signal makes a predominant contribution to our sense of angular motion. To experience your sense of angular motion, simply close your eyes and rotate your head from side to side as if to say "no." Because of contributions from your vestibular system, you should experience a perception of angular velocity that roughly matches the true angular velocity of your head.

The **otolith organs** transduce both **linear acceleration**, which is a change of linear velocity, and **gravity**. The otolith organs provide a predominant contribution to your sense of head tilt and a predominant contribution to your sense of linear motion, which is also referred to as your sense of translation. To experience your sense of tilt, simply close your eyes and nod your head as if to say "yes." Pitch your head forward and hold it there for several seconds; then pitch your head backward and hold it there. You should experience a perception of head tilt. Relatively pure linear motion is more difficult to achieve passively, but the experience of riding in a car, train, or bus provides an example. Try the following when you are a passenger in a car. With your eyes closed, pay attention to your sense of motion as the driver backs the car out of the garage, brings the car to a stop, and then begins to accelerate forward. Initially, you should perceive backward translation (backward linear motion). You should also perceive the cessation of translation as the car comes to a stop, and then forward translation as the car accelerates.

Two different types of sense organs—the semicircular canals and the otolith organs—establish at least two sensory modalities. But if we have only two types of sense organs, why do we say there are three modalities? As noted already, the otolith organs transduce both gravity and linear acceleration. Perception of tilt results from the brain's estimate of orientation with respect to gravity, and perception of linear motion results from the brain's estimate of linear acceleration. Personal experience suggests that tilt perception is fundamentally different from translation perception; these do not seem to be different sensory qualities like color and brightness.

Why is this so? This key question leads to the fundamental rationale for two modalities that arise from otolith signals, which is that classical physics teaches that the stimulation energies for gravity and linear acceleration are different; gravity and linear acceleration are distinct. Linear acceleration is not the same as gravity, and gravity is not a linear acceleration. Though Einstein hypothesized that gravity and linear acceleration have equivalent effects, he did not assert that they were the same. In fact, the brain does its best to separate the signals from the otolith organs into signals representative of

angular motion Rotational motion like the rotation of a spinning top or swinging saloon doors that rotate back and forth.

linear motion Translational motion like the predominant movement of a train car or bobblehead doll.

tilt Attaining a sloping position like that of the leaning tower of Pisa.

transduce To convert from one form of energy to another (e.g., from light to neural electrical energy, or from mechanical movement to neural electrical energy).

semicircular canal Any of three toroidal tubes in the vestibular system that sense angular motion.

angular acceleration The rate of change of angular velocity. Mathematically, the integral of angular acceleration is angular velocity, and the integral of angular velocity is angular displacement. Angular acceleration, angular velocity, and angular displacement all mathematically represent angular motion.

otolith organ Either of two mechanical structures (utricle and saccule) in the vestibular system that sense both linear acceleration and gravity.

linear acceleration The rate of change of linear velocity. Mathematically, the integral of linear acceleration is linear velocity, and the integral of linear velocity is linear displacement, which is also referred to as "translation." Linear acceleration, linear velocity, and linear displacement all mathematically represent linear motion.

gravity A force that attracts a body toward the center of the Earth.

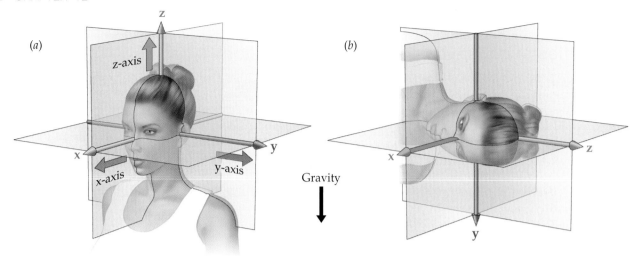

FIGURE 12.2 Movement of the head can be described in terms of a simple fixed coordinate system. The x-axis always points forward relative to the current orientation of the head, the y-axis always points out the left ear, and the z-axis always points out the top of the head. As part (*b*) illustrates, this coordinate system always moves with the head.

sense of angular motion The spatial orientation modality that senses rotation.

sense of linear motion The spatial orientation modality that senses translation.

sense of tilt The spatial orientation modality that senses head inclination with respect to gravity.

amplitude The size (increase or decrease) of a head movement (e.g., angular velocity, linear acceleration, tilt).

direction The line along which one faces or moves, with reference to the point or region toward which one is facing or moving.

gravity and linear acceleration. (See **Web Essay 12.1: Gravity versus Linear Acceleration** for more on the equivalence of these two forces.) Therefore, we assert three interacting sensory modalities—a **sense of angular motion**, a **sense of linear motion**, and a **sense of tilt**—paralleling the three different stimulation energies—angular acceleration, linear acceleration, and gravity (Guedry, 1974; Young, 1984).

Basic Qualities of Spatial Orientation: Amplitude and Direction

Each of our three spatial orientation modalities includes two qualities: **amplitude** and **direction**. As an example of amplitude, the speed of our perceived motion can be large (as in a jet just before takeoff) or small (as for a baby crawling). As an example of direction, perceived linear motion might be forward, up, and to the left.

AMPLITUDE For linear motion we can perceive translation having high velocity (think of a car speeding along a freeway) or low velocity (think of the same car inching forward in a traffic jam). Similarly, we can perceive rotation

FIGURE 12.3 Rotating bodies can move in three directions. The head can turn with a pure roll velocity around the x-axis (*a*), a pure pitch velocity around the y-axis (*b*), or a pure yaw velocity around the z-axis (*c*).

(*a*) **Roll:** Rotation around x-axis

(*b*) **Pitch:** Rotation around y-axis

(*c*) **Yaw:** Rotation around z-axis

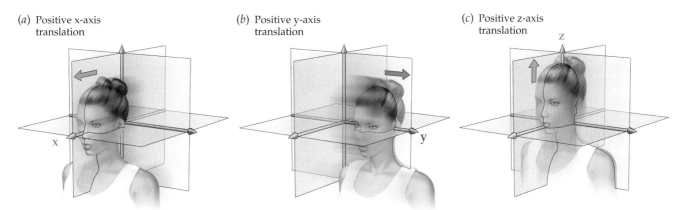

(a) Positive x-axis translation

(b) Positive y-axis translation

(c) Positive z-axis translation

FIGURE 12.4 Translating bodies can move in three directions. The head can translate forward and backward along the x-axis (a), left and right along the y-axis (b), or up and down along the z-axis (c).

velocity with high amplitude (think of vigorously shaking your head) or low amplitude (think of the glacial movement of minute or hour hands on a clock). Finally, tilt amplitude is also important. Tilt amplitudes can be small (as when you nod your head) or large (as when you lie down or hang upside down).

DIRECTION To help clearly classify direction, we first define a simple coordinate system that moves with the head (**Figure 12.2**). The x-axis always points forward, the y-axis always points out the left ear, and the z-axis always points out the top of the head.

Three directions define our sense of angular motion. That is, the head can rotate in three ways: (1) with a roll angular velocity (**Figure 12.3a**); (2) with a pitch angular velocity, as when you nod "yes" (Figure 12.3b); or (3) with a yaw angular velocity, as when you shake your head "no" (Figure 12.3c).

There are also three directions for our sense of linear motion. Imagine (1) stepping forward or backward along the x-axis (**Figure 12.4a**), (2) sliding from right to left along the y-axis (Figure 12.4b), and (3) translating up or down along the z-axis (Figure 12.4c).

Finally, each orientation has two tilt directions. For example, when you are upright, you might experience a pitch tilt forward or backward (**Figure 12.5a**). Or you might experience a roll tilt to the left or right (Figure 12.5b). What happened to the third dimension? The third rotation direction would be a yaw rotation, but this would not yield a change in the tilt of the head with respect to gravity (see Figure 12.3c). When head rotations align with gravity,

FIGURE 12.5 Tilting bodies can move in two directions. When you are initially upright with respect to gravity, there are two directions of tilt. You can pitch-tilt forward or backward (a), or you can roll-tilt to the left or right (b).

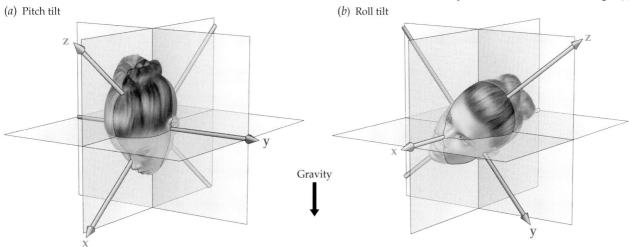

(a) Pitch tilt

(b) Roll tilt

Gravity

velocity The speed and direction in which something moves. Mathematically, velocity is the integral of *acceleration*. In words, linear velocity is the ratio of the distance moved divided by the time it takes to traverse that distance; angular velocity is the ratio of the angle rotated divided by the time it takes to traverse that angle.

acceleration A change in velocity. Mathematically, acceleration is the derivative of velocity. In words, linear acceleration indicates a change in linear velocity; angular acceleration indicates a change in angular velocity.

hair cell Any cell that has stereocilia for transducing mechanical movement in the inner ear into neural activity sent to the brain; some hair cells also receive inputs from the brain.

mechanoreceptor A sensory receptor that responds to mechanical stimulation (pressure, vibration, or movement).

FIGURE 12.6 (*a*) The vestibular labyrinth is a membranous, fluid-filled sac that occupies a cavity in the temporal bone, near the cochlea, and is the nonhearing part of the inner ear. (*b*) It consists of three semicircular canals (anterior, posterior, and horizontal) and two otolith organs (utricle and saccule) on each side of the head.

there is no change in head tilt. So there are three directions for angular velocity and translation, but only two directions for tilt.

The Mammalian Vestibular System

In this section we look at where and how motion signals are transduced by the vestibular organs. The vestibular organs are about the size of a large pea or a small marble and can be found in the inner ear right next to the cochlea (**Figure 12.6a**). They respond primarily to head motion—both linear and angular—and head tilt with respect to gravity. Each inner ear has one vestibular labyrinth, and each vestibular labyrinth includes five sense organs (Figure 12.6b): three semicircular canals that sense rotational motion, and two otolith organs that sense gravity and linear acceleration. (See **Web Activity 12.1: A Guided Tour of the Vestibular System**.)

Note that neither the otolith organs nor the semicircular canals respond to constant **velocity**. Rather, they respond to *changes* in velocity—called **acceleration**. The sensitivity of the vestibular system to acceleration—angular acceleration for the semicircular canals and linear acceleration for the otolith organs—demonstrates that the vestibular system is principally sensitive to *changes* in motion. Constant motion, whether angular or linear, does not result in vestibular signals that directly indicate motion.

As you will see again later, the otolith organs transduce both linear acceleration and gravity into a single neural signal sent to the brain. In fact, as Einstein asserted, no device can tell the difference between gravity and linear acceleration. Separating the otolith measurement of gravity and linear acceleration into estimates of gravity and linear acceleration is not easy and must be important, since the brain expends energy and effort to do so (Angelaki et al., 1999; Merfeld, Zupan, and Peterka, 1999). (See **Web Essay 12.2: Canal-Otolith Integration** for more on how the brain distinguishes gravity from linear acceleration.)

Hair Cells: Mechanical Transducers

Hair cells, which you read about in Chapter 9 when you began to learn about hearing (see Figure 9.9), act as **mechanoreceptors** in each of the five vestibular organs. Head motion causes hair cell stereocilia to deflect. Stereocilia deflection causes a change in the hair cell voltage, which alters neurotransmitter release, which, in turn, evokes action potentials in those vestibular nerve fibers that have one or more synapses on the hair cell. These afferent neurons carry these action potentials to the brain.

(*a*)

(*b*)

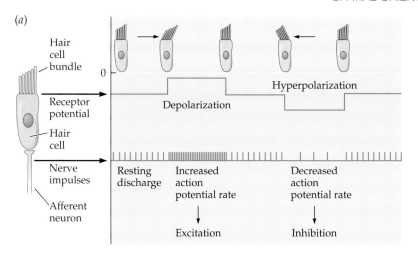

(a)

Hair cell bundle
Receptor potential
Hair cell
Nerve impulses
Afferent neuron

Hyperpolarization
Depolarization

Resting discharge | Increased action potential rate | Decreased action potential rate

Excitation | Inhibition

FIGURE 12.7 Hair cell responses. (*a*) When not stimulated, the hair cells have a negative voltage and release neurotransmitter at a constant rate, evoking a constant rate of action potentials in the afferent nerves. When they bend toward the kinocilium and tallest stereocilia, the hair cells become depolarized and more neurotransmitter is released (excitation); when they bend away, they become hyperpolarized and less transmitter is released (inhibition). (*b*) This cross-sectional view of a hair cell array shows the direction of deflection that causes depolarization. (*c*) Top view of a hair cell array. The black arrows indicate the excitatory direction of hair cell deflection.

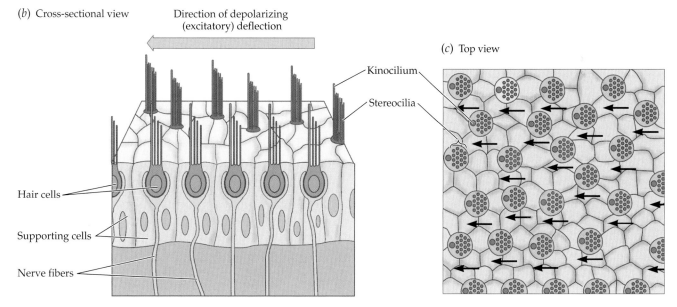

(b) Cross-sectional view

Direction of depolarizing (excitatory) deflection

Kinocilium
Stereocilia

Hair cells
Supporting cells
Nerve fibers

(c) Top view

Let's consider vestibular hair cell responses in a bit more detail. In the absence of stimulation, the hair cells have a negative voltage and release neurotransmitter at a constant rate, evoking a constant rate of action potentials in the afferent neurons (**Figure 12.7***a*). Changes in hair cell voltage—called the **receptor potential**—are proportional to the bending of the hair cell bundles and control the rate at which hair cells release neurotransmitter to the afferent neurons. When a hair cell bends toward the tallest stereocilia (Figures 12.7*b* and *c*), the hair cell voltage becomes less negative. This voltage change is also called a depolarization because the hair cell becomes less polarized than the negative resting potential (see Figure 12.7*a*). The hair cell depolarization increases the release of neurotransmitter, causing an increase in the action potential rate (called excitation). On the other hand, if the hair cell is bent away from the tallest stereocilia, the cell potential becomes more negative (hyperpolarizes), causing a decrease in the release of neurotransmitter and a decrease in the action potential rate (called inhibition). In summary, the rate of action potentials transmitted by afferent neurons increases or decreases following the hair cell receptor potential.

FURTHER DISCUSSION of the receptor potential of hair cells can be found in Chapter 9 on pages 253–254.

receptor potential A change in voltage across the membrane of a sensory receptor cell (in the vestibular system, a hair cell) in response to stimulation.

Thinking back to the fact that amplitude is one quality of our vestibular sense, we can begin to see how amplitude is encoded, since the rate of action potentials is proportional to the receptor potential, which in turn is proportional to the amount of hair cell deflection, which in turn is proportional to the amplitude of the motion.

The fact that the hair cells respond oppositely for deflections in opposite directions (see Figure 12.7*a*) is also crucial for the coding of vestibular stimuli. For example, as we'll discuss in detail in the following section, a yaw rotation to the left will increase the hair cell receptor potential for a hair cell located in the horizontal canal of the left ear, and a yaw rotation to the right will decrease the receptor potential for that same hair cell. A similar general principle applies for the otolith organs: acceleration in one direction increases the receptor potentials of some hair cells, while acceleration in the opposite direction decreases those receptor potentials.

Semicircular Canals

Each inner ear has three semicircular canals—horizontal (or lateral), anterior (or superior), and posterior (**Figure 12.8**) (the anterior and posterior canals are sometimes called the vertical canals). These canals are roughly orthogonal to one another. The name *semicircular canal* roughly reflects the gross anatomy of this structure, which has the circular shape of an incomplete toroid or dough-

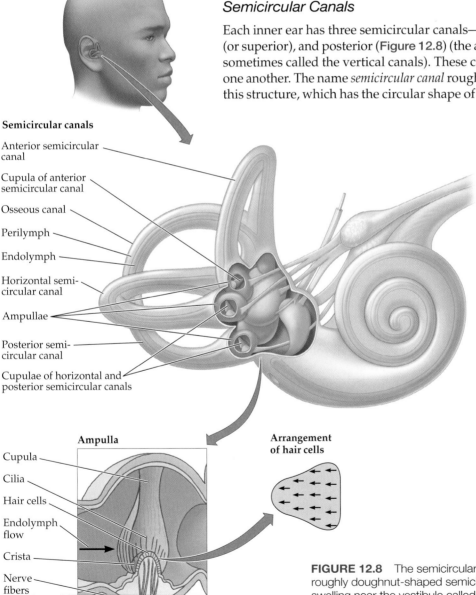

Semicircular canals

Anterior semicircular canal
Cupula of anterior semicircular canal
Osseous canal
Perilymph
Endolymph
Horizontal semicircular canal
Ampullae
Posterior semicircular canal
Cupulae of horizontal and posterior semicircular canals

Ampulla

Cupula
Cilia
Hair cells
Endolymph flow
Crista
Nerve fibers
Angular movement

Arrangement of hair cells

FIGURE 12.8 The semicircular canals. The inner ear has three roughly doughnut-shaped semicircular canals. Each canal has a swelling near the vestibule called an ampulla, where angular motion is transduced by hair cells in the crista. Within each crista, all of the hair cells are aligned.

nut. Specifically, about three-fourths of a toroid is formed by a bony tube approximately 15 millimeters (mm) long, with a cross section about 1.5 mm in diameter. This space—called the osseous ("bony") canal because it is a canal carved out of the mastoid bone—is colored tan in the figure and is filled with a fluid called perilymph. The remaining length of the toroid passes through the vestibule, which is opened up in the figure to allow a glimpse inside. A second, smaller toroid, appearing bluish in the figure, is found inside the larger toroid. This smaller toroid is formed by a membrane filled with a fluid called endolymph, and in cross section it has a diameter of about 0.3 mm, which is just a little thicker than a very thick human hair.

The cross section for each canal swells substantially near where the canals join the vestibule. Each swelling is called an **ampulla** (plural *ampullae*) (see Figure 12.8). Within the endolymph space of each ampulla, the angular-motion detectors are assembled into a sensory epithelium called the **crista** (plural *cristae*). Each crista consists of a small ridge, which has an epithelium made of about 7000 hair cells and is innervated by about 4000 nerve fibers. The stereocilia and kinocilia (collectively called **cilia**; singular *cilium*) of the hair cells project into a jellylike cupula (plural *cupulae*) that forms an elastic dam extending to the opposite wall of the ampulla, with endolymph on both sides of the dam.

When the head rotates, the inertia of the endolymph causes it to lag behind the motion of the head (Breuer, 1874; Brown, 1874; Mach, 1875/2001), leading to deflection of the cupula and thereby to tiny deflections of the stereocilia in the crista. As mentioned earlier, such deflections evoke voltage changes in the hair cells, which in turn cause changes in the firing rate of afferent neurons (see Figure 12.7a). For each individual semicircular canal, all of the hair cells are aligned (see Figure 12.8). Thus, rotations in one direction yield increases in the receptor potential of all hair cells in that semicircular canal, as well as concomitant increases in the action potential rate for all neurons that innervate that semicircular canal. Rotations in the opposite direction yield decreases in the hair cell receptor potentials and concomitant decreases in the rate of action potentials.

The three semicircular canals are maximally sensitive to rotations in different planes, thus yielding direction coding for head rotation. Specifically, each canal is maximally sensitive to rotations around the axis perpendicular to it, and insensitive to rotations about axes that fall in the plane of that canal (**Figure 12.9**). Think of each canal as a wheel that can spin about the axle. The canal is maximally sensitive to rotations aligned with the wheel axle and insensitive to rotations perpendicular to the wheel axle.

ampulla An expansion of each semicircular canal duct that includes that canal's cupula, crista, and hair cells, where transduction occurs.

crista Any of the specialized detectors of angular motion located in each semicircular canal in a swelling called the ampulla.

cilium Any of the hairlike structures that move as part of vestibular transduction. The vestibular system includes two types of cilia: kinocilia and stereocilia.

Maximum sensitivity of horizontal canal

Insensitive rotation axis of horizontal canal

Vestibular nerve

Cochlear nerve

Insensitive rotation axis of horizontal canal

Cochlea

FIGURE 12.9 Each semicircular canal is maximally sensitive to rotations perpendicular to the canal plane. Thinking of each semicircular canal as a wheel, we can see that the canals are maximally sensitive to rotations that align with the rotation axis (shown in green) and are insensitive to rotations that fall in the plane of the semicircular canal (e.g., purple and blue).

FIGURE 12.10 The semicircular canals function in pairs that have a push-pull relationship. (a) Bilateral stimulation of the horizontal semicircular canals as the head turns to the right (a yaw head rotation as shown in Figure 12.3c). This yaw rotation produces relative movement of the endolymph in the horizontal semicircular canals on both sides of the head. The movement of the fluid bends the hair cell bundles toward the tallest stereocilia on the right side, which depolarizes these hair cells and increases the rate of action potentials for neurons from the right side. The hair cell bundles move away from the tallest stereocilia on the left, hyperpolarizing the hair cells and decreasing the rate of action potentials for left-side neurons. This response—an increase on one side coupled with a decrease on the other side—is often called a "push-pull response." The two horizontal canals form one push-pull pair. (b) The axis of maximum sensitivity for the right horizontal canal. (c) The right anterior canal and the left posterior canal form another pair. Note that the maximum-sensitivity axes for the right anterior and left posterior canals are parallel. This means that they maximally respond to rotations around the same axis. The push-pull nature of this canal pair is a consequence of the opposite directions of their maximum-sensitivity rotations, as shown by the green arrows.

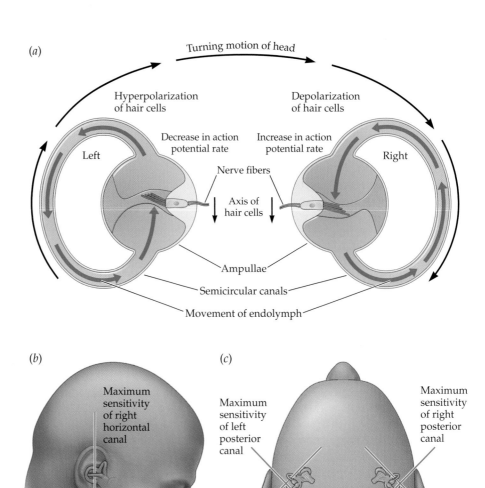

HOW AMPLITUDE IS CODED IN THE SEMICIRCULAR CANALS In the absence of any rotation, many afferent neurons from the semicircular canals respond with a nearly constant rate of action potentials (see Figure 12.7a); canal afferent firing rates at rest average about 100 action potentials ("spikes") per second (Goldberg and Fernandez, 1971), a rate that is high relative to spontaneous rates for nerve fibers for other sensory systems. For comparison, recall from Chapter 2 that retinal ganglion cells fire spontaneously at a rate of about one spike per second in the dark. The relatively high spontaneous firing rate of vestibular afferent neurons allows these neurons to decrease the firing rate for rotations in one direction and increase the firing rate for rotations in the opposite direction.

We already considered the fact that the hair cells and neurons for any individual canal increase their firing rate for rotations in one direction and decrease for rotations in the other direction (Goldberg and Fernandez, 1971). In fact, the semicircular canals are organized as functional pairs in what is called a push-pull arrangement. The two horizontal canals—one on the right side of the head and one on the left—lie roughly in the same plane and form one of the three functional canal pairs (**Figure 12.10**a and b) (Curthoys, Blanks, and Markham, 1977; V. J. Wilson and Melvill Jones, 1979). The horizontal-canal afferent neurons on the right all increase their firing rate for yaw head turns to the right (shaking "no"), and those on the left decrease their firing rate. For head turns to the left, the pattern is reversed, with left-canal afferent neurons increasing their firing rate and right-canal neurons decreasing their firing rate. The anterior and posterior canals are minimally sensitive to these yaw rotations.

In contrast to the horizontal-canal arrangement, the mirror symmetry of the semicircular canals in the left and right ears yields functional pairs that involve different vertical canals (Figure 12.10c); the maximum-sensitivity axis of the anterior semicircular canal on one side roughly parallels the maximum-sensitivity axis of the posterior semicircular canal on the opposite side. So the right anterior and left posterior canals form one canal pair, as do the left anterior and right posterior canals. These canal pairs work in a push-pull manner like that previously described for the horizontal canals.

The change in the firing rate is larger for large changes in the angular velocity of the head than for small changes (Goldberg and Fernandez, 1971). Since the change in the firing rate is proportional to angular velocity, we can think of the canals as somewhat similar to the speedometer in a car, with the change in neural activity proportional to the angular velocity of the head. As a specific example, if the afferent neurons from a horizontal canal suddenly change their firing rate, we know that the rotation includes a change in the velocity component aligned with the sensitive axis of that horizontal canal. The same is true for the other canals.

HOW DIRECTION IS CODED IN THE SEMICIRCULAR CANALS As previously discussed, the three semicircular canals are maximally sensitive to rotations in different planes; the result is direction coding of head rotations. Specifically, the head can rotate about any arbitrary rotation axis made up of roll, pitch, and yaw rotation velocity components. Each canal transduces the component of head velocity perpendicular to its plane. The brain then combines these signals to sense the rotation direction of the head movement.

SEMICIRCULAR-CANAL DYNAMICS If you suddenly begin to rotate at a constant velocity, the semicircular canals sensitive to that rotation will respond by causing a sudden change in afferent neural activity. But as the rotation continues at a constant velocity, the afferent neural activity will decay back to near zero after about 15 seconds. If you then suddenly decelerate to a stop, the canals will show a large response in the opposite direction (**Figure 12.11**). The afferent neural activity then decays with a time course similar to that during the constant-velocity rotation (Goldberg and Fernandez, 1971).

(*a*) Stimulus

(*b*) Neuron activity

FIGURE 12.11 Response of a semicircular-canal neuron to constant-velocity rotation. (*a*) The stimulus is a rotation that first accelerates to a constant angular velocity, then maintains that velocity, and then decelerates the head to a stop. (*b*) During the initial acceleration, the cupula deflects, causing the neuron activity to increase. During the constant angular velocity, the cupula returns to its nondeflected position, so the neuron activity returns to the baseline rate after about 15 seconds of constant-velocity rotation. During deceleration, the cupula is deflected in the opposite direction, causing a transient decrease in the firing rate. (After Goldberg and Fernandez, 1971.)

oscillatory Referring to back-and-forth movement that has a constant rhythm.

sinusoidal Referring to any oscillation, such as a sound wave or rotational motion, whose waveform is that of a sine curve. The period of a sinusoidal oscillation is the time that it takes for one full back-and-forth cycle of the motion to occur. The frequency of a sinusoidal oscillation is defined as the numeral 1 divided by the period.

Fourier analysis A mathematical procedure by which any signal—in this case motion trajectories as a function of time—can be separated into component sine waves at different frequencies. Combining these sine waves will reproduce the original motion trajectory.

utricle One of the two otolith organs. A saclike structure that contains the utricular macula. Also called *utriculus*.

saccule One of the two otolith organs. A saclike structure that contains the saccular macula. Also called *sacculus*.

macula Any of the specialized detectors of linear acceleration and gravity found in each otolith organ.

What happens for more natural head rotations—like the **oscillatory** back-and-forth movement when you shake your head "no"? (If you don't have a solid understanding of frequency analysis, now may be a good time to review the relevant discussion in Chapter 1. See also **Web Activity 12.2: Sinusoidal Motion.**) Figure 12.12*a* shows a **sinusoidal** motion trajectory at a frequency of 0.05 hertz (Hz)—a repeating back-and-forth motion that takes 20 seconds to complete. Figure 12.12*b* shows the oscillatory neural response evoked by this sinusoidal motion. More specifically, the firing rate of the afferent neuron increases and decreases as the angular velocity increases or decreases. This change in firing rate has the same frequency as the sinusoidal stimulus. We can calculate an estimate of afferent neuron sensitivity by taking the peak-to-peak amplitude of the change in the firing rate, in this example about 160 spikes/second, and dividing it by the peak-to-peak amplitude of the motion (160 degrees/second). The result is a sensitivity of about 1 spike/second per degree/second of motion. Experimentally, this process is often repeated at several different frequencies, yielding a number representing the neural sensitivity at each frequency tested.

Semicircular canals are not equally sensitive to all frequencies of rotation. Figure 12.12*c* shows a plot of response sensitivity as frequency is varied for a typical neuron innervating a semicircular canal; this plot indicates how the oscillatory-canal afferent firing rate changes with head rotation frequency. The data show that the amplitude of the canal afferent neuron's response is nearly constant for rotation frequencies above about 0.1 Hz. But when the frequency is less than about 0.1 Hz, the neuron responds less and less. For example, the response sensitivity at a frequency of 0.02 Hz (one cycle in 50 seconds) is only about 0.5 spike/second per degree/second—more than a 50% reduction from that observed at 1 Hz (one cycle in one second).

In summary, the canals are not very good transducers of low-frequency rotations—an effect that amusement park rides use to great advantage. (See **Web Essay 12.3: Amusement Park Rides—Vestibular Physics Is Fun.**)

WHY SINE WAVE MOTIONS? Now that we have described canal afferent responses to sinusoidal motion in some detail, you may wonder why anyone would care. We rarely experience perfect sinusoidal motion in the real world; we experience complex motions that vary with time. What do responses to sinusoidal motion at different frequencies tell us about how we sense motion?

One answer is that, although "pure" sine wave motions may be rare in the real world, patterns of oscillatory motions that have a predominant frequency are quite common: think again of shaking your head to say "no" or nodding your head to say "yes." More generally, **Fourier analysis** tells us that any complex motion can be broken down into some number of single-frequency components. Therefore, if we know responses to single frequencies, we know a good deal about responses to more complex motion. If this sounds familiar, that's because the same argument was made in Chapter 3 (see "Why Sine Wave Gratings?" on page 61), as well as in Chapter 9, when we talked about hearing.

Otolith Organs

As we mentioned earlier, the sensing of gravity and linear acceleration relies on two structures in each ear called the otolith organs: the **utricle** (or utriculus) and the **saccule** (or sacculus). Each of these organs consists of a small, oval-shaped, fluid-filled sac that is about 3 mm long in the longest direction and includes an area called the **macula** (plural *maculae*), which is where actual

(a)

(b)

(c)

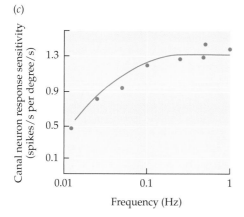

FIGURE 12.12   Sinusoidal motion trajectories. Stimulus (a) and response (b) for a single semicircular-canal afferent neuron at 0.05 Hz. Note that the neural firing rate increases and decreases nearly in tandem with the oscillating stimulus. The maximum is about 170 spikes/second; the minimum, about 10 spikes/second. So the peak-to-peak amplitude is about 160 spikes/second. The sensitivity of the neuron, defined as the average amplitude of the neural response (about 160 spikes/second) divided by the peak-to-peak amplitude of the stimulus (160 degrees/second), is about 1 spike/second per degree/second. (c) When this process is repeated at different stimulus frequencies, it can be seen that the sensitivity of the neuron changes with frequency. For this semicircular-canal neuron the response sensitivity averaged about 1.3 spikes/second per degree/second for frequencies above 0.1 Hz. The response sensitivity decreases substantially for frequencies below about 0.1 Hz. (Data from Fernandez and Goldberg, 1971.)

FIGURE 12.13 The otolith organs. (*a*) Orientation of the utricular and saccular maculae in the head. The saccules are oriented more or less vertically; the utricles, more or less horizontally. The striola is a structural landmark, that divides each otolith organ. The tallest stereocilia point toward the striola in the utricular macula and away from it in the saccular macula, as the arrows indicate. Because hair cells depolarize if they deflect toward the tallest stereocilia and hyperpolarize if they deflect away from the tallest, the arrows also show the movement direction that causes maximal neural excitation at each location on the maculae. Note that, given one utricle and one saccule on each side of the head, there is a continuous representation of all directions for sensing gravity and linear acceleration. (*b*) Cross section of the macula of an otolith organ. Hair bundles project into a gelatinous layer. (*c*) The otoconia shown in this scanning electron micrograph come from the utricular macula of a cat. Crystals are between 0.5 and 10 micrometers long. (*c* from Lindeman, 1973.)

sensory transduction occurs (**Figure 12.13***a*). Each human utricular macula contains about 30,000 hair cells; each saccular macula, about 16,000. The utricular and saccular maculae are innervated by about 4000 neurons each. Each macula is roughly planar and is primarily sensitive to shear forces—forces parallel to the macular plane. Perpendicular forces have little influence on neural response. Small movements caused by parallel shear forces, due to gravity and/or linear acceleration, deflect the hair cells and produce changes in the firing rate of afferent neurons.

The cilia of the otolith hair cells are encased in a gelatinous structure (Figure 12.13*b*) that contains calcium carbonate crystals called **otoconia** (singular *otoconium*) (Figure 12.13*c*). There are literally millions of these otoconia in the utricle and saccule. These small stones give the otolith organs their name: *oto* means "ear," and *lithos* means "stone" in Greek, so *otolith* translates as "ear stone." The otoconia are denser than the surrounding fluid. Like any dense object, they are pulled by both gravitational force and inertial force due to linear acceleration. The resulting displacement of the otoconia drags the gelatinous layer, thereby moving the hair cell stereocilia, leading to changes in the hair cell receptor potential, which in turn cause changes in the rate of action potentials in the afferent neurons.

otoconia Tiny calcium carbonate stones in the ear that provide inertial mass for the otolith organs, enabling them to sense gravity and linear acceleration.

HOW AMPLITUDE IS CODED IN THE OTOLITH ORGANS As in the semicircular canals, one aspect of amplitude coding in the otolith organs can be found in the response of a single neuron or single hair cell. Recall that (1) hair cell receptor potentials increase when hair bundle tips move toward the largest stereocilia, (2) receptor potentials decrease for movements in the opposite direction (see Figure 12.7), and (3) the direction of rotation is coded by excitation from a semicircular canal on one side and inhibition from the other side.

Similar mechanisms are at work in each otolith organ macula. Populations of hair cells on each macula have their stereocilia oriented in opposite directions (see Figure 12.13*a*). Both the utricle and the saccule include a central band called the striola (plural *striolae*). On opposite sides of the striola, hair cells are oriented in opposite directions. Remember that movement toward the tallest stereocilia excites the hair cells, and movement in the opposite direction inhibits the hair cells. Since the neuronal response arises from synapses to the hair cells, tilts (or linear accelerations) in opposite directions cause opposite changes in firing rate (**Figure 12.14**). So a tilt or an acceleration that maximally excites a hair cell and afferent neuron on one side of the striola will maximally inhibit a hair cell and afferent neuron on the opposite side.

Larger accelerations (or larger gravitational shear forces) move the otolith organs' otoconia more. This movement, in turn, leads to greater deflection of the hair cell bundles, which causes larger changes in the hair cell receptor potentials. The receptor potential evoked in a given hair cell is proportional to the component of gravity or linear acceleration that is aligned with the sensitive axis of that hair cell. Larger changes in the hair cell receptor potential lead to larger changes in the rate of action potentials sent to the brain via afferent neurons.

HOW DIRECTION IS CODED IN THE OTOLITH ORGANS Direction coding in the otolith organs arises, in part, from their anatomical orientation. The plane

(*a*)

(*b*)

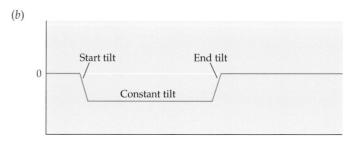

FIGURE 12.14 Activity of a vestibular neuron innervating the utricle (an otolith organ). (*a*) A change in head tilt is the stimulus (top). As shown in the histogram of the discharge rate (bottom), the neuron's activity increases in response to tilt in a particular direction. (*b*) The same neuron decreases its activity in response to tilt in the opposite direction. (After Goldberg and Fernandez, 1976.)

of the utricular macula is horizontal; the plane of the saccular macula, vertical (see Figure 12.13*a*). Since these maculae are exquisitely sensitive to gravity and linear acceleration in the plane of the macula and insensitive to gravity and acceleration perpendicular to the macula, the utricle will be sensitive primarily to horizontal linear accelerations and horizontal gravitational forces, while the saccule is sensitive to vertical linear accelerations and the vertical gravitational forces.

The other component of direction coding arises from variations in the orientation of the hair cells (Figure 12.13*a*, far right). Different hair cells respond maximally to different movement directions, with the direction of maximal sensitivity varying systematically across the plane of each macula. For example, hair cells in one region of the utricular macula will be maximally sensitive to forward-backward acceleration, while cells in another region will be maximally sensitive to side-to-side linear acceleration. In between, cells will maximally respond to linear acceleration that has both forward-backward and side-to-side components.

Spatial Orientation Perception

Long after it was known that we see with our eyes and hear with our ears, the primary source for our perception of spatial orientation remained a mystery. In fact, in the eighteenth century, gross fluid shifts in the head were accepted as an explanation for the source of our sense of spatial orientation. Once it was established that this sense degrades when the vestibular system is damaged, it became clear that the vestibular system provides crucial information regarding spatial orientation. For example, when patients with vestibular loss are moved in the dark, they have a much more difficult time correctly perceiving their motion than do people with normal vestibular function.

Today, three different techniques are frequently used to investigate spatial orientation perception: threshold estimation, magnitude estimation, and matching. For example, we can ask, What is the minimum motion (the "threshold") required for correctly perceiving the direction we are moved? Note that this is different from simply reporting *whether* we've moved, since vibration can provide a motion cue without informing about the direction of the motion. The vestibular system tells us more than whether motion is present or not; it actually informs us of the direction of motion—for example, whether we moved to the left or to the right.

In a magnitude estimation study, subjects might be asked to give verbal reports of how much they tilt, rotate, or translate using physical units like the number of degrees they rotated. Alternatively, magnitude estimation may utilize arbitrary scaling. For example, subjects may be trained to rotate a knob in proportion to their perceived velocity or provide a verbal indicator of their velocity on a scale of 1–10.

In a matching task, subjects might be asked to align a visual line with perceived Earth-vertical (which way is "down"). In such a task, the investigator could produce a vestibular stimulus by tilting the subject. That subject would be provided with a visible line in otherwise dark surroundings and with the ability to rotate the line to the perceived Earth-vertical. Alternatively, haptic sensation, which you will learn more about in Chapter 13, could be utilized instead of vision. For this technique, subjects might be asked to align a bar—that they hold but cannot see—with perceived vertical.

FURTHER DISCUSSION of similar matching tasks in connection with the sense of touch can be found in Chapter 13 on pages 387–389.

FIGURE 12.15 The red line on this graph shows the angular velocity of a person at rest, with eyes closed, who was suddenly rotated at a constant speed for 50 seconds and then was abruptly returned to rest. Initially, the subject's estimate of angular velocity was accurate (purple line at time 0), but then the perceived velocity dropped to near 0 after about 20 seconds. When stopped, the subject perceived an abrupt velocity in the opposite direction, which mimicked the initial perception but in the opposite direction. (After Young, 1984.) For comparison, we show a representation of the canal response in green, similar to that shown in Figure 12.11. Note the faster return to baseline for the canal response.

Rotation Perception

If you are spun on a barstool in the dark at a nearly constant velocity, you will initially perceive an angular velocity that is roughly the same as the actual rotation. However, if the constant-velocity rotation lasts more than a second or two, you will perceive that you are slowing down (**Figure 12.15**). If the constant-velocity rotation continues for more than 60 seconds or so, you will perceive that you are no longer rotating.

This description may remind you of the way the response of the semicircular canals decays during constant-velocity rotation (see Figure 12.11), and is another example of how the vestibular system is attuned to *changes* in motion. Interestingly, though, the time course of the perceptual decay is more gradual than that of the semicircular-canal signal sent to the brain. This effect is sometimes called "velocity storage" because the perception of rotation persists after the afferent signal from the semicircular canals has dissipated. The velocity storage phenomenon is interesting and important because it shows that the brain has improved on the incoming sensory information to yield a rotation perception that—while far from perfect—is closer to the actual rotation than if the perception simply followed the time course of the semicircular-canal afferent signal (Bertolini et al., 2011).

Later, if you are abruptly brought to a stop following extended rotation, you will perceive an angular velocity opposite the one you experienced while rotating (see Figure 12.15). This rotation illusion is one that many of us played with as children when we would spin ourselves for a while and then suddenly stop spinning and try to stand or walk. (And some amusement park junkies still play with this illusion!) The dizziness and imbalance that we experienced when we stopped rotating were due to an illusion of self-rotation caused by the semicircular-canal response.

One can develop an intuitive understanding of the reason for this illusion by considering the analogy of riding in a car. When you're riding at a constant velocity, you and the car are moving together. But when the car suddenly stops, you are thrown forward because you have momentum and keep moving even though the car has stopped. When you're rotating at a constant velocity, there

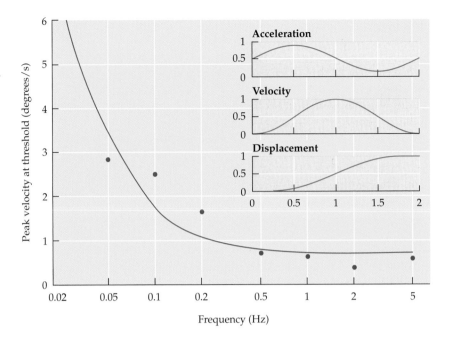

FIGURE 12.16 Mean velocity threshold as a function of frequency for seven subjects. Threshold velocity was the peak velocity achieved during a single cycle of sinusoidal acceleration at which subjects correctly recognized the direction of motion most of the time. The plotted curve shows a model fit to the data. The inset shows the angular acceleration, angular velocity, and angular displacement for a single cycle of sinusoidal acceleration at 0.5 Hz. For the example shown, the peak magnitude of the acceleration is 1.57 degrees/s^2, the peak velocity is 1 degree/s, and the peak displacement is 1 degree. (After Grabherr et al., 2008.)

is little or no hair cell deflection, because the endolymph and cupula are moving together. When the rotation is suddenly halted, however, the cupula stops moving quickly but the endolymph has momentum and tends to keep moving. The hair cells are therefore deflected, and the direction of the hair cell response is opposite the one measured when the constant-velocity rotation began.

THRESHOLDS　How sensitive are we to vestibular stimuli? Direction recognition thresholds for yaw rotation have been measured for rotational motion frequencies ranging from 0.05 Hz (one back-and-forth cycle of yaw acceleration in 20 seconds) to 5 Hz (one back-and-forth cycle of yaw acceleration in 1 second). For frequencies above 1 Hz (one back-and-forth cycle of yaw acceleration in 1 second), direction recognition thresholds are roughly constant; your head has to be moving at a speed of just a little below 1 degree per second. That is a rather slow turn of the head. It would take you 6 minutes to spin all the way around at an angular velocity of 1 degree per second. Clearly, we are very sensitive to rotation. For frequencies below 0.5 Hz (one back-and-forth yaw rotation in 2 seconds), thresholds increase with decreasing frequency (**Figure 12.16**). The important point here is to recognize that rotation thresholds vary as the frequency of the angular acceleration stimulus varies. (Recall that hearing thresholds changed with frequency too; see Figure 9.21.)

Translation Perception

When subjects are passively translated short distances while seated in a chair in the dark and then asked, while still seated in the chair, to use a joystick to actively move the chair to reproduce the distance that they had been passively translated, they do so accurately. But even though not asked to do so, they also reproduce the *velocity* of the passive-motion trajectory (Berthoz et al., 1995). The unrequested replication of velocity suggests that the brain remembers and replicates the velocity trajectory. Earlier we said that the otolith organs transduce linear acceleration, which is the change in linear velocity. Therefore, replication of the velocity trajectory means that the brain also seems to **mathematically integrate** the acceleration signal provided by the otolith organs to yield a perception of linear velocity. This apparent calculation suggests that while otolith organs sense linear acceleration, our brains turn this information into a perception of linear velocity.

mathematical integration Computing an integral—one of the two main operations in calculus (the other, the inverse operation, is differentiation). Velocity is the integral of acceleration. Change of position is the integral of velocity.

Measured thresholds for recognizing motion direction are also consistent with the idea that the brain integrates the linear acceleration transduced by the otolith organs to yield a perception of linear velocity. Data show that humans correctly recognize the direction of translation only when the linear velocity exceeds a few centimeters per second (cm/s). Average population thresholds as low as 3 cm/s have been reported for normal healthy subjects. For perspective, moving at that linear velocity for an entire minute would yield a translation of less than 2 meters.

Tilt Perception

How well do we perceive our tilt angle if we are positioned at a static orientation relative to gravity? For tilt angles less than 90 degrees—that is, body orientations between standing up (0 degrees) and lying down (90 degrees)—we are pretty good according to a variety of magnitude estimation techniques. Observers produce reliable and consistent answers if they indicate their perceived tilt verbally or if they align a handheld probe with perceived vertical (**Figure 12.17**).

We are not perfect, though. Some consistent errors appear, especially in the subjective visual vertical task described earlier (see p. 344). Back in 1861, Hermann Rudolf Aubert found that when he roll-tilted his head to the left or

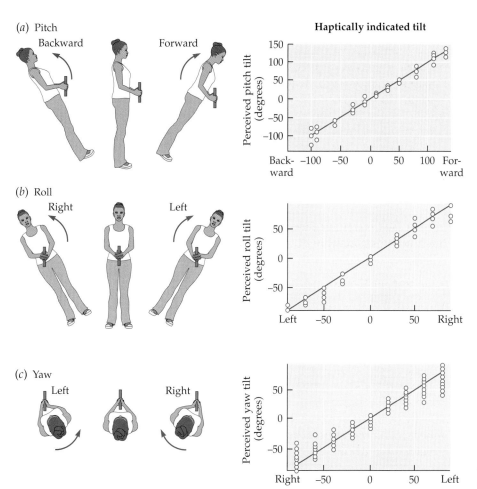

FIGURE 12.17 Subjects are generally pretty good at indicating how much they are tilted. Data (open circles) show tilt perception provided by subjects using a handheld haptic indicator (shown schematically at far left) for static pitch (a), roll (b), and yaw (c) tilts. Perceived tilt roughly reflects the actual tilt (solid lines) for all three tilt directions. (After Bortolami et al., 2006.)

sensory integration The process of combining different sensory signals. Typically, combining several signals yields more accurate and/or more precise information than can be obtained from individual sensory signals. This is *not* the mathematical process of integration learned in calculus (e.g., the integral of acceleration is velocity).

vection An illusory sense of self-motion caused by moving visual cues when you are not, in fact, actually moving.

right while looking at a vertical streak of light, the vertical line appeared to tilt in the direction opposite his head tilt. For tilt angles less than 90 degrees, the illusory tilt error is typically about 10 degrees, but the apparent tilt of the visual line can be as large as 45 degrees when the head is tilted 135 degrees. You can investigate this illusion in a completely dark room by leaving the door open just a crack—just enough to see a line of light in the doorway without illuminating the room at all—while you hold your head in a tilted position. Does the line appear to tilt when your head is tilted? Does it move in the direction of your tilted head or in the opposite direction?

Thresholds for recognizing the direction of tilt show that normal subjects correctly report the direction of a static tilt when tilted about 1 degree off vertical in the dark. This sensitivity serves our ability to stand upright, because the farther we are tilted from upright, the more difficult standing up is. For example, the amount of muscular effort required to maintain posture roughly doubles if we are tilted 2 degrees instead of 1 degree, so just imagine the effort of trying to stand tilted 20 degrees away from upright!

Sensory Integration

The senses do not operate independently. Instead, the brain combines signals from different sensory systems via neural processes of **sensory integration**. For example, visual cues influence sound localization—an effect utilized effectively by ventriloquists. Vestibular signals combine with information from numerous sensory systems to provide us with an understanding of the position and movements of the head and body.

> **FURTHER DISCUSSION** of a remarkable example of sensory integration—the McGurk effect on speech perception—can be found in Chapter 11 on page 316.

Visual-Vestibular Integration

Most of us have experienced illusions of self-motion caused by moving visual cues. Perhaps you've perceived self-motion while watching an IMAX movie. Or perhaps you've felt as if you were translating when you were stationary but the car (or train or bus) next to you began to move. Or perhaps you felt unsteady when standing on a bridge looking at the water flowing beneath. All of these situations can lead to perceptions of illusory self-motion called **vection**. Vection can be very compelling. For example, drivers stopped in traffic often press harder on the brake pedal when they perceive that they and their stationary car are moving, even though it is the cars around them that are moving.

To consider how vection contributes to spatial orientation, imagine a person standing upright while viewing the inside of a sphere rotating in roll (**Figure 12.18a**). At first, subjective perceptions match reality; humans initially perceive that they are stationary and that the sphere is rotating. But if they continue to observe the rotating visual display for 10 seconds or so, they usually begin to perceive that they're rotating in the direction opposite the sphere rotation (Figure 12.18b). This illusory rotational vection demonstrates the crucial contributions of vision to our sense of self-rotation. In fact, retinal signals converge with the semicircular-canal signals in the vestibular nuclei, which is the first place in the brain that vestibular information reaches. (**Web Essay 12.5: Canal-Otolith Integration** discusses a similar interaction of signals from the semicircular canals and otolith organs.)

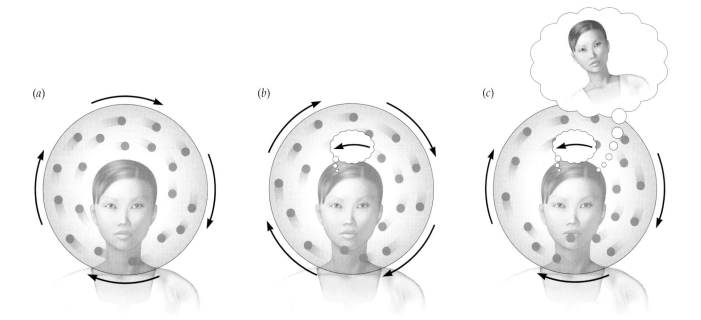

FIGURE 12.18 Rotational vection. A subject views a visual display rotating in roll. For demonstration purposes, the visual display is shown here as transparent. (*a*) Initially, the subject correctly senses that she is stationary and the visual display is rotating. (*b*) The subject begins to perceive vection, a sense of self-rotation in the direction opposite the rotation of the visual display. (*c*) Roll vection is often accompanied by an illusion of roll tilt that is induced by the perceived roll rotation. The direction of the perceived tilt is consistent with the tilt direction that would occur if the subject were truly rotating in roll. (After Young, Shelhamer, and Modestino, 1986.)

Paradoxically, subjects experiencing such rotational vection almost never report that they are tumbling head over heels as they would if they truly were rotating to the extent that they perceive. In fact, subjects typically experience a simultaneous illusory sensation of tilt that gradually builds up to a relatively constant level (Figure 12.18*c*). These perceptions—experienced as a sensation of motion without getting anywhere—are contradictory, since we cannot be rotating relative to gravity (as suggested by the visual cues) while also maintaining a constant orientation with respect to gravity (as indicated by the otolith organs). In addition to exemplifying sensory integration, this sensation of motion without getting anywhere demonstrates that our sense of spatial orientation is not constrained to combinations of motion and orientation that are physically possible.

In this example, the role played by the vestibular system is to put the brakes on visually induced vection. Patients suffering from severe vestibular damage generally report greater vection than do normal subjects. Astronauts experiencing rotational vection in space—in the absence of gravitational signals—report a head-over-heels tumbling sensation that is absent on Earth. These findings are explained by the fact that neither the patients nor the astronauts receive normal gravitational cues from the otolith organs to contradict their visual rotational cues. (**Web Essay 12.4: Space Motion Sickness** discusses another aspect of spaceflight that many astronauts experience.) Since illusory motion is greater when there are no otolith cues to contradict the visual cues, we can infer that, under normal circumstances, information from the vestibular system is combined with visual information to yield a "consensus" about our sense of spatial orientation.

Reflexive Vestibular Responses

vestibulo-ocular reflex (VOR) A short-latency reflex that helps stabilize vision by counterrotating the eyes when the vestibular system senses head movement.

balance system The sensory systems, neural processes, and muscles that contribute to postural control. Specific components include the vestibular labyrinth, proprioceptors, vestibulo-spinal pathways, and postural control muscles. Because of its crucial contributions to balance, some even informally refer to the vestibular system as the balance system and the vestibular organs as the balance organs. But the balance system is much more than just the vestibular system, and the vestibular system contributes to much more than just balance.

balance The neural processes of postural control by which weight is evenly distributed, enabling us to remain upright and stable.

As mentioned earlier, some crucial contributions of the vestibular system are automatic, or reflexive, doing their work outside of conscious awareness. For example, there is a set of automatic responses called **vestibulo-ocular reflexes—VORs** for short. We started the chapter with one of these. Remember looking at your finger as you shook your head? (If not, now might be a good time to go back and try this demonstration again; see Figure 12.1.) This task illustrates how the VOR contributes to visual stability by counterrotating the eyes in the head during head motion sensed by the vestibular system.

There is also a set of vestibulo-autonomic reflexes that contribute to autonomic responses like those that regulate blood pressure and help maintain adequate blood flow to the brain. Other vestibulo-autonomic reflexes lead to motion sickness. Finally, vestibulo-spinal reflexes contribute to postural control via the **balance system**. To demonstrate vestibular contributions to **balance**, try standing on one foot with your eyes closed. (When you start to feel unsteady, immediately open your eyes and put both feet on the ground!) Most healthy people with a normal balance system—including normal vestibular function—can do this for at least 5 seconds and often much longer. Patients without vestibular function, however, cannot stand on one foot in the dark for more than an instant.

Vestibulo-Ocular Responses

The angular VOR, the eye rotation that helps compensate for angular rotations of the head, is a robust reflex. In fact, this reflex is so robust that it is a standard part of clinical examinations of vestibular function. Furthermore, the VOR is certainly among the best-studied reflexes, dating as far back as the late 1700s with reports by William Charles Wells (1792).

The angular VOR is the compensatory eye rotation evoked by the semicircular canals when they sense head rotation. For example, when the head rotates to the left, the reflex pathways cause the eye to rotate to the right with respect to the head, so as to compensate—at least in part—for the head turn. When observing the eye, we see this eye rotation as movement of the pupil to the right. Of course, since the eye is really a spherical eyeball, it is really rotating in the eye socket, not moving laterally.

Recall that six ocular muscles—called "oculomotor muscles"—rotate the eyeball (see Chapter 8). Muscles can only pull; they cannot push. Muscles are paired to pull in opposite directions and are therefore called agonist-antagonist muscle pairs. For example, moving the left eye horizontally requires a coordination of the lateral rectus that pulls the eye to the left and the medial rectus that pulls the eye to the right. To make an eye movement to the right, the lateral rectus is inhibited and thus relaxes its pull, while the medial rectus is excited and thus increases its pull. The six oculomotor muscles are organized in three pairs that rotate the eye in each of three directions (see **Web Activity 12.3: Observing Torsional Eye Movement**). Eye movements result from a coordinated inhibition and excitation of the eye muscles.

When the vestibulo-ocular reflex is working effectively, it actively rotates the eye in the head such that the rotation of the eye roughly compensates for the rotation of the head in space. **Figure 12.19** demonstrates this with a simple example. In Figure 12.19*a*, the eyes rotate with the head; they do not counterrotate in the head. In Figure 12.19*b*, the eyes counterrotate in the head, which helps stabilize the visual field on the retina. If the eyes do not counterrotate in the head, the retinal image tends to blur during head rotation. (Remember how your fingers blurred when you rapidly moved them back and forth?)

FIGURE 12.19   Contribution of the angular VOR to visual stability. (*a*) When the eyes do not counterrotate, the image of the object is not foveated during head rotation. (*b*) When the eyes counterrotate during head rotation—with the amount of eye rotation roughly equal to the amount of head rotation—the image of an object can remain foveated even during head rotation. Because the eyes counterrotate in the head in (*b*) but not in (*a*), they continue to look at you in (*b*) but not in (*a*). This effect demonstrates how the angular VOR contributes to visual acuity, by helping to keep object images stationary on the retina, thereby reducing blurring.

The counterrotation of the eye in the head helps reduce this blur by reducing the motion of the image of an object across the retina. Note that because of eye counterrotation, the actual rotation of the eyes with respect to the external world is much less than that of the head.

The most direct neural path for the vestibulo-ocular reflexes consists of an arc of three neurons that yields reflexive eye responses with a latency of less than 10 milliseconds (ms) between the start of head motion and the eye movement. (That is really fast. Try doing anything else in less than 10 ms!) The first neurons in the arc are the afferent neurons (bottom right in **Figure 12.20**); these neurons transmit information from the vestibular periphery to the vestibular nuclei. There, the afferent neurons synapse on interneurons. These interneurons synapse on efferent oculomotor neurons in the ocular motor nuclei. These oculomotor neurons synapse with the oculomotor muscles to rotate the eyes with respect to the head.

FIGURE 12.20 Neural pathways for the angular-VOR three-neuron arc. Each type of neuron is depicted using a different color. Each of the vestibular afferent neurons (blue)—one branch for each of the three canals—projects to one of three vestibular nuclei: superior, medial, or lateral. Neurons that connect afferent and efferent neurons (green), called interneurons, project from the vestibular nuclei to the three ocular motor nuclei: abducens, trochlear, and oculomotor. (Note that one of the ocular motor nuclei is called the "oculomotor" nucleus.) The six efferent oculomotor neurons (red) project from these three ocular motor nuclei to the six oculomotor muscles: inferior oblique, superior oblique, inferior rectus, superior rectus, lateral rectus, and medial rectus. Recall that you previously were introduced to the oculomotor muscles in Figure 8.16

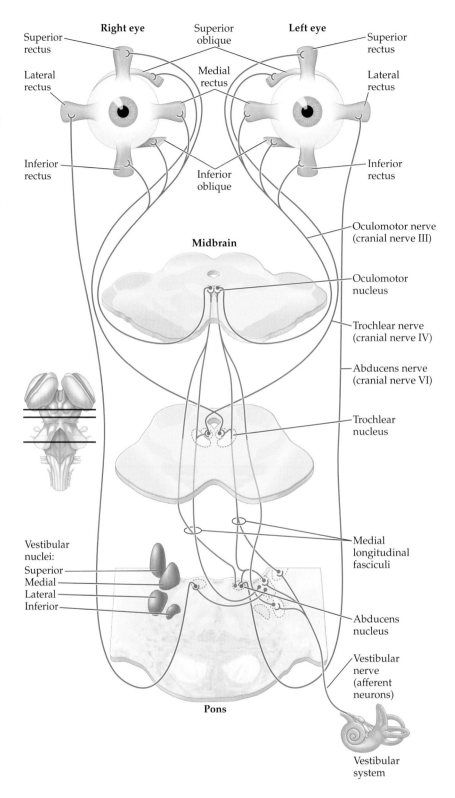

As you rotate your head from side to side, the angular VOR has properties similar to the characteristics that were discussed earlier for the semicircular canals, as illustrated in **Figures 12.21** and **12.22**. The VOR demonstrates a constant, relatively high amplitude at high frequencies, but it gets smaller and smaller as the frequency drops below about 0.05 Hz (Figure 12.21). Though the frequency characteristics of the VOR and canal afferents are qualitatively

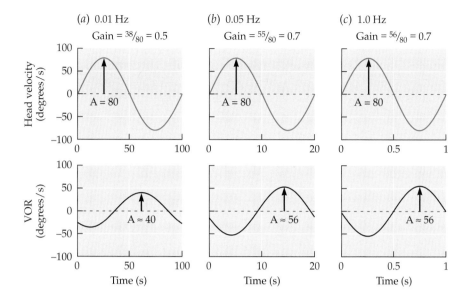

FIGURE 12.21 VOR responses in the dark at three frequencies. The stimulus (sinusoidal head rotation; top row) is shown for (a) 0.01, (b) 0.05, and (c) 1.0 Hz. Sinusoidal motion evokes an oscillatory VOR (bottom row), which opposes the head rotation such that head rotations to the right are accompanied by eye rotations to the left. If the VOR were perfect, it would have the same peak amplitude (labeled "A" in the figure) as the head rotation, meaning that the eye rotated at the same velocity as the head rotation. However, the peak compensatory eye velocity shown for 0.05 Hz and 1.0 Hz in the dark is about 70% of the peak head velocity (a gain of about 0.7). The remaining 30% is usually made up by visual contributions. At lower frequencies, the VOR is smaller; for example, at 0.01 Hz it is only about 50% of the peak head velocity (a gain of about 0.5). The gain of the VOR response is its peak amplitude divided by the peak amplitude of the stimulus.

similar, there is an interesting difference. As Figure 12.22 shows, the response of canal afferent neurons declines for frequencies below 0.2 Hz. In comparison, the VOR declines for frequencies below 0.05 Hz.

That difference is interesting because it means that, in some sense, the VOR is responding more accurately than a simple reading of its input signal would provide. This effect, analogous to what we saw earlier for rotation perception (see Figure 12.15), is called "velocity storage." It shows that the brain is not simply a relay station that passes sensory information to the muscles that yield the reflexive action. Instead, the brain helps shape the reflexes to be as effective as possible, given the available sensory information. In this specific case, central processing increases the effective VOR frequency range (Raphan, Matsuo, and Cohen, 1977; Robinson, 1977).

We also have a translational VOR that is evoked when the otolith organs sense head translation, especially high-frequency head translation. This translational VOR helps us keep our eyes pointed at an object when the head translates in one direction or the other.

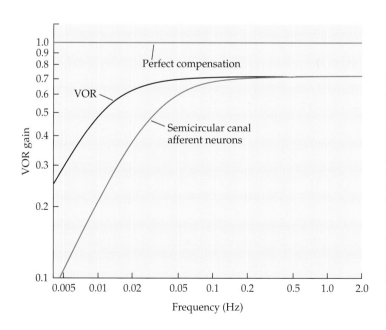

FIGURE 12.22 Dynamics of the VOR (black curve) are such that the response has a nearly constant gain—roughly a gain of 0.7, as calculated in Figure 12.21—at frequencies between about 0.05 and 2.0 Hz. In fact, while not shown in this figure, the VOR gain remains nearly constant for frequencies up to 25–30 Hz (Huterer and Cullen, 2002; R. Ramachandran and Lisberger, 2005). Perfectly compensatory response—having a gain of 1—is shown in red. See Figure 12.21 for examples of how this gain is calculated at each frequency. Below 0.05 Hz, the gain of the VOR decreases. For comparison, the normalized frequency response of semicircular-canal neurons that we saw in Figure 12.12 is indicated by the green curve. Since the green curve represents the information provided to the brain and the black line represents the VOR response at different frequencies, the difference between the black and green curves represents neural compensation performed by the brain.

autonomic nervous system The part of the nervous system that innervates glands, heart, digestive system, and so on, and that is responsible for regulating many involuntary actions.

Vestibulo-Autonomic Responses

The vestibular system also makes contributions to responses of the **autonomic nervous system**. Perhaps the most vivid of these responses is motion sickness, a vestibulo-autonomic ordeal that many of us wish we had never experienced. Severe symptoms of motion sickness include nausea and vomiting. Motion sickness typically results when there is a disagreement between the motion and orientation signals provided by the semicircular canals, otolith organs, and vision (Oman, 1990; Reason and Brand, 1975). For example, if you are below deck on a boat, your vestibular system will accurately record the motion of the boat while vision suggests no relative motion of the world, since you and the boat are moving together.

What is this response good for? One of several hypotheses is that it is a defense against some classes of poisons (M. Treisman, 1977). If you have been poisoned, you want to get rid of the poison before it gets rid of you. But how do you know if you have been poisoned? If the poison is a neurotoxin, disruption of the sensory systems is a good hint. How do you know that your senses have been disrupted? One way is to check whether senses that normally agree with one another have stopped doing so. Normally, if you move, your visual system and your vestibular system both register that fact. If the vestibular system says one thing and the visual system says another, the brain may decide that it is time to rid the body of a possible cause of the disagreement. This response could be a lifesaver if you just ate a bad mushroom. It is less desirable as a response to choppy weather at 35,000 feet.

Other vestibulo-autonomic responses are less spectacular and generally take the form of compensatory contributions. For example, consider the problem of regulating blood pressure. The heart pumps blood throughout the body, but maintaining oxygenation of the brain via blood flow is especially critical, because you will black out in just a few seconds if your brain does not receive adequate oxygen. Gravity pulls blood downward, so in the normal upright posture your heart has to work to maintain blood flow to the brain. When you're lying down, it takes much less work to pump blood to the brain. Now suppose you rapidly stand up. The cardiovascular system has to suddenly change the regulation of blood flow to maintain adequate oxygen supply to the brain. If these mechanisms fail, you will experience light-headedness or, in extreme cases, blackout. By informing the relevant parts of the autonomic nervous system about the position and motion of the head, the vestibular system contributes to the regulation of blood flow to the brain. As a result, one consequence of destructive lesions of the vestibular organs is that blood pressure regulation during whole-body tilts becomes much less stable (Figure 12.23).

Vestibulo-Spinal Responses

In the early 1800s, the French physiologist Jean Pierre Flourens reported abnormal head movements in pigeons after he had cut individual semicircular canals. The head movements he reported were in the plane of the lesioned canal. These studies demonstrated the presence of what we today consider to be the vestibular influences on posture control, and they initiated the formal study of vestibular influences on balance.

Vestibular reflexes keep us from falling over. Without vestibulo-spinal reflexes our balance would be severely degraded. We would be unable to stand in the dark. Part of the reason is that when we stand, we are inherently unstable. As two-legged creatures, we can be thought of as being composed of a series of inverted pendulums—pendulums in which the mass is above the

(a)

(b)

FIGURE 12.23 Vestibular influences on blood pressure. (*a*) This trace represents blood pressure in the head versus time in response to a nose-up tilt in a subject with a lesioned vestibular system. In the absence of vestibular contributions, a transient decrease in blood pressure can be observed immediately after the tilt. (*b*) Change in blood pressure is much greater for the subject without a functional vestibular system (lesioned) than for the subject with a normal vestibular system, demonstrating that the vestibular system helps maintain more constant blood pressure during whole-body tilts. (After Yates and Miller, 1998.)

pivot point. Balancing a pencil or broom on your palm demonstrates a simple inverted pendulum. These challenging tasks can be mastered with practice, but imagine trying to stabilize a series of at least four brooms or pencils on top of one another. At its essence, this is the task faced by our balance system, which works to keep the head, torso, thighs, and calves—each an inverted pendulum—upright with respect to gravity.

While a thorough discussion of the dynamics of the entire posture control system is beyond the scope of this book, investigators have been able to simplify the dynamics experimentally by strapping the head and body to a rigid board that converts the complex multijoint body into a single inverted pendulum pitching forward and backward about the ankle joint. When the foot plate that the subject stands on is gently rocked forward and backward while the subject's eyes are closed, normal subjects demonstrate body sway that is less than the amplitude of the applied rocking movement (Figure 12.24), indicating that the vestibular system is helping to compensate for the applied-movement disturbance. The vestibular system measures the movement of the head and sends commands to the postural control system that help reduce the amount of body sway. In contrast, patients with severe vestibular loss demonstrate body sway that exceeds the amplitude of the disturbance. This difference between postural responses of people with normal vestibular function and patients with vestibular loss is a clear indication of the importance of the vestibular system to balance and posture control (see Figure 12.24). A little later in the chapter we'll learn about mal de debarquement syndrome, an unusual disorder that causes imbalance and/or spatial disorientation.

FIGURE 12.24 The contributions of the vestibular system to balance are demonstrated by the comparison of postural responses of subjects with normal vestibular function to responses of patients suffering severe bilateral vestibular loss. Subjects were asked to maintain themselves upright in the presence of small angular displacements of their feet that were designed to challenge their balance control. For the purposes of illustration, a platform tilt of 20° is shown; in typical experiments the tilt would be much smaller (otherwise the subjects might fall off!).The values on the y-axis (the "gain") represent the amplitude of the subject's response divided by the amplitude of displacement. Gain is defined as tilt of the subject divided by tilt of the platform. As shown in the insets, if the subject did the task perfectly, the result would be a gain of 0 (0/θ). If the subject remained perpendicular to the platform, the gain would be 1 (θ/θ). If the subject tilted more than the platform, the gain would be greater than 1. The response gains for normal subjects were always near or below 1. On the other hand, vestibular-loss patients had response gains that often exceeded 1, indicating that their body tilt exceeded the platform tilt disturbance. Patients with vestibular loss exhibited much greater sway than normal subjects, clearly demonstrating the fundamental contributions of the vestibular system to balance control. (After Peterka, 2002.)

The vestibulo-spinal response can be thought of as a whole family of reflexes (**Figure 12.25**). In the vestibular nuclei, the primary afferent neurons synapse on descending interneurons that carry information through the lateral and medial vestibulo-spinal tracts. How far these neurons carry information down the spinal cord depends on their contribution to the balance system. If the interneuron synapses onto a neuron that controls a leg muscle, the information is transmitted beyond the bottom of the spinal cord. If the information contributes to postural control of the head, it is transmitted only as far as the neck.

Medial ⎫
Lateral ⎬ Vestibular
Inferior ⎭ nuclei

To cerebellum

Vestibular ganglion and nerve

Rostral medulla

Motor neurons (controlling neck muscles)

Vestibular system

Medial vestibulo-spinal fibers in medial longitudinal fasciculi

Lateral vestibulo-spinal tract

Lower part of **cervical spinal cord**

To flexor muscles
To extensor muscles

Lateral vestibulo-spinal tract

Inhibitory interneuron

Excitatory synapse

Lumbar spinal cord

To flexor muscles
To extensor muscles

FIGURE 12.25 Neural pathways for vestibulo-spinal reflexes. Most vestibular afferent neurons (blue) synapse in one of the vestibular nuclei, but some project to the cerebellum. From the vestibular nuclei, descending interneurons (green) carry the information via vestibulo-spinal tracts downward through the brain stem and spinal cord until they synapse on efferent neurons (red) that activate the muscles that control balance. (After Netter, 1983.)

Spatial Orientation Cortex

We have visual cortex and auditory cortex. Do we have a vestibular cortex? Some areas of the cortex certainly do respond to vestibular input, but these areas tend to respond to visual input as well. There does not appear to be an area of the cortex exclusively dedicated to vestibular signals. This is not shocking, since we learned earlier that perception of body motion and tilt result from multisensory convergence, including predominant contributions by the vestibular system and vision.

It may be that the cortex simply lacks a good reason to process vestibular information in isolation when other sensory information is available. For example, the visual system is responsive to constant-velocity visual motion—like that experienced during rotation in the light as you see the room spin around you—while the vestibular system responds primarily to changes in velocity and is relatively insensitive to constant-velocity motion. More specifically, recall that when rotated at a constant velocity in the dark, after about 30 seconds humans perceive that they are not rotating (see Figure 12.15). Therefore, when rotating with a nearly constant velocity in the light, it seems reasonable that the brain would utilize the visual information indicating motion to better estimate self-motion. It thus makes sense that areas of the cortex related to the perception of tilt and self-motion demonstrate a convergence of visual and vestibular information, as well as information from other sensory systems that contribute to spatial orientation.

Vestibular Thalamocortical Pathways

Vestibular information reaches the cortex via what are called the "thalamocortical pathways" (Figure 12.26). This means simply that the vestibular information, like most other sensory information, reaches the cortex via the thalamus. Neurons from the vestibular nuclei carry vestibular information to the thalamus, where that information is processed and relayed to the cortex. Compare this, for example, to the visual system, where the retinal ganglion cells synapse in the lateral geniculate nucleus of the thalamus (see the section on the LGN in Chapter 3). There the information is processed and passed on to visual cortex.

Evidence suggests that the temporo-parieto-insular cortex is involved in spatial orientation perception. This area of the cortex receives input from both the semicircular canals and the otolith organs. Furthermore, immediately after this part of the cortex is lesioned by a stroke, many patients report illusory tilts and/or illusory translation. Though more rare, rotational vertigo—an illusory sense of spinning—is reported by some of these patients.

Though more direct vestibular projections may exist, there is a vestibular pathway that leads to the hippocampus through the vestibular cortex, and neurons in the hippocampal formation respond to vestibular stimuli (Horii et al., 2004). These include a set of neurons called "direction cells" because they tend to spike vigorously when an animal's head is pointed toward a specific direction (Taube, 2007).

Cortical Influences

The areas of the cortex that receive projections from the vestibular system also project back to the vestibular nuclei. The existence of these pathways suggests that feedback from areas of the cortex that respond to vestibular stimulation likely modulates low-level vestibular processing in the brain stem. A specific role for these projections has not been proven, but it is known that higher cognitive knowledge can affect both perceptions and reflexive responses. For example, imagining whether an unseen visual target rotates with you alters the vestibulo-ocular reflex evoked by rotation. As is appropriate, the VOR is suppressed when subjects imagine that the target moves with them but is relatively large when subjects imagine that the target is Earth-fixed (Barr, Schultheis, and Robinson, 1976).

As another example of higher-order cortical influences, knowledge of the motion capabilities of a specific device can influence motion perceptions (Rader, Oman, and Merfeld, 2011; Wertheim, Mesland, and Bles, 2001). For example, if you were blindfolded and then taken to a merry-go-round that you had never ridden before, your perception of tilt and motion might differ from what you would experience if you were riding a merry-go-round that you had ridden many times before. The vestibular stimuli might be the same, but your knowledge and expectations—both of which are higher-level functions—would be different and could alter your spatial orientation perceptions.

FIGURE 12.26 Ascending vestibular (thalamocortical) pathways pass from the vestibular nuclei to the posterolateral thalamus on their way to the temporo-parieto-insular cortex. The brain is viewed from the right side. Cortex activation patterns shown at the top are PET (positron emission tomography) scans obtained during stimulation of the vestibular system on the right side. Red and yellow indicate activation, which occurs in the temporo-parieto-insular areas of both hemispheres. Unlike most other sensory systems, much of the vestibular activation is not visible on the outermost surface of the cortex but is found deeper in the brain, in the insular cortex. (Brain images from Dieterich and Brandt, 2008; courtesy of Marianne Dieterich.)

When the Vestibular System Goes Bad

We have learned that the vestibular system makes fundamental contributions to our sense of spatial orientation and also contributes to a number of reflexive responses. What happens when the vestibular system fails? Reflecting the widespread influence of the vestibular system, the bad news is that a lot of problems develop (Baloh and Halmagyi, 1996). Many patients develop

FIGURE 12.27 This button highlights how the symptoms of vestibular disorders could be misinterpreted.

spatial disorientation. Many experience imbalance. Many cannot see clearly unless they make an effort to hold their heads absolutely still. Many develop motion sickness that can lead to nausea or even vomiting. Some even develop cognitive problems. Because we are usually unaware of the vestibular system's contributions, it is possible to misinterpret the actions of people suffering from vestibular disorders (Figure 12.27).

The good news is that most patients partially adapt to the situation. For example, many patients quickly learn to curtail activities that lead to problems. This strategy is effective, but curtailing one's lifestyle is not an entirely satisfactory solution. Fortunately, in addition, most patients also learn to utilize other sensory information. As with the exquisite sense of hearing that is sometimes reported in blind patients, other sensory systems fill in to help reduce behavioral deficits caused by vestibular problems. This adaptation, coupled with physical rehabilitation and a curtailing of motion-related activities, yields an altered lifestyle that helps patients acclimate to their disability. Let's look at two illustrative vestibular disorders.

Mal de Debarquement Syndrome

Most travelers feel a little unbalanced after disembarking from a large boat following an extended cruise. This imbalance is sometimes accompanied by motion sickness and by swaying, rocking, or tilting perceptions. You may have experienced these sensations after spending just a few hours on a boat. After disembarking, as you lay in your bed, you might have felt the gentle rocking of the waves, even though you knew you were perfectly still. These symptoms are bothersome but typically dissipate within a few hours. It is generally believed that these perceptions are an aftereffect of adaptation. Specifically, you adapt to the rocking motion experienced while on the boat. This adaptation—"getting your sea legs"—is appropriate while you're on board the boat, but it is inappropriate once you're back on firm ground, leading to transient perceptions of disorientation, imbalance, and rocking that appear when you first disembark and then dissipate as you readapt to firm ground.

Relatively rarely, people are unable to readily readapt, and the condition sometimes leads to a clinical syndrome called mal de debarquement syndrome (meaning "disembarking sickness"). For these patients, the symptoms of spatial disorientation, imbalance, and rocking last a month or more after they disembark. In extreme cases, the symptoms can last for years and can be very debilitating. Why some individuals are unable to readapt to the normal situation of standing on firm ground remains a mystery.

Ménière's Syndrome

Imagine suddenly experiencing dizziness, imbalance, and spatial disorientation so severe that either you have to lie down (quickly!) or you fall down. Imagine that severe motion sickness ensues and leads to repeated vomiting. Now imagine that these symptoms can occur suddenly and more or less unexpectedly at any time. This is the plight experienced by some patients suffering from Ménière's syndrome, named after Prosper Ménière, the French physician who first described the syndrome in 1861.

Ménière's syndrome afflicts between one in 100 and one in 1000 people. It may strike at any age, but typically the syndrome first occurs in mid-adulthood. Other symptoms include tinnitus (an illusory ringing sound), hearing loss, and a feeling of pain or fullness in the ear—making this an inner-ear disorder and not just a vestibular disorder.

The vestibular symptoms of dizziness, imbalance, and disorientation are so debilitating that patients often are incapacitated when experiencing a Ménière's attack. Furthermore, the concern that these symptoms might return at any time can be terrifying; some patients become afraid to leave their homes even when they are symptom-free. Making matters worse, although the vestibular system is known to be the source for the spatial disorientation suffered, the specific cause of the symptoms remains elusive. While some think that excess fluid in the inner ear causes Ménière's syndrome, others think that several different inner-ear disorders yield this constellation of symptoms.

Treatments of the disease include medications to lower pressure in the inner ear, implanted devices that provide transtympanic micropressure pulses, and sometimes procedures that destroy the vestibular apparatus. Stop for a moment and imagine that! The transient Ménière's syndrome symptoms are so severe that patients (and their physicians) are willing to induce a permanent disability just to be rid of the symptoms. For those of us lucky enough to have never experienced severe vestibular problems, this provides a small hint at how disabling the symptoms can be when the vestibular system malfunctions, as well as a glimpse at the fundamental contributions provided by the vestibular system.

Summary

1. The vestibular organs are a set of sense organs located in the inner ear that sense head motion and gravity and contribute to our sense of spatial orientation.

2. The vestibular organs include three semicircular canals (horizontal, anterior, and posterior) that sense angular motion, and two otolith organs (utricle and saccule) that sense both gravity and linear acceleration.

3. Hair cells are the mechanoreceptors that convert both orientation with respect to gravity and head motion into signals that are sent to the brain.

4. The vestibular organs make a predominant contribution to our sense of spatial orientation, which includes three sensory modalities: linear motion, angular motion, and tilt. Direction and amplitude are qualities that define each of these three sensory modalities.

5. Our sense of spatial orientation results from a combination of information from multiple sensory systems. The vestibular and visual systems make predominant contributions to our sense of spatial orientation.

6. The vestibular system contributes to our sense of spatial orientation, but the brain processes the vestibular information to yield perceptions that differ substantially from the responses found on the afferent neurons.

7. We are exquisitely sensitive to head motion even in the dark, recognizing the directions of rotation, linear motion, and tilt at very low thresholds.

8. The vestibular system contributes to dynamic visual acuity by evoking compensatory vestibulo-ocular reflexes (VORs).

9. The vestibular system helps maintain balance via postural reflexes.

10. No area of the cortex exclusively devoted to processing vestibular information has been identified. Areas of the cortex that respond to vestibular stimuli also respond to visual and other sensory stimuli.

11. Vestibular problems are widespread, and treatments are limited. For Ménière's syndrome patients, for example, the symptoms may become so disabling that patients accept treatments that yield permanent disability just to be rid of the symptoms.

Refer to the
Sensation and Perception
Companion Website
sites.sinauer.com/wolfe3e
for activities, essays, study questions, and other study aids.

CHAPTER 13

Lia Cook, *Point of Touch: Bathsheba*, 1995

Touch

Having studied the perceptual systems for vision and hearing, you should recognize a number of questions that curious minds want asked and answered about any sense. In this chapter we consider the following questions regarding the sense of touch:

- What are the physical stimuli for touch? More precisely, what forms of energy lead to the sensation of being touched?
- What is touch good for? What might the evolutionary "niche" of this sensory modality be?
- What is the sensory apparatus for touch, and how do these structures change touch stimuli into neural signals?
- Which neurophysiological pathways connect touch receptors to higher-order perception and cognition in the brain?
- How do we use touch input to determine the identity (*what* tasks) and location (*where* tasks) of objects in the world?
- How does the sense of touch compare with and interact with other sensory modalities?

Let's start with the first two of these questions. By its most narrow definition, the term *touch* is used to refer to the sensations caused by mechanical displacements of the skin. These displacements occur when you are poked by your 4-year-old nephew, licked by your dog, or kissed by your significant other. They occur any time you grasp, wield, or otherwise make contact with an object. We will use the term *tactile* (the adjective form of *touch*) to refer to these mechanical interactions and will expand the definition of *touch* to include the perception of temperature changes (thermal sensation); the sensation of pain, which occurs when our body tissues are damaged (or potentially damaged) in some way; itchiness; and the internal sensations that inform us of the positions and movements of our limbs in space. Collectively, these internal sensations are known as **kinesthesis** when they arise from muscles, tendons, and joints; and they are part of a broader system known as **proprioception**, which includes the vestibular system as well (see Chapter 12). The technical term for all these senses put together is **somatosensation**.

It is difficult to conceive of our species surviving without a sense of touch. Pain serves as a sophisticated warning system that tells us when something might be internally wrong or when an external stimulus might be dangerous, enabling us to defend our bodies as quickly as possible (e.g., by rapidly moving away from the noxious stimulus). Temperature sensations enable us to seek or create a thermally safe environment. Mechanical sensations play an important role in our intimate sexual and reproductive activities, and they provide a powerful means of communicating our thoughts and emotions nonverbally.

kinesthesis Perception of the position and movement of our limbs in space.

proprioception Perception mediated by kinesthetic and vestibular receptors.

somatosensation Collectively, all sensory signals from the body.

FIGURE 13.1 Soapstone sculpture from Zimbabwe.

On a more fundamental level, touch is important because we can use it to identify and manipulate objects that cannot be seen or heard. Blindfold yourself for at least 10 minutes and try doing some routine tasks, like making a sandwich, getting dressed, or taking a shower. The first thing you will notice while doing this exercise is just how much our species normally relies on vision to inform us about the world around us. But you should also discover that touch can substitute for vision to a surprising degree: You probably won't have as much trouble distinguishing the peanut butter jar from the jelly jar as you might think. And if you pay attention, you will find that you don't actually use vision, or any sense other than touch, very much at all for some tasks (e.g., buttoning your shirt, brushing your teeth, opening that jar of peanut butter).

There is one more thing you may become acutely aware of during your experiment with the blindfold: Our eyes and ears can perceive signals from objects that are far from the body, but we must almost always be in direct contact with an object to perceive it by touch (exceptions to this rule include a jackhammer, whose vibrations on the street outside we can feel; and the sun, from which we feel warmth even though it is millions of miles away). Therefore, to use touch to learn about the world, we must act. If we want to know the weight of a beautiful soapstone sculpture like the one in Figure 13.1, we pick it up. We might also stroke it to feel its exquisite smoothness or press it to our forehead to feel its coolness. In sum, touch involves action, arguably to a greater degree than any of our other senses do.

Touch Physiology

The Skin and Its Tactile Receptors

The sites of our sensing equipment for vision, audition, olfaction, and gustation are all located in organs (the eyes, ears, nose, and mouth, respectively) that are more or less dedicated to sensory processing. Some other animals have analogous appendages: antennae. You might think that, for touch, humans do not have a readily apparent sense organ. In fact, the human sense of touch is housed in what is actually the largest and heaviest of the sense organs, the skin, which covers an area of approximately 1.8 square meters and weighs about 4 kilograms. Touch receptors are embedded all over the body, in both hairless and hairy skin, as well as within our mouths and our muscles, tendons, and joints.

Although the external quality of the skin varies across different parts of the body (it is thicker in some parts and thinner in others, smoother in some regions and coarser in others, and so on), most skin includes the basic substructures shown in Figure 13.2. The tactile receptors are embedded in both the outer layer, called the **epidermis**, and the underlying layer, known as the **dermis**. Just as the eye has its rods and three types of cones, the skin has multiple types of tactile receptors. These receptors form the basis for multiple "channels," specialized information-processing subsystems that each contribute to the overall sense of touch. For example, if we wrap our fingers around a cube of ice, different channels convey information about its temperature, its shape, and its texture.

We will discuss the receptors for these various channels in detail in the sections that follow (see also **Web Activity 13.1: Somatosensory Receptors**). In general, however, each type of receptor can be characterized by three attributes:

1. *Type of stimulation to which the receptor responds.* Receptors respond to different stimulus events—for example, to pressure, vibration, or temperature changes.

epidermis The outer of two major layers of skin.

dermis The inner of two major layers of skin, consisting of nutritive and connective tissues, within which lie the mechanoreceptors.

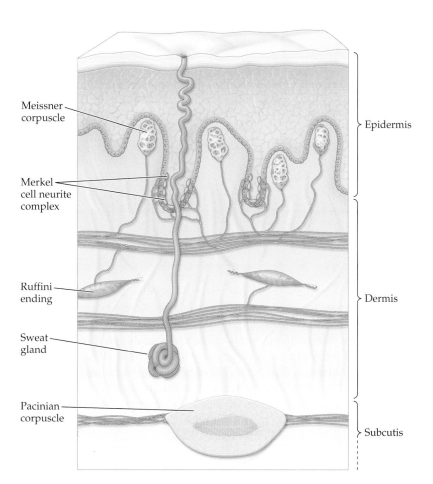

Meissner corpuscle

Merkel cell neurite complex

Ruffini ending

Sweat gland

Pacinian corpuscle

Epidermis

Dermis

Subcutis

FIGURE 13.2 A cross section of hairless skin of the human hand, schematically demonstrating the locations of the four types of mechanoreceptors—Meissner corpuscles, Merkel cell neurite complexes, Ruffini endings, and Pacinian corpuscles—and illustrating the two major layers of human skin. The subcutis, which underlies these outer two layers as shown here, is not usually included in the formal definition of "skin." (After R. S. Johansson and Vallbo, 1983.)

2. *Size of the receptive field.* Receptors are activated when stimulation is applied to a particular area of the body, which constitutes the receptors' *receptive field* (recall that the same term is used for the receptors of other sensory systems). The size of the receptive field is the extent of the body area that elicits a receptor response.

> FURTHER DISCUSSION of receptive fields as they relate to vision can be found in Chapter 2 on pages 44–46, and throughout Chapter 3.

3. *Rate of adaptation (fast versus slow).* A fast-adapting (FA) receptor responds with bursts of action potentials, first when its preferred stimulus is applied and then again when the stimulus is removed. It does not respond during the steady state between stimulus onset and offset. In contrast, a slowly adapting (SA) receptor remains active throughout the period during which the stimulus is in contact with its receptive field.

TACTILE RECEPTORS Tactile receptors are called **mechanoreceptors** because they respond to mechanical stimulation or pressure. A tactile receptor consists of a "nerve fiber" and an associated expanded ending. All tactile nerve fibers fall into a class called A-beta fibers, which have relatively wide diameters that permit very fast neural conduction. The four populations of tactile receptors that are found in the hairless skin on the palms are shown in Figure 13.2. (Note that there are also five major types of A-beta tactile receptors located in regions covered with hairy skin, such as the forearm. These mechanoreceptors and their associated afferent fibers have properties similar to those in hairless skin: two types are slowly adapting and three are fast adapting.) The tactile nerve fibers for the various types are assumed to terminate in different expanded endings. You may be surprised to learn that the specific kind of expanded

mechanoreceptor A sensory receptor that responds to mechanical stimulation (pressure, vibration, or movement).

TABLE 13.1 *Response characteristics of the four mechano-receptor populations*

Adaptation rate	Size of receptive field	
	Small	Large
Slow	SA I (Merkel)	SA II (Ruffini)
Fast	FA I (Meissner)	FA II (Pacinian)

Note: FA I = fast-adapting type I; FA II = fast-adapting type II; SA I = slowly adapting type I; SA II = slowly adapting type II. The terminal ending associated with each type of tactile nerve fiber is shown in parentheses.

Meissner corpuscle A specialized nerve ending associated with fast-adapting (FA I) fibers that have small receptive fields.

Merkel cell neurite complex A specialized nerve ending associated with slowly adapting (SA I) fibers that have small receptive fields.

Pacinian corpuscle A specialized nerve ending associated with fast-adapting (FA II) fibers that have large receptive fields.

Ruffini ending A specialized nerve ending associated with slowly adapting (SA II) fibers that have large receptive fields.

ending for each type of nerve fiber has provoked considerable controversy among tactile scientists for over a century now, because observing the physical connections directly has proved extremely difficult.

The expanded endings of the four different populations of tactile fibers in the hairless skin of the hand are named after the anatomists who first described them: **Meissner corpuscles**, **Merkel cell neurite complexes**, **Pacinian corpuscles**, and **Ruffini endings**. The endings of Meissner and Merkel receptors are located at the junction of the epidermis and dermis, whereas the Pacinian and Ruffini receptors are embedded more deeply in the dermis and underlying subcutaneous tissue. The fiber of a tactile mechanoreceptor extends all the way from its terminal to the dorsal root of the spinal cord, and it can sometimes be very long (stretching from the sole of your foot to your backbone, for example).

The four types of mechanoreceptors can be independently classified according to their adaptation rates and the sizes of their receptive fields, as measured from activity of the tactile nerve fibers. These two dimensions lead to a second set of labels for the mechanoreceptor types, listed in Table 13.1. Each type of tactile fiber is particularly sensitive to certain features of mechanical stimulation, rendering it suitable for particular types of functions, as shown in Table 13.2.

- SA I fibers respond best to steady downward pressure, fine spatial details, and very low frequency vibrations of less than about 5 Hz. They are especially important for texture and pattern perception. Some activities particularly dependent on this touch channel include reading Braille and determining the location and orientation of the

TABLE 13.2 *Mechanoreceptors: Feature sensitivity and associated function*

Mechanoreceptor population	Maximum feature sensitivity	Primary function(s)
SA I	Sustained pressure, very low frequency (< ~5 Hz)	Texture perception
	Spatial deformation	Pattern/form detection
SA II	Sustained downward pressure, lateral skin stretch, skin slip (low sensitivity to vibration across frequencies)	Finger position, stable grasp
FA I	Temporal changes in skin deformation (~5–50 Hz)	Low-frequency vibration detection
FA II	Temporal changes in skin deformation (~50–700 Hz)	High-frequency vibration detection

slot on the head of a screw that we can feel but not see. When a single SA I fiber is stimulated, people report feeling "pressure." These fibers are assumed to terminate in Merkel cell neurite complexes.

- SA II fibers in the skin (as well as in all fibrous tissues in the body) respond to sustained downward pressure, and particularly to lateral skin stretch, which occurs, for example, when we grasp an object. When you reach out for your coffee cup, the SA II fibers help determine when your fingers are shaped properly for picking up the cup. (Note that recent research has questioned whether the expanded terminals of the SA II fibers in the skin, the Ruffini endings, are as numerous as traditionally assumed.) When a single SA II fiber is stimulated, people experience no tactile sensation at all. Scientists have shown that for a stimulus to be detectable, more than a single SA II fiber must be stimulated. These fibers are assumed to terminate in Ruffini endings.

- FA I fibers respond best to low-frequency vibrations from about 5 to 50 Hz. If your coffee cup is heavier than you expected and begins to slip across your fingers, this motion across the skin will cause just such vibrations, and FA I fibers will help you correct your grip before your coffee spills all over you. When a lone SA I fiber is stimulated, people report a very localized sensation that they describe as "wobble" or "flutter." These fibers are assumed to terminate in Meissner corpuscles.

- FA II fibers respond best to high-frequency vibrations from about 50 to 700 Hz (the highest frequency tested to date). Such vibrations occur whenever an object first makes contact with the skin, as, for example, when a mosquito lands on your arm. Such vibrations are also generated when an object that you're holding contacts another object, so FA II fibers help you determine how hard you're tapping your pencil on your desk as you try to cram all this information into your brain. When a single FA II fiber is stimulated, people report a more diffuse sensation in the skin that corresponds to a "buzz." These fibers have been shown to terminate in Pacinian corpuscles.

Just as both rods and cones contribute to our perception of every individual visual stimulus, the four types of mechanoreceptors are always working together to inform us about every individual object we touch. K. O. Johnson (2002) gives the example of opening a door with a key. Feeling the shape of your key in your pocket requires the SA I (and maybe also the FA I) channel. Shaping your fingers to grasp the key involves the SA II channel. As you insert the key into the lock, your grip force increases so that the key does not slip, thanks to your FA I channel. Finally, your FA II channel tells you when the key has hit the end of the keyhole.

KINESTHETIC RECEPTORS   In addition to the tactile mechanoreceptors in the skin, yet other types of mechanoreceptors lie within muscles, tendons, and joints. These are collectively referred to as **kinesthetic** receptors, and they play an important role in sensing where our limbs are and what kinds of movements we're making (Clark and Horch, 1986; L. A. Jones, 1999). The angle formed by a limb at a joint is perceived primarily through muscle receptors called **muscle spindles** (Figure 13.3), which convey the rate at which the muscle fibers are changing in length. Receptors in the tendons provide signals about the tension in muscles attached to the tendons, and receptors directly in the joints themselves come into play particularly when a joint is bent to an extreme angle.

kinesthetic Referring to perception involving sensory mechanoreceptors in muscles, tendons, and joints.

muscle spindle A sensory receptor located in a muscle that senses its tension.

FIGURE 13.3 A muscle spindle embedded in main (extrafusal) muscle fibers contains inner (intrafusal) fibers. When the inner fibers contract, a sensory response from the spindle is sent back to the central nervous system, conveying information about muscle length and thus regulating muscle tension.

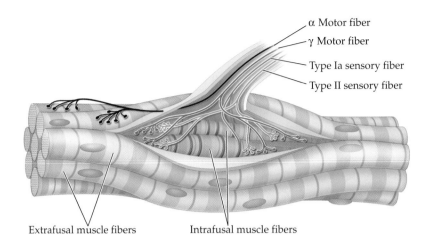

α Motor fiber
γ Motor fiber
Type Ia sensory fiber
Type II sensory fiber

Extrafusal muscle fibers   Intrafusal muscle fibers

The importance of kinesthetic receptors is graphically illustrated by the striking case of a neurological patient named Ian Waterman (read *Pride and a Daily Marathon* [1991] by Jonathan Cole for more about this interesting individual). The cutaneous nerves that connected Waterman's kinesthetic and other mechanoreceptors to his brain were destroyed by a viral infection when he was 19 years old. Lacking kinesthetic senses, Waterman is now completely dependent on vision to tell him about the positions of his limbs in space. If the lights are turned off, he cannot tie his shoes, walk up or down stairs, or even clap his hands, because he has no idea where his hands and feet are! Caught in an elevator when the lights went out, he was unable to remain standing and could not rise again until the illumination returned. (For additional details about Waterman's challenges, and the amazing degree to which he has compensated for his lack of kinesthetic receptors, see **Web Essay 13.1: Living without Kinesthesis**.)

THERMORECEPTORS **Thermoreceptors** located in both the epidermal and dermal layers of the skin (see Figure 13.2) inform us about changes in skin temperature. There are two distinct populations of thermoreceptors (**Figure 13.4**): **Warmth fibers** fire when the temperature of the skin surrounding the fibers rises. **Cold fibers** (which outnumber warmth fibers by a ratio of about 30:1) fire in response to decreases in skin temperature.

Our bodies are constantly working to regulate their internal temperature, so under normal conditions the skin is kept between 30°C and 36°C (86°F and 96°F), and neither cold nor warmth fibers respond much while skin temperature remains within this range. If you bundle up in your long underwear and snowsuit but then sit inside in front of the fire, your skin temperature will probably rise above 36°C, and your warmth fibers will begin to fire. If you then take the snowsuit off and walk out into the snow, your skin temperature will rapidly begin to fall, and as soon as it goes below 30°C, your cold receptors will start firing.

Thermoreceptors also kick into gear when we make contact with an object that is warmer or colder than our skin. Objects in the environment are typically cooler than 30°C, so it is usually the cold fibers that tell us about the object. For example, steel conducts heat more efficiently than stone. Your cold fibers will thus fire less rapidly and for a shorter period of time when you touch a steel object than when you touch a stone object (because the steel object will warm more quickly to match your skin temperature). If you've had prior experience with steel and stone, you can interpret the thermoreceptor responses to make this distinction.

thermoreceptor A sensory receptor that signals information about changes in skin temperature.

warmth fiber A sensory nerve fiber that fires when skin temperature increases.

cold fiber A sensory nerve fiber that fires when skin temperature decreases.

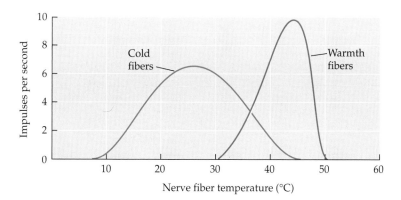

FIGURE 13.4 Thermal receptivity functions, showing the response of warmth and cold fibers to different temperatures. (After Guyton, 1991.)

NOCICEPTORS   Pain is the realm of touch that has the dubious honor of being home to the sensations we like the least. We may find some visual stimuli revolting and some olfactory or gustatory stimuli disgusting, but of all the sensations, it is pain that we take the most drastic actions to avoid. Pain begins with signals from **nociceptors**, touch receptors that have bare nerve endings and that respond to various forms of tissue damage or to stimuli that have the potential to damage tissue (including extreme skin temperatures lower than 15°C or higher than 45°C). (Pain receptors are also found in internal organs, but we will confine this discussion to touch.)

Nociceptors can be divided into two types by their nerve fibers, for which no specialized endings have been found: **A-delta fibers** respond primarily to strong pressure or heat and are myelinated, so they can conduct signals very rapidly. **C fibers** are unmyelinated and respond to intense stimulation of various sorts: pressure, heat or cold, or noxious chemicals. Both types of pain fibers are smaller in diameter than those coming from non-nociceptive mechanoreceptors in the skin—the wider-diameter fibers known as type *A-beta*. Many painful events seem to occur in two stages: a quick sharp burst of pain followed by a throbbing sensation. These two stages may reflect the onset of signals first from the A-delta fibers and then from the C fibers (Price et al., 1977).

It might seem that pain perception has no upside, but consider what would happen if we had no nociceptors. We wouldn't be able to sense dangerously sharp or hot objects. Lacking alarms, we might soon lack fingers! Some diseases, such as Hansen's disease (leprosy) and diabetes, are characterized by the loss of pain sensation and provide real-life examples of the consequences. The case of "Miss C," reported by Melzack and Wall (1988), shows what can happen to people born with insensitivity to pain. Not only did Miss C lack pain sensation, but she did not sneeze, cough, gag, or protect her eyes reflexively. She suffered childhood injuries from burning herself on a radiator and biting her tongue while chewing food. As an adult, she developed problems in her joints that were attributed to lack of discomfort, for example, from standing too long in the same position. She died at age 29 from infections that could probably have been prevented in someone who was alerted to injury by painful sensations.

From Skin to Brain

Because the receptors for sights, sounds, tastes, and smells are all located in the skull, the pathways that deliver information from these receptors to the brain are fairly short. Touch messages, on the other hand, must travel as far as 2 meters to get from the skin and muscles of the feet to the brain. To cross this distance, the information must move up through the spinal cord. Initially the axons of various tactile receptors are combined into single nerve trunks, in much the same way that retinal ganglion axons converge in the optic nerve

nociceptor A sensory receptor that transmits information about noxious (painful) stimulation that causes damage or potential damage to the skin.

A-delta fiber An intermediate-sized, myelinated sensory nerve fiber that transmits pain and temperature signals.

C fiber A narrow-diameter, unmyelinated sensory nerve fiber that transmits pain and temperature signals.

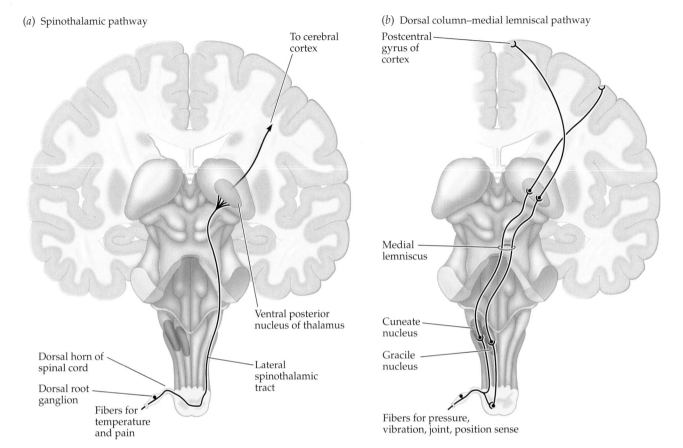

(a) Spinothalamic pathway

To cerebral cortex

Ventral posterior nucleus of thalamus

Dorsal horn of spinal cord

Dorsal root ganglion

Fibers for temperature and pain

Lateral spinothalamic tract

(b) Dorsal column–medial lemniscal pathway

Postcentral gyrus of cortex

Medial lemniscus

Cuneate nucleus

Gracile nucleus

Fibers for pressure, vibration, joint, position sense

FIGURE 13.5 Pathways from skin to cortex. (a) Spinothalamic pathway. (b) Dorsal column–medial lemniscal pathway. (After Levine, 2000.)

spinothalamic pathway The route from the spinal cord to the brain that carries most of the information about skin temperature and pain.

dorsal column–medial lemniscal (DCML) pathway The route from the spinal cord to the brain that carries signals from skin, muscles, tendons, and joints.

(see Chapter 2) and cochlear hair cells converge in the auditory nerve (see Chapter 9).

Right from the start, though, we see two major differences between the visual and auditory pathways and the pathways for touch. First, whereas there are only two optic nerves and two auditory nerves, there are a number of somatosensory nerve trunks, arising in the hands, arms, feet, legs, and other areas of the skin. Second, axons in the optic and auditory nerves go directly to the brain, whereas axons in the older nerve trunks, which we discuss next, synapse first in the spinal cord.

Once in the spinal cord, touch information proceeds upward toward the brain via two major pathways, as shown in **Figure 13.5**. The evolutionarily older **spinothalamic pathway** (Figure 13.5a) is the slower of the two and carries most of the information from thermoreceptors and nociceptors. This pathway includes a number of synapses within the spinal cord, thus slowing conduction while providing a mechanism for inhibiting pain perception when necessary, as will be discussed shortly. The **dorsal column–medial lemniscal (DCML) pathway** (Figure 13.5b) includes wider-diameter axons and fewer synapses and therefore conveys information more quickly to the brain. Tactile and kinesthetic information carried along this pathway is used for planning and executing rapid movements, where quick feedback is a must.

Neurons in the DCML pathway first synapse in the cuneate and gracile nuclei, near the base of the brain (see Figure 13.5b). Activity is then passed on to neurons that synapse in the ventral posterior nucleus of the thalamus. Recall from Chapters 3 and 9 that the visual and auditory pathways also pass through the thalamus, each synapsing in its own modality-specific nucleus. Because this portion of the brain is largely shut down when we are asleep, the brain does not register (and therefore does not attempt to respond to) the

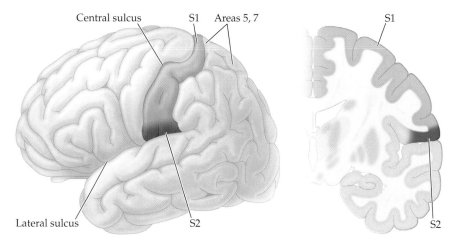

FIGURE 13.6 Primary somatosensory receiving areas in the brain. S1 includes Brodmann areas 1, 2, 3a, and 3b. Areas 5 and 7 are immediately posterior to S1. S2 lies within the lateral sulcus.

relatively gentle touch sensations that occur, for example, when we roll over in our sleep.

From the thalamus, much of the touch information is carried up to the cortex (**Figure 13.6**) into **somatosensory area 1** (**S1**), located in the parietal lobe just behind the postcentral gyrus. S1 is analogous to V1 in vision (see Chapter 3). Neurons in S1 communicate with **somatosensory area 2** (**S2**), which lies in the upper bank of the lateral sulcus, and with other cortical areas. The motor areas of the cortex, which control movements of body parts, are located just in front of the central sulcus. This adjacency enhances communication between the somatosensory and motor control systems.

Touch sensations that result from stimulation of the skin are spatially represented in area S1, and to some extent beyond, **somatotopically**. Somatotopy is analogous to the topographical spatial representation of events on the retina found in vision (see Chapter 3); adjacent areas on the skin are ultimately connected to adjacent areas in the brain (**Figure 13.7***a*). As a result, the somatosensory

somatosensory area 1 (S1) The primary receiving area for touch in the cortex.

somatosensory area 2 (S2) The secondary receiving area for touch in the cortex.

somatotopic Spatially mapped in the somatosensory cortex in correspondence to spatial events on the skin.

FIGURE 13.7 The sensory homunculus, showing brain regions that respond to stimulation of different parts of the body. (*a*) Multiple maps exist in primary and secondary somatosensory areas, three of which are shown within S1 and one within S2. (*b*) A schematic of the relative distribution of body parts in S1, as originally derived by Penfield and Rasmussen (1950).

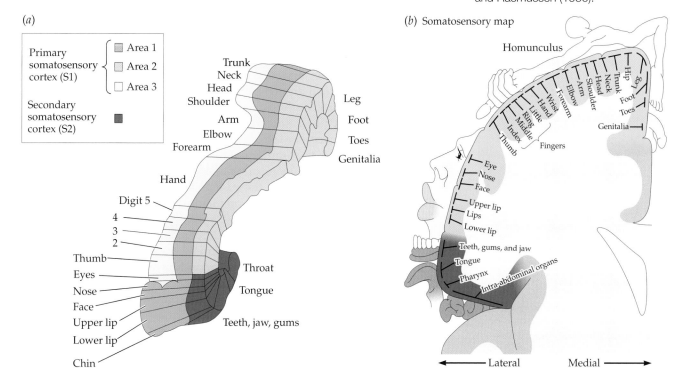

homunculus A maplike representation of regions of the body in the brain.

phantom limb Sensation perceived from a physically amputated limb of the body.

cortex is organized into a spatial map (or as we see below, multiple maps) of the layout of the skin. Each map has been called a sensory **homunculus** (plural *homunculi*) (Figure 13.7b), and actually has a twin homunculus because there are corresponding spatial maps in the left and right hemispheres.

The sensory homunculus is derived largely from the work of Canadian neurosurgeon Wilder Penfield, who charted the somatotopic map with the aid of patients undergoing brain surgery to alleviate epilepsy. Because there are no pain receptors in the brain, the patients did not need to be anesthetized and could remain responsive. During the operation, Dr. Penfield systematically stimulated different parts of a patient's somatosensory cortex with an electrode. As the probe was moved from one location in S1 to another, the patient reported feeling sensations in the arms, legs, face, and so on. The correspondence between the stimulation and the sensation gave rise to a map of the body in the brain (see **Web Activity 13.2: The Sensory Homunculus**). In fact, the brain contains multiple sensory maps of the body. Separate maps are now known to exist in the different subareas of S1, and additional maps exist in secondary areas, as shown in Figure 13.7a.

Like the retinotopic map in area V1 (see Figure 3.14), Penfield's somatotopic map in S1 is distorted. The thumb, for example, grabs a big piece of real estate relative to its size. In contrast, sensations from the leg are processed in a relatively small portion of S1. In the visual system, the foveal area is overrepresented in V1 (cortical magnification; see Chapter 3) because there are many more photoreceptors in the fovea than in peripheral parts of the retina. Similarly, a larger chunk of S1 is dedicated to processing information from the lips and the fingers than from the neck because tactile receptors are much more heavily concentrated in the lips than they are in the neck. The relatively tight correspondence between body parts and areas of S1 can have unfortunate side effects in cases of limb amputation. If an amputee's left arm is missing, obviously no mechanoreceptors are sending touch signals from that arm. However, sporadic activity can continue in the area of the amputee's right S1 corresponding to the arm, leading to the perception of a **phantom limb**. At times, patients may perceive their phantom limbs to be in uncomfortable positions, leading to persistent (and very real) pain.

The psychologist Vilayanur Ramachandran made the astonishing observation that amputees often report feeling sensations in their phantom arms and hands when their faces or remaining limbs are touched (**Figure 13.8**). The source of this somatosensory confusion can be traced to an idiosyncrasy in the homunculus. Note in Figure 13.7 that the area responding to the face is located (somewhat arbitrarily) adjacent to the area responding to the hand and arm. Apparently the hand and arm areas of S1 are, to some extent, "invaded" by neurons carrying information from touch receptors in the face. However, other parts of the brain listening to the hand and arm areas are not fully aware of these altered connections, and therefore they attribute activity in these areas to stimulation from the missing limb. (You can read more about Ramachandran's fascinating studies on phantom limbs in **Web Essay 13.2: Phantom Limbs.**)

Projections from S1 form the basis for further analysis of objects and surfaces by the cortex of the brain. The results of some recent studies suggest that, like vision (see Chapter 4), the sense of touch may show a division between *what* and *where* systems in higher cortical centers. A patient studied by Reed, Caselli, and Farah (1996) showed an impairment in her ability to recognize objects by touch (*what*), but she showed no deficit in her spatial ability (*where*). Another patient could locate and manipulate objects by touch without recognizing them (Rossetti, Rode, and Boisson, 1995). Activation of the brain, observed with fMRI (see Chapter 1), has been found in different areas, depending on

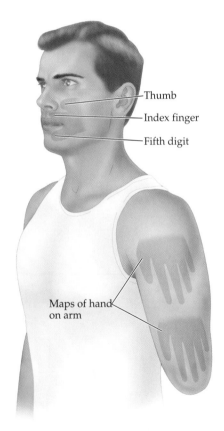

Thumb

Index finger

Fifth digit

Maps of hand on arm

FIGURE 13.8 Phantom limbs may appear on the face and stump subsequent to amputation. Amputees report feeling the amputated hand when their face or remaining limbs are stimulated. (After V. S. Ramachandran, 1993.)

whether the task is to locate an object or to recognize it tactually. And, as in vision, there is relatively more dorsal activation for locating objects and more ventral activation for recognizing objects (Reed, Klatzky, and Halgren, 2005; Reed, Shoham, and Halgren, 2004). You can learn more about the *what* versus *where* systems for touch by tapping into a lively debate on this topic among scientists interested in the neural circuitry that contributes to object processing (see Dijkerman and de Haan, 2007).

Lest you conclude that the neural organization of our brains for touch is permanent and unchanging, consider an experiment performed by Pascual-Leone and Hamilton (2001). These neuroscientists deprived normal, sighted volunteers of visual stimulation by having them wear a blindfold for 5 days. On each day the volunteers participated in an fMRI study during which pairs of Braille patterns were presented to the right index finger. Subjects were required to judge whether the two patterns within each pair were the same or different. Brain imaging found that on the first day, the Braille task activated only area S1 on the left side of the brain (which, you will recall, is activated by touching the right side of the body). But as the days progressed, the amount of activation in S1 declined while increasing in V1. Apparently area V1, which we think of as dedicated to vision, took over processing the spatial patterns introduced through the sense of touch. This change in V1 was transient: removing the blindfold resulted in a full return to what had been neurally observed before blindfolding.

Such results reveal the remarkable **neural plasticity** of the somatosensory system. Plasticity is a recurring theme in sensory systems. We saw something very similar at the end of Chapter 3 in the discussion of visual development and strabismus, in which abnormal experience alters the wiring of the visual system. Note that the example we're discussing here shows that plasticity is a property of the adult brain and is not limited to the immature nervous system.

The pathways from the skin to the brain tell just one part of the story of the transmission of signals in touch. Downward pathways from the brain can alter the sensations that stimulating the periphery produces. Some of the most surprising effects of these downward pathways relate to the feeling of pain, which we discuss next.

Pain

We tend to think of pain as an inevitable consequence of stress on or damage to our bodies, flowing from sensory levels to the conscious feeling of "ouch." The scientific study of pain, however, reveals it to be a highly subjective state with distinguishable components. What we think of as pain arises at multiple levels—sensory, emotional, and cognitive (Price, 2000)—which interact to create a conscious experience.

MULTIPLE LEVELS OF PAIN Pain sensations are triggered by the nociceptors (described earlier in this chapter). Neurons carrying nociceptive signals arrive at the spinal cord in an area called the **substantia gelatinosa** of the **dorsal horn**. Neurons there receive information *from* the brain, and they form synapses with the neurons that are conveying sensory information from nociceptors *to* the brain (see Figure 13.5). According to the very influential **gate control theory** (Melzack and Wall, 1988) (**Figure 13.9**), the bottom-up pain signals from the nociceptors can be blocked via a feedback circuit located in the dorsal horn. When these gate neurons send excitatory signals, the sensory information is allowed to go through, but inhibitory signals from the gate neurons cancel transmission to the brain. The results of these interactions at the spinal cord are transmitted to somatosensory areas S1 and S2.

neural plasticity The ability of neural circuits to undergo changes in function or organization as a result of previous activity.

substantia gelatinosa A jellylike region of interconnecting neurons in the dorsal horn of the spinal cord.

dorsal horn A region at the rear of the spinal cord that receives inputs from receptors in the skin.

gate control theory A description of the pain-transmitting system that incorporates modulating signals from the brain.

FIGURE 13.9 The gate control theory of Melzack and Wall (1988). Pain signals transmitted to the brain are moderated by activity in the substantia gelatinosa (SG) located in the dorsal horn of the spinal cord. The orange and green circles represent SG signals that decrease and increase pain, respectively, by their inhibitory and excitatory connections with transmission (T) cells. The transmission cells combine pain signals from the small-diameter fibers with signals inhibiting pain produced by stimulation of the large-diameter fibers. Direct excitatory pathways from both types of fibers are also found outside of the SG. As with the large-diameter fibers, the central control excites mechanisms in the SG that inhibit the activation of transmission cells, thus decreasing the pain response.

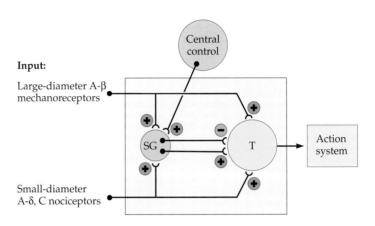

The signals arising at S1 and S2 don't tell the whole story, however. We have known for some time that these areas are responsible for the sensory aspects of pain, but researchers have used newer methods to identify other areas of the brain that correspond to the emotional aspects of painful experiences. In one study (Rainville et al., 1997) (**Figure 13.10**), participants were hypnotized and their hands were placed in lukewarm or very hot water (activating thermal nociceptors). The participants were sometimes told that the unpleasantness from the water was increasing or decreasing, and their brains were imaged during these periods by positron emission tomography (PET; see Chapter 1). The primary sensory areas of the cortex—S1 and S2—were activated by the hot water, but the suggestion of greater unpleasantness did not increase their response relative to the suggestion of decreased unpleasantness. In contrast, another area, the **anterior cingulate cortex** (**ACC**), did respond differentially to the two hypnotic suggestions, by increasing or decreasing its activity according to the suggestion of increased or decreased unpleasantness. The researchers concluded that the ACC processes raw sensory data from S1 and S2 in such a way as to produce an emotional response.

At a higher level still, pain can produce what Price (2000) called "secondary pain affect," which reflects the influence of cognition. Secondary affect is the emotional response associated with long-term suffering that occurs when

anterior cingulate cortex (ACC) A region of the brain associated with the perceived unpleasantness of a pain sensation.

FIGURE 13.10 PET signals showing the effect of hypnosis on the brain, as observed by Rainville et al. (1997). (a) Primary somatosensory cortex (S1) was not affected by the suggested unpleasantness of pain (high on the left, low on the right). (b) The anterior cingulate cortex (ACC, circled), however, showed significantly different activation, depending on suggested unpleasantness.

painful events are imagined or remembered. For example, cancer patients who face a second round of chemotherapy may remember the first and dread what is forthcoming. This component of pain is associated with the **prefrontal cortex**, an area concerned with cognition and executive control.

It may seem odd to associate pain with laughter, but at least some of the response people have to tickling seems to depend on nociceptors (Zotterman, 1939). And, just as signals from the brain can control pain perception, they appear to come into play when we try to tickle ourselves. Self-induced tickling not only produces less laughter; it also produces less activity in the somatosensory cortex, because of canceling signals from other brain areas that know where the tickling stimulation came from (S.-J. Blakemore, Wolpert, and Frith, 1998).

Some people may claim that itchiness is as great a pain as pain itself. In one extreme case, Mary Ellen Nilsen, over a period of a year after experiencing an outbreak of shingles (the same virus that causes chicken pox), scratched her scalp so intensively that she broke through the bone and damaged brain tissue. The issue of whether pain and itch have distinct neural pathways has been an elusive one, but recent work indicates that in mice at least, distinct neurons in the spinal cord lead to pain and itch sensations (Sun et al., 2009). Elimination of the itch neurons led to mice that didn't scratch, even when injected with stuff that drove normal mice into scratching frenzies. The animals' response to pain, in contrast, was unaffected. As for scratching, despite what you may have been told about "making it worse," it beneficially decreases activation at itch sites in the spinal cord and in the anterior cingulate, the site of emotional pain (S. Davidson et al., 2009).

MODERATING PAIN Pain experiences are the complex result of sensory signals interacting with many other factors that have moderating effects. Damping of pain sensations (without losing consciousness) is called **analgesia**. Responses to noxious stimulation can be affected by analgesic drugs, of course, but perhaps more surprising are the attenuating effects of anticipation, religious belief, prior experience, or excitement. Studies also highlight the importance of interpersonal and broader social influences on the emotional component of pain.

At the level of the spinal cord, the gate neurons that attenuate pain can be activated by "counterirritation" or "diffuse noxious inhibitory control"—extreme pressure, cold, or other noxious stimulation applied to another site distant from the source of the pain. For example, pain from electrically stimulating a tooth can be reduced by noxious stimulation of the hand (Motohashi and Umino, 2001). It appears that ascending signals from the counterirritation reach the brain stem and initiate a new set of signals that are sent back down to the pain-blocking gate in the spinal cord (Rollman, 1991).

A different, and certainly more pleasant, way of modulating pain is to use relatively benign counterstimulation—for example, rubbing the skin near a mosquito bite. This effect results from the stimulation of fibers other than the nociceptors and can be produced by interactions between neurons within the spinal cord.

There are many stories of soldiers in battle who did not feel painful wounds until the stress was over. The analgesic effect in such cases is probably caused by **endogenous opiates**, chemicals released by the body that block the release or uptake of neurotransmitters necessary to transmit pain sensations to the brain. Differences between individuals with respect to pain responsiveness (that is, pain "thresholds") may reflect differences in their baseline levels of these substances. Externally produced substances such as morphine, heroin, and codeine are similar in chemical structure to these endogenous opiates, and thus they have similar analgesic effects. Other drugs, such as acetaminophen

prefrontal cortex A region of the brain concerned with cognition and executive control.

analgesia Decreasing pain sensation during conscious experience.

endogenous opiate A chemical released by the body that blocks the release or uptake of neurotransmitters necessary to transmit pain sensations to the brain.

placebo effect Decreasing pain sensation when people think they're taking an analgesic drug but actually are not.

hyperalgesia An increased or heightened response to a normally painful stimulus.

and ibuprofen, alleviate pain at its source, by counteracting chemicals that would otherwise start the nociceptors firing.

Endogenous opiates may be responsible for **placebo effects**, the reduction of pain when people think they're taking an analgesic drug but are not actually doing so. The subjective reduction of pain by placebos is well documented, and recently, imaging of the spinal cord with functional MRI revealed that placebos actually inhibit nociceptive processing at the dorsal horn of the spinal cord, the site associated with gate control (Eippert et al., 2009).

Research has shown that contact with those we love reduces brain activation in areas that regulate our emotions and bodily arousal responses to the threat of painful stimulation. In an fMRI study by Coan, Schaefer, and Davidson (2006), women experienced the threat of electric shock while holding their husband's hand, the hand of a male with whom they were unacquainted, or no hand at all. The neural pain response was reduced by touching another's hand, and this effect increased with the closeness of the relationship. Broader social influences on pain have also been found. For example, reports of painful strains of the arm from tasks requiring repetitive motion spread rapidly in Australia during the 1980s—like a contagious disease—but they were communicated by workers who did nothing more than talk to one another about their experiences. The cross talk could have had multiple effects in this example, both heightening people's sensitivity to their suffering and providing a name for it.

PAIN SENSITIZATION   Nociceptors provide a signal when there is impending or ongoing damage to the body's tissue. This is called "nociceptive" pain. Once damage has occurred, the site can become more sensitive, triggering the feeling of pain more readily than before. This experience is **hyperalgesia** and reflects an increased or heightened response to a normally painful stimulus. The resulting pain is called *inflammatory*, and the heightened pain sensitivity usually goes away once the tissue heals.

Pain can also arise in the absence of immediate trauma, because of damage to or dysfunction of the nervous system. The resulting pain is called *neuropathic*. Some neuropathic pain reflects changes in the sensory fibers at the skin that do not normally produce pain but now become pain inducers (a phenomenon known as allodynia); other neuropathic pain arises from changes in the dorsal horn of the spinal cord. Changes at the level of the skin are called *peripheral*, and those at the level of the spinal cord are called *central*. The mechanisms by which neuropathic pain arises are increasingly understood at the cellular and molecular levels (Scholz and Woolf, 2002); an important implication of this research is that no single medication will alleviate all types of pain.

Pleasant Touch

The traditional way of classifying different bodily sensations, introduced at the beginning of this chapter, is in terms of tactile, thermal, pain, and itch experiences. Collectively, these classic sensations are known as *discriminative touch*. More recently, however, scientists uncovered a previously unknown fifth component that they named "pleasant" or "emotional" touch (McGlone et al., 2007). They argue that the emotional properties of nonpainful bodily touch are mediated in large part by a class of unmyelinated (and thus, slower) peripheral C fibers known as *C tactile afferents* (CT afferents for short) that are not related to either pain or itch. This type of C fiber, which differs from the C fiber associated with pain, seems to prefer mechanical stimulation in the form of slowly moving, lightly applied forces (like petting!).

Researchers have begun to think that CT afferents are located only in hairy skin, because a number of studies that have looked for them in hairless skin (e.g., palms and soles of the feet) have been unable to find any. It has been suggested, therefore, that these mechanical units form part of a neural subsystem that provides or supports emotional, hormonal, and behavioral responses to skin-to-skin contact with conspecifics, such as being stroked on the back of the hand, arm, or face by a girlfriend or boyfriend.

Pleasant touch and discriminative touch also are processed in different parts of the brain (S. T. Francis et al., 1999). Whereas primary somatosensory cortex is activated by the physical aspects of the stimulus (e.g., by the pressure it produces on the skin or a change in skin temperature), an area of the frontal lobes known to be involved in emotion—the orbitofrontal cortex—is activated by the pleasant qualities of the mechanical stimulation. The orbitofrontal cortex is activated by both painful and pleasant touch, suggesting that this region of the brain represents the emotional features of cutaneous stimulation, both rewarding and punitive (Rolls et al., 2003). There are indications that pleasant bodily contact promotes endorphin and oxytocin responses, which contribute to feelings of well-being, confidence, and calmness. Fearfulness can be reduced in rats by tactile stimulation such as stroking with a brush, and postnatal touch in premature human infants has similarly been found to have beneficial effects (T. M. Field et al., 1986).

> **FURTHER DISCUSSION** of the orbitofrontal cortex in the context of olfaction and taste can be found in Chapters 14 and 15, respectively.

Tactile Sensitivity and Acuity

Now that we've covered the physiological substrate of the touch system, we can turn to the psychological and psychophysical aspects. How sensitive are we to mechanical stimulation? What are the limits on tactile acuity in space and time? Put a bit differently, what are the smallest details that we can feel?

How Sensitive Are We to Mechanical Pressure?

To measure the minimum pressure that can be reliably sensed by a particular region of skin, we need a way to present well-defined amounts of pressure over and over again. In the nineteenth century, Max von Frey (1852–1932) developed an elegant and simple way to do this using carefully calibrated stimuli, including horse and human hairs. Modern researchers typically use nylon monofilaments (e.g., fishing lines) of varying diameters. The smaller the diameter, the less force the line applies to the skin before it buckles.

To replicate von Frey's method yourself, touch different parts of your skin with a hair from your head and a bristle from a hairbrush to reveal the relative skin sensitivity to these two different forces. With the thinner hair, you will probably find that you can feel it on the more sensitive areas, such as your lips and perhaps some parts of your hand. You probably will not feel it pushing into your thigh or upper arm. With the bristle, however, you should discover that your skin is sensitive to mechanical pressure all over, but not uniformly so. For example, if you explore the skin on the back of your hand, you should be able to convince yourself that there are spots of greater and lesser sensitivity (Geldard, 1972).

Data from a more controlled pressure sensitivity study reveal that for both men and women, thresholds vary across different sites of the body (a high threshold means that that part of the body is less sensitive). In general, tactile pressure sensitivity is highest on the face, followed by the trunk and upper extremities (arms and fingers) and then the lower extremities (thigh,

FIGURE 13.11 Results of an experiment measuring the minimal (threshold) amplitude of vibration at the fingertip that people can detect, as a function of the vibratory frequency. As labeled on the y-axis, the threshold is measured on a decibel scale relative to a reference vibration. The experimentally obtained function, portrayed by the solid line, is believed to reflect the contribution of three different mechanoreceptor populations (SA I, FA I, and FA II), which are shown as different colored segments. Each population is assumed to control the threshold in the limited frequency range where it is most sensitive. For comparison, the dashed lines in each color show the vibratory threshold for the corresponding mechanoreceptor population across the entire range of frequencies tested. These lines cannot be obtained from the experiment portrayed here, but rather are based on the results of neurophysiological studies of single-unit mechanoreceptor responses. Researchers have proposed that SA I units mediate our threshold for vibrations below about 5 Hz; FA I fibers, for frequencies from about 5 to 50 Hz; and FA II units, for frequencies above about 50 Hz. (After Löfvenberg and Johansson, 1984.)

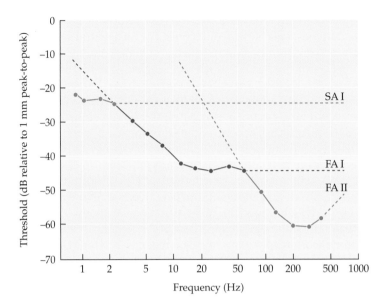

calf, and foot) (Weinstein, 1968). The pattern for males and females is very similar, except that women tend to be more sensitive to pressure than men. Sensitivity to temperature changes, as well as to pain, also varies markedly as a function of body site.

Another approach to measuring sensitivity is to ask what the smallest raised element is that we can feel as an otherwise completely smooth surface is passed over the skin. Like the storied princess who detected a pea under a pile of mattresses, we appear to be very sensitive to the pressure difference caused by a raised dot on a smooth surface. At a criterion of 75% detection, people can detect a dot only 1 micrometer (μm) high—that's a millionth of a meter, or 39 millionths of an inch! The dot seems to trigger detection by the FA I receptors, which also help us detect and correct for an object slipping within our grasp. Even more impressive, when a texture that is made of many raised dots only a very small fraction of a micrometer high moves across the skin, the resulting vibrations trigger the FA II receptors deep within the skin, enabling us to distinguish the dot from a perfectly smooth surface (LaMotte and Srinivasan, 1991).

People are also sensitive to changes in pressure over time—that is, to tactile vibration. **Figure 13.11** shows absolute vibratory threshold (the minimum amount that a vibrating stimulus displaces the skin in order to be detected) as a function of the frequency presented to the fingertip (Löfvenberg and Johansson, 1984). In this study, people could detect the presence of vibrations from below about 5 hertz (Hz; 5 cycles in 1 second) up to about 400 Hz, the highest frequency that was tested. Other studies have confirmed that people can detect vibrations up to 700 Hz (Verrillo, 1963), the highest frequency tested to date.

Although people can detect vibrations over a wide frequency range, they are not equally sensitive to all frequencies, as Figure 13.11 clearly shows. Scientists now believe that measurement of the threshold at a particular frequency of vibration depends only on the mechanoreceptor population that is most sensitive to that frequency. Since the various mechanoreceptor populations are sensitive to different frequencies, the overall psychophysical function for the detection of vibration reflects the contributions of different mechanoreceptor populations at different regions along it. Take a look at the corresponding vibration sensitivities of SA I, FA I, and FA II mechanoreceptor populations from less than 5 to 400 Hz, also shown in Figure 13.11. The SA I units would seem to mediate our absolute vibratory thresholds for frequencies below about 5 Hz; the FA I fibers, for frequencies from about 5 to 50 Hz; and the FA II units, for frequencies above about 50 Hz.

How Finely Can We Resolve Spatial Details?

Pressure detection is the tactile equivalent of detecting a spot of light, where the basic question is whether you can see or feel anything at all. For the tactile equivalent of visual acuity (can you make out the pattern of what you see or feel?), try measuring your **two-point touch threshold**. As the name suggests, this is the smallest separation at which we can tell that we're being touched by two points and not just one. This experiment is best done with a partner, although it will work to some degree if you test yourself. A compass (the kind that draws circles) is a useful stimulator, but you can use anything that enables you to vary the separation between two points, such as a bent paper clip. Pick one of your own or your partner's body regions and see if you can distinguish between a single point and two points. Then repeat the procedure with different separations of the two points (e.g., 0.5, 2, and 4 centimeters [cm]) and at different places on the skin (Figure 13.12).

Like sensitivity to pressure, spatial acuity varies across the body, but the extremities (fingertips, face, and toes) show the highest acuity. Results from a systematic study of two-point touch thresholds in females as a function of body site demonstrate this finding quite clearly (Figure 13.13), and the pat-

FIGURE 13.12 Two-point touch thresholds are determined primarily by the concentration and receptive-field sizes of tactile receptors in an area of the skin. The triangles represent point stimulators, and the circles represent the areas of skin that would respond to a single stimulation.

FIGURE 13.13 The minimal separation between two points needed to perceive them as separate (two-point threshold), when the points are applied at different sites on the body. (After Weinstein, 1968.)

tern for males is very similar. More sensitive psychophysical methods show that on the fingertips we are capable of resolving a separation of only about 1 millimeter (mm) (Loomis, 1981). These results place tactile acuity somewhere between vision and audition: it is worse than visual acuity, but better than auditory spatial resolution.

Note the correspondence between the pattern of two-point thresholds across the body in Figure 13.13 and the relative distortion of different body parts in the sensory homunculus of Figure 13.7. This match is not coincidental. The determination that two closely spaced points instead of just one are touching your skin requires that your brain receive two separate signals. This means that at the skin there must be a sufficient concentration of receptors, each with a small enough receptive field that the two contact points will elicit different responses. An additional constraint is that, as the signals are sent to the cortex, they must not converge. A chunk of cortical real estate large enough to receive them separately is necessary. In short, the two-point touch threshold is low (that is, the ability to discern two very close points as separate is high) only when the density of receptors is relatively high, the receptive fields are small, and cortical convergence does not occur. Tactile spatial acuity thresholds are mediated by the SA I (and possibly FA I) tactile receptors, which have relatively small receptive fields and high receptor densities. (See **Web Activity 13.3: Two-Point Touch Thresholds**.)

Although useful, the traditional two-point touch test has some drawbacks, as you may see when you try your own experiment. Even if the two stimulated points feel like one, it is not quite the same as stimulating the skin with a single continuous contact. Therefore, asking people whether they are really being touched by one point or two yields quite a different answer than does asking them if it *feels like* one point or two, especially in sensitive areas such as the fingertip. Alternatives that are more objective have been suggested, including judging whether an edge has a gap or indicating how a grating (a surface with alternating grooves and ridges) that is applied to the skin is oriented—along versus across the finger (Craig and Johnson, 2000).

How Finely Can We Resolve Temporal Details?

It is somewhat more difficult to perform your own measures of how well people can resolve fine temporal differences in tactile stimulation. Various psychophysical methods have been used to address this question. A common method requires subjects to decide whether two tactile pulses delivered to the skin appear to be either simultaneous or successive in time. With this method, subjects can resolve a temporal difference of only 5 milliseconds (ms) (Gescheider, 1974). Touch proves to be better than vision (which is 25 ms) but worse than audition (0.01 ms) (Sherrick and Cholewiak, 1986). As with spatial acuity, you will notice that touch falls somewhere between vision and audition; in this case, however, audition is the best and vision the worst.

Haptic Perception

With the physiology and basic psychophysics of the touch system now under our belts, we can turn to questions about how we use the information gathered by our thermoreceptors, muscle spindle fibers, Pacinian corpuscles, and so on. The term **haptic perception** refers to perceptual processing of inputs from multiple sensory subsystems, including those in skin, muscles, tendons, and joints. Haptic perception is usually active and information-seeking: the perceiver explores the world rather than passively receiving it.

haptic perception Knowledge of the world that is derived from sensory receptors in skin, muscles, tendons, and joints, usually involving active exploration.

Perception for Action

As mentioned earlier, touch relies on action to get information from the world. Expanding on this point a bit more, we can say that touch is active in two complementary ways. Using our hands to actively explore the world of surfaces and objects outside our bodies is *action for perception*. Using somatosensation to control our impressive ability to grasp and manipulate objects in a stable and highly coordinated manner and to maintain proper posture and balance involves *perception for action*.

In our discussion of kinesthetic receptors, we talked about how the loss of these internal tactile receptors leads to a devastating inability to know (without looking) where our limbs are positioned. Westling and Johansson (1984) showed that mechanoreceptors in the skin also play critical roles when we're interacting with objects (**Figure 13.14**). After these investigators anesthetized the skin on volunteers' hands, the volunteers could no longer maintain a stable grasp of objects that they could see perfectly well. Feedback from the mechanoreceptor populations in the skin appears to provide crucial information about when an object is about to slip on the skin. You may know this yourself from trying to unlock a door when your fingers are very cold!

Action for Perception

Let's now consider the action-for-perception side of haptic processing. Lederman and Klatzky (1987) coined the term **exploratory procedure** for a particular way of feeling an object in order to learn about one or more of its properties

exploratory procedure A stereotyped hand movement pattern used to touch objects in order to perceive their properties; each procedure is best for determining one (or more) object properties.

FIGURE 13.14 Force and position during lifting, grasping, and replacing a cube. Region a = grasping; b and c = lifting; d = holding; e = lowering; f and g = releasing. The load force (in newtons, abbreviated N) is in the gravitational direction, the grip force is imposed by the fingers pinching the cube, and the position is the height relative to the table. The ratio of grip force to load force is set so as to just prevent the cube from slipping. (After Westling and Johansson, 1984.)

FIGURE 13.15 Exploratory procedures described by Lederman and Klatzky, and the object properties associated with each procedure. (After Lederman and Klatzky, 1987.)

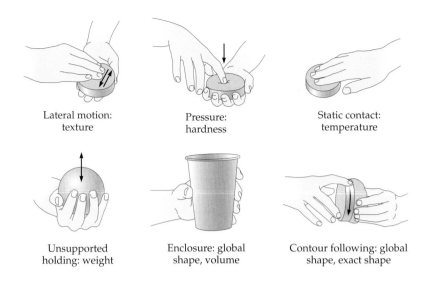

Lateral motion: texture

Pressure: hardness

Static contact: temperature

Unsupported holding: weight

Enclosure: global shape, volume

Contour following: global shape, exact shape

(Figure 13.15). Each exploratory procedure is optimal for obtaining precise details about one or two specific properties. For example, to find out how rough an object is, the best exploratory procedure is *lateral motion*—moving the fingers back and forth across the surface. This is the exploratory procedure that people freely choose when they wish to learn about roughness, and research indicates that it is also the one that works best.

To explain why each exploratory procedure is linked to a specific object property, we must consider both the neural structures that transduce information and the processes that operate on that information. For example, it has been shown that we adopt two different processes when judging the roughness of coarse as opposed to fine surfaces. K. O. Johnson and his colleagues (K. O. Johnson, 2002) have shown that the activity of slowly adapting mechanoreceptors (the SA I fibers) is a principal basis for the perception of surfaces that are at least moderately rough. These units are ten times as responsive when there is relative motion between the skin and the surface as when the fingers statically rest against the surface without motion.

As your finger sweeps across a surface, the pattern of force across the receptors varies with the hills and troughs on the object's surface, providing a kind of spatial map of the variations in skin deformation that is sensed by the SA I fibers (and for the coarser surfaces, possibly also by the FA I fibers). This map is passed on to higher-level neural structures, which integrate the lower-level information into an overall measure of the amount of variation. The brain then uses this neural measure to estimate the roughness of the surface. However, additional research has further shown that when surfaces are very fine, the mechanoreceptors responsive to high-frequency vibrations (the FA II fibers) appear to encode surface roughness, although stroking with the fingers is still needed to set up the vibration (see Hollins, 2002). Hollins suggested that scientific results obtained from the study of both coarse and fine surfaces support a dual-coding theory (as opposed to a single type of coding) for human roughness perception.

Hollins, Bensmaïa, and Washburn (2001) used a very clever psychophysical method known as selective adaptation to obtain scientific support for this dual-coding theory. They reasoned that if the high-frequency (FA II) mechanoreceptors are responsible for encoding the perceived roughness of fine surfaces, then if the fingertip is first selectively "adapted" (fatigued) to a very intense high-frequency vibration (e.g., 250 Hz), fine surfaces should subsequently not feel as rough as they do with the unadapted finger. In contrast, selectively adapting the fingertip to a high-intensity, low-frequency vibration (e.g., 10 Hz) should not affect how rough these same fine surfaces subsequently feel, because the mechanoreceptors that are most sensitive to such low-frequency vibration (SA I fibers, and possibly FA I fibers) do not encode the roughness of fine surfaces.

The results of this experiment nicely confirm the predictions, thus offering evidence in favor of dual-coding mechanisms for roughness. Selective adaptation has been more generally described as the "psychophysicist's microelectrode," in that this method offers a noninvasive complement to recording directly from neural fibers when studying a sensory system—in this case, somatosensation.

> FURTHER DISCUSSION of selective adaptation in spatial vision can be found in Chapter 3 on page 75.

Role of Fingerprints in Perception and Action

If you examine your finger pads, you will notice an elliptically shaped three-dimensional pattern of grooves and ridges that spirals inward toward the center of each pad surface (a closeup is shown in **Figure 13.16**). Those patterns are yours and yours alone (even if you have an identical twin). So what are they good for? Long before the hit show CSI became popular, the field of forensics used two-dimensional inked versions of these ridged "fingerprint" patterns to narrow down the field of suspects in a crime.

More recently, however, scientists have proposed that the finger pad ridges may play at least two other valuable functions in daily life as we manually explore, perceive, lift, transport, and manipulate objects. One is to enhance the tactual perception of fine surface textures. Research suggests that when finger pad–like ridges are used to actively explore very fine surface textures, they selectively amplify frequencies ranging from about 200 to 300 Hz by a factor of about 100, while filtering out other frequencies (Scheibert et al., 2009). However, neither of these effects has been observed in conjunction with coarse surface textures. If you recall our earlier discussion of the two processes for the manual perception of surface roughness (fine versus coarse), you will realize that the high-frequency selection and amplification implemented by the finger pad ridges dovetails with the maximum sensitivity of the FA II mechanoreceptors, which have been implicated in the neural processing that underlies the manual perception of fine surface textures. In short, the finger pads are tuning the signals from exploration of finely textured surfaces to the relevant neural processes.

FIGURE 13.16 Scanning electron micrograph of the skin ridges on a human index finger pad (field of view is 5 mm). (From Quilliam, 1978.)

Scientists have long speculated that fingerprint ridges play a second role, helping our fingers maintain a stable grasp on objects by increasing the amount of friction between our ridged skin and the object. In fact, these skin protrusions are often called "friction ridges." However, Peter Warman and Roland Ennos (2009) have challenged the validity of this function by experimentally showing that ridged fingertip skin produces less, not more, friction during contact by reducing the skin contact area. But take a look at Figure 13.16, showing a scanning electron micrograph of the skin ridges on a human finger pad, which suggests a different way that fingertip ridges could affect grasping. Notice the droplets of sweat that are produced along the tops of the ridges at short, regular intervals. Could moisture (which was not addressed in the previous study) help stabilize grasping by increasing the friction between the finger and the gripped object? Measurements of the slip threshold (see Figure 13.14) for different levels of grip force and skin moisture content suggest that moderate amounts of sweat could facilitate stable manipulation of objects by increasing friction (Andre et al., 2009).

The What System of Touch: Perceiving Objects and Their Properties

Chapter 4 described the processes that underlie visual object recognition. We need somatosensation to control simple actions such as standing or grasping and to warn of danger through pain, but how much value does somatosensation have as an object recognition system? You know the answer if you have ever gotten out of bed in the dark to use the bathroom. The designers of coins know that it is imperative to be able to identify change while it is still in your pocket—hence the failure of the Susan B. Anthony dollar, which felt too similar to the quarter. And the next time you get dressed, try to keep your gaze constantly focused on your hands as you button your shirt. This simple exercise should convince you that even when you can use vision, you sometimes rely on touch to recognize objects and their parts.

PERCEIVING MATERIAL VERSUS GEOMETRIC PROPERTIES People can perform haptic object recognition very well. Klatzky, Lederman, and Metzger (1985) asked people to identify each of 100 common objects (e.g., a fork, a brush, and a paper clip) placed in their hands. Not only did people perform almost perfectly without looking at the objects, but they also generally responded in less than about 2 seconds. However, the information used in haptic object recognition is quite different from that used in visual object recognition. Consider the difference between material properties—those that do not depend on the structure of a particular object, like its surface roughness—and geometric properties like size and shape. In haptic perception, the observer is in contact with the object being observed, so material properties of the object (is it soft? cold? fuzzy?) are easy to perceive and play a crucial role in the recognition process. In vision there is no physical contact, so thermal and textural properties of objects are much more difficult to perceive.

Therefore, the geometric properties of objects are the most important for visual recognition. Indeed, sparse line drawings may be quite easy to recognize visually, but they are hard to recognize when presented haptically as raised contours (**Figure 13.17**). To determine the overall shape of an object haptically, we usually must explore the object by tracing along its contours with our fingers. Integrating tactile information over time is possible but not very efficient, which is why the instantly recognizable material properties tend to be much more important in haptic recognition. (For more on this topic, see **Web Activity 13.4: Haptic Object Recognition**.)

FIGURE 13.17 Examples of common objects that, in two-dimensional form, are easy to recognize visually but, when raised for haptic presentation, are not easily recognized by touch. (After Lederman et al., 1990.)

HAPTIC SEARCH As we saw in Chapter 7, a number of so-called preattentive features in the visual domain are presumed to be critical in the visual object recognition process. These features can be identified by the extent to which they "pop out" in a visual search task. For example, if you are searching for a red object, you will be equally fast at finding it regardless of how many green objects are presented along with it. This result implies that the "redness" of an object is available to recognition processes before attentional mechanisms examine the objects in the display and integrate the various features of each one.

Does the sense of touch also support preattentive feature detection? To find out, Lederman and Klatzky (1997) constructed a set of surfaces somewhat like a tactile slot machine with one key for each of six fingers. The subject's right hand is shown in **Figure 13.18***a*. Stimulus patches were mounted around the planar

FIGURE 13.18 An experiment investigating whether touch supports preattentive feature detection. (*a*) The apparatus used to display targets to the fingertips. The rotating drums bring either a stimulus patch or a cutout (no stimulus) to the upper surface, and then rise as a whole to contact the middle three fingers of both hands (only one hand is shown). (*b*) The amount of time required to detect a rough target among smooth distractors as a function of the number of fingers stimulated. (*c*) A three-dimensional version, where a target object (sphere among cubes in the example shown) is detected among objects grasped in the hand (inset). (*a,b* after Lederman and Klatzky, 1997; *c* after Plaisier, Bergmann Tiest, and Kappers, 2009.)

edges of each of six stimulus wheels. On each trial, the wheels were rotated until the desired stimulus patches were facing upward to form the haptic display. The entire display was then moved up to contact different combinations of the middle three fingertips of each hand. Using this apparatus, Lederman and Klatzky found that a number of haptic features do indeed pop out. As Figure 13.18*b* shows, participants in these experiments were just as fast at detecting a rough surface when there was no smooth surface in the tactile "display" as when there were as many as five smooth surfaces. Similarly, a hard surface popped out of a group of soft surfaces, a cool surface popped out of warm surfaces, and a surface with an edge popped out of perfectly flat surfaces.

Plaisier, Bergmann Tiest, and Kappers (2009) developed a three-dimensional version of the haptic search paradigm in which clusters of objects were grasped in the hand, as shown in Figure 13.18*c*. Objects with different shapes had corresponding differences in the locations of edges, surface curvature, surface area, and height-to-width ratio. By means of a single grasp, subjects exhibited highly efficient search when targets and distractors differed in the type of shape; for example, a cube grasped within a handful of spheres tended to pop out.

However, not every haptic difference supports efficient search. For example, response times increased with the number of distractors when the task was to find a target with a horizontally oriented edge among distractors having vertical edges. Note that horizontal targets do pop out of vertical distractors in visual search tasks. This distinction fits nicely with the previous observation that haptic recognition relies extensively on material properties, but that the tactile system does not appear to be set up to efficiently differentiate object contours by their spatial layout.

PERCEIVING PATTERNS WITH THE SKIN   Even if pattern perception by touch is not terribly efficient, it can be done, especially if the patterns are small enough to be perceived by a single fingertip. Loomis (1990) suggested that, to some extent, touch acts like blurred vision when the fingertip explores a raised pattern. He tested people's ability to identify a set of patterns including Braille symbols, English and Japanese letters, and geometric forms—a few of which are shown in **Figure 13.19**. Sometimes the patterns were presented to the fingertips as raised elements. Other times they were presented visually behind a blurring screen that matched the resolution of the eye with the more limited acuity of fingertip skin. Interestingly, Loomis found very similar patterns of visual and tactile confusion errors—that is, responses in which one pattern was confused for another. This finding suggests that a common, amodal decision process operates on both haptically and visually perceived patterns.

In the Braille alphabet, shown in the first row of Figure 13.19, each letter is formed by raising some of the dots in a 2 × 3 array. For the letter *A*, for example, a single dot is raised in the top left position; and for the letter *Q*, all dots except for the one in the lower right position are raised. This design reflects a compromise between the skin's acuity and its "field of view," the area

FIGURE 13.19   Selected character recognition sets used by Loomis, including Braille (top). (After Loomis, 1990.)

of skin that we can take in all at once. It would be nice to include more than six dots in the array, but because of the spatial blurring imposed by the skin, denser patterns would be difficult to resolve and discriminate (remember that two-point thresholds on the fingertips are about 1 mm). Spreading a greater number of dots across a larger contact area would not work either, because then the pattern would extend beyond the fingertip. Unfortunately, people are unable to "read" more than one finger at a time, suggesting that our tactile field of view is very narrow.

TACTILE AGNOSIA   Just as lesions in the temporal lobe can produce visual agnosia (see Chapter 5), lesions of the parietal lobe can produce **tactile agnosia**, an inability to identify objects by touch. In making a diagnosis of tactile agnosia, the neurologist needs to be able to eliminate other possibilities. Is the problem impaired motor control, which would prevent the exploratory procedures needed to effectively learn about an object's properties? Or might the problem be a higher-level cognitive dysfunction, such as a loss of access to object names?

We already described a patient who could not recognize objects by touch but could locate them. She had tactile agnosia with her right hand, due to a lesion in the left inferior parietal region of her brain, but the deficit did not extend to her left hand. Reed and Caselli (1994) documented that, although the patient could not recognize objects such as a key chain or a combination lock with her right hand, she could easily recognize these objects visually or with her left hand, ruling out a general loss of knowledge about objects. Other capabilities were normal in both hands, including sensory threshold levels and the movements with which objects were explored. The patient could also discriminate between objects with different levels of weight and roughness using either hand. And she could answer questions about the haptic properties of named objects, such as whether an orange was harder than an apple, indicating that she had the ability to remember and imagine how objects felt.

Thus, the patient could acquire information with her impaired hand about an object's properties (e.g., its weight and roughness), and she had intact haptic knowledge about objects she had encountered in the past. What she lacked was a connection between these two components of object identification. That is, either she was unable to integrate the perceived properties into a coherent object representation, or she was unable to match perceived representations to stored representations in memory.

The Where System of Touch: Locating Objects

As with other sensory modalities, knowing *what* a haptic stimulus might be is only part of the perceptual problem. We also need to know *where* that stimulus is located because we often want to do something with it. If you are already touching an object, you obviously know where it is (a tree limb that you bump your head on is in the air; one that you stumble over has fallen to the ground). If you are not yet touching the object but can see it, your sense of vision can work out where the object is and guide your reaching behavior. But what about groping for the snooze button on your alarm clock when your eyes have not yet opened for the day? As mentioned already, there is evidence that touch, like vision, has a specialized neural pathway for dealing with questions of where objects are located, as compared to knowing what they are like.

HAPTIC OBJECT LOCALIZATION   Like visual and auditory localization, haptic object localization first requires that we establish a **frame of reference**. For vision, the center of the reference frame—the **egocenter**—is located near the

tactile agnosia The inability to identify objects by touch.

frame of reference The coordinate system used to define locations in space.

egocenter The center of a reference frame used to represent locations relative to the body.

FIGURE 13.20 Locating the haptic egocenter. One hand places a stylus on the target on the upper table surface, and the other hand attempts to match up underneath the table in the corresponding location. (After Haggard et al., 2000.)

(*a*) Top view

(*b*) Front view

bridge of the nose, between the two eyes; the auditory egocenter is a point smack in the middle of the head (between the two ears). One way to pinpoint your haptic egocenter is to place your left index finger on top of the edge of a desk or table, close your eyes, and try to match this location by placing your right index finger on the bottom of the desk. (**Figure 13.20** shows a version of this task using a stylus in each hand instead of the index finger.) If you do this many times, you may find that you consistently err to the left. Conversely, if you try to match the location of your right index finger with your left, you will be more likely to err to the right. A careful analysis of errors in a task of this type led Haggard et al. (2000) to conclude that there is, in fact, no single, fixed frame of reference for the haptic perception of locations. In the case of the index finger reaching task, the egocenter appears to be located at the shoulder of the arm doing the reaching. In other tasks, the egocenter may move to other positions on the body.

Although you might think you're pretty accurate at determining how external objects are oriented in haptic space, research has shown that people make surprisingly large and systematic errors. Try the following task, which is an informal demonstration of the experiment illustrated in **Figure 13.21** (Kappers, 2007). Have a friend place two pencils in front of you within reach, one far off to your left and the other far off to your right. Position your hands in a natural way on both pencils. The orientation of the left pencil should be fixed so that its length lies crosswise to the fingers of your left hand. The right pencil should be set in a random position beneath your right hand. Rotate the right-hand pencil until it feels parallel to the left-hand pencil. Now have a look at how the two pencils are aligned with respect to each other. Are they physically parallel?

FIGURE 13.21 Haptic perception of tabletop space. The two bars in this figure are arranged to represent how a typical experimental subject would orient two bars to appear close to "parallel." (After Kappers, 2007.)

In the actual experiment (Kappers, 2007), the rods at the two positions illustrated in Figure 13.21 were set to orientations differing by 40 degrees on average! Although individuals varied in their susceptibility to spatial errors in this haptic parallelism task (errors for the positions shown ranged from 8 to as much as 91 degrees), the average trends were quite consistent. Subjects tended to judge what was parallel by weighting their orientation judgments with respect to two different spatial frames of reference: one that was egocentric (with reference to the body, and commonly centered on the hand); the other, allocentric (with reference to external space).

BODY IMAGE Understanding how we haptically perceive space becomes even more fascinating when we find that the impression we have of our bodies in space (called the **body image**) is highly changeable. We have all heard of clinical reports of individuals with abnormal brain function who report "out-of-body" experiences in which the conscious sense of self lies outside the physical body. It is as if the observer were looking at his or her body, but from someone else's point of view.

A study by Ehrsson (2007) showed just how easy it is to induce an illusory out-of-body experience in healthy subjects. Here's how he did it. As depicted in Figure 13.22, the participant (let's call him "Frank") sat in front of two cameras placed beside each other. Frank wore virtual-reality goggles connected to the cameras for a stereo view. The experimenter stood at Frank's side and used a plastic rod to stroke his physical chest (unseen by the cameras). Being very careful to use exactly the same timing, the experimenter used a second rod to simultaneously "stroke" Frank's "phantom chest," an area in front of and just below the cameras (see Figure 13.22). Frank could see the back of his body sitting in the chair and the experimenter's hand moving down toward a point below the two cameras. When asked what he experienced, Frank reported viewing his own body from behind, with his head located at the site of the cameras (like the phantom's head in Figure 13.22). In addition he reported feeling the tap on the phantom's chest just below the cameras. Other subjects concurred. (Ehrsson was careful to address other control questions to ensure that the out-of-body experience could not be attributed to suggestibility or to the subjects' compliance with the task.) (See **Web Activity 13.5: The Rubber Hand Illusion** for another way to elicit an out-of-body experience.)

We are not the only primates who can modify their body schemas. Iriki, Tanaka, and Iwamura (1996) showed how quickly the body images of regular

body image The impression of our bodies in space.

FIGURE 13.22 The experimental setup used to induce an out-of-body experience. (After Ehrsson, 2007.)

Subject's view

tool-using Japanese monkeys could be modified. The monkeys practiced using a handheld tool, as they would a rake, to retrieve distant food objects. After this task was repeated for only 5 minutes, the visual receptive fields of bimodal cells that received converging inputs from both vision and touch actually grew in size to include the complete length of the tool in addition to the hand. The neuroscientists proposed that such neural modifications indicate that the monkey brain incorporated the tool into the body image as an extension of the monkey's own hand.

Tactile Spatial Attention

Although the last 50 years or so have produced a considerable amount of research on visual and auditory attention, only in the last decade have scientists begun to investigate the nature of the processes that underlie tactile attention. In this section we focus on tactile spatial (as opposed to nonspatial) attention.

> FURTHER DISCUSSION of attention as it relates to visual perception can be found in Chapter 7.

When people anticipate being touched in a particular location, they can voluntarily direct their attention to that location. Attention that is directed to the tactile modality in this way is known as **endogenous** (or top-down) control. In one study (Spence, Pavani, and Driver, 2000), participants were asked to indicate whether a sustained force or a series of pulses was delivered to a fingertip (Figure 13.23). The stimulated fingertip could be on the left or the right hand. A visual precue, in the form of an arrow, predicted which hand would receive the stimulation. If people could make use of this precue to direct attention to the predicted hand, it was expected that they would be faster at deciding whether the stimulus was sustained or pulsed. And indeed, this was the case: the precue

endogenous spatial attention A form of top-down (knowledge-driven) control of spatial attention in which attention is voluntarily directed toward the site where the observer anticipates a stimulus will occur.

Target lights

Tactile stimulators

Feedback lights

Cue light

Fixation light

FIGURE 13.23 Studying competition between sensory modalities. In each hand the subject holds a cube that has vibrotactile stimulators and lights, either of which can signal the required response. The arrows at fixation are used to direct attention. (After Spence, Pavani, and Driver, 2000.)

sped up responses relative to a no-cue control. Occasionally, however, the precue directed the participant's attention to the wrong hand, and on such trials people responded more slowly than in the no-cue condition.

These effects are exactly analogous to attentional cueing effects in vision and audition. Thus, we see that tactile attention, like visual and auditory attention, is a limited resource that must be allocated in one way or another. You will probably have realized that directing one's attention endogenously (voluntarily) to a stimulus event is not the only way in which people control spatial attention. It is also possible to reflexively direct one's spatial attention to an abruptly occurring tactile stimulus that takes place at a particular location or part of the body. Such reactive control of spatial attention is known as **exogenous** (or bottom-up) processing.

The sense of touch also demonstrates the attentional phenomenon of change blindness, described in Chapter 7. In a study mimicking the flicker paradigm used in visual change blindness, Gallace, Tan, and Spence (2007) stimulated subjects with vibrations at two or three sites on the body and asked them to detect when the number of vibrations changed from one presentation to the next. When the second presentation was preceded by a brief period in which multiple sites were stimulated, the ability to detect a change decreased dramatically. Even a single irrelevant vibratory stimulus, called a "mudsplash," between the two vibratory patterns substantially decreased the ability to detect differences between them.

Social Touch

Influences of touch extend beyond perception and action in sometimes surprising ways, to influence interactions with others. Incidental touch has been found, for example, to influence social judgments (J. M. Ackerman, Nocera,

exogenous spatial attention A form of bottom-up (stimulus-driven) spatial attention in which attention is reflexively (involuntarily) directed toward the site at which a stimulus has abruptly appeared.

and Bargh, 2010): When evaluators of job candidates hold their résumés on heavy clipboards, the candidates are judged to be more serious about the job. Similarly, people who sit in hard chairs while forming impressions of employees judge them to be more stable and less emotional than when they make the judgments while sitting in soft chairs. It seems that even when touch sensations are irrelevant to the task at hand, they shade interpersonal impressions. These implicit "haptic metaphors" reflect deep connections between touch experience and social constructs.

A quite different way in which touch affects social interactions is through individual characteristics that we think of as genetically determined, like personality. Work in the field of *epigenetics* has led to a model describing how the expression of genes related to social interaction is controlled by touch in the rat. Mother rats who lick and groom their pups produce offspring who tend to lick and groom their own pups as well. "Aha!" we might say, there must be a licking and grooming gene that is passed from one generation to the next. But to complicate matters, if, as in the old fable, pups from attentive and remote rat moms are switched at birth, they "inherit" the behavior of their adoptive, rather than biological, mothers (D. Francis et al., 1999). Their maternal behavior is governed not by their genetic makeup, but by the grooming behavior they have experienced.

Have the pups learned from their experience, then, to lick and groom? The mechanism for passing on the behavior is not what we normally think of as learning by association. There is instead an epigenetic process that turns licking-and-grooming genes off or on, according to the pup's experience with the same behaviors, by regulating neuroendocrine systems (Champagne, 2008). Complex behaviors are transmitted from one rat generation to the next by regulation of the genes, not control of their component DNA. Evidence for a similar mechanism in humans has been obtained (McGowan et al., 2009).

The rat mother's contact has consequences well beyond the maternal care exhibited by the offspring when they in turn have pups. Offspring of licking-and-grooming mothers turn out to be less timid than those of remote mothers.

Interactions between Touch and Other Modalities

Touch does not occur only in the absence of other sensory input, of course. We commonly touch objects that we see, and we hear the consequences of contact. How does the perceptual system as a whole deal with signals from multiple modalities? Sometimes they compete, and sometimes the whole is an integrated combination of the different inputs.

Competition can arise when resources are limited—that is, when attention comes into play in a particular task. Do the different modalities compete with each other for attentional resources as well? Consider the fact that the pressure stimulus of your posterior on your seat seems to have lost out to this visual text in the current competition for your attention (until now, that is). In the lab, Spence, Nicholls, and Driver (2001) did a cross-modal version of the same sort of cueing experiment that was described in the previous paragraph: They led participants to expect a stimulus to be presented via one modality and then sometimes presented it in a different modality. The participants were instructed to indicate with a foot pedal whether a target stimulus appeared on their left or right side. The stimulus could be noise from a loudspeaker (audition), a red circle at the location of the loudspeaker (vision), or a rod pressing the finger while it touched the loudspeaker (touch); and a cue could direct attention toward any of the three modalities.

Again, responses were faster when the cue was valid and slower when it was invalid. Interestingly, the greatest cost for an invalid cue occurred when observers expected a tactile stimulus but a visual or auditory stimulus was presented instead. This result may imply that the sense of touch has a particularly restricted attentional channel—that once attention is focused on the touch modality, it is relatively difficult to reallocate it. Or it may be that visual attention and auditory attention are shared to some extent, because expectancies in those modalities could be directed to a common location in external space, whereas the expectancy for touch is directed to a location on the body.

In contrast to attentional competition, intersensory integration can occur when different modalities receive information about the same object. Suppose, for example, that you're touching sandpaper. The roughness you feel also depends on the roughness you see. Participants in an experiment by Lederman, Thorne, and Jones (1986) saw one sandpaper surface and felt another, but were told the two surfaces were one and the same. When they were asked about how closely packed the elements in the surface were, they were more strongly influenced by vision. When asked about the roughness of the surface, however, touch became more important and vision less important.

In some circumstances, one modality may appear to dominate. In a classic study pitting vision against touch, Rock and Victor (1964) had people grasp a square while looking at it through a distorting lens. What these participants felt was pretty much what they saw: a rectangle. But dominance by one modality over the other is not the rule. A more general model is that people integrate the signals from two modalities, producing a weighted average. That is, they use x percent of the information from one modality and $(100 - x)$ percent from the other. The relative weighting reflects the quality of the signal from each modality.

Ernst and Banks (2002) demonstrated such integration with an apparatus that simultaneously created touch and sight of the same virtual display. The display consisted of a plane with a raised bar across the middle (**Figure 13.24**). The virtual visual display was produced with stereo glasses and an appropriate pair of random dot stereograms, one presented to each eye (see Figure 6.33), creating the visual illusion of a bar stepping up from a plane. The corresponding virtual touch display was created with a device that generated forces that pushed back on the hand whenever contact was made with the simulated surface. When the bar heights presented to the two modalities did not match (the touched bar was higher than the viewed bar, or vice versa), the perceived height of the bar was a weighted compromise between them, with vision more strongly weighted than touch. When the investigators made the information from vision less reliable by randomly changing the apparent height of some of the surface dots, the weight assigned to touch increased, and it played a greater role in determining the perceived height of the bar.

Multiple modalities may collaborate by signaling different, but complementary, sources of information about an object. Our discussion of object perception emphasized that vision and touch are intrinsically complementary: one well suited to convey an object's geometry; the other, its material.

FIGURE 13.24 Testing the integration of sensory modalities. The observer could see a virtual surface of dots through stereo goggles, which gave the appearance of a raised bar across the surface, and could touch the virtual surface and receive resisting forces consistent with the surface height. (After Ernst and Banks, 2002.)

CRT

Stereo glasses

Opaque mirror

Virtual surface

90°

Force-feedback device

Visual and haptic scene

3-cm-high bar

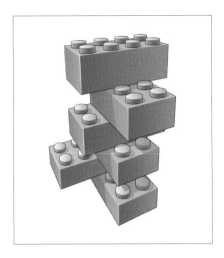

FIGURE 13.25 An example of the unfamiliar object shapes used in Newell's experiment. (After Newell et al., 2001.)

For a quite different example of intermodal cooperation, consider an intriguing study about the perception of object shape by Fiona Newell et al. (2001). In the learning phase of the experiment, observers studied a set of Lego shapes, each fixed in a particular orientation, using vision or touch (**Figure 13.25**). In the recognition phase, previously studied shapes were presented, oriented either as they had been during the study phase or reversed 180 degrees, along with unstudied shapes. Again using vision or touch, the subjects were required to indicate whether each tested shape was old (previously studied) or new. People who studied and were tested in the same modality, whether vision or touch, recognized old shapes better when they were presented in the same orientation as during the study phase, indicating that memory for the shapes was orientation-sensitive. But now for the surprise: for people who studied and were tested in different modalities—vision changed to touch, or vice versa—recognition was actually better when the studied shapes were reversed in orientation during the recognition phase! Why should this be?

The authors noticed that, when haptically exploring the shapes, subjects placed their thumbs on the front surface and their other fingers around the back surface, suggesting that they learned more about the back of the object. For people who studied with vision and were tested with touch, reversing the object meant that the previously visible (front) surface was then the one that was more accessible to manual exploration (back). For people who studied with touch and were tested with vision, reversing the object meant that the more effectively explored back surface was then what was accessible to vision. Thus, it would appear that two modalities might most efficiently process an object's shape by using two different, but highly complementary, sources of information: the object's front is processed best visually; its back, best haptically.

Haptic Virtual Environments

Anyone who has played a video game has been in a **haptic virtual environment**. The actions of the player (e.g., button presses or joystick movements) are sensed by the machine and filtered through a program that creates a simulated world, causing new events and outcomes that are fed back to the user through vision and audition. Although some joysticks employ crude vibration, what is missing from most of these environments at present is haptic feedback. However, interfaces have been developed that provide such feedback in the form of vibration or sustained forces to the hand, allowing diverse objects varying in shape, size, surface texture, and softness to be rendered.

Haptic virtual environments are useful in many applications other than video games. They enable an operator to manipulate objects with a remote robot and feel the forces the robot hand encounters. They are used to train novice surgeons for minimally invasive surgery, where the operator manipulates an implement inserted through a small incision while viewing the surgical site on a video display. In the haptic virtual training environment, the patient's body is replaced by a dummy, and the surgical tool connects to a computer that tracks the trainee's movements. The computer contains a simulation of the patient that describes body structures and their properties, such as slipperiness and softness. As the computer tracks the surgeon's actions with the tool, it determines the effect those actions would have on the simulated patient, and it generates high-precision graphics and forces to feed back to the surgeon (**Figure 13.26**). Commerce on the Internet is a potential domain for force-feedback devices that could allow products to be felt as well as seen.

haptic virtual environment A synthetic world that may be experienced haptically by operation of an electromechanical device that delivers forces to the hand of the user.

FIGURE 13.26 A virtual surgical trainer. A novice surgeon receives high-precision graphics and force feedback about a blood vessel that is being repaired. (After photographs from Boston Dynamics.)

Summary

1. The sense of touch produces a number of distinct sensory experiences. Each type of experience is mediated by its own sensory receptor system(s). Tactile receptors are responsive not only to pressure, but also to vibration, changes in temperature, and noxious stimulation. The kinesthetic system, which also contributes to our sense of touch, is further involved in sensing limb position and the movement of our limbs in space. Pleasant or emotional touch is another form of sensory specialization.

2. Four classes of pressure-sensitive (mechano-) receptors have been found within hairless skin, and another five classes within hairy skin. The organs used to sense limb position and movement (namely, our muscles, tendons, and joints) are more deeply situated within the body. Thermoreceptors respond to changes in skin temperature that occur, for example, when we contact objects that are warmer or cooler than our bodies. Nociceptors signal tissue damage (or its potential) and give rise to sensations of pain.

3. The pathways from touch receptors to the brain are complex. Two major pathways have been identified: a fast one (the dorsal column–medial lemniscal pathway) that carries information from mechanoreceptors, and a slower one (the spinothalamic pathway) that carries thermal and nociceptive information. Only the second pathway synapses when it first enters the spinal cord. These pathways project to the thalamus and from there to the primary somatosensory area, located in the parietal lobe just behind the central sulcus. This area contains several somatotopically organized subregions, in which adjacent areas of the body project to adjacent areas of the brain. The neural organization of the brain for touch has been shown to be remarkably plastic, even in adults.

4. Downward pathways from the brain play an important role in the perception of pain. According to the gate control theory, signals along these pathways interact at the spinal cord with those from the periphery of the body. Such interactions can block the pain signals that would otherwise be sent forward to the brain. The sensation of pain is further moderated by areas in the cortex.

Refer to the
Sensation and Perception
Companion Website
sites.sinauer.com/wolfe3e
for activities, essays, study questions, and other study aids.

5. Investigators have measured sensitivity to mechanical force by applying nylon hairs of different diameters to the skin. They determine spatial acuity of the skin by measuring the two-point touch threshold, and more precisely by discriminating the orientation of gratings applied to the skin. Tactile pressure sensitivity and spatial acuity vary with body site because of varying concentrations of different types of mechanoreceptors. The minimum depression of the skin needed to feel a stimulus vibrating at a particular rate (frequency) provides a measure of vibration sensitivity.

6. The sense of touch is intimately related to our ability to perform actions. Signals from the mechanoreceptors are necessary for simple actions such as grasping and lifting an object. Conversely, our own movements determine how touch receptors respond and, hence, which properties of the concrete world we can feel. Touch is better adapted to feeling the material properties of objects than it is to feeling their geometric features (e.g., shape), particularly when an object is large enough to extend beyond the fingertip.

7. Like other sensory modalities, touch gives rise to internal representations of the world, which convey the positions of objects using the body as a spatial reference system. Touch-derived representations are inputs to higher-level functions like allocation of attention and integration with information from other modalities.

8. The psychological study of touch is useful for a number of applications. Virtual touch environments that transmit forces to the touch receptors can provide a basis for training people to perform remote operations like surgery and perhaps, in the future, will convey the illusion of touched objects over the Internet.

CHAPTER 14

John Baldessari, *God Nose*, 2007

Olfaction

The story of the next two chapters begins at the dawn of life itself. When single-celled organisms first appeared on Earth, their basic purpose in life was to take in some substances (food) and avoid others (toxins). As these organisms evolved into multicellular creatures, detecting chemicals in the environment continued to be crucial for survival. Systems to detect and analyze environmental molecules were thus the first senses to evolve.

Humans have two main chemical detection systems: one for molecules floating in the air, and another for molecules that we put in our mouths. The technical names for these two systems are **olfaction** and **gustation**, respectively. The former, more commonly known as "smell," is the subject of this chapter. Gustation, which you probably know as "taste," will be explored in the next chapter (although, as you'll see, the distinction between tastes and smells is not as clear as you probably think). Another chemical sensing system that is important for our experiences of both smells and tastes is the trigeminal system, innervated by the trigeminal nerve. The trigeminal system enables us to *feel* gustatory and olfactory experiences, like burning and cooling. You will learn more about this system in this chapter and the next.

Olfactory Physiology

Odors and Odorants

Olfactory sensations are called **odors**. The stimuli for odors are chemical compounds called odorants. An analogy can be made with vision, where wavelengths of light are stimuli and colors are the visual sensations. However, not every chemical is an **odorant**. To be smelled, odorant molecules must be volatile (able to float through the air), small (less than about 5.8×10^{-22} grams), and hydrophobic (repellent to water). **Figure 14.1***a* shows the chemical structures of two odorant molecules. However, many molecules that would seem to meet the basic requirements still don't smell to us. Two examples are natural gas (methane) and a by-product of methane, carbon monoxide (Figure 14.1*b*). Our evolutionary ancestors would have had no reason to detect these substances, which are not dangerous in the concentrations found in nature. But because the buildup of carbon monoxide in enclosed spaces such as homes with gas furnaces can be fatal, gas companies add a compound (tertiary-butyl mercaptan) that we smell as rotten eggs, to act as a warning signal when a stove's pilot light goes out. We also can't smell the molecules that make up the air we breathe, such as oxygen and nitrogen.

olfaction The sense of smell.

gustation The sense of taste.

odor The translation of a chemical stimulus into a smell sensation. For example, "The cake has a chocolate *odor*."

odorant A molecule that is defined by its physicochemical characteristics, which are capable of being translated by the nervous system into the perception of a smell. For example, "You were given the *odorant* methyl salicylate to smell, which has the *odor* of wintergreen mint."

FIGURE 14.1 Odorants. Most small, volatile, and hydrophobic molecules activate the sense of smell (*a*), but there are notable exceptions to the rule, such as methane and carbon monoxide (*b*).

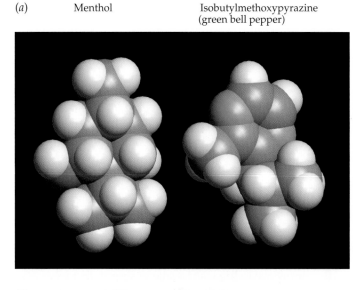

(*a*) Menthol   Isobutylmethoxypyrazine (green bell pepper)

(*b*) Methane   Carbon monoxide

olfactory cleft A narrow space at the back of the nose into which air flows and where the olfactory epithelium is located.

olfactory epithelium A secretory mucous membrane in the human nose whose primary function is to detect odorants in inhaled air. Located on both sides of the upper portion of the nasal cavity and the olfactory clefts, the olfactory epithelium contains three types of cells: olfactory sensory neurons, basal cells, and supporting cells.

nasal dominance The asymmetry characterizing the intake of air by the two nostrils, which corresponds to differing sensitivity to odorants between the two nostrils. Nasal dominance alternates nostrils throughout the day, but there is no predictability about when the nostrils alternate.

The Human Olfactory Apparatus

Unlike the visual and auditory systems, but like the systems of touch and taste, the human olfactory system is tacked onto an organ that serves another purpose. The primary function of the nose (**Figure 14.2**) is to filter, warm, and humidify the air that we breathe. But the inside of the nose has small ridges called turbinates that add turbulence to incoming air, causing a small puff of each breath to rise upward, pass through a narrow space called the **olfactory cleft**, and settle on a yellowish patch of mucous membrane called the **olfactory epithelium** (**Figure 14.3**). Notably, our two nostrils take in different amounts of air, and this **nasal dominance** alternates nostrils throughout the day. This means that the two nostrils continually vary in their sensitivities to odorants as a function of the amount of air inhaled.

FIGURE 14.2 The nose. Although the primary function of the nose is to warm and humidify the air that we breathe, the nose also directs odorants onto the olfactory epithelium.

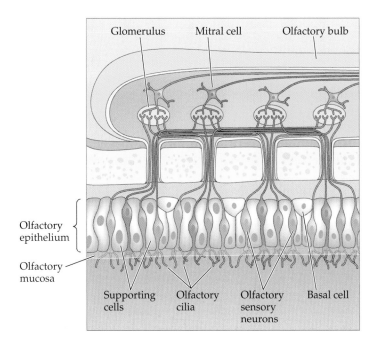

FIGURE 14.3 The retina of the nose. The olfactory epithelium contains three types of cells: olfactory sensory neurons (OSNs), basal cells, and supporting cells. The OSNs are located beneath a watery mucous layer on the epithelium; the hairlike olfactory cilia of the OSN dendrites project through the mucus and are the receptor sites for odorant molecules. The different colors of the OSNs in this illustration represent the glomeruli onto which they will converge. All blue OSNs go to blue glomeruli, all purple to purple, and so on. This schematic illustrates the fact that different OSNs expressing the same receptors converge on the same glomeruli, no matter where they are in the olfactory epithelium.

The olfactory epithelium is the "retina of the nose." We have an olfactory epithelium at the back of each nasal passage, about 2¾ inches up from the nostril. Each epithelium measures about 1–2 square inches (depending on the size of the nose) and contains three types of cells: **supporting cells**, **basal cells**, and **olfactory sensory neurons** (**OSNs**). (See **Web Activity 14.1: Olfactory Anatomy**.)

OSNs (**Figure 14.4**) are small neurons that have **cilia** (singular *cilium*) protruding into the mucus covering the olfactory epithelium. These cilia, which are actually the OSN's dendrites, have **olfactory receptors** (**ORs**) on their

supporting cell One of the three types of cells in the olfactory epithelium. Supporting cells provide metabolic and physical support for the olfactory sensory neurons.

basal cell One of the three types of cells in the olfactory epithelium. Basal cells are the precursor cells to olfactory sensory neurons.

olfactory sensory neuron (OSN) One of three cell types—the main one—in the olfactory epithelium. OSNs are small neurons located beneath a watery mucous layer in the epithelium. The cilia on the OSN dendrites contain the receptor sites for odorant molecules.

cilium Any of the hairlike protrusions on the dendrites of olfactory sensory neurons. The receptor sites for odorant molecules are on the cilia, which are the first structures involved in olfactory signal transduction.

olfactory receptor (OR) The region on the cilia of olfactory sensory neurons where odorant molecules bind.

FIGURE 14.4 A fluorescence image of an olfactory sensory neuron (lower right), with a schematic graph (upper right) of an action potential sequence following odorant application. The OSN collects odorant molecules via receptors on its dendrites and sends action potentials to the brain through its axons. pA = picoamperes. (Fluorescence image courtesy of C. Balmer and A. LaMantia.)

FIGURE 14.5 Tracking scents. (a) The path (red) of a dog following the scent trail (yellow) of a pheasant dragged through a field. (b) The path (red) of a human following a scent trail (yellow) of chocolate essential oil through a field. (After Porter et al., 2007.)

(a)

(b)

tips. The interaction between an odorant and the OR stimulates a cascade of biochemical events, ultimately producing an action potential that is transmitted along the axon of the OSN to the olfactory bulb (Schild and Restrepo, 1998). To initiate an action potential, about seven or eight odorant molecules must bind to a receptor, and it takes about 40 of these nerve impulses for a smell sensation to be reported.

We have approximately 20 million OSNs, split between the epithelia of our right and left nostrils. This is more sensory neurons than we have in any other sensory system except vision, and these OSNs enable us to distinguish thousands of different odors. However, the number of receptors we have is paltry compared to a bloodhound's 220 million OSNs. In addition, a much higher proportion of a dog's brain is dedicated to olfaction: about 5%, compared to 0.1% for humans. Researchers suspect that humans can smell about the same number of scents as dogs (the bloodhounds aren't talking, so we can't be sure), but dogs can sense odors at concentrations nearly 100 million times lower than the concentrations that humans can detect (Krestel et al., 1984; Willis et al., 2004). Nevertheless, in a recent study humans were able to follow a 10-meter-long scent track of chocolate aroma while on all fours in an open grass field (Porter et al., 2007), and the tracking pattern that the participants used was strikingly similar to that of a dog (**Figure 14.5**). Other amazing smellers include pigs, which can smell the scent of truffles (the mushroom, not the chocolate) under 6 inches of soil; and salmon, which use smell to find the waters of their birth from hundreds of miles away (Dittman and Quinn, 1996).

The axons on the ends of OSNs opposite the cilia (dendrites) pass through the tiny sievelike holes of the **cribriform plate**, a bony structure at the level of the eyebrows that separates the nose from the brain (**Figure 14.6**). A hard blow to the front of the head can cause the cribriform plate to be jarred back or fractured, slicing off the fragile olfactory axons, and consequently inducing **anosmia** ("smell blindness"), the total absence of a sense of smell. Stem cells

cribriform plate A bony structure riddled with tiny holes, at the level of the eyebrows, that separates the nose from the brain. The axons from the olfactory sensory neurons pass through the tiny holes of the cribriform plate to enter the brain.

anosmia The total inability to smell, most often resulting from sinus illness or head trauma.

(a)

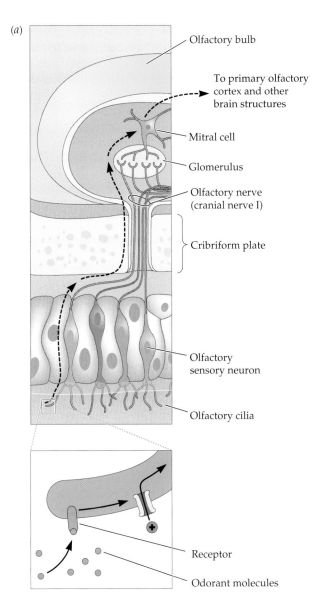

Olfactory bulb

To primary olfactory cortex and other brain structures

Mitral cell

Glomerulus

Olfactory nerve (cranial nerve I)

Cribriform plate

Olfactory sensory neuron

Olfactory cilia

Receptor

Odorant molecules

(b)

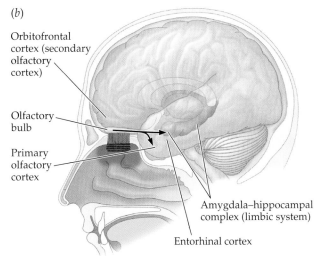

Orbitofrontal cortex (secondary olfactory cortex)

Olfactory bulb

Primary olfactory cortex

Amygdala–hippocampal complex (limbic system)

Entorhinal cortex

FIGURE 14.6 How smells are perceived. (a) The pathway of olfactory perception, from odorant molecule to the olfactory bulb. (b) A cross-sectional view of the neural organization of olfaction. Olfactory information is transmitted from the olfactory bulb to the primary olfactory cortex and the amygdala-hippocampal complex of the limbic system in the first stages of olfactory processing. The orbitofrontal cortex is considered to be the secondary olfactory cortex and is responsible for conscious odor perception.

in the olfactory epithelium can form new OSNs; indeed, all of our OSNs die and regenerate about once every 28 days. However, fractured cribriform plates typically scar over, preventing the new OSN axons from passing through to the brain, and crippling the sense of smell for life.

Head trauma is not the only way to produce anosmia. The most common cause of olfactory loss is upper respiratory tract infection (e.g., sinus infection); the second most common cause is sinonasal disease (such as polyps); only 30% of anosmias are caused by head trauma, the third most common cause. Certain medications can also cause smell loss or disturbance—particularly those used for treating high blood pressure or elevated cholesterol levels. The rarest form of anosmia is congenital; only 3% of people with anosmia were born anosmic. The likelihood of recovery is best when anosmia is caused by infection or disease, because often when the underlying illness is treated, normal smell function returns.

It is worth commenting here that compared to loss of vision or hearing, olfactory loss is paid little attention by both the medical and the general community. In a questionnaire administered to students at the University of

olfactory (I) nerves The first pair of cranial nerves. The axons of the olfactory sensory neurons bundle together after passing through the cribriform plate to form the olfactory nerve, which conducts impulses from the olfactory epithelia in the nose to the olfactory bulb.

olfactory bulb A blueberry-sized extension of the brain just above the nose, where olfactory information is first processed. There are two olfactory bulbs, one in each brain hemisphere, corresponding to the right and left nostrils.

ipsilateral Referring to the same side of the body (or brain).

glomerulus Any of the spherical conglomerates containing the incoming axons of the olfactory sensory neurons. Each OSN converges onto two glomeruli (one medial, one lateral).

Pennsylvania, loss of the sense of smell was ranked equal to losing one's big toe (Wrzesniewski, McCauley, and Rozin, 1999). However, anosmia can cause great suffering, because it affects many aspects of our lives, most noticeably our experience of taste, as we will discover in the next chapter. There is also a profound connection between psychiatric depression and our sense of smell. People who lose their sense of smell can fall into clinically depressive states, and people who are diagnosed with depression often concomitantly complain of a weakened sense of smell (Pause et al., 2001). The neurobiological connection between olfactory and emotional processing enables a bidirectional interaction between them (Herz, 2007).

Given the impact of anosmia on quality of life, treatment and attention are critical, especially since the incidence of anosmia is surprisingly high. From a survey by the National Institutes of Health (NIH) in 1994, it was conservatively estimated that one in every 100 people suffers from anosmia. However, more recent estimates indicate that as many as 14 million Americans over the age of 55 have a severely compromised sense of smell. Including younger adults, it appears that about one in 20 Americans may have some olfactory dysfunction. Olfactory loss can also be the first symptom of neurological disorders such as Alzheimer's and Parkinson's diseases. It is therefore very important to investigate olfactory loss when it occurs. Many smell and taste clinics throughout the country administer simple tests to determine the causes and treatment possibilities for olfactory loss and dysfunction.

In someone with a healthily functioning sense of smell, the OSN axons pass through the cribriform plate, bundle together to form the **olfactory nerve** (cranial nerve I), and enter a blueberry-sized extension of the brain just above the nose called the **olfactory bulb** (see Figure 14.6). We have two olfactory bulbs, one in each brain hemisphere. Unlike the other senses we've studied so far, olfaction is **ipsilateral**, meaning that the right olfactory bulb gets information from the right nostril and the left olfactory bulb gets information from the left nostril.

$C_8H_8O_3$, also known as the synthetic chemical *methyl salicylate*, has an odor that we identify as wintergreen mint. Like other odorants, methyl salicylate can activate several different types of odor receptors (ORs), and it does so with different degrees of "weighting" depending on the receptor's affinity to the wintergreen molecule. Humans have between 350 and 400 different types of functioning ORs. Most of these receptors won't be activated by methyl salicylate; a few will be weakly activated, and one or two will be strongly activated (this will become clearer as you read the following sections).

The first relay for the OSNs in the brain is in the olfactory bulb, where the sensory nerve endings gather together to form tiny spheres called **glomeruli** (singular *glomerulus*). Molecular genetic studies in mice have shown that all neurons expressing a particular OR type, no matter where they are on the nasal epithelium, send their axons to the same glomerulus pair (consisting of one medial and one lateral glomerulus) in the olfactory bulb (Mombaerts et al., 1996). The distinct pattern of OR activation for a specific odorant is then translated to a specific pattern of spatial activity across the glomeruli. Methyl salicylate, for example, will activate a set of specific ORs and consequently produce a pattern of glomerular activity that is unique to it. The compounds of rose aroma will initiate a different activity pattern, and so on. The specific pattern of glomeruli activity is then interpreted by the brain as indicating a specific odor.

However, this relatively simple picture is complicated by the fact that each glomerulus may receive axons from several different receptor types. Moreover, our personal experience with an odor can actually change the pattern of activity that is produced by the glomeruli in the olfactory bulb. For example, if you liked methyl salicylate (wintergreen) mints but one day became ill after eating one, causing you to thereafter find the scent very unpleasant (illustrating what is known as a learned taste aversion), the pattern of activity produced by the scent of methyl salicylate in the olfactory bulb would look different from what it did when you liked wintergreen mints. Astonishingly, what this means is that there is no fixed code for odor perception; rather, our personal experience with an odor determines how it will be processed by the olfactory system, even at very early levels (Wilson, Best, and Sullivan, 2004).

Still within the bulb, the glomeruli pass odor information on to **mitral cells** and **tufted cells**, nerve cells that coordinate information from the glomeruli for further processing and distribution to higher brain centers. Axons of the mitral and tufted cells of each bulb combine and form the **olfactory tract**, one in each hemisphere of the brain, that conveys odor information ipsilaterally to the **primary olfactory cortex**, also known as the **piriform cortex**. The primary olfactory cortex comprises the amygdala, parahippocampal gyrus, and interconnected areas; and it intimately interacts with the **entorhinal cortex** (see Figure 14.6*b*).

Though they number in the millions, OSNs converge onto a relatively small number of glomeruli. The mouse, whose brain and OR physiology are much more devoted to olfaction than are those of humans, has 2000 glomeruli. It was therefore speculated that humans with far fewer functioning ORs would have about 700 glomeruli (see the next section for more details). However, very recent immunohistochemistry research from Charles Greer's laboratory at Yale University revealed that humans have as many as 6000 glomeruli—three times as many as the mouse for only a third the number of receptors (Maresh et al., 2008). This discovery is quite a surprise and suggests that using the mouse olfactory system as a model for humans, which has been the traditional approach, may be inaccurate.

The central brain structures that process olfactory information are all part of a network of structures known as the **limbic system**, which is involved in many aspects of emotion and memory. As we will see later, these connections are key to the unique associative learning and emotional properties of olfaction.

Olfactory receptor cells are different from all other sensory receptor cells in that they are not mediated by a protective barrier and instead make direct contact with the brain. By contrast, visual receptors are protected by the cornea, receptors for hearing are protected by the eardrum, and taste buds are buried in papillae. One consequence of the fact that the olfactory sensory neurons are direct conduits into the brain is that many drugs can be inhaled.

In spite of their direct linkage into the brain, OSN axons are among the thinnest and slowest in the body. Therefore, even though the nose connects directly to the brain, the time it takes to perceive a stimulus (in this case an odor) is long compared to our other sensory experiences. The lag time between sniffing and the brain's registering a scent varies, averaging approximately 400 milliseconds (ms), almost half a second; compare this to the 45 ms it takes for the visual cortex to register an image presented to the retina. This half-second duration for odor registration does not take into account the time it takes to react to a scent, which effectively doubles the perceptual time, making olfaction a particularly slow sense. You yourself have probably observed that smells seem to *emerge* gradually, rather than flashing into your awareness.

These distinctions bring up the subtle differences between sensation and perception in olfaction. Sensation occurs when an odor is neurally registered; perception occurs when we become aware of detecting a scent. Similarly, odors tend to linger perceptually—because of both ambient airflow and receptor clearance speed. The relatively slow speed and lingering features of olfaction have been the central obstacles for developing effective "smell-o-vision" and olfactory virtual-reality technologies.

mitral cell Any of the main projective output neurons in the olfactory bulb.

tufted cell Any of a secondary class of output neurons in the olfactory bulb.

olfactory tract The bundle of axons of the mitral and tufted cells within the olfactory bulb that sends odor information to the primary olfactory cortex.

primary olfactory cortex or piriform cortex The neural area where olfactory information is first processed. It comprises the amygdala, parahippocampal gyrus, and interconnected areas; and it interacts closely with the entorhinal cortex.

entorhinal cortex A phylogenetically old cortical region that provides the major sensory association input into the hippocampus. The entorhinal cortex also receives direct projections from olfactory regions.

limbic system The encompassing group of neural structures that includes the olfactory cortex, the amygdala, the hippocampus, the piriform cortex, and the entorhinal cortex. The limbic system is involved in many aspects of emotion and memory. Olfaction is unique among the senses for its direct and intimate connection to the limbic system.

The Genetic Basis of Olfactory Receptors

In 1991, molecular biologists Linda Buck and Richard Axel (who were rewarded with a Nobel Prize for their efforts) showed that the mammalian genome contains between about 1000 and 2000 different olfactory receptor genes, depending on the species (rodents have the most), each of which codes for a single type of OR. All mammals appear to have pretty much this same set of genes, but some OR genes in each species are nonfunctional "pseudogenes": the genes are present on the chromosomes, but the proteins coded for by the genes never get produced. The latest figures suggest that dogs have 811 functional OR genes (Matsunami, 2011); therefore, about 19% of their OR genes are pseudogenes. In humans, the proportion of pseudogenes is much higher, between 60% and 70%.

We don't have a precise percentage of pseudogenes for humans, because researchers have found individual variability in the number of functional receptors expressed. One person may express 358 ORs while another expresses 388, but both have a "normal" sense of smell. This number reflects both which genes are expressed as functional receptors and how many copies of a specific receptor a person may have. The more copies of a specific receptor you have, the more sensitive you will be to certain odorants (that is, certain specific chemicals will smell stronger to one person than they do to another because of the number of receptor copies they have); and whether you have a pseudogene or a functional gene for a given receptor also alters odor perception (Keller et al., 2007). For example, people who "hate" the aroma of cilantro (also known as coriander) are missing the gene for detecting the herbal floral component of this aroma and therefore detect only the soapy note (Kurz, 2008). In olfaction, there may truly be different noses for different people (Menashe et al., 2003).

The number of particular receptors people express can also influence their liking for an odor, because having more receptors leads to a more intense smell, and strong scents in general tend to be perceived as less pleasant than the same scents at a lower intensity (see also the "Olfactory Hedonics" section of this chapter). We see this relationship with intensity in all our senses. Very bright lights and loud sounds are inherently more unpleasant than moderate-intensity lights and sounds, and our relative acuity in vision and hearing will individually affect how much we can tolerate (see Chapters 5 and 9 for more detail). Though genetic variation in receptor expression may contribute to inborn predispositions toward certain odorants, the lack of consistency across people, both in how receptors are expressed and in how other factors, such as personal experience, mediate the response, shows that there are no truly innate responses with the sense of smell.

Some researchers have recently suggested that the high proportion of OR pseudogenes in humans is the result of an evolutionary trade-off between vision and olfaction. Yoav Gilad et al. (2004) observed that Old World primate species such as gorillas and rhesus monkeys have about 30% OR pseudogenes, but most New World species (e.g., squirrel monkeys) have a lower proportion (about 18%). The one New World exception is the howler monkey, which also has about 30% OR pseudogenes. It turns out that the howler monkey has something in common with Old World primates that other New World monkeys do not: trichromatic color vision. Brains can get only so big, so to free up the brain space necessary to house human ancestors' evolving visual analysis tools (including trichromatic vision), we may have dropped the ability to analyze the odorants detected by certain OR genes, and they then became pseudogenes. For our evolutionary predecessors, the payoff from superior visual detection must have outweighed the disadvantages from diminished olfactory acuity.

FIGURE 14.7 The trigeminal nerve's role in the perception of odors. (*a*) The trigeminal nerve carries information from somatosensory receptors in the nose and face to the thalamus and then on to the somatosensory cortex. (*b*) The irritation or excitement (depending on your culinary preferences) caused by eating chili peppers is due to trigeminal nerve stimulation.

(*a*)

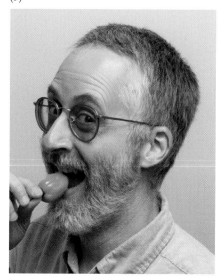

(*b*)

It may sound surprising, but new paleontological research has shown that mammalian brain evolution was precipitated by an increase in olfactory ability (Rowe, Macrinin, and Luo, 2011). That is, the first structures in mammalian brains to increase in size and complexity were those associated with the sense of smell. It is theorized that increased olfactory capacity enabled our 200-million-year-old predecessors to hunt at night, giving them the evolutionary edge they needed to develop further and eventually evolve our current brains, which, ironically along the way, traded off olfactory advantages for vision.

The Feel of Scent

As mentioned at the start of this chapter, our experience of odors often has a *feel* to it, as well as a smell. This is because most odorants stimulate the somatosensory system to some degree through polymodal nociceptors (touch, pain, and temperature receptors) inside the nose. For example, menthol feels cool and ammonia feels burning. These sensations are mediated by the **trigeminal nerve** (cranial nerve V) (Figure 14.7*a*). In many cases it is impossible to distinguish between the sensations traveling up cranial nerve I from olfactory receptors and those traveling up cranial nerve V from somatosensory receptors. For example, the nasal cooling (cranial nerve V) and specific scent (cranial nerve I) associated with the smell of peppermint fuse to produce a holistic sensory experience. Trigeminal stimulation accounts for why our eyes tear when we chop onions and why we sneeze when we sniff pepper. High levels of trigeminal stimulation (e.g., munching habanero peppers; Figure 14.7*b*) can produce a severe burning sensation, and trigeminal activity has been linked to the facial-head pain felt in migraine headaches. "Smelling salts" (made from ammonia combined with eucalyptus oil) revive us because of their trigeminal activation.

> FURTHER DISCUSSION of the trigeminal nerve, which also tells you about fat in your diet, can be found in Chapter 15 on page 448.

From Chemicals to Smells

Now that we know something about the physiological basis of olfaction, we can ask the following crucial question: How does the biochemical interaction between an odorant and an OR, and subsequent neurological processing in the olfactory bulbs and later brain structures, result in the psychological perception of a scent such as wintergreen mint? Buck and Axel's seminal discovery of olfactory receptor genes prompted an explosion of research surrounding this question over the past two decades, but a fully comprehensive theory of how we perceive scents has still not been realized.

Theories of Olfactory Perception

At present, the best-accepted biochemical theory (first proposed in its modern form in the 1950s by the British scientist John Amoore) is based on the match between the shapes of odorants and odor receptors. It was dubbed "shape

trigeminal (V) nerves The fifth pair of cranial nerves, which transmit information about the "feel" of an odorant (e.g., mint feels cool, cinnamon feels warm), as well as pain and irritation sensations (e.g., ammonia feels burning).

(a) Odorants   Odorant receptors   (b) Odorant compounds   Receptor arrays   Hypothetical receptor activation pattern

■ Best activation
□ Some activation

FIGURE 14.8 Odorant-receptor binding and odorant activation, as predicted by shape-pattern theory. (*a*) Chemicals of specific shapes fit receptors with shapes that best accommodate them. (*b*) Odorant molecules activate feature detectors on various receptor types. The specific pattern of activity elicited by a given set of receptors determines the specific scent perceived.

shape-pattern theory The current dominant biochemical theory for how chemicals come to be perceived as specific odors. Shape-pattern theory contends that different scents—as a function of the fit between odorant shape to OR shape—activate different arrays of olfactory receptors in the olfactory epithelia. These various arrays produce specific firing patterns of neurons in the olfactory bulb, which then determine the particular scent we perceive.

vibration theory An alternative to *shape-pattern theory* for describing how olfaction works. Vibration theory proposes that every odorant has a different vibrational frequency, and that molecules that produce the same vibrational frequencies will smell the same.

theory" but is better denoted as "shape-pattern theory." In a nutshell, **shape-pattern theory** contends that odorant molecules have different shapes and olfactory receptors have different shapes, and an odorant will be detected by a specific OR to the extent that the odorant's molecules fit into the OR (**Figure 14.8**). Gordon Shepherd and his students pioneered the idea that when a given odorant is sniffed, a particular pattern is generated across the glomeruli. Differences in those spatial patterns provide the basis for the array of odors that we perceive.

The most recent molecular research suggests that scents are detected by means of a combinatorial code, where one odorant may bind to several different receptors and one receptor may bind several different odorants to varying degrees (see Figure 14.8). This means that different scents activate different arrays of olfactory receptors in the olfactory epithelia, producing specific firing patterns of neurons in the olfactory bulb. The specific pattern of electrical activity in the olfactory bulb then determines the particular scent we perceive. That is, different patterns are elicited for the perception of rose, mint, urine, and skunk (for example), and the various patterns for specific scents turn out to be highly consistent across individuals (Zou, Li, and Buck, 2005). This theory was implied in the previous discussion of odor receptor-chemical interactions.

However, there are also alternative explanations of how olfaction works. The strongest alternative to shape-pattern theory is **vibration theory**, championed most recently by Luca Turin (Franco et al., 2011; Turin, 1996). In essence, vibration theory proposes that, because of atomic structure, every odorant has a different vibrational frequency, and molecules that produce the same vibrational frequencies have the same smell. Turin reported that various chemicals that have predictably similar vibrations because of their molecular composition also have similar smells. For example, all citrus odors fall into the same vibrational-frequency class. But other, independent researchers have not validated Turin's claims (Keller and Vosshall, 2004).

Much less research has focused on the vibration theory than on the shape-pattern theory, so current advances may unfairly bias our understanding. Nevertheless, vibration theory cannot explain several conundrums of olfactory perception, such as specific anosmias and the different scents produced by stereoisomers, which shape-pattern theory can explain.

A **specific anosmia** is the inability to smell one specific compound amid otherwise normal smell perception. Specific anosmias are due to faulty odorant-receptor interactions and not odorant vibrations. Most specific anosmias are to steroidal musk compounds, and the condition appears to be genetic. The most studied specific anosmia is an inability to smell the compound andro-stenone, which is found in armpit sweat and pork. A significant proportion of the population has a specific anosmia to androstenone; estimates range between 11% and 75%, but between 20% and 40% is more typical (Bremner et al., 2003). Interestingly, among those who can smell androstenone, the majority find it to be unpleasant and "urinous," while the rest describe it as a "sweet musky-floral" scent. A recent cloning study of human olfactory receptors showed that the variability in detection of the odorant androstenone, as well as its perceived pleasantness, is due to genetic differences in OR expression between individuals (Keller et al., 2007). The different anosmia rates obtained for adrostenone in different studies reflect the fact that the gene governing the ability to smell androstenone varies randomly within any given sample.

FURTHER DISCUSSION of specific sensory deficits amid otherwise normal perception—in this case vision (agnosias)—can be found in Chapter 4 on page 88.

Nonmusk odorants for which specific anosmias have also been found include the sulfur compound in asparagus—this is the "funny" smell in urine that some people detect after eating it, but in addition to variation in the ability to smell this compound, the amount of the compound that is excreted in urine varies genetically between individuals. Therefore, if you don't smell something "funny" after eating asparagus, it may be because you don't excrete the sulfur metabolite, not because you're missing the receptor to detect the odorant (Pelchat et al., 2011). If you really want to check whether you're among the approximately 6% of Americans who are anosmic to asparagus pee, you'll need to take a sniff after a friend who can smell it in her own urine and ate the same asparagus-containing meal as you goes to the bathroom. Approximately 10% of the population is anosmic to the scent of freesia flowers, and sensitivity to the sweaty-sock aroma of isovaleric acid also varies vastly among people, with about 3% of the population unable to detect it at all (Griff and Reed, 1995). These examples all further illustrate how individual variability in receptor expression determines each of our own unique olfactory experiences. Although the differences in perception may be small, ostensibly everyone has a different nose.

Vibration theory cannot explain the presence of specific anosmias or why the same odorant produces different scent sensations in different people, but shape-pattern theory can: these phenomena could arise from differing odorant–receptor interactions or the absence of certain receptors. Another mark in favor of shape-pattern theory comes from the study of stereoisomers. **Stereoisomers** are molecules that are mirror-image rotations of one another; and although they contain all the same atoms, they can smell completely different. For example, D-carvone (the right-handed isomer) smells like caraway (**Figure 14.9***a*), and L-carvone (the left-handed isomer) smells like spearmint (Figure 14.9*b*). According to shape-pattern theory, this difference arises because the rotated molecules do not fit the same receptors (as if you were trying to put your right hand into your left-hand glove); thus, different receptors are

specific anosmia The inability to smell one specific compound amid otherwise normal smell perception.

stereoisomers Isomers (molecules that can exist in different structural forms) in which the spatial arrangements of the atoms are mirror-image rotations of one another, like a right and left hand.

(a) D-carvone   (b) L-carvone

FIGURE 14.9 The stereoisomers D-carvone (a) and L-carvone (b) contain the same atoms, yet they smell completely different: D-carvone smells like caraway; L-carvone, like spearmint. Shape-pattern theory can account for this fact.

activated for these two molecules, causing different scents to be perceived. Vibration theory cannot explain why stereoisomers smell different, because the vibration of stereoisomers is the same. More recent, and more direct, evidence for shape-pattern theory comes from in vitro experiments using cloned olfactory receptors, which have revealed chemical-receptor interactions that show specific odorants binding with specific receptors.

At the same time, all molecules vibrate, and all receptors are made of atoms that vibrate. Moreover, recent work has shown that fruit flies are capable of distinguishing between two molecules that are identical in shape but have different vibrational frequencies (Franco et al., 2011). The same tests applied to humans have so far failed, but an interaction between the vibration and shape-pattern theories may yet be discovered for human olfaction. Stay tuned.

The Importance of Patterns

You may have noticed a potential discrepancy in how we've accounted for odor perception. As already noted, we can discriminate many thousands of odors, yet our genes code for only about 1000 olfactory receptors, and 600–700 of them are nonfunctional. How can we detect so many different scents? To start to see the way out of this conundrum, recall that, in vision, we can tell the difference between thousands of different colors, even though we have only *three* types of cones. Each type of olfactory receptor responds to the structure of certain molecules only. However, a molecule may have features that stimulate several different receptors. Moreover, each receptor appears to have various "feature detectors" that contribute to further specificity in OR activation. Thus, a different *set* of feature detectors is activated when we smell chocolate or wintergreen or rose (see Figure 14.8b).

As with color detection, we detect odors by the *pattern* of activity across various different receptor types. The intensity of an odor also changes which receptors (and hence patterns) will be activated, which is why weak and strong concentrations of an odorant do not smell quite the same. The fact that receptor activation is affected by odorant concentration likely explains why dogs with many more functional receptors than we have can perceive odorants of considerably lower concentrations. The timing of olfactory receptor activation also seems to be important; an odorant that activates several receptors will also stimulate them in a specific temporal sequence and speed. Another odorant might stimulate the same receptors in a different order and rate, and the difference might lead to the perception of a different smell (**Figure 14.10**).

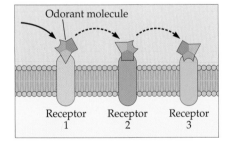

FIGURE 14.10 The hypothetical role of OR receptor activation timing and order. A single molecule binds first to receptor type 1, then a split second later to receptor type 2, and then to receptor type 3. Brains are especially well suited to recognizing patterns of responses such as this, so the number of odors we can recognize greatly exceeds the number of receptor types available.

Thus, different odor perceptions can be due to different OR firing patterns, or to firing of the same receptors at a different rate and/or in a different sequence.

The flip side of the pattern perception mechanism is that if two odorants, one molecularly simple and the other complex, activate the same receptors in the same way, we end up smelling the same thing. For example, the feature detectors for the odorant made up of the single molecule phenyl ethyl alcohol (used to make the artificial scent of rose) and a real live rose in the garden, whose scent is composed of more than 1000 different molecules, might both result in the same basic pattern of OR activation and hence the same perception of "rose" (this phenomenon should be reminiscent of metamers in color vision, discussed in Chapter 5).

Patterns are also important for odor processing at early stages in the olfactory cortex. Specific patterns of activity are produced by specific odors in the piriform cortex, and odors that are perceived as smelling similar produce similar patterns. For example, "minty" odors like wintergreen and spearmint produce patterns of activity that have a lot of overlap, but the pattern produced by a "citrus" odor like lemon does not overlap with the pattern elicited by wintergreen. Interestingly, distinctive patterns of activity by specific categories of odors (e.g., minty, citrus) are not seen farther downstream in olfactory processing, such as in the amygdala or orbitofrontal cortex (J. D. Howard et al., 2009). Patterns may be lacking in these regions of the brain because at these stages of processing, personal and emotional associations mediate activity patterns.

Odor Mixtures

Just as we rarely hear pure tones outside of auditory perception experiments, we rarely smell "pure odorants" outside of an olfactory perception lab. Almost all of the olfactory stimuli that we encounter in the real world are mixtures, like the 1000-molecule rose scent emanating from a flower bed that we discussed in the previous section. How do we process the components in an odorant mixture? There are two broad possibilities: *analysis* and *synthesis*. Auditory mixtures provide the classic example of analysis. A high note and a low note played simultaneously on a piano each can be analyzed out of the mix and perceived separately (**Figure 14.11***a*). Color mixtures provide the classic example of synthesis. If we mix red and green lights, the resulting color that we see is yellow (Figure 14.11*b*). Red and green cannot be analyzed out, because the two lights have been synthesized into something else. Is olfaction (Figure 14.11*c*) an analytical or a synthetic sense?

> **FURTHER DISCUSSION** of color mixture synthesis can be found in Chapter 5 on pages 123–124.

(*a*) Auditory mixture: analysis

(*b*) Color mixture: synthesis

(*c*) Olfactory mixture: analysis and synthesis

FIGURE 14.11 The roles of analysis and synthesis in sensory perception. We can separately perceive the three tones of the musical chord being played in (*a*), but not the high- and medium-wavelength light rays mixing in the center of (*b*). When we mix odorants (*c*), we perceive the mixture primarily synthetically, but some degree of analytical perception is possible. Analytical ability varies with prior training and with the odorants that constitute the mixture.

binaral rivalry Competition between the two nostrils for odor perception. When a different scent is presented to each nostril simultaneously, we perceive each scent to be alternating back and forth with the other, and not a blend of the two scents.

Although we are capable of discriminating thousands of different odors, intuition tells us that most mixtures are perceived as unitary wholes. For example, the smell of bacon is very distinctive, and most people would perceive it to be a unitary sensation. But, like the natural rose aroma, there is no single "bacon" odorant; the sensation we recognize as bacon is made up of a combination of many different volatile chemicals. To test the synthetic/analytical nature of olfactory perception, Laing and his colleagues (Laing and Francis, 1989; Laing and Glemarec, 1992) conducted a series of experiments in which they asked untrained participants, participants who had received preliminary "odor training," and experienced perfumers and flavorists to identify the constituents of mixtures containing between one and five common odorants. The average discrimination rate from all the participants combined was no more than three components in a five-component mixture. However, the more training the participants had, the better they did. Thus, it appears that olfaction is primarily a synthetic sense, but that a certain amount of analytical ability can be developed.

The synthetic and analytical qualities of olfaction are also evident in **binaral rivalry**. As you read in Chapter 6, when a different object is presented to each eye simultaneously, you don't see a blend of the two objects; rather, binocular rivalry occurs, and you see the two objects alternating. A similar phenomenon occurs in hearing when discrepant sounds are presented to each ear (see Chapter 10). It was recently found that binaral rivalry in olfaction does occur: when two different odors are presented to each of our nostrils, we alternate in our ability to smell one odor or the other (Zhou and Chen, 2009). Researchers presented a rose scent to one nostril and simultaneously an odor that smelled like marker pens to the other nostril and found that the participants alternated back and forth between saying that they smelled "markers" or "rose." The marker scent was perceived as more intense, and it was usually perceived first, which also occurs in binocular rivalry, where the "stronger" image tends to dominate. What's interesting is that this rivalry seems to occur in both the nose and the brain. When the same participants were later presented with a *mixture* scent of both rose and markers to each nostril simultaneously, most of them also reported smelling first markers and then rose and then markers again, and so on. This observation suggests that odor rivalry is occurring in the brain as well as in the nostrils, or perhaps only in the brain. Researchers continue to investigate the different contributions of the nostrils and the brain to odor perception.

An even closer connection between olfaction and vision has been shown by the recent discovery that odors can influence what we actually see (**Figure 14.12**). In a binocular rivalry task, Zhou and her colleagues presented participants with a picture of a rose to one eye and a picture of two Sharpie markers to the other. As expected, participants alternated back and forth between seeing the rose and the markers. Then the smell of rose or markers was presented (to both nostrils) while the participants looked at a rose and markers, and depending on what smell was given, participants saw the corresponding image longer than the other image. That is, although the images still alternated, participants' ability to *see* the rose lasted longer when they were also smelling

FIGURE 14.12 (*a*) Two images—one of two markers and the other of a rose—were shown to a subject, one image to each eye. The subject pressed one of two buttons to indicate when they switched between seeing predominantly the rose or predominantly the markers. (*b*) Subjects exposed to a rose scent spent more time predominantly seeing the rose. Exposure to a marker scent had the opposite effect. (After Zhou et al., 2010.)

(*a*)

Left eye

Right eye

(*b*)

rose, and their ability to *see* the Sharpie markers lasted longer when they were smelling markers (Zhou et al., 2010). In the brain it has also been shown that when olfactory input is received, the olfactory bulb executes early sensory transformations that are computationally analogous to those observed in other sensory systems, especially vision (Cleland, 2010). Thus, the most complex sense (vision) is profoundly and multiply connected to our most ancient sense (olfaction). Calling the olfactory epithelium "the retina of the nose" is more than just a simple metaphor.

The Power of Sniffing

When you smell something passively, you are breathing in air containing odorant molecules and detecting those molecules. By contrast, when you sniff, you are consciously and forcibly inhaling bursts of air into your nostrils, and sniffing increases the ability to detect odorants. Sniffing also produces greater activation in some parts of the brain, such as the cerebellum, than passive inhalation does. Exciting new research is currently exploring how active sniffing may enable severely physically disabled people to communicate with the outside world and to move independently. "Locked-in syndrome" is a horrendous neurological condition characterized by completely intact cognition and mentality but total physical paralysis, such that afflicted people are literally locked in their own bodies. Brain-computer interfaces would be an ideal solution for such individuals, but they have not yet been successfully implemented, and up to now these patients have had to rely on blinking as the sole means to communicate (it was recognized that the eyeblink response is still intact in these people).

Active sniffing has now also been discovered to be preserved in locked-in syndrome. Taking advantage of this intact physical function, researchers in Israel recently showed that by using precise, deliberate sniffing—changing sniff magnitude, duration, onset, and offset—locked-in patients can be successfully trained to control text-writing software and meaningfully communicate with loved ones. Using the same type of sniff technology, quadriplegic patients have also been trained to move their wheelchairs in complex circuits by using their nose alone (Plotkin et al., 2010). This may be the dawn of a nasally powered world.

Odor Imagery

One area where olfaction and our other senses diverge is imagery. We know that visual and auditory imagery is easy and readily accessible, and, though in somewhat different ways, imagery is also evident in touch (shivers, tingles, phantom limb), and taste (e.g., the sour salivation reaction). By contrast, humans appear to have little or no ability to conjure "odor images." For example, you can probably see the visual image of a Hershey's chocolate kiss in your mind's eye right now (you might even start salivating). But can you really reproduce the smell of chocolate in your "mind's nose"? Brain-imaging studies (e.g., Kosslyn et al., 1995) have shown that many of the same parts of the brain that would be involved in actually seeing the kiss are also involved in visually imaging it; with olfaction, however, similar studies suggest that the degree of overlap between smelling an odor and "imaging" it is much weaker (Djordjevic et al., 2005). Dreams with olfactory sensations are also very rare (Carskadon et al., 1989; Zadra, Nielsen, and Donderi, 1998).

Animals, such as rodents, that rely predominantly on smell as the sense to negotiate the world may well think and dream in smell. However, because we do not think in smell, it is not necessary to have stored representations of olfactory experiences. Nevertheless, recent functional neuroimaging research

psychophysics The science of defining quantitative relationships between physical and psychological (subjective) events.

suggests that although odor imagery among average people is very rare, expert perfumers may be able to acquire the ability to image odors through training. Functional MRI showed that perfumers produced activation in their piriform cortex when asked to image odors; and the greater their perfumery experience, the more their brains appeared to be reorganized to accommodate this task (Plailly, Delon-Martin, and Royet, 2011). This is another example of how the olfactory system is especially flexible and capable of neural reorganization on the basis of experience and learning.

Olfactory Psychophysics, Identification, and Adaptation

The subfield of psychology called **psychophysics** was introduced in Chapter 1. The goal of the psychophysicist is to quantify the psychological experience of our sensory world. In this section we will briefly discuss some of the nuts-and-bolts questions addressed by olfactory psychophysics; then we'll go on to consider the related and more interesting questions of how we identify and adapt to odors.

Detection, Discrimination, and Recognition

Perhaps the most basic question we can ask for any sense is, how much stimulation is required before we perceive something? As with other senses, our olfactory *detection thresholds* depend on a number of factors. For instance, odorant molecules with longer carbon chains, such as vanillin, are easier to detect (have lower detection thresholds) than those with shorter carbon chains, such as acetone (otherwise known as nail polish remover). Women also have generally lower olfactory detection thresholds than men, especially during the ovulatory phase of the menstrual cycle. But contrary to popular belief, research has shown that olfactory sensitivity is *not* heightened during pregnancy (Cameron, 2007; Hummel et al., 2002; Laska et al., 1996). Taste is another story, as we'll see in the next chapter.

Our ability to detect odorants also declines with age, because of a change in the proportion of cell regeneration to cell death in ORs: as we age, the number of odor receptors that die off rises beyond the number that are regenerated (Kern et al., 2004). This ratio continues to worsen in favor of cell death as we grow older, such that after the age of 85 it is estimated that about 50% of the population has effectively become anosmic (Hummel et al., 2007; J. C. Stevens and Cain, 1987). Taste and trigeminal perception do not decline in sensitivity as much with age, which explains why the elderly favor foods that are spicy (trigeminal) and salty (taste) (J. C. Stevens, Plantinga, and Cain, 1982, but see also Boesveldt et al., 2011).

The ability to detect an odorant can also be manipulated by experience. Serendipitous observation revealed that through repeated testing, sensitivity to androstenone (the steroidal musk compound that many people have a specific anosmia for) can be induced in about half of the people who are initially unable to detect it (Wysocki, Dorries, and Beauchamp, 1989). That is, a proportion of the people who are anosmic to this particular chemical develop an ability to smell androstenone through repeated exposure.

From other areas of biology, we know that genes can be "turned on" by environmental factors, and because each olfactory receptor is coded for by a specific gene, it is conceivable that the receptors for detecting androstenone can be activated through repeated presentation of the chemical. Other studies have shown that increased sensitivity to some common odorants, such as benzaldehyde (cherry-almond aroma) and citralva (lemon-orange scent), can be induced through repeated exposure to these chemicals, particularly among females (Dalton,

Doolittle, and Breslin, 2002; Diamond et al., 2005). Furthermore, recent studies in fruit flies have shown that genetically hardwired OSNs can be altered by exposure to specific chemicals (Sachse et al., 2007). Plasticity and modulation through environmental influences appear to be basic principles in olfaction.

As already noted, a healthy person can *discriminate* thousands of odors. The more "nose" training we have (e.g., professional perfumers and wine tasters), the more odors we can discriminate; some claims suggest that professionals can distinguish up to 100,000 odors (Dobb, 1989). Note, however, that discrimination is not the same thing as *recognition*, the ability to remember whether or not we've smelled an odor before. It takes as much as three times as many odorant molecules floating through the nose to recognize an odor as it does to simply detect the presence of an odor. You've probably experienced this phenomenon yourself: you register that you smell something before you realize that you know the smell. Interestingly, we don't need to know what a smell *is*, or be able to name it, in order to recognize it or even to have a memory triggered by it. The only requirement is that we have previously encountered the scent—that is, that the odor is familiar (Herz and Cupchik, 1992; Cleary et al., 2010). This is different from other sensory experiences among cognitively healthy adults. For example, we wouldn't be able to say that we "recognize," respond appropriately to, or have a memory elicited by something that we see without having some kind of label for it, even if the label is very vague or idiosyncratic, such as "food" or "uncle's weird hat." Brain-damaged patients with visual agnosia are the exception in that they often know how to use an object even if they don't know what it's called.

Another interesting feature of odor recognition is its durability. In controlled experiments, a 30-second delay between odor presentation and testing produces a precipitous drop in recognition accuracy, but what we remember after 30 seconds is very close to what we remember after 3 days, a month, or even a year (**Figure 14.13**) (Engen, Kuisma, and Eimas, 1973; Engen and Ross, 1973; Murphy et al., 1991; Rabin and Cain, 1984). Again, you probably recognize this phenomenon from your own life. If you smelled a certain perfume only once when you were a child, and you came upon that perfume again 20 years later, you might very well know that the odor was familiar. Our memory for odors is even more resilient if the initial exposure is accompanied by emotion (Herz, 1997).

FIGURE 14.13 Long-term memory for smells. The first point on this graph, at about 70%, indicates odor recognition accuracy with only a 30-second delay from learning. Note, however, that this accuracy level is the same after a week and has dropped only about 3% after a retention interval of a month. This retention rate remains relatively constant over intervals at least as long as one year. (From Engen and Ross, 1973.)

Psychophysical Methods for Detection and Discrimination

Researchers wanting to measure how perceptually sensitive people are to odors, or whether they can discriminate one odorant from another, use various psychophysical methods. A common olfactory technique for determining someone's odor detection threshold is called the **staircase method** (or "reverse staircase method"), and it is an example of what are known as "methods of limits" (see Chapter 1). There are various versions of the staircase method. In a typical procedure, an odorant is presented in ever-increasing concentration increments until the participant reports being able to "smell something" for several increments. Then the odorant's concentration is decreased incrementally until the participant reports no detection.

These reversals are repeated a number of times, and the odorant concentrations at the point where reversals occur are averaged to determine the approximate concentration needed for that person to detect the odorant. As a reversal point is reached, the increments by which an odorant's concentration is raised and lowered can be fine-tuned for precision. Staircase methods can be used to determine a general benchmark for olfactory sensitivity. They can also be used to determine detection thresholds across a range of odors to test individuals in specific ways.

staircase method A psychophysical method for determining the concentration of a stimulus required for detection at the threshold level. The staircase method is an example of a *method of limits*. A stimulus (e.g., odorant) is presented in an ascending concentration sequence until detection is indicated, and then the concentration is shifted to a descending sequence until the response changes to "no detection." This ascending and descending sequence is typically repeated several times, and the concentrations at which reversals occur are averaged to determine the threshold detection level of that odorant for a given individual. Also called *reverse staircase method*.

triangle test A test in which a participant is given three odorants to smell, of which two are the same and one is different. The participant is required to state which is the odd odor out. Typically, the order in which the three odorants are given (e.g., same, same, different; different, same, same; same, different, same) is manipulated and the test is repeated several times for greater accuracy.

tip-of-the-nose phenomenon The inability to name an odor, even though it is very familiar. Contrary to the tip-of-the-tongue phenomenon, one has no lexical access to the name of the odor, such as first letter, rhyme, number of syllables, and so on, when in the tip-of-the-nose state. This is an example of how language and olfactory perception are deeply disconnected.

To determine whether someone can discriminate between two odorants, the most common psychophysical test used is called the **triangle test**. In a triangle test, a participant is given three odorants to smell, of which two are the same and one is different. The participant is required to state which is the odd odor out. Typically, the order in which the three odorants are given (e.g., same, same, different; different, same, same; same, different, same) is manipulated and the test is repeated several times to establish accuracy.

Identification

Attaching a verbal label to a smell is yet another step beyond odor recognition. Olfaction has been called the "mute sense" because we are often so lost for words to describe our olfactory experiences (D. Ackerman, 1990). All of us have had the experience of not being able to come up with the name of something we know; for example, what was the name of your fourth-grade teacher? This experience is known as the "tip-of-the-tongue" phenomenon. In the olfactory domain, suppose you take a sniff of something from a bottle that provides no visual clues to what it contains and you immediately know that the scent is extremely familiar, but you just can't come up with the name for it. Borrowing from the verbal scenario, we call this experience the **tip-of-the-nose phenomenon** (Lawless and Engen, 1977), and it can be very frustrating.

There are some important differences between the tip-of-the-nose state and the tip-of-the-tongue state. For one, in the tip-of-the-tongue state we might not know the exact word we're looking for, but we might know its first letter, its general word configuration, the number of syllables in the word, and so on ("Starts with a *K*, two syllables, sounds like a sandwich roll … Aha, my fourth-grade teacher was Mrs. Kaiser!"). By contrast, in the tip-of-the-nose state, we typically know nothing about the label we're searching for. Anthropologists have found that in all known languages, there are fewer words that refer exclusively to our experience of smells than there are for any other sensation (Classen, Howes, and Synnott, 1994). In English, *aromatic*, *fragrant*, *pungent*, and *stinky* pretty much exhaust the list of adjectives that specifically describe olfactory stimuli and nothing else. More common terms used to describe odors, like *floral* or *fruity*, are references to the odor-producing objects (flowers and fruits), not the odorants themselves. We also borrow terms from other senses (chocolate smells *sweet*, grass smells *green*, and so on).

Various possibilities explain why our sense of smell and language are so disconnected. First, unlike what happens in other sensory systems, olfactory information does not need to be integrated in the thalamus prior to processing in the cortex, and it is argued that the thalamus has relevance for language. Second, a large body of evidence indicates that the majority of olfactory processing occurs in the right hemisphere of the brain, whereas language processing is known to be dominated by the left hemisphere (see Royet and Plailly, 2004, for a review). It has even been suggested that odors are hard to name because of competition between odor and language processing for cognitive resources that share the same neural substrates (Lorig, 1999). This latter theory was supported by a study using brain-imaging techniques, which showed that the presence of an odorant altered the semantic processing of words and degraded word encoding, but did not influence nonsemantic processing (Walla et al., 2003). (See also **Web Essays 14.1: Olfactory Lateralization** and **14.2: Verbal-Olfactory Interactions**.)

When odor identification is measured in a way that can trigger the tip-of-the-nose state, it is equivalent to a free-recall memory test: you have to come up with the name of the odor without any clues. Another way that odor identification is measured is by recognition, where, like a multiple-choice exam question, various alternates are given and the person must pick the correct name to go with that odor. Scratch-and-sniff odor recognition tests like this are very important in clinical contexts, particularly for detecting the early stages of neurological disorders like Alzheimer's disease. Prior to forgetting people's names or where the car keys are, people in the first stages of Alzheimer's are unable to correctly identify odors. This is because Alzheimer's is foremost a disease of semantic loss; and because language and smell are so weakly connected in the first place, the odor-naming system is the most vulnerable to semantic deterioration, so an inability to identify odors is likely to be one of the first signs of the disease. Testing for such a deficit is crucial, because the sooner people are correctly diagnosed with Alzheimer's disease and treated, the better their quality and duration of life will be.

Adaptation

Have you ever had the experience of noticing coworkers or classmates who seem to be pouring a bottle of cologne over their head every morning, leaving you choking on the overpowering aroma? Can't they smell anything? Or perhaps you've noticed that, after having a bottle of perfume for a few months, you can't smell the fragrance in it anymore. Or you've gone away on vacation and returned home to find that your house seems to have a "funny" smell that it didn't have when you left. What's going on? The answer has two parts: the first involves the nose, and the second involves the mind.

The sense of smell is a change detection system. When a new chemical comes along, your olfactory receptors fire in response to it, and you perceive a scent. For example, when you first enter a bakery, you notice the mouthwatering aromas of the cakes, cookies, pies, and breads. But if you stand inside inspecting the sweet baked goods for a while, you may find that by the time you've picked out what cake you want for dessert, you can no longer smell it. What has happened is that the odorant molecules that make up the bakery aroma have bound to the corresponding olfactory sensory neurons in your nose. When this happens the ORs retreat into the cell body (Firestein, 2001). The receptors are therefore no longer physically available to respond to the bakery scent molecules. This response is a process in "receptor recycling." Specifically, odorant binding to an OR causes the OR to be internalized into its cell body, where it becomes unbound from the odorant and is then recycled through the cell and emerges again in a number of minutes. Receptor recycling is a mechanism common to all receptors in the class to which ORs belong: **G protein–coupled receptors** (**GPCRs**).

G protein–coupled receptor (GPCR) Any of the class of receptors that are present on the surface of olfactory sensory neurons. All GPCRs are characterized by a common structural feature of seven membrane-spanning α-helices.

receptor adaptation The biochemical phenomenon, occurring after continual exposure to an odorant, whereby receptors stop responding to an odorant and detection ceases.

> **FURTHER DISCUSSION** of parallels to visual adaptation can be found in Chapter 2 on page 48.

This process is called **receptor adaptation**. The precise length of time required for adaptation varies as a function of both the individual (Dalton, 2002) and the odorant (Pierce et al., 1996). On average it takes about 15–20 minutes of continual exposure to an odorant for the molecules to stop eliciting an olfactory response, but adaptation can also occur in less than a minute. Receptor adaptation can also be undone relatively quickly. Stepping outside the bakery for a few minutes gives unbound olfactory receptors a chance to accumulate on the cell surface again, so when you walk back in you can enjoy the appetizing scents once more. The magnitude of adaptation is also affected by odor intensity (Kadohisa and Wilson, 2006). As the concentration of an odorant increases, the degree of adaptation decreases. For example, it takes

cross-adaptation The reduction in detection of an odorant following exposure to another odorant. Cross-adaptation is presumed to occur because the two odorants share one or more olfactory receptors for their transduction, but the order in which odorants are presented also plays a role.

longer to adapt to the aroma wafting from an apple pie baking in the oven than to the scent emanating from a cool slice of pie on the kitchen counter. This is because more molecules of apple pie aroma become volatile and are thus available to activate OR receptors when the pie is hot than when it is cold.

One way to prolong the effect of smelling a scent before adaptation kicks in is to dispense an odor intermittently. For example, bursts of air freshener alternated with no scent will draw out the time before your receptors are smothered by the air freshener molecules and duck for cover.

Dalton (1996) also showed that presumed danger can have an effect on adaptation rates. In one experiment, half the participants were told that an odor they were being exposed to was "healthful," while the other participants were told the odor was "hazardous." Twenty minutes after initial exposure, the participants smelling the supposedly healthful odor had adapted to it, whereas the participants who thought they were smelling a hazardous chemical actually became sensitized—they reported the smell as even more intense after 20 minutes than at the start of the experiment. However, when these participants were given a psychophysical test of odor detection, it was shown that they had adapted just as the people who were told it was healthful had adapted. Fear of odor exposure can even make people perceive an odor that does not exist (Engen, 1972). For example, people who believe that a factory must be emitting "dangerous chemicals" frequently complain that they can smell a malodor coming from the plant, regardless of what the factory produces or whether it is even functioning. These examples illustrate how psychological factors can often supersede physical reality in odor perception.

One of the benefits of olfactory adaptation is that it enables us to filter out stable background odors, and this filtering ability can be enhanced through active sniffing—that is, taking deliberate, quick inhalations (Kepecs, Uchida, and Mainen, 2007). Sniffing makes OR neurons less responsive to stable odors and more responsive to new odorants (Verhagen et al., 2007). For example, if we're at a car dealership and think we smell something burning, we typically engage in active sniffing to (1) see if we're right and (2) determine which BMW is smoldering. In vision and hearing, perceptual stimuli in the foreground can be segregated from stimuli in the background through spatial analysis of the scene. In olfaction, spatial analysis is compromised because background and foreground odors merge in the air. However, provided that background and foreground odors are at least briefly separated in time (new-car smell first and then the scent of burning plastic), sniffing enables us to separate components of an olfactory scene.

In some cases, exposure to one odorant can raise the odor detection threshold for a second, completely different odorant. For example, when you're picking out a perfume in a department store, your nose may become fairly useless at differentiating the fragrances after several samples, despite the salesperson's insistence that the perfumes are quite different from each other (Figure 14.14). This phenomenon is called **cross-adaptation**, and it is presumed to occur when the odorants in question rely on similar sets of olfactory receptors. However, this simple explanation is complicated by the fact that most cross-adaptation relationships

FIGURE 14.14 Do these five fragrances smell the same? No, but because of olfactory cross-adaptation, if you've smelled four of them in succession the subtleties of the fifth one may be lost to your nose.

are nonreciprocal. For example, smelling pentanol (a chemical used in some paints) seems to have a strong cross-adapting effect on next smelling propanol (used as an antiseptic and solvent), whereas smelling propanol first has only a small cross-adapting effect on then smelling pentanol (Cain and Engen, 1969). Furthermore, exposure to the first odorant can sometimes *enhance* sensitivity to the second odorant. (See **Web Activity 14.2: Odor Adaptation and Habituation**.)

Regardless of why they occur, cross-adaptation effects, like self-adaptation effects, usually go away after a few minutes. Professional perfumers, who may have to smell hundreds of scents per day and thus don't have a few minutes to spare, use a trick of sniffing their bare arm or cotton shirt sleeve between smelling odorants; doing this effectively clears the nose even at a fast pace of odorant presentation. Nobody knows why this works, but it does. The next time you find yourself suffering from numb nose in a department store, try it.

Cognitive Habituation

Receptor adaptation explains why you lose the delicious aroma of the bakery after you've been in the store for a while, but can smell it again after a short break outside. If you took a job at a bakery, however, a different process would take place. This is the phenomenon that your friend who can't smell his own cologne is experiencing, and it's the reason why you don't smell your house unless you go out of town for a couple weeks. It is a psychological effect called **cognitive habituation**.

In short, when we live with an odor, we cognitively habituate to it and no longer react to it, or we show a very diminished response to it. For example, textile workers exposed daily to acetone exhibited acetone detection thresholds that were eight times higher than those of a comparable group of control subjects. However, their thresholds to another chemical (butanol), to which neither group had been regularly exposed, were no different from each other (Wysocki et al., 1997). We habituate (that is, our receptors adapt) to some degree to stimuli presented to all our senses (for example, you stop hearing the ticktock of a grandfather clock after being in the room for a while), but attention can bring us out of habituation with every sense except smell. Unlike receptor adaptation, which can be undone in a few minutes, cognitive habituation requires weeks to reverse, even for pungent trigeminal stimulants like acetone (Dalton et al., 1997; Wysocki et al., 1997). For example, if you stopped wearing your cologne for 5 days, you would still *not* be able to smell it well once you put it back on. But if you abstained for 2 weeks or more, you would.

Dalton (2002) suggested that at least three mechanisms could be involved—either singularly or in combination—in producing olfactory habituation. First, the olfactory receptors that are internalized into their cell bodies during odor adaptation may be more hindered after continual exposure and take much longer to recycle than they normally would. Second, from continual exposure, odorant molecules may be absorbed into the bloodstream, and then transported to the olfactory receptors via nasal capillaries when we breathe out through the nose. As long as the odorant chemicals remain in the bloodstream, we will be constantly adapted (Maruniak, Silver, and Moulton, 1983). Finally, cognitive-emotional factors, like those demonstrated in the experiment in which participants were told that an odor was harmful and then *perceived* that they did not adapt, may be involved (but in the reverse direction) in cognitive habituation.

Another feature of olfactory perception that highlights the importance of conscious perception is that we cannot smell while we're asleep (Carskadon and Herz, 2004). Unlike what happens with auditory stimuli, presenting trigeminally activating odorants such as menthol and pyridine, even at high

cognitive habituation The psychological process by which, after long-term exposure to an odor, one no longer has the ability to detect that odor or has very diminished detection ability.

odor hedonics The liking dimension of odor perception, typically measured by ratings of an odors's perceived pleasantness, familiarity, and intensity.

concentrations, to participants who were in deep sleep—known as slow-wave sleep (SWS)—or who were dreaming (in REM sleep) did not awaken them or elicit electroencephalogram (EEG) sleep pattern changes. Nevertheless, a functional neuroimaging (fMRI) study reported that presenting an odor during SWS that had previously been present during an awake learning task produced hippocampal changes consistent with those observed in memory consolidation (B. Rasch et al., 2007). However, the odor had no effect if it was presented during other sleep stages, including REM sleep. This finding suggests that odors may be detected by the brain during SWS. However, other neuroimaging research on awake subjects during smell tasks indicates that attention to odors alters brain activity and odor detection ability (Zelano et al., 2005; Plailly et al., 2008). It may be that, because attention is effectively cut off during sleep, so is our ability to respond to odors. Note again the issue of sensation versus perception. Conscious olfactory perception depends on attention.

Olfactory Hedonics

The most immediate and basic response we have to an odor is whether we like it or not. Such affective evaluations are known as **odor hedonics**. In tests of odor hedonic evaluation, people are typically asked to rate how pleasant, familiar, and intense a given odor is. These measures are then used to determine the hedonic value of a specific smell. It is obvious that perceived pleasantness is related to our liking for an odor. But how are familiarity and intensity related?

Familiarity and Intensity

As with many other facets of life, we tend to like odors that we've smelled many times before. That is, we tend to like familiar odors better than unfamiliar odors. Moreover, we often perceive pleasant odors as familiar, even if we haven't smelled them before (Moskowitz, Dravnieks, and Klarman, 1976; Sulmont, Issanchou, and Koster, 2002). Thus, ratings of odor pleasantness and familiarity show a linear relationship with odor liking.

Intensity has a more complex relationship to odor liking that is often represented by an inverted-U function, but this depends on the odorant. A rose scent, like pheny ethyl alcohol, may be evaluated as more positive with increasing intensity, up to a point; then the function reverses, and as the scent becomes stronger it is judged to be more disagreeable (Figure 14.15a). By contrast, a fishy odor, like trimethylamine, may be acceptable at low concentrations, but as intensity increases, its perception becomes steadily more negative (Figure 14.15b). Note also that individual differences in the number and type of receptors expressed may influence one's sensitivity (intensity perception) and hence the predisposition to experience specific odors along a pleasantness continuum.

Nature or Nurture?

A long-standing debate in olfaction centers around whether hedonic responses to odors are innate or learned. Researchers on the *innate* side of the debate claim that we are born with a predisposition to like or dislike various smells. In other words, rose is inherently a good smell and skunk is inherently a bad smell, the way bitter taste is inherently unpleasant to us and sweet inherently pleasant (see Chapter 15). In contrast, researchers taking the *learned* view hold that we are born merely with a predisposition to learn to like or dislike smells, and that whether a smell is liked or not is determined by the emotional value

FIGURE 14.15 Pleasantness ratings of odorants plotted against intensity. (*a*) The relationship between odor intensity and pleasantness is often described by an inverted-*U* function, if the odorant is initially considered pleasant, as the synthetic rose scent (phenyl ethyl alcohol) usually is. (*b*) For an odorant that is initially considered tolerable (but not necessarily pleasant), such as fishy smelling trimethylamine, the relationship may more aptly be described by a linear graph like this.

(good or bad) of the experiences that have been associated with it. That is, if we like rose and dislike skunk, the reason is that we have a good and a bad association, respectively, with these two scents. We need not have direct contact with a skunk to form such an association, though, because cultural learning provides meaning to many unencountered stimuli.

If asked to take a position yourself, on the sole basis of your own personal experiences, it's pretty likely you would come down on the innate side of the debate. After all, who could like the smell of skunk, and who wouldn't like the smell of a rose? In fact, however, a great deal of evidence suggests that odor hedonics are almost exclusively learned. A good place to start looking for such evidence is with infants. If odor preferences are innate, then newborns should display them. However, researchers have repeatedly found that infants and children often display very different preferences from those of adults. For instance, infants do not find the smells of sweat and feces unpleasant (Engen, 1982; M. Stein, Ottenberg, and Roulet, 1958), and toddlers often do not hedonically differentiate between odorants that adults find either very unpleasant (e.g., butyric acid, which smells like dirty socks) or pleasant (e.g., amyl acetate, which smells like banana).

One difficulty with these types of studies is that the olfactory system is fully functional by the third month of **gestation** (6 months before the baby is born) (Schaal, Marlier, and Soussignan, 1995, 1998; Winberg and Porter, 1998), and odorant molecules do find their way into the womb. So it is difficult to know exactly how much exposure even a newborn infant has had to an odorant. But exposure to odors in utero has led to yet another line of evidence in support of the learned view of hedonics: Mennella and colleagues found that mothers who consumed distinctive-smelling volatiles (e.g., garlic, alcohol, and cigarette smoke) during pregnancy or breast-feeding had infants who showed greater preferences for these smells than did infants who had not been exposed to these scents (Mennella and Beauchamp, 1991, 1993; Mennella, Johnson, and Beauchamp, 1995). What we learn about odors prenatally and during infancy and early childhood can also go on to influence our food and flavor preferences in adulthood (Haller et al., 1999). This correlation suggests that it might be a good idea for women to eat lots of spinach and liver and other healthful foods during pregnancy and lactation.

Cross-cultural data provide further support for the idea that it's not hardwired responses, but rather associative learning, that is responsible for olfactory preferences. No scientific studies to date have found cross-cultural agreement for hedonic responses to common everyday odors, either "good" or "bad" (Ayabe-Kanamura et al., 1998; Schleidt, Hold, and Attila, 1981). And many anecdotal and observational examples illustrate the culturally polarized responses that we have to specific odors, especially food aromas. For example, many Asians consider the smell of cheese to be disgusting, yet most Westerners consider it anything from comfort food to an extravagant indulgence. In contrast, the Japanese often enjoy a meal for breakfast called *nattō* (a fermented soybean dish) (**Figure 14.16**) that most Westerners wouldn't bring near their mouths (some say it smells like burning rubber). Both cheese and *nattō* are high in protein and similarly nutritious; the reason they are preferred, or not, as foods has to do with our learned associations with their scents.

gestation Fetal development during pregnancy.

FIGURE 14.16 The Japanese regularly eat *nattō* (right) for breakfast, but Westerners do not equate the smell of this food with eating. In contrast, cheese, which most Westerners enjoy, is considered disgusting by most Japanese eaters.

In case you're thinking that the examples of odors given so far aren't really *that* bad, and that there must be consensus on really horrid stenches, this also doesn't seem to be the case. Fecal smells are not high on most North Americans' "best smells list," but the Masai of Africa like to dress their hair with cow dung as a cosmetic color treatment. And in a study undertaken by the US military to create a stink bomb (to be used in place of tear gas to disband riots), it was impossible to find an odor (including "US Army–issue latrine scent") that was unanimously considered repellent across ethnic groups (Dilks, Dalton, and Beauchamp, 1999). Recent laboratory studies directly aimed at testing the learning hypothesis have shown that a novel odor can be made to be perceived as good or bad as a function of the experiences (good or bad) that are associated with it (Herz, Beland, and Hellerstein, 2004). Note, however, that from an experimental perspective it is much easier to demonstrate that odor preferences can be learned than to prove that no odorants exist to which innate responses may be shown.

In an attempt to support the view that odor pleasantness has an innate basis, a recent study tested whether an odorant's physical and chemical structure could predict how pleasant (or not) it would be perceived to be (Khan et al., 2007). The researchers found that the molecular structure of odorants was able to account for 30% of the variance in participants' responses (70% was not accounted for this way) and therefore argued that a portion of odor pleasantness perception may be innate. More research is clearly needed, but as you will now read, it would actually be disadvantageous for us if our odor preferences were innate.

An Evolutionary Argument

Specialist animal species live in very specific habitats and thus have a limited number of food sources and predators. For such species, hardwired responses to particular odors are adaptive. California ground squirrels, for example, exhibit an instinctive defensive response the first time they are exposed to the odor of their natural predator, the Pacific rattlesnake, but they don't show the same response to the scent of Pacific gopher snakes, which are not their natural predators (Figure 14.17) (Coss et al., 1993; Poran and Coss, 1990). *Generalist* species (including humans, rats, and cockroaches), by contrast, can exploit many different habitats. For generalists, the available resources and potential predators can vary widely across environments, so it is not adaptive for these species to have predetermined olfactory responses to any particular odor. For

(a)

(b)

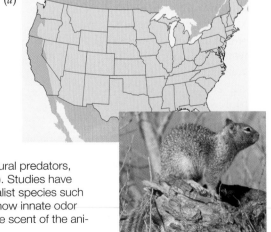

FIGURE 14.17 The California ground squirrel lives in a restricted habitat (a), so it has only a few natural predators, including the Pacific rattlesnake (b). Studies have shown that, unlike humans, specialist species such as the California ground squirrel show innate odor responses, in this case to avoid the scent of the animal that will try to eat them.

example, a certain odor in one locale may signal poisonous mushroom, but in another environment that same odor could mean nutritious food.

Clear evidence that learning is a critical mechanism by which generalists acquire odor responses is shown by **learned taste aversions**. Rats and humans can be made to avoid a flavor by being made sick after consumption. See Chapter 15 for an explanation of the critical role of olfaction in flavor perception. For example, presenting a rat with a sweet-tasting, banana-smelling drink and then injecting the rat with lithium causes nausea and creates a conditioned avoidance of this flavor in the future. Similarly, children who experienced chemotherapy after ingesting a novel flavor of ice cream (dubbed "mapletoff") subsequently refused to eat mapletoff ice cream (Bernstein, 1978).

Researchers have shown that in humans the conditioned aversion is to the smell, not the taste, of the substance (Bartoshuk and Wolfe, 1990). In rats, it remains unclear whether there is a discrete role for taste in this type of aversion learning. The long-term effects of learned taste aversion for humans are clearly adaptive. If poison is ingested, it is best to learn to immediately avoid it, rather than having to repeat the mistake until it kills you.

The special importance of initial associations in odor learning was further shown in a recent fMRI study where it was found that the first association made to an odor is etched into the brain and produces a unique neural signature in the **amygdala-hippocampal complex** that predicts later memory for that odor association. However, after the first association is made to an odor, subsequent associations do not produce a unique neural signature (Yeshurun et al., 2009). The bottom line is that the olfactory system of generalists does not come preprogrammed, but rather is geared to very effectively learn the meaning of smells based on experience.

Caveats

Although a great deal of evidence suggests that odor hedonics are learned, we must note two caveats. First, trigeminally irritating odorants may elicit pain responses, and all humans have an innate drive to avoid pain (although even this drive can be overcome by cultural influences, as attested by the popularity of chili peppers in many ethnic cuisines). Second, as has been mentioned several times, the potential variability in the receptor genes and pseudogenes that are expressed across individuals may influence odor intensity, and consequently the perceived pleasantness, of odors. For example, people who like the smell of skunk may exhibit this response in part because they are missing receptors for detecting some of the more pungent volatiles, whereas people who are particularly repulsed by this scent may be endowed with a greater number of receptors that are keenly attuned to the mercaptan and sulfide aspects of this bouquet. That is, how strong or weak an odor is perceived to be plays a role in its perceived (un)pleasantness. Recall that for many odors, an inverted-U function describes the relationship between liking and intensity (see Figure 14.15). Genetic differences in OR expression appear to extend to ethnicities as well (Menashe et al., 2003), which may help explain why it has been impossible to develop a universally effective stink bomb.

Olfaction, Memory, and Emotion

In the mid-1960s in Britain, adult respondents were asked to provide hedonic ratings for a battery of common odors (Moncrieff, 1966). A similar study was conducted in the United States in the late 1970s (Cain and Johnson, 1978). Included in both studies was the odorant methyl salicylate ("wintergreen"). In the British study, wintergreen was given one of the lowest pleasantness

learned taste aversion The avoidance of a novel flavor after it has been paired with gastric illness. The smell, not the taste, of the substance is key for the learned aversion response in humans.

amygdala-hippocampal complex The conjoined regions of the amygdala and hippocampus, which are key structures in the limbic system. This complex is critical for the unique emotional and associative properties of olfactory cognition.

FIGURE 14.18 The smell (a), sight (b), sound (c), feel (d), and verbal label (e) of popcorn elicit memories that are equivalent in terms of their accuracy. However, odor-induced recollections are more intensely emotional, and this quality has earned odors a reputation as particularly good cues for memory.

(a) Smell

(b) Sight

(c) Sound

(d) Feel

(e) Written label

Popcorn

Memory

Most intense emotional recollection

All equivalent recollection accuracy

ratings; in the American study, it was rated the most pleasant of the scents tested. There is a historical reason for this difference. In Britain, the smell of wintergreen is associated with medicine; in particular, wintergreen was added to analgesics used during World War II, a time that the adults in the 1966 study would not have remembered fondly. Conversely, in the United States the smell of wintergreen is exclusively a candy smell, so it has only sweet, positive connotations. As this example demonstrates, the key to olfactory associative learning is the experience when the odor is first encountered and, in particular, the emotional connotation of that experience (Bartoshuk, 1991; Engen, 1991; Herz, 2001).

When an odor is liked or disliked because of what it has been associated with in our past, we are also recalling a memory when we smell it. Many of our odor experiences, such as most Britons' and Americans' experiences with wintergreen, are too vague to conjure up specific memories, and only the feelings of good or bad remain. However, one of the most distinctive features of olfaction is its ability to elicit our most emotional and evocative personal recollections.

Odors have earned the reputation of being the "best cues" to memory, but are they? To address this question, Herz (1998, 2004) compared recollections stimulated by a familiar smell—for example, popcorn—with memories evoked by the sight of popcorn, the sound of popcorn popping, the feel of popcorn kernels, or simply the word *popcorn* (Figure 14.18). The take-home message from these studies was that, in terms of their vividness and accuracy, memories evoked by odors are as good as—but not any better than—memories evoked by sights, sounds, feel, or words. (See **Web Activity 14.3: Sensory Memory Cues.**) However, as already noted, memories triggered by odor cues are distinctive in one important way: their emotionality. Across a wide range of experiments that have assessed both laboratory-induced memories and naturalistic autobiographical memory using both behavioral and neuroimaging techniques, a consistent pattern of results has emerged. When a recollection is triggered by an odor, participants experience more emotionally intense memories and feel more transported back to the original time and place of the event than when memories are triggered by cues in any other modality (Chu and Downes, 2000; Herz, 1998, 2004; Herz and Cupchik, 1995; Willander and Larsson, 2007). In addition, the emotional regions of the brain (amygdala) are most activated when participants experience memories triggered by odors (Herz et al., 2004).

The emotional potency of odor-evoked memory, along with the emotional associative learning mechanisms that govern the hedonic perception of odors, also explains the truth behind aromatherapy effects. Proponents of **aromatherapy** contend that odors can influence and alter mood, performance, well-being, and the physiological correlates of emotion, such as heart rate, blood pressure, and sleep. Reliable research has in fact shown that certain odors can elicit various beneficial emotional, behavioral, and physical effects, *but only* if the aroma in question has previously been associated with the corresponding emotional experience. That is, an orange odor may indeed brighten your day, but only if you know and associate that odor with an uplifting and cheery emotional state. Odors do not exert any inherent druglike effects. If you had never smelled orange before or you disliked the scent of orange, it would produce either no effect or a negative one (Herz, 2009).

Neuroanatomical and Evolutionary Connections between Odor and Emotion

Neuroanatomy supports the proposition that our olfactory system is especially prepared to learn the affective significance of odors. The amygdala, which synapses directly with the olfactory nerve, is critical for emotional associative learning (M. Davis and Whalen, 2001). A recent neuroimaging study showed that when participants recalled a significant personal memory connected to the smell of a specific perfume, the amygdala was markedly more activated than when they recalled the same memory connected to the sight of the perfume bottle, or when they smelled or saw a nonmeaningful perfume (Herz et al., 2004).

The **orbitofrontal cortex** (**OFC**), which is located behind our eyes at the very front of the frontal lobes (see Figure 14.6b), is where we consciously experience and perceive odors, and it can be considered the "secondary olfactory cortex," just as the OFC has been labeled the "secondary taste cortex" (Rolls, 2006) because it is where pleasure and displeasure from food are integrated. Indeed, the OFC has been identified as the neural locus for assigning affective value—that is, our hedonic judgments in response to a wide range of stimuli (R. J. Davidson, Putnam, and Larson, 2000). Notably, the right OFC plays the most significant role

aromatherapy The contention that odors can influence, improve, and alter mood, performance, and well-being, as well as the physiological correlates of emotion such as heart rate, blood pressure, and sleep.

orbitofrontal cortex (OFC) The part of the frontal lobe of the cortex that lies behind the bone (orbit) containing the eyes. The OFC is responsible for the conscious experience of olfaction, as well as the integration of pleasure and displeasure from food; and it has been referred to as the *secondary olfactory cortex* and the *secondary taste cortex*. The OFC is also involved in many other functions, and it is critical for assigning affective value to stimuli—in other words, determining hedonic meaning.

in conscious olfactory perception (W. Li et al., 2010). This is important because the right hemisphere of the brain is dominant for emotional processing (R. J. Davidson, 1984) and odors are inherently hedonic—that is, emotional—stimuli (Herz, 2007). Furthermore, the most ancient part of the brain, the rhinencephalon—literally, the "nose brain"—which now comprises the primary olfactory cortex and the specific structures of the limbic system, developed first from tissue that was dedicated only to processing odors. It wasn't until later in evolution that limbic structures such as the amygdala and hippocampus developed. It is interesting to consider that our hedonic and emotional reactions to stimuli in general may have their origin in our sense of smell.

Almost all species of animals use smell or chemical communication for the most basic behaviors necessary for survival: recognizing kin, finding reproductively available mates, locating food, and determining whether an animal or object is dangerous (see the next section). Only in humans have visual and auditory information mostly replaced smell for imparting this kind of crucial knowledge about the world. Yet our olfactory system has retained some of its basic functions. The most immediate responses we have to odors are simple binary opposites: like or dislike, approach or avoid. Emotions convey similar messages: approach what is good, safe, and joyful; and avoid what is bad, dangerous, or liable to cause grief. Thus, emotions and olfaction are functionally analogous. Both enable the organism to react appropriately to its environment, maximizing its chances for basic survival and reproductive success. Viewed in this context, the human emotional system can be seen as a highly evolved, abstract cognitive version of the basic behavioral motivations instigated by the olfactory system in animals (Herz, 2000, 2004).

The Vomeronasal Organ, Human Pheromones, and Chemosignals

In animals that rely on smell for survival, the olfactory system consists of two subdivisions: the **main olfactory bulb** (**MOB**) and the **accessory olfactory bulb** (**AOB**) (**Figure 14.19**). The AOB is attached to the back of the MOB. Neurons from these two systems do not interconnect, and the two systems function separately in the integration of specific chemicals. In order for the AOB to be activated, a structure different from the nose needs to be engaged. This structure is called the **vomeronasal organ** (**VNO**), sometimes also referred to as "Jacobson's organ" after the Danish anatomist who discovered it.

The VNO is found in some amphibians, most reptiles (but not birds), and many mammals, including New World primates. When snakes open their mouths and appear to be licking the air, they are actually moving chemicals from the air into the vomeronasal organ. In mammals, the VNO is cigar-shaped and located at the base of the nasal cavity. The VNO can respond to some olfactory stimuli, but it responds primarily to chemicals that are higher in molecular weight than can be detected by the olfactory sensory neurons, as well as to chemicals that are nonvolatile. It also detects chemicals dissolved in water (as opposed to only in air). Whether humans possess a functioning VNO has been the focus of much debate, but it is now generally accepted that although human embryos may have a VNO, this tissue is not neurally connected and disappears shortly after birth. Moreover, we do not have an AOB for VNO neurons to connect to in the brain.

In animals that possess a VNO, its primary function is to detect **pheromones**. Pheromones are not odors. They are chemicals that may *or may not* have a smell. The word *pheromone* is derived from the Greek *pherein*, meaning "to carry," and *hormon*, meaning "to stimulate." It was first coined in 1959 by Peter Karlson (a German biochemist) and Martin Lüscher (a Swiss entomologist) to

main olfactory bulb (MOB) The olfactory bulb; the blueberry-sized extension of the brain just above the nose; the first region of the brain where smells are processed. In humans we refer simply to "olfactory bulb(s)"; in animals with accessory olfactory bulbs, we distinguish between "main" and "accessory."

accessory olfactory bulb (AOB) A smaller neural structure located behind the main olfactory bulb that receives input from the vomeronasal organ.

vomeronasal organ (VNO) A chemical sensing organ at the base of the nasal cavity with a curved tubular shape. The VNO evolved to detect chemicals that cannot be processed by the olfactory epithelium, such as large and/or aqueous molecules, the types of molecules that constitute pheromones. Also called *Jacobson's organ*.

pheromone A chemical emitted by one member of a species that triggers a physiological or behavioral response in another member of the same species. Pheromones are signals for chemical communication and do not need to have any smell.

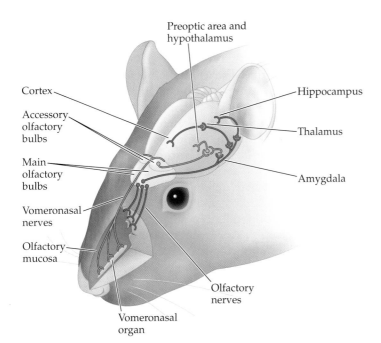

Preoptic area and
hypothalamus

Cortex

Accessory
olfactory
bulbs

Main
olfactory
bulbs

Vomeronasal
nerves

Olfactory
mucosa

Hippocampus

Thalamus

Amygdala

Olfactory
nerves

Vomeronasal
organ

FIGURE 14.19 The olfactory system of a hamster, showing the location of the vomeronasal organ and accessory olfactory bulbs. Note that no functional vomeronasal organ or accessory olfactory bulbs have been found in humans. (After an illustration by Dr. Michael Meredith.)

describe a chemical substance that carries a message about the physiological or behavioral state of one insect to another, and that in turn leads to a specific reaction in the receiver insect. That is, pheromones are a means of chemical communication. Today, the more generalized definition of a pheromone is *a chemical compound produced by one animal that elicits a specific behavioral or physiological response in another animal of the same species.*

Pheromones are most important for communication in the social insects, like ants, termites, and bees, but they also convey important information for many noninsect species, including primates. There are many examples of this form of chemical communication. Pheromones are used to identify territory. For example, a tiger will rub a tree with glands from its cheeks to claim it—just as a cat rubs your leg with its eyebrow and rump glands to mark you as its territory! Pheromones also initiate alarm or defense reactions. When a honeybee stings us, the chemical released from the stinger (which happens to smell like banana) is a cue to other bees to join in—unfortunately for us. Most important, for many animals pheromones are critically involved in communication about reproductive behavior. They can provide signals to males about when a female is fertile and provide signals to females to initiate sexual behavior. For example, a male rhesus monkey will ignore a female rhesus in heat if his nose is blocked, and a female pig will not go into **lordosis** (the position necessary for impregnation) if she isn't exposed to the male pig pheromone androstenone.

Pheromones have two kinds of effects. The two types of pheromones that cause these effects are known as **releaser pheromones** and **primer pheromones**. Primer pheromone effects are slow and produce a physiological change in the recipient over time. For example, female rodents that are housed together will come into estrus at the same time after several cycles. Releaser pheromone effects are fast and always produce behavioral responses. The consequence of the banana aroma from a bee sting is one example. Sexual cues and behavioral responses to those cues, such as lordosis, are other examples of releaser pheromone effects. In contrast, primer pheromones may produce no behavioral consequences and may be noticeable only in terms of physiological changes.

lordosis The position that females of some species (e.g., pigs and rats) need to assume in order to be impregnated. It involves the inward curving of the spinal column and exposure of the genitals.

releaser pheromone A pheromone that triggers an immediate behavioral response among conspecifics.

primer pheromone A pheromone that triggers a physiological (often hormonal) change among conspecifics. This effect usually involves prolonged pheromone exposure.

chemosignal Any of various chemicals emitted by humans that are detected by the olfactory system and that may have some effect on the mood, behavior, hormonal status, and/or sexual arousal of other humans.

The most frequently mentioned example of a primer pheromone effect in humans is known as the "McClintock effect" after the physiological psychologist Martha McClintock, who identified this phenomenon in college while pursuing her undergraduate degree. The McClintock effect is shown when women who are in physical proximity (e.g., live together) over time start to have menstrual cycles that coincide. That is, women who move into college dormitories together at the beginning of the school term often find that by the end of the semester they're having their periods in sync with one another. The McClintock effect is believed to be caused by chemicals present in human sweat that are capable of priming the hormonal systems of other individuals. However, other research suggests that human pheromones are a myth (Doty, 2010), and even the McClintock effect has come under sharp criticism. For one, McClintock's former collaborator, Jeffrey Schank, recently followed 186 Chinese students living in dormitories for an entire year and saw no evidence of menstrual synchrony (Yang and Schank, 2006). Other researchers have argued convincingly for decades that the McClintock effect is no more than a statistical artifact (H. C. Wilson, 1992). Finally, we do not have a functioning VNO or AOB. Therefore, it is unknown how this effect could be happening, if indeed it truly is. Some have suggested that, presuming the effect is real, hormonal information may be transmitted from sweat through another system altogether, such as absorption through the skin from physical contact (Herz, 2007). Nonetheless, until the chemicals responsible for menstrual synchrony, or any other putative pheromone, are identified and their biochemical pathways determined, the validity of human pheromones remains dubious.

Since the existence of human pheromones is highly uncertain, a more impartial way to discuss human chemical communication is to use the term **chemosignal**. Here, *chemosignals* refers to chemicals emitted by humans that *are* detected by the olfactory system and that may have some effect on the mood or behavior of other humans.

The chemical androstadienone is a steroid derivative of the male sex hormone testosterone (it is chemically related to androstenone, which was mentioned earlier), and it is present in male body fluids (e.g., sweat) at higher concentrations than in females. In several studies, androstadienone has been observed to improve women's mood, *but* only when women are in the presence of men (Jacob, Hayreh, and McClintock, 2001; Lundstrom and Olsson, 2005). In the presence of a female experimenter, androstadienone had no effect on female participants' mood. Another study with a male experimenter found that androstadienone also increased self-rated sexual arousal and cortisol (a stress/arousal hormone) levels (Wyert et al., 2007). Note, however, that the levels of androstadienone that women were exposed to in these studies were a million times higher than the amount a normal male actually emits. Thus, the ecological validity of androstadienone as an aphrodisiac chemosignal is questionable.

With respect to chemicals emitted by females, a recent study (G. Miller, Tybur, and Jordan, 2007) found that professional exotic lap dancers earned almost twice as much in tips (averaging $335 a night versus $185) when they performed during the ovulatory phase of their menstrual cycles compared to the menstrual phase of their cycles. Moreover, dancers who were taking birth control pills (and were thus hormonally infertile) showed *no* change in tip earnings over time and also earned less overall than did dancers who were not using hormonal contraception (average earnings $193 versus $276). Since the dancers all claimed they performed the same way every day and that their behavior to the patrons was consistent, the explanation offered is that the women were *perceived* as more attractive by the male patrons when they were most fertile through some mechanism other than behavioral or visual cues. This other mechanism is proposed to be chemical. Note, though, that the degree to which conscious smelling by the male patrons was involved was not tested. However, a recent study found that when men *smelled* T-shirts that had been worn by ovulating women, their testosterone levels were higher than they were after they sniffed T-shirts worn by nonovulating women or a clean, unworn T-shirt (S. L. Miller and Maner, 2010). It has also been shown that the odors emitted by a breast-feeding woman could increase sexual desire in another woman—by 24% if the woman smelling had a partner (whether male or female) and by 17% if she was single (Spencer et al., 2004).

However, not all female chemosignals increase sexual desire. Indeed, a recent study found that chemicals present in the tears of women dampen the sexual desire of men (Gelstein et al., 2011). When men were exposed to a strip placed under their nose containing emotional tears from women, though they knew nothing about the source of the compound, a significant decrease was observed in self-rated sexual desire, rated sexual attractiveness of female faces, testosterone level, and brain activity associated with sexual arousal. Are the tears of a distressed woman a direct turnoff, or is the effect due to something else? The authors suggested that the drop in testosterone and sexual arousal may be a by-product of a drop in aggression, which is also manifested by lowered testosterone, and there are good evolutionary reasons to hope for a decrease in testosterone from potential aggressors when they are exposed to your tears. With that in mind, the authors speculated that the effect would also be seen if the tears came from a man.

In sum, chemicals present in human body fluids may modulate sexual arousal to some extent. These findings can be interpreted as illustrating a biological basis for olfactory influences on behavior, but they are also consistent with the view that through past associations, odors acquire meaning and then affect emotional and behavioral responses accordingly. Therefore, the scent of ovulating women may be arousing to men because of the men's past sexual experiences; and despite not having a distinctive odor, past associations with tears and their connection with sadness may explain why tears are the anti-Viagra. The degree to which perceptible odors and/or imperceptible chemical signals influence human sexuality is an exciting field of current and future research.

Summary

1. Olfaction is one of the two chemical senses; the other is taste (discussed in the next chapter). To be perceived as scent, a chemical must possess certain physical properties; however, even some molecules that have these characteristics cannot be smelled. Olfaction has some unique physiological properties, one of which is that only about 35% of the genes that code for olfactory receptors in humans are functional. Another unusual feature is that most odorants also stimulate the somatosensory system via the trigeminal nerve, and it is often impossible to distinguish the contribution of olfactory sensation from trigeminal stimulation.

2. The dominant biochemical theory of odor perception—shape-pattern theory—contends that the fit between a molecule and an olfactory receptor (OR) determine which molecules are detected as scents, and that specific odorants activate a combinatorial code of ORs, producing specific patterns of spatial and temporal neural activation for each perceived scent. However, this theory is not universally accepted, and alternate explanations exist (e.g., vibration theory).

3. Recently, researchers demonstrated a closer connection between the visual system and olfaction than has ever before been thought to exist. Two examples are binaral rivalry and the observation that what we're smelling influences what we concomitantly register as seeing. There is also a difference between active sniffing and passive inhalation of odors at both neurological

> Refer to the
> **Sensation and Perception**
> Companion Website
> **sites.sinauer.com/wolfe3e**
> for activities, essays, study
> questions, and other study aids.

and functional levels. Active sniffing may even have therapeutic applications for patients suffering from extreme physical disabilities.

4. Almost all odors that we encounter in the real world are mixtures, and we appear not to be very good at analyzing the discrete chemical components of scent mixtures. Olfaction is thus primarily a synthetic, as opposed to analytical, sense. However, analytical olfactory ability can be developed with training. True odor imagery is also weak (or nonexistent) for most people, but training, as in the case of odor experts, appears to facilitate this ability.

5. The psychophysical study of smell has shown that various odorant intensity levels and various cognitive functions are required for odor detection, discrimination, and recognition. Identification differs from odor recognition in that, in the former, one must come up with a name for the olfactory sensation. It is very difficult to name even very familiar odors—an experience known as the tip-of-the-nose phenomenon—one of several indications that linguistic processing is highly disconnected from olfactory experience. Unlike the case with other sensory experiences, however, we do not need to access any semantic information about an odor in order to respond to it appropriately, as long as it is familiar.

6. Another important discrepancy between the physical experience and the psychological experience of odors is the difference between receptor adaptation and cognitive habituation. Receptor adaptation occurs after continual odorant exposure over a number of minutes, can be undone after a few minutes away from the odorant, and is explained by a basic biochemical mechanism. By contrast, cognitive habituation occurs after long-term exposure (e.g., in a living or work environment) to an odor and takes weeks away from the odor to undo. Psychological influences can have strong effects on both perceived odor adaptation and habituation. At present, the physiological mechanisms responsible for cognitive habituation are not fully understood.

7. The most immediate and basic response we have to an odor is whether we like it or not; this is hedonic evaluation. Odor hedonics are measured by pleasantness, familiarity, and intensity ratings. Pleasantness and familiarity are linearly related to odor liking; odor intensity has a more complex relationship with hedonic perception. Substantial evidence suggests that our hedonic responses to odors are learned and not innate, even for so-called stenches. That we have learned to like or dislike various odors rather than being born with hardwired responses is evolutionarily adaptive for generalist species like humans. The caveats to the learned proposition are odors that are highly trigeminally irritating (pain-inducing) and the potential genetic variability in the number and types of receptors expressed across individuals, which may influence olfactory sensitivity (intensity) and hence odor hedonic perception.

8. The key to olfactory associative learning is the emotional value of the context in which the odor is first encountered. If the emotional context is good, the odor will be liked; if it is bad, the odor will be disliked. Previously acquired emotional associations with odors also underlie validated aromatherapy effects. Emotional potency further distinguishes odor-evoked memories from memories triggered by other sensory cues. The neuroanatomy of the olfactory and limbic systems and their neuroevolutionary development illustrate how emotional processing and olfactory processing are uniquely and intimately interrelated.

9. Pheromones are chemicals emitted by individuals that affect the physiology and/or behavior of other members of the same species and may or may not have any smell. In all mammals that have been shown to use pheromones for communication, detection is mediated through the vomeronasal organ and processed by the accessory olfactory bulb. Humans do not possess a functional VNO or AOB, and evidence for human pheromones is controversial. However, human chemosignals that are processed through the olfactory system appear to have some influence on hormonal status and sexual arousal.

CHAPTER 15

Matt Sesow, *Meat*, 2007

Taste

C alvin Trillin, a writer who makes wonderful observations about the joys of eating, described his 4-year-old daughter's reaction to "polishing off a particularly satisfying dish of chocolate ice cream." She said, "My tongue is smiling."

What makes tongues smile? As with our noses, the basic answer to this question is molecules. Olfaction and gustation are often grouped together as the chemical senses, and in terms of physiology, these two sensory systems are in some ways quite similar. But the chemicals we taste have already entered our mouths and are about to move even farther into our bodies. Thus, taste serves the most specific function of any of the senses: discerning which chemicals we need to ingest because they are nutritious and which we need to spit out because they may be poisonous. Perhaps this is why something about our liking or disliking of tastes and flavors seems to be very different from the liking or disliking that one might associate with the color red or the sound of middle C on the piano. Nature has equipped us to care passionately about food because that passion holds the key to our survival.

Taste versus Flavor

Before delving any further into the gustatory system, we need to clear up a very old misunderstanding. According to the early Greeks, sensations perceived from foods and beverages in the mouth were tastes, and sensations perceived by sniffing were smells. In fact, however, food molecules are almost always perceived by both our gustatory and our olfactory systems. The molecules we taste are dissolved in our saliva and stimulate the taste receptors on our taste buds, as we'll discuss in this chapter. But when we chew and swallow foods, other molecules are released into the air inside our mouths and forced up behind the palate into the nasal cavity, where they contact the olfactory epithelium and stimulate our olfactory receptors (Figure 15.1). The brain then knits these **retronasal olfactory sensations** together with our gustatory sensations into a kind of metasensation that goes by the name **flavor**.

It is quite easy to prevent the airflow that carries odorants through the retronasal passage. Children do it all the time when they hold their noses while eating spinach. Try the following experiment now—but use a piece of chocolate if you're still not crazy about spinach. Pinch your nose before putting the chocolate in your mouth, and then chew it and note the sensation, which will be almost pure taste (sweet with a bit of bitter). Then, just before swallowing, release your nose. The volatile molecules responsible for the chocolate sensation will immediately flow up behind your palate and into the nasal cavity, and you will understand the difference between taste and flavor. You've probably noticed before that flavor is similarly impoverished when

retronasal olfactory sensation The sensation of an odor that is perceived when chewing and swallowing force an odorant in the mouth up behind the palate into the nose. Such odor sensations are perceived as originating from the mouth, even though the actual contact of odorant and receptor occurs at the olfactory mucosa.

flavor The combination of true taste (sweet, salty, sour, bitter) and retronasal olfaction.

FIGURE 15.1 Molecules released into the air inside our mouths as we chew and swallow food travel up through the retronasal passage into the nose, where they then move upward and contact the olfactory epithelium.

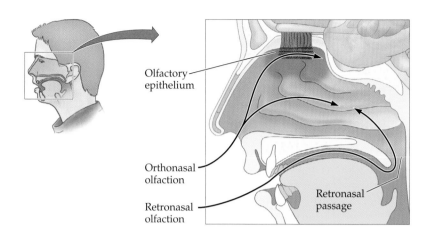

Olfactory epithelium

Orthonasal olfaction

Retronasal olfaction

Retronasal passage

you have a stuffy nose. **Web Activity 15.1: Taste without Smell** asks you to test this phenomenon with other stimuli.

Foods are also perceived by the somatosensory system via touch, temperature, and pain receptors in the tongue and mouth. Some of these sensations have protective functions: the burn of acid (which might damage your stomach if swallowed), the heat pain from scalding coffee, the pain of biting the tongue, and so on. Somatosensations also provide information about the nature of foods and beverages. For example, we get information about the fat content of foods from tactile sensations such as oily, viscous, thick, and creamy.

Localizing Flavor Sensations

You should have realized something else when you performed the chocolate experiment described in the previous section: even though you now know that the chocolate sensation originates from the olfactory receptors in your nose, you probably still perceived the flavor as coming entirely from your mouth. This perception is due in part to the tactile sensations evoked by chewing and swallowing, and in part to taste. Because you taste and feel the food only in your mouth (not in your nose), your brain concludes that the sensations must have arisen entirely from the mouth. Exceptions include foods such as horseradish, wasabi, and spicy mustard, which give off volatile chemicals that activate pain receptors all the way up through the retronasal passage. But these exceptions prove the rule: when we eat these foods, we experience the sensations as coming from our noses as well as our mouths.

Now consider the following curious case. A patient with normal olfaction but damaged taste and oral touch reported that she could smell lasagna, but when she ate it, it had no flavor. A similar effect was produced in a laboratory using a small amount of lidocaine and a large amount of blueberry yogurt. Subjects in this study had their left **chorda tympani** (a branch of the facial nerve, one of the **cranial nerves** that carries information from taste receptors to the brain) anesthetized with the lidocaine while they tasted the yogurt. In this situation the subjects reported that the blueberry sensation—which is due entirely to retronasal olfaction—seemed to come only from the right side of the mouth. Moreover, the intensity of the blueberry sensation was reduced, and this intensity was reduced even further when both taste nerves were blocked (D. J. Snyder et al., 2001).

In both the patient and the experimental subjects, the pathway from the mouth to the nasal cavity was completely intact. Why, then, were their retronasal lasagna and blueberry sensations reduced? Recent brain-imaging research by

chorda tympani The branch of cranial nerve VII (the facial nerve) that carries taste information from the anterior, mobile tongue (the part that can be stuck out). The chorda tympani exits the tongue with the lingual branch of the trigeminal nerve (cranial nerve V) and then passes through the middle ear on its way to the brain.

cranial nerves Twelve pairs of nerves (one for each side of the body) that originate in the brain stem and reach sense organs and muscles through openings in the skull.

Dana Small appears to answer this question: the brain processes odors differently, depending on whether they come from the mouth or through the nostrils. This distinction makes good sense functionally because the significance of odors in the mouth is very different from that of odors sniffed from the outside world. Without the proper cues to tell us where an odorant is coming from, input from the olfactory receptors apparently cannot be routed to the proper brain area to connect the smell sensation with the food stimulus.

The connections between taste and smell have been understood by the food industry for many years (Noble, 1996). For example, if a company is marketing pear juice and wants to intensify the sensation of pear, it will add sugar. The increase in sweetness (a pure taste sensation) will increase the perceived olfactory sensation of pear. However, this will work only for pairs of taste and retronasal olfaction that are commonly experienced. If our pear juice company were to add salt, the pear sensation would not increase. Thus, learning plays a role in this phenomenon.

The pervasiveness of food additives such as carrageenan, guar gum, and other thickening agents shows that the food industry also has a good handle on how somatosensation affects food perception. And the ingredient lists of most processed foods include at least one artificial coloring, testifying to the importance of yet another sense, vision, in how we perceive foods.

Anatomy and Physiology of the Gustatory System

Taste perception consists of the following sequence of events (the structures involved are illustrated in **Figure 15.2**): Chewing breaks down food substances into molecules, which are dissolved in saliva. The saliva-borne food molecules flow into a taste pore that leads to the **taste buds** housed in structures

taste bud A globular cluster of cells that has the function of creating neural signals conveyed to the brain by the taste nerves. Some of the cells in a taste bud have specialized sites on their apical projections that interact with taste stimuli. Some of the cells form synapses with taste nerve fibers.

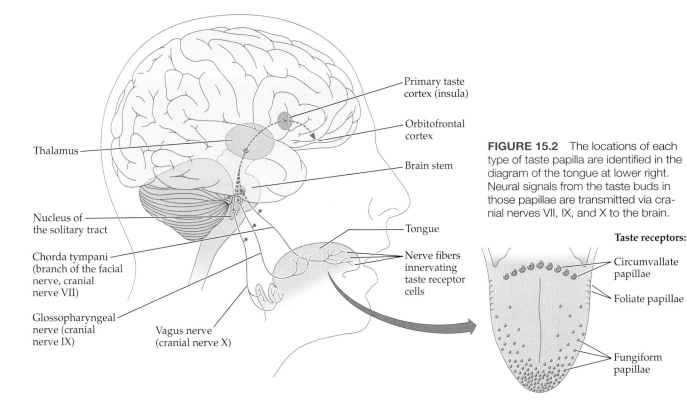

FIGURE 15.2 The locations of each type of taste papilla are identified in the diagram of the tongue at lower right. Neural signals from the taste buds in those papillae are transmitted via cranial nerves VII, IX, and X to the brain.

Primary taste cortex (insula)

Orbitofrontal cortex

Thalamus

Brain stem

Nucleus of the solitary tract

Tongue

Chorda tympani (branch of the facial nerve, cranial nerve VII)

Nerve fibers innervating taste receptor cells

Glossopharyngeal nerve (cranial nerve IX)

Vagus nerve (cranial nerve X)

Taste receptors:

Circumvallate papillae

Foliate papillae

Fungiform papillae

papilla Any of multiple structures that give the tongue its bumpy appearance. From smallest to largest, the papilla types that contain taste buds are fungiform, foliate, and circumvallate; filiform papillae, which do not contain taste buds, are the smallest and most numerous.

taste receptor cell A cell within the taste bud that contains sites on its apical projection that can interact with taste stimuli. These sites fall into two major categories: those interacting with charged particles (e.g., sodium and hydrogen ions), and those interacting with specific chemical structures.

filiform papillae Small structures on the tongue that provide most of the bumpy appearance. Filiform papillae have no taste function.

fungiform papillae Mushroom-shaped structures (maximum diameter 1 millimeter) that are distributed most densely on the edges of the tongue, especially the tip. Taste buds (an average of six per papilla) are buried in the surface.

called **papillae** (singular *papilla*) that are located mostly on the edges of the tongue in a rough oval (if the olfactory epithelium is the retina of the nose, the tongue is the retina of the mouth). Taste buds, in turn, contain multiple **taste receptor cells**, each of which responds to a limited number of molecule types. When it comes in contact with one of its preferred molecules, the taste receptor cell produces action potentials that send information along one of the cranial nerves to the brain. See **Web Activity 15.2: Gustatory Anatomy** for an interactive overview of the system, which is described in greater detail in the sections that follow.

Papillae

Papillae give the tongue its bumpy appearance and come in four major varieties: filiform, fungiform, foliate, and circumvallate. The latter three of these contain taste buds.

Filiform papillae, the ones *without* any taste function, are located on the anterior portion of the tongue (the part we stick out when giving someone a raspberry) and come in different shapes in different species. In cats, they are shaped like tiny spoons with sharp edges. The filiform papillae on our tongues do not have these sharp edges, which is why you will find lapping milk from a bowl considerably more difficult than your cat does.

Fungiform papillae, so named because they resemble tiny button mushrooms, are also located on the anterior part of the tongue. They are visible to the naked eye, but blue food coloring swabbed onto the tongue makes them particularly easy to see (blue food coloring stains filiform papillae much better than fungiform papillae, so the fungiform papillae appear as light circles against a darker blue background). Fungiform papillae vary in diameter, but the maximum is about 1 millimeter (mm). On average, about six taste buds are buried in the surface of each fungiform papilla. If we stain the tongues of many individuals, we see a large amount of variation (Figure 15.3). Some tongues have so few fungiform papillae that their stained tongues appear to have polka dots on them. Other tongues have so many that the polka dots are wall-to-wall.

FIGURE 15.3 Examples showing typical variability in the density of fungiform papillae from one individual to the next. The circles show the 6-mm template area used for counting fungiform papillae on tongues stained with blue food coloring. (*a*) This supertaster's tongue (supertasters are discussed later in the chapter) has 60 fungiform papillae in that area. (*b*) The tongue of another individual (not a supertaster) has 16 fungiform papillae. In extreme cases, normal individuals may have as few as 5 fungiform papillae in that area or as many as 60.

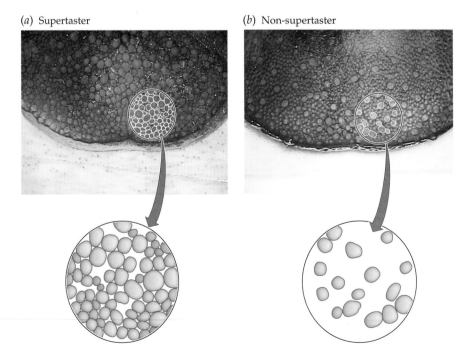

(*a*) Supertaster   (*b*) Non-supertaster

Foliate papillae are located on the sides of the tongue at the point where the tongue is attached. Under magnification, they look like a series of folds. Taste buds are buried in the folds.

Finally, **circumvallate papillae** are relatively large, circular structures forming an inverted *V* on the rear of the tongue. These papillae look like tiny islands surrounded by moats. The taste buds are buried in the sides of the moats.

Although most people don't realize this, there are also taste buds on the roof of the mouth where the hard and soft palates meet. To demonstrate these, wet your finger and dip it into salt crystals. Touch the roof of your mouth and move your finger back until you feel the bone end (the margin between the hard and soft palates). You will experience a flash of saltiness as you move the salt crystals onto the taste buds arrayed on that margin.

In sum, the taste buds are distributed in a line across the roof of the mouth and in papillae distributed in an oval on the tongue. Fungiform papillae make up the front of the oval, and foliate and circumvallate papillae make up its rear. Note that we have no subjective awareness of this distribution of taste buds. (For more on this topic, see **Web Essay 15.1: Scientific Urban Legend—The Bogus Tongue Map**.)

Taste Buds and Taste Receptor Cells

Each taste bud is a cluster of elongated cells, organized much like the segments of an orange (**Figure 15.4***a*). The tips of some of the cells—the taste receptor cells—end in slender **microvilli** (singular *microvillus*) containing the sites that bind to taste substances. In an earlier era, these microvilli were mistakenly thought to be tiny hairs; we now know that microvilli are extensions of the cell membrane.

Taste nerve fibers were once believed to be connected to receptors on one end and nerve fibers that convey taste information to the brain at the other end. But at least some receptors are on cells that do not synapse with taste nerve fibers; the information they convey must travel to the nerve fibers in some other way (Herness et al., 2005; Roper, 2006). Details of how this happens are beginning to emerge. Anatomically, taste bud cells fall into three different groups that appear to mediate different taste qualities (Figure 15.4*b*): Type I cells may respond to salt (very little is known about these); they do not have synapses. Type II cells respond to sweet, bitter, or umami (more about that later); these cells have receptor sites on the microvilli but, like type I cells, do not have synapses. Type III cells carry sourness and saltiness, and they look much like our older view of taste receptor cells.

In fungiform papillae, the taste nerve fibers that enter the taste buds branch so that an individual cell can be innervated by more than one taste fiber and an individual taste fiber can innervate more than one cell. Taste receptors have a limited life span. After a matter of days they die and are replaced by new cells. This constant renewal enables the taste system to recover from a variety of sources of damage, and it explains why our taste systems remain robust even into old age. Recordings from taste nerve fibers show that different receptor cells contacted by branches of a single fiber show similar specificities

foliate papillae Folds of tissue containing taste buds. Foliate papillae are located on the rear of the tongue lateral to the circumvallate papillae, where the tongue attaches to the mouth.

circumvallate papillae Circular structures that form an inverted *V* on the rear of the tongue (three to five on each side, with the largest in the center). Circumvallate papillae are mound-like structures surrounded by a trench (like a moat). These papillae are much larger than fungiform papillae.

microvilli Slender projections of the cell membrane on the tips of some taste bud cells that extend into the taste pore.

(*a*)

(*b*)

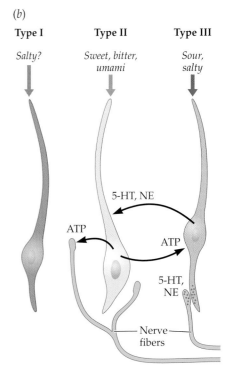

FIGURE 15.4 Taste buds. (*a*) A taste bud buried in the tissue of a fungiform papilla. (*b*) Stimulation of the three taste receptor cell types results in responses in the taste nerves. Type III cells have synapses. ATP (adenosine triphosphate), 5-HT (5-hydroxytryptamine, or serotonin), and NE (norepinephrine) are neurotransmitters that may be secreted by cells without synapses. These neurotransmitters may act on adjacent cells, as well as taste nerve fibers, to ultimately produce neural signals that will travel to the brain. (After Roper and Chaudhari, 2009.)

tastant Any stimulus that can be tasted.

to taste stimuli. In other words, it appears that the nerve fibers are somehow able to select the cells with which they will synapse so that the message they convey remains stable, even though the receptor cells are continually replaced.

The mechanisms that permit a taste cell to recognize a taste stimulus (known as a **tastant**) that is contacting its microvillus can be divided into two large categories. One class of tastants is made up of small, charged molecules that taste salty or sour. Small openings, called "ion channels," in microvillus membranes allow some types of charged particles to enter cells but bar others. When the charged particles in salty and sour foods enter salty and sour receptor cells, these cells signal their respective tastes.

Tastants in the second class, which produce sensations that we label as sweet or bitter, are perceived via a mechanism similar to that in the olfactory system, using G protein–coupled receptors (GPCRs). The GPCRs wind back and forth across microvillus membranes, and when a particular tastant molecule "key" is fitted into the "lock" portion of a GPCR on the outside of the membrane, the portion of the GPCR inside the cell starts a cascade of molecular events that eventually causes an action potential to be sent to the brain.

> FURTHER DISCUSSION of GPCRs in the context of olfaction can be found in Chapter 14 on page 417.

FIGURE 15.5 Taste information projects from the tongue to the medulla (via cranial nerves VII, IX, and X), then to the thalamus (shown in cross section 1 of the brain), then to the insula (cross section 2), and finally to the orbitofrontal cortex (cross section 3).

Taste Processing in the Central Nervous System

After leaving the taste buds through the cranial nerves, gustatory information travels through way stations in the medulla and thalamus before reaching the cortex (**Figure 15.5**) (Pritchard and Norgren, 2004). The primary cortical processing area for taste—the part of the cortex that first receives taste information—is the insula, or **insular cortex** (also referred to as the gustatory cortex). The **orbitofrontal cortex** receives projections from the insular cortex. Some orbitofrontal neurons are multimodal; that is, they respond to temperature, touch, and smell, as well as to taste, suggesting that the orbitofrontal cortex may be an integration area.

Inhibition plays an important role in the processing of taste information in the brain. One of the functions of this inhibition may be to protect our whole-mouth perception of taste in the face of injuries to the taste system. Our brains receive taste input from several nerves (see Figure 15.5). Damage to one of them diminishes its contribution to the whole; however, that damage also releases the inhibition that is normally produced by the damaged nerve. The result is that whole-mouth taste intensities are relatively unchanged. Unfortunately, this preserved whole-mouth perception comes at a cost in some cases. Localized taste damage is often accompanied by "phantom taste" sensations (recall the phantom limbs experienced by many limb amputees, described in Chapter 13), as if the release of inhibition permits even noise in the nervous system to be perceived as a taste.

Descending inhibition from the taste cortex to a variety of other structures (DiLorenzo and Monroe, 1995) may also serve other functions. For example, mouth injuries that lead to oral pain make it harder to eat. The inhibition of such pain perceptions by taste-processing parts of the brain would make eating easier and thus increase the likelihood of survival (because no matter how much the mouth hurts, we still have to eat). Consistent with this principle, patients with a serious oral pain disorder (burning mouth syndrome) were shown to have localized taste damage as well (Grushka and Bartoshuk, 2000). Furthermore, women who have taste damage are more likely to suffer from severe nausea and vomiting during pregnancy (Sipiora et al., 2000); and cancer patients whose chemotherapy and radiation therapy is known to damage the taste system are more likely to experience coughing, gagging, hiccups, and oral pain. In all these cases, inhibitory signals from the taste cortex that normally help prevent eating-disruptive symptoms (oral pain, vomiting, hiccuping, and so on) may have been turned off because of the damage to the taste system.

The Four Basic Tastes

We learned in the previous chapter that we are able to distinguish many different odorants. Already in this chapter, however, we have seen that when olfaction is taken out of the equation, much of the complexity of the sensations evoked by foods vanishes. Thus we are led to believe that the number of basic taste qualities is quite small. In fact, the current universally accepted list includes only the four **basic tastes** previously mentioned in the section on taste buds and taste receptor cells: **salty**, **sour**, **bitter**, and **sweet**. As we discuss these in the sections that follow, note that one of the most important features of these basic tastes is that our liking (or disliking) for them is "hardwired" in the brain; that is, we are essentially born liking or disliking these tastes. This is very different from the way we learn to like or dislike odors.

Salty

Salts are made up of two charged particles: a cation (positively charged) and an anion (negatively charged). For example, common table salt is NaCl; the sodium is the cation (Na^+), and the chloride is the anion (Cl^-). The source of the salty taste is the cation (**Figure 15.6**a). Although all salts taste at least a little salty to humans, pure NaCl is the saltiest-tasting salt around. Sodium

insular cortex The primary cortical processing area for taste—the part of the cortex that first receives taste information. Also called *insula* or *gustatory cortex*.

orbitofrontal cortex (OFC) The part of the frontal lobe of the cortex that lies behind the bone (orbit) containing the eyes. The OFC is responsible for the conscious experience of olfaction, as well as the integration of pleasure and displeasure from food; and it has been referred to as the *secondary olfactory cortex* and *secondary taste cortex*. The OFC is also involved in many other functions, and it is critical for assigning affective value to stimuli—in other words, determining hedonic meaning.

basic taste Any of the four taste qualities that are generally agreed to describe human taste experience: sweet, salty, sour, bitter.

salty One of the four basic tastes; the taste quality produced by the cations of salts (e.g., the sodium in sodium chloride produces the salty taste). Some cations also produce other taste qualities (e.g., potassium tastes bitter as well as salty). The purest salty taste is produced by sodium chloride (NaCl), common table salt.

sour One of the four basic tastes; the taste quality produced by the hydrogen ion in acids.

bitter One of the four basic tastes; the taste quality, generally considered unpleasant, produced by substances like quinine or caffeine.

sweet One of the four basic tastes; the taste quality produced by some sugars, such as glucose, fructose, and sucrose. These three sugars are particularly biologically useful to us, and our sweet receptors are tuned to them. Some other compounds (e.g., saccharin, aspartame) are also sweet.

FIGURE 15.6 Diagram of a taste receptor cell illustrating the different receptor mechanisms for ionic stimuli (salty and sour). (a) Salty taste is produced by the cation in a salt. In NaCl, the sodium cation is admitted to the receptor cell by sodium channels (ENaC). (b) Sour taste is produced by hydrogen ions (H⁺), which can enter the cell in two ways (see the text for details). (After Chaudhari and Roper, 2010.)

must be available in relatively large quantities in the body to maintain nerve and muscle function, and loss of body sodium leads to a swift death.

Our ability to perceive saltiness is not static. Gary Beauchamp and his colleagues (Bertino, Beauchamp, and Engelman, 1982) showed that diet can affect the perception of saltiness. Fortunately for those on low-sodium diets, reduced sodium intake increases the intensity of saltiness over time. Individuals who are initially successful in reducing their sodium intake will find that foods they used to love may now taste too salty. This adjustment in perception helps them keep their sodium intake down.

Our liking for saltiness is not static either. Early experiences can modify salt preference. In 1978 and 1979, several hundred infants were fed soy formulas that were accidentally deficient in chloride because of an error in formulation. Chloride deficiency has effects on human physiology that mimic the effects of sodium deficiency. Thus, the infants who were chloride-deficient offered an important way to study sodium deficiency in humans. The Centers for Disease Control and Prevention (CDC) in Atlanta monitored these infants, and a variety of studies were done to assess any potential damage. One of the consequences was that the salt preference of the children increased (L. J. Stein et al., 1996). Experiences during gestation can also affect salt preference. Crystal and Bernstein (1995) found an increased preference for salty snacks among college students whose mothers had experienced moderate to severe morning sickness during pregnancy. The exact mechanisms by which these abnormal metabolic events enhance salt preference are still not understood.

Sour

As you may remember from high school chemistry, a solution containing hydrogen ions (H⁺) and hydroxide ions (OH⁻) in equal proportions produces water (HOH, or H_2O). As the relative proportion of H⁺ increases (decreasing the pH level), the solution becomes more *acidic*. Why do you need to be reminded of all this? Because sour taste is produced by hydrogen ions. Hydrogen ions enter the receptor cell through ion channels; however, an additional mechanism for sour allows undissociated acid molecules (those that have not split into the two charged particles that make up the acid molecule) to enter as well. The undissociated acid molecules dissociate inside the cell. Ultimately, the stimulus that triggers sour taste is the hydrogen concentration inside the receptor cell (see Figure 15.6b) (DeSimone et al., 2011).

Some individuals like the sourness of acids in relatively low concentrations. Many adults enjoy pickles and sauerkraut, both of which get their sour tastes from lactic acid. In addition, many children in particular like sour candies (Liem and Mennella, 2003). At high concentrations, however, acids will damage both external and internal body tissues.

Bitter

The Human Genome Project revealed a multigene family responsible for about 25 different bitter receptors. The HUGO Gene Nomenclature Committee has established the rules for naming genes. (HUGO stands for Human Genome Organisation, an international organization of scientists involved in human genetic and genomic research.) The bitter gene family is *TAS2R* ("*TAS*" stands for taste, with the "2" indicating bitter—we will see shortly that a "1" indicates sweet and umami); numbers following the *R* indicate the particular gene that is a member of that family. The 25 bitter genes are located on three different chromosomes: 5, 7, and 12. The receptors these genes express are designated without using italics (e.g., TAS2R# or T2R#).

The bitter receptors expressed by these genes face a formidable task. Wolfgang Meyerhof, one of the world's experts on bitter genes, estimates that there are thousands of bitter molecules (many coming from plants that protect themselves from predators by tasting bitter). How can only 25 bitter receptors handle the job? Part of the answer is that some of the T2 receptors respond only to specific compounds (e.g., the PROP [propylthiouracil] receptor [see Figure 15.13*b*] responds to a small group of chemically related compounds), but others (bitter "generalists") respond to many compounds (Figure 15.7). This also means that some bitter stimuli stimulate many bitter receptors (e.g., quinine stimulates 9 of the 25 bitter receptors).

Tonic water (which contains quinine), was originally formulated as a treatment for malaria; now, however, we know that unfortunately it does not contain enough quinine for that purpose. But tonic water does contain enough quinine to taste very bitter, and for this reason lots of sugar was added to make the tonic water palatable. This approach works because sweet and bitter tastes inhibit one another; tonic water tastes much less bitter than the quinine content alone would, and it also tastes much less sweet than the sugar content alone would. Tonic water actually contains about the same amount of sugar that sodas have.

Although a great many different compounds taste bitter, we generally do not distinguish between the tastes of these compounds; we simply avoid them all. The diversity of receptors for bitterness enables species or even individuals in a given species to have varying responses to an array of bitter compounds. One of the most famous of these is "taste blindness" to PTC (phenylthiocarbamide) found in humans—a phenomenon we will revisit later in this chapter.

Not coincidentally, compounds that taste bitter to us tend to be poisonous. However, some bitter stimuli are actually good for us. For example, bitter compounds in some vegetables help protect against cancer. We would like to be able to "turn off" these bitter sensations to make it easier for people to eat their vegetables. In pursuit of this goal, Robert Margolskee, a pioneer in studies of bitter transduction, used his understanding of the bitter system to identify a substance that can inhibit some bitter sensations: adenosine monophosphate

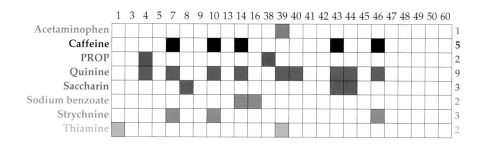

FIGURE 15.7 Bitter receptors are designated by TAS2R#, where # is the number of the receptor. The receptor numbers are shown at the top of the table. Examples of common bitter compounds are listed at the left. A filled box indicates a receptor that responds to the bitter compound on the left. The total number of receptors stimulated by a given compound is shown on the right. (After Meyerhof et al., 2010.)

(AMP) (Ming, Ninomiya, and Margolskee, 1999). AMP may actually function as a natural bitter inhibitor in mother's milk. A number of compounds in milk, such as casein (milk protein) and calcium salts, taste bitter; and, as we will see later, aversions to bitter tastes are present at birth. The presence of AMP in mother's milk may suppress those bitter tastes enough to allow milk to be palatable to babies who are particularly responsive to them.

Bitter perception is also affected by hormone levels in women. Sensitivity to bitterness intensifies during pregnancy and diminishes after menopause (Duffy et al., 1998). These differences make sense in the context of the function of bitterness as a poison detection mechanism. Intensifying the perception of bitter early in pregnancy, when toxins exert their maximum effects, has clear biological value. Consistent with this correlation, some of the aversions during pregnancy occur with foods or beverages that have bitter tastes (e.g., coffee).

One of the most interesting recent developments concerning bitter is the discovery that bitter receptors can be found on locations other than the tongue. For example, bitter receptors in the gut appear to slow absorption (Jeon et al., 2008). Thus, if toxins get past the mouth, the gut can still prevent poisoning.

Sweet

Sweetness is evoked by sugars, simple carbohydrates that generally conform to the chemical formula $(CH_2O)_n$, where n is a number between 3 and 7. Glucose, one of the sweetest-tasting sugars, is the principal source of energy in humans (as well as nearly every other living thing on Earth). Common table sugar, sucrose (**Figure 15.8**)—which is a combination of glucose and yet another sugar, fructose—tastes even sweeter.

The biological function of sweet is different from that of bitter, and the way taste receptors are tuned supports that biological difference. Many different molecules taste bitter. Our biological task is not to distinguish among them but rather to avoid them all. Thus, we have multiple bitter receptors to encompass the chemical diversity of poisons, but they all feed into a common line leading to rejection. With regard to sweet, some biologically useless sugars have structures very similar to those of glucose, fructose, and sucrose. In this case, then, the task of the taste system is to tune receptors so specifically that the biologically important sugars stimulate sweet taste but the others do not.

Consistent with the biological purpose of sweet, the family of genes expressing sweet receptors is very small, consisting of only *TAS1R1*, *TAS1R2*, and *TAS1R3*. (We will discuss *TAS1R1* later.) These genes express three different G protein–coupled receptors: T1R1, T1R2, and T1R3.

FIGURE 15.8 The molecular structure of sucrose, common table sugar. This disaccharide is formed from a combination of a glucose molecule and a fructose molecule. Glucose, which is easily extracted from sucrose by the digestive system, is the main fuel that powers almost every biological engine (including the human brain currently reading this book).

FIGURE 15.9 Structure of the T1R2-T1R3 heterodimer sweet receptor, showing binding sites for both large and small sweet molecules. (After Temussi, 2007.)

Simple molecules (monomers) can form chains of varying length (polymers). When the chain has only two units, it is called a **dimer**; when the two units are different, it is called a **heterodimer**. Receptors T1R2 and T1R3 combine to form the heterodimer that is now known to be a sweet receptor (**Figure 15.9**). The complex extracellular portion of the receptors that form this combination (which resembles the shape of a Venus flytrap) provides a variety of positions at which sweeteners with very different chemical structures can bind. For example, sweet proteins are very large compared to smaller sweeteners like sucrose, and these sweet proteins can act like wedges that insert into the trap of the Venus flytrap domain and trigger the receptor. Smaller sweeteners (sugars, saccharin, aspartame, and so on) can interact with this same site or with other sites on the receptor.

Initially, the T1R2-T1R3 heterodimer was thought to be responsible for all sweetness, but it introduced a new puzzle: No matter how the heterodimer is stimulated, the receptor produces only one signal. Therefore, we would expect all sweeteners—sugars and artificial sweeteners alike—to produce the same sweetness. However, artificial sweeteners like saccharin and aspartame do not taste exactly like sugar; if they did, there would be no need to continually search for better artificial sweeteners. Some claim that artificial sweeteners produce additional tastes that account for the difference. For example, saccharin tastes bitter as well as sweet to many. But some of us (the author included) do not taste the bitterness of saccharin at all; we are quite convinced that it is the nature of the sweetness that differs. Genetic studies may offer some help here. The receptor T1R3 appears to be able to function alone to respond only to high concentrations of sucrose (Zhao et al., 2003). In addition, Margolskee and colleagues (Yee et al., 2011) have identified yet another mechanism in addition to the heterodimer that can mediate sweetness. Thus we can explain why many of us perceive differences between the sweetness of sucrose and that of artificial sweeteners.

Since our taste system can produce sweet receptors so precisely tuned to the biologically useful sugars, what is going on with artificial sweeteners? Are these nonsugar molecules sweet because they accidentally stimulate the sweet heterodimer? We don't know. Are artificial sweeteners medically useful? Certainly they enable diabetics to enjoy a sweet taste without the dangers of sugar, but the early hopes that artificial sweeteners would be a panacea for weight loss now appear wrong.

Saccharin was discovered in 1879 when the chemist Ira Remsen, working on coal tar derivatives, failed to wash up before dinner and subsequently noticed that the tar residue on his hands tasted sweet. Another artificial sweetener was discovered in 1937, by a graduate student working in what must have been a messy lab. When he tasted sweet while smoking a cigarette, he realized that

dimer A chain of two molecules.

heterodimer A chain of two molecules that are different from each other.

some compound in the lab must be responsible. In this way, cyclamate was discovered. Cyclamate was very popular for a few years, but suspicions were raised that it was carcinogenic. Although those suspicions were challenged and cyclamate remains legal in a number of other countries, the Food and Drug Administration (FDA) banned it in the United States. Artificial sweeteners are attractive to dieters because their sweet taste comes with essentially no calories. Millions of dieters count on this property to help them watch their weight, but a 1986 epidemiological study showed that women who consumed artificial sweeteners actually gained weight (Stellman and Garfinkel, 1986).

Also in 1986, John Blundell, an English expert on weight regulation, published a provocative article suggesting that aspartame (the artificial sweetener sold as NutraSweet) increases appetite (Blundell and Hill, 1986). Was the benefit of the reduced calories lost when individuals using aspartame actually increased their caloric intake in subsequent meals? T. L. Davidson and S. E. Swithers (2004) elaborated on this kind of thinking with studies using rats. The earlier work with humans was discounted by many; after all, those with weight problems may be the individuals who choose to consume artificial sweeteners and it is not surprising that they gain weight. However, the same criticism could not be made when the rats fed artificial sweeteners gained weight. Davidson and Swithers point to the fact that the "obesity epidemic" occurred over the same years as the introduction of low-calorie foods into the American market. They argue that the uncoupling of the sensory properties of these diet foods from their metabolic consequences disrupts regulation, leading to weight gain.

Incidentally, the so-called "obesity epidemic" deserves closer study. Katherine Flegal, an epidemiologist who monitors weight changes in the United States, showed that the data tell a rather different story (Flegal et al., 2002). Weight gain over time affects obese more than thin adults. Stated more accurately, those who are overweight are getting even heavier.

The Survival Value of Taste

Like olfactory receptors, taste receptors detect specific features of molecules. But the two associated senses evolved to serve quite different functions. In olfaction, specific features of molecules interact with receptors tuned to them. All receptors of a given type project to individual glomeruli in the olfactory brain. The pattern across the glomeruli paints a picture of the chemical structure of the molecule. These pictures help us identify objects in our environment. Indeed, for many animals (e.g., rodents), olfaction is the primary means for knowing what surrounds them in the world. Consistent with this purpose, the olfactory system is capable of distinguishing among a large number of different molecules, and an individual animal can learn about whatever olfactory stimuli exist in the environment where it happens to live.

FURTHER DISCUSSION of the sensing of molecular structure as it relates to olfaction can be found in Chapter 14 starting on page 407.

On the other hand, we've just seen that the gustatory system responds to a fixed and much smaller set of molecules that nature knows we will encounter. This precise tuning is consistent with the role of taste as a system for detecting nutrients and "antinutrients" (substances that are either helpful or harmful, respectively, to our bodies) before we ingest them.

Each of the four basic tastes is responsible for a different nutrient or antinutrient, and has evolved according to its purpose. For example, the bitter taste subsystem is nature's poison detector. In terms of chemical structure, poisons are quite diverse. Thus the bitter receptors must be diverse as well.

On the other hand, given that we don't really care if we can discriminate among poisons (since we just want to avoid them all), we could hook all of those receptors up to a few common lines to the brain. As we saw earlier, this is exactly how the bitter subsystem is set up.

Similarly, the sour subsystem is configured to reject any highly acidic solution without distinguishing exactly what is causing the acidity of the solution to be so high. The other two taste subsystems enable us to detect, and therefore selectively ingest, foods that our bodies need: sodium (salty) and sugars (sweet).

The Pleasures of Taste

Carl Pfaffmann wrote a famous paper in 1960 entitled "The Pleasures of Sensation," in which he underlined unique features of the sense of taste with regard to affective experience. Taste provides sensory information not only about certain nutrients, but also about pleasure (sweet, salty, and, for children, sour) and displeasure (bitter). The pleasure or displeasure that these tastes evoke is present at birth. That is, with no experience an infant will like sweet and dislike bitter and strong sour. Salty receptors are not completely mature at birth, but when they do become functional, infants will like relatively dilute salts.

Some of the most impressive evidence for this hardwired affect with taste came from the work of Jacob Steiner on facial expressions in newborn infants (Steiner, 1973). Steiner found that infants responded with stereotyped facial expressions when sweet, salty, sour, and bitter solutions were applied to their tongues. Sweet evoked a "smilelike" expression followed by sucking (**Figure 15.10***a*). Sour produced pursing and protrusion of the lips (Figure 15.10*b*). Bitter produced gaping, movements of spitting, and in some cases, vomiting movements. Even infants born without cerebral hemispheres (a condition known as anencephaly) showed the same facial expressions, suggesting that these expressions are mediated by very primitive parts of the brain.

This hardwired affect responds to body need. For example, craving for salt was demonstrated by a dramatic case described in 1940. A 3½-year-old boy with an intense craving for salt died when his salt intake was restricted during a hospital stay. An autopsy revealed a tumor of his adrenal gland that had caused his body to lose sodium. His salt craving had enabled his body to retain enough sodium to keep him alive (Wilkins and Richter, 1940).

The fact that the basic tastes provide both information and affective experience enables organisms to solve critical nutritional problems immediately, without having to learn (which takes time). The newborn baby can nurse because the sweet taste of mother's milk is pleasurable. The baby can also reject poisons because the

FIGURE 15.10 The two toddlers' facial expressions reveal the taste qualities that they're experiencing. (*a*) Sweet potato produces the typical smile associated with the acceptance of sweet. (*b*) Green apple produces the puckery face associated with sour.

(*a*)

(*b*)

bitter tastes they evoke are aversive. The athlete who sweats or the new mother who loses blood can replace lost sodium because the taste of salt is pleasant.

Specific Hungers

specific hungers theory The idea that deficiency of a given nutrient produces craving (a specific hunger) for that nutrient. Curt Richter first proposed this theory and demonstrated that cravings for salty or for sweet are associated with deficiencies in those substances. However, the idea proved wrong for other nutrients (e.g., vitamins).

Early on, Curt Richter proposed a simple mechanism for the regulation of nutrients: the **specific hungers theory**. According to this view, the need for a nutrient causes the body to crave it. Ingestion of the nutrient reduces the craving and brings the body back into balance. The case of the boy with the salt craving described in the previous section provided support for this theory. Another source of support was a treatment for schizophrenia that was popular in the 1940s. At the time, some experts believed that the brain, which depends on glucose for fuel, could be forcibly rested if blood glucose were driven to very low values with insulin. Intense cravings for sweet were an unexpected by-product of the therapy. Subsequent laboratory studies confirmed that insulin injections produce increased liking for sweet.

Even more support for the idea of specific hungers seemed to come from the work of a pediatrician, Clara Davis. She allowed a group of 6-month-old infants to eat whatever they liked, to see if they would choose wisely (C. M. Davis, 1928). The infants thrived, leading Davis to conclude that, when allowed to choose among a variety of healthy foods, infants had the ability to select a healthy diet.

The success of the specific hungers theory spurred further investigations that ultimately proved that the theory was limited only to sweet and salty. In one of the early studies, rats were fed a diet deficient in vitamin B_{12}, which made them sick. When the rats were offered a choice of remaining on the same diet or switching to a diet containing B_{12}, they immediately switched. But Paul Rozin conducted a crucial control. He gave the control rats the choice of the original diet or a different diet that was also deficient in B_{12}. These rats also immediately switched to the different diet. Thus, the rats in the original study had not specifically sought B_{12}; they had simply learned to avoid the diet that made them ill (Rozin, 1967).

Rozin's work ended belief in specific hungers as an explanation of dietary regulation for anything beyond sugar and salt. In retrospect, we can see that the theory lacked an important ingredient. For craving to cause an animal to seek out and take in a needed nutrient, a sensory cue would have to be unambiguously associated with the nutrient. The saltiness of salt and the sweetness of sugar could serve as such cues, but the B_{12} molecule does not produce a detectable cue in food (**Figure 15.11**).

We were left with a problem, though. How did Clara Davis's infants know how to select a healthy diet if specific hungers do not operate for all nutrients? It turned out that they were not selecting a healthy diet at all. They were simply eating a variety of the foods presented because they got bored eating single foods. Because all of the choices were healthy, all the infants needed to do was eat a variety. In the modern world, eating whatever we like will not produce good health, because too many of the available foods are not healthy. In fact, the specific hungers that are genuine can do us considerable harm; just think about our love for sweet and salty junk foods.

If specific hungers don't control all of what we eat, what does? Our likes and dislikes of food depend very much on our likes and dislikes of the retronasal olfactory sensations associated with foods. As we saw in the previous chapter, these olfactory likes and dislikes are not hardwired as those for taste are. Thus, our affect toward foods is made up of the hardwired affect contributed by taste, combined with the learned affect contributed by retronasal smell. By the way, evidence up to now tells us that all olfactory affect is learned; however, not all

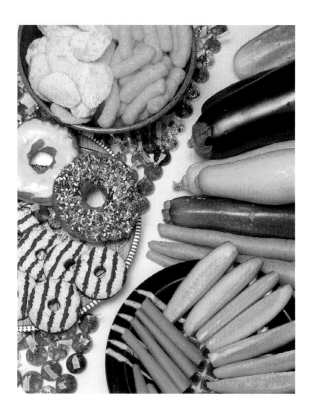

FIGURE 15.11 In our evolutionary past, when food was scarce and we had to expend considerable physical effort to get it, specific hungers for sugar and salt were adaptive. In the current era, in which foods are plentiful and easily obtained, these specific hungers (combined with the profit motive for the food industry) lead many to consume too much junk food. The nutrients in vegetables are, alas, largely undetectable, so we cannot develop specific hungers for them.

odorants have been appropriately tested. Could there be a few that, like taste, have hardwired affect? One suggestion is that certain odorants produced by vegetables and fruits are cues to important nutrients. Harry Klee, an expert on the odorants produced by tomatoes, thinks this might be the case. If there are some hardwired odorants, we could make vegetables and fruits more palatable.

The gastrointestinal tract (commonly referred to as the gut) plays a crucial role in this learning. The macronutrients (nutrients that provide calories) are carbohydrates (long chains of sugar molecules), proteins (chains of amino acids), and fats (chains of fatty acids attached to glycerol). Except for the special case of sugar (a very short chain), these macronutrient molecules are too large to be sensed by taste or olfactory receptors. When foods containing these macronutrients enter the gut, however, the macronutrients are broken into their constituent pieces. These pieces stimulate chemoreceptors in the gut, and the brain makes us like the sensory properties (primarily the retronasal olfactory sensations) of the foods (conditioned food preferences). On the other hand, if we experience nausea after eating, the brain makes us dislike the sensory properties of the foods (conditioned food aversions). Thus, we regulate our intake through a combination of hardwired basic tastes and learned responses to food flavors.

The Special Case of Umami

Umami arose as a candidate for a fifth basic taste as part of advertising claims by manufacturers of **monosodium glutamate** (**MSG**), the sodium salt of glutamic acid. Identified by Japanese chemists in the early 1900s, MSG was initially marketed as a flavor enhancer, said to suppress unpleasant tastes and enhance pleasant ones. When taste experts expressed skepticism, MSG manufacturers went on to claim that MSG was a fifth basic taste, speculating that it signaled protein and thus played an important role in nutrition. However, the umami

umami The taste sensation produced by monosodium glutamate.

monosodium glutamate (MSG) The sodium salt of glutamic acid (an amino acid).

taste is not perceptible in many foods containing proteins. Another reason why umami is an unlikely candidate for a fifth basic taste is that some individuals like it and some do not. The four basic tastes, in contrast, are distinguished by their hardwired affect.

There is an emerging and interesting distinction between the physiology and the psychophysics of taste. Physiologically, it seems that there are glutamate receptors in the mouth and the gut and that reception of glutamate has consequences. Psychophysically, it seems less likely that stimulation of these receptors gives rise to sensations that would qualify umami as a basic taste along with the classical sweet, sour, salty, and bitter.

Because glutamate is an important neurotransmitter, receptors for the molecule are common throughout the body. The argument that such receptors might have been harnessed by the taste system to signal umami gained respectability when neuroscientists Nirupa Chaudhari and Steve Roper identified a version of a glutamate receptor in rat taste papillae (Chaudhari, Landin, and Roper, 2000). There may be several kinds of receptors that respond to glutamate. Sweet compounds stimulate the T1R2-T1R3 heterodimer; umami stimulates another heterodimer, T1R1-T1R3.

Of special interest, Robert Margolskee (whose pioneering studies focused on not only the bitter receptor but also the sweet receptor) discovered that many taste receptors, including the glutamate receptor, are found in the gut. This exciting discovery suggests a different function for umami. Protein molecules are too large to be sensed by taste or smell, but proteins are made up of amino acids, including glutamic acid. When eaten, proteins are broken down into their constituent amino acids, providing stimuli for the glutamate receptors in the gut. These receptors can signal the brain that protein has been consumed. In this way, glutamate receptors can fulfill the function attributed to umami, but this is done in the gut, not the mouth. Consistent with this finding, John Prescott (a cognitive psychologist who studies the chemical senses) showed that consuming a novel-flavored soup with MSG added to it produces a conditioned preference for the novel flavor, while simply holding the soup in the mouth does not (Prescott, 2004).

Because glutamate is a neurotransmitter, concerns have been raised about its safety in the human diet. MSG became particularly notorious in the 1960s. First it became associated with Chinese restaurant syndrome—a constellation of symptoms including numbness, headache, flushing, tingling, sweating, and tightness in the chest—that was reported by some individuals after consuming MSG (R. H. M. Kwok, 1968). Then Dr. John Olney, a toxicologist, suggested that MSG might induce brain lesions, particularly in infants (Olney and Sharpe, 1969). In response to these concerns, MSG was removed from baby foods in the 1970s. The final conclusion (see Walker and Lupien, 2000) is that MSG in large doses may be a problem for some sensitive individuals, but apparently it does not present a serious problem for the general population. For those who are sensitive, however, MSG can pose a serious risk.

The Special Case of Fat

Like protein, fat is a very important nutrient. Also like protein, fat molecules are too large to stimulate either taste or olfaction but are broken into their constituent parts by digestion in the gut. Fat molecules are made up of fatty acids attached to a support structure. Whole fat molecules stimulate the trigeminal nerve in the mouth, evoking tactile sensations like oily, viscous, creamy, and so on; but some fat molecules may be partially digested while still in the mouth, thus releasing fatty acids. Neurobiologist Tim Gilbertson's discovery of fatty acid receptors on the tongues of rats led to the idea that stimulation of these fatty acid receptors might play a hardwired role in our love of fat. Just as with glutamate, however, nature uses a more general method to ensure that we love fat-containing foods. Anthony Sclafani (a learning theorist who is an expert on conditioned food preferences) showed that fat in the gut produces conditioned preferences for the sensory properties of the food containing fat. Once we understand the role of conditioning in food preferences, we should have a healthy skepticism about the value of so-called diet foods. Mimicking the sensory properties of normal foods but reducing the caloric content disrupts normal regulatory mechanisms, as noted by Davidson and Swithers (see the discussion of sweet earlier in this chapter).

Coding of Taste Quality

A major source of historical controversy in the taste literature revolved around whether tastes are coded mainly via **labeled lines**, in which each taste neuron would unambiguously signal the presence of a certain basic taste, or via patterns of activity across many different taste neurons. We've seen examples of both types of coding in other senses. For example, color vision and olfaction use pattern coding. A single type of cone cannot tell us the wavelength of a light ray, but the pattern of activity across our three cone types can give us this information. Hearing, on the other hand, uses a mechanism more akin to the labeled-line approach: certain neurons always respond best to 5000-hertz (Hz) tones, others always respond best to 5100-Hz tones, and so on. Which scheme is used in the gustatory system?

labeled lines A theory of taste coding in which each taste nerve fiber carries a particular taste quality. For example, the quality evoked from a sucrose-best fiber is sweet, that from an NaCl-best fiber is salty, and so on.

> FURTHER DISCUSSION of the coding of colors, sounds, and odors, can be found in Chapters 5, 9, and 14, respectively.

Given what we've already learned about the functions of the four basic tastes, it is easy to construct an evolutionary argument for labeled-line coding. Recall that in olfaction, which uses pattern coding, mixtures of different compounds very often produce a new smell sensation; the components cannot be recognized. Such a coding system would be disastrous for the purpose of the taste system. For example, poisonous plants contain components with a variety of tastes. If bitterness were to synthesize with these other tastes, we would not be able to parse it out and thus avoid the poison. The functions of the four tastes are well served by their independence from each other. In addition, studies have shown that we are, in fact, very good at analyzing taste mixtures. For example, in tonic water, which contains a combination of quinine and sugar, we have no difficulty identifying its two components—bitter and sweet.

The historical controversy arose because initial research seemed to indicate that most neurons coming from taste buds respond to more than one of the four basic tastes. How could such a system code sweet, sour, salt, and bitter without confusion? Pfaffmann initially concluded that taste qualities were coded by a pattern across taste fibers, but he changed his mind because of observations of squirrel monkey behavior (Pfaffmann, 1974b). By this time Marion Frank (one of Pfaffmann's students) had shown that most taste nerve fibers have a clear "favorite" stimulus (e.g., "NaCl-best" or "sucrose-best"). Thus, taste quality might be coded by a noisy labeled-line system (NaCl-best fibers producing a salty taste, sucrose-best fibers producing a sweet taste, and so on) (Frank, 1973). Alternatively, taste quality could still be produced by the pattern of responses across a population of taste fibers.

Pfaffmann (1974a) ultimately decided in favor of labeled lines. Squirrel monkeys love sweet. Their taste nerves produce larger responses to fructose than to sucrose, suggesting that fructose tastes sweeter. However, given a

FIGURE 15.12 The tastes that human subjects perceive for each of four stimuli: sucrose, NaCl, HCl, and quinine. Also shown are the tastes that a monkey would perceive if the monkey's sweet-best fibers coded sweetness, NaCl-best fibers coded saltiness, HCl-best fibers coded sourness, and quinine-best fibers coded bitterness. (Monkey data from Sato, Ogawa, and Yamashita, 1975; human data from Bartoshuk, 1975.)

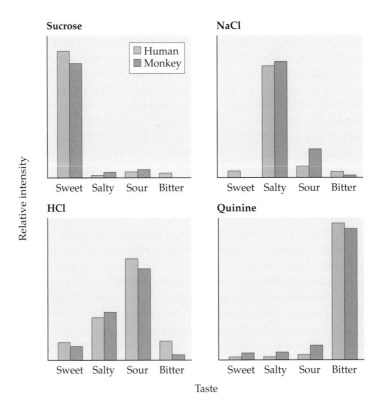

choice between sucrose and fructose, they choose sucrose. The answer came from single-fiber recording: sucrose-best fibers responded better to sucrose than to fructose, and NaCl-best fibers responded better to fructose than to sucrose. Labeled-line theory explained the monkeys' behavior. Tasting sucrose evoked a sweet taste from the sucrose-best fibers; tasting fructose evoked both a sweet taste from the sucrose-best fibers and a salty taste from the NaCl-best fibers. The monkeys preferred the pure sweet taste to the sweet + salty taste.

By the way, the fact that taste nerve fibers are not exclusively tuned to single basic tastes means that we rarely, if ever, experience "pure tastes." For example, sour tastes are perceived when acid-best fibers are activated, but acids also activate NaCl-best fibers (**Figure 15.12**). Thus, a solution of hydrochloric acid (HCl) will taste primarily sour, but also salty.

Taste Adaptation and Cross-Adaptation

As we've seen throughout this book, all sensory systems show adaptation effects, in which constant application of a certain stimulus temporarily weakens subsequent perception of that stimulus. In taste, our constant adaptation to the salt in saliva affects our ability to taste salt; in addition, adaptation to certain components in one food can change the perception of a second food. (See **Web Essay 15.2: Water Tastes**.) You've experienced cross-adaptation yourself if you've ever noticed that a beverage like lemonade tastes too sour after you eat a sweet dessert. The sugar in the dessert adapts the sweet receptors so that the subsequent lemonade tastes less sweet and more sour than normal.

Genetic Variation in Taste Experience

In 1931 a chemist named Arthur Fox discovered that we do not all live in the same taste worlds (A. L. Fox, 1931). Fox was synthesizing the compound phenylthiocarbamide (PTC) (**Figure 15.13a**), when some spilled and flew into the air. A colleague nearby noticed a bitter taste, but Fox tasted nothing. A test of additional colleagues revealed a few more **nontasters** like Fox who tasted little bitterness in the compound, but most (**tasters**) perceived it as bitter. The next year, Albert Blakeslee (a famous geneticist of the day) and Fox took PTC crystals to a meeting of the American Association for the Advancement of Science and set up a voting booth for attendees to register their perceptions. About one-third of those polled found the crystals to be tasteless, while two-thirds found them to be bitter. These proportions captured the imagination of many researchers, and for several years the *Journal of Heredity* sold papers impregnated with PTC for further studies. Family studies eventually confirmed that taster status is an inherited trait (e.g., the Dionne quintuplets were all found to be tasters in 1941). Nontasters carry two recessive alleles, whereas tasters have either one or both dominant alleles.

Initially, individuals were simply classified according to whether they could taste PTC, but eventually threshold studies came into vogue. In a threshold method invented specifically for PTC studies, subjects were given eight cups, four containing water and four containing a given concentration of PTC. Correct sorting determined the threshold. The distribution of thresholds was bimodal, with nontasters showing very high thresholds and tasters showing low thresholds. This distribution varied by sex and race: women had lower thresholds than men, and Asians had lower thresholds than Caucasians.

In the 1960s, Roland Fischer shifted studies to a chemical relative of PTC that was safer to test—propylthiouracil (PROP) (Figure 15.13*b*)—and focused on the nutritional implications of the genetic variation in taster status (Fischer and Griffin, 1964). Fischer suggested that tasters were more finicky eaters: because bitter tastes are more intense to these individuals, they tend to dislike foods high in bitter compounds, such as many vegetables, that nontasters find more palatable. Fischer also related taster status to body type (e.g., weight) and health. Alcoholics and smokers were found to contain a lower proportion of tasters than would be expected by chance, presumably because unpleasant sensations (e.g., bitterness) produced by alcoholic beverages and tobacco act as deterrents. The effect of genetic variation in taste is even related to cancer risk, as will be described shortly.

In 2003, Dennis Drayna and his colleagues discovered the location of the gene that expresses PTC/PROP receptors (Kim et al., 2003). This gene is a member of the bitter family introduced earlier and is designated *TAS2R38*. Individuals with two recessive alleles are nontasters; those with either one or both dominant alleles are tasters.

Supertasters

By the 1970s, the "direct" psychophysical methods introduced by Harvard's S. S. Stevens led to a new look at genetic variation in taste. Instead of measuring thresholds—the dimmest sensations—investigators could look at suprathreshold taste and plot the psychophysical functions showing how perceived taste intensity varies with concentration. You may remember from Chapter 1 that Stevens and his students documented what is now known as Stevens' power law. It holds that perceived sensations rise as the stimulus raised to some power. Written as an equation, this is

$$S = aI^b$$

where S is sensation, I is stimulus intensity (concentration of a solution if we're talking about taste, and we are), and b takes on different values for different sensory modalities (S. S. Stevens and Galanter, 1957). Of special interest for our present purposes, b takes on different values for different taste qualities.

(a) Phenylthiocarbamide

(b) Propylthiouracil

FIGURE 15.13 The chemical structures of PTC (*a*) and PROP (*b*). The portions shaded in blue are those responsible for the bitter taste.

nontaster (of PTC/PROP) An individual born with two recessive alleles for the *TAS2R38* gene and unable to taste the compounds phenylthiocarbamide and propylthiouracil.

taster (of PTC/PROP) An individual born with one or both dominant alleles for the *TAS2R38* gene and able to taste the compounds phenylthiocarbamide and propylthiouracil. PTC/PROP tasters who also have a high density of fungiform papillae are PROP supertasters.

FIGURE 15.14 Psychophysical functions for quinine and sucrose. The logarithm of the perceived taste intensity is plotted against the logarithm of the concentration. In this plot, *b* is the slope of the function. The value of *b* for quinine is 0.3; for sucrose, 0.8. (Data from Bartoshuk, 1979.)

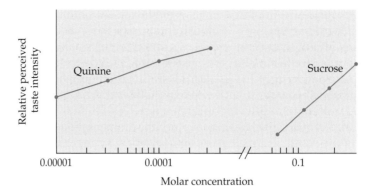

For example, bitterness grows more slowly with concentration than sweet does (Figure 15.14). That is, the value of *b* for bitter is smaller than the value of *b* for sweet.

Unfortunately, knowing how taste intensity grows with concentration does not permit comparisons of perceived taste intensity across individuals; *b* can be equal for two people even if one experiences taste intensities twice as great as the other. Fortunately, two of S. S. Stevens' students—Joseph Stevens and Lawrence Marks—made another fundamental discovery in this era. As we discussed in Chapter 1, humans are surprisingly good at **cross-modality matching** (J. C. Stevens, 1959). For example, we can match the loudness of a sound to the brightness of a light, and we can match both of these to the intensity of a taste. This finding ultimately led to the discovery of supertasters. Katherine Fast, one of Bartoshuk's students, asked subjects to match the bitterness of PROP to other sensations completely unrelated to taste (see Figure 1.9). For example, nontasters matched the taste of PROP to very weak sensations (the sound of a watch or a whisper). Tasters proved to be a heterogeneous lot. For some, PROP was likened to very intense sensations, such as the brightness of the sun or the most intense pain ever experienced. These individuals were labeled **supertasters**. "Medium tasters" matched PROP to weaker stimuli, such as the smell of frying bacon or the pain of a mild headache (Bartoshuk, Fast, and Snyder, 2005).

Armed with genotypes, ratings of the bitterness of PROP, and counts of fungiform papillae, Valerie Duffy (a pioneer in the modern movement among nutritionists to evaluate food behavior in terms of the sensory properties of foods instead of only their nutrient content), along with her student John Hayes and colleagues (Hayes et al., 2008), was able to show that a combination of PROP genotype and tongue anatomy divided individuals into the three groups already described: nontasters, tasters, and supertasters. This research showed that PROP status and number of fungiform papillae are independent. The combination of ability to taste PROP and possession of a very large number of fungiform papillae produces a PROP supertaster; PROP tasters with fewer fungiform papillae are medium PROP tasters. Among PROP nontasters, the number of fungiform papillae varies across the whole range. Thus, a person can be a PROP nontaster but be a supertaster in all other ways.

Those with the most numerous fungiform papillae experience not only the most intense taste sensations in general, but also the most intense sensations of oral burn (e.g., from chili peppers) and oral touch (from fats or thickeners in foods), because fungiform papillae are innervated by nerve fibers that convey burn and touch sensations, as well as those that convey taste sensations. In addition, because of central connections between taste and retronasal olfaction, those who experience the most intense taste sensations also perceive more intense retronasal olfaction and thus more intense flavor.

cross-modality matching The ability to match the intensities of sensations that come from different sensory modalities. This ability enables insight into sensory differences. For example, a listener might adjust the brightness of a light until it matches the loudness of a tone.

supertaster An individual whose perception of taste sensations is the most intense. A variety of factors may contribute to this heightened perception; among the most important is the density of fungiform papillae.

Pathology adds yet another source of variation in our oral sensations. Surprisingly, removing input from one of the taste nerves (by anesthesia or damage) can actually intensify taste sensations (Lehman et al., 1995). This intensification results because inputs from the different taste nerves inhibit one another in the brain. Loss of input from one nerve releases others from that inhibition. In some cases, the result is actual intensification of whole-mouth taste. When damage is more widespread, not surprisingly, taste perception diminishes.

In sum, taste experience is the outcome of genetic variation, pathology, and interactions among all of the cranial nerves innervating the mouth.

Health Consequences of Taste Sensation

With these new insights, the potential links between responsiveness to PROP and health have become the focus of renewed interest. The new psychophysical methods permitted Duffy to show that variation in the sensory properties of foods and beverages affects food preferences and thus diet. Because diet is a major risk factor for a variety of diseases, genetic variation in taste plays a role in these diseases. For instance, some vegetables produce unpleasant sensations (e.g., bitter) to medium tasters and supertasters, leading these individuals to eat fewer of them. Reduced vegetable intake is in turn a risk factor for colon cancer.

Sure enough, Duffy and her colleagues found that, in a sample of older men getting routine colonoscopies at a Department of Veterans Affairs hospital, those tasting PROP as most bitter had the most colon polyps, a precursor to colon cancer (Basson et al., 2005). On the other hand, fats can produce unpleasantly intense sensations in supertasters, leading them to eat fewer high-fat foods and thereby lowering their risk of cardiovascular disease (Duffy, Lucchina, and Bartoshuk, 2004). These sensory links to behavior that affects health are not limited to diet. Fischer's early suggestion that nontasters are more likely to smoke and consume alcohol has proved correct (Duffy et al., 2004; D. J. Snyder et al., 2005).

Pleasure and Retronasal versus Orthonasal Olfaction

There is still much that is not understood about the links between retronasal and orthonasal (through the nostrils) olfaction, including the pleasure or displeasure associated with these sensations. We know that we learn to like or dislike smells, but do we learn these preferences separately for retro- and orthonasal olfaction? Bartoshuk recounts getting carsick on a childhood vacation while simultaneously eating chocolate-covered cherries. She now not only avoids the cherries, but finds cherry-scented soaps disgusting as well.

Chili Peppers

The pleasure that some people experience from chili peppers deserves special attention. We are not born liking chili peppers. Rozin studied the acquisition of chili pepper preference in Mexico and found that the process depends on social influences. Chili is gradually added to the diet of young children beginning at about age 3, and the children observe their family members enjoying it. By age 5 or 6, children voluntarily add chili to their own food. At some point the chili is liked for its own sake.

A variety of arguments based on presumed health benefits have been introduced to account for our love of chili peppers. For example, some have argued that chilis kill microorganisms in food, thus acting as a preservative. Others have argued that chilis contain vitamins A and C, which give them adaptive value (in other words, the pain of the chili serves as a cue for the presence of

FIGURE 15.15 Do these images inspire fear or delight in your taste buds?

the vitamins). The pleasure that some people experience from chilis has also been linked to the idea that the resulting burn leads to the release of endorphins, the brain's internal painkillers.

One of the most interesting features of the liking for the burn of chili peppers is its near total restriction to humans. Rozin has documented a few cases on record of animals showing a liking for chilis, but in all cases these were pets fed chili pepper by their human companions. When Rozin tried to produce liking for chilis in rats, he failed. But one of Rozin's students, Bennett Galef, who is famous for the study of social interactions among rats, was finally able to get rats to like a diet seasoned with a mild level of cayenne pepper, by exposing the rats to a "demonstrator" rat that had just eaten the diet. It seems that growing to like chili peppers is a social phenomenon for rats as well.

The burn that we experience from chili peppers is highly variable across individuals (Figure 15.15). The variability has two sources. First, as noted earlier, individuals with the largest number of fungiform papillae (supertasters) have the most fibers mediating pain, and thus they perceive the most intense oral burn from chilis. Second, capsaicin, the chemical that produces the burn in chilis, desensitizes pain receptors. This means that individuals who consume chilis quite often (once every 48 hours is sufficient) are chronically desensitized. Chili peppers produce considerably less burn to those who are desensitized.

Desensitization can come to your rescue if you accidentally order a meal that proves to be overspiced for your palate. After the first mouthful, wait until the burn has subsided. The mistake many diners make is to keep trying to eat. As long as the capsaicin continues to be applied, desensitization does not occur. Desensitization occurs during the decline of the burn (B. G. Green, 1993). Once the initial burn has faded, the rest of the meal can be consumed with relative comfort.

Capsaicin desensitization has important clinical value. The ancient Mayan Indians used a concoction made of chilis to treat the pain of mouth sores. In the 1990s, Wolffe Nadoolman, then a medical student at Yale working in Bartoshuk's laboratory, created a similar remedy by adding cayenne pepper to a recipe for taffy. Cancer patients often develop painful mouth sores from chemotherapy and radiation therapy, and if these patients suck on the capsaicin candies, capsaicin is brought into contact with the pain receptors stimulated by the sores. The pain receptors are then desensitized and the pain is dramatically reduced (Berger et al., 1995). Although capsaicin can be used to reduce pain at any body site, the skin is a potent barrier that prevents capsaicin from contacting pain receptors. Thus, capsaicin remedies for disorders like arthritis are rarely very satisfactory. In the mouth, the mucous membrane permits capsaicin to easily contact pain receptors, so there, desensitization is fast and powerful.

Summary

1. Flavor is produced by the combination of taste and retronasal olfaction (olfactory sensations produced when odorants in the mouth are forced up behind the palate into the nose). Flavor sensations are localized to the mouth, even though the retronasal olfactory sensations come from the olfactory receptors high in the nasal cavity.

2. Taste buds are globular clusters of cells (like the segments in an orange). The tips of some of the cells (microvilli) contain sites that interact with taste molecules. Those sites fall into two groups: ion channels that mediate responses

Refer to the
Sensation and Perception
Companion Website
sites.sinauer.com/wolfe3e
for activities, essays, study
questions, and other study aids.

to salts and acids, and G protein–coupled receptors that bind to sweet and bitter compounds.

3. The tongue has a bumpy appearance because of structures called papillae. Filiform papillae (the most numerous) have no taste buds. Taste buds are found in the fungiform papillae (front of the tongue), foliate papillae (rear edges of the tongue), and circumvallate papillae (rear center of the tongue), as well as on the roof of the mouth.

4. Taste projects ipsilaterally from the tongue to the medulla, thalamus, and cortex. It projects first to the insula in the cortex, and from there to the orbito-frontal cortex, an area where taste can be integrated with other sensory input (e.g., retronasal olfaction).

5. Taste and olfaction play very different roles in the perception of foods and beverages. Taste is the true nutritional sense; taste receptors are tuned to molecules that function as important nutrients. Bitter taste is a poison detection system. Sweet taste enables us to respond to the sugars that are biologically useful to us: sucrose, glucose, and fructose. Salty taste enables us to identify sodium, a mineral crucial to survival because of its role in nerve conduction and muscle function. Sour taste permits us to avoid acids in concentrations that might injure tissue.

6. Umami, the taste produced by monosodium glutamate, has been suggested as a fifth basic taste that detects protein. However, umami lacks one of the most important properties of a basic taste: hardwired affect. Some individuals like umami, but others do not. The presence of glutamate receptors in the gut suggests that proteins are detected there. Digestion breaks down proteins into their constituent amino acids, and the glutamate released stimulates gut glutamate receptors, leading to conditioned preferences for the sensory properties of the foods containing the protein.

7. The importance of taste to survival requires that we be able to recognize each taste quality independently, even when it is present in a mixture. By coding taste quality with labeled lines in much the same way that frequencies are coded in hearing, nature has ensured that we have this important capability. These labeled lines are noisy. For example, acids are able to stimulate fibers mediating saltiness, as well as those mediating sourness. Thus, acids tend to taste both salty and sour.

8. Foods do not taste the same to everyone. The Human Genome Project revealed that we carry about 25 genes for bitter taste. The most studied bitter receptor responds to PROP and shows allelic variation in humans leading to the designations "PROP nontaster" for those who taste the least bitterness and "PROP taster" for those who taste the most. In addition, humans vary in the number of fungiform papillae (and thus taste buds) they possess. Those with the most taste buds are called supertasters and live in a "neon" taste world; those with the fewest taste buds live in a "pastel" taste world. Psychologists discovered these differences by testing people's ability to match sensory intensities of stimuli from different modalities. For example, the bitterness of black coffee matches the pain of a mild headache to nontasters but resembles a severe headache to supertasters. The way foods taste affects palatability, which in turn affects diet. Poor diet contributes to diseases like cancer and cardiovascular disease.

9. For taste, unlike olfaction, liking and disliking are hardwired; for example, babies are born liking sweet and salty and disliking bitter. When we become deficient in salt or sucrose, liking for salty and sweet tastes, respectively, increases. Junk foods are constructed to appeal to these preferences. Liking the burn of chili peppers, on the other hand, is acquired and, with the exception of some pets, is essentially limited to humans. Because taste buds are surrounded by pain fibers, supertasters perceive much greater burn from chilis than do nontasters.

Glossary

A

A-delta fiber An intermediate-sized, myelinated sensory nerve fiber that transmits pain and temperature signals. Compare *C fiber*.

A1 See *primary auditory cortex*.

abducens (VI) nerves The sixth pair of cranial nerves, which innervate the lateral rectus muscle of each eye.

absolute metrical depth cue A depth cue that provides quantifiable information about distance in the third dimension (e.g., his nose sticks out 4 centimeters in front of his face). Compare *relative metrical depth cue*.

absolute threshold The minimum amount of stimulation necessary for a person to detect a stimulus 50% of the time.

absorb To take up light, noise, or energy and not transmit it at all.

ACC See *anterior cingulate cortex*.

acceleration A change in velocity. Mathematically, acceleration is the derivative of *velocity*. In words, linear acceleration indicates a change in linear velocity; angular acceleration indicates a change in angular velocity.

accessory olfactory bulb (AOB) A smaller neural structure located behind the *main olfactory bulb* that receives input from the vomeronasal organ.

accidental viewpoint A viewing position that produces some regularity in the visual image that is not present in the world (e.g., the sides of two independent objects lining up perfectly). Compare *nonaccidental feature*.

accommodation The process by which the eye changes its focus (in which the lens gets fatter as gaze is directed toward nearer objects).

achromatic Referring to any color that lacks a chromatic (hue) component. Black, white, or gray.

achromatopsia An inability to perceive colors that is caused by damage to the central nervous system.

acoustic reflex A reflex that protects the ear from intense sounds, via contraction of the stapedius and tensor tympani muscles.

acuity The smallest spatial detail that can be resolved.

adaptation A reduction in response caused by prior or continuing stimulation.

adapting stimulus A stimulus whose removal produces a change in visual perception or sensitivity.

additive color mixture A mixture of lights. If light A and light B are both reflected from a surface to the eye, in the perception of color the effects of those two lights add together. Compare *subtractive color mixture*.

aerial perspective A depth cue based on the implicit understanding that light is scattered by the atmosphere. More light is scattered when we look through more atmosphere. Thus, more distant objects are subject to more scatter and appear fainter, bluer, and less distinct. Also called *haze*.

afferent fiber A neuron that carries sensory information to the central nervous system. Compare *efferent fiber*.

afterimage A visual image seen after the stimulus has been removed.

aging-related macular degeneration (AMD) A disease associated with aging that affects the macula. AMD gradually destroys sharp central vision, making it difficult to read, drive, and recognize faces. There are two forms of AMD: wet and dry.

agnosia A failure to recognize objects in spite of the ability to see them. Agnosia is typically due to brain damage. Compare *anomia*.

akinetopsia A rare neuropsychological disorder in which the affected individual has no perception of motion.

aliasing Misperception of a grating due to undersampling.

amacrine cell A retinal cell found in the inner synaptic layer that makes synaptic contacts with bipolar cells, ganglion cells, and other amacrine cells.

ambiguous figure A visual stimulus that gives rise to two or more interpretations of its identity or structure.

amblyopia A developmental disorder characterized by reduced spatial vision in an otherwise healthy eye, even with proper correction for refractive error. Also known as *lazy eye*.

AMD See *aging-related macular degeneration*.

amplitude The size (increase or decrease) of a sound pressure wave or of a head movement (e.g., angular velocity, linear acceleration, tilt). In hearing, amplitude is also called *intensity*, and it is perceived as *loudness*.

ampulla An expansion of each semicircular canal duct that includes that canal's cupula, crista, and hair cells, where transduction occurs.

amygdala-hippocampal complex The conjoined regions of the amygdala and hippocampus, which are key structures in the limbic system. This complex is critical for the unique emotional and associative properties of olfactory cognition.

analgesia Decreasing pain sensation during conscious experience.

anamorphosis (or anamorphic projection) Use of the rules of linear perspective to create a two-dimensional image so distorted that it looks correct only when viewed from a special angle or with a mirror that counters the distortion.

angular acceleration The rate of change of angular velocity. Mathematically, the integral of angular acceleration is angular velocity, and the integral of angular velocity is angular displacement. Angular acceleration, angular velocity, and angular displacement all mathematically represent angular motion. Compare *linear acceleration*.

angular motion Rotational motion like the rotation of a spinning top or swinging saloon doors that rotate back and forth. Compare *linear motion*.

anisometropia A condition in which the two eyes have different refractive errors (e.g., one eye is farsighted and the other not).

anomia An inability to name objects in spite of the ability to see and recognize them (as shown by usage). Anomia is typically due to brain damage. Compare *agnosia*.

anosmia The total inability to smell, most often resulting from sinus illness or head trauma.

anterior cingulate cortex (ACC) A region of the brain associated with the perceived unpleasantness of a pain sensation.

AOB See *accessory olfactory bulb*.

aperture An opening that allows only a partial view of an object.

aperture problem The fact that when a moving object is viewed through an aperture (or a receptive field), the direction of motion of a local feature or part of the object may be ambiguous.

apparent motion The illusory impression of smooth motion resulting from the rapid alternation of objects that appear in different locations in rapid succession.

aqueous humor The watery fluid in the anterior chamber of the eye. Compare *vitreous humor*.

area 17 See *primary visual cortex*.

aromatherapy The contention that odors can influence, improve, and alter mood, performance, and well-being, as well as the physiological correlates of emotion such as heart rate, blood pressure, and sleep.

articulation The act or manner of producing a speech sound using the vocal tract.

astigmatism A visual defect caused by the unequal curving of one or more of the refractive surfaces of the eye, usually the cornea.

attack In hearing, the part of a sound during which amplitude increases (onset). Compare *decay*.

attention Any of the very large set of selective processes in the brain. To deal with the impossibility of handling all inputs at once, the nervous system has evolved mechanisms that are able to restrict processing to a subset of things, places, ideas, or moments in time.

attentional blink The tendency not to perceive or respond to the second of two different target stimuli amid a rapid stream of distracting stimuli if the observer has responded to the first target stimulus within 200–500 milliseconds before the second stimulus is presented. Compare *repetition blindness*.

audibility threshold The lowest sound pressure level that can be reliably detected at a given frequency.

auditory (VIII) nerves See *vestibulocochlear nerve*.

auditory nerve fiber A collection of neurons that convey information from hair cells in the cochlea to (afferent) and from (efferent) the brain stem.

auditory scene analysis See *source segregation*.

auditory stream segregation The perceptual organization of a complex acoustic signal into separate auditory events for which each stream is heard as a separate event.

autonomic nervous system The part of the nervous system that innervates glands, heart, digestive system, and so on, and that is responsible for regulating many involuntary actions.

azimuth The angle of a sound source on the horizontal plane relative to a point in the center of the head between the ears. Azimuth is measured in degrees, with 0 degrees being straight ahead. The angle increases clockwise toward the right, with 180 degrees being directly behind.

B

balance The neural processes of postural control by which weight is evenly distributed, enabling us to remain upright and stable.

balance system The sensory systems, neural processes, and muscles that contribute to postural control. Specific components include the vestibular labyrinth, proprioceptors, vestibulo-spinal pathways, and postural control muscles. Because of its crucial contributions to balance, some even informally refer to the vestibular system as the balance system and the vestibular organs as the balance organs. But the balance system is much more than just the vestibular system, and the vestibular system contributes to much more than just balance.

basal cell One of the three types of cells in the olfactory epithelium. Basal cells are the precursor cells to olfactory sensory neurons. Compare *olfactory sensory neuron* and *supporting cell*.

basic taste Any of the four taste qualities that are generally agreed to describe human taste experience: sweet, salty, sour, bitter.

basilar membrane A plate of fibers that forms the base of the cochlear partition and separates the middle and tympanic canals in the cochlea.

Bayesian approach A way of formalizing the idea that our perception is a combination of the current stimulus and our knowledge about the conditions of the world—what is and is not likely to occur. The Bayesian approach is stated mathematically as Bayes' theorem—$P(A|O) = P(A) \times P(O|A)/P(O)$—which enables us to calculate the probability (P) that the world is in a particular state (A) given a particular observation (O).

belt area A region of cortex, directly adjacent to the primary auditory cortex (A1), with inputs from A1, where neurons respond to more complex characteristics of sounds. Compare *parabelt area*.

binaral rivalry Competition between the two nostrils for odor perception. When a different scent is presented to each nostril simultaneously, we perceive each scent to be alternating back and forth with the other, and not a blend of the two scents.

binding problem The challenge of tying different attributes of visual stimuli (e.g., color, orientation, motion), which are handled by different brain circuits, to the appropriate object so that we perceive a unified object (e.g., red, vertical, moving right).

binocular With two eyes. Compare *monocular*.

binocular depth cue A depth cue that relies on information from both eyes. Stereopsis is the primary example in humans, but convergence and the ability of two eyes to see more of an object than one eye sees are also binocular depth cues. Compare *monocular depth cue*.

binocular disparity The differences between the two retinal images of the same scene. Disparity is the basis for stereopsis, a vivid perception of the three-dimensionality of the world that is not available with monocular vision.

binocular rivalry The competition between the two eyes for control of visual perception, which is evident when completely different stimuli are presented to the two eyes.

binocular summation The combination (or "summation") of signals from each eye in ways that make performance on many tasks better with both eyes than with either eye alone.

binocular vision See *correspondence problem*.

biological motion The pattern of movement of living beings (humans and animals).

bipolar cell A retinal cell that synapses with either rods or cones (not both) and with horizontal cells, and then passes the signals on to ganglion cells.

bitter One of the four basic tastes; the taste quality, generally considered unpleasant, produced by substances like quinine or caffeine. Compare *salty*, *sour*, and *sweet*.

blood oxygen level–dependent (BOLD) signal The ratio of oxygenated to deoxygenated hemoglobin that permits the localization of brain neurons that are most involved in a task.

body image The impression of our bodies in space.

BOLD See *blood oxygen level–dependent signal*.

brightness The perceptual consequence of the physical intensity of a light. Compare *hue* and *saturation*.

C

C fiber A narrow-diameter, unmyelinated sensory nerve fiber that transmits pain and temperature signals. Compare *A-delta fiber*.

cataract An opacity of the crystalline lens.

categorical perception For speech as well as other complex sounds and images, the phenomenon by which the discrimination of items is no better than the ability to label items.

CF See *characteristic frequency*.

change blindness The failure to notice a change between two scenes. If the gist, or meaning, of the scene is not altered, quite large changes can pass unnoticed.

characteristic frequency (CF) The frequency to which a particular auditory nerve fiber is most sensitive.

chemosignal Any of various chemicals emitted by humans that are detected by the olfactory system and that may have some effect on the mood, behavior, hormonal status, and/or sexual arousal of other humans. Compare *pheromone*.

chord A combination of three or more musical notes with different pitches played simultaneously.

chorda tympani The branch of cranial nerve VII (the facial nerve) that carries taste information from the anterior, mobile tongue (the part that can be stuck out). The chorda tympani exits the tongue with the lingual branch of the trigeminal nerve (cranial nerve V) and then passes through the middle ear on its way to the brain.

chromophore The light-catching part of the visual pigments of the retina.

cilium (pl. cilia) 1. Any of the hairlike structures that move as part of vestibular transduction. The vestibular system includes two types of cilia: kinocilia and stereocilia. 2. Any of the hairlike protrusions on the dendrites of olfactory sensory neurons. The receptor sites for odorant molecules are on the cilia, which are the first structures involved in olfactory signal transduction.

circumvallate papillae Circular structures that form an inverted *V* on the rear of the tongue (three to five on each side, with the largest in the center). Circumvallate papillae are moundlike structures surrounded by a trench (like a moat). These papillae are much larger than fungiform papillae. Compare *filiform papillae*, *foliate papillae*, and *fungiform papillae*.

CO See *cytochrome oxidase*.

coarticulation The phenomenon in speech whereby attributes of successive speech units overlap in articulatory or acoustic patterns.

cochlea A spiral structure of the inner ear containing the organ of Corti.

cochlear nucleus The first brain stem nucleus at which afferent auditory nerve fibers synapse.

cochlear partition The combined basilar membrane, tectorial membrane, and organ of Corti, which are together responsible for the transduction of sound waves into neural signals.

cognitive habituation The psychological process by which, after long-term exposure to an odor, one no longer has the ability to detect that odor or has very diminished detection ability. Compare *receptor adaptation*.

cold fiber A sensory nerve fiber that fires when skin temperature decreases. Compare *warmth fiber*.

color-anomalous A better term for what is usually called "color-blind." Most "color-blind" individuals can still make discriminations based on wavelength.

Those discriminations are different from the norm—that is, *anomalous*.

color assimilation A color perception effect in which two colors bleed into each other, each taking on some of the chromatic quality of the other.

color constancy The tendency of a surface to appear the same color under a fairly wide range of illuminants.

color contrast A color perception effect in which the color of one region induces the opponent color in a neighboring region.

color space The three-dimensional space, established because color perception is based on the outputs of three cone types, that describes the set of all colors.

column A vertical arrangement of neurons.

comparator An area of the visual system that receives one copy of the command issued by the motor system when the eyes move (the other copy goes to the eye muscles). The comparator compares the image motion signal with the eye motion signal and can compensate for the image changes caused by the eye movement.

complex cell A neuron whose receptive-field characteristics cannot be easily predicted by mapping with spots of light. Compare *simple cell*.

computed tomography (CT) An imaging technology that uses X-rays to create images of slices through volumes of material (e.g., the human body).

conductive hearing loss Hearing loss caused by problems with the bones of the middle ear. Compare *sensorineural hearing loss*.

cone A photoreceptor specialized for daylight vision, fine visual acuity, and color. Compare *rod*.

cone monochromat An individual with only one cone type. Cone monochromats are truly color-blind. Compare *rod monochromat*.

cone of confusion A region of positions in space where all sounds produce the same time and level (intensity) differences (ITDs and ILDs).

cone-opponent cell A cell type—found in the retina, lateral geniculate nucleus, and visual cortex—that, in effect, subtracts one type of cone input from another. Also called *single-opponent cell*. Compare *double-opponent cell*.

congenital prosopagnosia A form of "face blindness" apparently present from birth, as opposed to "acquired prosop-

prosopagnosia," which would typically be the result of an injury to the nervous system.

conjunction search Search for a target defined by the presence of two or more attributes (e.g., a *red*, *vertical* target among *red* horizontal and blue *vertical* distractors). Compare *feature search*.

continuity constraint In stereopsis, the observation that, except at the edges of objects, neighboring points in the world lie at similar distances from the viewer. This is one of several constraints that have been proposed to help solve the correspondence problem.

contralateral Referring to the opposite side of the body (or brain). Compare *ipsilateral*.

contralesional field The visual field on the side opposite a brain lesion. For example, points to the left of fixation are contralesional to damage in the right hemisphere of the brain. Compare *ipsilesional field*.

contrast The difference in luminance between an object and the background, or between lighter and darker parts of the same object.

contrast-defined object See *texture-defined object*.

contrast sensitivity function (CSF) A function describing how the sensitivity to contrast (defined as the reciprocal of the contrast threshold) depends on the spatial frequency (size) of the stimulus.

contrast threshold The smallest amount of contrast required to detect a pattern.

convergence The ability of the two eyes to turn inward, often used in order to place the two images of a feature in the world on corresponding locations in the two retinal images (typically on the fovea of each eye). Convergence reduces the disparity of that feature to zero (or nearly zero). Compare *divergence*.

cornea The transparent "window" into the eyeball.

correspondence problem 1. In binocular vision, the problem of figuring out which bit of the image in the left eye should be matched with which bit in the right eye. The problem is particularly vexing when the images consist of thousands of similar features, like dots in random dot stereograms. 2. In motion detection, the problem faced by the motion detection system of knowing which feature in frame 2 corresponds to a particular feature in frame 1.

corresponding retinal points A geometric concept stating that points on the retina of each eye where the monocular retinal images of a single object are formed are at the same distance from the fovea in each eye. The two foveas are also corresponding points.

cortical magnification The amount of cortical area (usually specified in millimeters) devoted to a specific region (e.g., 1 degree) in the visual field.

cranial nerves Twelve pairs of nerves (one for each side of the body) that originate in the brain stem and reach sense organs and muscles through openings in the skull.

cribriform plate A bony structure riddled with tiny holes, at the level of the eyebrows, that separates the nose from the brain. The axons from the olfactory sensory neurons pass through the tiny holes of the cribriform plate to enter the brain.

crista (pl. cristae) Any of the specialized detectors of angular motion located in each semicircular canal in a swelling called the ampulla.

criterion In signal detection theory, an internal threshold that is set by the observer. If the internal response is above criterion, the observer gives one response (e.g., "yes, I hear that"). Below criterion, the observer gives another response (e.g., "no, I hear nothing").

critical bandwidth The range of frequencies conveyed within a channel in the auditory system.

critical period A period of time during development when the organism is particularly susceptible to developmental change. There are critical periods in the development of binocular vision, human language, and so on.

cross-adaptation The reduction in detection of an odorant following exposure to another odorant. Cross-adaptation is presumed to occur because the two odorants share one or more olfactory receptors for their transduction, but the order in which odorants are presented also plays a role.

cross-modality matching The ability to match the intensities of sensations that come from different sensory modalities. This ability enables insight into sensory differences. For example, a listener might adjust the brightness of a light until it matches the loudness of a tone.

crossed disparity The sign of disparity created by objects in front of the plane of fixation (the horopter). The term *crossed* is used because images of objects located in front of the horopter appear to be displaced to the left in the right eye,

and to the right in the left eye. Compare *uncrossed disparity*.

crystalline lens The lens inside the eye that enables the changing of focus.

CSF See *contrast sensitivity function*.

CT See *computed tomography*.

cue A stimulus that might indicate where (or what) a subsequent stimulus will be. Cues can be valid (giving correct information), invalid (incorrect), or neutral (uninformative).

cultural relativism In sensation and perception, the idea that basic perceptual experiences (e.g., color perception) may be determined in part by the cultural environment.

cycle For a grating, a pair consisting of one dark bar and one bright bar.

cycles per degree The number of pairs of dark and bright bars per degree of visual angle.

Cyclopean Referring to stimuli that are defined by binocular disparity alone. Named after the one-eyed Cyclops of Homer's *Odyssey*.

cytochrome oxidase (CO) An enzyme used to reveal the regular array of "CO blobs," which are spaced about 0.5 millimeter apart in the primary visual cortex.

D

dB See *decibel*.

DCML pathway See *dorsal column–medial lemniscal pathway*.

decay In hearing, the part of a sound during which amplitude decreases (offset). Compare *attack*.

decibel (dB) A unit of measure for the physical intensity of sound. Decibels define the difference between two sounds as the ratio between two sound pressures. Each 10:1 sound pressure ratio equals 20 dB, and a 100:1 ratio equals 40 dB.

depth cues Information about the third dimension (depth) of visual space. Depth cues may be monocular or binocular.

dermis The inner of two major layers of skin, consisting of nutritive and connective tissues, within which lie the mechanoreceptors. Compare *epidermis*.

deuteranope An individual who suffers from color blindness that is due to the absence of M-cones. Compare *protanope* and *tritanope*.

dichoptic Referring to the presentation of two different stimuli, one to each eye. Different from binocular presentation, which could involve both eyes looking at a single stimulus.

difference threshold See *just noticeable difference*.

diffuse bipolar cell A bipolar retinal cell whose processes are spread out to receive input from multiple cones. Compare *midget bipolar cell*.

dimer A chain of two molecules. Compare *heterodimer*.

diplopia Double vision. If visible in both eyes, stimuli falling outside of Panum's fusional area will appear diplopic.

direction The line along which one faces or moves, with reference to the point or region toward which one is facing or moving.

directional transfer function (DTF) A measure that describes how the pinna, ear canal, head, and torso change the intensity of sounds with different frequencies that arrive at each ear from different locations in space (azimuth and elevation).

distractor In visual search, any stimulus other than the *target*.

divergence The ability of the two eyes to turn outward, often used in order to place the two images of a feature in the world on corresponding locations in the two retinal images (typically on the fovea of each eye). Divergence reduces the disparity of that feature to zero (or nearly zero). Compare *convergence*.

dizziness A commonly used lay term that nonspecifically indicates any form of perceived spatial disorientation, with or without instability.

doctrine of specific nerve energies A doctrine, formulated by Johannes Müller, stating that the nature of a sensation depends on which sensory fibers are stimulated, not on how fibers are stimulated.

dorsal column–medial lemniscal (DCML) pathway The route from the spinal cord to the brain that carries signals from skin, muscles, tendons, and joints. Compare *spinothalamic pathway*.

dorsal horn A region at the rear of the spinal cord that receives inputs from receptors in the skin.

double dissociation The phenomenon in which one of two functions, such as hearing and sight, can be damaged without harm to the other, and vice versa.

double-opponent cell A cell type, found in the visual cortex, in which one region is excited by one cone type, combination of cones, or color and inhibited by the opponent cones or color (e.g., R+/G–). Another adjacent region would be inhibited by the first input and excited by the second (thus, in this example, R–/G+). Compare *cone-opponent cell*.

DTF See *directional transfer function*.

dualism The idea that the mind has an existence separate from the material world of the body. Compare *materialism* and *panpsychism*.

duplex In reference to the retina, consisting of two parts: the rods and cones, which operate under different conditions.

E

ear canal The canal that conducts sound vibrations from the pinna to the tympanic membrane and prevents damage to the tympanic membrane.

EBA See *extrastriate body area*.

eccentricity The distance between the retinal image and the fovea.

EEG See *electroencephalography*.

efferent fiber A neuron that carries information from the central nervous system to the periphery. Compare *afferent fiber*.

egocenter The center of a reference frame used to represent locations relative to the body.

electroencephalography (EEG) A technique that, using many electrodes on the scalp, measures electrical activity from populations of many neurons in the brain. Compare *magnetoencephalography*.

emmetropia The condition in which there is no refractive error, because the refractive power of the eye is perfectly matched to the length of the eyeball.

end stopping The process by which a cell in the cortex first increases its firing rate as the bar length increases to fill up its receptive field, and then decreases its firing rate as the bar is lengthened further.

endogenous opiate A chemical released by the body that blocks the release or uptake of neurotransmitters necessary to transmit pain sensations to the brain.

endogenous spatial attention A form of top-down (knowledge-driven) control of spatial attention in which attention is voluntarily directed toward the site where the observer anticipates a stimulus will occur. Compare *exogenous spatial attention*.

ensemble statistics The average and distribution of properties like orientation or color over a set of objects or over a region in a scene.

entorhinal cortex A phylogenetically old cortical region that provides the major sensory association input into the hippocampus. The entorhinal cortex also receives direct projections from olfactory regions.

entry-level category For an object, the label that comes to mind most quickly when we identify it (e.g., "bird"). At the subordinate level, the object might be more specifically named (e.g., "eagle"); at the superordinate level, it might be more generally named (e.g., "animal").

epidermis The outer of two major layers of skin. Compare *dermis*.

equal-loudness curve A graph plotting sound pressure level (dB SPL) against the frequency for which a listener perceives constant loudness.

ERP See *event-related potential*.

esotropia Strabismus in which one eye deviates inward. Compare *exotropia*.

Euclidean Referring to the geometry of the world, so named in honor of Euclid, the ancient Greek geometer of the third century BCE. In Euclidean geometry, parallel lines remain parallel as they are extended in space, objects maintain the same size and shape as they move around in space, the internal angles of a triangle always add to 180 degrees, and so forth.

event-related potential (ERP) A measure of electrical activity from a subpopulation of neurons in response to particular stimuli that requires averaging many EEG recordings.

exogenous spatial attention A form of bottom-up (stimulus-driven) spatial attention in which attention is reflexively (involuntarily) directed toward the site at which a stimulus has abruptly appeared. Compare *endogenous spatial attention*.

exotropia Strabismus in which one eye deviates outward. Compare *esotropia*.

exploratory procedure A stereotyped hand movement pattern used to touch objects in order to perceive their properties; each procedure is best for determining one (or more) object properties.

extinction In visual attention, the inability to perceive a stimulus to one side of the point of fixation (e.g., to the right) in the presence of another stimulus, typically in a comparable position in the other visual field (e.g., on the left side). Compare *neglect*.

extrastriate body area (EBA) A region of extrastriate visual cortex in humans that is specifically and reliably activated by images of the body other than the face.

extrastriate cortex The region of cortex bordering the primary visual cortex and containing multiple areas involved in visual processing.

F

familiar size A depth cue based on knowledge of the typical size of objects like humans or pennies.

feature integration theory Anne Treisman's theory of visual attention, which holds that a limited set of basic features can be processed in parallel preattentively, but that other properties, including the correct binding of features to objects, require attention. Compare *guided search*.

feature search Search for a target defined by a single attribute, such as a salient color or orientation. Compare *conjunction search*.

Fechner's law A principle describing the relationship between stimulus and resulting sensation that says the magnitude of subjective sensation increases proportionally to the logarithm of the stimulus intensity. Compare *Stevens' power law* and *Weber's law*.

feed-forward process A process that carries out a computation (e.g., object recognition) one neural step after another, without need for feedback from a later stage to an earlier stage.

FFA See *fusiform face area*.

figure-ground assignment The process of determining that some regions of an image belong to a foreground object (figure) and other regions are part of the background (ground).

filiform papillae Small structures on the tongue that provide most of the bumpy appearance. Filiform papillae have no taste function. Compare *circumvallate papillae, foliate papillae,* and *fungiform papillae*.

filter An acoustic, electrical, electronic, or optical device, instrument, computer program, or neuron that allows the passage of some frequencies or digital elements and blocks the passage of others.

first-order motion The motion of an object that is defined by changes in luminance. Compare *second-order motion*.

flavor The combination of true taste (sweet, salty, sour, bitter) and retronasal olfaction.

fMRI See *functional magnetic resonance imaging*.

focus of expansion The point in the center of the horizon from which, when we're in motion (e.g., driving on the highway), all points in the perspective image seem to emanate. The focus of expansion is one aspect of optic flow.

foliate papillae Folds of tissue containing taste buds. Foliate papillae are located on the rear of the tongue lateral to the circumvallate papillae, where the tongue attaches to the mouth. Compare *circumvallate papillae, filiform papillae,* and *fungiform papillae*.

formant A resonance of the vocal tract. Formants are specified by their center frequency and are denoted by integers that increase with relative frequency.

Fourier analysis A mathematical procedure by which any signal can be separated into component sine waves at different frequencies. Combining these sine waves will reproduce the original signal.

fovea A small pit, near the center of the macula, that contains the highest concentration of cones, and no rods. It is the portion of the retina that produces the highest visual acuity and serves as the point of fixation.

frame of reference The coordinate system used to define locations in space.

free fusion The technique of converging (crossing) or diverging the eyes in order to view a stereogram without a stereoscope.

frequency For sound, the number of times per second that a pattern of pressure change repeats. Frequency is perceived as *pitch*.

functional magnetic resonance imaging (fMRI) A variant of magnetic resonance imaging that makes it possible to measure localized patterns of activity in the brain. Activated neurons provoke increased blood flow, which can be quantified by measuring changes in of the response of oxygenated and deoxygenated blood to strong magnetic fields. Compare *positron emission tomography*.

fundamental frequency The lowest-frequency component of a complex periodic sound.

fundus (pl. fundi) The back layer of the retina—what the eye doctor sees through an ophthalmoscope.

fungiform papillae Mushroom-shaped structures (maximum diameter 1 millimeter) that are distributed most densely on the edges of the tongue, especially the tip. Taste buds (an average of six per papilla) are buried in the surface. Compare *circumvallate papillae, filiform papillae,* and *foliate papillae*.

fusiform face area (FFA) A region of extrastriate visual cortex in humans that is specifically and reliably activated by human faces. Compare *parahippocampal place area*.

G

G protein–coupled receptor (GPCR) Any of the class of receptors that are present on the surface of olfactory sensory neurons. All GPCRs are characterized by a common structural feature of seven membrane-spanning α-helices.

ganglion cell A retinal cell that receives visual information from photoreceptors via two intermediate neuron types (bipolar cells and amacrine cells) and transmits information to the brain and midbrain.

gate control theory A description of the pain-transmitting system that incorporates modulating signals from the brain.

geon In Biederman's *recognition-by-components model*, any of the "geometric ions" out of which perceptual objects are built.

Gestalt In German, literally "form." In perception, a school of thought stressing that the perceptual whole could be greater than the apparent sum of the parts. Compare *structuralism*.

Gestalt grouping rules A set of rules describing which elements in an image will appear to group together. The original list was assembled by members of the Gestalt school of thought.

gestation Fetal development during pregnancy.

global superiority effect The finding in various experiments that the properties of the whole object take precedence over the properties of parts of the object.

glomerulus (pl. glomeruli) Any of the spherical conglomerates containing the incoming axons of the olfactory sensory neurons. Each OSN converges onto two glomeruli (one medial, one lateral).

good continuation A Gestalt grouping rule stating that two elements will tend to group together if they seem to lie on the same contour.

GPCR See *G protein–coupled receptor*.

graded potential An electrical potential that can vary continuously in amplitude.

gravity A force that attracts a body toward the center of the Earth.

guided search Search in which attention can be restricted to a subset of possible items on the basis of information about the target item's basic features (e.g., its color). Compare *feature integration theory*.

gustation The sense of taste.

gustatory cortex See *insular cortex*.

H

hair cell Any cell that has stereocilia for transducing mechanical movement in the inner ear into neural activity sent to the brain; some hair cells also receive inputs from the brain.

haptic perception Knowledge of the world that is derived from sensory receptors in skin, muscles, tendons, and joints, usually involving active exploration.

haptic virtual environment A synthetic world that may be experienced haptically by operation of an electromechanical device that delivers forces to the hand of the user.

harmonic spectrum The spectrum of a complex sound in which energy is at integer multiples of the fundamental frequency.

haze See *aerial perspective*.

helicotrema The opening that connects the tympanic and vestibular canals at the apex of the cochlea.

hertz (Hz) A unit of measure for frequency. One hertz equals one cycle per second.

heterodimer A chain of two molecules that are different from each other. Compare *dimer*.

heuristic A mental shortcut.

high-spontaneous fiber An auditory nerve fiber that has a high rate (more than 30 spikes per second) of spontaneous firing; high-spontaneous fibers increase their firing rate in response to relatively low levels of sound. Compare *low-spontaneous fiber* and *mid-spontaneous fiber*.

homologous regions Brain regions that appear to have the same function in different species.

homunculus (pl. homunculi) A map-like representation of regions of the body in the brain.

horizontal cell A specialized retinal cell that contacts both photoreceptor and bipolar cells.

horopter The location of objects whose images lie on corresponding points. The surface of zero disparity. Compare *Vieth-Müller circle*.

hue The chromatic (colorful) aspect of color (red, blue, green, yellow, and so on). Compare *brightness* and *saturation*.

hyperalgesia An increased or heightened response to a normally painful stimulus.

hypercolumn A 1-millimeter block of striate cortex containing two sets of columns, each covering every possible orientation (0–180 degrees), with one set preferring input from the left eye and one set preferring input from the right eye.

hyperopia Farsightedness, a common condition in which light entering the eye is focused behind the retina and accommodation is required in order to see near objects clearly. Compare *myopia*.

hyperpolarization An increase in membrane potential such that the inner membrane surface becomes more negative than the outer membrane surface.

Hz See *hertz*.

I

ideal observer A theoretical observer with complete access to the best available information and the ability to combine different sources of information in the optimal manner. It can be useful to compare human performance to that of an ideal observer.

ILD See *interaural level difference*.

illuminant The light that illuminates a surface.

illusory conjunction An erroneous combination of two features in a visual scene—for example, seeing a red *X* when the display contains red letters and *X*s but no red *X*s.

illusory contour A contour that is perceived even though nothing changes from one side of it to the other in an image.

image A picture or likeness.

imbalance Lack of balance; unsteadiness; nearly falling over.

inattentional blindness A failure to notice—or at least to report—a stimulus that would be easily reportable if it were attended.

incus The middle of the three ossicles, connecting the malleus and the stapes.

inferior colliculus A midbrain nucleus in the auditory pathway. Compare *superior colliculus*.

inferotemporal (IT) cortex Part of the cerebral cortex in the lower portion of the temporal lobe, important in object recognition.

inner ear A hollow cavity in the temporal bone of the skull, and the structures within this cavity: the cochlea and the semicircular canals of the vestibular system. Compare *middle ear* and *outer ear*.

inner segment The part of a photoreceptor that lies between the outer segment and the cell nucleus. Compare *outer segment*.

insular cortex (or insula) The primary cortical processing area for taste—the part of the cortex that first receives taste information. Also called *gustatory cortex*.

intensity See *amplitude*.

interaural level difference (ILD) The difference in level (intensity) between a sound arriving at one ear versus the other. Compare *interaural time difference*.

interaural time difference (ITD) The difference in time between a sound arriving at one ear versus the other. Compare *interaural level difference*.

interocular transfer The transfer of an effect (such as adaptation) from one eye to the other.

inverse-square law A principle stating that as distance from a source increases, intensity initially decreases much faster than distance increases, such that the decrease in intensity is equal to the increase in distance squared. This general law also applies to optics and other forms of energy.

ipsilateral Referring to the same side of the body (or brain). Compare *contralateral*.

ipsilesional field The visual field on the same side as a brain lesion. Compare *contralesional field*.

iris The colored part of the eye, consisting of a muscular diaphragm surrounding the pupil and regulating the light entering the eye by expanding and contracting the pupil.

isointensity curve A map plotting the firing rate of an auditory nerve fiber against varying frequencies at a steady intensity.

IT See *inferotemporal cortex*.

ITD See *interaural time difference*.

J

Jacobson's organ See *vomeronasal organ*.

JND See *just noticeable difference*.

just noticeable difference (JND) The smallest detectable difference between two stimuli, or the minimum change in a stimulus that enables it to be correctly judged as different from a reference stimulus. Also called *difference threshold*.

K

kinesthesis Perception of the position and movement of our limbs in space.

kinesthetic Referring to perception involving sensory mechanoreceptors in muscles, tendons, and joints.

koniocellular cell A neuron located between the magnocellular and parvocellular layers of the lateral geniculate nucleus. This layer is known as the koniocellular layer.

L

L-cone A cone that is preferentially sensitive to long wavelengths; colloquially (but not entirely accurately) known as a "red cone." Compare *M-cone* and *S-cone*.

labeled lines A theory of taste coding in which each taste nerve fiber carries a particular taste quality. For example, the quality evoked from a sucrose-best fiber is sweet, that from an NaCl-best fiber is salty, and so on.

lateral geniculate nucleus (LGN) A structure in the thalamus, part of the midbrain, that receives input from the retinal ganglion cells and has input and output connections to the visual cortex. Compare *medial geniculate nucleus*.

lateral inhibition Antagonistic neural interaction between adjacent regions of the retina.

lateral superior olive (LSO) A relay station in the brain stem where inputs from both ears contribute to detection of the interaural level difference. Compare *medial superior olive*.

lazy eye See *amblyopia*.

learned taste aversion The avoidance of a novel flavor after it has been paired with gastric illness. The smell, not the taste, of the substance is key for the learned aversion response in humans.

lesion In neuropsychology: 1. (n) A region of damaged brain. 2. (v) To destroy a section of the brain.

LGN See *lateral geniculate nucleus*.

limbic system The encompassing group of neural structures that includes the olfactory cortex, the amygdala, the hippocampus, the piriform cortex, and the entorhinal cortex. The limbic system is involved in many aspects of emotion and memory. Olfaction is unique among the senses for its direct and intimate connection to the limbic system.

linear acceleration The rate of change of linear velocity. Mathematically, the integral of linear acceleration is linear velocity, and the integral of linear velocity is linear displacement, which is also referred to as "translation." Linear acceleration, linear velocity, and linear displacement all mathematically represent linear motion. Compare *angular acceleration*.

linear motion Translational motion like the predominant movement of a train car or bobblehead doll. Compare *angular motion*.

linear perspective A depth cue based on the fact that lines that are parallel in the three-dimensional world will appear to converge in a two-dimensional image.

lordosis The position that females of some species (e.g., pigs and rats) need to assume in order to be impregnated. It involves the inward curving of the spinal column and exposure of the genitals.

loudness The psychological aspect of sound related to perceived intensity (*amplitude*). Compare *pitch*.

low-spontaneous fiber An auditory nerve fiber that has a low rate (less than 10 spikes per second) of spontaneous firing; low-spontaneous fibers require relatively intense sound before they will fire at higher rates. Compare *high-spontaneous fiber* and *mid-spontaneous fiber*.

LSO See *lateral superior olive*.

luminance-defined object An object that is delineated by changes in reflected light.

M

M-cone A cone that is preferentially sensitive to middle wavelengths; colloquially (but not entirely accurately) known as a "green cone." Compare *L-cone* and *S-cone*.

M ganglion cell A ganglion cell resembling a little umbrella that receives excitatory input from diffuse bipolar cells and feeds the magnocellular layer of the lateral geniculate nucleus. Compare *P ganglion cell*.

macula (pl. maculae) 1. The central part of the retina that has a high concentration of cones. 2. Any of the specialized detectors of linear acceleration and gravity found in each otolith organ.

MAE See *motion aftereffect*.

magnetic resonance imaging (MRI) An imaging technology that uses the responses of atoms to strong magnetic fields to form images of structures like the brain. The method can be adapted to measure activity in the brain, as well (see *functional magnetic resonance imaging*).

magnetoencephalography (MEG) A technique, similar to electroencephalography, that measures changes in magnetic activity across populations of many neurons in the brain. Compare *electroencephalography*.

magnitude estimation A psychophysical method in which the participant assigns values according to perceived magnitudes of the stimuli.

magnocellular layer Either of the bottom two neuron-containing layers of the lateral geniculate nucleus, the cells of which are physically larger than those in the top four layers. Compare *parvocellular layer*.

main olfactory bulb (MOB) The olfactory bulb; the blueberry-sized extension of the brain just above the nose; the first region of the brain where smells are processed. In humans we refer simply to "olfactory bulb(s)"; in animals with *accessory olfactory bulbs*, we distinguish between "main" and "accessory."

malleus One of the three ossicles. The malleus receives vibration from the tympanic membrane and is attached to the incus.

masking Using a second sound, frequently noise, to make the detection of another sound more difficult.

materialism The idea that the only thing that exists is matter, and that all things, including the mind and consciousness, are the results of interaction between bits of matter. Compare *dualism* and *panpsychism*.

mathematical integration Computing an integral—one of the two main operations in calculus (the other, the inverse operation, is differentiation). Velocity is the integral of acceleration. Change of position is the integral of velocity. Compare *sensory integration*.

mechanoreceptor A sensory receptor that responds to mechanical stimulation (pressure, vibration, or movement).

medial geniculate nucleus The part of the thalamus that relays auditory signals to the temporal cortex and receives input from the auditory cortex. Compare *lateral geniculate nucleus*.

medial superior olive (MSO) A relay station in the brain stem where inputs from both ears contribute to detection of the interaural time difference. Compare *lateral superior olive*.

MEG See *magnetoencephalography*.

Meissner corpuscle A specialized nerve ending associated with fast-adapting (FA I) fibers that have small receptive fields. Compare *Merkel cell neurite complex*, *Pacinian corpuscle*, and *Ruffini ending*.

melanopsin A photopigment that is sensitive to ambient light.

melody A sequence of notes or chords perceived as a single coherent structure.

Merkel cell neurite complex A specialized nerve ending associated with slowly adapting (SA I) fibers that have small receptive fields. Compare *Meiss-*

ner corpuscle, *Pacinian corpuscle*, and *Ruffini ending*.

metamers Different mixtures of wavelengths that look identical. More generally, any pair of stimuli that are perceived as identical in spite of physical differences.

method of adjustment A method of limits in which the subject controls the change in the stimulus.

method of constant stimuli A psychophysical method in which many stimuli, ranging from rarely to almost always perceivable (or rarely to almost always perceivably different from a reference stimulus), are presented one at a time. Participants respond to each presentation: "yes/no," "same/different," and so on.

method of limits A psychophysical method in which the particular dimension of a stimulus, or the difference between two stimuli, is varied incrementally until the participant responds differently. See also *method of adjustment* and *staircase method*.

metrical depth cue A depth cue that provides quantitative information about distance in the third dimension. Compare *nonmetrical depth cue*.

microsaccade An involuntary, small, jerklike eye movement.

microvilli (s. microvillus) Slender projections of the cell membrane on the tips of some taste bud cells that extend into the taste pore.

middle canal One of three fluid-filled passages in the cochlea. The middle canal is sandwiched between the *tympanic* and *vestibular canals* and contains the cochlear partition. Also called *scala media*.

middle ear An air-filled chamber containing the middle bones, or ossicles. The middle ear conveys and amplifies vibration from the tympanic membrane to the oval window. Compare *inner ear* and *outer ear*.

middle temporal area (MT) An area of the brain thought to be important in the perception of motion.

middle vision A loosely defined stage of visual processing that comes after basic features have been extracted from the image (low-level, or early, vision) and before object recognition and scene understanding (high-level vision). Also called *midlevel vision*.

midget bipolar cell A small bipolar cell in the central retina that receives input from a single cone. Compare *diffuse bipolar cell*.

midlevel vision See *middle vision*.

mid-spontaneous fiber An auditory nerve fiber that has a medium rate (10–30 spikes per second) of spontaneous firing. The characteristics of mid-spontaneous fibers are intermediate between *low-* and *high-spontaneous fibers*.

mitral cell Any of the main projective output neurons in the olfactory bulb. Compare *tufted cell*.

MOB See *main olfactory bulb*.

monocular With one eye. Compare *binocular*.

monocular depth cue A depth cue that is available even when the world is viewed with one eye alone. Compare *binocular depth cue*.

monosodium glutamate (MSG) The sodium salt of glutamic acid (an amino acid).

motion aftereffect (MAE) The illusion of motion of a stationary object that occurs after prolonged exposure to a moving object.

motion parallax An important depth cue that is based on head movement. The geometric information obtained from an eye in two different positions at two different times is similar to the information from two eyes in different positions in the head at the same time.

MRI See *magnetic resonance imaging*.

MSG See *monosodium glutamate*.

MSO See *medial superior olive*.

MT See *middle temporal area*.

muscle spindle A sensory receptor located in a muscle that senses its tension.

myopia Nearsightedness, a common condition in which light entering the eye is focused in front of the retina and distant objects cannot be seen sharply. Compare *hyperopia*.

N

naïve template theory The proposal that the visual system recognizes objects by matching the neural representation of the image with a stored representation of the same "shape" in the brain.

nasal dominance The asymmetry characterizing the intake of air by the two nostrils, which corresponds to differing sensitivity to odorants between the two nostrils. Nasal dominance alternates nostrils throughout the day, but there is no predictability about when the nostrils alternate.

Necker cube An outline that is perceptually bi-stable. Unlike the situation with most stimuli, two interpretations continually battle for perceptual dominance.

negative afterimage An afterimage whose polarity is the opposite of the original stimulus. Light stimuli produce dark negative afterimages. Colors are complementary; for example, red produces green, and yellow produces blue.

neglect As a neurological symptom, (1) in visual attention the inability to attend to or respond to stimuli in the contralesional visual field (typically, the left field after right parietal damage); (2) ignoring half of the body or half of an object. Compare *extinction*.

neural plasticity The ability of neural circuits to undergo changes in function or organization as a result of previous activity.

neurotransmitter A chemical substance used in neuronal communication at synapses.

neutral point The point at which an opponent color mechanism is generating no signal. If red-green and blue-yellow mechanisms are at their neutral points, a stimulus will appear achromatic. (The black-white process has no neutral point.)

nociceptor A sensory receptor that transmits information about noxious (painful) stimulation that causes damage or potential damage to the skin.

nonaccidental feature A feature of an object that is not dependent on the exact (or accidental) viewing position of the observer. Compare *accidental viewpoint*.

nonmetrical depth cue A depth cue that provides information about the depth order (relative depth) but not depth magnitude (e.g., his nose is in front of his face). Compare *metrical depth cue*.

nontaster (of PTC/PROP) An individual born with two recessive alleles for the *TAS2R38* gene and unable to taste the compounds phenylthiocarbamide and propylthiouracil. Compare *taster* and *supertaster*.

O

occlusion A cue to relative depth order in which, for example, one object obstructs the view of part of another object.

octave The interval between two sound frequencies having a ratio of 2:1.

ocular dominance The property of the receptive fields of striate cortex neurons by which they demonstrate a preference, responding somewhat more rapidly when a stimulus is presented in one eye than when it is presented in the other.

oculomotor (III) nerves The third pair of cranial nerves, which innervate all the extrinsic muscles of the eye except the lateral rectus and the superior oblique muscles, and which innervate the elevator muscle of the upper eyelid, the ciliary muscle, and the sphincter muscle of the pupil.

odor The translation of a chemical stimulus into a smell sensation. For example, "The cake had a chocolate *odor*." Compare *odorant*.

odor hedonics The liking dimension of odor perception, typically measured by ratings of an odor's perceived pleasantness, familiarity, and intensity.

odorant A molecule that is defined by its physicochemical characteristics, which are capable of being translated by the nervous system into the perception of a smell. For example, "You were given the *odorant* methyl salicylate to smell, which has the *odor* of wintergreen mint." Compare *odor*.

OFC See *orbitofrontal cortex*.

OFF bipolar cell A bipolar cell that responds to a decrease in light captured by the cones. Compare *ON bipolar cell*.

OFF-center cell A cell that depolarizes in response to a decrease in light intensity in its receptive-field center. Compare *ON-center cell*.

olfaction The sense of smell.

olfactory bulb A blueberry-sized extension of the brain just above the nose, where olfactory information is first processed. There are two olfactory bulbs, one in each brain hemisphere, corresponding to the right and left nostrils. See also *main olfactory bulb*.

olfactory cleft A narrow space at the back of the nose into which air flows and where the olfactory epithelium is located.

olfactory epithelium A secretory mucous membrane in the human nose whose primary function is to detect odorants in inhaled air. Located on both sides of the upper portion of the nasal cavity and the olfactory clefts, the olfactory epithelium contains three types of cells: olfactory sensory neurons, basal cells, and supporting cells.

olfactory (I) nerves The first pair of cranial nerves. The axons of the olfactory sensory neurons bundle together after passing through the cribriform plate to form the olfactory nerve, which conducts impulses from the olfactory epithelia in the nose to the olfactory bulb.

olfactory receptor (OR) The region on the cilia of olfactory sensory neurons where odorant molecules bind.

olfactory sensory neuron (OSN) One of three cell types—the main one—in the olfactory epithelium. OSNs are small neurons located beneath a watery mucous layer in the epithelium. The cilia on the OSN dendrites contain the receptor sites for odorant molecules. Compare *basal cell* and *supporting cell*.

olfactory tract The bundle of axons of the mitral and tufted cells within the olfactory bulb that sends odor information to the primary olfactory cortex.

ON bipolar cell A bipolar cell that responds to an increase in light captured by the cones. Compare *OFF bipolar cell*.

ON-center cell A cell that depolarizes in response to an increase in light intensity in its receptive-field center. Compare *OFF-center cell*.

opponent color theory The theory that perception of color is based on the output of three mechanisms, each of them resulting from an opponency between two colors: red-green, blue-yellow, and black-white.

optic array The collection of light rays that interact with objects in the world that are in front of a viewer. Term coined by J. J. Gibson.

optic flow The changing angular positions of points in a perspective image that we experience as we move through the world.

optic (II) nerves The second pair of cranial nerves, which arise from the retina and carry visual information to the thalamus and other parts of the brain.

OR See *olfactory receptor*.

orbitofrontal cortex (OFC) The part of the frontal lobe of the cortex that lies behind the bone (orbit) containing the eyes. The OFC is responsible for the conscious experience of olfaction, as well as the integration of pleasure and displeasure from food; and it has been referred to as the *secondary olfactory cortex* and the *secondary taste cortex*. The OFC is also involved in many other functions, and it is critical for assigning affective value to stimuli—in other words, determining hedonic meaning. Compare *primary olfactory cortex*.

organ of Corti A structure on the basilar membrane of the cochlea that is composed of hair cells and dendrites of auditory nerve fibers.

orientation tuning The tendency of neurons in striate cortex to respond optimally to certain orientations and less to others.

oscillatory Referring to back-and-forth movement that has a constant rhythm.

OSN See *olfactory sensory neuron*.

ossicle Any of three tiny bones of the middle ear: malleus, incus, and stapes.

otitis media Inflammation of the middle ear, commonly in children as a result of infection.

otoconia (s. otoconium) Tiny calcium carbonate stones in the ear that provide inertial mass for the otolith organs, enabling them to sense gravity and linear acceleration.

otolith organ Either of two mechanical structures (utricle and saccule) in the vestibular system that sense both linear acceleration and gravity.

otosclerosis Abnormal growth of the middle-ear bones that causes hearing loss.

ototoxic Producing adverse effects on cochlear or vestibular organs or nerves.

outer ear The external sound-gathering portion of the ear, consisting of the pinna and the ear canal. Compare *inner ear* and *middle ear*.

outer segment The part of a photoreceptor that contains photopigment molecules. Compare *inner segment*.

oval window The flexible opening to the cochlea through which the stapes transmits vibration to the fluid inside.

P

P ganglion cell A small ganglion cell that receives excitatory input from single midget bipolar cells in the central retina and feeds the parvocellular layer of the lateral geniculate nucleus. Compare *M ganglion cell*.

Pacinian corpuscle A specialized nerve ending associated with fast-adapting (FA II) fibers that have large receptive fields. Compare *Meissner corpuscle*, *Merkel cell neurite complex*, and *Ruffini ending*.

panpsychism The idea that the mind exists as a property of all matter—that is, that all matter has consciousness. Compare *dualism* and *materialism*.

Panum's fusional area The region of space, in front of and behind the horopter, within which binocular single vision is possible. See also *diplopia*.

papilla (pl. papillae) Any of multiple structures that give the tongue its bumpy appearance. From smallest to largest, the papilla types that contain taste buds are fungiform, foliate, and circumvallate; filiform papillae, which do not contain taste buds, are the smallest and most numerous.

parabelt area A region of cortex, lateral and adjacent to the belt area, where neurons respond to more complex characteristics of sounds, as well as to input from other senses. Compare *belt area*.

parahippocampal place area (PPA) A region of extrastriate visual cortex in humans that is specifically and reliably activated more by images of places than by other stimuli. Compare *fusiform face area*.

parallel search A search in which multiple stimuli are processed at the same time. Compare *serial self-terminating search*.

parallelism A rule for figure-ground assignment stating that parallel contours are likely to belong to the same figure.

parietal lobe In each cerebral hemisphere, a lobe that lies toward the top of the brain between the frontal and occipital lobes.

parvocellular layer Any of the top four neuron-containing layers of the lateral geniculate nucleus, the cells of which are physically smaller than those in the bottom two layers. Compare *magnocellular layer*.

perception The act of giving meaning to a detected sensation. Compare *sensation*.

period The time (or space) required for one cycle of a repeating waveform. Also called *wavelength*.

PET See *positron emission tomography*.

phantom limb Sensation perceived from a physically amputated limb of the body.

phase 1. In vision, the relative position of a grating. 2. In hearing, the relative timing of a sine wave.

phase locking Firing of a single neuron at one distinct point in the period (cycle) of a sound wave at a given frequency. (The neuron need not fire on every cycle, but each firing will occur at the same point in the cycle).

pheromone A chemical emitted by one member of a species that triggers a physiological or behavioral response in another member of the same species. Pheromones are signals for chemical communication and do not need to have any smell. Compare *chemosignal*.

phonation The process through which vocal folds are made to vibrate when air pushes out of the lungs.

photoactivation Activation by light.

photon A quantum of visible light or other form of electromagnetic radiation demonstrating both particle and wave properties.

photopic Referring to light intensities that are bright enough to stimulate the cone receptors and bright enough to "saturate" the rod receptors (that is,

drive them to their maximum responses). Compare *scotopic*.

photoreceptor A light-sensitive receptor in the retina.

pictorial depth cue A cue to distance or depth used by artists to depict three-dimensional depth in two-dimensional pictures.

pinna (pl. pinnae) The outer, funnel-like part of the ear.

piriform cortex See *primary olfactory cortex*.

pitch The psychological aspect of sound related mainly to perceived *frequency*. Compare *loudness*.

place code Tuning of different parts of the cochlea to different frequencies, in which information about the particular frequency of an incoming sound wave is coded by the place along the cochlear partition that has the greatest mechanical displacement. Compare *temporal code*.

placebo effect Decreasing pain sensation when people think they're taking an analgesic drug but actually are not.

polysensory Blending multiple sensory systems.

positivism A philosophical position arguing that all we really have to go on is the evidence of the senses, so the world might be nothing more than an elaborate hallucination. Compare *realism*.

positron emission tomography (PET) An imaging technology that enables us to define locations in the brain where neurons are especially active by measuring the metabolism of brain cells using safe radioactive isotopes. Compare *functional magnetic resonance imaging*.

PPA See *parahippocampal place area*.

preattentive stage The processing of a stimulus that occurs before selective attention is deployed to that stimulus.

prefrontal cortex A region of the brain concerned with cognition and executive control.

presbyopia Literally "old sight." The loss of near vision because of insufficient accommodation.

primary auditory cortex (A1) The first area within the temporal lobes of the brain responsible for processing acoustic information.

primary olfactory cortex The neural area where olfactory information is first processed. It comprises the amygdala, parahippocampal gyrus, and interconnected areas; and it interacts closely with the entorhinal cortex. Also called *piriform cortex*. Compare *orbitofrontal cortex*.

primary visual cortex (V1) The area of the cerebral cortex of the brain that receives direct inputs from the lateral geniculate nucleus, as well as feedback from other brain areas, and is responsible for processing visual information. Also called *area 17* or *striate cortex*.

primer pheromone A pheromone that triggers a physiological (often hormonal) change among conspecifics. This effect usually involves prolonged pheromone exposure. Compare *releaser pheromone*.

problem of univariance The fact that an infinite set of different wavelength-intensity combinations can elicit exactly the same response from a single type of photoreceptor. One photoreceptor type cannot make color discriminations based on wavelength.

projective geometry For purposes of studying perception of the three-dimensional world, the geometry that describes the transformations that occur when the three-dimensional world is *projected* onto a two-dimensional surface. For example, parallel lines do not converge in the real world, but they do in the two-dimensional projection of that world.

proprioception Perception mediated by kinesthetic and vestibular receptors.

prosopagnosia An inability to recognize faces.

protanope An individual who suffers from color blindness that is due to the absence of L-cones. Compare *deuteranope* and *tritanope*.

proto-object A loose collection of unbound features (size, color, and so forth) that will be a recognizable object, once attended.

proximity A Gestalt grouping rule stating that the tendency of two features to group together will increase as the distance between them decreases.

psychoacoustics The study of the psychological correlates of the physical dimensions of acoustics; a branch of psychophysics.

psychophysics The science of defining quantitative relationships between physical and psychological (subjective) events.

pupil The dark, circular opening at the center of the iris in the eye, where light enters the eye.

pure tone See *sine wave* (definition 1).

Q

quale (pl. qualia) In philosophy, a private conscious experience of sensation or perception.

R

random dot stereogram (RDS) A stereogram made of a large number (often in the thousands) of randomly placed dots. Random dot stereograms contain no monocular cues to depth. Stimuli visible stereoscopically in random dot stereograms are Cyclopean stimuli.

rapid serial visual presentation (RSVP) An experimental procedure in which stimuli appear in a stream at one location (typically the point of fixation) at a rapid rate (typically about eight per second).

rate-intensity function A graph plotting the firing rate of an auditory nerve fiber in response to a sound of constant frequency at increasing intensities.

rate saturation The point at which a nerve fiber is firing as rapidly as possible and further stimulation is incapable of increasing the firing rate.

RDS See *random dot stereogram*.

reaction time (RT) A measure of the time from the onset of a stimulus to a response.

realism A philosophical position arguing that there is a real world to sense. Compare *positivism*.

receiver operating characteristic (ROC) curve In studies of signal detection, the graphical plot of the hit rate as a function of the false-alarm rate. If these are the same, points fall on the diagonal, indicating that the observer cannot tell the difference between the presence and absence of the signal. As the observer's sensitivity increases, the curve bows upward toward the upper left corner. That point represents a perfect ability to distinguish signal from noise (100% hits, 0% false alarms).

receptive field The region on the retina in which visual stimuli influence a neuron's firing rate.

receptor adaptation The biochemical phenomenon, occurring after continual exposure to an odorant, whereby receptors stop responding to an odorant and detection ceases. Compare *cognitive habituation*.

receptor potential A change in voltage across the membrane of a sensory receptor cell (in the vestibular system, a hair cell) in response to stimulation.

recognition-by-components model Biederman's model of object recognition, which holds that objects are recognized by the identities and relationships of their component parts. See also *geon*.

reflect To redirect something that strikes a surface—especially light, sound, or heat—usually back toward its point of origin.

reflectance The percentage of light hitting a surface that is reflected and not absorbed into the surface. Typically reflectance is given as a function of wavelength.

reflexive eye movement A movement of the eye that is automatic and involuntary.

refract 1. To alter the course of a wave of energy that passes into something from another medium, as water does to light entering it from the air. 2. To measure the degree of refraction in a lens or eye.

Reissner's membrane A thin sheath of tissue separating the vestibular and middle canals in the cochlea.

relatability The degree to which two line segments appear to be part of the same contour.

related color A color, such as brown or gray, that is seen only in relation to other colors. For example, a "gray" patch in complete darkness appears white. Compare *unrelated color*.

relative height As a depth cue, the observation that objects at different distances from the viewer on the ground plane will form images at different heights in the retinal image. Objects farther away will be seen as higher in the image.

relative metrical depth cue A depth cue that could specify, for example, that object A is twice as far away as object B without providing information about the absolute distance to either A or B. Compare *absolute metrical depth cue*.

relative size A comparison of size between items without knowing the absolute size of either one.

releaser pheromone A pheromone that triggers an immediate behavioral response among conspecifics. Compare *primer pheromone*.

repetition blindness A failure to detect the second occurrence of an identical letter, word, or picture in a rapidly presented stream of stimuli when the second occurrence falls within 200–500 milliseconds of the first. Compare *attentional blink*.

response enhancement An effect of attention on the response of a neuron in which the neuron responding to an attended stimulus gives a bigger response.

retina A light-sensitive membrane in the back of the eye that contains rods and cones, which receive an image from the lens and send it to the brain through the optic nerve.

retinitis pigmentosa (RP) A progressive degeneration of the retina that affects night vision and peripheral vision. RP commonly runs in families and can be caused by defects in a number of different genes that have recently been identified.

retronasal olfactory sensation The sensation of an odor that is perceived when chewing and swallowing force an odorant in the mouth up behind the palate into the nose. Such odor sensations are perceived as originating from the mouth, even though the actual contact of odorant and receptor occurs at the olfactory mucosa.

reverse staircase method See *staircase method*.

rhodopsin The visual pigment found in rods.

ROC curve See *receiver operating characteristic curve*.

rod A photoreceptor specialized for night vision. Compare *cone*.

rod monochromat An individual with no cones of any type. In addition to being truly color-blind, rod monochromats are badly visually impaired in bright light. Compare *cone monochromat*.

round window A soft area of tissue at the base of the tympanic canal that releases excess pressure remaining from extremely intense sounds.

RP See *retinitis pigmentosa*.

RSVP See *rapid serial visual presentation*.

RT See *reaction time*.

Ruffini ending A specialized nerve ending associated with slowly adapting (SA II) fibers that have large receptive fields. Compare *Meissner corpuscle*, *Merkel cell neurite complex*, and *Pacinian corpuscle*.

S

S-cone A cone that is preferentially sensitive to short wavelengths; colloquially (but not entirely accurately) known as a "blue cone." Compare *L-cone* and *M-cone*.

S1 See *somatosensory area 1*.

S2 See *somatosensory area 2*.

saccade A type of eye movement, made both voluntarily and involuntarily, in which the eyes rapidly change fixation from one object or location to another. Compare *smooth pursuit* and *vergence*.

saccadic suppression The reduction of visual sensitivity that occurs when we make saccadic eye movements. Saccadic suppression eliminates the smear from retinal image motion during an eye movement.

saccule (or sacculus) One of the two otolith organs. A saclike structure that contains the saccular macula. Compare *utricle*.

salience The vividness of a stimulus relative to its neighbors.

salty One of the four basic tastes; the taste quality produced by the cations of salts (e.g., the sodium in sodium chloride produces the salty taste). Some cations also produce other taste qualities (e.g., potassium tastes bitter as well as salty). The purest salty taste is produced by sodium chloride (NaCl), common table salt. Compare *bitter*, *sour*, and *sweet*.

saturation The chromatic strength of a hue. White has zero saturation, pink is more saturated, and red is fully saturated. Compare *brightness* and *hue*.

scala media See *middle canal*.

scala tympani See *tympanic canal*.

scala vestibuli See *vestibular canal*.

scatter To disperse light in an irregular fashion.

scene-based guidance Information in our understanding of scenes that helps us find specific objects in scenes (e.g., objects do not float in air, faucets are near sinks).

scotoma A blind spot in the visual field.

scotopic Referring to light intensities that are bright enough to stimulate the rod receptors but too dim to stimulate the cone receptors. Compare *photopic*.

second-order motion The motion of an object that is defined by changes in contrast or texture, but not by luminance. Compare *first-order motion*.

secondary olfactory cortex See *orbitofrontal cortex*.

secondary taste cortex See *orbitofrontal cortex*.

selective attention The form of attention involved when processing is restricted to a subset of the possible stimuli.

semicircular canal Any of three toroidal tubes in the vestibular system that sense angular motion.

sensation The ability to detect a stimulus and, perhaps, to turn that detection into a private experience. Compare *perception*.

sense of angular motion The spatial orientation modality that senses rotation.

sense of linear motion The spatial orientation modality that senses translation.

sense of tilt The spatial orientation modality that senses head inclination with respect to gravity.

sensitivity 1. The ability to perceive via the sense organs. 2. Extreme responsiveness to radiation, especially to light of a specific wavelength. 3. The ability to respond to transmitted signals. 4. In signal detection theory, a value that defines the ease with which an observer can tell the difference between the presence and absence of a stimulus or the difference between stimulus 1 and stimulus 2.

sensorineural hearing loss Hearing loss due to defects in the cochlea or auditory nerve. Compare *conductive hearing loss*.

sensory integration The process of combining different sensory signals. Typically, combining several signals yields more accurate and/or more precise information than can be obtained from individual sensory signals. This is *not* the mathematical process of integration learned in calculus (e.g., the integral of acceleration is velocity). Compare *mathematical integration*.

serial self-terminating search A search from item to item, ending when a target is found. Compare *parallel search*.

set size The number of items in a visual display.

shape-pattern theory The current dominant biochemical theory for how chemicals come to be perceived as specific odors. Shape-pattern theory contends that different scents—as a function of the fit between odorant shape to OR shape—activate different arrays of olfactory receptors in the olfactory epithelia. These various arrays produce specific firing patterns of neurons in the olfactory bulb, which then determine the particular scent we perceive. Compare *vibration theory*.

sharper tuning An effect of attention on the response of a neuron in which the neuron responding to an attended stimulus responds more precisely. For example, a neuron that responds to lines with orientations from –20 degrees to +20 degrees might come to respond to ±10-degree lines.

signal detection theory A psychophysical theory that quantifies the response of an observer to the presentation of a signal in the presence of noise. Measures obtained from a series of presentations are sensitivity (d') and criterion of the observer.

similarity A Gestalt grouping rule stating that the tendency of two features to group together will increase as the similarity between them increases.

simple cell A cortical neuron with clearly defined excitatory and inhibitory regions. Compare *complex cell*.

simultagnosia An inability to perceive more than one object at a time. Simultagnosia is a consequence of bilateral damage to the parietal lobes (Balint syndrome).

sine wave 1. In hearing, a waveform for which variation as a function of time is a sine function. Also called *pure tone*. 2. In vision, a pattern for which variation in a property like brightness or color as a function of space is a sine function.

sine wave grating A grating with a sinusoidal luminance profile.

single-opponent cell See *cone-opponent cell*.

sinusoidal Referring to any oscillation, such as a sound wave or rotational motion, whose waveform is that of a sine curve. The period of a sinusoidal oscillation is the time that it takes for one full back-and-forth cycle of the motion to occur. The frequency of a sinusoidal oscillation is defined as the numeral 1 divided by the period.

smooth pursuit A type of voluntary eye movement in which the eyes move smoothly to follow a moving object. Compare *saccade* and *vergence*.

SOA See *stimulus onset asynchrony*.

somatosensation Collectively, all sensory signals from the body.

somatosensory area 1 (S1) The primary receiving area for touch in the cortex. Compare *somatosensory area 2*.

somatosensory area 2 (S2) The secondary receiving area for touch in the cortex. Compare *somatosensory area 1*.

somatotopic Spatially mapped in the somatosensory cortex in correspondence to spatial events on the skin.

sour One of the four basic tastes; the taste quality produced by the hydrogen ion in acids. Compare *bitter*, *salty*, and *sweet*.

source segregation Processing an auditory scene consisting of multiple sound sources into separate sound images. Also called *auditory scene analysis*.

spatial disorientation Any impairment of spatial orientation. More specifically, any impairment of our sense of linear motion, angular motion, or tilt.

spatial frequency The number of cycles of a grating per unit of visual angle (usually specified in cycles per degree).

spatial-frequency channel A pattern analyzer, implemented by an ensemble of cortical neurons, in which each set of neurons is tuned to a limited range of spatial frequencies.

spatial layout The description of the structure of a scene (e.g., enclosed, open, rough, smooth) without reference to the identity of specific objects in the scene.

spatial orientation A sense consisting of three interacting sensory modalities: the senses of linear motion, angular motion, and tilt.

specific anosmia The inability to smell one specific compound amid otherwise normal smell perception.

specific hungers theory The idea that deficiency of a given nutrient produces craving (a specific hunger) for that nutrient. Curt Richter first proposed this theory and demonstrated that cravings for salty or for sweet are associated with deficiencies in those substances. However, the idea proved wrong for other nutrients (e.g., vitamins).

spectral power distribution The physical energy in a light as a function of wavelength.

spectral reflectance function The percentage of a particular wavelength that is reflected from a surface.

spectrogram In sound analysis, a three-dimensional display that plots time on the horizontal axis, frequency on the vertical axis, and amplitude (intensity) on a color or gray scale.

spectrum (pl. spectra) A representation of the relative energy (intensity) present at each frequency.

spinothalamic pathway The route from the spinal cord to the brain that carries most of the information about skin temperature and pain. Compare *dorsal column–medial lemniscal pathway*.

staircase method A psychophysical method for determining the concentration of a stimulus required for detection at the threshold level. The staircase method is an example of a *method of limits*. A stimulus (e.g., odorant) is presented in an ascending concentration sequence until detection is indicated, and then the concentration is shifted to a descending sequence until the response changes to "no detection." This ascending and descending sequence is typically repeated several times, and the concentrations at which reversals occur are averaged to determine the threshold detection level of that odorant for a given individual. Also called *reverse staircase method*.

stapedius The muscle attached to the stapes; tensing the stapedius decreases vibration. See also *tensor tympani*.

stapes One of the three ossicles. Connected to the incus on one end, the sta-pes presses against the oval window of the cochlea on the other end.

stereoacuity A measure of the smallest binocular disparity that can generate a sensation of depth.

stereoblindness An inability to make use of binocular disparity as a depth cue. This term is typically used to describe individuals with vision in both eyes. Someone who has lost one (or both) eyes is not typically described as "stereoblind."

stereocilium (pl. stereocilia) Any of the hairlike extensions on the tips of hair cells in the cochlea that, when flexed, initiate the release of neurotransmitters.

stereoisomers Isomers (molecules that can exist in different structural forms) in which the spatial arrangements of the atoms are mirror-image rotations of one another, like a right and left hand.

stereopsis The ability to use binocular disparity as a cue to depth.

stereoscope A device for simultaneously presenting one image to one eye and another image to the other eye. Stereoscopes can be used to present dichoptic stimuli for stereopsis and binocular rivalry.

Stevens' power law A principle describing the relationship between stimulus and resulting sensation that says the magnitude of subjective sensation is proportional to the stimulus magnitude raised to an exponent. Compare *Fechner's law* and *Weber's law*.

stimulus onset asynchrony (SOA) The time between the onset of one stimulus and the onset of another.

strabismus A misalignment of the two eyes such that a single object in space is imaged on the fovea of one eye, and on a nonfoveal area of the other (turned) eye.

striate cortex See *primary visual cortex*.

structural description A description of an object in terms of the nature of its constituent parts and the relationships between those parts.

structuralism A school of thought believing that complex objects or perceptions could be understood by analysis of the components. Compare *Gestalt*.

substantia gelatinosa A jellylike region of interconnecting neurons in the dorsal horn of the spinal cord.

subtractive color mixture A mixture of pigments. If pigments A and B mix, some of the light shining on the surface will be subtracted by A, and some by B. Only the remainder contributes to the perception of color. Compare *additive color mixture*.

superior colliculus A structure in the midbrain that is important in initiating and guiding eye movements. Compare *inferior colliculus*.

superior olive An early brain stem region in the auditory pathway where inputs from both ears converge.

supertaster An individual whose perception of taste sensations is the most intense. A variety of factors may contribute to this heightened perception; among the most important is the density of fungiform papillae. Compare *nontaster* and *taster*.

supporting cell One of the three types of cells in the olfactory epithelium. Supporting cells provide metabolic and physical support for the olfactory sensory neurons. Compare *basal cell* and *olfactory sensory neuron*.

suppression In vision, the inhibition of an unwanted image. Suppression occurs frequently in persons with strabismus.

surroundedness A rule for figure-ground assignment stating that if one region is entirely surrounded by another, it is likely that the surrounded region is the figure.

sweet One of the four basic tastes; the taste quality produced by some sugars, such as glucose, fructose, and sucrose. These three sugars are particularly biologically useful to us, and our sweet receptors are tuned to them. Some other compounds (e.g., saccharin, aspartame) are also sweet. Compare *bitter*, *salty*, and *sour*.

symmetry A rule for figure-ground assignment stating that symmetrical regions are more likely to be seen as figure.

synapse The junction between neurons that permits information transfer.

synaptic terminal The location where axons terminate at the synapse for transmission of information by the release of a chemical transmitter.

syncopation Any deviation from a regular rhythm.

T

tactile agnosia The inability to identify objects by touch.

target The goal of a visual search. Compare *distractor*.

tastant Any stimulus that can be tasted.

taste bud A globular cluster of cells that has the function of creating neural signals conveyed to the brain by the taste nerves. Some of the cells in a taste bud have specialized sites on their apical projections that interact with taste stimuli. Some of the cells form synapses with taste nerve fibers.

taste receptor cell A cell within the taste bud that contains sites on its apical projection that can interact with taste stimuli. These sites fall into two major categories: those interacting with charged particles (e.g., sodium and hydrogen ions), and those interacting with specific chemical structures.

taster (of PTC/PROP) An individual born with one or both dominant alleles for the *TAS2R38* gene and able to taste the compounds phenylthiocarbamide and propylthiouracil. PTC/PROP tasters who also have a high density of fungiform papillae are PROP supertasters. Compare *nontaster* and *supertaster*.

tau (τ) Information in the optic flow that could signal time to collision (TTC) without the necessity of estimating either absolute distances or rates. The ratio of the retinal image size at any moment to the rate at which the image is expanding is tau, and TTC is proportional to tau.

tectorial membrane A gelatinous structure, attached on one end, that extends into the middle canal of the ear, floating above inner hair cells and touching outer hair cells.

tempo The perceived speed of the presentation of sounds.

temporal code Tuning of different parts of the cochlea to different frequencies, in which information about the particular frequency of an incoming sound wave is coded by the timing of neural firing as it relates to the period of the sound. Compare *place code*.

temporal integration The process by which a sound at a constant level is perceived as being louder when it is of greater duration. The term also applies to perceived brightness, which depends on the duration of light.

tensor tympani The muscle attached to the malleus; tensing the tensor tympani decreases vibration. See also *stapedius*.

texture-defined object An object that is defined by changes in contrast, or texture, but not by luminance. Also called *contrast-defined object*.

texture gradient A depth cue based on the geometric fact that items of the same size form smaller images when they are farther away. An array of items that change in size smoothly across the image will appear to form a surface tilted in depth.

texture segmentation Carving an image into regions of common texture properties.

thermoreceptor A sensory receptor that signals information about changes in skin temperature.

threshold tuning curve A graph plotting the thresholds of a neuron or fiber in response to sine waves with varying frequencies at the lowest intensity that will give rise to a response.

tilt Attaining a sloping position like that of the leaning tower of Pisa.

tilt aftereffect The perceptual illusion of tilt, produced by adaptation to a pattern of a given orientation.

timbre The psychological sensation by which a listener can judge that two sounds with the same loudness and pitch are dissimilar. Timbre quality is conveyed by harmonics and other high frequencies.

time to collision (TTC) The time required for a moving object (such as a cricket ball) to hit a stationary object (such as a batsman's head). TTC = distance/rate.

tip link A tiny filament that stretches from the tip of a stereocilium to the side of its neighbor.

tip-of-the-nose phenomenon The inability to name an odor, even though it is very familiar. Contrary to the tip-of-the-tongue phenomenon, one has no lexical access to the name of the odor, such as first letter, rhyme, number of syllables, and so on, when in the tip-of-the-nose state. This is an example of how language and olfactory perception are deeply disconnected.

tone chroma A sound quality shared by tones that have the same octave interval.

tone height A sound quality corresponding to the level of pitch. Tone height is monotonically related to frequency.

tonotopic organization An arrangement in which neurons that respond to different frequencies are organized anatomically in order of frequency.

topographical mapping The orderly mapping of the world in the lateral geniculate nucleus and the visual cortex.

transduce To convert from one form of energy to another (e.g., from light to neural electrical energy, or from mechanical movement to neural electrical energy).

transmit To convey something (e.g., light) from one place or thing to another.

transparent Allowing light to pass through with no interruption, so that

objects on the other side can be clearly seen.

triangle test A test in which a participant is given three odorants to smell, of which two are the same and one is different. The participant is required to state which is the odd odor out. Typically, the order in which the three odorants are given (e.g., same, same, different; different, same, same; same, different, same) is manipulated and the test is repeated several times for greater accuracy.

trichromatic theory of color vision (or trichromacy) The theory that the color of any light is defined in our visual system by the relationships of three numbers—the outputs of three receptor types now known to be the three cones. Also known as *Young-Helmholtz theory*.

trigeminal (V) nerves The fifth pair of cranial nerves, which transmit information about the "feel" of an odorant (e.g., mint feels cool, and cinnamon feels warm), as well as pain and irritation sensations (e.g., ammonia feels burning).

tritanope An individual who suffers from color blindness that is due to the absence of S-cones. Compare *deuteranope* and *protanope*.

trochlear (IV) nerves The fourth pair of cranial nerves, which innervate the superior oblique muscles of the eyeballs.

TTC See *time to collision*.

tufted cell Any of a secondary class of output neurons in the olfactory bulb. Compare *mitral cell*.

two-point touch threshold The minimum distance at which two stimuli (e.g., two simultaneous touches) are just perceptible as separate.

two-tone suppression A decrease in the firing rate of one auditory nerve fiber due to one tone, when a second tone is presented at the same time.

tympanic canal One of three fluid-filled passages in the cochlea. The tympanic canal extends from the round window at the base of the cochlea to the helicotrema at the apex. Also called *scala tympani*. Compare *middle canal* and *vestibular canal*.

tympanic membrane The eardrum; a thin sheet of skin at the end of the outer ear canal. The tympanic membrane vibrates in response to sound.

U

umami The taste sensation produced by monosodium glutamate.

uncrossed disparity The sign of disparity created by objects behind the plane of fixation (the horopter). The term *uncrossed* is used because images of objects located behind the horopter will appear to be displaced to the right in the right eye, and to the left in the left eye. Compare *crossed disparity*.

unique hue Any of four colors that can be described with only a single color term: red, yellow, green, blue. Other colors (e.g., purple or orange) can be described as compounds (reddish blue, reddish yellow).

uniqueness constraint In stereopsis, the observation that a feature in the world is represented exactly once in each retinal image. This constraint simplifies the correspondence problem.

unrelated color A color that can be experienced in isolation. Compare *related color*.

utricle (or utriculus) One of the two otolith organs. A saclike structure that contains the utricular macula. Compare *saccule*.

V

V1 See *primary visual cortex*.

vanishing point The apparent point at which parallel lines receding in depth converge. See also *Euclidean* and *linear perspective*.

vection An illusory sense of self-motion caused by moving visual cues when you are not, in fact, actually moving.

velocity The speed and direction in which something moves. Mathematically, velocity is the integral of *acceleration*. In words, linear velocity is the ratio of the distance moved divided by the time it takes to traverse that distance; angular velocity is the ratio of the angle rotated divided by the time it takes to traverse that angle.

vergence A type of eye movement in which the two eyes move in opposite directions; for example, both eyes turn toward the nose (convergence) or away from the nose (divergence). Compare *saccade* and *smooth pursuit*.

vertigo A sensation of rotation or spinning. The term is sometimes used erroneously to mean any form of dizziness.

vestibular canal One of three fluid-filled passages in the cochlea. The vestibular canal extends from the oval window at the base of the cochlea to the helicotrema at the apex. Also called *scala vestibuli*. Compare *middle canal* and *tympanic canal*.

vestibular labyrinth See *vestibular organs*.

vestibular organs The set of five organs—three semicircular canals and two otolith organs—located in each inner ear that sense head motion and head orientation with respect to gravity. These organs are also sometimes called the *vestibular system* or the *vestibular labyrinth*, but the name *vestibular system* is often used more generally to refer to the vestibular organs and their neural pathways.

vestibular system See *vestibular organs*.

vestibulocochlear nerve The eighth pair of cranial nerves, which connect the inner ear with the brain, transmitting impulses concerned with hearing and spatial orientation. The vestibulocochlear nerve is composed of the cochlear nerve branch and the vestibular nerve branch.

vestibulo-ocular reflex (VOR) A short-latency reflex that helps stabilize vision by counterrotating the eyes when the vestibular system senses head movement.

vibration theory An alternative to *shape-pattern theory* for describing how olfaction works. Vibration theory proposes that every odorant has a different vibrational frequency, and that molecules that produce the same vibrational frequencies will smell the same.

Vieth-Müller circle The location of objects whose images fall on geometrically corresponding points in the two retinas. If life were simple, this circle would be the *horopter*, but life is not simple.

viewpoint invariance 1. A property of an object that does not change when observer viewpoint changes. 2. A class of theories of object recognition that proposes representations of objects that do not change when viewpoint changes.

visual acuity A measure of the finest detail that can be resolved by the eyes.

visual angle The angle subtended by an object at the retina.

visual crowding The deleterious effect of clutter on peripheral object recognition.

visual-field defect A portion of the visual field with no vision or with abnormal vision, typically resulting from damage to the visual nervous system.

visual search Search for a target in a display containing distracting elements.

vitalism The idea that there is a force in life that is distinct from physical entities.

vitreous humor The transparent fluid that fills the vitreous chamber in the posterior part of the eye. Compare *aqueous humor*.

VNO See *vomeronasal organ*.

vocal tract The airway above the larynx used for the production of speech. The vocal tract includes the oral tract and nasal tract.

volley principle The idea that multiple neurons can provide a temporal code for frequency if each neuron fires at a distinct point in the period of a sound wave but does not fire on every period.

vomeronasal organ (VNO) A chemical sensing organ at the base of the nasal cavity with a curved tubular shape. The VNO evolved to detect chemicals that cannot be processed by the olfactory epithelium, such as large and/or aqueous molecules, the types of molecules that constitute pheromones. Also called *Jacobson's organ*.

VOR See *vestibulo-ocular reflex*.

W

warmth fiber A sensory nerve fiber that fires when skin temperature increases. Compare *cold fiber*.

wave An oscillation that travels through a medium by transferring energy from one particle or point to another without causing any permanent displacement of the medium.

wavelength See *period*.

Weber fraction The constant of proportionality in Weber's law.

Weber's law The principle describing the relationship between stimulus and resulting sensation that says the just noticeable difference (JND) is a constant fraction of the comparison stimulus. Compare *Fechner's law* and *Stevens' power law*.

white noise Noise consisting of all audible frequencies in equal amounts. White noise in hearing is analogous to white light in vision, for which all wavelengths are present.

Y

Young-Helmholtz theory See *trichromatic theory of color vision*.

References

Ackerman, D. (1990). *A Natural History of the Senses.* New York: Random House.

Ackerman, J. M., Nocera, C. C., and Bargh, J. (2010). Incidental haptic sensations influence social judgments and decisions. *Science* 328: 1712–1714.

Addams, R. (1834). An account of a peculiar optical phenomenon seen after having looked at a moving body, etc. *Lond Edinb Philos Mag J Sci* 5: 373–374.

Adelson, E. H. (1993). Perceptual organization and the judgment of brightness. *Science* 262: 2042–2044.

Adelson, E. H., and Bergen, J. R. (1985). Spatiotemporal energy models perception of motion. *J Opt Soc Am A* 2: 284–299.

Ahissar, M., and Hochstein, S. (2004). The reverse hierarchy theory of visual perceptual learning. *Trends Cogn Sci* 8: 457–464.

Alais, D., and Blake, R. (2005). *Binocular Rivalry and Perceptual Ambiguity.* Cambridge, MA: MIT Press.

Alpern, M., Kitahara, K., and Krantz, D. H. (1983). Classical tritanopia. *J Physiol* 335: 655–681.

Alvarez, G. A. (2011). Representing multiple objects as an ensemble enhances visual cognition. *Trends Cogn Sci* 15: 122–131.

Amano, K., Wandell, B. A., and Dumoulin, S. O. (2009). Visual field maps, population receptive field sizes, and visual field coverage in the human MT+ complex. *J Neurophysiol* 102: 2704–2718.

American Standards Association. (1960). *Acoustical Terminology SI, 1-1960.* New York: American Standards Association.

Anderson, J. A., Silverstein, J. W., Ritz, S. A., and Jones, R. S. (1977). Distinctive features, categorical perception, and probability learning: Some applications of a neural model. *Psychol Rev* 84: 413–451.

Anderson, J. S., Lampl, I., Gillespie, D. C., and Ferster, D. (2000). Contribution of noise to contrast invariance of orientation tuning in cat visual cortex. *Science* 290: 1968–1972.

Andre, T., Lefèvre, P., and Thonnard, J. L. (2009). A continuous measure of finger-tip friction during precision grip. *J Neurosci Methods* 179: 224–229.

Angelaki, D., McHenry, M., Dickman, J. D., Newlands, S., and Hess, B. (1999). Computation of inertial motion: Neural strategies to resolve ambiguous otolith information. *J Neurosci* 19: 316–327.

Attneave, F., and Olson, R. K. (1971). Pitch as a medium: A new approach to psychophysical scaling. *Am J Psychol* 84: 147–166.

Aubert, H. (1861). Eine scheinbare bedeutende Drehung von Objekten bei Neigung des Kopfes nach rechts oder links. *Virchows Arch.* 20: 381–393.

Aubert, H. (1886). Die Bewegungsempfindung. *Arch Ges Physiol* 39: 347–370.

Ayabe-Kanamura, S., Schicker, I., Laska, M., Hudson, R., Distel, H., Kobayakawa, T., and Saito, S. (1998). Differences in perception of everyday odors: A Japanese-German cross-cultural study. *Chem Senses* 23: 31–38.

Babadi, B., Casti, A., Xiao, Y., Kaplan, E., and Paninski, L. (2010). A generalized linear model of the impact of direct and indirect inputs to the lateral geniculate nucleus. *J Vis* 10(10): 22.

Bahill, A. T., and Stark, L. (1979). The trajectories of saccadic eye movements. *Sci Am* 240(1): 108–117.

Baloh, R., and Halmagyi, G. M. (Eds.). (1996). *Disorders of the Vestibular System.* Oxford, UK: Oxford University Press.

Banks, M. S., Aslin, R. N., and Letson, R. D. (1975). Sensitive period for the development of human binocular vision. *Science* 190: 675–677.

Barclay, C. D., Cutting, J. E., and Kozlowski, L. T. (1978). Temporal and spatial factors in gait perception that influence gender recognition. *Percept Psychophys* 23: 145–152.

Baringa, M. (2002). How the brain's clock gets daily enlightenment. *Science* 295: 955–957.

Barlow, H. B. (1972). Single units and sensation: A neuron doctrine for perceptual psychology. *Perception* 1: 371–394.

Barlow, H. B. (1995). The neuron doctrine in perception. In M. S. Gazzaniga (Ed.), *The Cognitive Neurosciences* (pp. 415–435). Cambridge, MA: MIT Press.

Barlow, H. B., Blakemore, C., and Pettigrew, J. D. (1967). The neural mechanism of binocular depth discrimination. *J Physiol* 193: 327–342.

Barlow, H. B., and Levick, W. R. (1965). The mechanism of directionally selective units in rabbit's retina. *J Physiol* 178: 477–504.

Barr, C. C., Schultheis, L. W., and Robinson, D. A. (1976). Voluntary, non-visual control of the human vestibulo-ocular reflex. *Acta Otolaryngol* 81: 365–375.

Bartoshuk, L. M. (1977). Psychophysical studies of taste mixtures. In J. LeMagnen (Ed.), *Olfaction and Taste* (Vol. VI, pp. 377–384). London: Information Retrieval.

Bartoshuk, L. M. (1979). Bitter taste of saccharin: Related to the genetic ability to taste the bitter substance 6-*n*-propylthiouracil (PROP). *Science* 205: 934–935.

Bartoshuk, L. M. (1991). Taste, smell and pleasure. In R. C. Bolles (Ed.), *The Hedonics of Taste* (pp. 15–28). Hillsdale, NJ: Erlbaum.

Bartoshuk, L. M., Fast, K., and Snyder, D. (2005). Differences in our sensory worlds: Invalid comparisons with labeled scales. *Curr Dir Psychol Sci* 14: 122–125.

Bartoshuk, L. M., and Wolfe, J. M. (1990). Conditioned taste aversions in humans: Are they olfactory aversions? *Chem Senses* 15: 551.

Bashford, J. A., and Warren, R. M. (1987). Multiple phonemic restorations follow the rules for auditory induction. *Percept Psychophys* 42: 114–121.

Basson, M. D., Bartoshuk, L. M., Dichello, S. Z., Panzini, L., Weiffenbach, J. M., and Duffy, V. B. (2005). Association between 6-*n*-propylthiouracil (PROP) bitterness and colonic neoplasms. *Dig Dis Sci* 50: 483–489.

Bautista, D. M., Siemens, J., Glazer, J. M., Tsuruda, P. R., Basbaum, A. I., Stucky, C. L., Jordt, S. E., and Julius, D. (2007). The menthol receptor TRPM8 is the principal detector of environmental cold. *Nature* 448: 204–208.

Beck, J. (1982). Textural segmentation. In J. Beck (Ed.), *Organization and Representation in Perception* (pp. 285–317). Hillsdale, NJ: Erlbaum.

Behrmann, M., and Avidan, G. (2005). Congenital prosopagnosia: Face-blind from birth. *Trends Cogn Sci* 9: 180–187.

Bergen, J. R., and Adelson, E. H. (1988). Early vision and texture perception. *Nature* 333: 363–364.

Berger, A., Henderson, M., Nadoolman, W., Duffy, V. B., Cooper, D., Saberski, L., and Bartoshuk, L. (1995). Oral capsaicin provides temporary relief for oral mucositis pain secondary to chemotherapy/radiation therapy. *J Pain Symptom Manage* 10: 243–248.

Berlin, B., and Kay, P. (1969). *Basic Color Terms: Their Universality and Evolution.* Berkeley: University of California Berkeley.

Bernstein, I. L. (1978). Learned taste aversions in children receiving chemotherapy. *Science* 200: 1302–1303.

Berthoz, A., Israel, I., Georges-Francois, P., Grasso, R., and Tsuzuku, T. (1995). Spatial memory of body linear displacement: What is being stored? *Science* 269: 95–98.

Bertino, M., Beauchamp, G. K., and Engelman, K. (1982). Long-term reduction in dietary sodium alters the taste of salt. *Am J Clin Nutr* 36: 1134–1144.

Bertolini, G., Ramat, S., Laurens, J., Bockisch, C. J., Marti, S., Straumann, D., and Palla, A. (2011). Velocity storage contribution to vestibular self-motion perception in healthy human subjects. *J Neurophysiol* 105: 209–223.

Bialystok, E., and Hakuta, K. (1994). *In Other Words: The Science and Psychology of Second-Language Acquisition.* New York: Basic Books.

Biederman, I. (1987). Recognition-by-components: A theory of human image understanding. *Psychol Rev* 94: 115–147.

Binder, J. R. (2000). The neuroanatomy of speech perception (Editorial). *Brain* 123: 2371–2372.

Birch, E. E. (1993). Stereopsis in infants and its developmental relation to visual acuity. In K. Simons (Ed.), *Early Visual Development Normal and Abnormal* (pp. 224–234). New York: Oxford University Press.

Birch, E., and Petrig, B. (1996). FPL and VEP measures of fusion, stereopsis and stereoacuity in normal infants. *Vision Res* 36: 1321–1326.

Blake, R. (1988). Cat spatial vision. *Trends Neurosci* 11: 78–83.

Blake, R., and Logothetis, N. K. (2002). Visual competition. *Nat Rev Neurosci* 3: 13–21.

Blake, R., Sloane, M., and Fox, R. (1981). Further developments in binocular summation. *Percept Psychophys* 30: 266–276.

Blake, R., and Wilson, H. (2011). Binocular vision. *Vision Res* 51: 754–770.

Blakemore, C., and Campbell, F. W. (1969). On the existence of neurons in the human visual system selectively sensitive to the orientation and size of images. *J Physiol* 203: 237–260.

Blakemore, S.-J., Wolpert, D. M., and Frith, C. D. (1998). Central cancellation of self-produced tickle sensation. *Nat Neurosci* 1: 635–640.

Blasdel, G. G., and Salama, G. (1986). Voltage-sensitive dyes reveal a modular organization in monkey striate cortex. *Nature* 321: 579–585.

Bloj, M. G., Kersten, D., and Hurlbert, A. C. (1999). Perception of three-dimensional shape influences colour perception through mutual illumination. *Nature* 402: 877–880.

Blood, A. J., and Zatorre, R. J. (2001). Intensely pleasurable responses to music correlate with activity in brain regions implicated in reward and emotion. *Proc Natl Acad Sci USA* 98: 11818–11823.

Blumenfeld, H. (2010). *Neuroanatomy through Clinical Cases* (2nd ed.). Sunderland, MA: Sinauer.

Blundell, J., and Hill, A. J. (1986). Paradoxical effects of an intense sweetener (aspartame) on appetite. *Lancet* 1: 1092–1093.

Boesveldt, S., Lindau, S. T., McClintock, M. K., Hummel, T., and Lundstrom, J. N. (2011). Gustatory and olfactory dysfunction in older adults: A national probability study. *Rhinology*, 49: 324–330.

Bolton, T. L. (1894). Rhythm. *Am J Psychol* 6: 145–238.

Boothe, R. G., Dobson, V., and Teller, D. Y. (1985). Postnatal development of vision in human and non-human primates. *Annu Rev Neurosci* 8: 495–545.

Boring, E. G. (1950). *A History of Experimental Psychology* (2nd ed.). New York: Appleton-Century-Crofts.

Bortolami, S. B., Pierobon, A., DiZio, P., and Lackner, J. R. (2006). Localization of the subjective vertical during roll, pitch, and recumbent yaw body tilt. *Exp Brain Res* 173: 364–373.

Boycott, B. B., and Dowling, J. E. (1969). Organization of the primate retina: Light microscopy. *Philos Trans R Soc Lond B Biol Sci* 255: 109–176.

Brady, T. F., Konkle, T., Alvarez, G. A., and Oliva, A. (2008). Visual long-term memory has a massive storage capacity for object details. *Proc Natl Acad Sci USA* 105: 14325–14329.

Brainard, D. H. (2009). Bayesian approaches to color vision. In M. S. Gazzaniga (Ed.), *The Cognitive Neurosciences* (4th ed., pp. 395–408). Cambridge, MA: MIT Press.

Brainard, D. H., and Freeman, W. T. (1997). Bayesian color constancy. *J Opt Soc Am A* 14: 1393–1411.

Brand, A., Behrend, O., Marquardt, T., McAlpine, D., and Grothe, B. (2002). Precise inhibition is essential for microsecond interaural time difference coding. *Nature* 417: 543–547.

Breedlove, S. M., Rosenzweig, M. R., and Watson, N. V. (2007). *Biological Psychology: An Introduction to Behavioral, Cognitive, and Clinical Neuroscience* (5th ed.). Sunderland, MA: Sinauer.

Breedlove, S. M., Watson, N. V., and Rosenzweig, M. R. (2010). *Biological Psychology: An Introduction to Behavioral, Cognitive, and Clinical Neuroscience* (6th ed.). Sunderland, MA: Sinauer.

Brefczynski, J. A., and DeYoe, E. A. (1999). A physiological correlate of the "spotlight" of visual attention. *Nat Neurosci* 2: 370–374.

Bremner, E. A., Mainland, J .D., Khan, R. M., and Sobel, N. (2003). The prevalence of androstenone anosmia. *Chem Senses* 28: 423–432.

Breuer, J. (1874). Ueber die Funktion der Bogengänge des Ohrlabyrinths [About the functions of the semicircular canals of the ear labyrinth]. *Med Jahrbücher* 2nd series 4: 72–124.

Brown, A. C. (1874). The sense of rotation and the anatomy and physiology of the semicircular canals of the internal ear. *J Anat Physiol* 8: 327–331.

Brugge, J. F., and Howard, M. A. (2002). Hearing. In V. S. Ramachandran (Ed.), *Encyclopedia of the Human Brain* (pp. 429–448). New York: Academic Press.

Brungart, D. S., Durlach, N. I., and Rabinowitz, W. M. (1999). Auditory localization of nearby sources. II. Localization of a broadband source. *J Acoust Soc Am* 106: 1956–1968.

Buchsbaum, G. (1980). A spatial processor model for object colour perception. *J Franklin Inst* 310: 1–26.

Buchsbaum, G., and Gottschalk, A. (1983). Trichromacy, opponent colours coding and optimum colour information transmission in the retina. *Proc R Soc Lond B Biol Sci* 220: 89–113.

Buck, L., and Axel, R. (1991). A novel multigene family may encode odorant receptors: A molecular basis for odor recognition. *Cell* 65: 175–187.

Burgess, A. E. (2010). Signal detection in radiology. In E. Samei and E. A. Krupinski (Eds.), *The Handbook of Medical Image Perception and Techniques* (pp. 26–46). Cambridge, UK: Cambridge University Press.

Busskamp, V., Duebel, J., Balya, D., Fradot, M., Viney, T. J., Siegert, S., Groner, A. C., Cabuy, E., Forster, V., Seeliger, M., Biel, M., Humphries, P., Paques, M., Mohand-Said, S., Trono, D., Deisseroth, K., Sahel, J. A., Picaud, S., and Roska, B. (2010). Genetic reactivation of cone photoreceptors restores visual responses in retinitis pigmentosa. *Science* 329: 413–417.

Cain, W. S., and Engen, T. (1969). Olfactory adaptation and the scaling of odor intensity. In C. Pfaffmann (Ed.), *Olfaction and Taste III* (pp. 127–141). New York: Rockefeller University Press.

Cain, W. S., and Johnson, F., Jr. (1978). Lability of odor pleasantness: Influence of mere exposure. *Perception* 7: 459–465.

Cameron, E. L. (2007). Measures of human olfactory perception during pregnancy. *Chem Senses* 32: 775–782.

Campbell, F. W., and Green, D. G. (1965). Optical and retinal factors affecting visual resolution. *J Physiol* 181: 576–593.

Campbell, F. W., and Robson, J. G. (1968). Application of Fourier analysis to the visibility of gratings. *J Physiol* 197: 551–556.

Campbell, R., Pascalis, O., Coleman, M., Wallace, B., and Benson, P. J. (1997). Are faces of different species perceived categorically by human observers? *Proc R Soc Lond B Biol Sci* 264: 1429–1434.

Carrasco, M. (2011). Visual attention: The past 25 years. *Vision Res* 51: 1484–1525.

Carskadon, M., and Herz, R. S. (2004). Minimal olfactory perception during sleep: Why odor alarms will not work for humans. *Sleep* 27: 402–405.

Carskadon, M. A., Wyatt, J., Etgen, G., and Rosekind, M. R. (1989). Nonvisual sensory experiences in dreams of college students. *Sleep Res* 18: 159.

Casagrande, V. A., Yazar, F., Jones, K. D., and Ding, Y. (2007). The morphology of the koniocellular axon pathway in the macaque monkey. *Cereb Cortex* 17: 2334–2345.

Castelhano, M. S., and Heaven, C. (2010). The relative contribution of scene context and target features to visual search in scenes. *Atten Percept Psychophys* 72: 1283–1297.

Castet, E., Jeanjean, S., and Masson, G. S. (2001). "Saccadic suppression"—no need for an active extra-retinal mechanism. *Trends Neurosci* 24: 316–318.

Cavanagh, P., Hunt, A. R., Afraz, A., and Rolfs, M. (2010). Visual stability based on remapping of attention pointers. *Trends Cogn Sci* 14: 147–153.

Cavanagh, P., and Leclerc, Y. G. (1989). Shape from shadows. *J Exp Psychol Hum Percept Perform* 15: 3–27.

Cave, K. R., and Bichot, N. P. (1999). Visuospatial attention: Beyond a spotlight model. *Psychon Bull Rev* 6: 204–223.

Chabris, C. F., and Simons, D. J. (2011). You do not talk about Fight Club if you do not notice Fight Club: Inattentional blindness for a simulated real-world assault. *i-Perception* 2, http://i-perception.perceptionweb.com.

Champagne, F. A. (2008). Epigenetic mechanisms and the transgenerational effects of maternal care. *Front Neuroendocrinol* 29: 386–397.

Chang, E. F., Rieger, J. W., Johnson, K., Berger, M. S., Barbaro, N. M., and Knight, R. T. (2010). Categorical speech representation in human superior temporal gyrus. *Nat Neurosci* 13: 1428–1432.

Changizi, M. A., Zhang, Q., and Shimojo, S. (2006). Bare skin, blood and the evolution of primate colour vision. *Biol Lett* 2: 217–221.

Chaudhari, N., Landin, A. M., and Roper, S. D. (2000). A metabotropic glutamate receptor variant functions as a taste receptor. *Nat Neurosci* 3: 113–119.

Chaudhari, N., and Roper, S. D. (2010) The cell biology of taste. *J Cell Biol* 190: 285–296.

Chino, Y. M., Smith, E. L., III, Hatta, S., and Cheng, H. (1997). Postnatal development of binocular disparity sensitivity in neurons of the primate visual cortex. *J Neurosci* 17: 296–307.

Chong, S. C., and Treisman, A. (2003). Representation of statistical properties. *Vision Res* 43: 393–404.

Chu, S., and Downes, J. J. (2000). Long live Proust: The odour-cued autobiographical memory bump. *Cognition* 75: B41–B50.

Chubb, C., and Landy, M. S. (1994). Orthogonal distribution analysis: A new approach to the study of texture perception. In M. S. Landy and J. A. Movshon (Eds.), *Computational Models of Visual Processing* (pp. 291–301). Cambridge, MA: MIT Press.

Chun, M. M. (1997). Types and tokens in visual processing: A double dissociation between the attentional blink and repetition blindness. *J Exp Psychol Hum Percept Perform* 23: 738–755.

Chun, M. M., Golomb, J. D., and Turk-Browne, N. B. (2011). A taxonomy of external and internal attention. *Annu Rev Psychol* 62: 73–101.

Chun, M. M., and Potter, M. C. (1995). A two-stage model for multiple target detection in RSVP. *J Exp Psychol Hum Percept Perform* 21: 109–127.

Clark, F. J., and Horch, K. W. (1986). Kinesthesia. In K. R. Boff, L. Kaufman, and J. P. Thomas (Eds.), *Handbook of Perception & Human Performance*, Vol. 1: *Sensory Processes and Perception* (pp. 13-1 to 13-62). New York: Wiley.

Classen, C., Howes, D., and Synnott, A. (1994). *Aroma: The Cultural History of Smell*. London: Routledge.

Cleary, A. M., Konkel, K. E., Nomi, J. S., and McCabe, D. P. (2010). Odor recognition without identification. *Mem Cognit* 38: 452–460.

Cleland, T. A. (2010). Early transformation in odor representation. *Trends Neurosci* 33: 130–139.

Clifford, C. W. G. (2009). Binocular rivalry. *Curr Biol* 19: R1022–R1023. doi: 10.1016/j.cub.2009.09.006.

Coady, J. A., Kluender, K. R., and Rhode, W. S. (2003). Effects of contrast between onsets of speech and other complex spectra. *J Acoust Soc Am* 114: 2225–2235.

Coan, J. A., Schaefer, H. S., and Davidson, R. J. (2006). Lending a hand: Social regulation of the natural response to threat. *Psychol Sci* 17: 1032–1039.

Cole, J. (1991). *Pride and a Daily Marathon*. Boston: MIT Press.

Conard, N., Malina, M., and Münzel, S. (2009). New flutes document the earliest musical tradition in southwestern Germany. *Nature* 460: 737–740.

Conway, B. R., Kitaoka, A., Yazdanbakhsh, A., Pack, C. C., and Livingstone, M. S. (2005). Neural basis for a powerful static motion illusion. *J Neurosci* 25: 5651–5656.

Cornsweet, T. N. (1970). *Visual Perception*. New York: Academic Press.

Coss, R. G., Gusé, K. L., Poran, N. S., and Smith, D. (1993). Development of anti-snake defense in California ground squirrels (*Sperophilus beecheyi*). II. Microevolutionary effects of relaxed selection from rattlesnakes. *Behavior* 124: 137–165.

Craft, E., Schütze, H., Niebur, E., and von der Heydt, R. (2007). A neural model of figure-ground organization. *J Neurophysiol* 97: 4310–4326.

Craig, J. C., and Johnson, K. O. (2000). The two-point threshold: Not a measure of tactile spatial resolution. *Curr Dir Psychol Sci* 9: 29–32.

Cronin, T. W., Jarvilehto, M., Weckstrom, M., and Lall, A. B. (2000). Tuning of photoreceptor spectral sensitivity in fireflies (Coleoptera: Lampyridae). *J Comp Physiol A* 186: 1–12.

Crystal, S. R., and Bernstein, I. L. (1995). Morning sickness: Impact on offspring salt preference. *Appetite* 25: 231–240.

Curcio, C. A., Sloan, K. R., Kalina, R. E., and Hendrickson, A. E. (1990). Human photoreceptor topography. *J Comp Neurol* 292: 497–523.

Curthoys, I., Blanks, R., and Markham, C. (1977). Semicircular canal functional anatomy in cat, guinea pig, and man. *Acta Otolaryngol* 83: 258–265.

Dalton, P. (1996). Odor perception and beliefs about risk. *Chem Senses* 21: 447–458.

Dalton, P. (2002). Olfaction. In H. Pashler, S. Yantis, D. Medin, R. Gallistel, and J. Wixted (Eds.), *Stevens' Handbook of Experimental Psychology* (3rd ed.), Vol. 1: *Sensation and Perception* (pp. 691–746). New York: Wiley.

Dalton, P., Doolittle, N., and Breslin, P. A. S. (2002). Gender-specific induction of enhanced sensitivity to odors. *Nat Neurosci* 5: 199–200.

Dalton, P., Wysocki, C. J., Brody, M. J., and Lawley, H. J. (1997). Perceived odor, irritation and health symptoms following short-term exposure to acetone. *Am J Ind Med* 31: 558–569.

Damasio, A. R., Damasio, H., and Van Hoesen, G. W. (1982). Prosopagnosia. *Neurology* 32: 331.

Damper, R. I., and Harnad, S. R. (2000). Neural network models of categorical perception. *Percept Psychophys* 62: 843–867.

Darwin, C. (1859). *The Origin of Species, by Means of Natural Selection or the Preserva-*

tion of Favoured Races in the Struggle for Life. New York: New York American Library.

Darwin, C. (1871). *The Descent of Man, and Selection in Relation to Sex.* New York: Burt.

Darwin, C. J. (1984). Perceiving vowels in the presence of another sound: Constraints on formant perception. *J Acoust Soc Am* 76: 1636–1647.

Davidoff, J., Davies, I., and Roberson, D. (1999). Is colour categorisation universal? New evidence from a stone-age culture. *Nature* 398: 203–204.

Davidson, R. J. (1984). Affect, cognition, and hemispheric specialization. In S. E. Izard, J. Kagan, and R. Zajonc, (Eds.). *Emotions, Cognition and Behavior* (pp. 320–365). Cambridge, UK: Cambridge University Press.

Davidson, R. J., Putnam, K. M., and Larson, C. L. (2000). Dysfunction in the neural circuitry of emotion regulation—A possible prelude to violence. *Science* 289: 591–594.

Davidson, S., Zhang, X., Khasabov, S. G., Simone D. A., and Giesler, G. J., Jr. (2009). Relief of itch by scratching: State-dependent inhibition of primate spinothalamic tract neurons. *Nat Neurosci* 12: 544–546.

Davidson, T. L., and Swithers, S. E. (2004). A Pavlovian approach to the problem of obesity. *Int J Obes Relat Metab Disord* 28: 933–935.

Davis, C. M. (1928). Self selection of diet by newly weaned infants: An experimental study. *Am J Dis Child* 36: 651–679.

Davis, M. and Whalen, P. J. (2001). The amygdala: Vigilance and emotion. *Mol Psychiatry* 6: 13–34.

DeCasper, A. J., and Fifer, W. P. (1980). Of human bonding: Newborns prefer their mother's voices. *Science* 208: 1174–1176.

DeCasper, A. J., and Spence, M. J. (1986). Prenatal maternal speech influences newborns' perception of speech sounds. *Infant Behav Dev* 9: 133–150.

De Gelder, B., Teunisse, J. P., and Benson, P. J. (1997). Categorical perception of facial expressions: Categories and their internal structure. *Cogn Emot* 11: 1–23.

Descartes, R. (1664). *Le Monde.* Paris: Jacques Le Gras.

DeSimone, J. A., Phan, T.-H. T., Heck, G. L., Ren, Z., Coleman, J., Mummalaneni, S., Melone, P., and Lyall, V. (2011). Involvement of NADPH-dependent and cAMP-PKA sensitive H$^+$ channels in the chorda tympani nerve responses to strong acids. *Chem Senses* 36: 389–403.

De Valois, R. L., Abramov, I., and Jacobs, G. H. (1966). Analysis of response patterns of LGN cells. *J Opt Soc Am A* 56: 966–977.

De Valois, R. L., Albrecht, D. G., and Thorell, L. G. (1982). Spatial frequency selectivity of cells in macaque visual cortex. *Vision Res* 22: 545–559.

De Valois, R. L., Yund, E. W., and Hepler, N. (1982). The orientation and direction se-

lectivity of cells in macaque visual cortex. *Vision Res* 22: 531–544.

DeWitt, L. A., and Samuel, A. G. (1990). The role of knowledge-based expectations in music perception: Evidence from musical restoration. *J Exp Psychol Gen* 119: 123–144.

Diamond, J., Dalton, P., Doolittle, N., and Breslin, P. A. (2005). Gender-specific olfactory sensitization: Hormonal and cognitive influences. *Chem Senses* Supp.1: i224–i225.

DiCarlo, J. J., and Maunsell, J. H. (2003). Anterior inferotemporal neurons of monkeys engaged in object recognition can be highly sensitive to object retinal position. *J Neurophysiol* 89: 3264–3278.

Dieterich, M., and Brandt, T. (2008). Functional brain imaging of peripheral and central vestibular disorders. *Brain* 131(Pt.10): 2538–2552.

Dijkerman, C., and de Haan, E. (2007). Somatosensory processes subserving perception and action. *Behav Brain Sci* 30: 189–239.

Dilks, D. D., Dalton, P., and Beauchamp, G. K. (1999). Cross-cultural variation in responses to malodors. *Chem Senses* 24: 599.

Di Lollo, V., Enns, J. T., and Rensink, R. A. (2000). Competition for consciousness among visual events: The psychophysics of reentrant visual pathways. *J Exp Psychol Gen* 129: 481–507.

Di Lollo, V., Kawahara, J., Shahab Ghorashi, S. M., and Enns, J. T. (2005). The attentional blink: Resource depletion or temporary loss of control? *Psychol Res* 69: 191–200.

DiLorenzo, P. M., and Monroe, S. (1995). Corticofugal influence on taste responses in the nucleus of the solitary tract in the rat. *J Neurophysiol* 74: 258–272.

Dittman, A., and Quinn, T. (1996). Homing in Pacific salmon: Mechanisms and ecological basis. *J Exp Biol* 199(Pt.1): 83–91.

Djordjevic, J., Zatorre, R. J., Petrides, M., Boyle, J. A., and Jones-Gotman, M. (2005). Functional neuroimaging of odor imagery. *Neuroimage* 24: 791–801.

Dobb, E. (1989). The scents around us. *Sciences* 29(6): 46–53.

Dorr, S., and Neumeyer, C. (1996). The goldfish—A colour-constant animal. *Perception* 25: 243–250.

Doty, R. L. (2010). *The Great Pheromone Myth.* Baltimore: Johns Hopkins University Press.

Downing, P., Liu, J., and Kanwisher, N. (2001). Testing cognitive models of visual attention with fMRI and MEG. *Neuropsychologia* 39: 1329–1342.

Driver, J. (1998). The neuropsychology of spatial attention. In H. Pashler (Ed.), *Attention* (pp. 297–340). Hove, East Sussex, UK: Psychology Press.

Dubin, M. W., and Cleland, B. G. (1977). Organization of visual inputs to interneu-

rons of lateral geniculate nucleus of the cat. *J Neurophysiol* 40: 410–427.

Duffy, V. B., Bartoshuk, L. M., Striegel-Moore, R., and Rodin, J. (1998). Taste changes across pregnancy. In C. Murphy (Ed.), *Olfaction and Taste XIX: An International Symposium* (Vol. 855, pp. 805–809). New York: Annals of the New York Academy of Sciences.

Duffy, V. B., Davidson, A. C., Kidd, J. R., Kidd, K. K., Speed, W. C., Pakstis, A. J., Reed, D. R., Snyder, D. J., and Bartoshuk, L. M. (2004). Bitter receptor gene (TAS2R38), 6-*n*-propylthiouracil (PROP) bitterness and alcohol intake. *Alcohol Clin Exp Res* 28: 1629–1637.

Duffy, V. B., Lucchina, L. A., and Bartoshuk, L. M. (2004). Genetic variation in taste: Potential biomarker for cardiovascular disease risk? In J. Prescott and B. J. Tepper (Eds.), *Genetic Variations in Taste Sensitivity: Measurement, Significance and Implications* (pp. 195–228). New York: Dekker.

Durgin, F. H., Proffitt, D. R., Olson, T. J., and Reinke, K. S. (1995). Comparing depth from motion with depth from binocular disparity. *J Exp Psychol Hum Percept Perform* 21: 679–699.

Ehinger, K. A., Hidalgo-Sotelo, B., Torralba, A., and Oliva, A. (2009). Modelling search for people in 900 scenes: A combined source model of eye guidance. *Vis Cogn* 17: 945–978.

Ehrsson, H. H. (2007). The experimental induction of out-of-body experiences. *Science* 317: 1048.

Eich, E. (1995). Mood as a mediator of place dependent memory. *J Exp Psychol* 124: 293–308.

Eippert, F., Finsterbusch, J., Bingel, U., and Büchel, C. (2009). Direct evidence for spinal cord involvement in placebo analgesia. *Science* 326: 404.

Engen, T. (1972). The effect of expectation on judgments of odor. *Acta Psychol* 36: 450–458.

Engen, T. (1982). *The Perception of Odors.* Toronto: Academic Press.

Engen, T. (1991). *Odor Sensation and Memory.* New York: Praeger.

Engen, T., Kuisma, J. E., and Eimas, P. D. (1973). Short-term memory of odors. *J Exp Psychol* 99: 222–225.

Engen, T., and Ross, B. M. (1973). Long-term memory odours with and without verbal descriptions. *J Exp Psychol* 100: 221–227.

Enns, J. T., and Rensink, R. A. (1990). Scene based properties influence visual search. *Science* 247: 721–723.

Enroth-Cugell, C., and Robson, J. G. (1984). Functional characteristics and diversity of cat retinal ganglion cells: Basic characteristics and quantitative description. *Invest Ophthalmol Vis Sci* 25: 250–267.

Epshtein, B., Lifshitz, I., and Ullman, S. (2008). Image interpretation by a single bottom-up top-down cycle. *Proc Natl Acad Sci USA* 105: 14298–14303.

Epstein, R., Harris, A., Stanley, D., and Kanwisher, N. (1999). The parahippocampal place area: Recognition, navigation, or encoding? *Neuron* 23: 115–125.

Epstein, R., and Kanwisher, N. (1998). A cortical representation of the local visual environment. *Nature* 392: 598–601.

Eriksen, C. W., and Yeh, Y. Y. (1985). Allocation of attention in the visual field. *J Exp Psychol Hum Percept Perform* 11: 583–597.

Ernst, M. O., and Banks, M. S. (2002). Humans integrate visual and haptic information in a statistically optimal fashion. *Nature* 415: 429–433.

Eskew, R. T., Jr. (2008). Chromatic detection and discrimination. In R. H. Masland and T. D. Albright (Eds.), *The Senses: A Comprehensive Reference*, Vol. 2: *Vision II* (pp. 101–117). New York: Academic Press.

Evers, S., and Suhr, B. (2000). Changes of the neurotransmitter serotonin but not of hormones during short time music perception. *Eur Arch Psychiatry Clin Neurosci* 250: 144–147.

Fahle, M. (1982). Binocular rivalry: Suppression depends on orientation and spatial frequency. *Vision Res* 22: 787–800.

Farah, M. (1992). Is an object an object an object? Cognitive and neuropsychological investigations of domain specificity in visual object recognition. *Curr Dir Psychol Sci* 1: 165–169.

Fast, K. (2004). *Developing a Scale to Measure Just About Anything: Comparisons across Groups and Individuals*. New Haven, CT: Yale University School of Medicine.

Fedderson, W. E., Sandel, T. T., Teas, D. C., and Jeffress, L. A. (1957). Localization of high frequency tones. *J Acoust Soc Am* 29: 988–991.

Federer, F., Ichida, J. M., Jeffs, J., Schiessl, I., McLoughlin, N., and Angelucci, A. (2009). Four projection streams from primate V1 to the cytochrome oxidase stripes of V2. *J Neurosci* 29: 15455–15471.

Felleman, D. J., and Van Essen, D. C. (1991). Distributed hierarchical processing in the primate cerebral cortex. *Cereb Cortex* 1: 1–47.

Fernandez, C., and Goldberg, J. (1971). Physiology of peripheral neurons innervating semicircular canals of the squirrel monkey. II. Response to sinusoidal stimulation and dynamics of peripheral vestibular system. *J Neurophysiol* 34: 661–675.

Fettiplace, R., and Hackney, C. M. (2006). The sensory and motor roles of auditory hair cells. *Nature* 7: 19–29.

Field, D. J., Hayes, A., and Hess, R. F. (1992). Contour integration by the human visual system: Evidence for a local "association field." *Vision Res* 33: 173–193.

Field, T. M., Schanberg, S. M., Scafidi, F., Bauer, C. R., Vega-Lahr, N., Garcia, R., Nystrom, J., and Kuhn, C. M. (1986).

Tactile/kinesthetic stimulation effects on preterm neonates. *Pediatrics* 77: 654–658.

Firestein, S. (2001). How the olfactory system makes sense of scents. *Nature* 413: 211–218.

Fischer, R., and Griffin, F. (1964). Pharmacogenetic aspects of gustation. *Drug Res* 14: 673–686.

Fisher, S. K., and Ciuffreda, K. J. (1988). Accommodation and apparent distance. *Perception* 17: 609–621.

Flegal, K. M., Carroll, M. D., Ogden, C. L., and Johnson, C. L. (2002). Prevalence and trends in obesity among U.S. adults, 1999–2000. *JAMA* 14: 1723–1727.

Flege, J. E., Bohn, O. S., and Jang, S. (1997). Effects of experience on non-native speakers' production and perception of English vowels. *J Phon* 25: 437–470.

Fletcher, H. (1940). Auditory patterns. *Rev Mod Phys* 12: 47–65.

Fletcher, H., and Galt, R. H. (1950). The perception of speech and its relation to telephony. *J Acoust Soc Am* 22: 89–151.

Foster, D. H. (2011). Color constancy. *Vision Res* 51: 674–700.

Fox, A. L. (1931). Six in ten "tasteblind" to bitter chemical. *Sci News Lett* 9: 249.

Fox, R., and Blake, R. R. (1971). Stereoscopic vision in the cat. *Nature* 233: 55–56.

Francis, D., Diorio, J., Liu, D., and Meaney, M. J. (1999). Nongenomic transmission across generations of maternal behavior and stress responses in the rat. *Science* 286: 1155–1158.

Francis, S. T., Rolls, E. T., Bowtell, R., McGlone, F., O'Doherty, J. O., Browning, A., Clare, S., and Smith, E. (1999). The representation of pleasant touch in the brain and its relationship with taste and olfactory areas. *Neuroreport* 10: 453–459.

Franco, M. I., Turin, L., Mershin, A., and Skoulakis, E. M. C. (2011). Molecular vibration sensing component in *Drosophila melanogaster* olfaction. *Proc Natl Acad Sci USA* 108: 3797–3802.

Frank, M. (1973). An analysis of hamster afferent taste nerve response function. *J. Gen. Physiol.* 61: 588–618.

Freedman, D. J., Riesenhuber, M., Poggio, T., and Miller, E. K. (2001). Categorical perception of visual stimuli in the primate prefrontal cortex. *Science* 291: 312–316.

Freire, A., Lewis, T. L., Maurer, D., and Blake, R. (2006). The development of sensitivity to biological motion in noise. *Perception* 35: 647–657.

Friedman-Hill, S. R., Robertson, L. C., and Treisman, A. (1995). Parietal contributions to visual feature binding: Evidence from a patient with bilateral lesions. *Science* 269: 853–855.

Frisby, J. P. (1980). *Seeing: Illusion, Brain and Mind*. Oxford, UK: Oxford University Press.

Galanter, E. (1962). Direct measurement of utility and subjective probability. *Am J Psychol* 75: 208–220.

Gallace, A., Tan, H. Z., and Spence, C. (2007). Do "mudsplashes" induce tactile change blindness? *Percept Psychophys* 69: 477–486.

Gallant, J. L., Braun, B., and Van Essen, D. C. (1993). Selectivity for polar, hyperbolic, and cartesian gratings in macaque visual cortex. *Science* 259: 100–103.

Gandhi, S. P., Heeger, D. J., and Boynton, G. M. (1998). Spatial attention affects brain activity in human primary visual cortex. *Proc Natl Acad Sci USA* 96: 3314–3319.

Gangrade, A. (2011). The effect of music on the production of neurotransmitters, hormones, cytokines, and peptides: A review. *Music Med* 3(3) [Published online before print]. doi: 10.1177/1943862111415117.

Gauthier, I., Behrmann, M., and Tarr, M. J. (1999). Can face recognition really be dissociated from object recognition? *J Cogn Neurosci* 11: 349–370.

Gauthier, I., Williams, P., Tarr, M. J., and Tanaka, J. (1998). Training "greeble" experts: A framework for studying expert object recognition processes. *Vision Res* 38: 2401–2428.

Gegenfurtner, K. R. (2003). Cortical mechanisms of colour vision. *Nat Rev Neurosci* 4: 563–572.

Geisler, C. D. (1998). *From Sound to Synapse: Physiology of the Mammalian Ear*. New York: Oxford University Press.

Geisler, W. S. (1989). Sequential ideal-observer analysis of visual discriminations. *Psychol Rev* 96: 267–314.

Geisler, W. S., and Perry, J. S. (2009). Contour statistics in natural images: Grouping across occlusions. *Vis Neurosci* 26: 109–121.

Geldard, F. A. (1972). *The Human Senses* (2nd ed.). New York: Wiley.

Gelstein, S., Yeshurun, Y., Rozenkrantz, L., Shushan, S., Frumin, I., Roth, Y., and Sobel, N. (2011). Human tears contain chemosignal. *Science* 331: 226–230.

Gescheider, G. A. (1974). *Temporal Relations in Cutaneous Stimulation* (Conference on Cutaneous Communication Systems and Devices). Oxford, UK: Psychonomic Society.

Getty, D. J., D'Orsi, C., and Pickett, R. M. (2008). Stereoscopic digital mammography: Improved accuracy of lesion detection in breast cancer screening. In E. A. Krupinski (Ed.), *Digital Mammography: 9th International Workshop, IWDM 2008 Tucson, AZ, USA, July 20–23, 2008 Proceedings* (Lecture Notes in Computer Science, no. 5116) (pp. 74–79). Berlin: Springer.

Gibson, J. J. (1957). Optical motions and transformations as stimuli for visual perception. *Psychol Rev* 64: 288–295.

Gilad, Y., Wiebe, V., Przeworski, M., Lancet, D., and Paabo, S. (2004). Loss of olfactory receptors genes coincides with the acquisition of full trichromatic vision in primates. *PLoS Biol* 2: 120–125.

Gillam, B. (1980). Geometrical illusions. *Sci Am* 242(1): 102–111.

Goldberg, J. (2008). The quivering bundles that let us hear: The goal: Extreme sensitivity and speed. *Seeing, Hearing, and Smelling the World: A Report from the Howard Hughes Medical Institute*, http://www.hhmi.org/senses/c120.html.

Goldberg, J. M., and Fernandez, C. (1971). Physiology of peripheral neurons innervating semicircular canals of the squirrel monkey, Parts 1, 2, 3. *J Neurophysiol* 34: 635–684.

Goldberg, J. M., and Fernandez, C. (1976). Physiology of peripheral neurons innervating otolith organs of the squirrel monkey, Parts 1, 2, 3. *J Neurophysiol* 39: 970–1008.

Govardovskii, V. I. (1983). On the role of oil drops in colour vision. *Vision Res* 23: 1739–1740.

Goycoolea, M. V., Goycoolea, H. G., Farfan, C. R., Rodriguez, L. G., Martinez, G. C., and Vidal, R. (1986). Effect of life in industrialized societies on hearing in natives of Easter Island. *Laryngoscope* 96: 1391–1396.

Grabherr, L., Nicoucar, K., Mast, F. W., and Merfeld, D. M. (2008). Direction detection thresholds for yaw rotation about an earth-vertical axis as a function of frequency. *Exp Brain Res* 186: 677–681.

Gracheva, E. O., Cordero-Morales, J. F., González-Carcacía, J. A., Ingolia, N. T., Manno, C., Aranguren, C. I., Weissman, J. S., and Julius, D. (2011). Ganglion-specific splicing of TRPV1 underlies infrared sensation in vampire bats. *Nature* 476: 88–91.

Graham, N., and Nachmias, J. (1971). Detection of grating patterns containing two spatial frequencies: A comparison of single-channel and multiple-channel models. *Vision Res* 11: 251–259.

Green, B. G. (1993). Evidence that removal of capsaicin accelerates desensitization on the tongue. *Neurosci Lett* 150: 44–48.

Green, C. S., and Bavelier, D. (2003). Action video game modifies visual attention. *Nature* 423: 534–537.

Green, D. M., and Swets, J. (1966). *Signal Detection Theory and Psychophysics*. New York: Wiley.

Greene, M. R., and Oliva, A. (2009). The briefest of glances: The time course of natural scene understanding. *Psychol Sci* 20: 464–472.

Gregory, R. L. (1966). *Eye and Brain*. New York: World University Library.

Gregory, R. L. (1970). *The Intelligent Eye*. London: Weidenfeld and Nicolson.

Griff, I. C., and Reed, R. R. (1995). The generic basis for specific anosmia to isovaleric acid in the mouse. *Cell* 83: 407–414.

Grill-Spector, K., and Malach, R. (2004). The human visual cortex. *Annu Rev Neurosci* 27: 649–677.

Gross, C. G., Rocha-Miranda, C. E., and Bender, D. B. (1972). Visual properties of neurons in inferotemporal cortex of the macaque. *J Neurophysiol* 35: 96–111.

Grushka, M., and Bartoshuk, L. M. (2000). Burning mouth syndrome and oral dysesthesias. *Can J Diagn* 17: 99–109.

Guedry, F. (1974). Psychophysics of vestibular sensation. In H. H. Kornhuber (Ed.), *Vestibular System* (Handbook of Sensory Physiology, vol. 6) (pp. 1–154). New York: Springer.

Guyton, A. C. (1991). *Textbook of Medical Physiology* (8th ed). Philadelphia: Saunders.

Haenny, P. E., and Schiller, P. H. (1988). State dependent activity in monkey visual cortex. I. Single cell activity in V1 and V4 on visual tasks. *Exp Brain Res* 69: 225–244.

Haggard, P., Newman, C., Blundell, J., and Andrew, H. (2000). The perceived position of the hand in space. *Percept Psychophys* 68: 363–377.

Haller, R., Rummel, C., Henneberg, S., Pollmer, U., and Koster, E. P. (1999). The influence of early experience with vanillin on food preference in later life. *Chem Senses* 24: 465–467.

Han, S. E., Sundarajan, J., Bowling, D. L., Lake, J., and Purves, D. (2011). Co-variation of tonality in the music and speech of different cultures. *PLoS One* 6: e20160–e20160.

Handel, S. (1989). *Listening: An Introduction to the Perception of Auditory Events*. Cambridge, MA: MIT Press.

Handel, S., and Oshinsky, J. S. (1981). The meter of syncopated auditory polyrhythms. *Percept Psychophys* 30: 1–9.

Harkness, L. (1977). Chameleons use accommodation cues to judge distance. *Nature* 267: 346–349.

Hartline, H. K. (1940). The nerve messages in the fibers of the visual pathway. *J Opt Soc Am* 30: 239–247.

Hayes, J. E., Bartoshuk, L. M., Kidd, J. R., and Duffy, V. B. (2008). Supertasting and PROP bitterness depends on more than the *Tas2r38* gene. *Chem Senses* 33: 255–265.

Hayward, W. G., and Williams, P. (2000). Viewpoint dependence and object discriminability. *Psychol Sci* 11: 7–12.

Heider, E. R. (1972). Universals in color naming and memory. *J Exp Psychol* 93: 10–20.

Heise, G. A., and Miller, G. A. (1951). An experimental study of auditory patterns. *Am J Psychol* 64: 68–77.

Held, R. T., and Hui, T. T. (2011). A guide to stereoscopic 3D displays in medicine. *Acad Radiol* 18: 1035–1048.

Helmholtz, H. von. (1924). *Helmholtz's Treatise on Physiological Optics* (translated from the 3rd German ed.; edited by J. P. C.

Southall). Rochester, NY: Optical Society of America.

Hendry, S. H., and Reid, R. C. (2000). The koniocellular pathway in primate vision. *Annu Rev Neurosci* 23: 127–153.

Hering, E. (1878). *Zur Lehre vom Lichtsinn*. Vienna: Gerold.

Herness, S., Zhao, F.-L., Kaya, N., Shen, T., Lu, S.-G., and Cao, Y. (2005). Communication routes within the taste bud by neurotransmitters and neuropeptides. *Chem Senses* 30(Suppl.1): i37–i38.

Herz, R. S. (1997). Emotion experienced during encoding enhances odor retrieval cue effectiveness. *Am J Psychol* 110: 489–505.

Herz, R. S. (1998). Are odors the best cues to memory? A cross-modal comparison of associative memory stimuli. *Ann NY Acad Sci* 855: 670–674.

Herz, R. S. (2000). Scents of time. *Sciences* 40(4): 34–39.

Herz, R. S. (2001). Ah, sweet skunk: Why we like or dislike what we smell. *Cerebrum* 3(4): 31–47.

Herz, R. S. (2004). A comparison of autobiographical memories triggered by olfactory, visual and auditory stimuli. *Chem Senses* 29: 217–224.

Herz, R. (2007). *The Scent of Desire: Discovering Our Enigmatic Sense of Smell*. New York: Morrow.

Herz, R. S. (2009). Aromatherapy facts and fictions: A scientific analysis of olfactory effects on mood, physiology and behavior. *Int J Neurosci* 119: 263–290.

Herz, R. S., Beland, S. L., and Hellerstein, M. (2004). Changing odor hedonic perception through emotional associations in humans. *Int J Comp Psychol* 17: 315–339.

Herz, R. S., and Cupchik, G. C. (1992). An experimental characterization of odor-evoked memories in humans. *Chem Senses* 17: 519–528.

Herz, R. S., and Cupchik, G. C. (1995). The emotional distinctiveness of odor-evoked memories. *Chem Senses* 20: 517–528.

Herz, R. S., Eliassen, J. C., Beland, S. L., and T. Souza. (2004). Neuroimaging evidence for the emotional potency of odor-evoked memory. *Neuropsychologia* 42: 371–378.

Hillis, J., Watt, S., Landy, M., and Banks, M. (2004). Slant from texture and disparity cues: Optimal cue combination. *J Vis* 4: 967–992.

Hoffman, D. D., and Richards, W. A. (1984). Parts of recognition. *Cognition* 18: 65–96.

Hofman, P. M., Van Riswick, J. G. A., and Van Opsal, A. J. (1998). Relearning sound localization with new ears. *Nat Neurosci* 1: 417–421.

Hohmann A., and Creutzfeldt, O. D. (1975). Squint and the development of binocularity in humans. *Nature* 254: 613–614.

Hollins, M. (2002). Touch and haptics. In H. Pashler and S. Yantis (Eds.), *Stevens Handbook of Experimental Psychology* (3rd ed.), Vol. 1: *Sensation and Perception* (pp. 585–618). New York: Wiley.

Hollins, M., Bensmaïa, S., and Washburn, S. (2001). Vibrotactile adaptation impairs discrimination of fine, but not coarse, textures. *Somatosens Mot Res* 18: 253–262.

Horii, A., Russell, N. A., Smith, P. F., Darlington, C. L., and Bilkey, D. K. (2004). Vestibular influences on CA1 neurons in the rat hippocampus: An electrophysiological study in vivo. *Exp Brain Res* 155: 245–250.

Horton, J. C., and Hocking, D. R. (1996). An adult-like pattern of ocular dominance columns in striate cortex of newborn monkeys prior to visual experience. *J Neurosci* 16: 1791–1807.

Horton, J. C., and Hoyt, W. F. (1991). The representation of the visual field in human striate cortex. A revision of the classic Holmes map. *Arch Ophthalmol* 109: 816–824.

Horton, J. C., and Trobe, J. D. (1999). Akinetopsia from nefazodone toxicity. *Am J Ophthalmol* 128: 530–531.

Howard, I. P., and Rogers, B. J. (1995). *Binocular Vision and Stereopsis.* New York: Oxford University Press.

Howard, I. P., and Rogers, B. J. (2001). *Seeing in Depth.* Toronto: Porteous.

Howard, J. D., Plailly, J., Grueschow, M., Hayens, J.-D., and Gottfried, J. A. (2009). Odor quality coding and categorization in human posterior piriform cortex. *Nat Neurosci* 12: 932–938.

Hubel, D. H. (1982). Exploration of the primary visual cortex, 1955–78. *Nature* 299: 515–524.

Hubel, D. H. (1988). *Eye, Brain, and Vision.* New York: Scientific American Library.

Hubel, D. H., and Wiesel, T. N. (1962). Receptive fields, binocular interaction and functional architecture in the cat's visual cortex. *J Physiol* 160: 106–154.

Hubel, D. H., and Wiesel, T. N. (1973). A re-examination of stereoscopic mechanisms in area 17 of the cat. *J Physiol* 232: 29P–30P.

Hubel, D. H., Wiesel, T. N., and Stryker, M. P. (1978). Anatomical demonstration of orientation columns in macaque monkey. *J Comp Neurol* 177: 361–380.

Hudspeth, A. J. (1997). How hearing happens. *Neuron* 19: 947–950.

Hughes, A. (1977). The topography of vision in mammals of contrasting life styles: Comparative optics and retinal organization. In F. Crescitelli (Ed.), *Handbook of Sensory Physiology,* Vol. VII/5: *The Visual System in Vertebrates* (pp. 613–756). New York: Springer.

Huk, A. C., Ress, D., and Heeger, D. J. (2001). Neuronal basis of the motion aftereffect reconsidered. *Neuron* 32: 161–172.

Hummel, T., Kobel, G., Gudziol, H., and Mackay-Sim, A. (2007). Normative data for the "Sniffin' Sticks" including tests of odor identification, odor discrimination, and olfactory thresholds: An upgrade based on a group of more than 3,000 subjects. *Eur Arch Otorhinolaryngol* 264: 237–243.

Hummel, T., von Mering, R., Huch, R., and Kolble, N. (2002). Olfactory modulation of nausea during early pregnancy? *BJOG* 109: 1394–1397.

Hurvich, L., and Jameson, D. (1957). An opponent process theory of color vision. *Psychol Rev* 64: 384–404.

Huterer, M., and Cullen, K. E. (2002). Vestibuloocular reflex dynamics during high-frequency and high-acceleration rotations of the head on body in rhesus monkey. *J Neurophysiol* 88: 13–28.

Imai, S., Flege, J., and Wayland, R. (2002). Perception of cross-language vowel differences: A longitudinal study of native Spanish learners of English. *J Acoust Soc Am* 111: 2364–2364.

Ingle, D. J. (1985). The goldfish as a retinex animal. *Science* 227: 651–654.

Intraub, H. (1981). Rapid conceptual identification of sequentially presented pictures. *J Exp Psychol Hum Learn Mem* 7: 604–610.

Iriki, A., Tanaka, M., and Iwamura, Y. (1996). Coding of modified body schema during tool use by macaque postcentral neurons. *Neuroreport* 7: 2325–2330.

Irwin, D. E., Zacks, J. L., and Brown, J. S. (1990). Visual memory and the perception of a stable visual environment. *Percept Psychophys* 47: 35–46.

Jacob, S., Hayreh, D. J. S, and McClintock, M. (2001). Context-dependent effects of steroid chemosignals on human physiology and mood. *Physiol Behav* 74: 15–27.

James, W. (1890). *The Principles of Psychology* (2 vols.). New York: Holt.

Jeon, T.-I., Zhu, B., Larson, J. L., and Osborne, T. F. (2008). SREBP-2 regulates gut peptide secretion through intestinal bitter taste receptor signaling in mice. *J Clin Invest* 118: 3693–3700.

Johansson, G. (1975). Visual motion perception. *Sci Am* 232(6): 76–88.

Johansson, R. S., and Vallbo, A. B. (1983). Tactile sensory coding in the glabrous skin of the human hand. *Trends Neurosci* 6: 27–32.

Johnson, E. N., Hawken, M. J., and Shapley, R. (2001). The spatial transformation of color in the primary visual cortex of the macaque monkey. *Nat Neurosci* 4: 409–416.

Johnson, K. O. (2002). Neural basis of haptic perception. In H. Pashler and S. Yantis (Eds.), *Stevens Handbook of Experimental Psychology* (3rd ed.), Vol. 1: *Sensation and Perception* (pp. 537–583). New York: Wiley.

Jolicoeur, P., Gluck, M. A., and Kosslyn, S. M. (1984). Pictures and names: Making the connection. *Cogn Psychol* 16: 243–275.

Jones, H. G., Koka, K., Thornton, J. L., and Tollin, D. J. (2011). Concurrent development of the head and pinnae and the acoustic cues to sound location in a precocious species, the chinchilla (*Chincilla lanigera*). *J Assoc Res Otolaryngol* 12: 127–140.

Jones, L. A. (1999). Somatic senses 3: Proprioception. In H. Cohen (Ed.), *Neuroscience for Rehabilitation* (2nd ed.), pp. 111–130. Philadelphia: Lippincott.

Jones, M., and Love, B. C. (2011). Bayesian Fundamentalism or Enlightenment? On the explanatory status and theoretical contributions of Bayesian models of cognition. *Behav Brain Sci* 34: 169–188.

Jones, R. K., and Lee, D. N. (1981). Why two eyes are better than one: The two views of binocular vision. *J Exp Psychol Hum Percept Perform* 7: 30–40.

Julesz, B. (1964). Binocular depth perception without familiarity cues. *Science* 45: 356–362.

Julesz, B. (1971). *Foundations of Cyclopean Perception.* Chicago: University of Chicago Press.

Kadohisa, M., and Wilson, D. A. (2006). Olfactory cortical adaptation facilitates detection of odors against background. *J Neurophysiol* 95: 1888–1896.

Kanwisher, N. (1987). Repetition blindness: Type recognition without token individuation. *Cognition* 27: 117–143.

Kanwisher, N. (2010). Functional specificity in the human brain: A window into the functional architecture of the mind. *Proc Natl Acad Sci USA* 107: 11163–11170.

Kanwisher, N., McDermott, J., and Chun, M. M. (1997). The fusiform face area: A module in human extrastriate cortex specialized for face perception. *J Neurosci* 17: 4302–4311.

Kapfer, C., Seidl, A. H., Schweizer, H., and Grothe, B. (2002). Experience-dependent refinement of inhibitory inputs to auditory coincidence-detector neurons. *Nat Neurosci* 5: 247–253.

Kappers, S. (2007). Haptic space perception. *Can J Exp Psychol* 61: 208–218.

Keller, A., and Vosshall, L. B. (2004). A psychophysical test of the vibration theory of olfaction. *Nat Neurosci* 7: 337–338.

Keller, A., Zhuang, H., Chi, Q., Vosshall, L. B., and Matsunami, H. (2007). Genetic variation in a human odorant receptor alters odour perception. *Nature* 449: 468–472.

Kellman, P. J. (1998). An update on gestalt psychology. In *Perception, Cognition, and Language: Essays in Honor of Henry and Lila Gleitman* (pp. 157–190). Cambridge, MA: MIT Press.

Kellman, P. J., and Shipley, T. F. (1991). A theory of visual interpolation in object perception. *Cogn Psychol* 23: 141–221.

Kepecs, A., Uchida, N., and Mainen, Z. F. (2007). Rapid and precise control of sniffing during olfactory discrimination in rats. *J Neurophysiol* 98: 205–213.

Kern, R. C., Conley, D. B., Haines, G. K., and Robinson, A. M. (2004). Pathology of the olfactory mucosa: Implications for the treatment of olfactory dysfunction. *Laryngoscope* 114: 279–285.

Kessel, R. G., and Kardon, R. H. (1979). *Tissues and Organs: A Text-Atlas of Scanning Electron Microscopy.* San Francisco: Freeman.

Khan, R. M., Luk, C. H., Flinker, A., Aggarwal, A., Lapid, H., Haddad, R., and Sobel, N. (2007). Predicting odor pleasantness from odorant structure: Pleasantness as a reflection of the physical world. *J Neurosci* 27: 1–9.

Kiefte, M., and Kluender, K. R. (2005). The relative importance of spectral tilt in monopthongs and diphthongs. *J Acoust Soc Am* 117: 1395–1404.

Kiefte, M., and Kluender, K. R. (2008). Absorption of reliable spectral characteristics in auditory perception. *J Acoust Soc Am* 123: 366–376.

Kim, U. K., Jorgenson, E., Coon, H., Leppert, M., Risch, N., and Drayna, D. (2003). Positional cloning of the human quantitative trait locus underlying taste sensitivity to phenylthiocarbamide. *Science* 299: 1221–1225.

Kirchner, H., and Thorpe, S. J. (2006). Ultra-rapid object detection with saccadic eye movements: Visual processing speed revisited. *Vision Res* 46: 1762–1776.

Kistler, D. J., and Wightman, F. L. (1992). The dominant role of low-frequency interaural time differences in sound localization. *J Acoust Soc Am* 91: 1648–1661.

Klatzky, R. L., Lederman, S. J., and Metzger, V. (1985). Identifying objects by touch: An "expert system." *Percept Psychophys* 37: 299–302.

Kluender, K. R., and Alexander, J. M. (2008). Perception of speech sounds. In A. I. Basbaum, A. Kaneko, G. M. Shepard, and G. Westheimer (Eds.), *The Senses: A Comprehensive Reference*, Vol. 3: *Audition* (P. Dallos and D. Oertel, Eds.) (pp. 829–860). San Diego: Academic Press.

Kluender, K. R., Diehl, R. L., and Killeen, P. R. (1987). Japanese quail can learn phonetic categories. *Science* 237: 1195–1197.

Kluender, K. R., and Jenison, R. L. (1992). Effects of glide slope, noise intensity, and noise duration on the extrapolation of FM glides through noise. *Percept Psychophys* 51: 231–238.

Kluender, K. R., Lotto, A. J., and Holt, L. L. (2005). Contributions of nonhuman animal models to understanding human speech perception. In S. Greenberg and W. Ainsworth (Eds.), *Listening to Speech: An Auditory Perspective* (pp. 203–220). Mahwah, NJ: Erlbaum.

Kluender, K. R., Lotto, A. J., Holt, L. L., and Bloedel, S. L. (1998). Role of experience for language-specific functional mapping of vowel sounds. *J Acoust Soc Am* 104: 3596–3582.

Klumpp, R. G., and Eady, H. R. (1956). Some measurements of interaural time-difference thresholds. *J Acoust Soc Am* 28: 859–860.

Klüver, H., and Bucy, P. C. (1938). An analysis of certain effects of bilateral temporal lobectomy in the rhesus monkey, with special reference to "psychic blindness." *J Psychol* 5: 33–54.

Klüver, H., and Bucy, P. C. (1939). Preliminary analysis of functions of the temporal lobes in monkeys. *Arch Neurol Psychiatry* 42: 979–1000.

Ko, H. K., Poletti, M., and Rucci, M. (2010). Microsaccades precisely relocate gaze in a high visual acuity task. *Nat Neurosci* 13: 1549–1553.

Koenigsberger, L. (1906/1965). *Hermann von Helmholtz* (translated by F. A. Welby). Repr. New York: Dover.

Konen, C. S., and Kastner, S. (2008). Two hierarchically organized neural systems for object information in human visual cortex. *Nat Neurosci* 11: 224–231.

Kosslyn, S. M., Thompson, W. L., Kim, I. J., and Alpert, A. M. (1995). Topographic representations of mental images in primary visual cortex. *Nature* 378: 496–498.

Kourtzi, Z., and Connor, C. E. (2011). Neural representations for object perception: Structure, category, and adaptive coding. *Annu Rev Neurosci* 34: 45–67.

Kovacs, I., and Julesz, B. (1993). A closed curve is much more than an incomplete one: Effect of closure in figure-ground segmentation. *Proc Natl Acad Sci USA* 90: 7495–7497.

Kovacs, I., Papathomas, T., Yang, M., and Feher, A. (1996). When the brain changes its mind: Interocular grouping during binocular rivalry. *Proc Natl Acad Sci USA* 93: 15508–15511.

Kowler, E., and Collewijn, H. (2010). The eye on the needle. *Nat Neurosci* 13: 1443–1444.

Krauskopf, J., Williams, D. R., and Heeley, D. W. (1982). Cardinal directions of color space. *Vision Res* 22: 1123–1131.

Krestel, D., Passe, D., Smith, J. C., and Jonsson, L. (1984). Behavioral determinants of olfactory thresholds to amyl acetate in dogs. *Neurosci Biobehav Rev* 8: 169–174.

Kubovy, M., and Cohen, D. J. (2001). What boundaries tell us about binding. *Trends Cogn Sci* 5: 93–95.

Kuffler, S. W. (1953). Discharge patterns and functional organization of mammalian retina. *J Neurophysiol* 16: 37–68.

Kuhl, P. K. (1981). Discrimination of speech by nonhuman animals: Basic sensitivities conducive to the perception of speech sound categories. *J Acoust Soc Am* 70: 340–349.

Kuhl, P. K., and Miller, J. D. (1978). Speech perception by the chinchilla: Identification functions for synthetic VOT stimuli. *J Acoust Soc Am* 63: 905–917.

Kuhl, P. K., Williams, K. A., Lacerda, F., Stevens, K. N., and Lindblom, B. (1992). Linguistic experience alters phonetic perception in infants six months of age. *Science* 255: 606–608.

Kuhn, G., and Kingstone, A. (2009). Look away! Eyes and arrows engage oculomotor responses automatically. *Atten Percept Psychophys* 71: 314–327.

Kumagami, T., Zhang, B., Smith, E. L., III, and Chino, Y. M. (2000). Effect of onset age of strabismus on the binocular responses of neurons in the monkey visual cortex. *Invest Ophthalmol Vis Sci* 41: 948–954.

Kurz, J. (2008, December 26). Getting to the root of the great cilantro divide. *National Public Radio*, http://www.npr.org.

Kwok, R. H. M. (1968). Chinese-restaurant syndrome. *N Engl J Med* 278: 796.

Kwok, V., Niu, Z., Kay, P., Zhou, K., Mo, L., Jin, Z., So, K.-W., and Tan, L. H. (2011). Learning new color names produces rapid increase in gray matter in the intact adult human cortex. *Proc Natl Acad Sci USA* 108: 6686–6688.

Laing, D. G., and Francis, G. W. (1989). The capacity of humans to identify odors in mixtures. *Physiol Behav* 46: 809–814.

Laing, D. G., and Glemarec, A. (1992). Selective attention and the perceptual analysis of odor mixtures. *Physiol Behav* 33: 309–319.

LaMotte, R. H., and Srinivasan, M. A. (1991). Surface microgeometry: Tactile perception and neural encoding. In O. Franzen and J. Westman (Eds.), *Information Processing in the Somatosensory System* (pp. 49–58). London: Macmillan.

Land, E. H., and McCann, J. J. (1971). Lightness and retinex theory. *J Opt Soc Am* 61: 1–11.

Laska, M., Koch, B., Heid, B., and Hudson, R. (1996). Failure to demonstrate systematic changes in olfactory perception in the course of pregnancy: A longitudinal study. *Chem Senses* 21: 567–571.

Lawless, H., and Engen, T. (1977). Associations to odors: Interference, mnemonics, and verbal labelling. *J Exp Psychol* 3: 52–59.

Lecanuet, J. P., Granier-Deferre, C., Cohen, C., Le Houezec, R., and Busnel, M. C. (1986). Fetal responses to acoustic stimulation depend on heart rate variability pattern stimulus intensity and repetition. *Early Hum Dev* 13: 269–283.

Lederman, S. J., and Klatzky, R. L. (1987). Hand movements: A window into haptic object recognition. *Cogn Psychol* 19: 342–368.

Lederman, S. J., and Klatzky, R. L. (1997). Relative availability of surface and object properties during early haptic processing. *J Exp Psychol Hum Percept Perform* 23: 1680–1707.

Lederman, S., Klatzky, R., Chataway, C., and Summers, C. (1990). Visual mediation and the haptic recognition of two-dimensional pictures of common objects. *Percept Psychophys* 47: 54–64.

Lederman, S. J., Thorne, G., and Jones, B. (1986). The perception of texture by vision and touch: Multidimensionality and intersensory integration. *J Exp Psychol Hum Percept Perform* 12: 169–180.

Ledgeway, T. (1994). Adaptation to second-order motion results in a motion aftereffect for directionally-ambiguous test stimuli. *Vision Res* 34: 2879–2889.

Ledgeway, T., and Smith, A. T. (1994). The duration of the motion aftereffect following adaptation to first-order and second-order motion. *Perception* 23: 1211–1219.

Lee, D. N. (1976). A theory of visual control of braking based on information about time-to-collision. *Perception* 5: 437–459.

Lee, S.-H., and Blake, R. (1999). Visual form created solely from temporal structure. *Science* 284: 1165–1168.

Lehman, C. D., Bartoshuk, L. M., Catalanotto, F. C., Kveton, J. F., and Lowlicht, R. A. (1995). The effect of anesthesia of the chorda tympani nerve on taste perception in humans. *Physiol Behav* 57: 943–951.

LeVay, S., Hubel, D. H., and Wiesel, T. N. (1975). The pattern of ocular dominance columns in macaque visual cortex revealed by a reduced silver stain. *J Comp Neurol* 159: 559–576.

Levi, D. M. (2008). Crowding—an essential bottleneck for object recognition: A mini-review. *Vision Res* 48: 635–654.

Levi, D. M., Klein, S. A., and Aitsebaomo, A. P. (1985). Vernier acuity, crowding and cortical magnification. *Vision Res* 25: 963–977.

Levi, D. M., and Li, R. W. (2009). Perceptual learning as a potential treatment for amblyopia: A mini review. *Vision Res* 49: 2535–2549.

Levin, D. T., and Beale, J. M. (2000). Categorical perception occurs in newly learned faces, other-race faces, and inverted faces. *Atten Percept Psychophys* 62: 386–401.

Levine, M. W. (2000). *Levine & Shefner's Fundamentals of Sensation and Perception* (3rd ed.). Oxford, UK: Oxford University Press.

Li, B., Peterson, M. R., and Freeman, R. D. (2003). Oblique effect: A neural basis in the visual cortex. *J Neurophysiol* 90: 204–217.

Li, W., Lopez, L., Osher, J., Howard, J. D., Parrish, T. B., and Gottfried, J. A. (2010). Right orbitofrontal cortex mediates conscious olfactory perception. *Psychol Sci* 21: 1454–1463.

Liberman, A. M., Cooper, F. S., Shankweiler, D. P., and Studdert Kennedy, M. (1967). Perception of the speech code. *Psychol Rev* 74: 431–461.

Liberman, A. M., and Mattingly, I. G. (1985). The motor theory of speech perception revised. *Cognition* 21: 1–36.

Lieberman, P. (1984). *The Biology and Evolution of Language.* Cambridge, MA: Harvard University Press.

Liem, D. G., and Mennella, J. A. (2003). Heightened sour preferences during childhood. *Chem Senses* 28: 173–180.

Lindeman, H. H. (1973). Anatomy of the otolith organs. *Adv Otorhinolaryngol* 20: 404–433.

Lindsey, D. T., and Brown, A. M. (2006). Universality of color names. *Proc Natl Acad Sci USA* 103: 16608–16613.

Linhares, J. M. M., Pinto, P. D., and Nascimento, S. M. C. (2008). The number of discernible colors in natural scenes. *J Opt Soc Am A Opt Image Sci Vis* 25: 2918–2924.

Lisker, L. (1978). Rapid versus rabid: A catalogue of acoustical features that may cue the distinction. *Haskins Lab Status Rep Speech Res* SR 54: 127–132.

Livingstone, M., and Hubel, D. (1988). Segregation of form, color, movement, and depth: Anatomy, physiology, and perception. *Science* 240: 740–749.

Löfvenberg, J., and Johansson, R. S. (1984). Regional differences and interindividual variability in sensitivity to vibration in the glabrous skin of the human hand. *Brain Res* 301: 65–72.

Logothetis, N. K., Pauls, J., and Poggio, T. (1995). Shape representation in the inferior temporal cortex of monkeys. *Curr Biol* 5: 552–563.

Logothetis, N. K., and Schall, J. D. (1989). Neuronal correlates of subjective visual perception. *Science* 245: 761–763.

Loomis, J. M. (1981). On the tangibility of letters and braille. *Percept Psychophys* 29: 37–46.

Loomis, J. M. (1990). A model of character recognition and legibility. *J Exp Psychol Hum Percept Perform* 16: 106–120.

Lorig, T. (1999). On the similarity of odor and language perception. *Neurosci Biobehav Rev* 23: 391–398.

Lowe, D. G. (1985). *Perceptual Organization and Visual Recognition.* Boston: Kluwer.

Lu, Z.-L., and Dosher, B. A. (1998). External noise distinguishes attention mechanisms. *Vision Res* 38: 1183–1198.

Lundstrom, J. N., and Olsson, M. J. (2005). Subthreshold amounts of a social odorant affect mood, but not behavior, in heterosexual women when tested by a male, but not a female experimenter. *Biol Psychol* 60: 197–204.

Lynch, M. P., and Eilers, R. E. (1990). Innateness, experience, and music perception. *Psychol Sci* 1: 272–276.

Mach, E. (1875/2001). *Fundamentals of the Theory of Movement Perception.* New York: Kluwer/Plenum. (Republished with translations in 2001.)

MacLeod, D. I., and Lennie, P. (1976). Red-green blindness confined to one eye. *Vision Res* 16: 691–702.

Macmillan, N. A., and Creelman, C. D. (2005). *Detection Theory.* Mahwah, NJ: Erlbaum.

Maddieson, I. (1984). *Patterns of Sound.* Cambridge, UK: Cambridge University Press.

Maffei, L., and Fiorentini, A. (1973). The visual cortex as a spatial frequency analyzer. *Vision Res* 13: 1255–1267.

Malik, J., and Perona, P. (1990). Preattentive texture discrimination with early vision mechanisms. *J Opt Soc Am A* 7: 923–932.

Maloney, L. T. (1986). Evaluation of linear models of surface spectral reflectance with small numbers of parameters. *J Opt Soc Am A* 3: 1673–1683.

Maquet, P., Peters, J., Aerts, J., Delfiore, G., Degueldre, C., Luxen, A., and Franck, G. (1996). Functional neuroanatomy of human rapid-eye-movement sleep and dreaming. *Nature* 383: 163–166.

Maresh, A., Gil, D. R., Whitman, M. C., and Greer, C. A. (2008). Principles of glomerular organization in the human olfactory bulb—Implications for odor processing. *PLoS ONE* 3: 1–6.

Marks, L. E., Stevens, J. C., Bartoshuk, L. M., Gent, J. G., Rifkin, B., and Stone, V. K. (1988). Magnitude matching: The measurement of taste and smell. *Chem Senses* 13: 63–87.

Marr, D., and Nishihara, H. K. (1977). Representation and recognition of the spatial organization of three-dimensional shapes. *Proc R Soc Lond B Biol Sci* 200: 269–294.

Marr, D., and Poggio, T. (1979). A computational theory of human stereo vision. *Proc R Soc Lond B Biol Sci* 204: 301–328.

Martinez, A., Anllo-Vento, L., Sereno, M. I., Frank, L. R., Buxton, R. B., Dubowitz, D. J., Wong, E. C., Hinrichs, H., Heinze, H. J., and Hillyard, S. A. (1999). Involvement of striate and extrastriate visual cortical areas in spatial attention. *Nat Neurosci* 2: 364–369.

Maruniak, J. A., Silver, W. L., and Moulton, D. G. (1983). Olfactory receptors respond to blood-borne odorants. *Brain Res* 265: 312–316.

Mather, G., and Murdoch, L. (1994). Gender discrimination in biological motion displays based on dynamic cues. *Proc R Soc Lond B Biol Sci* 258: 273–279.

Matin, L., Picoult, E., Stevens, J. K., Edwards, M. W., Jr., Young, D., and MacArthur, R. (1982). Oculoparalytic illusion: Visual-field dependent spatial mislocalizations by humans partially paralyzed with curare. *Science* 216: 198–201.

Matsunami, H. (2011). Recent advances in understanding olfactory molecular biological mechanisms. Paper presented at the AChemS Annual Meeting, St. Petersburg, FL.

Maurer, D., Lewis, T. L., Brent, H. P., and Levin, A. V. (1999). Rapid improvement in the acuity of infants after visual input. *Science* 286: 108–110.

Mays, L. E., and Sparks, D. L. (1980). Dissociation of visual and saccade-related responses in superior colliculus neurons. *J Neurophysiol* 43: 207–232.

McConkie, G. W., and Currie, C. (1996). Visual stability across saccades while viewing complex pictures. *J Exp Psychol Hum Percept Perform* 22: 563–581.

McDermott, J. H., Wroblewski, D., and Oxenham, A. J. (2011). Recovering sound sources from embedded repetition. *Proc Natl Acad Sci USA* 108: 1188–1193.

McGlone, F., Vallbo, A. B., Olausson, H., Loken, L. S., and Wessberg, J. (2007). Discriminative touch and emotional touch. *Can J Exp Psychol* 61: 173–183.

McGowan, P. O., Sasaki, A., D'Alessio, A. C., Dymov, S., Labonté, B., Szy, M., Turecki, G., and Meaney, M. J. (2009). Epigenetic regulation of the glucocorticoid receptor in human brain associates with childhood abuse. *Nat Neurosci* 12: 342–348.

McGurk, H., and MacDonald, J. (1976). Hearing lips and seeing voices. *Nature* 264: 746–748.

McMains, S. A., and Somers, D. C. (2004). Multiple spotlights of attentional selection in human visual cortex. *Neuron* 42: 677–686.

Mehler, J., Jusczyk, P., Lambertz, C., Halsted, N., Bertoncini, J., and Amiel-Tison, C. (1988). A precursor of language acquisition in young infants. *Cognition* 29: 143–178.

Melzack, R., and Wall, P. D. (1988). *The Challenge of Pain* (2nd ed.). New York: Penguin.

Menashe, I., Man, O., Lancet, D., and Gilad, Y. (2003). Different noses for different people. *Nat Genet* 34: 143–144.

Mennella, J. A., and Beauchamp, G. K. (1991). The transfer of alcohol to human milk: Effects on flavor and the infant's behavior. *N Engl J Med* 325: 981–985.

Mennella, J. A., and Beauchamp, G. K. (1993). The effects of repeated exposure to garlic-flavored milk on the nursling's behavior. *Pediatr Res* 34: 805–808.

Mennella, J. A., Johnson, A., and Beauchamp, G. K. (1995). Garlic ingestion by pregnant women alters the odor of amniotic fluid. *Chem Senses* 20: 207–209.

Merfeld, D., Zupan, L., and Peterka, R. (1999). Humans use internal models to estimate gravity and linear acceleration. *Nature* 398: 615–618.

Meyerhof, W., Batram, C., Kuhn, C., Brockhoff, A., Chudoba, E., Bufe, B., Appendino, G., and Behrens, M. (2010). The molecular receptive ranges of human TAS2R bitter taste receptors. *Chem Senses* 35: 157–170.

Miller, G., Tybur, J. M., and Jordan, B. D. (2007). Ovulatory cycle effects on tip earnings by lap dancers: Economic evidence for human estrus? *Evol Hum Behav* 28: 375–381.

Miller, G. A., and Heise, G. A. (1950). The trill threshold. *J Acoust Soc Am* 22: 637–638.

Miller, S. L., and Maner J. K. (2010). Scent of a woman: Men's testosterone responses to olfactory ovulation cues. *Psychol Sci* 21: 276–283.

Ming, D., Ninomiya, Y., and Margolskee, R. F. (1999). Blocking taste receptor activation of gustducin inhibits gustatory responses to bitter compounds. *Proc Natl Acad Sci USA* 96: 9903–9908.

Mombaerts, P., Wang, F., Dulac, C., Chao, S. K., Nemes, A., Mendelsohn, M., Edmondson, J., and Axel, R. (1996). Visualizing an olfactory sensory map. *Cell* 87: 675–686.

Moncrieff, R. W. (1966). *Odour Preferences.* New York: Wiley.

Moore, B. C. J. (2003). *An Introduction to the Psychology of Hearing* (5th ed.). London: Academic Press.

Moran, J., and Desimone, R. (1985). Selective attention gates visual processing in the extrastriate cortex. *Science* 229: 782–784.

Moskowitz, H. R., Dravnieks, A., and Klarman, L. A. (1976). Odor intensity and pleasantness for a diverse set of odorants. *Percept Psychophys* 19: 122–128.

Motohashi, K., and Umino, M. (2001). Heterotopic painful stimulation decreases the late component of somatosensory evoked potentials induced by electrical tooth stimulation. *Brain Res Cogn Brain Res* 11: 39–46.

Motoyoshi, I., Nishida, S., Sharan, L., and Adelson, E. H. (2007). Image statistics and the perception of surface qualities. *Nature* 447: 206–209.

Mounts, J. R. (2000). Evidence for suppressive mechanisms in attentional selection: Feature singletons produce inhibitory surrounds. *Percept Psychophys* 62: 969–983.

Mozer, M. C. (1991). *The Perception of Multiple Objects: A Connectionist Approach.* Cambridge, MA: MIT Press.

Müller, J. (1838/1912). *Handbook of Physiology* (translation from B. Rand [1912], *The Classical Psychologists*). Repr. Boston: Houghton-Mifflin.

Murphy, C., Cain, W. S., Gilmore, M. M., and Skinner, R. B. (1991). Sensory and semantic factors in recognition memory for odors and graphic stimuli: Elderly versus young persons. *Am J Psychol* 104: 161–192.

Nagy, A. L., MacLeod, D. I., Heyneman, N. E., and Eisner, A. (1981). Four cone pigments in women heterozygous for color deficiency. *J Opt Soc Am* 71: 719–722.

Nathans, J. (1986). Molecular genetics of inherited variation in human color vision. *Science* 232: 203–210.

Nathans, J., Thomas, D., and Hogness, D. S. (1986). Molecular genetics of human color vision: The genes encoding blue, green, and red pigments. *Science* 232: 193–202.

National Eye Institute, "Facts about age-related macular degeneration," August 2010, http://www.nei.nih.gov/health/maculardegen/armd_facts.asp.

Nauhaus, I., Benucci, A., Carandini, M., and Ringach, D. L. (2008). Neuronal selectivity and local map structure in visual cortex. *Neuron* 57: 673–679.

Navon, D. (1977). Forest before the trees: The precedence of global features in visual perception. *Cogn Psychol* 9: 353–383.

Neitz, J., Geist, T., and Jacobs, G. H. (1989). Color vision in the dog. *Vis Neurosci* 3: 119–125.

Nerger, J. L., Volbrecht, V. J., and Ayde, C. J. (1995). Unique hue judgments as a function of test size in the fovea and at 20-deg temporal eccentricity. *J Opt Soc Am A Opt Image Sci Vis* 12: 1225–1232.

Neri, P., Luu, J. Y., and Levi, D. M. (2006). Meaningful interactions can enhance visual discrimination of human agents. *Nat Neurosci* 9: 1186–1192.

Neri, P., Morrone, M. C., and Burr, D. C. (1998). Seeing biological motion. *Nature* 395: 894–896.

Netter, F. (1983). *Nervous System: Anatomy and Physiology.* West Caldwell, NJ: CIBA Pharmaceutical Company.

Newcombe, F., and de Haan, E. H. F. (1994). Category specificity in visual recognition. In M. J. Farah and G. Ratcliff (Eds.), *The Neuropsychology of High-Level Vision: Collected Tutorial Essays* (Carnegie Mellon Symposia on Cognition) (pp. 103–132). Hillsdale, NJ: Erlbaum.

Newell, F. N., and Bülthoff, H. H. (2002). Categorical perception of familiar objects. *Cognition* 85: 113–143.

Newell, F. N., Ernst, M. O., Tjan, B. S., and Bulthoff, H. (2001). Viewpoint dependence in visual and haptic object recognition. *Psychol Sci* 12: 37–42.

Newsome, W. T., and Pare, E. B. (1988). A selective impairment of motion perception following lesions of the middle temporal visual area (MT). *J Neurosci* 8: 2201–2211.

Noble, A. C. (1996). Taste-aroma interactions. *Trends Food Sci Technol* 7: 439–444.

Nodine, C. F., Mello-Thoms, C., Kundel, H. L., and Weinstein, S. P. (2002). Time course of perception and decision making during mammographic interpretation. *Am J Roentgenol* 179: 917–923.

Norcia, A. M., Tyler, C. W., and Hamer, R. D. (1990). Development of contrast sensitivity in the human infant. *Vision Res* 30: 1475–1486.

O'Craven, K. M., and Kanwisher, N. (2000). Mental imagery of faces and places activates corresponding stimulus-specific brain regions. *J Cogn Neurosci* 12: 1013–1023.

O'Dell, C., and Boothe, R. G. (1997). The development of stereoacuity in infant rhesus monkeys. *Vision Res* 37: 2675–2684.

Ohzawa, I., and Freeman, R. D. (1986a). The binocular organization of simple cells in the cat's visual cortex. *J Neurophysiol* 56: 221–242.

Ohzawa, I., and Freeman, R. D. (1986b). The binocular organization of complex cells in the cat's visual cortex. *J Neurophysiol* 56: 243–259.

Okano, T., Fukada, Y., and Yoshizawa, T. (1995). Molecular basis for tetrachromatic color vision. *Comp Biochem Physiol B* 112: 405–414.

Oliva, A., and Torralba, A. (2001). Modeling the shape of the scene: A holistic representation of the spatial envelope. *Int J Comput Vis* 42: 145–175.

Olivers, C. N., and Meeter, M. (2008). A boost and bounce theory of temporal attention. *Psychol Rev* 115: 836–863.

Olney, J. W., and Sharpe, L. G. (1969). Brain lesions in an infant rhesus monkey treated with monosodium glutamate. *Science* 166: 386–388.

Oman, C. (1990). Motion sickness: A synthesis and evaluation of the sensory conflict theory. *Can J Physiol Pharmacol* 68: 294–303.

Ooi, T., and He, Z. (1999). Binocular rivalry and visual awareness: The role of attention. *Perception* 28: 551–574.

O'Regan, K. (1992). Solving the "real" mysteries of visual perception: The world as an outside memory. *Can J Psychol* 46: 461–488.

Owens, D. A. (1987). Oculomotor information and perception of three-dimensional space. In H. Heuer and A. F. Sanders (Eds.), *Perspectives on Perception and Action* (pp. 215–248). Hillside, NJ: Erlbaum.

Oxbury, J. M., Oxbury, S. M., and Humphrey, N. K. (1969). Varieties of colour anomia. *Brain* 92: 847–860.

Oyster, C. W. (1999). *The Human Eye: Structure and Function.* Sunderland, MA: Sinauer.

Paik, S. B., and Ringach, D. L. (2011). Retinal origin of orientation maps in visual cortex. *Nat Neurosci* 14: 919–925.

Palmer, J. (1995). Attention in visual search: Distinguishing four causes of a set size effect. *Curr Dir Psychol Sci* 4: 118–123.

Palmer, S. E. (1992). Common region: A new principle of perceptual grouping. *Cogn Psychol* 24: 436–447.

Palmer, S. E., and Ghose, T. (2008). Extremal edges: A powerful cue to depth perception and figure-ground organization. *Psychol Sci* 19: 77–84.

Palmeri, T. J., and Gauthier, I. (2004). Visual object understanding. *Nat Rev Neurosci* 5: 291–303.

Panum, P. L. (1940). *Physiological Investigations Concerning Vision with Two Eyes* (translated from German by C. Hubscher). Hanover, NH: Dartmouth Eye Institute. (Original work published 1858.)

Parker, A. J. (2007). Binocular depth perception and the cerebral cortex. *Nat Rev Neurosci* 8: 379–391.

Parrish, E. E., Giaschi, D. E., Boden, C., and Dougherty, R. (2005). The maturation of form and motion perception in school age children. *Vision Res* 45: 827–837.

Pascual-Leone, A., and Hamilton, R. (2001). The metamodal organization of the brain. *Prog Brain Res* 134: 427–445.

Patterson, R. D., and Johnsrude, I. S. (2008). Functional imaging of the auditory processing applied to speech sounds. *Philos Trans R Soc B Biol Sci* 363: 1023–1035.

Pause, B. M., Miranda, A., Goder, R., Aldenhoff, J. B., and Ferstl, R. (2001). Reduced olfactory performance in patients with major depression. *J Psychiatr Res* 35: 271–277.

Pelchat, M. L., Bykowski, C., Duke, F. F., and Reed, D. R. (2011). Excretion and perception of a characteristic odor in urine after asparagus ingestion: A psychophysical and genetic study. *Chem Senses* 36: 9–17.

Penfield, W., and Rasmussen, T. (1950). *The Cerebral Cortex of Man: A Clinical Study of Localization of Function.* New York: Macmillan.

Perlman, M., and Krumhansl, C. L. (1996). An experimental study of internal interval standards in Javanese and Western musicians. *Music Percept* 14: 95–116.

Pessoa, L. (1996). Mach bands: How many models are possible? Recent experimental findings and modeling attempts. *Vision Res* 36: 3205–3227.

Peterhans, E., von der Heydt, R., Baumgartner, G., Pettigrew, J. D., Sanderson, K. J., and Levick, W. R. (1986). Neuronal responses to illusory contour stimuli reveal stages of visual cortical processing. In J. D. Pettigrew, K. J. Sanderson, and W. R. Levick (Eds.), *Visual Neuroscience* (pp. 343–351). Cambridge, UK: Cambridge University Press.

Peterka, R. J. (2002). Sensorimotor integration in human postural control. *J Neurophysiol* 88: 1097–1118.

Peterson, M. A., and Rhodes, G. (Eds.). (2003). *Analytic and Holistic Processes.* London: Oxford University Press.

Peterson, M. A., and Skow, E. (2008). Inhibitory competition between shape properties in figure-ground perception. *J Exp Psychol Hum Percept Perform* 34: 251–267.

Petkov, C. I., O'Connor, K. N., and Sutter, M. L. (2003). Illusory sound perception in macaque monkeys. *J Neurosci* 23: 9155–9161.

Petkov, C. I., O'Connor, K. N., and Sutter, M. L. (2007). Encoding of illusory continuity in primary auditory cortex. *Neuron* 54: 153–165.

Pettigrew, J. D., Nikara, T., and Bishop, P. O. (1968). Binocular interaction on single units in cat striate cortex: Simultaneous stimulation by single moving slit with receptive fields in correspondence. *Exp Brain Res* 6: 391–410.

Pfaffmann, C. (1960). The pleasures of sensation. *Psychol Rev* 67: 253–268.

Pfaffmann, C. (1974a). The sensory coding of taste quality. *Chem Senses Flavor* 1: 5–8.

Pfaffmann, C. (1974b). Specificity of the sweet receptors of the squirrel monkey. *Chem Senses Flavor* 1, 61–67.

Pierce, J. D., Jr., Wysocki, C. J., Aronov, E. V., Webb, J. B., and Boden, R. M. (1996). The role of perceptual and structural similarity in cross-adaptation. *Chem Senses* 21: 223–237.

Pignatiello, M. F., Camp, C. J., and Rasar, L. A. (1986). Musical mood induction: An alternative to the Velten technique. *J Abnorm Psychol* 95: 295–297.

Plailly, J., Delon-Martin, C., and Royet, J.-P. (2011). Experience induces functional reorganization in brain regions involved in odor imagery in perfumers. *Human Brain Mapping* [Epub ahead of print]. doi: 10.1002/hbm.21207.

Plailly, J., Howard, J. D., Gitelman, D. R., and Gottfried, J. A. (2008). Attention to odor modulates thalamocortical connectivity in the human brain. *J Neurosci* 28: 5257–5267.

Plaisier, M. A., Bergmann Tiest, W. M., and Kappers, A. M. L. (2009). Salient features in 3-D haptic shape perception. *Atten Percept Psychophys* 71: 421–430.

Plomp, R. (1976). *Aspects of Tone Sensation— A Psychophysical Study.* New York: Academic Press.

Plotkin, A., Sela, L., Weissbord, A., Kahana, R., Haviv, L., Yeshurun, Y., and Soroker, N. (2010). Sniffing enables communication and environmental control for the severely disabled. *Proc Natl Acad Sci USA* 107: 14413–14418.

Poggio, G. F., and Talbot, W. H. (1981). Mechanisms of static and dynamic stereopsis in foveal cortex of the rhesus monkey. *J Physiol* 315: 469–492.

Pointer, M. R., and Attridge, G. G. (1998). The number of discernible colours. *Color Res Appl* 23: 52–54.

Polat, U., and Sagi, D. (1993). Lateral interactions between spatial channels: Suppression and facilitation revealed by lateral masking experiments. *Vision Res* 33: 993–999.

Poletti, M., Listorti, C., and Rucci, M. (2010). Stability of the visual world during eye drift. *J Neurosci* 30: 11143–11150.

Ponzo, M. (1913). Rapports entre quelque illusions visuelles de contraste angulaire et l'appreciation de grandeur astres a l'horizon. *Arch Ital Biol* 58: 327–329.

Poran N. S., and Coss, R. G. (1990). Development of antisnake defenses in California ground squirrels (*Spermaphilus beecheyi*): I. Behavioral and immunological relationships. *Behavior* 112: 222–245.

Porter, J., Carven, B., Khan, R. M., Chang, S. J., Kang, I., Judkewicz, B., Volpe, J., Settles, G., and Sobel, N. (2007). Mechanisms of scent-tracking in humans. *Nat Neurosci* 10: 27–29.

Posner, M. I. (1980). Orienting of attention. *Q J Exp Psychol* 32: 3–25.

Potter, M. C. (1975). Meaning in visual search. *Science* 187: 965–966.

Potter, M. C. (1976). Short-term conceptual memory for pictures. *J Exp Psychol Hum Learn Mem* 2: 509–522.

Prescott, J. (2004). Effects of added glutamate on liking for novel flavors. *Appetite* 42: 143–150.

Preston, T. J., Li, S., Kourtzi, Z., and Welchman, A. E. (2008). Multivoxel pattern selectivity for perceptually relevant binocular disparities in the human brain. *J Neurosci* 28: 11315–1132.

Price, D. D. (2000). Psychological and neural mechanisms of the affective dimension of pain. *Science* 288: 1769–1772.

Price, D. D., Wu, J. W., Dubner, R., and Gracely, R. H. (1977). Peripheral suppression of first pain and central summation of second pain evoked by noxious heat pulses. *Pain* 3: 57–68.

Prinzmetal, W., and Beck, D. M. (2001). The tilt-constancy theory of visual illusions. *J Exp Psychol Hum Percept Perform* 27: 206–217.

Prinzmetal, W., Shimamura, A. P., and Mikolinski, M. (2001). The Ponzo illusion and the perception of orientation. *Percept Psychophys* 63: 99–114.

Pritchard, T. C., and Norgren, R. (2004). Gustatory system. In G. Paxinos and J. K. Mai (Eds.), *The Human Nervous System* (2nd ed., pp. 1171–1196). Amsterdam: Elsevier.

Pugh, M. C., Ringach, D. L., Shapley, R., and Shelley, M. J. (2000). Computational modeling of orientation tuning dynamics in monkey primary visual cortex. *J Comput Neurosci* 8: 143–159.

Purves, D., Augustine, G. J., Fitzpatrick, D., Hall, W. C., LaMantia, A.–S., McNamara, J. O., and White, L. E. (2008). *Neuroscience* (4th ed.). Sunderland, MA: Sinauer.

Quilliam, T. A. (1978), The structure of finger print skin. In G. Gordon (Ed.), *Active Touch: The Mechanisms of Recognition of Objects by Manipulation. A Multidisciplinary Approach* (pp. 1–15). Oxford, UK: Pergamon.

Quiroga, R. Q., Kreiman, G., Koch, C., and Fried, I. (2008). Sparse but not "grandmother-cell" coding in the medial temporal lobe. *Trends Cogn Sci* 12: 87–91.

Quiroga, R. Q., Reddy, L., Kreiman, G., Koch, C., and Fried, I. (2005). Invariant visual representation by single neurons in the human brain. *Nature* 435: 1102–1107.

Rabin, M. D., and Cain, W. S. (1984). Odor recognition, familiarity, identifiability and encoding consistency. *J Exp Psychol Learn Mem Cogn* 10: 316–325.

Rader, A. A., Oman, C. M., and Merfeld, D. M. (2011). Perceived tilt and translation during variable-radius swing motion with congruent or conflicting visual and vestibular cues. *Exp Brain Res* 210: 173–184.

Rainville, P., Duncan, G. H., Price, D. D., Carrier, B., and Bushnell, M. C. (1997). Pain affect encoded in human anterior cingulate but not somatosensory cortex. *Science* 277: 968–971.

Ramachandran, R., and Lisberger, S. G. (2005). Normal performance and expression of learning in the vestibulo-ocular reflex (VOR) at high frequencies. *J Neurophysiol* 93: 2028–2038.

Ramachandran, V. S. (1993). Behavioral and magnetoencephalographic correlates of plasticity in the adult human brain. *Proc Natl Acad Sci USA* 90: 10413–10420.

Raphan, T., Matsuo, V., and Cohen, B. (1977). A velocity storage mechanism responsible for optokinetic nystagmus (OKN), optokinetic after-nystagmus (OKAN) and vestibular nystagmus. In R. Baker and A. Berthoz (Eds.), *Control of Gaze by Brain Stem Neurons: Proceedings of the Symposium Held in the Abbaye de Royaumont, Paris, France on July 12–15, 1977* (Developments in Neuroscience, vol. 1) (pp. 37–47). Amsterdam: Elsevier/North Holland.

Rasch, B., Buchel, C., Gais, S., and Born, J. (2007). Odor cues during slow-wave sleep prompt declarative memory consolidations. *Science* 315: 1426–1429.

Rasch, R. A. (1978). The perception of simultaneous notes such as in polyphonic music. *Acustica* 40: 1–72.

Raymond, J. E. (1993). Complete interocular transfer of motion adaptation effects on motion coherence thresholds. *Vision Res* 33: 1865–1870.

Rayner, K. (1978). Eye movements in reading and information processing. *Psychol Bull* 85: 618–660.

Rayner, K., Liversedge, S. P., White, S. J., and Vergilino-Perez, D. (2003). Reading disappearing text: Cognitive control of eye movements. *Psychol Sci* 14: 385–388.

Reale, R. A., Calvert, G. A., Thesen, T., Jenison, R. L., Kawasaki, H., Oya, H., Howard, M. A., and Brugge, J. F. (2007). Auditory-visual processing represented in the human superior temporal gyrus. *Neuroscience* 145: 162–184.

Reason, J., and Brand, J. (1975). *Motion Sickness*. London: Academic Press.

Reed, C. L., and Caselli, R. J. (1994). The nature of tactile agnosia: A case study. *Neuropsychologia* 32: 527–539.

Reed, C. L., Caselli, R. J., and Farah, M. J. (1996). Tactile agnosia: Underlying impairment and implications for normal tactile object recognition. *Brain* 119: 875–888.

Reed, C. L., Klatzky, R. L., and Halgren, E. (2005). What versus where in touch: An fMRI study. *Neuroimage* 25: 718–726.

Reed, C. L., Shoham, S., and Halgren, E. (2004). Neural substrates of tactile object recognition: A fMRI study. *Hum Brain Mapp* 21: 236–246.

Regan, D. (1991). Depth from motion and motion in depth. In D. Regan (Ed.), *Binocular Vision* (pp. 137–169). London: Macmillan.

Reichardt, W. (1986). Processing of optical information by the visual system of the fly. *Vision Res* 26: 113–126.

Rensink, R. A. (2000). Seeing, sensing, and scrutinizing. *Vision Res* 40: 1469–1487.

Rensink, R. A., O'Regan, J. K., and Clark, J. J. (1997). To see or not to see: The need for attention to perceive changes in scenes. *Psychol Sci* 8: 368–373.

Reynolds, J. H., and Chelazzi, L. (2004). Attentional modulation of visual processing. *Annu Rev Neurosci* 27: 611–647.

Reynolds, J. H., and Heeger, D. J. (2009). The normalization model of attention. *Neuron* 61: 168–185.

Rhode, W. S., and Cooper, N. P. (1993). Two-tone suppression and distortion production on the basilar membrane in the hook region of the cat and guinea pig cochleae. *Hear Res* 66: 31–45.

Riecke, L., Esposito, F., Bonte, M., and Formisano, E. (2009). Hearing illusory sounds in noise: The timing of sensory-perceptual transformations in auditory cortex. *Neuron* 64: 550–561.

Riecke, L., van Opstal, A. J., Goebel, R., and Formisano, E. (2007). Hearing illusory sounds in noise: Sensory-perceptual transformations in primary auditory cortex. *J Neurosci* 27: 12684–12689.

Rind, F. C., and Simmons, P. J. (1999). Seeing what is coming: Building collision-sensitive neurones. *Trends Neurosci* 22: 215–220.

Robinson, D. (1977). Vestibular and optokinetic symbiosis: An example of explaining by modelling. In R. Baker and A. Berthoz (Eds.), *Control of Gaze by Brain Stem Neurons: Proceedings of the Symposium Held in the Abbaye de Royaumont, Paris, France on July 12–15, 1977* (Developments in Neuroscience, vol. 1) (pp. 49–58). Amsterdam: Elsevier/North Holland.

Robson, J., and Campbell, F. (1997). A quick demonstration of your own contrast sensitivity function. In D. G. Pelli and A. M. Torres, *Thresholds: Limits of Perception*. New York: NY Arts Magazine.

Rock, I., and Victor, J. (1964) Vision and touch: An experimentally created conflict between the two senses. *Science* 143: 594–596.

Rodieck, R. W. (1998). *The First Steps in Seeing*. Sunderland, MA: Sinauer.

Rogers, B. J., and Collett, T. S. (1989). The appearance of surfaces specified by motion parallax and binocular disparity. *Q J Exp Psychol A* 41: 697–717.

Rollman, G. B. (1991). Pain responsiveness. In M. A. Heller and W. Schiff (Eds.), *The*

Psychology of Touch (pp. 91–114). Hillsdale, NJ: Erlbaum.

Rolls, E. T. (2006). Brain mechanisms underlying flavor and appetite. *Philos Trans R Soc Lond B Biol Sci* 361: 1123–1136.

Rolls, E. T., O'Doherty, J. O., Kringelbach, M. L., Francis, S., Bowtell, R., and McGlone, F. (2003). Representations of pleasant and painful touch in the human orbitofrontal and cingulate cortex. *Cereb Cortex* 13: 308–317.

Roorda, A., and Williams, D. R. (1999). The arrangement of the three cone classes in the living human eye. *Nature* 397: 520–522.

Roper, S. D. (2006). Cell communication in taste buds. *Cell Mol Life Sci* 63: 1494–1500.

Roper, S. D., and Chaudhari, N. (2009). Processing umami and other tastes in mammalian taste buds. *Ann NY Acad Sci* 1170: 60–65.

Rosen, S., Wise, R. J. S., Chadha, S., Conway, E.-J., and Scott, S. K. (2011). Hemispheric asymmetries in speech perception: Sense, nonsense, and modulations. *PLoS One, in press*.

Rosenzweig, M. R., Breedlove, S. M., and Watson, N. V. (2005). *Biological Psychology: An Introduction to Behavioral and Cognitive Neuroscience* (4th ed.). Sunderland, MA: Sinauer.

Rossetti, Y., Rode, G., and Boisson, D. (1995). Implicit processing of somaesthetic information: A dissociation between where and how? *Neuroreport* 15: 506–510.

Rowe, T. B., Macrinin, T. E., and Luo, Z.-X. (2011). Fossil evidence on origin of the mammalian brain. *Science* 332: 955–957.

Roy, M., Peretz, I., and Rainville, P. (2007). Emotional valence contributes to music-induced analgesia. *Pain* 1–2: 140–147.

Royden, C. S., Banks, M. S., and Crowell, J. A. (1992). The perception of heading during eye movements. *Nature* 360: 583–585.

Royet, J.-P, and Plailly, J. (2004). Lateralization of olfactory processes. *Chem Senses* 29: 731–745.

Rozin, P. (Ed.). (1967). *Thiamin Specific Hunger* (Vol. 1). Washington, DC: American Physiological Society.

Rushton, W. (1972). Visual pigments in man. In H. Dartnall (Ed.), *Photochemistry of Vision* (Vol. VII/1, pp. 364–394). New York: Springer.

Sachse, S., Rueckert, E., Keller, A., Okada, R., Tanaka, N. K., Ito, K., and Vosshall, L. B. (2007). Activity dependent plasticity in an olfactory circuit. *Neuron* 56: 838–850.

Sacks, O. (2006, June 19). A neurologist's notebook: "Stereo Sue." *New Yorker*, 64.

Saffran, J. R. (2001). Words in a sea of sounds: The output of statistical learning. *Cognition* 81: 149–169.

Saffran, J. R. (2002). Constraints on statistical language learning. *J Mem Lang* 47: 172–196.

Saffran, J. R., Aslin, R. N., and Newport, E. L. (1996). Statistical learning by 8-month-old infants. *Science* 274: 1926–1928.

Saffran, J. R., Johnson, E. K., Aslin, R. N., and Newport, E. L. (1999). Statistical learning of tone sequences by human infants and adults. *Cognition* 70: 27–52.

Saffran, J. R., Loman, M. M., and Robertson, R. R. W. (2000). Infant memory for musical experiences. *Cognition* 77: B15–B23.

Salzman, C. D., Britten, K. H., and Newsome, W. T. (1990). Cortical microstimulation influences perceptual judgements of motion direction. *Nature* 346: 174–177.

Sato, M., Ogawa, H., and Yamashita, S. (1975). Response properties of macaque monkey chorda tympani fibers. *J Gen Physiol* 66: 781–810.

Sceniak, M. P., Ringach, D. L., Hawken, M. J., and Shapley, R. (1999). Contrast's effect on spatial summation by macaque V1 neurons. *Nat Neurosci* 2: 733–739.

Schaal, B., Marlier, L., and Soussignan, R. (1995). Responsiveness to the odor of amniotic fluid in the human neonate. *Biol Neonate* 671: 397–406.

Schaal, B., Marlier, L., and Soussignan, R. (1998). Olfactory function in the human fetus: Evidence from selective neonatal responsiveness to the odor of amniotic fluid. *Behav Neurosci* 112: 1438–1449.

Scheibert, J., Leurent, S., Prevost, A., and Debrégeas, G. (2009). The role of fingerprints in the coding of tactile information probed with a biomimetic sensor. *Science* 323: 1503–1506.

Schild, D., and Restrepo, D. (1998). Transduction mechanism in vertebrate olfactory receptor cells. *Physiol Rev* 37: 369–375.

Schiller, P. H., and Sandell, J. H. (1983). Interactions between visually and electrically elicited saccades before and after superior colliculus and frontal eye field ablations in the rhesus monkey. *Exp Brain Res* 49: 381–392.

Schleidt, M., Hold, B., and Attila, G. (1981). A cross-cultural study on the attitude towards personal odors. *J Chem Ecol* 7: 19–31.

Schnapf, J. L., Kraft, T. W., and Baylor, D. A. (1987). Spectral sensitivity of human cone photoreceptors. *Nature* 325: 439–441.

Scholz, J., and Woolf, C. J. (2002). Can we conquer pain? *Nat Neurosci* 5 Suppl.: 1062–1067.

Schoonevelt, G. P., and Moore, B. C. J. (1989). Comodulation masking release (CMR) as a function of masker bandwidth, modulator bandwidth, and signal duration. *J Acoust Soc Am* 85: 273–281.

Schor, C. M., and Badcock, D. R. (1985). A comparison of stereo and vernier acuity within spatial channels as a function of distance from fixation. *Vision Res* 25: 1113–1119.

Seay, C. F. (1975). *First Thoughts on a Theology of Music from the Psalter*. Dallas, TX: Dallas Theological Seminary.

Seeba, F., and Klump, G. M. (2009). Stimulus familiarity affects perceptual restoration in the European starling (*Sturnus vulgaris*). *PLoS ONE* 4: e5974. doi:10.1371/journal.pone.0005974.

Seidl, A. H., and Grothe, B. (2005). Development of sound localization mechanisms in the Mongolian gerbil is shaped by early acoustic experience. *J Neurophysiol* 94: 1028–1036.

Selfridge, O. G. (1959). Pandemonium: A paradigm for learning. In D. V. Blake and A. M. Uttley (Eds.), *Proceedings of the Symposium on the Mechanisation of Thought Processes* (pp. 511–529). London: Her Majesty's Stationery Office.

Serences, J. T., and Yantis, S. (2006). Selective visual attention and perceptual coherence. *Trends Cogn Sci* 10: 38–45.

Shapiro, K. L. (1994). The attentional blink: The brain's eyeblink. *Curr Dir Psychol Sci* 3: 86–89.

Shapley, R., and Hawken, M. J. (2011). Color in the cortex: Single- and double-opponent cells. *Vision Res* 51: 701–717.

Shepard, R. N. (1967). Recognition memory for words, sentences, and pictures. *J Verbal Learn Verbal Behav* 6: 156–163.

Sherrick C., and Cholewiak, R. (1986). Cutaneous sensitivity. In K. R. Boff, L. Kaufman, and J. P. Thomas (Eds.), *Handbook of Perception and Human Performance* (Vol 1., pp. 12-1 to 12-58). New York: Wiley.

Shevell, S. K. (2003). Color appearance. In S. K. Shevell (Ed.), *The Science of Color* (2nd ed., pp. 149–190). Oxford, UK: Elsevier.

Simon, R., Holderied, M. W., Koch, C. U., and von Helversen, O. (2011). Floral acoustics: Conspicuous echoes of a dish-shaped leaf attract bat pollinators. *Science* 333: 631–633.

Simons, D. J., and Chabris, C. F. (1999). Gorillas in our midst: Sustained inattentional blindness for dynamic events. *Perception* 28: 1059–1074.

Simons, D. J., and Levin, D. T. (1997). Change blindness. *Trends Cogn Sci* 1: 261–267.

Sipiora, M. L., Murtaugh, M. A., Gregoire, M. B., and Duffy, V. B. (2000). Bitter taste perception and severe vomiting during pregnancy. *Physiol Behav* 69: 259–267.

Sloboda, J. A. (1999). Music: Where cognition and emotion meet. *Psychologist* 12: 450–455.

Smith, J. D., Kemler Nelson, D. G., Grohskopf, L. A., and Appleton, T. (1994). What child is this? What interval was that? Familiar tunes and music perception in novice listeners. *Cognition* 52: 23–54.

Smithson, H. E. (2005). Sensory, computational and cognitive components of human colour constancy. *Philos Trans R Soc Lond B Biol Sci* 360: 1329–1346.

Snyder, D. J., Davidson, A. C., Kidd, J. R., Kidd, K. K., Speed, W. C., Pakstis, A. J., Cubells, J. F., O'Malley, S. S., and Bartoshuk, L. M. (2005). Oral sensation influences tobacco use: Genetic and psychophysical evidence. Paper presented at the Society for Research on Nicotine and Tobacco, Prague, Czech Republic.

Snyder, D. J., Dwivedi, N., Mramor, A., Bartoshuk, L. M., and Duffy, V. B. (2001). Taste and touch may contribute to the localization of retronasal olfaction: Unilateral and bilateral anesthesia of cranial nerves V/VII. Paper presented at the Society of Neuroscience Abstract, San Diego, CA.

Snyder, J. S., and Alain, C. (2007). Toward a neurophysiological theory of auditory stream segregation. *Psychol Bull* 133: 780–799.

Sollberger, B., Reber, R., and Eckstein, D. (2003). Musical chords as affective priming context in a word-evaluation task. *Music Percept* 20: 263–283.

Spence, C., Nicholls, M. E. R., and Driver, J. (2001). The cost of expecting events in the wrong sensory modality. *Percept Psychophys* 63: 330–336.

Spence, C., Pavani, F., and Driver, J. (2000). Crossmodal links between vision and touch in covert endogenous spatial attention. *J Exp Psychol Hum Percept Perform* 26: 1298–1319.

Spencer, N. A., McClintock, M. K., Sellergren, S. A., Bullivant, S., Jacob, S., and Mennella, J. A. (2004). Social chemosignals from breastfeeding women increase sexual motivation. *Hum Behav* 46: 362–370.

Sperling, G., and Weichselgartner, E. (1995). Episodic theory of the dynamics of spatial attention. *Psychol Rev* 102: 503–532.

Spiridon, M., Fischl, B., and Kanwisher, N. (2006). Location and spatial profile of category-specific regions in human extrastriate cortex. *Hum Brain Mapp* 27: 77–89.

Stabell, B., and Stabell, U. (2002). Effects of rod activity on color perception with light adaptation. *J Opt Soc Am A Opt Image Sci Vis* 19: 1249–1258.

Stager, D. R., and Birch, E. (1986). Preferential-looking acuity and stereopsis in infantile esotropia. *J Pediatr Ophthalmol Strabismus* 23: 160–165.

Standing, L. (1973). Learning 10,000 pictures. *Q J Exp Psychol* 25: 207–222.

Standing, L., Conezio, J., and Haber, R. N. (1970). Perception and memory for pictures: Single trial learning of 2500 visual stimuli. *Psychon Sci* 19: 73–74.

Stein, L. J., Cowart, B. J., Epstein, A. N., Pilot, L. J., Laskin, C. R., and Beauchamp, G. K. (1996). Increased liking for salty foods in adolescents exposed during infancy to a chloride-deficient feeding formula. *Appetite* 27: 65–77.

Stein, M., Ottenberg, M. D., and Roulet, N. (1958). A study of the development of olfactory preferences. *Arch Neurol Psychiatry* 80: 264–266.

Steiner, J. E. (1973). The gustofacial response: Observation on normal and anencephalic newborn infants. In J. F. Bosma (Ed.), *Development in the Fetus and Infant* (pp. 254–278). Washington, DC: U.S. Government Printing Office.

Stellman, S. D., and Garfinkel, L. (1986). Artificial sweetener use and one-year weight change among women. *Prev Med* 15: 195–202.

Stevens, J. C. (1959). Cross-modality validation of subjective scales for loudness, vibration, and electric shock. *J Exp Psychol* 57: 201–209.

Stevens, J. C., and Cain, W. S. (1987). Old-age deficits in the sense of smell as gauged by thresholds, magnitude matching and odor identification. *Psychol Aging* 2: 36–42.

Stevens, J. C., Plantinga, A., and Cain, W. S. (1982). Reduction of odor and nasal pungency associated with aging. *Neurobiol Aging* 3: 125–132.

Stevens, S. S. (1962). The surprising simplicity of sensory metrics. *Am Psychol* 17: 29–39.

Stevens, S. S. (1975). *Psychophysics.* New York: Academic Press.

Stevens, S. S., Carton, A. S., and Shickman, G. M. (1958). A scale of apparent intensity of electric shock. *J Exp Psychol* 56: 328–334.

Stevens, S. S., and Galanter, E. H. (1957). Ratio scales and category scales for a dozen perceptual continua. *J Exp Psychol* 54: 377–411.

Stilp, C. E., Alexander, J. M., Kiefte, M., and Kluender, K. R. (2010). Auditory color constancy: Calibration to reliable spectral characteristics across speech and nonspeech contexts and targets. *Atten Percept Psychophys* 72: 470–480.

Stockman, A., and Brainard, D. H. (2010). Color vision mechanisms. In M. Bass (Ed.), *OSA Handbook of Optics* (3rd ed., pp. 11.11–11.104.). New York: McGraw-Hill.

Stryker, M. P., and, Schiller, P. H. (1975). Eye and head movements evoked by electrical stimulation of monkey superior colliculus. *Exp Brain Res* 23: 103–112.

Sulmont, C., Issanchou, S., and Koster, E. P. (2002). Selection of odorants for memory tests on the basis of familiarity, perceived complexity, pleasantness, similarity and identification. *Chem Senses* 27: 307–317.

Sun, Y.-G., Zhao, Z.-Q., Meng, X.-L., Yin, J., Liu, X.-Y., and Chen, Z.-F. (2009). Cellular basis of itch sensation. *Science* 325: 1531–1534.

Suzuki, Y., and Takeshima, H. (2004). Equal-loudness-level contours for pure tones. *J Acoust Soc Am* 116: 918–933.

Svaetichin, G., and Macnichol, E. F., Jr. (1959). Retinal mechanisms for chromatic and achromatic vision. *Ann NY Acad Sci* 74: 385–404.

Szmajda, B. A., Grünert, U., and Martin, P. R. (2008). Retinal ganglion cell inputs to the koniocellular pathway. *J Comp Neurol* 510: 251–268.

Tanaka, J. W., and Taylor, M. (1991). Object categories and expertise: Is the basic level in the eye of the beholder? *Cogn Psychol* 23: 457–482.

Tarr, M. J., and Pinker, S. (1990). When does human object recognition use a viewer-centered reference frame? *Psychol Sci* 1: 253–256.

Taube, J. S. (2007). The head direction signal: Origins and sensory-motor integration. *Annu Rev Neurosci* 30: 181–207.

Teller, D. Y., and Movshon, J. A. (1986). Visual development. *Vision Res* 26: 1483–1506.

Temussi, P. (2007). The sweet taste receptor: A single receptor with multiple sites and modes of interaction. In S. Taylor (Ed.), *Advances in Food and Nutrition Research* (Vol. 53, pp. 199–239). Elsevier, New York.

Thompson, P. (1980). Margaret Thatcher: A new illusion. *Perception* 9: 482–484.

Thorpe, S., Fize, D., and Marlot, C. (1996). Speed of processing in the human visual system. *Nature* 381: 520–552.

Tipper, S. P., and Behrmann, M. (1996). Object-centered not scene-based visual neglect. *J Exp Psychol Hum Percept Perform* 22: 1261–1278.

Tong, F., Meng, M., and Blake, R. (2006). Neural bases of binocular rivalry. *Trends Cogn Sci* 10: 502–511.

Tong, F., Nakayama, K., Vaughan, J. T., and Kanwisher, N. (1998). Binocular rivalry and visual awareness in human extrastriate cortex. *Neuron* 21: 753–759.

Treisman, A. (1986a). Features and objects in visual processing. *Sci Am* 255(5): 114–125.

Treisman, A. (1986b). Properties, parts, and objects. In K. R. Boff, L. Kaufmann, and J. P. Thomas (Eds.), *Handbook of Perception and Human Performance, Vol. 2: Cognitive Processes and Performance* (pp. 35.31–35.70). New York: Wiley.

Treisman, A. (1996). The binding problem. *Curr Opin Neurobiol* 6: 171–178.

Treisman, A., and Gelade, G. (1980). A feature-integration theory of attention. *Cogn Psychol* 12: 97–136.

Treisman, A. M., and Schmidt, H. (1982). Illusory conjunctions in the perception of objects. *Cogn Psychol* 14: 107–141.

Treisman, M. (1977). Motion sickness: An evolutionary hypothesis. *Science* 197: 493–495.

Tresilian, J. R. (1999). Visually timed action: Time-out for "tau"? *Trends Cogn Sci* 3: 301–310.

Treue, S., and Trujillo, J. C. M. (1999). Feature-based attention influences motion processing gain in macaque visual cortex. *Nature* 399: 575–579.

Tsotsos, J. K. (1990). Analyzing vision at the complexity level. *Behav Brain Sci* 13: 423–469.

Turin, L. (1996). A spectroscopic mechanism for primary olfactory reception. *Chem Senses* 21: 773–791.

Tyler, C. W. (1991). Cyclopean vision. In D. Regan (Ed.), *Binocular Vision* (Vol. 9, pp. 38–74). Boca Raton, FL: CRC Press.

Ungerleider, L. G., and Bell, A. H. (2011). Uncovering the visual "alphabet": Advances in our understanding of object perception. *Vision Res* 51: 782–799.

Ungerleider, L. G., and Mishkin, M. (1982). Two cortical visual systems. In D. J. Ingle, M. A. Goodale, and R. J. W. Mansfield (Eds.), *Analysis of Visual Behavior* (pp. 549–586). Cambridge, MA: MIT Press.

Uppenkamp, S., Johnsrude, I. S., Norris, D., Marslen-Wilson, W., and Patterson, R. D. (2006). Locating the initial stages of speech-sound processing in human temporal cortex. *Neuroimage* 31: 1284–1296.

Vaina, L. M., and Cowey, A. (1996). Impairment of the perception of second order motion but not first order motion in a patient with unilateral focal brain damage. *Proc R Soc Lond B Biol Sci* 263: 1225–1232.

Vaina, L. M., Makris, N., Kennedy, D., and Cowey, A. (1998). The selective impairment of the perception of first-order motion by unilateral cortical brain damage. *Vis Neurosci* 15: 333–348.

van Noorden, L. P. A. S. (1975). *Temporal Coherence in the Perception of Tone Sequences.* PhD diss., Technical University, Eindhoven, Netherlands.

Verhagen, J. V., Wesson, D. W., Netoff, T. I., White, J. A., and Wachowiak, M. (2007). Sniffing controls an adaptive filter of sensory input to the olfactory bulb. *Nat Neurosci* 10: 631–639.

Verrillo, R. T. (1963). Effect of contactor area on the vibrotactile threshold. *J Acoust Soc Am* 35: 1962–1966.

Vickery, T. J., King, L.-W., and Jiang, Y. (2005). Setting up the target template in visual search. *J Vis* 5: 81–92.

Vishwanath, D., Girshik, A. R., and Banks, M. (2005). Why pictures look right when viewed from the wrong place. *Nat Neurosci* 8: 1401–1410.

von der Heydt, R., Peterhans, E., and Baumgartner, G. (1984). Illusory contours and cortical neuron responses. *Science* 224: 1260–1262.

von der Malsburg, C. (1981). *The Correlation Theory of Brain Function.* Göttingen, Germany: Max-Planck-Institute for Biophysical Chemistry.

Wade, N. J. (2000). William Charles Wells (1757–1817) and vestibular research before Purkinje and Flourens. *J Vestib Res* 10: 127–137.

Walker, R., and Lupien, J. R. (2000). The safety evaluation of monosodium glutamate. *J Nutr* 130(4S Suppl.): 1049S–1052S.

Walla, P., Hufnagl, B., Lehern, J., Mayer, D., Lindinger, G., Imhof, H., Deeke, L., and Lang, W. (2003). Olfaction and depth of word processing: A magnetoencephalographic study. *Neuroimage* 18: 104–116.

Wandell, B. A., and Winawer, J. (2011). Imaging retinotopic maps in the human brain. *Vision Res* 51: 718–737.

Wang, Y., and Frost, B. J. (1992). Time to collision is signalled by neurons in the nucleus rotundus of pigeons. *Nature* 356: 236–238.

Ward, W. D. (1954). Subjective musical pitch. *J Acoust Soc Am* 26: 369–380.

Warman, P. H., and Ennos, A. R. (2009). Fingerprints are unlikely to increase the friction of primate fingerpads. *J Exp Biol* 212: 2016–2022.

Warren, R. M. (1984). Perceptual restoration of obliterated sounds. *Psychol Rev* 96: 371–385.

Warren, R. M., and Obusek, C. J. (1971). Speech perception and phonemic restorations. *Percept Psychophys* 9: 358–362.

Warren, R. M., and Sherman, G. L. (1974). Phonemic restorations based on subsequent context. *Percept Psychophys* 16: 150–156.

Warren, W. H., Jr., and Hannon, D. J. (1990). Eye movements and optical flow. *J Opt Soc Am A* 7: 160–169.

Warren, W. H., Jr., Morris, M. W., and Kalish, M. (1988). Perception of translational heading from optical flow. *J Exp Psychol Hum Percept Perform* 14: 646–660.

Warren, W. H., Jr., and Saunders, J. A. (1995). Perceiving heading in the presence of moving objects. *Perception* 24: 315–331.

Warren, W. H., Jr., and Verbrugge, R. R. (1984). Auditory perception of breaking and bouncing events: A case study in ecological acoustics. *J Exp Psychol Hum Percept Perform* 10: 704–712.

Weinstein, S. (1968). Intensive and extensive aspects of tactile sensitivity as a function of body part, sex, and laterality. In D. R. Kenshalo (Ed.), *The Skin Senses* (pp. 195–222). Springfield, IL: Thomas.

Wells, G. L., and Olson, E. A. (2003). Eyewitness testimony. *Annu Rev Psychol* 54: 277–295.

Wells, W. (1792). *An Essay upon Single Vision with Two Eyes: Together with Experiments and Observations on Several Other Subjects in Optics.* London: Cadell.

Werker, J. F., and Tees, R. C. (1984). Phonemic and phonetic factors in adult cross-language speech perception. *J Acoust Soc Am* 75: 1866–1878.

Werner, A., Menzel, R., and Wehrhahn, C. (1988). Color constancy in the honeybee. *J Neurosci* 8: 156–159.

Werner, J. S., Peterzell, D. H., and Scheetz, A. J. (1990). Light, vision, and aging. *Optom Vision Sci* 67: 214–229.

Wertheim, A. H., Mesland, B. S., and Bles, W. (2001). Cognitive suppression of tilt sensations during linear horizontal self-motion in the dark. *Perception* 30: 733–741.

Wessel, D. L. (1979). Timbre space as a musical control structure. *Comput Music J* 3: 45–52.

Westling, G., and Johansson, R. S. (1984). Factors influencing the force control during precision grip. *Exp Brain Res* 53: 277–284.

Wever, E. G. (1949). *Theory of Hearing.* New York: Wiley.

Wheatstone, C. (1852). Some remarkable and hitherto unobserved phenomena of binocular vision: Part two. *Philos Mag* 4: 504–523.

Whitney, D., and Levi, D. M. (2011). Visual crowding: A fundamental limit on conscious perception and object recognition. *Trends Cogn Sci* 15: 160–168.

Wiesel, T. N. (1982). Postnatal development of the visual cortex and the influence of environment. *Nature* 299: 583–591.

Wightman, F. L., and Jenison, R. (1995). Auditory spatial layout. In W. Epstein and S. Rogers (Eds.), *Perception of Space and Motion* (pp. 365–400). San Diego, CA: Academic Press.

Wightman, F., and Kistler, D. (1998). Of Vulcan ears, human ears and "earprints." *Nat Neurosci* 1: 337–339.

Wilkins, L., and Richter, C. P. (1940). A great craving for salt by a child with cortico-adrenal insufficiency. *J Am Med Assoc* 114: 866–868.

Willander, J., and Larsson, M. (2007). Olfaction and emotion: The case of autobiographical memory. *Mem Cognit* 35: 1659–1663.

Willis, C. M., Church, S. M., Guest, C. M., Cook, W. A., McCarthy, N., Bransbury, A. J., Church, M. R. T., and Church J. C. T. (2004). Olfactory detection of human bladder cancer by dogs: Proof of principle study. *Br Med J* 329: 712–714.

Wilson, D. A., Best, A. R., and Sullivan, R. M. (2004). Plasticity in the olfactory system: Lessons for the neurobiology of memory. *Neuroscientist* 10: 513–524.

Wilson, H. C. (1992). A critical review of menstrual synchrony research. *Psychoneuroendocrinology* 17: 565–591.

Wilson, V. J., and Melvill Jones, G. (1979). *Mammalian Vestibular Physiology.* New York: Plenum.

Winawer, J., Witthoft, N., Frank, M. C., Wu, L., Wade, A. R., and Boroditsky, L. (2007). Russian blues reveal effects of language on color discrimination. *Proc Natl Acad Sci USA* 104: 7780–7785.

Winberg, J., and Porter, R. H. (1998). Olfaction and human neonatal behaviour: Clinical implications. *Acta Paediatr* 87: 6–10.

Wolfe, J. M. (1994). Guided Search 2.0: A revised model of visual search. *Psychon Bull Rev* 1: 202–238.

Wolfe, J. M., and Bennett, S. C. (1997). Preattentive object files: Shapeless bundles of basic features. *Vision Res* 37: 25–43.

Wolfe, J. M., Cave, K. R., and Franzel, S. L. (1989). Guided search: An alternative to the feature integration model for visual search. *J Exp Psychol Hum Percept Perform* 15: 419–433.

Wolfe, J. M., and Held, R. (1981). A purely binocular mechanism in human vision. *Vision Res* 21: 1755–1759.

Wolfe, J. M., and Horowitz, T. S. (2004). What attributes guide the deployment of visual attention and how do they do it? *Nat Rev Neurosci* 5: 495–501.

Wolfe, J. M., Reinecke, A., and Brawn, P. (2006). Why don't we see changes? The role of attentional bottlenecks and limited visual memory. *Vis Cogn* 14: 749–780.

Wolfe, J. M., Vo, M. L.-H., Evans, K. K., and Greene, M. R. (2011). Visual search in scenes involves selective and non-selective pathways. *Trends Cogn Sci* 15: 77–84.

Womelsdorf, T., Anton-Erxleben, K., Pieper, F., and Treue, S. (2006). Dynamic shifts of visual receptive fields in cortical area MT by spatial attention. *Nat Neurosci* 9: 1156–1160.

Woodrow, H. (1909). A quantitative study of rhythm. *Arch Psychol* 14: 1–66.

Wrzesniewski, A., McCauley, C., and Rozin, P. (1999). Odor and affect: Individual differences in the impact of odor on liking for places, things and people. *Chem Senses* 24: 713–721.

Wyert, C., Webster, W. W., Chen, J. H., Wilson, S. R., McClary, A., Khan, R. M., and Sobel, N. (2007). Smelling a single component of male sweat alters levels of cortisol in women. *J Neurosci* 27: 1261–1265.

Wysocki, C. J., Dalton, P., Brody, M. J., and Lawley, H. J. (1997). Acetone odor and irritation thresholds obtained from acetone-exposed factory workers and from control (occupationally non-exposed) subjects. *Am Ind Hyg Assoc J* 58: 704–712.

Wysocki, C. J., Dorries, K. M., and Beauchamp, G. K. (1989). Ability to perceive androstenone can be acquired by ostensibly anosmic people. *Proc Natl Acad Sci USA* 86: 7976–7978.

Yabuta, N. H., and Callaway, E. M. (1998). Functional streams and local connections of layer 4C neurons in primary visual cortex of the macaque monkey. *J Neurosci* 18: 9489–9499.

Yamane, Y., Carlson, E. T., Bowman, K. C., Wang, Z., and Connor, C. E. (2008). A neural code for three-dimensional object shape in macaque inferotemporal cortex. *Nat Neurosci* 11: 1352–1360.

Yang, Z., and Schank, J. C. (2006). Women do not synchronize their menstrual cycles. *Hum Nat* 17: 433–447.

Yantis, S. (1993). Stimulus-driven attentional capture. *Curr Dir Psychol Sci* 2: 156–161.

Yarbus, A. L. (1967). *Eye Movements and Vision*. New York: Plenum.

Yates, B., and Miller, A. (1998). Physiological evidence that the vestibular system participates in autonomic and respiratory control. *J Vestib Res* 8: 17–26.

Yee, K. K., Sukumaran, S. K., Kotha, R., Gilbertson, T. A., and Margolskee, R. F. (2011). Glucose transporters and ATP-gated K^+ (K_{ATP}) metabolic sensors are present in type 1 taste receptor 3 (T1r3)-expressing taste cells. *Proc Natl Acad Sci USA* 108: 5431–5436.

Yeshurun, Y., Lapid, H., Dudai, Y., and Sobel, N. (2009). The privileged brain representation of first olfactory associations. *Curr Biol* 19: 1869–1874.

Yesilyurt, B., Whittingstall, K., Ugurbil, K., Logothetis, N. K., and Uludag, K. (2009). Relationship of the BOLD signal with VEP for ultrashort duration visual stimuli (0.1 to 5 ms) in humans. *J Cereb Blood Flow Metab* 30: 449–458.

Yin, C., Kellman, P. J., and Shipley, T. F. (1997). Surface completion complements boundary interpolation in the visual integration of partly occluded objects. *Perception* 26: 1459–1479.

Yin, T. C., and Chan, J. C. (1990). Interaural time sensitivity in medial superior olive of cat. *J Neurophysiol* 65: 465–488.

Yonas, A., Craton, L. G., and Thompson, W. B. (1987). Relative motion: Kinetic information for the order of depth at an edge. *Percept Psychophys* 41: 53–59.

Young, L. R. (1984). Perception of the body in space: Mechanisms. In I. Darian-Smith (Ed.), *Handbook of Physiology—The Nervous System* (Vol. 3[2], pp. 1023–1066). Bethesda, MD: American Physiological Society.

Young, L. R., Shelhamer, M., and Modestino, S. (1986) M.I.T./Canadian vestibular experiments on the Spacelab-1 mission. 2. Visual vestibular tilt interaction in weightlessness. *Exp Brain Res* 64: 299–307.

Yu, K., and Blake, R. (1992). Do recognizable figures enjoy an advantage in binocular rivalry? *J Exp Psychol Hum Percept Perform* 18: 1158–1173.

Yuille, A., and Kersten, D. (2006). Vision as Bayesian inference: Analysis by synthesis? *Trends Cogn Sci* 10: 301–308.

Yuodelis, C., and Hendrickson, A. (1986). A qualitative and quantitative analysis of the human fovea during development. *Vision Res* 26: 847–855.

Zadra, A., Nielsen, T. A., and Donderi, D. C. (1998). Prevalence of auditory, olfactory, and gustatory experiences in home dreams. *Percept Mot Skills* 87: 819–826.

Zahorik, P. (2002). Assessing auditory distance perception using virtual acoustics. *J Acoust Soc Am* 111: 1832–1846.

Zaidi, Q. (1997). Decorrelation of L- and M-cone signals. *J Opt Soc Am A Opt Image Sci Vis* 14: 3430–3431.

Zatorre, R. J. (2001). Do you see what I'm saying? Interactions between auditory and visual cortices in cochlear implant users. *Neuron* 1: 13–14.

Zeki, S. (1983a). Colour coding in the cerebral cortex: The reaction of cells in monkey visual-cortex to wavelengths and colours. *Neuroscience* 9: 741–765.

Zeki, S. (1983b). Colour coding in the cerebral cortex: The responses of wavelength-selective and colour-coded cells in monkey visual cortex to changes in wavelength composition. *Neuroscience* 9: 767–781.

Zeki, S. (1990). A century of cerebral achromatopsia. *Brain* 113(Pt.6): 1721–1777.

Zelano, C., Bensafi, M., Porter, J., Mainland, J., Johnson, B., Bremner, E., Telles, C., Khan, R., and Sobel, N. (2005). Attentional modulation in human primary olfactory cortex. *Nat Neurosci* 8: 114–120.

Zhang, B., Zheng, J., Watanabe, I., Maruko, I., Bi, H., Smith, E. L., III, and Chino, Y. (2005). Delayed maturation of receptive field center/surround mechanisms in V2. *Proc Natl Acad Sci USA* 102: 5862–5867.

Zhao, G. Q., Zhang, Y., Hoon, M. A., Chandrashekar, J., Erlenbach, I., Ryba, N. J., and Zuker, C. S. (2003). The receptors for mammalian sweet and umami taste. *Cell* 115: 255–266.

Zheng, J., Zhang, B., Bi, H., Maruko, I., Watanabe, I., Nakatsuka, C., Smith, E. L., III, and Chino, Y. M. (2007). Development of temporal response properties and contrast sensitivity of V1 and V2 neurons in macaque monkeys. *J Neurophysiol* 97: 3905–3916.

Zhou, W., and Chen, D. (2009). Binaral rivalry between the nostrils and the cortex. *Curr Biol* 19: 1561–1565.

Zhou, W., Jiang, Y., He, S., and Chen, D. (2010). Olfaction modulates visual perception in binocular rivalry. *Curr Biol* 20: 1356–1358.

Zipser, K., Lamme, V. A., and Schiller, P. H. (1996). Contextual modulation in primary visual cortex. *J Neurosci* 16: 7376–7389.

Zotterman, Y. (1939). Touch, pain and tickling: An electrophysiological investigation on cutaneous sensory nerves. *J Physiol* 95: 1–28.

Zou, Z., Li, F., and Buck, L. B. (2005). Odor maps in the olfactory cortex. *Proc Natl Acad Sci USA* 102: 7724–7729.

Photo Credits

Index

Entries in *italic* type indicate that the information will be found in an illustration.